150 Best Federal Jobs

Part of JIST's Best Jobs® Series

Laurence Shatkin, Ph.D.

JIST Works
America's Career Publisher®

10-11

150 Best Federal Jobs

© 2012 by JIST Publishing

Published by JIST Works, an imprint of JIST Publishing
7321 Shadeland Station, Suite 200
Indianapolis, IN 46256-3923

Phone: 800-648-JIST   Fax: 877-454-7839
E-mail: info@jist.com   Website: www.jist.com

Other books by Laurence Shatkin

The Sequel	40 Best Fields for Your Career
Best Jobs for the 21st Century	225 Best Jobs for Baby Boomers
200 Best Jobs for College Graduates	250 Best-Paying Jobs
300 Best Jobs Without a Four-Year Degree	150 Best Jobs for a Better World
200 Best Jobs Through Apprenticeships	200 Best Jobs for Introverts
50 Best Jobs for Your Personality	

Quantity discounts are available for JIST products. Please call 800-648-JIST or visit www.jist.com for a free catalog and more information.

Visit www.jist.com for information on JIST, free job search information, tables of contents and sample pages, and ordering information on our many products.

Acquisitions Editor: Susan Pines
Development Editor: Stephanie Koutek
Cover and Interior Designer: Aleata Halbig
Interior Layout: Toi Davis
Proofreader: Laura Bowman, Jeanne Clark
Indexer: Cheryl Ann Lenser

Printed in the United States of America

16 15 14 13 12 11   9 8 7 6 5 4 3 2 1

Library of Congress Cataloging-in-Publication Data

Shatkin, Laurence.
  150 best federal jobs / Laurence Shatkin.
      p. cm.
  Includes index.
  ISBN 978-1-59357-891-6 (alk. paper)
1. Civil service positions--United States. I. Title. II. Title: One hundred fifty best federal jobs.
  JK716.S48 2011
  351.73023--dc23

                    2011029756

ISBN 978-1-59357-891-6

The Nation's Largest Employer Wants You!

The federal government offers good salaries, great benefits, job security, and flexible work schedules in locations across the country. Many federal workers are approaching the age when they'll retire and create job openings—maybe one to suit you.

But some federal jobs offer better pay and more opportunities than others. This book will help you target the most rewarding federal jobs and the ones that can suit you in other ways, such as fitting your personality or meeting your geographical preference. Easy-to-scan "best federal jobs" lists, 64 in all, organize the jobs in many useful ways. Fact-packed job descriptions break down large occupations into specific federal job titles.

You'll also learn how the government fills jobs, how to search and apply for federal jobs, and how the pay systems work. You'll get a detailed explanation of opportunities for veterans and people with disabilities.

Table of Contents

Summary of Major Sections

Introduction. A short overview to help you better understand and use the book. *Starts on Page 1.*

Part I—How to Get a Federal Job. Explains where and how to search for a federal job, how to apply, the special arrangements for veterans and applicants with disabilities, and the pay scales used for federal jobs. *Starts on Page 17.*

Part II—The Best Jobs Lists. Very useful for exploring federal career options! Lists are arranged into easy-to-use groups. The first group of lists presents the best overall federal jobs—jobs with the highest earnings, projected growth, and number of openings. More-specialized lists follow, presenting the best jobs for workers age 16–29, workers 55 and over, women, men, and part-time workers. Other lists sort the best jobs in six regions of the United States, at various GS (pay-scale) levels, in 16 career clusters, and linked to six personality types. The column starting at right presents all the list titles within the groups. *Starts on Page 27.*

Part III—The Job Descriptions. Provides complete descriptions of the 150 federal jobs that met my criteria for high pay, fast growth, or large number of openings. Each description contains information on earnings, projected growth, job duties, skills, related job titles, education and training required, and many other details. Much of the information is derived from a database of facts about federal workers. *Starts on Page 97.*

Appendix A—Definitions of Skills Referenced in This Book. Defines the 35 skill names that are used in the job descriptions in this book. *Starts on Page 353.*

Appendix B—Categories of GS Series. Lists the 59 categories of federal jobs in the GS system. You can use this to search for families of jobs in the database of federal job openings. *Starts on Page 357.*

Appendix C—Best Jobs with Largest Workforces, by State. Lists the 20 best jobs with the largest number of federal workers in each state plus the District of Columbia. *Starts on Page 361.*

Appendix D—Best Jobs with Largest Workforces, by Agency. Lists the 20 best jobs with the largest number of workers in each of 15 federal agencies plus the Postal Service. *Starts on Page 397.*

Appendix E—Foreign Job Opportunities. Explains how foreign federal jobs are filled and lists the occupations and locations with the most workers. *Starts on Page 409.*

Detailed Table of Contents

Introduction

Not everybody will want to read this introduction. You may want to skip this background information and go directly to Part I, which explains how to get a federal job, or Part II, which lists the best federal jobs.

But if you want to understand how (and why) I put this book together, where the information comes from, and what makes a job "best," this introduction can answer many questions.

Why Seek a Federal Job?

The federal government is one of the few industries that was not badly hurt by the recent recession. It continues to offer jobs in a wide variety of fields.

Jobs with the federal government have many advantages compared to jobs in the private sector:

⚜ Federal jobs tend to be more secure. When agencies need to reduce their size, they usually do so by attrition (that is, not replacing people who leave). Employees can challenge termination or other personnel decisions through a formal appeals process.

⚜ Hiring and promotion in federal jobs are guided by a stronger commitment to diversity and inclusion than you'll find in most private-sector worksites.

⚜ Federal jobs offer a wider selection of health-insurance plans than do private-sector employers. Retirees can continue their health-insurance coverage for the same fee they paid while working.

⚜ Federal jobs offer better retirement benefits than many jobs in the private sector.

⚜ Federal jobs offer 10 holidays per year.

⚜ Federal jobs offer 13 vacation days per year to beginning workers, 20 days after 3 years, and 26 days after 15 years. To this, add 13 days of sick leave per year.

⚜ Federal jobs often permit flexible work arrangements. For example, you may be able to work four 10-hour days per week or do some work from home. Workers are rarely required to work more than 40 hours. This can make a huge difference in some fields, such as law and accounting.

⁕ High-quality day care for children is often available at federal job sites or sometimes is subsidized at off-site centers.

⁕ Federal jobs can give you the satisfaction of serving the nation.

Federal employment is not a worker's paradise, however:

⁕ Competition for some federal jobs is intense.

⁕ Contrary to what you may have heard about the growth of the federal workforce, it is not a fast-growing field. The Bureau of Labor Statistics projects 0.6 percent growth from 2008–2018, compared to 10.1 percent for all industries. If you don't count Postal Service jobs, federal growth is a healthier 3.4 percent, but that still does not compare well to the average across all career fields.

⁕ A few federal jobs require security clearance, which may require background investigations that can drag on for months.

⁕ The workplace structure tends to be more bureaucratic than in small private-sector businesses. In high-tech jobs, the workplace may be slower to adopt the newest technologies.

⁕ Sometimes political pressures prevent workers from doing their jobs as they see fit.

⁕ Although the many rules are designed to promote fairness, some workers find ways to manipulate the rules to gain an advantage.

What about pay? The answer depends on how you analyze the data. Federal workers earn more than private-sector workers, but they also are better educated. Most individual federal workers would earn more in an equivalent private-sector job. On the other hand, federal pay is extremely fair. In many private-sector jobs, you have to negotiate your salary and don't know what other workers' salaries are based on. The pay for federal jobs is supposed to be comparable to what is current in the private sector, with adjustments for local cost of living, and it is based on your salary grade.

The high level of competition for federal jobs, though listed here as a disadvantage, is an indication that work for the federal government is, on balance, very rewarding.

How This Book Can Help You Plan for a Federal Job

This book is targeted at readers who have not yet made a firm decision about a career goal but who want to know what highly rewarding careers have the extra advantage of offering employment by the federal employment. That's why this book focuses on *occupations* rather than on federal departments and agencies. This book will start you on the road to choosing and planning for a satisfying and productive career. What matters most is that you choose an occupation that is a good fit for your interests, abilities, and other preferences. Later, after you have made your choice and have started to prepare for it or to hunt for job openings, you may or may not decide to pursue that career in the federal government. But it's nice to know that federal employment, with its many advantages, will be an option for you.

In addition to the many lists in Part II that help you find rewarding federal jobs that have certain characteristics (such as a large number of opportunities for part-time work), you can use Appendix C to find outstanding federal jobs located in your state or Appendix D to identify jobs in 16 federal agencies. If overseas work interests you, read Appendix E to learn about foreign job opportunities.

Where the Information Came From

The information I used in creating the job lists in Part II and the job descriptions in Part III came mostly from databases created by the U.S. Department of Labor and the Office of Personnel Management (OPM):

* The Bureau of Labor Statistics (BLS) provided detailed economic data about the jobs. Figures on earnings, job growth, and job openings are reported under a classifying system called Standard Occupational Classification (SOC), which organizes the U.S. workforce into approximately 800 job titles. You'll find figures that provide averages (for example, earnings) for both federal jobs and jobs with all employers. The lists in Part II are all based on SOC titles.

* A table on the website of the BLS's Office of Occupational Statistics and Employment Projections (www.bls.gov/emp/ep_table_111.htm) was my source for information about the level of education required. These levels apply to the occupation as a whole, not just to federal jobs within the occupation.

* The spring 2010 issue of the BLS publication *Occupational Outlook Quarterly* provided the information for the statements about "Other Considerations for Job Outlook." These statements also apply to the occupation as a whole, not just to federal jobs within the occupation.

* The Office of Personnel Management classifies occupations as *General Schedule (GS) series*. Some of the SOC titles in the Part II lists are linked to a single GS series; for example, the SOC title Foresters is linked to OPM's Forestry series. In other cases, a single SOC title links to two or more GS series; for example, the SOC title Agricultural Inspectors is linked to the Agricultural Warehouse Inspection series and also to the Food Inspection series. Definitions of the GS series are based on materials from the OPM. The OPM also provided skill or knowledge requirements for each GS series. In Appendix B, you can find a complete list of the 59 categories of GS series.

* For information about workers in specific federal jobs—that is, GS series—I used the FedScope database of the OPM (www.fedscope.opm.gov). I used data from

September 2010 and limited it to the federal workforce employed within the United States so it would be comparable with the BLS data.

⁕ To obtain additional information about occupations, I linked the SOC job titles to titles in the O*NET (Occupational Information Network) database, which is now the primary source of detailed information on occupations. The Labor Department updates the O*NET regularly, and I used the most recent version available: O*NET release 15.1. Data from the O*NET was the basis of the information about the personality types associated with jobs, as well as the important skills, types of knowledge, and work conditions. Because the O*NET uses a slightly different set of job titles than SOC, I matched similar titles. In a few cases, data was not available about each of these topics for every occupation. Nevertheless, the information reported here is the most reliable data obtainable. Note, however, that these information topics apply to the occupation as a whole, not just to federal jobs within the occupation.

⁕ The Classification of Instructional Programs, a system developed by the U.S. Department of Education, is the basis of the cross-references to the education or training programs related to each job. I linked programs to jobs by following the crosswalk developed jointly by the BLS and the National Center for Education Statistics (NCES).

Of course, information in a database format can be boring and even confusing, so I did many things to help make the data useful and present it to you in a form that is easy to understand.

How the Best Federal Jobs Were Selected

Like other books in the *Best Jobs* series, this one identifies occupations that have the best combination of three economic factors: earnings, job growth, and job openings. Whereas other books in this series use data that applies to *all* industries, in this book I wanted to use data on the earnings, job growth, and openings for jobs in the federal government. For one of these factors, job openings, the BLS projects only the openings in all industries, so I developed a formula for computing a rough estimate of the job openings in federal jobs, as explained later in this introduction.

I obtained all three federal-specific economic measures—earnings, projected job growth, and projected job openings—for 296 occupations. Some occupations that might have been promising choices had to be excluded because the BLS did not provide the full range of information. For example, I was able to obtain the earnings for the roughly 27,000 federally employed Physicians and Surgeons, but not the projected job growth and openings for this occupation. For the set of occupations with full information, I followed this procedure for sorting them to identify the 150 best jobs:

1. I eliminated 23 occupations because I was unable to identify equivalent job titles in the federal government's OPM classification. (I did not eliminate 4 Postal Service jobs, although they are not in the OPM system.)

2. I eliminated 37 occupations because their employment is not expected to grow and they are expected to offer fewer than 100 federal job openings per year. I eliminated an additional 15 jobs that have fewer than 10 projected federal job openings per year. These cannot be considered best jobs.

3. I ranked the remaining 221 occupations three times, based on the three major economic measures.

4. I then added the three numerical rankings for each occupation to calculate its overall score.

5. To emphasize federal jobs that tend to pay more, are likely to grow more rapidly, and have more job openings, I selected the 150 job titles with the best total overall scores.

For example, the job with the best combined score for earnings, growth, and number of job openings is Financial Examiners, so this job is listed first even though it is not the best-paying job (which is Public Relations Managers), the fastest-growing job (which is Biomedical Engineers), or the job with the most openings (which is Postal Service Mail Carriers).

Understand the Limits of the Data in This Book

In this book, I used the most reliable and up-to-date information available on earnings, projected growth, number of openings, and other topics. The earnings data came from the U.S. Department of Labor's Bureau of Labor Statistics. As you look at the figures, keep in mind that they are estimates. They give you a general idea about the number of workers employed, annual earnings, rate of job growth, and annual job openings.

Understand that a problem with such data is that it describes an average. Just as there is no precisely average person, there is no such thing as a statistically average example of a particular job, even within a single employer such as the federal government. I say this because data, while helpful, can also be misleading.

Take, for example, the yearly earnings information in this book. This is highly reliable data obtained from a very large U.S. working population sample by the Bureau of Labor Statistics. It reports the average annual pay received as of May 2009 by people in various job titles (actually, it is the median annual pay, which means that half earned more and half less). It is available for both federal workers and workers in all industries.

This sounds great, except that half of all people in the occupation earned less than that amount. For example, people who are new to the occupation or with only a few years of work experience often earn much less than the median amount. In federal jobs, pay is sometimes adjusted to reflect the local cost of living, which varies across the country.

Also keep in mind that the figures for job growth and number of openings are projections by labor economists—their best guesses about what we can expect between now and 2018. (The projections for job openings in federal jobs are particularly rough, as explained later in this introduction.) These projections are not guarantees. A catastrophic economic downturn, war, or technological breakthrough could change the actual outcome. The projections are also averages over a ten-year period. During economic slowdowns, you can expect job growth and openings to be lower; during recoveries, both will be higher. Political developments, such as attempts to downsize the government, may change the outlook for federal employment in some occupations.

Finally, don't forget that the job market consists of both job openings and job *seekers*. The figures on job growth and openings don't tell you how many people will be competing with you to be hired. The Department of Labor and the Office of Personnel Management do not publish figures on the supply of job candidates, so I can't provide a number that tells how much competition you can expect. Competition is an important issue that you should research for any tentative career goal. Each job description in Part III includes a brief statement about outlook that may include a comment about competition. You can find additional discussion in the *Occupational Outlook Handbook*. You also should speak to people who educate or train tomorrow's workers; they probably have a good idea of how many graduates find rewarding employment and how quickly. People in the workforce, especially in federal jobs, can provide insights into this issue. Use your critical thinking skills to evaluate what people tell you. For example, educators or trainers may be trying to recruit you, whereas people in the workforce may be trying to discourage you from competing. Get a variety of opinions to balance out possible biases.

So, in reviewing the information in this book, please understand the limitations of the data. You need to use common sense in career decision making as in most other things in life. I hope that, by using that approach, you find the information helpful and interesting.

The Data Complexities

If you are curious about details, the following section explains some of the complexities inherent in the sources of information I used and what I did to make sense of them. You don't need to know this to use the book, so jump to the "How This Book Is Organized" section if you are bored with details.

As explained earlier, I selected the jobs on the basis of economic data specific to federal jobs. You'll find information on earnings, projected growth, and number of job openings for each job throughout this book.

Earnings

The employment security agency of each state gathers information on earnings for various jobs and forwards it to the U.S. Bureau of Labor Statistics. This information is organized in standardized ways by a BLS program called Occupational Employment Statistics (OES). To keep the earnings for the various jobs and regions comparable, the OES screens out certain types of earnings and includes others, so the OES earnings I use in this book represent straight-time gross pay exclusive of premium pay. More specifically, the OES earnings include the job's base rate; cost-of-living allowances; guaranteed pay; hazardous-duty pay; incentive pay, including commissions and production bonuses; on-call pay; and tips. They do not include back pay, jury duty pay, overtime pay, severance pay, shift differentials, nonproduction bonuses, or tuition reimbursements.

For each job, you'll find four facts related to earnings, all based on the OES survey:

* The two Annual Earnings figures show the median earnings (half earn more, half earn less) for federal workers and for all workers.

* The two Earnings Growth Potential statements—again, one each for federal workers and all workers—represent the gap between the 10th percentile and the median. This information answers the question, "If I compared the wages of the low earners to the median, how much of a pay difference (in percentage terms) would I find?" If the difference is large, the job has great potential for increasing your earnings as you gain experience and skills. If the difference is small, you probably will need to move on to another occupation to improve your earnings substantially. Because a percentage figure, by itself, might be hard to interpret, I follow the figure with an easy-to-understand verbal tag that expresses the Earnings Growth Potential: "very low" when the percentage is less than 25%, "low" for 25%–35%, "medium" for 35%–40%, "high" for 40%–50%, and "very high" for any figure higher than 50%. You may notice in some cases that the job has better Earnings Growth Potential for federal workers than for all workers or vice versa.

The median earnings for all workers in all occupations in all industries were $33,190 in May 2009. Federal workers, however, tend to be paid better (on average) than those in other industries, largely because they are better educated. Their median earnings were $53,880. The 150 jobs in this book were chosen partly on the basis of good earnings, so their average is a respectable $54,383 for workers in all industries and $66,174 for federal workers. (These are weighted averages, which means that jobs with larger workforces are given greater weight in the computations.)

Projected Growth and Number of Job Openings

This information comes from the Office of Occupational Statistics and Employment Projections, a program within the Bureau of Labor Statistics that develops information about projected trends in the nation's labor market for the next ten years. As mentioned earlier, the most recent projections available cover the years 2008 to 2018. The projections are based on information about people moving into and out of occupations. The BLS uses data from various sources in projecting the growth and number of openings for each job title; some data comes from the Census Bureau's Current Population Survey and some comes from an OES survey. In making the projections, the BLS economists assume that there will be no major war, depression, or other economic upheaval. They do assume that recessions may occur, in keeping with the business cycles we have experienced for several decades, but because the projections cover ten years, they are intended to provide an average of both the good times and the bad times.

Like the earnings figures, the figures on projected growth and job openings are reported for each occupation both for workers in all industries and for federal workers.

While salary figures are fairly straightforward, you may not know what to make of job-growth figures. For example, is a projected growth of 15 percent good or bad? Keep in mind that the average (mean) growth in all occupations for all kinds of employers, as projected by the Bureau of Labor Statistics, is 10.1 percent. One-quarter of the SOC occupations have a growth projection of 0.3 percent or lower. Growth of 9.1 percent is the median, meaning that half of the occupations have more, half less. Only one-quarter of the occupations have growth projected at more than 15.4 percent.

Now, let's see how these figures compare to the outlook for federal workers. As mentioned previously, the average (mean) growth in federal employment projected by the BLS for all occupations is 0.5 percent. One-quarter of the SOC occupations have a federal growth projection of 4.0 percent or lower. The median is 7.6 percent. Only one-quarter of the occupations have federal growth projected at more than 10.0 percent.

It's interesting to compare these two distributions. For all industries, the growth projected for the middle 50 percent of jobs ranges from 0.3 to 15.4 percent. For the federal jobs, however, the middle 50 percent ranges from 4.0 percent to 10.0 percent, a much smaller spread. This indicates that the federal jobs have a growth rate that, although slower, is more consistent.

But not *all* federal jobs were selected for this book, and the ones that are included were chosen partly on the basis of job growth. That's why their mean growth is 4.8 percent, which is considerably lower than the mean of 10.1 percent for all jobs, but also quite a bit higher than the mean of 0.5 percent for all federal jobs. Among these 150 jobs, the job ranked 37th by projected growth has a figure of 13.5 percent, the job ranked 75th (the median) has a projected growth of 8.0 percent, and the job ranked 112th has a projected growth of 7.5 percent.

The BLS's job-growth projections are presented as a matrix of occupations and industries; that is, for each occupation, BLS offers a separate growth figure for each industry in the economy. For projections of job *openings*, however, BLS offers only one figure for each occupation: the figure for openings in all industries. Nevertheless, I was able to compute a rough estimate of the job openings that can be expected in one industry—the federal government—by following this procedure:

1. First, for each occupation, I obtained the Department of Labor's estimate of the size of the workforce employed by the federal government. I divided this by the size of the workforce employed in *all* industries to get a percentage for the federal government workforce—the "federal portion" of the workforce. For each occupation, I multiplied this percentage by the number of projected job openings in all industries to get a preliminary estimate of the federal portion of these projected openings.

2. Second, I addressed the concern that job turnover in the federal government tends to be slower than in other industries, resulting in fewer openings than the federal portion would indicate. Each month, the Job Openings and Labor Turnover Survey by the Department of Labor measures the *job opening rate* for major industries—that is, the monthly number of jobs in the industry expressed as a percentage of the total workforce. These monthly figures can be summed to determine an annual job-opening rate. For federal employment during the years 2001–2009, this rate ranged from a low of 20.2 percent in 2002 to a high of 30.5 percent in 2009. The average rate over those 9 years was 23.7 percent. (It makes sense to ignore 2010, because temporary Census Bureau hiring that year was an anomaly.) The percent average for all industries over that same time period was 33.5. I divided 23.7 by 33.5 to get 0.7, the *job turnover ratio* for federal jobs.

3. For each occupation, I multiplied the preliminary estimated federal portion of projected openings (from step 1) by this job turnover ratio (from step 2). The product was a somewhat better estimate of the federal job openings that can be expected for the occupation. Because this estimate is still rough (turnover probably varies among occupations, even within the same industry), I rounded this figure to the nearest 10.

4. For six occupations with more than 75 percent federally employed workers, I used the Department of Labor's projection for job openings in all industries.

When job openings are calculated this way, one-quarter of the SOC occupations are projected to have 10 or fewer annual federal job openings. The median is 40 job openings. Only one-quarter of the occupations have 170 or more projected job openings.

Of course, the outlook is much better for the occupations selected for this book. Of these, only one-quarter are projected to have 50 or fewer annual federal job openings.

The median is 120 job openings. One-quarter of the occupations have 300 or more projected job openings.

Perhaps you're wondering why this book offers figures on both job growth *and* number of openings. Aren't these two ways of saying the same thing? Actually, you need to know both. Consider the occupation Biomedical Engineers, which is projected to grow at the phenomenal rate of 62.8 percent in the federal government. There should be lots of opportunities in such a fast-growing job, right? Not exactly. This is a tiny occupation, with only about 400 federal workers currently employed, so although it is growing rapidly, it will not create many new jobs (about 30 per year). Now consider Postal Service Mail Sorters, Processors, and Processing Machine Operators. Because automation has taken over most tasks of this job, this occupation actually has a *negative* growth rate, with the alarming figure of –30.4 percent. Nevertheless, this is a very large occupation that employs more than 175,000 workers, so although it is shrinking, it is expected to take on more than 1,660 new workers each year as existing workers retire, die, or move on to other jobs. That's why I based my selection of the best jobs on both of these economic indicators and why you should pay attention to both when you scan the lists of best federal jobs.

How This Book Is Organized

The information in this book about best federal jobs moves from the general to the highly specific.

Part I. How to Get a Federal Job

Part I explains the policies that federal agencies follow when they advertise and fill jobs. This includes the policies that provide special consideration for veterans and applicants with disabilities. You'll learn what information to look for in the announcements of federal job openings and how to apply. You'll also get an explanation of the GS and FWS systems for federal pay.

Part II. The Best Jobs Lists

For many people, the 64 lists in Part II are the book's most interesting feature. Here you can see the titles of federal jobs with high salaries, fast growth, and plentiful job openings. You can see which jobs are best in terms of each of these factors combined and considered separately. Additional lists highlight federal jobs with a high percentage of female, male, and part-time workers. Look in the Table of Contents for a complete list of lists. Although there are a lot of lists, they are not difficult to understand because they have clear titles and are organized into groupings of related lists.

Depending on your situation, some of the lists in Part II will interest you more than others. For example, if you are young, you may be interested in the best-paying federal jobs that employ high percentages of people age 16–29. Other lists show jobs within personality types, by levels of education, or in other ways that you might find helpful in exploring your career options.

Whatever your situation, I suggest you use the lists that make sense for you to help explore career options. Following are the names of each group of lists along with short comments on each group. You will find additional information in a brief introduction provided at the beginning of each group of lists in Part II.

Best Federal Jobs Overall: Lists of Jobs with the Highest Pay, Fastest Growth, and Most Openings

These four lists are the ones that most people want to see first. The list presents the top 150 occupation titles in order of their combined scores for earnings, growth, and number of job openings. (These economic statistics apply specifically to workers employed by the federal government.) Additional lists are extracted from the best jobs and present the 50 jobs with the highest earnings, the 50 jobs projected to grow most rapidly, and the 50 jobs with the most openings.

Best Jobs Lists by Demographic

Like other books in the *Best Jobs* series, this one includes lists that show what sorts of jobs different types of people are most likely to have. For example, you can see which federal jobs have the highest percentage of men or young workers. I'm not saying that men or young people should consider these jobs over others based solely on this information, but it is interesting information to know.

In some cases, the lists can give you ideas for jobs to consider that you might otherwise overlook. For example, perhaps women should consider some jobs that traditionally have high percentages of men in them. Or older workers might consider some jobs typically held by young people. Although these aren't obvious ways of using these lists, the lists may give you some good ideas of jobs to consider. The lists may also help you identify jobs that work well for others in your situation—for example, jobs with plentiful opportunities for part-time work, if that's something you want to do.

All lists in this section were created through a similar process. I began with the 150 best jobs and sorted those jobs in order of the primary criterion for each set of lists. For example, I sorted the 150 jobs based on the percentage of workers under age 30 from highest to lowest percentage and then selected the jobs with a high percentage (33 jobs with a percentage greater than 15). From this initial list of jobs with a high percentage of each type of worker, I created four more-specialized lists:

❋ 25 Best Jobs Overall (the subset of jobs that have the highest combined scores for earnings, growth rate, and number of openings)

❋ 25 Best-Paying Jobs

❋ 25 Fastest-Growing Jobs

❋ 25 Jobs with the Most Openings

Again, each of these four lists includes only jobs that have high percentages of different types of workers. The same basic process was used to create all the lists in this section. The lists are very interesting, and I hope you find them helpful.

Best Federal Jobs by Location

Some federal jobs are concentrated in one part of the nation. For example, Detectives and Criminal Investigators are concentrated in the Southwest because many of the 20,000 Border Patrol agents are stationed there. If you have a strong regional preference, knowing about geographic concentrations may help you decide which federal jobs to seek or avoid. That's why I assembled six lists of the best jobs based on geographic concentrations:

❋ Best Federal Jobs Concentrated in the DC Area

❋ Best Federal Jobs Concentrated in the Northeast

❋ Best Federal Jobs Concentrated in the Southeast

❋ Best Federal Jobs Concentrated in the Midwest

❋ Best Federal Jobs Concentrated in the Southwest

❋ Best Federal Jobs Concentrated in the West

Best Federal Jobs Based on GS Levels

Because GS levels are based on the level of education or training that is expected of job applicants, I thought you would be interested in seeing lists of jobs at various GS levels (as well as the blue-collar jobs not in the GS system). Here are the lists that I created for this purpose:

❋ Best Federal Jobs Not in the GS System

❋ Best Federal Jobs at GS Levels 5 through 8

❋ Best Federal Jobs at GS Levels 9 through 11

❋ Best Federal Jobs at GS Level 12

❋ Best Federal Jobs at GS Level 13

❋ Best Federal Jobs at GS Levels 14 through 15

Best Federal Jobs Based on Career Clusters

These lists organize the 150 best federal jobs into the 16 career clusters that are used by many educational institutions and career information resources to divide up the world of work. In the private sector, you might think of these clusters—for example, Health Science or Manufacturing—as major industry groups. However, all 16 of these clusters offer job opportunities in the industry we call the federal government. For each cluster, you can see the jobs ordered by the combination of their scores for earnings, growth, and number of openings. This information may help you link federal jobs to educational programs available to you or may give you ideas about what private-sector career fields lead to opportunities for federal employment—and vice versa.

Best Federal Jobs Based on Personality Types

These lists organize the 150 best federal jobs into six personality types described in the introduction to the lists: Realistic, Investigative, Artistic, Social, Enterprising, and Conventional. In each of the six lists, the jobs are presented in order of their combined scores for earnings, growth, and number of openings.

Part III: The Job Descriptions

This part contains descriptions of the 150 best federal jobs, using a format that is informative yet compact and easy to read. The descriptions contain statistics such as earnings and projected percent of growth; lists such as major skills and work conditions; as well as important work tasks and personality type. Because the jobs in this section are arranged in alphabetical order, you can easily find a job that you've identified from Part II and that you want to learn more about.

As explained earlier in this introduction, the job titles used in the lists are based on the Standard Occupational Classification (SOC), but in Part III each SOC title is linked to one or more General Schedule (GS) Series, which is how the Office of Personnel Management (OPM) classifies federal jobs (other than Postal Service jobs). The job descriptions in Part III are based partly on information from the Department of Labor that applies to the SOC title and partly on information from the OPM that applies to each related GS Series.

Although I've tried to make the descriptions easy to understand, the sample that follows—with an explanation of each of its parts—may help you better understand and use the descriptions.

Job Title →

Clergy

Data Elements

- ❀ Education/Training Required: Master's degree
- ❀ Annual Earnings (Federal): $74,360
- ❀ Annual Earnings (All Industries): $42,950
- ❀ Earnings Growth Potential (Federal): 24.1% (very low)
- ❀ Earnings Growth Potential (All Industries): 46.6% (high)
- ❀ Job Growth (Federal): 10.2%
- ❀ Job Growth (All Industries): 12.7%
- ❀ Annual Job Openings (Federal): 310
- ❀ Annual Job Openings (All Industries): 21,770

Summary Description and Tasks →

Conduct religious worship and perform other spiritual functions associated with beliefs and practices of religious faith or denomination. Provide spiritual and moral guidance and assistance to members. Pray and promote spirituality. Read from sacred texts such as the Bible, Torah, or Koran. Prepare and deliver sermons and other talks. Organize and lead regular religious services. Share information about religious issues by writing articles, giving speeches, or teaching. Instruct people who seek conversion to a particular faith. Visit people in homes, hospitals, and prisons to provide them with comfort and support. Counsel individuals and groups concerning their spiritual, emotional, and personal needs. Train leaders of church, community, and youth groups. Administer religious rites or ordinances. Study and interpret religious laws, doctrines, and/or traditions. Conduct special ceremonies such as weddings, funerals, and confirmations. Plan and lead religious education programs for their congregations. Respond to requests for assistance during emergencies or crises. Devise ways in which congregation membership can be expanded. Collaborate with committees and individuals to address financial and administrative issues pertaining to congregations. Prepare people for participation in religious ceremonies. Perform administrative duties such as overseeing building management, ordering supplies, contracting for services and repairs, and supervising the work of staff members and volunteers. Refer people to community support services, psychologists, and/or doctors as necessary. Participate in fundraising activities to support congregation activities and facilities.

Considerations for Job Outlook: About average employment growth is projected.

Personality Type: Social-Enterprising-Artistic. **Skills:** Management of Financial Resources; Social Perceptiveness; Persuasion; Negotiation; Learning Strategies; Management of Material Resources; Service Orientation; Systems Evaluation. **Education and Training Program:** Clinical Pastoral Counseling/Patient Counseling; Divinity/Ministry (BD, MDiv); Pastoral Counseling and Specialized Ministries, Other; Pastoral Studies/Counseling; Philosophy; Pre-Theology/Pre-Ministerial Studies; Rabbinical Studies (M.H.L./Rav); Religion/Religious Studies; Theological and Ministerial Studies, Other; Theology and Religious Vocations, Other; Theology/Theological Studies; Youth Ministry. **Work Environment:** Indoors; sitting.

OTHER FEDERAL JOB FACTS

RELATED GS SERIES: 0060 CHAPLAIN

- ❀ U.S. Federal Workforce: 1,157
- ❀ Average Length of Service: 9.6 years
- ❀ Percent Part-Time: 24.9%
- ❀ Percent Women: 13.7%
- ❀ Largest Age Bracket: 65 or more (20.7%)
- ❀ GS Level with Most Workers: 12
- ❀ Agency with Most Workers: Veterans Affairs
- ❀ States with Most Workers: California, Texas

Advise on, administer, supervise, or perform professional work involved in a program of spiritual welfare and religious guidance for patients of government hospitals and homes, for inmates of government correctional and penal or other institutions, or for persons in other government activities where civilian chaplain service is needed.

Requirements: Ordination by a recognized ecclesiastical body.

Margin labels (right): Considerations for Job Outlook; Personality Type; Skills; Education and Training Program; Work Environment; Other Federal Job Facts

Here are some details on each of the major parts of the job descriptions you will find in Part III:

* **Job Title:** This is the title for the job as defined by the Standard Occupational Classification (SOC) taxonomy.

* **Data Elements:** The information comes from various U.S. Department of Labor databases, as explained elsewhere in this introduction.

* **Summary Description and Tasks:** The boldfaced sentence provides a summary description of the occupation. It is followed by a listing of tasks generally performed by people who work in this job. This information comes from the O*NET database but, where necessary, has been edited to avoid exceeding 1,500 characters.

* **Considerations for Job Outlook:** This information, based on statements by the BLS's Office of Occupational Statistics and Employment Projections, explains some factors that are expected to affect opportunities for job-seekers. Note that these comments apply to the period of time from 2008 to 2018. Like all the following topics, except "Other Federal Job Facts," these apply to the occupation as a whole, not just to federal jobs in the occupation.

* **Personality Type:** The O*NET database assigns each job to a primary personality type and to as many as two secondary types. The job descriptions include the name of the related personality types as well as a brief definition of the primary type.

* **Skills:** For each job, I included the skills whose level-of-performance scores exceeded the average for all jobs by the greatest amount and whose ratings on the importance scale were higher than very low. I included as many as six such skills for each job, and I ranked them by the extent to which their rating exceeds the average. You'll find a definition for each skill in Appendix A.

* **Education and Training Program:** This part of the job description provides the name of the educational or training program(s) for the job. It will help you identify sources of formal or informal training for a job that interests you. To get this information, I adapted a crosswalk created by the National Center for O*NET Development to connect information in the Classification of Instructional Programs (CIP) to the O*NET job titles I used in this book. I made various changes to connect the O*NET job titles to the education or training programs related to them and also modified the names of some education and training programs so that they would be more easily understood. In 19 cases, I abbreviated the listing of related programs for the sake of space; such entries end with "others."

* **Work Environment:** I included any work condition with a rating that exceeds the midpoint of the rating scale. The order does not indicate their frequency on the job. Consider whether you like these conditions and whether any of these conditions would make you uncomfortable. Keep in mind that when hazards are present (such as contaminants), protective equipment and procedures are provided to keep you safe.

❊ **Other Federal Job Facts:** This information applies to a group of federal jobs that the Office of Personnel Management (OPM) classifies into a GS series. The data elements that begin this section are derived from OPM's FedScope database and are based on the most recent data available, which applies to September 2010 and to federal jobs within the United States. The title and definition of the GS series and the statement about its requirements are based on text obtained from the OPM website, rewritten for clarity and brevity. In some cases, you'll find an alternate title that is used on the USAJobs site (www.USAJobs.gov) and that will help you to search for current job openings there.

Getting all the information I used in the job descriptions was not a simple process, and it is not always perfect. Even so, I used the best and most recent sources of data I could find, and I think that my efforts will be helpful to many people.

PART I

How to Get a Federal Job

Applying for a federal job used to be a drawn-out nightmare of paperwork, but the Office of Personnel Management (OPM) has overhauled this process and made it much more like applying for a private-sector job. In addition, the federal government tries much harder than many private-sector employers to make the job-application process as fair as possible, to provide opportunities for people who often encounter discrimination elsewhere (such as people with disabilities), and to reward people who have served their country in uniform.

How Federal Jobs Are Filled

In the private sector, the most effective way to get a job usually is to find unadvertised job openings. But that's not true for federal jobs. Almost all of them are announced on the USAJobs site (www.usajobs.gov). A few agencies, such as the FBI, Congress, the judiciary, and the Postal Service, are not required to announce there or to follow the standard federal hiring procedures. But even these agencies often follow those procedures anyway. So the way to find most federal jobs is to search on USAJobs for an announced opening and apply for it according to the specifications listed in the job announcement.

When a job is open for application, the hiring managers review the submitted resumes and any other supporting documentation and score each applicant on how well he or she meets the requirements for the job. Many veterans get extra points, as is explained in greater detail later in this chapter.

Some federal jobs are not filled through the normal competitive process. For example, the president gets to choose ambassadors and Supreme Court justices. The military has its own procedures for filling jobs with service members. (For details, see my book *150 Best Jobs Through Military Training.*) However, all the jobs included in this book are civilian jobs that are filled through the competitive process, so that's what this chapter describes. (Veterans sometimes can be appointed for positions in some of these jobs.)

How to Search for and Apply for a Federal Job

Before you go to the USAJobs site, you should begin to narrow down your search by scanning the lists in Part II of this book. When you find an appealing job there, be sure to read the job description in Part III, where the jobs from the lists are ordered alphabetically. Note the related GS titles listed there. Each GS title is actually the name of a GS series, which means a family of more-specific job titles.

Searching at the USAJobs Site

You do not need to establish an account at the USAJobs site to search and apply for jobs, but an account is free and allows you to save searches, create an online resume, store supporting documents online, and apply online.

When you search at USAJobs, the job titles in the announcements you retrieve may be somewhat different from the titles used in either Part II or Part III. For example, Business Operations Specialists, All Other, is one of the occupations that appears in the Part II lists. One of the related GS series you'll find in the Part III job description is 2032 Packaging, with the equivalent USAJobs title Packaging Specialist. If you plug the keyword "Packaging" into the search box on the USAJobs site (or refine your search by specifying the GS series 2032 Packaging Specialist), one of the job titles you'll retrieve might be "Packing Specialist (HAZMAT)."

One of the strengths of the search page at USAJobs is that it allows you to refine your search. For example, you can specify a certain geographical area, a salary range, a particular agency, and a work schedule (such as part-time), among other criteria. If you're interested in some specialized task or other feature of the job (for example, working with HAZMATs), you can specify one or more keywords.

In the advanced search, you can retrieve jobs from an entire category of jobs—for example, all jobs related to human resource management—by using the first two digits of the code for the GS category that interests you. See Appendix B for the full list of these categories.

Once you have decided on a suitable combination of search terms (maybe more than one), you can save these criteria and be informed when future jobs meeting these criteria are posted. If you have an account with USAJobs, click "Save this search and email me jobs." You can save as many as 10 searches. Another way is to click "RSS Feed Of This Search," copy the address (URL) of the page that appears, and paste it into whatever website or application serves as your RSS aggregator. (Google Reader, My MSN, My Yahoo, and many e-mail readers can serve this function.) RSS, which stands for Really Simple Syndication, is a summary of Web content that is updated on a regular basis.

Once you retrieve a list of open jobs, browse the list and click interesting postings for detailed information. The job overview usually includes the following:

- Dates when the job is open for application
- The salary range and benefits
- Where the job is located (sometimes multiple locations)
- The work schedule (for example, full-time)
- Major work duties and tasks
- Qualifications, such as education, work experience, or licensure
- Other requirements, such as citizenship, security clearance, or a test you must pass
- Required supporting documents
- How applicants are evaluated
- How to apply
- What to expect next

Note that these facts are now much more relevant to your job search than the information in Part III of this book. The job description in Part III introduced you to a group of jobs (one or more GS series), but you now need to focus on one particular position.

Applying at the USAJobs Site

Once you find a job that you want to apply for, the "How to Apply" topic will explain the appropriate procedure. In many cases, an "Apply Online" button will appear; in all cases, you can also pursue the entire application process offline. Before you apply, you should print out the information you retrieved about the job, read it carefully to make sure you are qualified and can provide all the necessary supporting documentation, and save the printout for your records.

Whether you apply online or offline, you need a resume. If you apply for more than one federal job, especially if the jobs are very different from each other, you may find it useful to create more than one resume and tailor each resume for the specific job target. The USAJobs site provides an online tool for creating and storing as many as five resumes.

One way to tailor a resume is to choose appropriate language to describe your work experiences and perhaps also your educational programs. The human resource managers who will evaluate your application may be looking for keywords indicating that your background is appropriate for this job. Carefully reread the job description that you retrieved in your search to find some clues to relevant keywords. The knowledge, skills, and work tasks listed in the Part III job description in this book, although they refer to a GS series rather than to a particular job, may provide additional clues. Read the "Resume and Application Tips" on the USAJobs site (www.usajobs.gov/ei/ resumeandapplicationtips.asp) for further suggestions about creating an effective resume. *Federal Resume Guidebook* (JIST) has many useful examples that you can use as models for your resume.

Many jobs require supporting documents, such as a college transcript or a record of previous federal employment or military service. If you have these documents in electronic form, you can upload them to your USAJobs account and submit them with the online job application.

Although the federal government is trying to simplify the job-application process, some jobs still require one step that takes some time and care: writing brief statements indicating your relevant knowledge, skills, and abilities (KSAs). The USAJobs site features a fact sheet with valuable suggestions for writing effective KSA statements: "Ten Tips for Letting Federal Employers Know Your Worth," at www.usajobs.gov/ei/tentips. asp. You'll find even more ideas in *Federal Resume Guidebook*.

Once you submit your application, either by clicking the button that submits it, by mailing it, or by faxing it, you begin a four-stage process. You are supposed to be notified at each stage:

* When your application is received
* When your application is assessed
* When your application is referred or not referred to a selection official
* When you have been selected or not selected

Each agency operates on a different schedule, but you should expect to start getting feedback within two to four weeks after the closing date for applications. If you have not heard from the agency, inquire about your application using the contact address listed on the job description. With an online application, you can check its status on the USAJobs site.

If you are called for an interview, remember that the same principles that apply to any job interview are relevant here:

* Just as you would research a company before interviewing for a job there, you should research the agency that announced the job. This will help prepare you to ask good questions and to understand what you're being told about the job. It also will demonstrate your interest in the job.
* Dress in appropriate business clothes.
* Be prepared to give a one-minute answer to the question, "Tell me about yourself." Your remarks should summarize your background and why you're the right person for the job.

❋ Make eye contact with the interviewer and show a positive attitude.

❋ Tangible evidence of your work, such as sample output, a photograph of the results, or a testimonial letter, can be very effective props.

❋ It's also useful to bring along a copy of the job description on which you have underlined the topics that you want to ask questions about. This will jog your memory and help you sustain the conversation.

❋ The job interview is not the time to negotiate your salary or your benefits. Wait until they have offered you the job.

❋ Follow up the interview with a thank-you note. Besides showing good manners, it gives you an extra chance to mention why you're a good fit for the job. An e-mail is acceptable, but a handwritten note is much more effective.

Who Qualifies for Federal Jobs

Most federal jobs are open only to United States citizens. (For a full discussion of the exceptions, see www.usajobs.gov/EI/noncitizensemployment.asp.) For most federal jobs, male applicants of ages 18 through 25 must be registered with the Selective Service System. With rare exceptions, you cannot hold a federal job while simultaneously holding a civilian job that creates a conflict of interest or that causes your total work schedule to exceed 40 hours per week.

Any other restrictions for a particular job opening are listed under the "Who May Apply" or "Who May Be Considered" heading in the job announcement. Some jobs are open only to "status applicants." These people are current or former federal civilian employees, but veterans can also apply in some cases.

Opportunities for Veterans

The federal government has a long history of giving hiring preference to people who have served our country in the armed forces. About one-quarter of the federal workforce consists of vets, compared to less than one-tenth of the civilian workforce. If you're a veteran, you can get help in your job search from a website called Feds Hire Vets (www.fedshirevets.gov). The discussion that follows is a summary of the more-detailed information you can find at that website.

Being a veteran does not guarantee you a federal job, nor does your advantage apply to internal agency actions such as promotions and transfers. You must have been discharged from active duty under an honorable or general discharge, be disabled, or have retired below the rank of major.

When you compete for a job at an agency that uses a numerical rating and ranking system to identify the best-qualified applicants, your record of service earns you extra points. If you served during certain timeframes, most of which are eras associated with military conflict, you receive a bonus of 5 points. Veterans who have a service-related disability or who have been awarded the Purple Heart receive a 10-point bonus.

Some agencies don't use a numerical rating system and instead divide qualified job applicants into "quality categories" that indicate their level of qualification for the job. In this hiring process (except for scientific or professional positions at the GS-9 level or higher), veterans with a disability rating of at least 10 percent are placed at the top of the highest category. Veterans with a lower disability rating or no disability are placed at the top of their assigned category.

In some cases, disabled veterans can submit a job application after the deadline that applies to other applicants.

Agencies can give veterans preference in some additional ways that are called special hiring authorities for veterans. For example, under the Veterans' Recruitment Appointment authority, an agency can directly appoint a qualified veteran to a position that normally would be competitive. Other authorities allow agencies to appoint veterans who have a disability rating of 30 percent or higher and veterans who have been trained for the job by the agency as part of a Veterans Affairs vocational rehabilitation program. Still another authority, the Veterans Employment Opportunity Act, allows qualified veterans to apply for jobs that otherwise are open only to "status applicants" (as explained in the previous section). If one of these special hiring authorities applies to a job, you'll see this mentioned in the job announcement.

One way to identify job openings with special opportunities for veterans is to add the word "veteran" when you search for jobs on the USAJobs site. For example, instead of simply searching for the keyword "mechanic," you might search for "mechanic veteran."

To take advantage of your veteran's preference in the job-application process, you need to submit appropriate documentation of your veteran status and disability rating, if any. The job announcement identifies the appropriate documents. To get a veteran's preference letter from the Department of Veterans Affairs, contact your local VA regional office at 800-827-1000 or at www.va.gov.

Opportunities for People with Disabilities

Under an authority called Schedule A, people with disabilities (not just veterans) can be appointed to a federal position that normally would be competitive. These applicants are not guaranteed a job, and they must be qualified for the position (for example, with the appropriate education or experience) and be able to perform the essential duties of the job with reasonable accommodation. The U.S. Office of Personnel Management maintains a website (www.opm.gov/disability) that explains the relevant policies. The discussion that follows is a summary of the more-detailed information you can find at that website.

Your disability can be considered as part of the hiring decision if it falls into one of these three categories: an intellectual disability, a psychiatric disability, or a severe physical disability. You need to get a statement that confirms your disability from your physician, from a licensed rehabilitation professional, or from a government agency that provides disability benefits. This statement, often called a Schedule A letter, does not need to detail your medical history or explain any need for accommodation. The simpler the letter, the better.

A second statement you need to submit with your job application is something that certifies your job readiness. This does not need to be a formal certificate—for example, the kind awarded after completion of a training program. It is simply a statement that you can do the work. It can be issued by any of the authorities that can furnish the Schedule A letter—in fact, a single document can cover both purposes. You also can get an appropriate certificate from a licensed career counselor, from a public or private vocational rehabilitation counselor, or from a Veterans Administration counselor. Sometimes an agency determines the job readiness of a Schedule A applicant by hiring the person as a temporary employee.

When you apply, you should contact the Disability Program Manager (DPM) or Selective Placement Coordinator (SPC) at the agency where you wish to work. You can identify the appropriate person by speaking to the human resources department at the agency. Note that Schedule A applies to more than just people with disabilities, so make clear that this is your interest. This DPM or SPC will explain the best way to use Schedule A in the hiring process.

Understand that applying for the job under Schedule A can be complicated and can take more time than seems reasonable. You may find help and support not only at the OPM website but also at www.disability.gov or at the website of an organization that deals with your particular disability, such as the American Council of the Blind (www.acb.org) or the National Alliance on Mental Illness (www.nami.org).

Pay Systems for Federal Jobs

Salaries in federal jobs are governed by systems that can seem mysterious to outsiders. However, they are designed so that people start at a fair wage and earn pay increases as they acquire experience.

When you retrieve a job announcement on the USAJobs site, look at the "Pay Plan" heading to see which wage system is being used for the job. For white-collar jobs, the pay plan usually begins with GS, which means the job falls under the General Schedule system. The salary range for GS jobs is expressed in terms of annual pay. For blue-collar jobs, the pay plan usually begins with WG (Wage Grade), WL (Wage Leader), or WS (Wage Supervisor), meaning that the job is governed by the Federal Wage System (FWS). For FWS jobs, the salary range is expressed as hourly wages.

Some agencies administer their own pay systems. For example, you may see nursing positions within the Department of Veterans Affairs that have a pay plan beginning with VN. Positions with the Senior Executive Service use the ES pay plan. For details about these specialized wage systems, you should contact the employing agency. The discussion that follows focuses on the most common wage systems, GS and FWS.

Most of the jobs included in this book are paid under the GS system, which has 15 salary grades. For example, GS-5 and GS-7 typically are used when the job requires a bachelor's degree or its equivalent; in a job requiring a master's degree, you would probably start at GS-9. Within each GS salary grade are 10 steps. You generally are assigned to the lowest step in your grade when you are first hired. As you handle your job successfully and gain experience in it, you usually will be raised to higher steps and eventually to a higher grade. Each occupation has a GS ceiling that you cannot rise above.

If you're working in a GS position in the continental United States, your pay is also determined by which of the 32 localities (geographical areas) you live in. Employees outside the continental United States in nonforeign areas (Alaska, Hawaii, Puerto Rico, Guam, and the U.S. Virgin Islands) are not governed by locality rates but rather receive cost-of-living allowances. The current salary tables for the GS and locality pay areas are available at www.opm.gov/oca/06tables/index.asp.

The FWS has 15 salary grades for the WG and WL pay schedules and 19 grades for WS. Each grade is divided into five steps, with step 2 designed to be comparable to what private industry pays for a similar job in the same geographical area. For each wage area, the federal agency that employs the most FWS workers is responsible for setting the wage rates. The Department of Defense most often serves this function, and you may find the current FWS wage rates on a military website, www.cpms.osd.mil/wage/wage_schedules. aspx. Unfortunately, two different schemes are used to divide the United States into geographical areas that determine your wage rate. One scheme is for jobs that are paid out of "appropriated funds," and the other is for jobs paid out of "nonappopriated funds." The job announcement on the USAJobs site won't tell you which scheme applies, but you can ask the agency that posted the job.

These pay systems may give you the mistaken impression that you can't negotiate your earnings when you're offered a federal job. But notice that the salary listed in the job announcement is always expressed as a range. The human resources manager who offers you the job will probably offer you the salary at the lowest step in your pay grade, but you can bargain for a higher rate. What's true for any hiring situation is true here: It helps to have some arguments for better pay other than just the fact that you want it. For example, you can point out an unusual skill, experience, or educational background you have that will boost the agency's mission. If you must relocate and the agency is not authorized to pay for this directly, you can ask to have your salary offset these costs. The best argument of all is a better-paying job offer from another employer.

PART II

The Best Jobs Lists

This part contains a lot of interesting lists, and it's a good place for you to start using the book. Here are some suggestions for using the lists to explore career options:

⊛ The table of contents at the beginning of this book presents a complete listing of the list titles in this section. You can browse the lists or use the table of contents to find those that interest you most.

⊛ I gave the lists clear titles, so most require little explanation. I provide comments for each group of lists.

⊛ As you review the lists of jobs, one or more of the jobs may appeal to you enough that you want to seek additional information. As this happens, mark that job (or, if someone else will be using this book, write it on a separate sheet of paper) so that you can look up the description of the job in Part III.

⊛ Keep in mind that all jobs in these lists meet my basic criteria for being included in this book, as explained in the introduction. All lists, therefore, contain jobs that have high pay, high growth, or large numbers of openings. These measures are easily quantified and are often presented in lists of best jobs in the newspapers and other media. Although earnings, growth, and openings are important, you also should consider other factors in your career planning, such as amount of variety, liking the people you work with, and having opportunities to be creative. Many other factors that may help define the ideal job for you are difficult or impossible to quantify and thus aren't used in this book, so you will need to consider the importance of these issues yourself.

⊛ All data used to create these lists comes from the U.S. Department of Labor and the Office of Personnel Management. The earnings figures are based on the average annual pay received by full-time federal workers in the United States. Because the earnings represent the national averages, actual pay rates can vary greatly by location, specialized job function, amount of previous work experience, and other factors.

Some Details on the Lists

The sources of the information I used in constructing these lists are presented in this book's introduction. Here are some additional details on how I created the lists:

⚹ Some jobs have the same scores for one or more data elements. For example, in the category of fastest-growing, two jobs (Loan Officers and Registered Nurses) are expected to grow at the same rate, 14.0 percent. Therefore I ordered these two jobs alphabetically, and their order in relation to each other has no other significance. Avoiding these ties was impossible, so understand that the difference of several positions on a list may not mean as much as it seems.

⚹ Likewise, it is unwise to place too much emphasis on small differences in outlook information: projections for job growth and job openings. For example, Detectives and Criminal Investigators are projected to have 1,160 federal job openings per year, whereas 1,060 openings are projected for Tax Examiners, Collectors, and Revenue Agents. This is a difference of only 100 jobs spread over the entire United States, and it is only a rough estimate based on a projection. So, again, keep in mind that small differences of position on a list aren't very significant.

Best Federal Jobs Overall: Lists of Jobs with the Highest Pay, Fastest Growth, and Most Openings

The four lists that follow are this book's premier lists. They are the lists that are most often mentioned in the media and the ones that most readers want to see.

In the introduction, I explain how I created the initial list of 150 best jobs. In the sections that follow, I explain the rationale for each specialized list and why you may find it useful.

The first list presents all 150 best federal jobs according to their combined rankings for pay, growth, and number of openings. Three additional lists present the 40 jobs with the top scores for each of three measures: annual earnings, projected percentage growth through 2018, and number of annual openings. Descriptions for all the jobs in these lists are included in Part III.

The 150 Best Federal Jobs Overall—Jobs with the Best Combination of Pay, Growth, and Openings

This list arranges all 150 federal jobs that were selected for this book in order of their overall scores for pay, growth, and number of openings, as explained in the introduction.

The job with the best overall score was Financial Examiners. Other jobs follow in order of their total scores for pay, growth, and openings. These 150 federal jobs are the ones I use throughout this book: in the other lists in Part II and in the descriptions found in Part III.

As you look over the list, remember that jobs near the top of the list are not necessarily "good" jobs—nor are jobs toward the end of the list necessarily "bad" ones for you to consider. Their positions in the list are simply a result of each one's total score based on pay, growth, and number of openings. This means, for example, that some jobs with low pay and modest growth but a high number of openings appear higher on the list than some jobs with higher pay and modest growth but a low number of openings. A "right" job for you could be anywhere on this list.

Also, remember that almost all of these occupations may be pursued outside of the federal government. (Air Traffic Controllers; Postal Service Mail Carriers; Postal Service Mail Sorters, Processors, and Processing Machine Operators; Postal Service Clerks; and Postmasters and Mail Superintendents are the notable exceptions.) So if you prepare for an occupation that has only a small number of federal openings per year and you fail to get hired into one of those openings, you may still have many job opportunities in the private sector. For example, I estimate only 10 federal job openings per year for Actuaries, but 1,000 annual job openings are projected for the same occupation in the private sector. (The bonus list at the end of this chapter identifies the 25 jobs with the best rewards *outside of* federal government.)

The 150 Best Federal Jobs Overall

Job	Annual Earnings	Percent Growth	Annual Openings
1. Financial Examiners	$101,770	41.5%	260
2. Air Traffic Controllers	$113,840	10.7%	780
3. Lawyers	$131,410	8.4%	960
4. Detectives and Criminal Investigators	$73,320	29.8%	1,160
5. Computer and Information Research Scientists	$99,730	19.5%	200
6. Social Scientists and Related Workers, All Other	$75,540	19.3%	800
7. Accountants and Auditors	$87,730	11.1%	740
8. Aerospace Engineers	$109,190	12.0%	200
9. Logisticians	$76,000	17.8%	730
10. Political Scientists	$113,050	18.4%	120
11. Purchasing Agents, Except Wholesale, Retail, and Farm Products	$75,050	17.8%	950
12. Registered Nurses	$74,790	14.0%	1,790
13. Biological Scientists, All Other	$69,860	19.6%	670

(continued)

(continued)

The 150 Best Federal Jobs Overall

Job	Annual Earnings	Percent Growth	Annual Openings
14. Claims Adjusters, Examiners, and Investigators	$66,580	19.5%	1,050
15. Operations Research Analysts	$103,780	15.4%	160
16. Transportation Inspectors	$100,100	18.3%	150
17. Budget Analysts	$73,120	19.9%	300
18. Management Analysts	$83,140	8.4%	1,970
19. Engineers, All Other	$110,860	7.6%	520
20. Tax Examiners, Collectors, and Revenue Agents	$56,420	19.5%	1,060
21. Medical Scientists, Except Epidemiologists	$110,260	29.0%	50
22. Public Relations Specialists	$83,440	18.0%	180
23. Natural Sciences Managers	$106,160	7.7%	290
24. Mechanical Engineers	$91,520	8.5%	240
25. Dentists	$137,950	9.9%	80
26. Paralegals and Legal Assistants	$60,500	18.2%	420
27. Clergy	$74,360	10.2%	310
28. Compliance Officers, Except Agriculture, Construction, Health and Safety, and Transportation	$45,720	29.8%	3,080
29. Computer and Information Systems Managers	$133,440	8.3%	100
30. Pharmacists	$107,330	7.7%	190
31. Physical Scientists, All Other	$104,480	7.6%	230
32. Psychologists, All Other	$91,110	7.8%	240
33. Materials Engineers	$108,670	19.4%	30
34. Physician Assistants	$83,370	18.3%	90
35. Medical and Health Services Managers	$104,530	7.6%	190
36. Civil Engineers	$87,900	7.6%	320
37. Health Diagnosing and Treating Practitioners, All Other	$85,610	7.6%	340
38. Electronics Engineers, Except Computer	$102,730	7.5%	300
39. Environmental Scientists and Specialists, Including Health	$91,550	7.6%	230
40. Engineering Managers	$125,730	7.6%	110
41. Biomedical Engineers	$87,830	62.8%	30
42. Chemists	$98,860	7.7%	150
43. Industrial Engineers	$86,260	18.9%	40
44. Writers and Authors	$80,410	9.7%	110
45. Anthropologists and Archeologists	$70,400	19.9%	70
46. Astronomers	$136,010	10.9%	20
47. Fire Fighters	$46,630	19.1%	310
48. Petroleum Engineers	$96,480	30.0%	10

The 150 Best Federal Jobs Overall

Job	Annual Earnings	Percent Growth	Annual Openings
49. Nuclear Engineers	$91,050	11.6%	50
50. Financial Managers	$117,190	7.0%	210
51. Real Estate Sales Agents	$73,050	8.5%	170
52. Computer Hardware Engineers	$100,560	7.6%	110
53. Actuaries	$113,020	14.8%	10
54. Engineering Technicians, Except Drafters, All Other	$67,080	7.6%	340
55. Physicists	$111,370	7.5%	110
56. Business Operations Specialists, All Other	$72,120	7.3%	4,290
57. Electrical and Electronics Repairers, Commercial and Industrial Equipment	$53,870	12.0%	160
58. Market Research Analysts	$87,720	13.5%	30
59. Environmental Engineers	$98,760	7.5%	150
60. Captains, Mates, and Pilots of Water Vessels	$63,620	28.8%	50
61. Geographers	$74,890	17.8%	40
62. Loan Officers	$69,920	14.0%	70
63. Marine Engineers and Naval Architects	$100,920	8.9%	30
64. Eligibility Interviewers, Government Programs	$46,430	8.6%	670
65. First-Line Supervisors/Managers of Police and Detectives	$93,390	6.8%	240
66. Media and Communication Equipment Workers, All Other	$77,920	7.6%	150
67. Arbitrators, Mediators, and Conciliators	$119,740	9.5%	10
68. Industrial Machinery Mechanics	$54,090	24.7%	70
69. Forensic Science Technicians	$95,620	16.7%	10
70. Artists and Related Workers, All Other	$70,520	7.6%	200
71. Podiatrists	$110,850	9.4%	10
72. Electrical Engineers	$89,130	7.7%	70
73. Physical Therapists	$75,960	9.7%	50
74. Administrative Law Judges, Adjudicators, and Hearing Officers	$125,360	7.4%	70
75. Animal Scientists	$101,350	10.0%	10
76. Purchasing Managers	$119,840	7.4%	70
77. Conservation Scientists	$69,580	8.0%	110
78. Directors, Religious Activities and Education	$89,210	10.5%	20
79. Social and Community Service Managers	$91,140	12.2%	10
80. Agricultural Inspectors	$44,460	19.7%	140
81. Aircraft Mechanics and Service Technicians	$53,750	7.6%	330
82. Correctional Officers and Jailers	$53,360	7.6%	350
83. Instructional Coordinators	$83,910	7.6%	80

(continued)

(continued)

The 150 Best Federal Jobs Overall

Job	Annual Earnings	Percent Growth	Annual Openings
84. Airline Pilots, Copilots, and Flight Engineers	$97,290	7.5%	90
85. Pharmacy Technicians	$38,870	18.5%	210
86. Teachers and Instructors, All Other	$62,840	7.4%	430
87. Statisticians	$92,720	6.9%	140
88. Speech-Language Pathologists	$81,130	7.9%	40
89. Funeral Directors	$67,620	22.5%	10
90. Interpreters and Translators	$67,600	18.4%	20
91. Installation, Maintenance, and Repair Workers, All Other	$49,640	7.8%	270
92. Technical Writers	$73,340	10.0%	30
93. Chemical Engineers	$97,350	7.8%	20
94. Life, Physical, and Social Science Technicians, All Other	$48,280	7.7%	310
95. Microbiologists	$92,580	7.4%	80
96. Geoscientists, Except Hydrologists and Geographers	$92,410	7.4%	80
97. Occupational Health and Safety Specialists	$74,370	6.5%	260
98. Ship Engineers	$47,570	29.8%	50
99. Librarians	$77,970	7.8%	40
100. Medical and Clinical Laboratory Technologists	$61,630	7.7%	120
101. Industrial Engineering Technicians	$64,910	18.1%	20
102. Veterinarians	$81,130	7.6%	50
103. Recreational Therapists	$63,780	11.4%	30
104. Zoologists and Wildlife Biologists	$70,190	7.4%	160
105. Optometrists	$76,720	9.1%	20
106. Construction and Building Inspectors	$63,330	7.8%	80
107. Economists	$104,530	−1.5%	110
108. Licensed Practical and Licensed Vocational Nurses	$43,160	7.6%	590
109. Surveyors	$81,140	8.0%	20
110. Transportation, Storage, and Distribution Managers	$94,890	−5.7%	160
111. Foresters	$60,630	10.8%	30
112. Museum Technicians and Conservators	$38,450	18.1%	120
113. Procurement Clerks	$41,920	7.6%	380
114. Sheet Metal Workers	$50,890	7.7%	160
115. Agricultural Engineers	$74,380	9.5%	10
116. Sailors and Marine Oilers	$37,300	19.6%	80
117. Mathematicians	$104,540	6.6%	40
118. Painters, Construction and Maintenance	$47,470	7.9%	140
119. Radiologic Technologists and Technicians	$55,600	7.6%	90

The 150 Best Federal Jobs Overall

Job	Annual Earnings	Percent Growth	Annual Openings
120. Coaches and Scouts	$56,190	17.9%	10
121. Biological Technicians	$32,850	7.6%	470
122. Orthotists and Prosthetists	$65,800	10.2%	10
123. Postal Service Mail Carriers	$52,200	–1.1%	10,720
124. Soil and Plant Scientists	$71,460	7.5%	70
125. Healthcare Support Workers, All Other	$40,020	7.6%	280
126. Graphic Designers	$73,130	7.4%	70
127. Hydrologists	$83,370	5.4%	80
128. Combined Food Preparation and Serving Workers, Including Fast Food	$29,720	8.1%	210
129. Set and Exhibit Designers	$67,080	7.9%	20
130. Postmasters and Mail Superintendents	$58,780	–15.1%	520
131. Plant and System Operators, All Other	$56,520	7.9%	30
132. Public Relations Managers	$140,970	5.9%	10
133. Veterinary Technologists and Technicians	$46,440	12.5%	30
134. Architects, Except Landscape and Naval	$89,070	5.7%	50
135. Administrative Services Managers	$75,950	5.2%	90
136. Forest and Conservation Technicians	$31,390	7.5%	960
137. Medical Records and Health Information Technicians	$44,460	7.6%	150
138. Health Technologists and Technicians, All Other	$52,080	7.6%	80
139. Precision Instrument and Equipment Repairers, All Other	$54,550	7.6%	60
140. Producers and Directors	$77,300	7.3%	40
141. Education, Training, and Library Workers, All Other	$38,860	7.6%	210
142. Maintenance and Repair Workers, General	$52,920	–0.1%	420
143. Postal Service Clerks	$52,530	–18.3%	1,610
144. Social and Human Service Assistants	$42,210	11.4%	50
145. Postal Service Mail Sorters, Processors, and Processing Machine Operators	$52,520	–30.4%	1,170
146. Electrical and Electronic Engineering Technicians	$61,500	–2.9%	220
147. Motor Vehicle Operators, All Other	$44,020	7.7%	110
148. Security Guards	$35,410	8.3%	120
149. Avionics Technicians	$51,650	7.9%	40
150. First-Line Supervisors/Managers of Correctional Officers	$69,570	7.5%	40

The 50 Best-Paying Federal Jobs

I sorted all 150 best federal jobs based on their annual median earnings from highest to lowest. *Median earnings* means that half of all federal workers in each of these jobs earn more than that amount and half earn less. I then selected the 50 jobs with the highest earnings to create the list that follows.

It shouldn't be a big surprise to learn that most of the highest-paying jobs require advanced levels of education, training, or experience. For example, most of the 10 jobs with the highest earnings require a doctoral or professional degree, and others, such as Purchasing Managers and Engineering Managers, require extensive training and experience beyond the bachelor's degree. Although the top 10 jobs may not appeal to you for various reasons, you are likely to find others that will among the top 50 jobs with the highest earnings.

Keep in mind that the earnings reflect the national average for all federal workers in the occupation. This is an important consideration, because starting pay in the job is usually much less than the pay that workers can earn with several years of experience. Some of these job titles are linked to two or more federal job categories with differing earnings levels. For example, Lawyers is linked to the GS series Law Clerk, with median earnings of about $60,000 (exact median figures are not available for GS series), and also to Patent Attorney, with median earnings of about $150,000. Earnings also vary by region of the country, so actual pay in your area could be substantially different.

The 50 Best-Paying Federal Jobs

Job	Annual Earnings
1. Public Relations Managers	$140,970
2. Dentists	$137,950
3. Astronomers	$136,010
4. Computer and Information Systems Managers	$133,440
5. Lawyers	$131,410
6. Engineering Managers	$125,730
7. Administrative Law Judges, Adjudicators, and Hearing Officers	$125,360
8. Purchasing Managers	$119,840
9. Arbitrators, Mediators, and Conciliators	$119,740
10. Financial Managers	$117,190
11. Air Traffic Controllers	$113,840
12. Political Scientists	$113,050
13. Actuaries	$113,020

The 50 Best-Paying Federal Jobs

Job	Annual Earnings
14. Physicists	$111,370
15. Engineers, All Other	$110,860
16. Podiatrists	$110,850
17. Medical Scientists, Except Epidemiologists	$110,260
18. Aerospace Engineers	$109,190
19. Materials Engineers	$108,670
20. Pharmacists	$107,330
21. Natural Sciences Managers	$106,160
22. Mathematicians	$104,540
23. Economists	$104,530
24. Medical and Health Services Managers	$104,530
25. Physical Scientists, All Other	$104,480
26. Operations Research Analysts	$103,780
27. Electronics Engineers, Except Computer	$102,730
28. Financial Examiners	$101,770
29. Animal Scientists	$101,350
30. Marine Engineers and Naval Architects	$100,920
31. Computer Hardware Engineers	$100,560
32. Transportation Inspectors	$100,100
33. Computer and Information Research Scientists	$99,730
34. Chemists	$98,860
35. Environmental Engineers	$98,760
36. Chemical Engineers	$97,350
37. Airline Pilots, Copilots, and Flight Engineers	$97,290
38. Petroleum Engineers	$96,480
39. Forensic Science Technicians	$95,620
40. Transportation, Storage, and Distribution Managers	$94,890
41. First-Line Supervisors/Managers of Police and Detectives	$93,390
42. Statisticians	$92,720
43. Microbiologists	$92,580
44. Geoscientists, Except Hydrologists and Geographers	$92,410
45. Environmental Scientists and Specialists, Including Health	$91,550
46. Mechanical Engineers	$91,520
47. Social and Community Service Managers	$91,140
48. Psychologists, All Other	$91,110
49. Nuclear Engineers	$91,050
50. Directors, Religious Activities and Education	$89,210

The 50 Fastest-Growing Federal Jobs

I created this list by sorting all 150 best federal jobs by their projected growth over the ten-year period from 2008 to 2018. Growth rates are one measure to consider in exploring career options, as jobs with higher growth rates tend to provide more job opportunities. But don't forget the warning in the introduction: Even a fast-growing occupation will not provide many job openings if it has a tiny workforce. If a job interests you, check its figure for projected job openings in Part III.

The 50 Fastest-Growing Federal Jobs

Job	Percent Growth
1. Biomedical Engineers	62.8%
2. Financial Examiners	41.5%
3. Petroleum Engineers	30.0%
4. Compliance Officers, Except Agriculture, Construction, Health and Safety, and Transportation	29.8%
5. Detectives and Criminal Investigators	29.8%
6. Ship Engineers	29.8%
7. Medical Scientists, Except Epidemiologists	29.0%
8. Captains, Mates, and Pilots of Water Vessels	28.8%
9. Industrial Machinery Mechanics	24.7%
10. Funeral Directors	22.5%
11. Anthropologists and Archeologists	19.9%
12. Budget Analysts	19.9%
13. Agricultural Inspectors	19.7%
14. Biological Scientists, All Other	19.6%
15. Sailors and Marine Oilers	19.6%
16. Claims Adjusters, Examiners, and Investigators	19.5%
17. Computer and Information Research Scientists	19.5%
18. Tax Examiners, Collectors, and Revenue Agents	19.5%
19. Materials Engineers	19.4%
20. Social Scientists and Related Workers, All Other	19.3%
21. Fire Fighters	19.1%
22. Industrial Engineers	18.9%
23. Pharmacy Technicians	18.5%
24. Interpreters and Translators	18.4%
25. Political Scientists	18.4%
26. Physician Assistants	18.3%
27. Transportation Inspectors	18.3%
28. Paralegals and Legal Assistants	18.2%

The 50 Fastest-Growing Federal Jobs

Job	Percent Growth
29. Industrial Engineering Technicians	18.1%
30. Museum Technicians and Conservators	18.1%
31. Public Relations Specialists	18.0%
32. Coaches and Scouts	17.9%
33. Geographers	17.8%
34. Logisticians	17.8%
35. Purchasing Agents, Except Wholesale, Retail, and Farm Products	17.8%
36. Forensic Science Technicians	16.7%
37. Operations Research Analysts	15.4%
38. Actuaries	14.8%
39. Loan Officers	14.0%
40. Registered Nurses	14.0%
41. Market Research Analysts	13.5%
42. Veterinary Technologists and Technicians	12.5%
43. Social and Community Service Managers	12.2%
44. Aerospace Engineers	12.0%
45. Electrical and Electronics Repairers, Commercial and Industrial Equipment	12.0%
46. Nuclear Engineers	11.6%
47. Recreational Therapists	11.4%
48. Social and Human Service Assistants	11.4%
49. Accountants and Auditors	11.1%
50. Astronomers	10.9%

The 50 Federal Jobs with the Most Openings

I created this list by sorting all 150 best jobs by the number of federal job openings that each is expected to have per year. (The introduction explains why this figure is a rough estimate.) Jobs with large numbers of openings often provide easier entry for new workers, make it easier to move from one position to another, or are attractive for other reasons. Some of these jobs may also appeal to people re-entering the labor market, part-time workers, and workers who want to move to federal employment from another employer. And some of these jobs pay quite well or have other advantages.

The 50 Federal Jobs with the Most Openings

Job	Annual Openings
1. Postal Service Mail Carriers	10,720
2. Business Operations Specialists, All Other	4,290
3. Compliance Officers, Except Agriculture, Construction, Health and Safety, and Transportation	3,080
4. Management Analysts	1,970
5. Registered Nurses	1,790
6. Postal Service Clerks	1,610
7. Postal Service Mail Sorters, Processors, and Processing Machine Operators	1,170
8. Detectives and Criminal Investigators	1,160
9. Tax Examiners, Collectors, and Revenue Agents	1,060
10. Claims Adjusters, Examiners, and Investigators	1,050
11. Forest and Conservation Technicians	960
12. Lawyers	960
13. Purchasing Agents, Except Wholesale, Retail, and Farm Products	950
14. Social Scientists and Related Workers, All Other	800
15. Air Traffic Controllers	780
16. Accountants and Auditors	740
17. Logisticians	730
18. Biological Scientists, All Other	670
19. Eligibility Interviewers, Government Programs	670
20. Licensed Practical and Licensed Vocational Nurses	590
21. Engineers, All Other	520
22. Postmasters and Mail Superintendents	520
23. Biological Technicians	470
24. Teachers and Instructors, All Other	430
25. Maintenance and Repair Workers, General	420
26. Paralegals and Legal Assistants	420
27. Procurement Clerks	380
28. Correctional Officers and Jailers	350
29. Engineering Technicians, Except Drafters, All Other	340
30. Health Diagnosing and Treating Practitioners, All Other	340
31. Aircraft Mechanics and Service Technicians	330
32. Civil Engineers	320
33. Clergy	310
34. Fire Fighters	310
35. Life, Physical, and Social Science Technicians, All Other	310
36. Budget Analysts	300

The 50 Federal Jobs with the Most Openings

Job	Annual Openings
37. Electronics Engineers, Except Computer	300
38. Natural Sciences Managers	290
39. Healthcare Support Workers, All Other	280
40. Installation, Maintenance, and Repair Workers, All Other	270
41. Financial Examiners	260
42. Occupational Health and Safety Specialists	260
43. First-Line Supervisors/Managers of Police and Detectives	240
44. Mechanical Engineers	240
45. Psychologists, All Other	240
46. Environmental Scientists and Specialists, Including Health	230
47. Physical Scientists, All Other	230
48. Electrical and Electronic Engineering Technicians	220
49. Combined Food Preparation and Serving Workers, Including Fast Food	210
50. Education, Training, and Library Workers, All Other	210

Best Jobs Lists by Demographic

One way to learn about jobs is to find those where certain kinds of people are concentrated. You can use this information in various ways. You can look for jobs with *many* people like you, assuming that these jobs attract these workers for some good reason and that you'll probably fit in well. You can look for jobs with *few* people like you, assuming that you'll find less competition there. In some cases, the lists can give you ideas for jobs to consider that you might otherwise overlook.

All lists in this section were created through a similar process. I began with the 150 best federal jobs and sorted them in order of the primary criterion for each set of lists, producing a list of jobs with a high percentage of workers who fit the criterion, ordered from highest to lowest percentage. For example, when I sorted the 150 jobs based on the percentage of workers age 16 to 29, I set the cutoff point at 15 percent and produced a list of 33 jobs, ranging from a high of 42.5 percent to a low of 15.1 percent. For other criteria, such as number of part-time workers or female workers, I used other cutoff points. From this initial list of jobs with a high percentage of each type of worker, I created four more-specialized lists:

* 25 Best Federal Jobs Overall (the subset of jobs that have the highest combined scores for earnings, growth rate, and number of openings)
* 25 Best-Paying Federal Jobs

⁂ 25 Fastest-Growing Federal Jobs

⁂ 25 Federal Jobs with the Most Openings

Again, each of these four lists includes only federal jobs that have high percentages of different types of workers. The same basic process was used to create all the lists in this section. The lists are very interesting, and I hope you find them helpful.

Best Federal Jobs with the Highest Percentage of Workers Age 16–29

From the starting list of 150 jobs used in this book, this list contains jobs with the highest percentage of federal workers age 16 to 29 (higher than 15 percent), presented in order of the percentage of these young workers in each job. Federal workers typically need more education or training than their counterparts in the private sector, so they tend to be older. Nevertheless, in 35 of the 150 best federal jobs, more than 15 percent of the workers are under age 30.

Best Federal Jobs with the Highest Percentage of Workers Age 16–29	
Job	Percent Age 16–29
1. Forest and Conservation Technicians	40.5%
2. Biological Technicians	38.1%
3. Biomedical Engineers	29.0%
4. Mechanical Engineers	26.1%
5. Nuclear Engineers	24.9%
6. Marine Engineers and Naval Architects	23.5%
7. Life, Physical, and Social Science Technicians, All Other	21.8%
8. Chemical Engineers	21.0%
9. Optometrists	20.8%
10. Financial Examiners	20.8%
11. Museum Technicians and Conservators	20.4%
12. Avionics Technicians	20.2%
13. Air Traffic Controllers	20.0%
14. Computer Hardware Engineers	19.0%
15. Security Guards	18.9%
16. Industrial Engineers	18.5%
17. Aircraft Mechanics and Service Technicians	17.7%
18. Podiatrists	17.6%
19. Statisticians	17.5%

Best Federal Jobs with the Highest Percentage of Workers Age 16–29

Job	Percent Age 16–29
20. Actuaries	17.4%
21. Pharmacy Technicians	17.2%
22. Agricultural Engineers	17.1%
23. Mathematicians	17.0%
24. Correctional Officers and Jailers	17.0%
25. Speech-Language Pathologists	16.8%
26. Installation, Maintenance, and Repair Workers, All Other	16.6%
27. Pharmacists	16.6%
28. First-Line Supervisors/Managers of Police and Detectives	16.4%
29. Computer and Information Research Scientists	16.1%
30. Computer and Information Systems Managers	16.1%
31. Engineers, All Other	16.1%
32. Sailors and Marine Oilers	16.0%
33. Sheet Metal Workers	15.7%
34. Fire Fighters	15.4%
35. Accountants and Auditors	15.1%

The jobs in the following four lists are derived from the preceding list of the federal jobs with the highest percentage of workers age 16–29.

Best Federal Jobs Overall with a High Percentage of Workers Age 16–29

Job	Percent Age 16–29	Annual Earnings	Percent Growth	Annual Openings
1. Air Traffic Controllers	20.0%	$113,840	10.7%	780
2. Financial Examiners	20.8%	$101,770	41.5%	260
3. Computer and Information Research Scientists	16.1%	$99,730	19.5%	200
4. Accountants and Auditors	15.1%	$87,730	11.1%	740
5. Engineers, All Other	16.1%	$110,860	7.6%	520
6. Computer and Information Systems Managers	16.1%	$133,440	8.3%	100
7. Fire Fighters	15.4%	$46,630	19.1%	310
8. Actuaries	17.4%	$113,020	14.8%	10
9. Mechanical Engineers	26.1%	$91,520	8.5%	240
10. Biomedical Engineers	29.0%	$87,830	62.8%	30
11. Pharmacists	16.6%	$107,330	7.7%	190
12. Nuclear Engineers	24.9%	$91,050	11.6%	50
13. Industrial Engineers	18.5%	$86,260	18.9%	40

(continued)

(continued)

Best Federal Jobs Overall with a High Percentage of Workers Age 16–29

Job	Percent Age 16–29	Annual Earnings	Percent Growth	Annual Openings
14. Pharmacy Technicians	17.2%	$38,870	18.5%	210
15. Aircraft Mechanics and Service Technicians	17.7%	$53,750	7.6%	330
16. Podiatrists	17.6%	$110,850	9.4%	10
17. Marine Engineers and Naval Architects	23.5%	$100,920	8.9%	30
18. Correctional Officers and Jailers	17.0%	$53,360	7.6%	350
19. Museum Technicians and Conservators	20.4%	$38,450	18.1%	120
20. Sailors and Marine Oilers	16.0%	$37,300	19.6%	80
21. First-Line Supervisors/Managers of Police and Detectives	16.4%	$93,390	6.8%	240
22. Computer Hardware Engineers	19.0%	$100,560	7.6%	110
23. Installation, Maintenance, and Repair Workers, All Other	16.6%	$49,640	7.8%	270
24. Life, Physical, and Social Science Technicians, All Other	21.8%	$48,280	7.7%	310
25. Chemical Engineers	21.0%	$97,350	7.8%	20

Best-Paying Federal Jobs with a High Percentage of Workers Age 16–29

Job	Percent Age 16–29	Annual Earnings
1. Computer and Information Systems Managers	16.1%	$133,440
2. Air Traffic Controllers	20.0%	$113,840
3. Actuaries	17.4%	$113,020
4. Engineers, All Other	16.1%	$110,860
5. Podiatrists	17.6%	$110,850
6. Pharmacists	16.6%	$107,330
7. Mathematicians	17.0%	$104,540
8. Financial Examiners	20.8%	$101,770
9. Marine Engineers and Naval Architects	23.5%	$100,920
10. Computer Hardware Engineers	19.0%	$100,560
11. Computer and Information Research Scientists	16.1%	$99,730
12. Chemical Engineers	21.0%	$97,350
13. First-Line Supervisors/Managers of Police and Detectives	16.4%	$93,390
14. Statisticians	17.5%	$92,720
15. Mechanical Engineers	26.1%	$91,520
16. Nuclear Engineers	24.9%	$91,050

Best-Paying Federal Jobs with a High Percentage of Workers Age 16–29

Job	Percent Age 16–29	Annual Earnings
17. Biomedical Engineers	29.0%	$87,830
18. Accountants and Auditors	15.1%	$87,730
19. Industrial Engineers	18.5%	$86,260
20. Speech-Language Pathologists	16.8%	$81,130
21. Optometrists	20.8%	$76,720
22. Agricultural Engineers	17.1%	$74,380
23. Aircraft Mechanics and Service Technicians	17.7%	$53,750
24. Correctional Officers and Jailers	17.0%	$53,360
25. Avionics Technicians	20.2%	$51,650

Fastest-Growing Federal Jobs with a High Percentage of Workers Age 16–29

Job	Percent Age 16–29	Percent Growth
1. Biomedical Engineers	29.0%	62.8%
2. Financial Examiners	20.8%	41.5%
3. Sailors and Marine Oilers	16.0%	19.6%
4. Computer and Information Research Scientists	16.1%	19.5%
5. Fire Fighters	15.4%	19.1%
6. Industrial Engineers	18.5%	18.9%
7. Pharmacy Technicians	17.2%	18.5%
8. Museum Technicians and Conservators	20.4%	18.1%
9. Actuaries	17.4%	14.8%
10. Nuclear Engineers	24.9%	11.6%
11. Accountants and Auditors	15.1%	11.1%
12. Air Traffic Controllers	20.0%	10.7%
13. Agricultural Engineers	17.1%	9.5%
14. Podiatrists	17.6%	9.4%
15. Optometrists	20.8%	9.1%
16. Marine Engineers and Naval Architects	23.5%	8.9%
17. Mechanical Engineers	26.1%	8.5%
18. Computer and Information Systems Managers	16.1%	8.3%
19. Security Guards	18.9%	8.3%
20. Avionics Technicians	20.2%	7.9%
21. Speech-Language Pathologists	16.8%	7.9%

(continued)

(continued)

Fastest-Growing Federal Jobs with a High Percentage of Workers Age 16–29

Job	Percent Age 16–29	Percent Growth
22. Chemical Engineers	21.0%	7.8%
23. Installation, Maintenance, and Repair Workers, All Other	16.6%	7.8%
24. Life, Physical, and Social Science Technicians, All Other	21.8%	7.7%
25. Pharmacists	16.6%	7.7%

Federal Jobs with the Most Openings with a High Percentage of Workers Age 16–29

Job	Percent Age 16–29	Annual Openings
1. Forest and Conservation Technicians	40.5%	960
2. Air Traffic Controllers	20.0%	780
3. Accountants and Auditors	15.1%	740
4. Engineers, All Other	16.1%	520
5. Biological Technicians	38.1%	470
6. Correctional Officers and Jailers	17.0%	350
7. Aircraft Mechanics and Service Technicians	17.7%	330
8. Fire Fighters	15.4%	310
9. Life, Physical, and Social Science Technicians, All Other	21.8%	310
10. Installation, Maintenance, and Repair Workers, All Other	16.6%	270
11. Financial Examiners	20.8%	260
12. First-Line Supervisors/Managers of Police and Detectives	16.4%	240
13. Mechanical Engineers	26.1%	240
14. Pharmacy Technicians	17.2%	210
15. Computer and Information Research Scientists	16.1%	200
16. Pharmacists	16.6%	190
17. Sheet Metal Workers	15.7%	160
18. Statisticians	17.5%	140
19. Museum Technicians and Conservators	20.4%	120
20. Security Guards	18.9%	120
21. Computer Hardware Engineers	19.0%	110
22. Computer and Information Systems Managers	16.1%	100
23. Sailors and Marine Oilers	16.0%	80
24. Nuclear Engineers	24.9%	50
25. Avionics Technicians	20.2%	40

Best Federal Jobs with a High Percentage of Workers Age 55 and Over

In this set of lists, all the jobs have more than 35 percent of workers age 55 and over. Older workers don't change careers as often as younger ones do, and on average, they tend to have been in their jobs for quite some time. Many of the federal jobs with the highest percentages of workers age 55 and over—and those with the highest earnings— require considerable preparation, either through experience or through education and training. The highly skilled workers in these jobs, after investing a lot of time and money in lengthy career preparation, tend to resist career change or retirement so they can recoup more of their investment. Many of these jobs also have modest physical demands that older workers can handle easily.

Highly skilled older workers who are interested in changing careers may also want to consider some of the jobs on the following list. Some of these jobs would make good "retirement" jobs that a worker could continue to pursue, perhaps part time, after leaving federal employment. Others may be long-term targets for younger workers because the high percentage of older workers indicates the likelihood of future job openings.

Best Federal Jobs with the Highest Percentage of Workers Age 55 and Over

Job	Percent Age 55 and Over
1. Clergy	55.7%
2. Directors, Religious Activities and Education	55.7%
3. Librarians	54.2%
4. Transportation Inspectors	48.7%
5. Construction and Building Inspectors	46.1%
6. Dentists	46.1%
7. Astronomers	45.1%
8. Veterinarians	43.9%
9. Interpreters and Translators	43.2%
10. Instructional Coordinators	42.5%
11. Geoscientists, Except Hydrologists and Geographers	42.2%
12. Arbitrators, Mediators, and Conciliators	41.3%
13. Administrative Law Judges, Adjudicators, and Hearing Officers	41.3%
14. Motor Vehicle Operators, All Other	40.9%
15. Architects, Except Landscape and Naval	40.3%
16. Medical Scientists, Except Epidemiologists	40.0%

(continued)

(continued)

Best Federal Jobs with the Highest Percentage of Workers Age 55 and Over

Job	Percent Age 55 and Over
17. Transportation, Storage, and Distribution Managers	39.8%
18. Social and Community Service Managers	39.6%
19. Animal Scientists	38.5%
20. Soil and Plant Scientists	37.9%
21. Petroleum Engineers	37.7%
22. Funeral Directors	37.5%
23. Physicists	36.6%
24. Real Estate Sales Agents	36.3%
25. Chemists	35.9%
26. Writers and Authors	35.5%
27. Medical and Health Services Managers	35.2%
28. Anthropologists and Archeologists	35.1%
29. Technical Writers	35.1%

The jobs in the following four lists are derived from the preceding list of the federal jobs with the highest percentage of workers age 55 and over.

Best Federal Jobs Overall with a High Percentage of Workers Age 55 and Over

Job	Percent Age 55 and Over	Annual Earnings	Percent Growth	Annual Openings
1. Transportation Inspectors	48.7%	$100,100	18.3%	150
2. Dentists	46.1%	$137,950	9.9%	80
3. Medical Scientists, Except Epidemiologists	40.0%	$110,260	29.0%	50
4. Medical and Health Services Managers	35.2%	$104,530	7.6%	190
5. Astronomers	45.1%	$136,010	10.9%	20
6. Clergy	55.7%	$74,360	10.2%	310
7. Chemists	35.9%	$98,860	7.7%	150
8. Physicists	36.6%	$111,370	7.5%	110
9. Petroleum Engineers	37.7%	$96,480	30.0%	10
10. Real Estate Sales Agents	36.3%	$73,050	8.5%	170
11. Writers and Authors	35.5%	$80,410	9.7%	110

Best Federal Jobs Overall with a High Percentage of Workers Age 55 and Over

Job	Percent Age 55 and Over	Annual Earnings	Percent Growth	Annual Openings
12. Administrative Law Judges, Adjudicators, and Hearing Officers	41.3%	$125,360	7.4%	70
13. Animal Scientists	38.5%	$101,350	10.0%	10
14. Anthropologists and Archeologists	35.1%	$70,400	19.9%	70
15. Arbitrators, Mediators, and Conciliators	41.3%	$119,740	9.5%	10
16. Transportation, Storage, and Distribution Managers	39.8%	$94,890	–5.7%	160
17. Directors, Religious Activities and Education	55.7%	$89,210	10.5%	20
18. Social and Community Service Managers	39.6%	$91,140	12.2%	10
19. Instructional Coordinators	42.5%	$83,910	7.6%	80
20. Geoscientists, Except Hydrologists and Geographers	42.2%	$92,410	7.4%	80
21. Construction and Building Inspectors	46.1%	$63,330	7.8%	80
22. Technical Writers	35.1%	$73,340	10.0%	30
23. Funeral Directors	37.5%	$67,620	22.5%	10
24. Interpreters and Translators	43.2%	$67,600	18.4%	20
25. Motor Vehicle Operators, All Other	40.9%	$44,020	7.7%	110

Best-Paying Federal Jobs with a High Percentage of Workers Age 55 and Over

Job	Percent Age 55 and Over	Annual Earnings
1. Dentists	46.1%	$137,950
2. Astronomers	45.1%	$136,010
3. Administrative Law Judges, Adjudicators, and Hearing Officers	41.3%	$125,360
4. Arbitrators, Mediators, and Conciliators	41.3%	$119,740
5. Physicists	36.6%	$111,370
6. Medical Scientists, Except Epidemiologists	40.0%	$110,260
7. Medical and Health Services Managers	35.2%	$104,530
8. Animal Scientists	38.5%	$101,350
9. Transportation Inspectors	48.7%	$100,100
10. Chemists	35.9%	$98,860
11. Petroleum Engineers	37.7%	$96,480

(continued)

(continued)

Best-Paying Federal Jobs with a High Percentage of Workers Age 55 and Over

Job	Percent Age 55 and Over	Annual Earnings
12. Transportation, Storage, and Distribution Managers	39.8%	$94,890
13. Geoscientists, Except Hydrologists and Geographers	42.2%	$92,410
14. Social and Community Service Managers	39.6%	$91,140
15. Directors, Religious Activities and Education	55.7%	$89,210
16. Architects, Except Landscape and Naval	40.3%	$89,070
17. Instructional Coordinators	42.5%	$83,910
18. Veterinarians	43.9%	$81,130
19. Writers and Authors	35.5%	$80,410
20. Librarians	54.2%	$77,970
21. Clergy	55.7%	$74,360
22. Technical Writers	35.1%	$73,340
23. Real Estate Sales Agents	36.3%	$73,050
24. Soil and Plant Scientists	37.9%	$71,460
25. Anthropologists and Archeologists	35.1%	$70,400

Fastest-Growing Federal Jobs with a High Percentage of Workers Age 55 and Over

Job	Percent Age 55 and Over	Percent Growth
1. Petroleum Engineers	37.7%	30.0%
2. Medical Scientists, Except Epidemiologists	40.0%	29.0%
3. Funeral Directors	37.5%	22.5%
4. Anthropologists and Archeologists	35.1%	19.9%
5. Interpreters and Translators	43.2%	18.4%
6. Transportation Inspectors	48.7%	18.3%
7. Social and Community Service Managers	39.6%	12.2%
8. Astronomers	45.1%	10.9%
9. Directors, Religious Activities and Education	55.7%	10.5%
10. Clergy	55.7%	10.2%
11. Animal Scientists	38.5%	10.0%
12. Technical Writers	35.1%	10.0%
13. Dentists	46.1%	9.9%

Fastest-Growing Federal Jobs with a High Percentage of Workers Age 55 and Over

Job	Percent Age 55 and Over	Percent Growth
14. Writers and Authors	35.5%	9.7%
15. Arbitrators, Mediators, and Conciliators	41.3%	9.5%
16. Real Estate Sales Agents	36.3%	8.5%
17. Construction and Building Inspectors	46.1%	7.8%
18. Librarians	54.2%	7.8%
19. Chemists	35.9%	7.7%
20. Motor Vehicle Operators, All Other	40.9%	7.7%
21. Instructional Coordinators	42.5%	7.6%
22. Medical and Health Services Managers	35.2%	7.6%
23. Veterinarians	43.9%	7.6%
24. Physicists	36.6%	7.5%
25. Soil and Plant Scientists	37.9%	7.5%

Federal Jobs with the Most Openings with a High Percentage of Workers Age 55 and Over

Job	Percent Age 55 and Over	Annual Openings
1. Clergy	55.7%	310
2. Medical and Health Services Managers	35.2%	190
3. Real Estate Sales Agents	36.3%	170
4. Transportation, Storage, and Distribution Managers	39.8%	160
5. Chemists	35.9%	150
6. Transportation Inspectors	48.7%	150
7. Motor Vehicle Operators, All Other	40.9%	110
8. Physicists	36.6%	110
9. Writers and Authors	35.5%	110
10. Construction and Building Inspectors	46.1%	80
11. Dentists	46.1%	80
12. Geoscientists, Except Hydrologists and Geographers	42.2%	80
13. Instructional Coordinators	42.5%	80
14. Administrative Law Judges, Adjudicators, and Hearing Officers	41.3%	70
15. Anthropologists and Archeologists	35.1%	70

(continued)

(continued)

Federal Jobs with the Most Openings with a High Percentage of Workers Age 55 and Over		
Job	Percent Age 55 and Over	Annual Openings
16. Soil and Plant Scientists	37.9%	70
17. Architects, Except Landscape and Naval	40.3%	50
18. Medical Scientists, Except Epidemiologists	40.0%	50
19. Veterinarians	43.9%	50
20. Librarians	54.2%	40
21. Technical Writers	35.1%	30
22. Astronomers	45.1%	20
23. Directors, Religious Activities and Education	55.7%	20
24. Interpreters and Translators	43.2%	20
25. Animal Scientists	38.5%	10

Best Federal Jobs Employing a High Percentage of Women

Among all the federal workers in the United States, 55.1 percent are female and 44.8 percent male. To create the lists that follow, I sorted the 150 best jobs according to the percentages of women and men in the workforce. I created one set of lists for jobs with more than 60 percent women and another set of lists for jobs with more than 80 percent men.

It's important to understand that these lists are not meant to restrict women or men from considering job options; my reason for including these lists is exactly the opposite. I hope the lists help people see possibilities that they might not otherwise have considered. The federal government is committed to achieving a better gender balance in jobs that have traditionally been held by one sex only. That means that, all else being equal, you may find better job opportunities in an occupation that presently is dominated by the opposite sex.

It's interesting to note that female federal workers earned an average (mean) of $57,664 in 2005, which was 87 percent of the $66,334 earned by male federal workers. Compare that to the economy as a whole, where women earned only 77 percent as much as men that year. In federal jobs, the wage disparity had narrowed to 90 percent by 2010. When you compare federally employed women with men *in the same occupation,* you find the women earning about 83 percent of the wages of the men. Much of this pay difference may happen because the women in federal jobs have an average of about 7 percent fewer years of service.

Best Federal Jobs Employing the Highest Percentage of Women

Job	Percent Women
1. Medical Records and Health Information Technicians	86.1%
2. Registered Nurses	84.7%
3. Licensed Practical and Licensed Vocational Nurses	84.1%
4. Speech-Language Pathologists	80.4%
5. Paralegals and Legal Assistants	76.7%
6. Librarians	74.4%
7. Pharmacy Technicians	72.9%
8. Budget Analysts	71.9%
9. Eligibility Interviewers, Government Programs	71.8%
10. Medical and Clinical Laboratory Technologists	71.2%
11. Recreational Therapists	70.2%
12. Purchasing Managers	68.9%
13. Writers and Authors	67.0%
14. Claims Adjusters, Examiners, and Investigators	65.7%
15. Education, Training, and Library Workers, All Other	63.2%
16. Physical Therapists	61.7%
17. Tax Examiners, Collectors, and Revenue Agents	61.6%
18. Postmasters and Mail Superintendents	61.0%
19. Pharmacists	60.5%

The jobs in the following four lists are derived from the preceding list of the federal jobs employing the highest percentage of women. Keep in mind that the earnings estimates in the following lists apply to *all* federal workers in these jobs, not just women. The earnings differences for the occupations in the following lists may be significantly higher or lower.

Best Federal Jobs Overall Employing a High Percentage of Women

Job	Percent Women	Annual Earnings	Percent Growth	Annual Openings
1. Registered Nurses	84.7%	$74,790	14.0%	1,790
2. Budget Analysts	71.9%	$73,120	19.9%	300
3. Paralegals and Legal Assistants	76.7%	$60,500	18.2%	420
4. Purchasing Managers	68.9%	$119,840	7.4%	70

(continued)

(continued)

Best Federal Jobs Overall Employing a High Percentage of Women

Job	Percent Women	Annual Earnings	Percent Growth	Annual Openings
5. Speech-Language Pathologists	80.4%	$81,130	7.9%	40
6. Physical Therapists	61.7%	$75,960	9.7%	50
7. Claims Adjusters, Examiners, and Investigators	65.7%	$66,580	19.5%	1,050
8. Licensed Practical and Licensed Vocational Nurses	84.1%	$43,160	7.6%	590
9. Recreational Therapists	70.2%	$63,780	11.4%	30
10. Medical Records and Health Information Technicians	86.1%	$44,460	7.6%	150
11. Pharmacy Technicians	72.9%	$38,870	18.5%	210
12. Eligibility Interviewers, Government Programs	71.8%	$46,430	8.6%	670
13. Librarians	74.4%	$77,970	7.8%	40
14. Tax Examiners, Collectors, and Revenue Agents	61.6%	$56,420	19.5%	1,060
15. Writers and Authors	67.0%	$80,410	9.7%	110
16. Pharmacists	60.5%	$107,330	7.7%	190
17. Postmasters and Mail Superintendents	61.0%	$58,780	−15.1%	520
18. Medical and Clinical Laboratory Technologists	71.2%	$61,630	7.7%	120
19. Education, Training, and Library Workers, All Other	63.2%	$38,860	7.6%	210

Best-Paying Federal Jobs Employing a High Percentage of Women

Job	Percent Women	Annual Earnings
1. Purchasing Managers	68.9%	$119,840
2. Pharmacists	60.5%	$107,330
3. Speech-Language Pathologists	80.4%	$81,130
4. Writers and Authors	67.0%	$80,410
5. Librarians	74.4%	$77,970
6. Physical Therapists	61.7%	$75,960
7. Registered Nurses	84.7%	$74,790
8. Budget Analysts	71.9%	$73,120
9. Claims Adjusters, Examiners, and Investigators	65.7%	$66,580
10. Recreational Therapists	70.2%	$63,780
11. Medical and Clinical Laboratory Technologists	71.2%	$61,630
12. Paralegals and Legal Assistants	76.7%	$60,500
13. Postmasters and Mail Superintendents	61.0%	$58,780

Best-Paying Federal Jobs Employing a High Percentage of Women

Job	Percent Women	Annual Earnings
14. Tax Examiners, Collectors, and Revenue Agents	61.6%	$56,420
15. Eligibility Interviewers, Government Programs	71.8%	$46,430
16. Medical Records and Health Information Technicians	86.1%	$44,460
17. Licensed Practical and Licensed Vocational Nurses	84.1%	$43,160
18. Pharmacy Technicians	72.9%	$38,870
19. Education, Training, and Library Workers, All Other	63.2%	$38,860

Fastest-Growing Federal Jobs Employing a High Percentage of Women

Job	Percent Women	Percent Growth
1. Budget Analysts	71.9%	19.9%
2. Claims Adjusters, Examiners, and Investigators	65.7%	19.5%
3. Tax Examiners, Collectors, and Revenue Agents	61.6%	19.5%
4. Pharmacy Technicians	72.9%	18.5%
5. Paralegals and Legal Assistants	76.7%	18.2%
6. Registered Nurses	84.7%	14.0%
7. Recreational Therapists	70.2%	11.4%
8. Physical Therapists	61.7%	9.7%
9. Writers and Authors	67.0%	9.7%
10. Eligibility Interviewers, Government Programs	71.8%	8.6%
11. Speech-Language Pathologists	80.4%	7.9%
12. Librarians	74.4%	7.8%
13. Medical and Clinical Laboratory Technologists	71.2%	7.7%
14. Pharmacists	60.5%	7.7%
15. Education, Training, and Library Workers, All Other	63.2%	7.6%
16. Licensed Practical and Licensed Vocational Nurses	84.1%	7.6%
17. Medical Records and Health Information Technicians	86.1%	7.6%
18. Purchasing Managers	68.9%	7.4%
19. Postmasters and Mail Superintendents	61.0%	−15.1%

Federal Jobs with the Most Openings Employing a High Percentage of Women

Job	Percent Women	Annual Openings
1. Registered Nurses	84.7%	1,790
2. Tax Examiners, Collectors, and Revenue Agents	61.6%	1,060
3. Claims Adjusters, Examiners, and Investigators	65.7%	1,050
4. Eligibility Interviewers, Government Programs	71.8%	670
5. Licensed Practical and Licensed Vocational Nurses	84.1%	590
6. Postmasters and Mail Superintendents	61.0%	520
7. Paralegals and Legal Assistants	76.7%	420
8. Budget Analysts	71.9%	300
9. Education, Training, and Library Workers, All Other	63.2%	210
10. Pharmacy Technicians	72.9%	210
11. Pharmacists	60.5%	190
12. Medical Records and Health Information Technicians	86.1%	150
13. Medical and Clinical Laboratory Technologists	71.2%	120
14. Writers and Authors	67.0%	110
15. Purchasing Managers	68.9%	70
16. Physical Therapists	61.7%	50
17. Librarians	74.4%	40
18. Speech-Language Pathologists	80.4%	40
19. Recreational Therapists	70.2%	30

Best Federal Jobs Employing a High Percentage of Men

If you haven't already read the intro to the previous group of lists, "Best Federal Jobs Employing a High Percentage of Women," consider doing so. Much of the content there applies to these lists as well.

I didn't include these groups of lists with the assumption that men should consider only jobs with high percentages of men or that women should consider only jobs with high percentages of women. Instead, these lists are here because I think they are interesting and perhaps helpful in considering nontraditional career options. For example, some men would do very well in and enjoy some of the jobs with high percentages of women but may not have considered them seriously. Similarly, some women would very much enjoy and do well in some jobs that traditionally have been held by high percentages of men. I hope that these lists help you consider options that you simply didn't seriously consider because of gender stereotypes.

In the jobs in the following lists, more than 80 percent of the workers are men, but increasing numbers of women are entering many of these jobs.

Best Federal Jobs Employing the Highest Percentage of Men

Job	Percent Men
1. Airline Pilots, Copilots, and Flight Engineers	97.8%
2. Captains, Mates, and Pilots of Water Vessels	97.4%
3. Fire Fighters	97.4%
4. Plant and System Operators, All Other	96.6%
5. Ship Engineers	96.5%
6. Aircraft Mechanics and Service Technicians	95.7%
7. Construction and Building Inspectors	94.6%
8. Industrial Machinery Mechanics	94.3%
9. Maintenance and Repair Workers, General	94.0%
10. Sailors and Marine Oilers	93.7%
11. Avionics Technicians	93.1%
12. Transportation Inspectors	92.6%
13. Installation, Maintenance, and Repair Workers, All Other	92.5%
14. Motor Vehicle Operators, All Other	92.2%
15. Electrical and Electronics Repairers, Commercial and Industrial Equipment	91.8%
16. First-Line Supervisors/Managers of Police and Detectives	91.3%
17. Electrical and Electronic Engineering Technicians	90.7%
18. Engineering Technicians, Except Drafters, All Other	90.3%
19. Mechanical Engineers	89.9%
20. Engineers, All Other	89.8%
21. Precision Instrument and Equipment Repairers, All Other	89.7%
22. Electronics Engineers, Except Computer	89.1%
23. Electrical Engineers	88.7%
24. Industrial Engineering Technicians	88.6%
25. Nuclear Engineers	88.2%
26. Security Guards	87.8%
27. Marine Engineers and Naval Architects	86.6%
28. Clergy	86.3%
29. Directors, Religious Activities and Education	86.3%
30. Petroleum Engineers	86.0%
31. Correctional Officers and Jailers	85.9%
32. Detectives and Criminal Investigators	85.1%
33. Physicists	85.0%
34. Aerospace Engineers	84.2%

(continued)

(continued)

Best Federal Jobs Employing the Highest Percentage of Men

Job	Percent Men
35. Funeral Directors	84.0%
36. Air Traffic Controllers	83.9%
37. Engineering Managers	83.9%
38. Coaches and Scouts	82.9%
39. Civil Engineers	82.6%
40. Materials Engineers	82.3%
41. Computer Hardware Engineers	82.1%
42. Media and Communication Equipment Workers, All Other	81.9%
43. Astronomers	80.8%
44. Surveyors	80.7%
45. Forest and Conservation Technicians	80.5%
46. Agricultural Engineers	80.4%

The jobs in the following four lists are derived from the preceding list of the federal jobs employing the highest percentage of men. Keep in mind that the earnings estimates in the following lists are based on a survey of *all* workers, not just men. The earnings differences for the occupations in the following lists may be significantly higher or lower.

Best Federal Jobs Overall Employing a High Percentage of Men

Job	Percent Men	Annual Earnings	Percent Growth	Annual Openings
1. Air Traffic Controllers	83.9%	$113,840	10.7%	780
2. Detectives and Criminal Investigators	85.1%	$73,320	29.8%	1,160
3. Aerospace Engineers	84.2%	$109,190	12.0%	200
4. Engineers, All Other	89.8%	$110,860	7.6%	520
5. Transportation Inspectors	92.6%	$100,100	18.3%	150
6. Materials Engineers	82.3%	$108,670	19.4%	30
7. Mechanical Engineers	89.9%	$91,520	8.5%	240
8. Clergy	86.3%	$74,360	10.2%	310
9. Engineering Managers	83.9%	$125,730	7.6%	110
10. Astronomers	80.8%	$136,010	10.9%	20
11. Petroleum Engineers	86.0%	$96,480	30.0%	10
12. Civil Engineers	82.6%	$87,900	7.6%	320
13. Electronics Engineers, Except Computer	89.1%	$102,730	7.5%	300
14. Fire Fighters	97.4%	$46,630	19.1%	310

Best Federal Jobs Overall Employing a High Percentage of Men

Job	Percent Men	Annual Earnings	Percent Growth	Annual Openings
15. Computer Hardware Engineers	82.1%	$100,560	7.6%	110
16. Nuclear Engineers	88.2%	$91,050	11.6%	50
17. Captains, Mates, and Pilots of Water Vessels	97.4%	$63,620	28.8%	50
18. Engineering Technicians, Except Drafters, All Other	90.3%	$67,080	7.6%	340
19. Electrical and Electronics Repairers, Commercial and Industrial Equipment	91.8%	$53,870	12.0%	160
20. Marine Engineers and Naval Architects	86.6%	$100,920	8.9%	30
21. Physicists	85.0%	$111,370	7.5%	110
22. Industrial Machinery Mechanics	94.3%	$54,090	24.7%	70
23. Media and Communication Equipment Workers, All Other	81.9%	$77,920	7.6%	150
24. First-Line Supervisors/Managers of Police and Detectives	91.3%	$93,390	6.8%	240
25. Correctional Officers and Jailers	85.9%	$53,360	7.6%	350

Best-Paying Federal Jobs Employing a High Percentage of Men

Job	Percent Men	Annual Earnings
1. Astronomers	80.8%	$136,010
2. Engineering Managers	83.9%	$125,730
3. Air Traffic Controllers	83.9%	$113,840
4. Physicists	85.0%	$111,370
5. Engineers, All Other	89.8%	$110,860
6. Aerospace Engineers	84.2%	$109,190
7. Materials Engineers	82.3%	$108,670
8. Electronics Engineers, Except Computer	89.1%	$102,730
9. Marine Engineers and Naval Architects	86.6%	$100,920
10. Computer Hardware Engineers	82.1%	$100,560
11. Transportation Inspectors	92.6%	$100,100
12. Airline Pilots, Copilots, and Flight Engineers	97.8%	$97,290
13. Petroleum Engineers	86.0%	$96,480
14. First-Line Supervisors/Managers of Police and Detectives	91.3%	$93,390
15. Mechanical Engineers	89.9%	$91,520
16. Nuclear Engineers	88.2%	$91,050
17. Directors, Religious Activities and Education	86.3%	$89,210

(continued)

(continued)

Best-Paying Federal Jobs Employing a High Percentage of Men

Job	Percent Men	Annual Earnings
18. Electrical Engineers	88.7%	$89,130
19. Civil Engineers	82.6%	$87,900
20. Surveyors	80.7%	$81,140
21. Media and Communication Equipment Workers, All Other	81.9%	$77,920
22. Agricultural Engineers	80.4%	$74,380
23. Clergy	86.3%	$74,360
24. Detectives and Criminal Investigators	85.1%	$73,320
25. Funeral Directors	84.0%	$67,620

Fastest-Growing Federal Jobs Employing a High Percentage of Men

Job	Percent Men	Percent Growth
1. Petroleum Engineers	86.0%	30.0%
2. Detectives and Criminal Investigators	85.1%	29.8%
3. Ship Engineers	96.5%	29.8%
4. Captains, Mates, and Pilots of Water Vessels	97.4%	28.8%
5. Industrial Machinery Mechanics	94.3%	24.7%
6. Funeral Directors	84.0%	22.5%
7. Sailors and Marine Oilers	93.7%	19.6%
8. Materials Engineers	82.3%	19.4%
9. Fire Fighters	97.4%	19.1%
10. Transportation Inspectors	92.6%	18.3%
11. Industrial Engineering Technicians	88.6%	18.1%
12. Coaches and Scouts	82.9%	17.9%
13. Aerospace Engineers	84.2%	12.0%
14. Electrical and Electronics Repairers, Commercial and Industrial Equipment	91.8%	12.0%
15. Nuclear Engineers	88.2%	11.6%
16. Astronomers	80.8%	10.9%
17. Air Traffic Controllers	83.9%	10.7%
18. Directors, Religious Activities and Education	86.3%	10.5%
19. Clergy	86.3%	10.2%
20. Agricultural Engineers	80.4%	9.5%
21. Marine Engineers and Naval Architects	86.6%	8.9%

Fastest-Growing Federal Jobs Employing a High Percentage of Men

Job	Percent Men	Percent Growth
22. Mechanical Engineers	89.9%	8.5%
23. Security Guards	87.8%	8.3%
24. Surveyors	80.7%	8.0%
25. Avionics Technicians	93.1%	7.9%

Federal Jobs with the Most Openings Employing a High Percentage of Men

Job	Percent Men	Annual Openings
1. Detectives and Criminal Investigators	85.1%	1,160
2. Forest and Conservation Technicians	80.5%	960
3. Air Traffic Controllers	83.9%	780
4. Engineers, All Other	89.8%	520
5. Maintenance and Repair Workers, General	94.0%	420
6. Correctional Officers and Jailers	85.9%	350
7. Engineering Technicians, Except Drafters, All Other	90.3%	340
8. Aircraft Mechanics and Service Technicians	95.7%	330
9. Civil Engineers	82.6%	320
10. Clergy	86.3%	310
11. Fire Fighters	97.4%	310
12. Electronics Engineers, Except Computer	89.1%	300
13. Installation, Maintenance, and Repair Workers, All Other	92.5%	270
14. First-Line Supervisors/Managers of Police and Detectives	91.3%	240
15. Mechanical Engineers	89.9%	240
16. Electrical and Electronic Engineering Technicians	90.7%	220
17. Aerospace Engineers	84.2%	200
18. Electrical and Electronics Repairers, Commercial and Industrial Equipment	91.8%	160
19. Media and Communication Equipment Workers, All Other	81.9%	150
20. Transportation Inspectors	92.6%	150
21. Security Guards	87.8%	120
22. Computer Hardware Engineers	82.1%	110
23. Engineering Managers	83.9%	110
24. Motor Vehicle Operators, All Other	92.2%	110
25. Physicists	85.0%	110

Best Federal Jobs Employing a High Percentage of Part-Time Workers

The following lists of part-time federal jobs includes those in which 10 percent or more of the federal workers either are on a schedule that is intermittent or have a workday that is less than full time. This definition, which fits 6.5 percent of federal workers, includes job-sharers but does not include full-time seasonal workers.

Some part-time workers want the freedom of time this arrangement can provide, but others may be in this category because they can't find full-time employment. These folks may work in other full- or part-time jobs to make ends meet. If you want to work part time now or in the future, these lists will help you identify federal jobs that are more likely to provide that opportunity. If you want full-time work, the lists may also help you identify jobs for which such opportunities are more difficult to find. In either case, it's good information to know in advance.

Best Federal Jobs Employing the Highest Percentage of Part-Time Workers

Job	Percent Part-Time
1. Funeral Directors	93.2%
2. Dentists	32.5%
3. Clergy	24.9%
4. Directors, Religious Activities and Education	24.9%
5. Veterinary Technologists and Technicians	23.3%
6. Podiatrists	23.1%
7. Biological Technicians	22.1%
8. Optometrists	19.4%
9. Healthcare Support Workers, All Other	18.3%
10. Agricultural Inspectors	17.2%
11. Medical Scientists, Except Epidemiologists	17.2%
12. Pharmacists	16.1%
13. Interpreters and Translators	15.0%
14. Speech-Language Pathologists	14.9%
15. Health Diagnosing and Treating Practitioners, All Other	14.4%
16. Education, Training, and Library Workers, All Other	14.1%
17. Life, Physical, and Social Science Technicians, All Other	14.0%
18. Museum Technicians and Conservators	13.8%
19. Physician Assistants	12.4%
20. Physical Therapists	11.3%
21. Veterinarians	11.0%
22. Registered Nurses	10.8%

The jobs in the following four lists are derived from the preceding list of the federal jobs employing the highest percentage of part-time workers. Keep in mind that the earnings estimates in the following lists are based on a survey of *full-time* federal workers.

Best Federal Jobs Overall Employing a High Percentage of Part-Time Workers

Job	Percent Part-Time	Annual Earnings	Percent Growth	Annual Openings
1. Medical Scientists, Except Epidemiologists	17.2%	$110,260	29.0%	50
2. Registered Nurses	10.8%	$74,790	14.0%	1,790
3. Physician Assistants	12.4%	$83,370	18.3%	90
4. Dentists	32.5%	$137,950	9.9%	80
5. Clergy	24.9%	$74,360	10.2%	310
6. Health Diagnosing and Treating Practitioners, All Other	14.4%	$85,610	7.6%	340
7. Pharmacists	16.1%	$107,330	7.7%	190
8. Agricultural Inspectors	17.2%	$44,460	19.7%	140
9. Directors, Religious Activities and Education	24.9%	$89,210	10.5%	20
10. Life, Physical, and Social Science Technicians, All Other	14.0%	$48,280	7.7%	310
11. Physical Therapists	11.3%	$75,960	9.7%	50
12. Podiatrists	23.1%	$110,850	9.4%	10
13. Funeral Directors	93.2%	$67,620	22.5%	10
14. Interpreters and Translators	15.0%	$67,600	18.4%	20
15. Museum Technicians and Conservators	13.8%	$38,450	18.1%	120
16. Speech-Language Pathologists	14.9%	$81,130	7.9%	40
17. Veterinarians	11.0%	$81,130	7.6%	50
18. Biological Technicians	22.1%	$32,850	7.6%	470
19. Optometrists	19.4%	$76,720	9.1%	20
20. Veterinary Technologists and Technicians	23.3%	$46,440	12.5%	30
21. Healthcare Support Workers, All Other	18.3%	$40,020	7.6%	280
22. Education, Training, and Library Workers, All Other	14.1%	$38,860	7.6%	210

Best-Paying Federal Jobs Employing a High Percentage of Part-Time Workers

Job	Percent Part-Time	Annual Earnings
1. Dentists	32.5%	$137,950
2. Podiatrists	23.1%	$110,850
3. Medical Scientists, Except Epidemiologists	17.2%	$110,260
4. Pharmacists	16.1%	$107,330
5. Directors, Religious Activities and Education	24.9%	$89,210
6. Health Diagnosing and Treating Practitioners, All Other	14.4%	$85,610
7. Physician Assistants	12.4%	$83,370
8. Speech-Language Pathologists	14.9%	$81,130
9. Veterinarians	11.0%	$81,130
10. Optometrists	19.4%	$76,720
11. Physical Therapists	11.3%	$75,960
12. Registered Nurses	10.8%	$74,790
13. Clergy	24.9%	$74,360
14. Funeral Directors	93.2%	$67,620
15. Interpreters and Translators	15.0%	$67,600
16. Life, Physical, and Social Science Technicians, All Other	14.0%	$48,280
17. Veterinary Technologists and Technicians	23.3%	$46,440
18. Agricultural Inspectors	17.2%	$44,460
19. Healthcare Support Workers, All Other	18.3%	$40,020
20. Education, Training, and Library Workers, All Other	14.1%	$38,860
21. Museum Technicians and Conservators	13.8%	$38,450
22. Biological Technicians	22.1%	$32,850

Fastest-Growing Federal Jobs Employing a High Percentage of Part-Time Workers

Job	Percent Part-Time	Percent Growth
1. Medical Scientists, Except Epidemiologists	17.2%	29.0%
2. Funeral Directors	93.2%	22.5%
3. Agricultural Inspectors	17.2%	19.7%
4. Interpreters and Translators	15.0%	18.4%
5. Physician Assistants	12.4%	18.3%
6. Museum Technicians and Conservators	13.8%	18.1%
7. Registered Nurses	10.8%	14.0%

Fastest-Growing Federal Jobs Employing a High Percentage of Part-Time Workers

Job	Percent Part-Time	Percent Growth
8. Veterinary Technologists and Technicians	23.3%	12.5%
9. Directors, Religious Activities and Education	24.9%	10.5%
10. Clergy	24.9%	10.2%
11. Dentists	32.5%	9.9%
12. Physical Therapists	11.3%	9.7%
13. Podiatrists	23.1%	9.4%
14. Optometrists	19.4%	9.1%
15. Speech-Language Pathologists	14.9%	7.9%
16. Life, Physical, and Social Science Technicians, All Other	14.0%	7.7%
17. Pharmacists	16.1%	7.7%
18. Biological Technicians	22.1%	7.6%
19. Education, Training, and Library Workers, All Other	14.1%	7.6%
20. Health Diagnosing and Treating Practitioners, All Other	14.4%	7.6%
21. Healthcare Support Workers, All Other	18.3%	7.6%
22. Veterinarians	11.0%	7.6%

Federal Jobs with the Most Openings Employing a High Percentage of Part-Time Workers

Job	Percent Part-Time	Annual Openings
1. Registered Nurses	10.8%	1,790
2. Biological Technicians	22.1%	470
3. Health Diagnosing and Treating Practitioners, All Other	14.4%	340
4. Clergy	24.9%	310
5. Life, Physical, and Social Science Technicians, All Other	14.0%	310
6. Healthcare Support Workers, All Other	18.3%	280
7. Education, Training, and Library Workers, All Other	14.1%	210
8. Pharmacists	16.1%	190
9. Agricultural Inspectors	17.2%	140
10. Museum Technicians and Conservators	13.8%	120
11. Physician Assistants	12.4%	90
12. Dentists	32.5%	80
13. Medical Scientists, Except Epidemiologists	17.2%	50
14. Physical Therapists	11.3%	50

(continued)

(continued)

Federal Jobs with the Most Openings Employing a High Percentage of Part-Time Workers

Job	Percent Part-Time	Annual Openings
15. Veterinarians	11.0%	50
16. Speech-Language Pathologists	14.9%	40
17. Veterinary Technologists and Technicians	23.3%	30
18. Directors, Religious Activities and Education	24.9%	20
19. Interpreters and Translators	15.0%	20
20. Optometrists	19.4%	20
21. Funeral Directors	93.2%	10
22. Podiatrists	23.1%	10

Best Federal Jobs by Location

Some people are willing to move to any location where they can find work. If, however, you have a strong preference for a particular region of the United States, you may be interested in one of the lists in the following set. These lists identify federal occupations for which a large percentage of the workforce is located in a particular region. Unlike the previous sets of lists, these offer only a single "best federal jobs overall" list for each geographical region, ordered by a combination of the usual three economic criteria (earnings, job growth, and job openings), and with no more than 25 jobs in each list.

You probably will not be surprised to learn that many federal jobs are concentrated in the District of Columbia and in its adjacent states. Because so many jobs are located in this dynamic region, I provide a list selected from the 35 best jobs for which 35 percent or more of the federal workers are located in DC and those two states. In the other lists in this set, I assigned an occupation to a region if 20 percent or more of the federal workers are located in that region. Here are the regions that are included and the states assigned to each:

Region	States
DC Area	District of Columbia, Maryland, and Virginia
Northeast	Connecticut, Delaware, Maine, Massachusetts, New Hampshire, New Jersey, New York, Pennsylvania, Rhode Island, and Vermont
Southeast	Alabama, Arkansas, Florida, Georgia, Kentucky, Louisiana, Mississippi, North Carolina, South Carolina, Tennessee, and West Virginia
Midwest	Illinois, Indiana, Iowa, Kansas, Michigan, Minnesota, Missouri, Nebraska, North Dakota, Ohio, South Dakota, and Wisconsin

Region	States
Southwest	Arizona, New Mexico, Oklahoma, and Texas
West	Alaska, California, Colorado, Hawaii, Idaho, Montana, Nevada, Oregon, Utah, Washington, and Wyoming

Best Federal Jobs Concentrated in the DC Area

Job	Percent of Fed Workers in This Region	Annual Earnings	Percent Growth	Annual Openings
1. Financial Examiners	82.9%	$101,770	41.5%	260
2. Lawyers	39.4%	$131,410	8.4%	960
3. Political Scientists	95.2%	$113,050	18.4%	120
4. Medical Scientists, Except Epidemiologists	74.6%	$110,260	29.0%	50
5. Operations Research Analysts	62.9%	$103,780	15.4%	160
6. Budget Analysts	37.0%	$73,120	19.9%	300
7. Computer and Information Systems Managers	39.4%	$133,440	8.3%	100
8. Public Relations Specialists	38.7%	$83,440	18.0%	180
9. Management Analysts	53.0%	$83,140	8.4%	1,970
10. Financial Managers	36.5%	$117,190	7.0%	210
11. Paralegals and Legal Assistants	35.3%	$60,500	18.2%	420
12. Physical Scientists, All Other	36.4%	$104,480	7.6%	230
13. Astronomers	61.4%	$136,010	10.9%	20
14. Biomedical Engineers	47.0%	$87,830	62.8%	30
15. Physicists	58.1%	$111,370	7.5%	110
16. Chemists	47.9%	$98,860	7.7%	150
17. Actuaries	89.5%	$113,020	14.8%	10
18. Writers and Authors	63.6%	$80,410	9.7%	110
19. Museum Technicians and Conservators	56.6%	$38,450	18.1%	120
20. Marine Engineers and Naval Architects	47.9%	$100,920	8.9%	30
21. Forensic Science Technicians	55.8%	$95,620	16.7%	10
22. Economists	73.0%	$104,530	−1.5%	110
23. Statisticians	80.1%	$92,720	6.9%	140
24. Healthcare Support Workers, All Other	46.8%	$40,020	7.6%	280
25. Interpreters and Translators	36.4%	$67,600	18.4%	20
26. Mathematicians	55.6%	$104,540	6.6%	40
27. Chemical Engineers	48.0%	$97,350	7.8%	20
28. Public Relations Managers	38.7%	$140,970	5.9%	10
29. Social and Community Service Managers	37.8%	$91,140	12.2%	10
30. Microbiologists	38.0%	$92,580	7.4%	80

(continued)

(continued)

Best Federal Jobs Concentrated in the DC Area

Job	Percent of Fed Workers in This Region	Annual Earnings	Percent Growth	Annual Openings
31. Librarians	55.1%	$77,970	7.8%	40
32. Graphic Designers	46.0%	$73,130	7.4%	70
33. Producers and Directors	48.9%	$77,300	7.3%	40
34. Set and Exhibit Designers	51.1%	$67,080	7.9%	20
35. Administrative Services Managers	35.4%	$75,950	5.2%	90

Best Federal Jobs Concentrated in the Northeast

Job	Percent of Fed Workers in This Region	Annual Earnings	Percent Growth	Annual Openings
1. Detectives and Criminal Investigators	24.9%	$73,320	29.8%	1,160
2. Aerospace Engineers	20.5%	$109,190	12.0%	200
3. Social Scientists and Related Workers, All Other	31.8%	$75,540	19.3%	800
4. Engineers, All Other	32.2%	$110,860	7.6%	520
5. Accountants and Auditors	33.8%	$87,730	11.1%	740
6. Biological Scientists, All Other	32.3%	$69,860	19.6%	670
7. Logisticians	22.8%	$76,000	17.8%	730
8. Claims Adjusters, Examiners, and Investigators	27.8%	$66,580	19.5%	1,050
9. Compliance Officers, Except Agriculture, Construction, Health and Safety, and Transportation	25.9%	$45,720	29.8%	3,080
10. Tax Examiners, Collectors, and Revenue Agents	25.4%	$56,420	19.5%	1,060
11. Materials Engineers	35.0%	$108,670	19.4%	30
12. Natural Sciences Managers	36.6%	$106,160	7.7%	290
13. Engineering Managers	32.2%	$125,730	7.6%	110
14. Mechanical Engineers	41.6%	$91,520	8.5%	240
15. Biomedical Engineers	58.4%	$87,830	62.8%	30
16. Medical and Health Services Managers	20.3%	$104,530	7.6%	190
17. Psychologists, All Other	25.4%	$91,110	7.8%	240
18. Clergy	23.3%	$74,360	10.2%	310
19. Electronics Engineers, Except Computer	29.5%	$102,730	7.5%	300
20. Nuclear Engineers	26.9%	$91,050	11.6%	50
21. Arbitrators, Mediators, and Conciliators	34.4%	$119,740	9.5%	10
22. Computer Hardware Engineers	32.1%	$100,560	7.6%	110

Best Federal Jobs Concentrated in the Northeast

Job	Percent of Fed Workers in This Region	Annual Earnings	Percent Growth	Annual Openings
23. Health Diagnosing and Treating Practitioners, All Other	42.7%	$85,610	7.6%	340
24. Industrial Engineers	34.1%	$86,260	18.9%	40
25. Marine Engineers and Naval Architects	45.6%	$100,920	8.9%	30

Best Federal Jobs Concentrated in the Southeast

Job	Percent of Fed Workers in This Region	Annual Earnings	Percent Growth	Annual Openings
1. Air Traffic Controllers	28.0%	$113,840	10.7%	780
2. Social Scientists and Related Workers, All Other	25.8%	$75,540	19.3%	800
3. Aerospace Engineers	34.7%	$109,190	12.0%	200
4. Biological Scientists, All Other	25.1%	$69,860	19.6%	670
5. Claims Adjusters, Examiners, and Investigators	24.1%	$66,580	19.5%	1,050
6. Registered Nurses	25.7%	$74,790	14.0%	1,790
7. Accountants and Auditors	23.1%	$87,730	11.1%	740
8. Logisticians	34.6%	$76,000	17.8%	730
9. Engineers, All Other	34.3%	$110,860	7.6%	520
10. Transportation Inspectors	24.8%	$100,100	18.3%	150
11. Tax Examiners, Collectors, and Revenue Agents	21.8%	$56,420	19.5%	1,060
12. Compliance Officers, Except Agriculture, Construction, Health and Safety, and Transportation	23.0%	$45,720	29.8%	3,080
13. Natural Sciences Managers	25.1%	$106,160	7.7%	290
14. Mechanical Engineers	21.3%	$91,520	8.5%	240
15. Pharmacists	29.2%	$107,330	7.7%	190
16. Materials Engineers	23.6%	$108,670	19.4%	30
17. Clergy	29.9%	$74,360	10.2%	310
18. Psychologists, All Other	25.8%	$91,110	7.8%	240
19. Medical and Health Services Managers	25.8%	$104,530	7.6%	190
20. Petroleum Engineers	42.7%	$96,480	30.0%	10
21. Physician Assistants	32.7%	$83,370	18.3%	90
22. Civil Engineers	31.9%	$87,900	7.6%	320
23. Engineering Managers	34.3%	$125,730	7.6%	110

(continued)

(continued)

Best Federal Jobs Concentrated in the Southeast

Job	Percent of Fed Workers in This Region	Annual Earnings	Percent Growth	Annual Openings
24. Health Diagnosing and Treating Practitioners, All Other	29.3%	$85,610	7.6%	340
25. Environmental Scientists and Specialists, Including Health	27.8%	$91,550	7.6%	230

Best Federal Jobs Concentrated in the Midwest

Job	Percent of Fed Workers in This Region	Annual Earnings	Percent Growth	Annual Openings
1. Air Traffic Controllers	21.7%	$113,840	10.7%	780
2. Registered Nurses	20.4%	$74,790	14.0%	1,790
3. Accountants and Auditors	20.3%	$87,730	11.1%	740
4. Claims Adjusters, Examiners, and Investigators	21.3%	$66,580	19.5%	1,050
5. Biomedical Engineers	22.1%	$87,830	62.8%	30
6. Materials Engineers	26.7%	$108,670	19.4%	30
7. Pharmacists	21.0%	$107,330	7.7%	190
8. Medical and Health Services Managers	20.2%	$104,530	7.6%	190
9. Loan Officers	26.9%	$69,920	14.0%	70
10. Captains, Mates, and Pilots of Water Vessels	22.6%	$63,620	28.8%	50
11. Arbitrators, Mediators, and Conciliators	33.3%	$119,740	9.5%	10
12. Agricultural Inspectors	28.0%	$44,460	19.7%	140
13. Pharmacy Technicians	21.3%	$38,870	18.5%	210
14. Physical Therapists	22.2%	$75,960	9.7%	50
15. Funeral Directors	21.2%	$67,620	22.5%	10
16. Transportation, Storage, and Distribution Managers	20.2%	$94,890	−5.7%	160
17. Veterinarians	24.9%	$81,130	7.6%	50
18. Conservation Scientists	27.6%	$69,580	8.0%	110
19. Postal Service Mail Carriers	24.8%	$52,200	−1.1%	10,720
20. Optometrists	21.6%	$76,720	9.1%	20
21. Agricultural Engineers	35.4%	$74,380	9.5%	10
22. Licensed Practical and Licensed Vocational Nurses	21.3%	$43,160	7.6%	590
23. Postal Service Clerks	20.5%	$52,530	−18.3%	1,610
24. Combined Food Preparation and Serving Workers, Including Fast Food	22.3%	$29,720	8.1%	210
25. Postmasters and Mail Superintendents	32.3%	$58,780	−15.1%	520

Best Federal Jobs Concentrated in the Southwest

Job	Percent of Fed Workers in This Region	Annual Earnings	Percent Growth	Annual Openings
1. Detectives and Criminal Investigators	35.7%	$73,320	29.8%	1,160
2. Environmental Scientists and Specialists, Including Health	20.6%	$91,550	7.6%	230
3. Aircraft Mechanics and Service Technicians	29.8%	$53,750	7.6%	330
4. Instructional Coordinators	26.4%	$83,910	7.6%	80
5. Industrial Engineering Technicians	29.2%	$64,910	18.1%	20
6. Sheet Metal Workers	31.4%	$50,890	7.7%	160
7. Veterinary Technologists and Technicians	29.8%	$46,440	12.5%	30
8. Medical Records and Health Information Technicians	21.3%	$44,460	7.6%	150

Best Federal Jobs Concentrated in the West

Job	Percent of Fed Workers in This Region	Annual Earnings	Percent Growth	Annual Openings
1. Air Traffic Controllers	23.8%	$113,840	10.7%	780
2. Transportation Inspectors	24.6%	$100,100	18.3%	150
3. Biological Scientists, All Other	20.9%	$69,860	19.6%	670
4. Tax Examiners, Collectors, and Revenue Agents	25.2%	$56,420	19.5%	1,060
5. Natural Sciences Managers	20.7%	$106,160	7.7%	290
6. Compliance Officers, Except Agriculture, Construction, Health and Safety, and Transportation	21.2%	$45,720	29.8%	3,080
7. Mechanical Engineers	20.3%	$91,520	8.5%	240
8. Psychologists, All Other	20.1%	$91,110	7.8%	240
9. Electronics Engineers, Except Computer	27.3%	$102,730	7.5%	300
10. Petroleum Engineers	29.7%	$96,480	30.0%	10
11. Civil Engineers	30.2%	$87,900	7.6%	320
12. Environmental Scientists and Specialists, Including Health	21.4%	$91,550	7.6%	230
13. Real Estate Sales Agents	33.6%	$73,050	8.5%	170
14. Anthropologists and Archeologists	52.9%	$70,400	19.9%	70
15. Fire Fighters	28.2%	$46,630	19.1%	310
16. Nuclear Engineers	37.9%	$91,050	11.6%	50
17. Marine Engineers and Naval Architects	23.7%	$100,920	8.9%	30

(continued)

(continued)

Best Federal Jobs Concentrated in the West

Job	Percent of Fed Workers in This Region	Annual Earnings	Percent Growth	Annual Openings
18. Eligibility Interviewers, Government Programs	23.0%	$46,430	8.6%	670
19. Environmental Engineers	24.2%	$98,760	7.5%	150
20. Engineering Technicians, Except Drafters, All Other	27.8%	$67,080	7.6%	340
21. Business Operations Specialists, All Other	20.2%	$72,120	7.3%	4,290
22. Media and Communication Equipment Workers, All Other	21.1%	$77,920	7.6%	150
23. Industrial Machinery Mechanics	39.5%	$54,090	24.7%	70
24. Airline Pilots, Copilots, and Flight Engineers	20.7%	$97,290	7.5%	90
25. Artists and Related Workers, All Other	22.4%	$70,520	7.6%	200

Best Federal Jobs Based on GS Levels

No federal job is "at" a specific General Schedule (GS) level; every job includes workers at various levels. An individual worker may climb up several levels after many years on the job. Nevertheless, if you're thinking of entering a federal job, it's useful to know which GS level is *most frequent,* because it gives you an idea of how much education is typically expected of job applicants. As Part I explains, the GS system is a 15-point scale, with GS-2 jobs requiring a high school diploma and GS-11 jobs requiring a doctoral or professional degree. Many blue-collar jobs are not in the GS system, and relevant work experience or training would be appropriate preparation for these jobs.

These lists can help you identify a federal job with higher earnings or upward mobility that requires a similar level of education to the job you now hold or to another job you have been considering. You can also use these lists to explore possible job options if you were to get additional training, education, or work experience. For example, you can use these lists to identify occupations that offer high potential and then look into the education or training required to get the jobs that interest you most.

Keep in mind that for some jobs, you may start at a lower GS level than the most-frequent level that is listed here. That can happen if a large number of workers in the job have climbed the GS ladder over many years of service.

In the following lists (and in the job descriptions in Part III), I assigned some jobs to multiple GS levels. For some of these jobs, two adjacent GS levels were virtually tied for having the most workers (less than a 10 percent difference). For other jobs, the two highest collections of workers were not at adjacent GS levels, indicating a very diverse set of specific job titles and requirements. A good example of the latter is Tax Examiners, Collectors, and Revenue Agents, a SOC job title that is linked to six federal job series. Among these are some 15,000 Internal Revenue Agents, who are most commonly at GS-13, as well as some 12,000 Tax Examiners, who are most commonly at GS-7. Given this split, I assigned this occupation to both GS-7 and GS-13.

To keep the number of lists from getting too large, I based some lists on a range of GS levels rather than on a single level. In those lists, I include a column that identifies the most frequent GS level of each occupation.

All the lists in this set show the 25 (or fewer) best jobs overall for each level or group of levels, based on earnings, job growth, and job openings.

Best Federal Jobs Not in the GS System

Job	Annual Earnings	Percent Growth	Annual Openings
1. Captains, Mates, and Pilots of Water Vessels	$63,620	28.8%	50
2. Electrical and Electronics Repairers, Commercial and Industrial Equipment	$53,870	12.0%	160
3. Industrial Machinery Mechanics	$54,090	24.7%	70
4. Postmasters and Mail Superintendents	$58,780	–15.1%	520
5. Aircraft Mechanics and Service Technicians	$53,750	7.6%	330
6. Maintenance and Repair Workers, General	$52,920	–0.1%	420
7. Postal Service Mail Carriers	$52,200	–1.1%	10,720
8. Postal Service Clerks	$52,530	–18.3%	1,610
9. Installation, Maintenance, and Repair Workers, All Other	$49,640	7.8%	270
10. Precision Instrument and Equipment Repairers, All Other	$54,550	7.6%	60
11. Postal Service Mail Sorters, Processors, and Processing Machine Operators	$52,520	–30.4%	1,170
12. Sheet Metal Workers	$50,890	7.7%	160
13. Painters, Construction and Maintenance	$47,470	7.9%	140
14. Ship Engineers	$47,570	29.8%	50
15. Sailors and Marine Oilers	$37,300	19.6%	80
16. Avionics Technicians	$51,650	7.9%	40
17. Motor Vehicle Operators, All Other	$44,020	7.7%	110

Best Federal Jobs at GS Levels 5 through 8

Job	Most Frequent GS Level(s)	Annual Earnings	Percent Growth	Annual Openings
1. Tax Examiners, Collectors, and Revenue Agents	7	$56,420	19.5%	1,060
2. Fire Fighters	7	$46,630	19.1%	310
3. Eligibility Interviewers, Government Programs	8	$46,430	8.6%	670
4. Correctional Officers and Jailers	7, 8	$53,360	7.6%	350
5. Agricultural Inspectors	5, 7	$44,460	19.7%	140
6. Forensic Science Technicians	8	$95,620	16.7%	10
7. Life, Physical, and Social Science Technicians, All Other	7	$48,280	7.7%	310
8. Coaches and Scouts	7	$56,190	17.9%	10
9. Social and Community Service Managers	8	$91,140	12.2%	10
10. First-Line Supervisors/Managers of Police and Detectives	6	$93,390	6.8%	240
11. Licensed Practical and Licensed Vocational Nurses	6	$43,160	7.6%	590
12. Pharmacy Technicians	6	$38,870	18.5%	210
13. Biological Technicians	5, 7	$32,850	7.6%	470
14. Veterinary Technologists and Technicians	8	$46,440	12.5%	30
15. Health Technologists and Technicians, All Other	8	$52,080	7.6%	80
16. Procurement Clerks	7	$41,920	7.6%	380
17. Purchasing Managers	7	$119,840	7.4%	70
18. Healthcare Support Workers, All Other	6, 7	$40,020	7.6%	280
19. Radiologic Technologists and Technicians	8	$55,600	7.6%	90
20. Administrative Services Managers	7	$75,950	5.2%	90
21. Medical Records and Health Information Technicians	7, 8	$44,460	7.6%	150
22. Education, Training, and Library Workers, All Other	5	$38,860	7.6%	210
23. Social and Human Service Assistants	5, 7	$42,210	11.4%	50
24. Forest and Conservation Technicians	5, 7	$31,390	7.5%	960
25. Security Guards	5	$35,410	8.3%	120

Best Federal Jobs at GS Levels 9 through 11

Job	Most Frequent GS Level(s)	Annual Earnings	Percent Growth	Annual Openings
1. Social Scientists and Related Workers, All Other	11	$75,540	19.3%	800
2. Air Traffic Controllers	11	$113,840	10.7%	780

Best Federal Jobs at GS Levels 9 through 11

Job	Most Frequent GS Level(s)	Annual Earnings	Percent Growth	Annual Openings
3. Registered Nurses	11	$74,790	14.0%	1,790
4. Budget Analysts	11	$73,120	19.9%	300
5. Claims Adjusters, Examiners, and Investigators	11	$66,580	19.5%	1,050
6. Physician Assistants	11	$83,370	18.3%	90
7. Compliance Officers, Except Agriculture, Construction, Health and Safety, and Transportation	9	$45,720	29.8%	3,080
8. Anthropologists and Archeologists	11	$70,400	19.9%	70
9. Paralegals and Legal Assistants	9, 11	$60,500	18.2%	420
10. Real Estate Sales Agents	11	$73,050	8.5%	170
11. Physical Therapists	11	$75,960	9.7%	50
12. Social and Community Service Managers	9	$91,140	12.2%	10
13. Transportation, Storage, and Distribution Managers	9, 11	$94,890	−5.7%	160
14. Engineering Technicians, Except Drafters, All Other	11	$67,080	7.6%	340
15. Instructional Coordinators	11	$83,910	7.6%	80
16. Conservation Scientists	11	$69,580	8.0%	110
17. Librarians	11	$77,970	7.8%	40
18. Museum Technicians and Conservators	11	$38,450	18.1%	120
19. Industrial Engineering Technicians	11	$64,910	18.1%	20
20. Teachers and Instructors, All Other	9, 11	$62,840	7.4%	430
21. Zoologists and Wildlife Biologists	11	$70,190	7.4%	160
22. Graphic Designers	11	$73,130	7.4%	70
23. Combined Food Preparation and Serving Workers, Including Fast Food	11	$29,720	8.1%	210
24. Life, Physical, and Social Science Technicians, All Other	9	$48,280	7.7%	310
25. Medical and Clinical Laboratory Technologists	9, 11	$61,630	7.7%	120

Best Federal Jobs at GS Level 12

Job	Annual Earnings	Percent Growth	Annual Openings
1. Accountants and Auditors	$87,730	11.1%	740
2. Logisticians	$76,000	17.8%	730

(continued)

(continued)

Best Federal Jobs at GS Level 12

Job	Annual Earnings	Percent Growth	Annual Openings
3. Public Relations Specialists	$83,440	18.0%	180
4. Purchasing Agents, Except Wholesale, Retail, and Farm Products	$75,050	17.8%	950
5. Mechanical Engineers	$91,520	8.5%	240
6. Management Analysts	$83,140	8.4%	1,970
7. Pharmacists	$107,330	7.7%	190
8. Budget Analysts	$73,120	19.9%	300
9. Compliance Officers, Except Agriculture, Construction, Health and Safety, and Transportation	$45,720	29.8%	3,080
10. Electronics Engineers, Except Computer	$102,730	7.5%	300
11. Civil Engineers	$87,900	7.6%	320
12. Nuclear Engineers	$91,050	11.6%	50
13. Biological Scientists, All Other	$69,860	19.6%	670
14. Industrial Engineers	$86,260	18.9%	40
15. Clergy	$74,360	10.2%	310
16. Writers and Authors	$80,410	9.7%	110
17. Marine Engineers and Naval Architects	$100,920	8.9%	30
18. Electrical Engineers	$89,130	7.7%	70
19. Directors, Religious Activities and Education	$89,210	10.5%	20
20. Market Research Analysts	$87,720	13.5%	30
21. Geoscientists, Except Hydrologists and Geographers	$92,410	7.4%	80
22. Microbiologists	$92,580	7.4%	80
23. Geographers	$74,890	17.8%	40
24. Instructional Coordinators	$83,910	7.6%	80
25. Media and Communication Equipment Workers, All Other	$77,920	7.6%	150

Best Federal Jobs at GS Level 13

Job	Annual Earnings	Percent Growth	Annual Openings
1. Aerospace Engineers	$109,190	12.0%	200
2. Political Scientists	$113,050	18.4%	120
3. Computer and Information Research Scientists	$99,730	19.5%	200
4. Engineers, All Other	$110,860	7.6%	520
5. Natural Sciences Managers	$106,160	7.7%	290
6. Operations Research Analysts	$103,780	15.4%	160

Best Federal Jobs at GS Level 13

Job	Annual Earnings	Percent Growth	Annual Openings
7. Dentists	$137,950	9.9%	80
8. Detectives and Criminal Investigators	$73,320	29.8%	1,160
9. Computer and Information Systems Managers	$133,440	8.3%	100
10. Transportation Inspectors	$100,100	18.3%	150
11. Tax Examiners, Collectors, and Revenue Agents	$56,420	19.5%	1,060
12. Accountants and Auditors	$87,730	11.1%	740
13. Engineering Managers	$125,730	7.6%	110
14. Physical Scientists, All Other	$104,480	7.6%	230
15. Electronics Engineers, Except Computer	$102,730	7.5%	300
16. Management Analysts	$83,140	8.4%	1,970
17. Financial Managers	$117,190	7.0%	210
18. Materials Engineers	$108,670	19.4%	30
19. Psychologists, All Other	$91,110	7.8%	240
20. Public Relations Specialists	$83,440	18.0%	180
21. Chemists	$98,860	7.7%	150
22. Arbitrators, Mediators, and Conciliators	$119,740	9.5%	10
23. Computer Hardware Engineers	$100,560	7.6%	110
24. Environmental Scientists and Specialists, Including Health	$91,550	7.6%	230
25. Physicists	$111,370	7.5%	110

Best Federal Jobs at GS Levels 14 through 15

Job	Most Frequent GS Level(s)	Annual Earnings	Percent Growth	Annual Openings
1. Lawyers	15	$131,410	8.4%	960
2. Astronomers	15	$136,010	10.9%	20
3. Medical Scientists, Except Epidemiologists	14	$110,260	29.0%	50
4. Actuaries	14	$113,020	14.8%	10
5. Financial Managers	14	$117,190	7.0%	210
6. Health Diagnosing and Treating Practitioners, All Other	14	$85,610	7.6%	340
7. Medical and Health Services Managers	14, 15	$104,530	7.6%	190
8. Physicists	15	$111,370	7.5%	110
9. Podiatrists	14	$110,850	9.4%	10
10. Animal Scientists	14	$101,350	10.0%	10
11. First-Line Supervisors/Managers of Correctional Officers	14	$69,570	7.5%	40

Best Federal Jobs Lists Based on Career Clusters

This group of lists organizes the 150 best federal jobs into 16 career clusters. The U.S. Department of Education's Office of Vocational and Adult Education developed these career clusters in 1999, and many states now use them to organize their career-oriented programs and career information. You can use these lists to identify jobs quickly based on your interests. Within each cluster, jobs are listed by combined score for earnings, job growth, and job openings, from highest to lowest.

Find the cluster or clusters that appeal to you most and review the jobs in those lists. When you find jobs you want to explore in more detail, look up their descriptions in Part III. You can also review clusters in which you've had past experience, education, or training to see whether other jobs in those clusters would meet your current requirements. Some of the 150 best federal jobs appear on more than one cluster's list. For example, Administrative Services Managers work in both the private sector and in government, so this job appears on the list for 04 Management and also on the list for 07 Governance.

Descriptions for the 16 Career Clusters

Brief descriptions follow for the 16 career clusters, defining them in terms of interests. Some of them refer to jobs (as examples) that aren't included in this book.

* **Agriculture and Natural Resources:** *An interest in working with plants, animals, forests, or mineral resources for agriculture, horticulture, conservation, extraction, and other purposes.* You can satisfy this interest by working in farming, landscaping, forestry, fishing, mining, and related fields. You may like doing physical work outdoors, such as on a farm or ranch, in a forest, or on a drilling rig. If you have a scientific curiosity, you could study plants and animals or analyze biological or rock samples in a lab. If you have management ability, you could own, operate, or manage a fish hatchery, a landscaping business, or a greenhouse.

* **Architecture and Construction:** *An interest in designing, assembling, and maintaining components of buildings and other structures.* You may want to be part of the team of architects, drafters, and others who design buildings and render plans. If construction interests you, you might find fulfillment in the many building projects that are being undertaken at all times. If you like to organize and plan, you can find careers in managing these projects. Or you can play a more direct role in putting up and finishing buildings by doing jobs such as plumbing, carpentry, masonry, painting, or roofing, either as a skilled craftsworker or as a helper. You can prepare the building site by operating heavy equipment or installing, maintaining, and repairing vital building equipment and systems such as electricity and heating.

❋ **Arts and Communication:** *An interest in creatively expressing feelings or ideas, in communicating news or information, or in performing.* You can satisfy this interest in creative, verbal, or performing activities. For example, if you enjoy literature, perhaps writing or editing would appeal to you. Journalism and public relations are other fields for people who like to use their writing or speaking skills. Do you prefer to work in the performing arts? If so, you could direct or perform in drama, music, or dance. If you especially enjoy the visual arts, you could create paintings, sculpture, or ceramics or design products or visual displays. A flair for technology might lead you to specialize in photography, broadcast production, or dispatching.

❋ **Business and Administration:** *An interest in making a business organization or function run smoothly.* You can satisfy this interest by working in a position of leadership or by specializing in a function that contributes to the overall effort in a business, nonprofit organization, or government agency. If you especially enjoy working with people, you may find fulfillment from working in human resources. An interest in numbers may lead you to consider accounting, finance, budgeting, billing, or financial record-keeping. A job as an administrative assistant may interest you if you like a variety of tasks in a busy environment. If you are good with details and word processing, you may enjoy a job as a secretary or data-entry clerk. Or perhaps you would do well as the manager of a business.

❋ **Education and Training:** *An interest in helping people learn.* You can satisfy this interest by teaching students, who may be preschoolers, retirees, or any age in between. You may specialize in a particular academic field or work with learners of a particular age, with a particular interest, or with a particular learning problem. Working in a library or museum may give you an opportunity to expand people's understanding of the world.

❋ **Finance and Insurance:** *An interest in helping businesses and people be assured of a financially secure future.* You can satisfy this interest by working in a financial or insurance business in a leadership or support role. If you like gathering and analyzing information, you may find fulfillment as an insurance adjuster or financial analyst. Or you may deal with information at the clerical level as a banking or insurance clerk or in person-to-person situations providing customer service. Another way to interact with people is to sell financial or insurance services that will meet their needs.

❋ **Government and Public Administration:** *An interest in helping a government agency serve the needs of the public.* You can satisfy this interest by working in a position of leadership or by specializing in a function that contributes to the role of government. You may help protect the public by working as an inspector or examiner to enforce standards. If you enjoy using clerical skills, you could work as a clerk in a law court or government office. Or perhaps you prefer the top-down perspective of a government executive or urban planner.

❋ **Health Science:** *An interest in helping people and animals be healthy.* You can satisfy this interest by working on a health-care team as a doctor, therapist, or nurse. You might specialize in one of the many different parts of the body (such as the teeth or eyes) or in one of the many different types of care. Or you may want to be a generalist who deals with the whole patient. If you like technology, you might find satisfaction working with X-rays or new diagnostic methods. You might work with relatively healthy people, helping them to eat better. If you enjoy working with animals, you might care for them and keep them healthy.

❀ **Hospitality, Tourism, and Recreation:** *An interest in catering to the personal wishes and needs of others so that they can enjoy a clean environment, good food and drink, comfortable lodging away from home, and recreation.* You can satisfy this interest by providing services for the convenience, care, and pampering of others in hotels, restaurants, airplanes, beauty parlors, and so on. You may want to use your love of cooking as a chef. If you like working with people, you may want to provide personal services by being a travel guide, a flight attendant, a concierge, a hairdresser, or a waiter. You may want to work in cleaning and building services if you like a clean environment. If you enjoy sports or games, you could work for an athletic team or casino.

❀ **Human Service:** *An interest in improving people's social, mental, emotional, or spiritual well-being.* You can satisfy this interest as a counselor, social worker, or religious worker who helps people sort out their complicated lives or solve personal problems. You may work as a caretaker for very young people or the elderly. Or you may interview people to help identify the social services they need.

❀ **Information Technology:** *An interest in designing, developing, managing, and supporting information systems.* You can satisfy this interest by working with hardware, software, multimedia, or integrated systems. If you like to use your organizational skills, you might work as a systems or database administrator. Or you can solve complex problems as a software engineer or systems analyst. If you enjoy getting your hands on hardware, you might find work servicing computers, peripherals, and information-intense machines such as cash registers and ATMs.

❀ **Law and Public Safety:** *An interest in upholding people's rights or in protecting people and property by using authority, inspecting, or investigating.* You can satisfy this interest by working in law, law enforcement, fire fighting, the military, and related fields. For example, if you enjoy mental challenge and intrigue, you could investigate crimes or fires for a living. If you enjoy working with verbal skills and research skills, you may want to defend citizens in court or research deeds, wills, and other legal documents. If you want to help people in critical situations, you may want to fight fires, work as a police officer, or become a paramedic. Or, if you want more routine work in public safety, perhaps a job in guarding, patrolling, or inspecting would appeal to you. If you have management ability, you could seek a leadership position in law enforcement and the protective services. Work in the military gives you a chance to use technical and leadership skills while serving your country.

⚜ **Manufacturing:** *An interest in processing materials into intermediate or final products or maintaining and repairing products by using machines or hand tools.* You can satisfy this interest by working in one of many industries that mass-produce goods or by working for a utility that distributes electrical power or other resources. You might enjoy manual work, using your hands or hand tools in highly skilled jobs such as assembling engines or electronic equipment. If you enjoy making machines run efficiently or fixing them when they break down, you could seek a job installing or repairing such devices as copiers, aircraft engines, cars, or watches. Perhaps you prefer to set up or operate machines that are used to manufacture products made of food, glass, or paper. You could enjoy cutting and grinding metal and plastic parts to desired shapes and measurements. Or you may want to operate equipment in systems that provide water and process wastewater. You may like inspecting, sorting, counting, or weighing products. Another option is to work with your hands and machinery to move boxes and freight in a warehouse. If leadership appeals to you, you could manage people engaged in production and repair.

⚜ **Marketing, Sales, and Service:** *An interest in bringing others to a particular point of view by personal persuasion and by sales and promotional techniques.* You can satisfy this interest in various jobs that involve persuasion and selling. If you like using knowledge of science, you may enjoy selling pharmaceutical, medical, or electronic products or services. Real estate offers several kinds of sales jobs as well. If you like speaking on the phone, you could work as a telemarketer. Or you may enjoy selling apparel and other merchandise in a retail setting. If you prefer to help people, you may want a job in customer service.

⚜ **Scientific Research, Engineering, and Mathematics:** *An interest in discovering, collecting, and analyzing information about the natural world; in applying scientific research findings to problems in medicine, the life sciences, human behavior, and the natural sciences; in imagining and manipulating quantitative data; and in applying technology to manufacturing, transportation, and other economic activities.* You can satisfy this interest by working with the knowledge and processes of the sciences. You may enjoy researching and developing new knowledge in mathematics, or perhaps solving problems in the physical, life, or social sciences would appeal to you. You may want to study engineering and help create new machines, processes, and structures. If you want to work with scientific equipment and procedures, you could seek a job in a research or testing laboratory.

⚜ **Transportation, Distribution, and Logistics:** *An interest in operations that move people or materials.* You can satisfy this interest by managing a transportation service, by helping vehicles keep on their assigned schedules and routes, or by driving or piloting a vehicle. If you enjoy taking responsibility, perhaps managing a rail line would appeal to you. If you work well with details and can take pressure on the job, you might consider being an air traffic controller. Or would you rather get out on the highway, on the water, or up in the air? If so, you could drive a truck from state to state, be employed on a ship, or fly a crop duster over a cornfield. If you prefer to stay closer to home, you could drive a delivery van, taxi, or school bus. You can use your physical strength to load freight and arrange it so that it gets to its destination in one piece.

Best Federal Jobs for People Interested in Agriculture and Natural Resources

Job	Annual Earnings	Percent Growth	Annual Openings
1. Biological Scientists, All Other	$69,860	19.6%	670
2. Environmental Scientists and Specialists, Including Health	$91,550	7.6%	230
3. Animal Scientists	$101,350	10.0%	10
4. Engineering Technicians, Except Drafters, All Other	$67,080	7.6%	340
5. Agricultural Inspectors	$44,460	19.7%	140
6. Life, Physical, and Social Science Technicians, All Other	$48,280	7.7%	310
7. Conservation Scientists	$69,580	8.0%	110
8. Occupational Health and Safety Specialists	$74,370	6.5%	260
9. Economists	$104,530	–1.5%	110
10. Forest and Conservation Technicians	$31,390	7.5%	960
11. Veterinarians	$81,130	7.6%	50
12. Zoologists and Wildlife Biologists	$70,190	7.4%	160
13. Foresters	$60,630	10.8%	30
14. Graphic Designers	$73,130	7.4%	70
15. Soil and Plant Scientists	$71,460	7.5%	70

Best Federal Jobs for People Interested in Architecture and Construction

Job	Annual Earnings	Percent Growth	Annual Openings
1. Social Scientists and Related Workers, All Other	$75,540	19.3%	800
2. Engineers, All Other	$110,860	7.6%	520
3. Engineering Managers	$125,730	7.6%	110
4. Surveyors	$81,140	8.0%	20
5. Engineering Technicians, Except Drafters, All Other	$67,080	7.6%	340
6. Painters, Construction and Maintenance	$47,470	7.9%	140
7. Construction and Building Inspectors	$63,330	7.8%	80
8. Architects, Except Landscape and Naval	$89,070	5.7%	50
9. Maintenance and Repair Workers, General	$52,920	–0.1%	420

Best Federal Jobs for People Interested in Arts and Communication

Job	Annual Earnings	Percent Growth	Annual Openings
1. Public Relations Specialists	$83,440	18.0%	180
2. Writers and Authors	$80,410	9.7%	110
3. Media and Communication Equipment Workers, All Other	$77,920	7.6%	150
4. Artists and Related Workers, All Other	$70,520	7.6%	200
5. Museum Technicians and Conservators	$38,450	18.1%	120
6. Technical Writers	$73,340	10.0%	30
7. Graphic Designers	$73,130	7.4%	70
8. Producers and Directors	$77,300	7.3%	40
9. Set and Exhibit Designers	$67,080	7.9%	20

Best Federal Jobs for People Interested in Business and Administration

Job	Annual Earnings	Percent Growth	Annual Openings
1. Financial Examiners	$101,770	41.5%	260
2. Accountants and Auditors	$87,730	11.1%	740
3. Operations Research Analysts	$103,780	15.4%	160
4. Logisticians	$76,000	17.8%	730
5. Natural Sciences Managers	$106,160	7.7%	290
6. Management Analysts	$83,140	8.4%	1,970
7. Budget Analysts	$73,120	19.9%	300
8. Public Relations Specialists	$83,440	18.0%	180
9. Computer and Information Systems Managers	$133,440	8.3%	100
10. Financial Managers	$117,190	7.0%	210
11. Business Operations Specialists, All Other	$72,120	7.3%	4,290
12. Purchasing Managers	$119,840	7.4%	70
13. Market Research Analysts	$87,720	13.5%	30
14. Public Relations Managers	$140,970	5.9%	10
15. Social and Community Service Managers	$91,140	12.2%	10
16. Statisticians	$92,720	6.9%	140
17. Economists	$104,530	−1.5%	110
18. Postal Service Mail Carriers	$52,200	−1.1%	10,720
19. Procurement Clerks	$41,920	7.6%	380
20. Transportation, Storage, and Distribution Managers	$94,890	−5.7%	160
21. Postal Service Clerks	$52,530	−18.3%	1,610
22. Technical Writers	$73,340	10.0%	30

(continued)

(continued)

Best Federal Jobs for People Interested in Business and Administration

Job	Annual Earnings	Percent Growth	Annual Openings
23. Postal Service Mail Sorters, Processors, and Processing Machine Operators	$52,520	−30.4%	1,170
24. Administrative Services Managers	$75,950	5.2%	90

Best Federal Jobs for People Interested in Education and Training

Job	Annual Earnings	Percent Growth	Annual Openings
1. Chemists	$98,860	7.7%	150
2. Physicists	$111,370	7.5%	110
3. Instructional Coordinators	$83,910	7.6%	80
4. Interpreters and Translators	$67,600	18.4%	20
5. Librarians	$77,970	7.8%	40
6. Teachers and Instructors, All Other	$62,840	7.4%	430
7. Coaches and Scouts	$56,190	17.9%	10

Best Federal Jobs for People Interested in Finance and Insurance

Job	Annual Earnings	Percent Growth	Annual Openings
1. Budget Analysts	$73,120	19.9%	300
2. Claims Adjusters, Examiners, and Investigators	$66,580	19.5%	1,050
3. Financial Managers	$117,190	7.0%	210
4. Actuaries	$113,020	14.8%	10
5. Loan Officers	$69,920	14.0%	70

Best Federal Jobs for People Interested in Government and Public Administration

Job	Annual Earnings	Percent Growth	Annual Openings
1. Financial Examiners	$101,770	41.5%	260
2. Compliance Officers, Except Agriculture, Construction, Health and Safety, and Transportation	$45,720	29.8%	3,080

Best Federal Jobs for People Interested in Government and Public Administration

Job	Annual Earnings	Percent Growth	Annual Openings
3. Political Scientists	$113,050	18.4%	120
4. Tax Examiners, Collectors, and Revenue Agents	$56,420	19.5%	1,060
5. Accountants and Auditors	$87,730	11.1%	740
6. Transportation, Storage, and Distribution Managers	$94,890	–5.7%	160
7. Social and Community Service Managers	$91,140	12.2%	10
8. Postmasters and Mail Superintendents	$58,780	–15.1%	520
9. Administrative Services Managers	$75,950	5.2%	90

Best Federal Jobs for People Interested in Health Science

Job	Annual Earnings	Percent Growth	Annual Openings
1. Biological Scientists, All Other	$69,860	19.6%	670
2. Computer and Information Research Scientists	$99,730	19.5%	200
3. Registered Nurses	$74,790	14.0%	1,790
4. Engineers, All Other	$110,860	7.6%	520
5. Medical Scientists, Except Epidemiologists	$110,260	29.0%	50
6. Public Relations Specialists	$83,440	18.0%	180
7. Dentists	$137,950	9.9%	80
8. Physician Assistants	$83,370	18.3%	90
9. Psychologists, All Other	$91,110	7.8%	240
10. Health Diagnosing and Treating Practitioners, All Other	$85,610	7.6%	340
11. Pharmacists	$107,330	7.7%	190
12. Medical and Health Services Managers	$104,530	7.6%	190
13. Physical Scientists, All Other	$104,480	7.6%	230
14. Pharmacy Technicians	$38,870	18.5%	210
15. Podiatrists	$110,850	9.4%	10
16. Life, Physical, and Social Science Technicians, All Other	$48,280	7.7%	310
17. Physical Therapists	$75,960	9.7%	50
18. Speech-Language Pathologists	$81,130	7.9%	40
19. Licensed Practical and Licensed Vocational Nurses	$43,160	7.6%	590
20. Occupational Health and Safety Specialists	$74,370	6.5%	260
21. Recreational Therapists	$63,780	11.4%	30
22. Medical and Clinical Laboratory Technologists	$61,630	7.7%	120
23. Optometrists	$76,720	9.1%	20

(continued)

(continued)

Best Federal Jobs for People Interested in Health Science

Job	Annual Earnings	Percent Growth	Annual Openings
24. Healthcare Support Workers, All Other	$40,020	7.6%	280
25. Orthotists and Prosthetists	$65,800	10.2%	10
26. Veterinary Technologists and Technicians	$46,440	12.5%	30
27. Social and Human Service Assistants	$42,210	11.4%	50
28. Health Technologists and Technicians, All Other	$52,080	7.6%	80
29. Veterinarians	$81,130	7.6%	50
30. Medical Records and Health Information Technicians	$44,460	7.6%	150
31. Radiologic Technologists and Technicians	$55,600	7.6%	90

Best Federal Jobs for People Interested in Hospitality, Tourism, and Recreation

Job	Annual Earnings	Percent Growth	Annual Openings
1. Combined Food Preparation and Serving Workers, Including Fast Food	$29,720	8.1%	210

Best Federal Jobs for People Interested in Human Service

Job	Annual Earnings	Percent Growth	Annual Openings
1. Social Scientists and Related Workers, All Other	$75,540	19.3%	800
2. Public Relations Specialists	$83,440	18.0%	180
3. Directors, Religious Activities and Education	$89,210	10.5%	20
4. Psychologists, All Other	$91,110	7.8%	240
5. Social and Community Service Managers	$91,140	12.2%	10
6. Clergy	$74,360	10.2%	310
7. Funeral Directors	$67,620	22.5%	10
8. Writers and Authors	$80,410	9.7%	110
9. Interpreters and Translators	$67,600	18.4%	20
10. Eligibility Interviewers, Government Programs	$46,430	8.6%	670

Best Federal Jobs for People Interested in Information Technology

Job	Annual Earnings	Percent Growth	Annual Openings
1. Biological Scientists, All Other	$69,860	19.6%	670
2. Computer and Information Research Scientists	$99,730	19.5%	200
3. Computer and Information Systems Managers	$133,440	8.3%	100
4. Engineering Managers	$125,730	7.6%	110
5. Physical Scientists, All Other	$104,480	7.6%	230
6. Computer Hardware Engineers	$100,560	7.6%	110
7. Life, Physical, and Social Science Technicians, All Other	$48,280	7.7%	310
8. Graphic Designers	$73,130	7.4%	70

Best Federal Jobs for People Interested in Law and Public Safety

Job	Annual Earnings	Percent Growth	Annual Openings
1. Detectives and Criminal Investigators	$73,320	29.8%	1,160
2. Lawyers	$131,410	8.4%	960
3. Compliance Officers, Except Agriculture, Construction, Health and Safety, and Transportation	$45,720	29.8%	3,080
4. Paralegals and Legal Assistants	$60,500	18.2%	420
5. Fire Fighters	$46,630	19.1%	310
6. Arbitrators, Mediators, and Conciliators	$119,740	9.5%	10
7. Physical Scientists, All Other	$104,480	7.6%	230
8. Forensic Science Technicians	$95,620	16.7%	10
9. Administrative Law Judges, Adjudicators, and Hearing Officers	$125,360	7.4%	70
10. Correctional Officers and Jailers	$53,360	7.6%	350
11. First-Line Supervisors/Managers of Police and Detectives	$93,390	6.8%	240
12. First-Line Supervisors/Managers of Correctional Officers	$69,570	7.5%	40
13. Security Guards	$35,410	8.3%	120

Best Federal Jobs for People Interested in Manufacturing

Job	Annual Earnings	Percent Growth	Annual Openings
1. Engineering Technicians, Except Drafters, All Other	$67,080	7.6%	340
2. Industrial Machinery Mechanics	$54,090	24.7%	70

(continued)

(continued)

Best Federal Jobs for People Interested in Manufacturing

Job	Annual Earnings	Percent Growth	Annual Openings
3. Electrical and Electronics Repairers, Commercial and Industrial Equipment	$53,870	12.0%	160
4. Industrial Engineering Technicians	$64,910	18.1%	20
5. Aircraft Mechanics and Service Technicians	$53,750	7.6%	330
6. Occupational Health and Safety Specialists	$74,370	6.5%	260
7. Plant and System Operators, All Other	$56,520	7.9%	30
8. Installation, Maintenance, and Repair Workers, All Other	$49,640	7.8%	270
9. Life, Physical, and Social Science Technicians, All Other	$48,280	7.7%	310
10. Biological Technicians	$32,850	7.6%	470
11. Electrical and Electronic Engineering Technicians	$61,500	−2.9%	220
12. Avionics Technicians	$51,650	7.9%	40
13. Sheet Metal Workers	$50,890	7.7%	160
14. Precision Instrument and Equipment Repairers, All Other	$54,550	7.6%	60

Best Federal Jobs for People Interested in Marketing, Sales, and Service

Job	Annual Earnings	Percent Growth	Annual Openings
1. Purchasing Agents, Except Wholesale, Retail, and Farm Products	$75,050	17.8%	950
2. Market Research Analysts	$87,720	13.5%	30
3. Real Estate Sales Agents	$73,050	8.5%	170

Best Federal Jobs for People Interested in Scientific Research, Engineering, and Mathematics

Job	Annual Earnings	Percent Growth	Annual Openings
1. Political Scientists	$113,050	18.4%	120
2. Aerospace Engineers	$109,190	12.0%	200
3. Medical Scientists, Except Epidemiologists	$110,260	29.0%	50
4. Engineers, All Other	$110,860	7.6%	520
5. Operations Research Analysts	$103,780	15.4%	160
6. Natural Sciences Managers	$106,160	7.7%	290
7. Social Scientists and Related Workers, All Other	$75,540	19.3%	800

Best Federal Jobs for People Interested in Scientific Research, Engineering, and Mathematics

Job	Annual Earnings	Percent Growth	Annual Openings
8. Biological Scientists, All Other	$69,860	19.6%	670
9. Materials Engineers	$108,670	19.4%	30
10. Electronics Engineers, Except Computer	$102,730	7.5%	300
11. Mechanical Engineers	$91,520	8.5%	240
12. Engineering Managers	$125,730	7.6%	110
13. Physical Scientists, All Other	$104,480	7.6%	230
14. Chemists	$98,860	7.7%	150
15. Astronomers	$136,010	10.9%	20
16. Psychologists, All Other	$91,110	7.8%	240
17. Civil Engineers	$87,900	7.6%	320
18. Physicists	$111,370	7.5%	110
19. Computer Hardware Engineers	$100,560	7.6%	110
20. Biomedical Engineers	$87,830	62.8%	30
21. Petroleum Engineers	$96,480	30.0%	10
22. Anthropologists and Archeologists	$70,400	19.9%	70
23. Environmental Engineers	$98,760	7.5%	150
24. Marine Engineers and Naval Architects	$100,920	8.9%	30
25. Museum Technicians and Conservators	$38,450	18.1%	120
26. Industrial Engineers	$86,260	18.9%	40
27. Nuclear Engineers	$91,050	11.6%	50
28. Economists	$104,530	–1.5%	110
29. Statisticians	$92,720	6.9%	140
30. Geographers	$74,890	17.8%	40
31. Education, Training, and Library Workers, All Other	$38,860	7.6%	210
32. Chemical Engineers	$97,350	7.8%	20
33. Electrical Engineers	$89,130	7.7%	70
34. Market Research Analysts	$87,720	13.5%	30
35. Geoscientists, Except Hydrologists and Geographers	$92,410	7.4%	80
36. Mathematicians	$104,540	6.6%	40
37. Microbiologists	$92,580	7.4%	80
38. Zoologists and Wildlife Biologists	$70,190	7.4%	160
39. Industrial Engineering Technicians	$64,910	18.1%	20
40. Agricultural Engineers	$74,380	9.5%	10
41. Hydrologists	$83,370	5.4%	80

Best Federal Jobs for People Interested in Transportation, Distribution, and Logistics

Job	Annual Earnings	Percent Growth	Annual Openings
1. Air Traffic Controllers	$113,840	10.7%	780
2. Compliance Officers, Except Agriculture, Construction, Health and Safety, and Transportation	$45,720	29.8%	3,080
3. Logisticians	$76,000	17.8%	730
4. Transportation Inspectors	$100,100	18.3%	150
5. Aircraft Mechanics and Service Technicians	$53,750	7.6%	330
6. Captains, Mates, and Pilots of Water Vessels	$63,620	28.8%	50
7. Environmental Scientists and Specialists, Including Health	$91,550	7.6%	230
8. Environmental Engineers	$98,760	7.5%	150
9. Installation, Maintenance, and Repair Workers, All Other	$49,640	7.8%	270
10. Transportation, Storage, and Distribution Managers	$94,890	–5.7%	160
11. Airline Pilots, Copilots, and Flight Engineers	$97,290	7.5%	90
12. Ship Engineers	$47,570	29.8%	50
13. Sailors and Marine Oilers	$37,300	19.6%	80
14. Avionics Technicians	$51,650	7.9%	40
15. Motor Vehicle Operators, All Other	$44,020	7.7%	110

Best Federal Jobs Lists Based on Personality Types

These lists organize the 150 best federal jobs into groups matching six personality types. Within each personality type, I ranked the jobs based on each one's total combined score for earnings, growth, and annual job openings.

The personality types are Realistic, Investigative, Artistic, Social, Enterprising, and Conventional (RIASEC). This system was developed by John Holland and is used in the *Self-Directed Search (SDS)* and other career assessment inventories and information systems. If you have used one of these career inventories or systems, the lists will help you identify jobs that most closely match these personality types. Even if you have not used one of these systems, the concept of personality types and the jobs that are related to them can help you identify jobs that suit the type of person you are.

Unlike the set of lists for the career clusters, this set assigns each of the best federal jobs to only one list: the list for the primary personality type that describes the job. Nevertheless, you should be aware that most jobs also are linked to one or two secondary personality types. The job descriptions in Part III indicate all relevant personality types.

Consider reviewing the jobs for more than one personality type so you don't overlook possible jobs that would interest you. (Note: There is no RIASEC information for Engineers, All Other, and 18 others of the best federal jobs that have "All Other" in their title.)

Descriptions of the Six Personality Types

Following are brief descriptions for each of the six personality types used in the lists. Select the two or three descriptions that most closely describe you and then use the lists to identify jobs that best fit these personality types.

- ❋ **Realistic:** These occupations frequently involve work activities that include practical, hands-on problems and solutions. They often deal with plants; animals; and real-world materials such as wood, tools, and machinery. Many of the occupations require working outside and don't involve a lot of paperwork or working closely with others.

- ❋ **Investigative:** These occupations frequently involve working with ideas and require an extensive amount of thinking. These occupations can involve searching for facts and figuring out problems mentally.

- ❋ **Artistic:** These occupations frequently involve working with forms, designs, and patterns. They often require self-expression, and the work can be done without following a clear set of rules.

- ❋ **Social:** These occupations frequently involve working with, communicating with, and teaching people. These occupations often involve helping or providing service to others.

- ❋ **Enterprising:** These occupations frequently involve starting up and carrying out projects. These occupations can involve leading people and making many decisions. They sometimes require risk taking and often deal with business.

- ❋ **Conventional:** These occupations frequently involve following set procedures and routines. These occupations can include working with data and details more than with ideas. Usually there is a clear line of authority to follow.

Best Federal Jobs for People with a Realistic Personality Type

Job	Annual Earnings	Percent Growth	Annual Openings
1. Transportation Inspectors	$100,100	18.3%	150
2. Civil Engineers	$87,900	7.6%	320
3. Captains, Mates, and Pilots of Water Vessels	$63,620	28.8%	50

(continued)

(continued)

Best Federal Jobs for People with a Realistic Personality Type

Job	Annual Earnings	Percent Growth	Annual Openings
4. Electrical and Electronics Repairers, Commercial and Industrial Equipment	$53,870	12.0%	160
5. Fire Fighters	$46,630	19.1%	310
6. Conservation Scientists	$69,580	8.0%	110
7. Industrial Machinery Mechanics	$54,090	24.7%	70
8. Aircraft Mechanics and Service Technicians	$53,750	7.6%	330
9. Agricultural Inspectors	$44,460	19.7%	140
10. Correctional Officers and Jailers	$53,360	7.6%	350
11. Ship Engineers	$47,570	29.8%	50
12. Airline Pilots, Copilots, and Flight Engineers	$97,290	7.5%	90
13. Construction and Building Inspectors	$63,330	7.8%	80
14. Electrical and Electronic Engineering Technicians	$61,500	–2.9%	220
15. Maintenance and Repair Workers, General	$52,920	–0.1%	420
16. Surveyors	$81,140	8.0%	20
17. Foresters	$60,630	10.8%	30
18. Museum Technicians and Conservators	$38,450	18.1%	120
19. Sheet Metal Workers	$50,890	7.7%	160
20. Biological Technicians	$32,850	7.6%	470
21. Painters, Construction and Maintenance	$47,470	7.9%	140
22. Sailors and Marine Oilers	$37,300	19.6%	80
23. Radiologic Technologists and Technicians	$55,600	7.6%	90
24. Security Guards	$35,410	8.3%	120
25. Forest and Conservation Technicians	$31,390	7.5%	960
26. Avionics Technicians	$51,650	7.9%	40
27. Veterinary Technologists and Technicians	$46,440	12.5%	30

Best Federal Jobs for People with an Investigative Personality Type

Job	Annual Earnings	Percent Growth	Annual Openings
1. Political Scientists	$113,050	18.4%	120
2. Aerospace Engineers	$109,190	12.0%	200
3. Computer and Information Research Scientists	$99,730	19.5%	200
4. Operations Research Analysts	$103,780	15.4%	160
5. Medical Scientists, Except Epidemiologists	$110,260	29.0%	50

Best Federal Jobs for People with an Investigative Personality Type

Job	Annual Earnings	Percent Growth	Annual Openings
6. Dentists	$137,950	9.9%	80
7. Pharmacists	$107,330	7.7%	190
8. Electronics Engineers, Except Computer	$102,730	7.5%	300
9. Materials Engineers	$108,670	19.4%	30
10. Astronomers	$136,010	10.9%	20
11. Mechanical Engineers	$91,520	8.5%	240
12. Chemists	$98,860	7.7%	150
13. Physicists	$111,370	7.5%	110
14. Management Analysts	$83,140	8.4%	1,970
15. Environmental Scientists and Specialists, Including Health	$91,550	7.6%	230
16. Biomedical Engineers	$87,830	62.8%	30
17. Computer Hardware Engineers	$100,560	7.6%	110
18. Environmental Engineers	$98,760	7.5%	150
19. Petroleum Engineers	$96,480	30.0%	10
20. Anthropologists and Archeologists	$70,400	19.9%	70
21. Industrial Engineers	$86,260	18.9%	40
22. Nuclear Engineers	$91,050	11.6%	50
23. Podiatrists	$110,850	9.4%	10
24. Marine Engineers and Naval Architects	$100,920	8.9%	30
25. Economists	$104,530	–1.5%	110
26. Animal Scientists	$101,350	10.0%	10
27. Forensic Science Technicians	$95,620	16.7%	10
28. Geographers	$74,890	17.8%	40
29. Market Research Analysts	$87,720	13.5%	30
30. Electrical Engineers	$89,130	7.7%	70
31. Geoscientists, Except Hydrologists and Geographers	$92,410	7.4%	80
32. Mathematicians	$104,540	6.6%	40
33. Chemical Engineers	$97,350	7.8%	20
34. Microbiologists	$92,580	7.4%	80
35. Occupational Health and Safety Specialists	$74,370	6.5%	260
36. Medical and Clinical Laboratory Technologists	$61,630	7.7%	120
37. Industrial Engineering Technicians	$64,910	18.1%	20
38. Zoologists and Wildlife Biologists	$70,190	7.4%	160
39. Veterinarians	$81,130	7.6%	50
40. Hydrologists	$83,370	5.4%	80
41. Optometrists	$76,720	9.1%	20
42. Agricultural Engineers	$74,380	9.5%	10
43. Soil and Plant Scientists	$71,460	7.5%	70

Best Federal Jobs for People with an Artistic Personality Type

Job	Annual Earnings	Percent Growth	Annual Openings
1. Writers and Authors	$80,410	9.7%	110
2. Technical Writers	$73,340	10.0%	30
3. Architects, Except Landscape and Naval	$89,070	5.7%	50
4. Graphic Designers	$73,130	7.4%	70
5. Interpreters and Translators	$67,600	18.4%	20
6. Set and Exhibit Designers	$67,080	7.9%	20

Best Federal Jobs for People with a Social Personality Type

Job	Annual Earnings	Percent Growth	Annual Openings
1. Physician Assistants	$83,370	18.3%	90
2. Registered Nurses	$74,790	14.0%	1,790
3. Clergy	$74,360	10.2%	310
4. Arbitrators, Mediators, and Conciliators	$119,740	9.5%	10
5. Instructional Coordinators	$83,910	7.6%	80
6. Physical Therapists	$75,960	9.7%	50
7. Eligibility Interviewers, Government Programs	$46,430	8.6%	670
8. Recreational Therapists	$63,780	11.4%	30
9. Speech-Language Pathologists	$81,130	7.9%	40
10. Coaches and Scouts	$56,190	17.9%	10
11. Orthotists and Prosthetists	$65,800	10.2%	10
12. Licensed Practical and Licensed Vocational Nurses	$43,160	7.6%	590

Best Federal Jobs for People with an Enterprising Personality Type

Job	Annual Earnings	Percent Growth	Annual Openings
1. Lawyers	$131,410	8.4%	960
2. Air Traffic Controllers	$113,840	10.7%	780
3. Financial Examiners	$101,770	41.5%	260
4. Detectives and Criminal Investigators	$73,320	29.8%	1,160
5. Logisticians	$76,000	17.8%	730
6. Natural Sciences Managers	$106,160	7.7%	290
7. Computer and Information Systems Managers	$133,440	8.3%	100
8. Engineering Managers	$125,730	7.6%	110

Best Federal Jobs for People with an Enterprising Personality Type

Job	Annual Earnings	Percent Growth	Annual Openings
9. Public Relations Specialists	$83,440	18.0%	180
10. Medical and Health Services Managers	$104,530	7.6%	190
11. Financial Managers	$117,190	7.0%	210
12. Administrative Law Judges, Adjudicators, and Hearing Officers	$125,360	7.4%	70
13. Purchasing Managers	$119,840	7.4%	70
14. First-Line Supervisors/Managers of Police and Detectives	$93,390	6.8%	240
15. Real Estate Sales Agents	$73,050	8.5%	170
16. Directors, Religious Activities and Education	$89,210	10.5%	20
17. Social and Community Service Managers	$91,140	12.2%	10
18. Public Relations Managers	$140,970	5.9%	10
19. Funeral Directors	$67,620	22.5%	10
20. Transportation, Storage, and Distribution Managers	$94,890	−5.7%	160
21. Postmasters and Mail Superintendents	$58,780	−15.1%	520
22. Producers and Directors	$77,300	7.3%	40
23. First-Line Supervisors/Managers of Correctional Officers	$69,570	7.5%	40
24. Administrative Services Managers	$75,950	5.2%	90

Best Federal Jobs for People with a Conventional Personality Type

Job	Annual Earnings	Percent Growth	Annual Openings
1. Claims Adjusters, Examiners, and Investigators	$66,580	19.5%	1,050
2. Compliance Officers, Except Agriculture, Construction, Health and Safety, and Transportation	$45,720	29.8%	3,080
3. Tax Examiners, Collectors, and Revenue Agents	$56,420	19.5%	1,060
4. Budget Analysts	$73,120	19.9%	300
5. Purchasing Agents, Except Wholesale, Retail, and Farm Products	$75,050	17.8%	950
6. Accountants and Auditors	$87,730	11.1%	740
7. Paralegals and Legal Assistants	$60,500	18.2%	420
8. Actuaries	$113,020	14.8%	10
9. Loan Officers	$69,920	14.0%	70
10. Postal Service Clerks	$52,530	−18.3%	1,610
11. Postal Service Mail Carriers	$52,200	−1.1%	10,720
12. Statisticians	$92,720	6.9%	140
13. Librarians	$77,970	7.8%	40

(continued)

(continued)

Best Federal Jobs for People with a Conventional Personality Type

Job	Annual Earnings	Percent Growth	Annual Openings
14. Postal Service Mail Sorters, Processors, and Processing Machine Operators	$52,520	–30.4%	1,170
15. Pharmacy Technicians	$38,870	18.5%	210
16. Procurement Clerks	$41,920	7.6%	380
17. Combined Food Preparation and Serving Workers, Including Fast Food	$29,720	8.1%	210
18. Medical Records and Health Information Technicians	$44,460	7.6%	150
19. Social and Human Service Assistants	$42,210	11.4%	50

Bonus List: The 25 Federal Jobs with the Best Industry-Wide Rewards

It's possible that you may prepare for one of the occupations in this book but fail to be hired by the federal government. Or you may start in a federal job but later leave it to work in the private sector. Given these possibilities, you may want to know which of these 150 jobs have the best rewards across *all* industries, not just in the federal government. To create the following list, I first removed five occupations that are available *only* in federal government: Air Traffic Controllers; Postal Service Clerks; Postal Service Mail Carriers; Postal Service Mail Sorters, Processors, and Processing Machine Operators; and Postmasters and Mail Superintendents. Then I sorted the 145 remaining jobs by their combined scores for earnings, growth, and job openings in *all* industries (including the federal government) and listed the best 25 jobs.

The 25 Federal Jobs with the Best Industry-Wide Rewards

Job	Annual Earnings	Percent Growth	Annual Openings
1. Management Analysts	$75,250	23.9%	30,650
2. Civil Engineers	$76,590	24.3%	11,460
3. Pharmacists	$109,180	17.0%	10,580
4. Computer and Information Systems Managers	$113,720	16.9%	9,710
5. Medical Scientists, Except Epidemiologists	$74,590	40.4%	6,620
6. Physical Therapists	$74,480	30.3%	7,860
7. Physician Assistants	$84,420	39.0%	4,280
8. Lawyers	$113,240	13.0%	24,040

The 25 Federal Jobs with the Best Industry-Wide Rewards

Job	Annual Earnings	Percent Growth	Annual Openings
9. Dentists	$142,090	15.6%	6,150
10. Accountants and Auditors	$60,340	21.6%	49,750
11. Veterinarians	$80,510	32.9%	3,020
12. Medical and Health Services Managers	$81,850	16.0%	9,940
13. Environmental Engineers	$77,040	30.6%	2,790
14. Optometrists	$96,140	24.4%	2,010
15. Environmental Scientists and Specialists, Including Health	$61,010	27.9%	4,840
16. Instructional Coordinators	$58,780	23.2%	6,060
17. Compliance Officers, Except Agriculture, Construction, Health and Safety, and Transportation	$49,750	31.0%	10,850
18. Public Relations Specialists	$51,960	24.0%	13,130
19. Biomedical Engineers	$78,860	72.0%	1,490
20. Industrial Engineers	$75,110	14.2%	8,540
21. Logisticians	$67,960	19.5%	4,190
22. Financial Managers	$101,190	7.6%	13,820
23. Operations Research Analysts	$70,070	22.0%	3,220
24. Paralegals and Legal Assistants	$46,980	28.1%	10,400
25. Speech-Language Pathologists	$65,090	18.5%	4,380

PART III

The Job Descriptions

This part of the book provides descriptions for all the federal jobs included in the lists in Part II. The introduction gives more details on how to use and interpret the job descriptions, but here is some additional information:

* Job descriptions are arranged in alphabetical order by job title. This approach allows you to quickly find a description if you know its correct title from one of the lists in Part II.

* If you are using this section to browse for interesting options, I suggest you begin with the table of contents. Part II features many interesting lists that will help you identify federal jobs to explore in more detail. If you have not browsed the lists in Part II, consider spending some time there. The lists are interesting and will help you identify job titles you can find described in the material that follows. The job titles in Part III are also listed in the table of contents.

Accountants and Auditors

- ❋ Education/Training Required: Bachelor's degree
- ❋ Annual Earnings (Federal): $87,730
- ❋ Annual Earnings (All Industries): $60,340
- ❋ Earnings Growth Potential (Federal): 40.0% (high)
- ❋ Earnings Growth Potential (All Industries): 37.5% (medium)
- ❋ Job Growth (Federal): 11.1%
- ❋ Job Growth (All Industries): 21.6%
- ❋ Annual Job Openings (Federal): 740
- ❋ Annual Job Openings (All Industries): 49,750

Examine, analyze, and interpret accounting records for the purpose of giving advice or preparing statements. Install or advise on systems of recording costs or other financial and budgetary data.

Considerations for Job Outlook: An increase in the number of businesses, a more stringent regulatory environment, and increased corporate accountability are expected to drive job growth for accountants and auditors. Opportunities should be favorable; job seekers with professional certification, especially a CPA, should have the best prospects.

JOB SPECIALIZATION: ACCOUNTANTS

Analyze financial information and prepare financial reports to determine or maintain record of assets, liabilities, profit and loss, tax liability, or other financial activities within an organization. Prepare, examine, or analyze accounting records, financial statements, or other financial reports to assess accuracy, completeness, and conformance to reporting and procedural standards. Report to management regarding the finances of establishment. Establish tables of accounts and assign entries to proper accounts. Develop, implement, modify, and document recordkeeping and accounting systems, making use of current computer technology. Compute taxes owed and prepare tax returns, ensuring compliance with payment, reporting, or other tax requirements. Maintain or examine the records of government agencies. Advise clients in areas such as compensation, employee health-care benefits, the design of accounting or data-processing systems, or long-range tax or estate plans. Develop, maintain, and analyze budgets, preparing periodic reports that compare budgeted costs to actual costs. Provide internal and external auditing services for businesses or individuals. Analyze business operations, trends, costs, revenues, financial commitments, and obligations to project future revenues and expenses or to provide advice. Advise management about issues such as resource utilization, tax strategies, and the assumptions underlying budget forecasts. Represent clients before taxing authorities and provide support during litigation involving financial issues. Prepare forms and manuals for accounting and bookkeeping personnel and direct their work activities.

Personality Type: Conventional-Enterprising. **Skills:** Operations Analysis; Mathematics; Systems Analysis; Management of Financial Resources; Systems Evaluation; Critical Thinking; Judgment and Decision Making; Negotiation. **Education and Training Program:** Accounting; Accounting and Business/Management; Accounting and Computer Science; Accounting and Finance; Auditing; Taxation. **Work Environment:** Indoors; sitting; making repetitive motions.

JOB SPECIALIZATION: AUDITORS

Examine and analyze accounting records to determine financial status of establishment and prepare financial reports concerning operating procedures. Collect and analyze data to detect deficient controls; duplicated effort; extravagance;

fraud; or non-compliance with laws, regulations, and management policies. Prepare detailed reports on audit findings. Supervise auditing of establishments and determine scope of investigation required. Report to management about asset utilization and audit results and recommend changes in operations and financial activities. Inspect account books and accounting systems for efficiency, effectiveness, and use of accepted accounting procedures to record transactions. Examine records and interview workers to ensure recording of transactions and compliance with laws and regulations. Examine and evaluate financial and information systems, recommending controls to ensure system reliability and data integrity. Review data about material assets, net worth, liabilities, capital stock, surplus, income, and expenditures. Confer with company officials about financial and regulatory matters. Examine whether the organization's objectives are reflected in its management activities and whether employees understand the objectives. Prepare, analyze, and verify annual reports, financial statements, and other records, using accepted accounting and statistical procedures to assess financial condition and facilitate financial planning. Inspect cash on hand, notes receivable and payable, negotiable securities, and canceled checks to confirm records are accurate.

Personality Type: Conventional-Enterprising-Investigative. **Skills:** Systems Evaluation; Systems Analysis; Management of Financial Resources; Mathematics; Writing; Operations Analysis; Active Learning; Management of Personnel Resources. **Education and Training Program:** Accounting; Accounting and Business/Management; Accounting and Computer Science; Accounting and Finance; Auditing; Taxation. **Work Environment:** Indoors; sitting.

OTHER FEDERAL JOB FACTS
RELATED GS SERIES: 0510 ACCOUNTING
TITLE ON USAJOBS: ACCOUNTANT

- ✸ U.S. Federal Workforce: 13,815
- ✸ Average Length of Service: 15.4 years
- ✸ Percent Part-Time: 1.4%
- ✸ Percent Women: 58.0%
- ✸ Largest Age Bracket: 50–54 (17.0%)
- ✸ GS Level with Most Workers: 12
- ✸ Agency with Most Workers: Defense
- ✸ State with Most Workers: District of Columbia

Advise on or administer, supervise, or perform professional accounting work; design, develop, operate, or inspect accounting systems; prescribe accounting standards, policies, and requirements; examine, analyze, and interpret accounting data, records, and reports; or advise or assist management on accounting and financial management matters.

Requirements: Knowledge of accounting theories, concepts, principles, and standards as they apply to the financial activities of governmental, quasi-governmental, or private-sector organizations.

RELATED GS SERIES: 0511 AUDITING
TITLE ON USAJOBS: AUDITOR

- ✸ U.S. Federal Workforce: 12,012
- ✸ Average Length of Service: 13.5 years
- ✸ Percent Part-Time: 1.3%
- ✸ Percent Women: 48.1%
- ✸ Largest Age Bracket: 45–49 (14.8%)
- ✸ GS Levels with Most Workers: 13, 12
- ✸ Agency with Most Workers: Defense
- ✸ States with Most Workers: District of Columbia, Virginia

Systematically examine and appraise financial records, financial and management reports, management controls, and policies and practices affecting or reflecting the financial condition and operating results of an activity; analyze work related to developing and executing audit policies and programs; conduct performance audits; or conduct activities related to the detection of fraud, waste, and abuse.

Requirements: Professional knowledge of accounting and auditing standards and principles.

Actuaries

- ⊛ Education/Training Required: Bachelor's or higher degree, plus work experience
- ⊛ Annual Earnings (Federal): $113,020
- ⊛ Annual Earnings (All Industries): $87,210
- ⊛ Earnings Growth Potential (Federal): 35.3% (median)
- ⊛ Earnings Growth Potential (All Industries): 40.4% (medium)
- ⊛ Job Growth (Federal): 14.8%
- ⊛ Job Growth (All Industries): 21.3%
- ⊛ Annual Job Openings (Federal): 10
- ⊛ Annual Job Openings (All Industries): 1,000

Analyze statistical data, such as mortality, accident, sickness, disability, and retirement rates, and construct probability tables to forecast risk and liability for payment of future benefits. May ascertain premium rates required and cash reserves necessary to ensure payment of future benefits. Determine or help determine company policy and explain complex technical matters to company executives, government officials, shareholders, policyholders, or the public. Design, review, and help administer insurance, annuity, and pension plans, determining financial soundness and calculating premiums. Analyze statistical information to estimate mortality, accident, sickness, disability, and retirement rates. Provide advice to clients on a contract basis, working as a consultant. Collaborate with programmers, underwriters, accounts, claims experts, and senior management to help companies develop plans for new lines of business or improving existing business. Provide expertise to help financial institutions manage risks and maximize returns associated with investment products or credit offerings. Construct probability tables for events such as fires, natural disasters, and unemployment, based on analysis of statistical data and other pertinent information. Determine equitable basis for distributing surplus earnings under participating insurance and annuity contracts in mutual companies. Testify before public agencies on proposed legislation affecting businesses. Determine policy contract provisions for each type of insurance.

Considerations for Job Outlook: Employment growth is projected as industries not traditionally associated with actuaries, such as financial services and consulting, employ these workers to assess risk. Keen competition is expected.

Personality Type: Conventional-Investigative-Enterprising. **Skills:** Mathematics; Management of Financial Resources; Systems Evaluation; Systems Analysis; Programming; Judgment and Decision Making; Operations Analysis; Complex Problem Solving. **Education and Training Program:** Actuarial Science. **Work Environment:** Indoors; sitting.

OTHER FEDERAL JOB FACTS
Related GS Series: 1510 Actuarial Science
Title on USAJobs: Actuary

- ⊛ U.S. Federal Workforce: 276
- ⊛ Average Length of Service: 12.2 years
- ⊛ Percent Part-Time: 4.3%
- ⊛ Percent Women: 33.3%
- ⊛ Largest Age Bracket: 45–49 (14.9%)
- ⊛ GS Level with Most Workers: 14

- Agency with Most Workers: Health and Human Services
- State with Most Workers: District of Columbia

Apply knowledge of actuarial science to programs or problems related to the financial risks posed by life, health, retirement/pension, and property/casualty entities and contingencies.

Requirements: Professional knowledge of the disciplines of mathematics, statistics, business, finance, economics, and insurance.

Administrative Law Judges, Adjudicators, and Hearing Officers

- Education/Training Required: Bachelor's or higher degree, plus work experience
- Annual Earnings (Federal): $125,360
- Annual Earnings (All Industries): $83,920
- Earnings Growth Potential (Federal): 33.7% (low)
- Earnings Growth Potential (All Industries): 52.2% (very high)
- Job Growth (Federal): 7.4%
- Job Growth (All Industries): 8.1%
- Annual Job Openings (Federal): 70
- Annual Job Openings (All Industries): 380

Conduct hearings to decide or recommend decisions on claims concerning government programs or other government-related matters and prepare decisions. Determine penalties or the existence and the amount of liability or recommend the acceptance or rejection of claims or compromise settlements. Prepare written opinions and decisions. Review and evaluate data on documents such as claim applications, birth or death certificates, and physician or employer records. Research and analyze laws, regulations, policies, and precedent decisions to prepare for hearings and to determine conclusions. Confer with individuals or organizations involved in cases to obtain relevant information. Recommend the acceptance or rejection of claims or compromise settlements according to laws, regulations, policies, and precedent decisions. Explain to claimants how they can appeal rulings that go against them. Monitor and direct the activities of trials and hearings to ensure that they are conducted fairly and that courts administer justice while safeguarding the legal rights of all involved parties. Authorize payment of valid claims and determine method of payment. Conduct hearings to review and decide claims regarding issues such as social program eligibility, environmental protection, and enforcement of health and safety regulations. Rule on exceptions, motions, and admissibility of evidence. Determine existence and amount of liability according to current laws, administrative and judicial precedents, and available evidence. Issue subpoenas and administer oaths in preparation for formal hearings. Conduct studies of appeals procedures in field agencies to ensure adherence to legal requirements and to facilitate determination of cases.

Considerations for Job Outlook: Budget pressures are expected to limit the hiring of new judges, particularly in federal courts. Alternatives to litigation are usually faster and less expensive, spurring employment growth for other judicial workers, such as arbitrators, mediators, and conciliators.

Personality Type: Enterprising-Investigative-Social. **Skills:** Active Listening; Critical Thinking; Reading Comprehension; Speaking; Operations Analysis; Writing; Judgment and Decision Making; Negotiation. **Education and Training Program:** Law (LL.B., J.D.); Legal Professions and Studies, Other; Legal Studies, General. **Work Environment:** Indoors; sitting.

OTHER FEDERAL JOB FACTS

RELATED GS SERIES: 0930 HEARINGS AND APPEALS

TITLE ON USAJOBS: HEARINGS AND APPEALS OFFICER

- U.S. Federal Workforce: 2,026
- Average Length of Service: 20.6 years
- Percent Part-Time: 0.6%
- Percent Women: 53.6%
- Largest Age Bracket: 55–59 (21.1%)
- GS Level with Most Workers: 13
- Agency with Most Workers: Treasury
- State with Most Workers: California

Adjudicate cases; conduct formal or informal hearings; conduct appellate reviews of prior decisions.

Requirements: The ability to review and evaluate investigative reports and case records, conduct hearings in an orderly and impartial manner, determine credibility of witnesses, sift and evaluate evidence, analyze complex issues, apply agency rules and regulations and court decisions, prepare clear and concise statements of fact, and exercise sound judgment in arriving at decisions. For additional information, see www.usajobs.gov/EI/administrativelawjudges.asp.

Administrative Services Managers

- Education/Training Required: Bachelor's or higher degree, plus work experience
- Annual Earnings (Federal): $75,950
- Annual Earnings (All Industries): $75,520
- Earnings Growth Potential (Federal): 37.6% (median)
- Earnings Growth Potential (All Industries): 48.8% (high)
- Job Growth (Federal): 5.2%
- Job Growth (All Industries): 12.5%
- Annual Job Openings (Federal): 90
- Annual Job Openings (All Industries): 8,660

Plan, direct, or coordinate supportive services of an organization, such as recordkeeping, mail distribution, telephone operator/receptionist, and other office support services. May oversee facilities planning and maintenance and custodial operations. Monitor the facility to ensure that it remains safe, secure, and well-maintained. Direct or coordinate the supportive services department of a business, agency, or organization. Set goals and deadlines for the department. Prepare and review operational reports and schedules to ensure accuracy and efficiency. Analyze internal processes and recommend and implement procedural or policy changes to improve operations such as supply changes or the disposal of records. Acquire, distribute, and store supplies. Plan, administer, and control budgets for contracts, equipment, and supplies. Oversee construction and renovation projects to improve efficiency and to ensure that facilities meet environmental, health, and security standards and comply with government regulations. Hire and terminate clerical and administrative personnel. Oversee the maintenance and repair of machinery, equipment, and electrical and mechanical systems. Manage leasing of facility space. Participate in architectural and engineering planning and design, including space and installation management. Conduct classes to teach procedures to staff. Dispose of, or oversee the disposal of, surplus or unclaimed property.

Considerations for Job Outlook: Employment of these workers is projected to increase as companies strive to maintain, secure, and efficiently operate their facilities. Competition should be keen for top managers; better opportunities are expected at the entry level.

Personality Type: Enterprising-Conventional. **Skills:** Management of Financial Resources;

Management of Material Resources; Management of Personnel Resources; Negotiation; Coordination; Time Management; Social Perceptiveness; Service Orientation. **Education and Training Program:** Business Administration and Management, General; Business/Commerce, General; Medical Staff Services Technology/Technician; Medical/Health Management and Clinical Assistant/Specialist Training; Public Administration; Purchasing, Procurement/Acquisitions and Contracts Management; Transportation/Mobility Management. **Work Environment:** Indoors; sitting.

OTHER FEDERAL JOB FACTS

RELATED GS SERIES: 1654 PRINTING SERVICES

TITLE ON USAJOBS: PRINTING OFFICER

* U.S. Federal Workforce: 615
* Average Length of Service: 21.9 years
* Percent Part-Time: 0.3%
* Percent Women: 45.7%
* Largest Age Bracket: 55–59 (21.5%)
* GS Levels with Most Workers: 12, 13
* Agency with Most Workers: Treasury
* State with Most Workers: District of Columbia

Operate and maintain a printing program.

Requirements: Knowledge and skill in printing; printing processes; reprographics; printing procurement; and applying relevant laws, regulations, methods, and techniques.

RELATED GS SERIES: 0342 SUPPORT SERVICES ADMINISTRATION

TITLE ON USAJOBS: SUPPORT SERVICES ADMINISTRATOR

* U.S. Federal Workforce: 2,354
* Average Length of Service: 19.7 years
* Percent Part-Time: 0.7%
* Percent Women: 62.4%

* Largest Age Bracket: 50–54 (22.6%)
* GS Levels with Most Workers: 7, 12
* Agencies with Most Workers: Treasury, Defense
* State with Most Workers: District of Columbia

Supervise, direct, or plan and coordinate a variety of service functions that are principally work-supporting; such service functions include (but are not limited to) communications, procurement of administrative supplies and equipment, printing, reproduction, property management, space management, records management, mail service, facilities and equipment maintenance, and transportation.

Requirements: Technical and administrative ability necessary to effectively manage or supervise the function.

Aerospace Engineers

* Education/Training Required: Bachelor's degree
* Annual Earnings (Federal): $109,190
* Annual Earnings (All Industries): $94,780
* Earnings Growth Potential (Federal): 32.6% (low)
* Earnings Growth Potential (All Industries): 37.2% (medium)
* Job Growth (Federal): 12.0%
* Job Growth (All Industries): 10.4%
* Annual Job Openings (Federal): 200
* Annual Job Openings (All Industries): 2,230

Perform a variety of engineering work in designing, constructing, and testing aircraft, missiles, and spacecraft. May conduct basic and applied research to evaluate adaptability of materials and equipment to aircraft design

and manufacture. **May recommend improvements in testing equipment and techniques.** Direct and coordinate activities of engineering or technical personnel designing, fabricating, modifying, or testing aircraft or aerospace products. Formulate conceptual design of aeronautical or aerospace products or systems to meet customer requirements. Plan and coordinate activities concerned with investigating and resolving customers' reports of technical problems with aircraft or aerospace vehicles. Plan and conduct experimental, environmental, operational, and stress tests on models and prototypes of aircraft and aerospace systems and equipment. Analyze project requests and proposals and engineering data to determine feasibility, productibility, cost, and production time of aerospace or aeronautical product. Evaluate product data and design from inspections and reports for conformance to engineering principles, customer requirements, and quality standards. Maintain records of performance reports for future reference. Write technical reports and other documentation, such as handbooks and bulletins, for use by engineering staff, management, and customers. Develop design criteria for aeronautical or aerospace products or systems, including testing methods, production costs, quality standards, and completion dates. Review performance reports and documentation from customers and field engineers and inspect malfunctioning or damaged products to determine problem.

Considerations for Job Outlook: Aerospace engineers are expected to have 10 percent growth in employment from 2008–2018, about as fast as the average for all occupations. New technologies and new designs for commercial and military aircraft and spacecraft produced during the next decade should spur demand for aerospace engineers. The employment outlook for aerospace engineers appears favorable. Although the number of degrees granted in aerospace engineering has begun to increase after many years of declines, new graduates continue to be needed to replace aerospace engineers who retire or leave the occupation for other reasons.

Personality Type: Investigative-Realistic. **Skills:** Science; Operations Analysis; Technology Design; Mathematics; Quality Control Analysis; Reading Comprehension; Systems Analysis; Writing. **Education and Training Program:** Aerospace, Aeronautical, and Astronautical/Space Engineering. **Work Environment:** Indoors; sitting.

OTHER FEDERAL JOB FACTS

RELATED GS SERIES: 0861 AEROSPACE ENGINEERING

TITLE ON USAJOBS: ENGINEER, AEROSPACE

- U.S. Federal Workforce: 9,379
- Average Length of Service: 15.2 years
- Percent Part-Time: 0.6%
- Percent Women: 15.8%
- Largest Age Bracket: 45–49 (21.3%)
- GS Level with Most Workers: 13
- Agency with Most Workers: Defense
- States with Most Workers: Maryland, Alabama

Manage, supervise, lead, and/or perform professional engineering and scientific work concerning the integration of the aeronautics and astronautics sciences within the broad arena of aviation and space exploration; includes related materials, equipment, systems, applications, and components.

Requirements: Professional knowledge of and skills in aerospace engineering.

Agricultural Engineers

- Education/Training Required: Bachelor's degree
- Annual Earnings (Federal): $74,380
- Annual Earnings (All Industries): $69,560

❋ Earnings Growth Potential (Federal): 24.8% (very low)

❋ Earnings Growth Potential (All Industries): 38.2% (medium)

❋ Job Growth (Federal): 9.5%

❋ Job Growth (All Industries): 11.9%

❋ Annual Job Openings (Federal): 10

❋ Annual Job Openings (All Industries): 90

Apply knowledge of engineering technology and biological science to agricultural problems concerned with power and machinery, electrification, structures, soil and water conservation, and processing of agricultural products. Visit sites to observe environmental problems, to consult with contractors, or to monitor construction activities. Design agricultural machinery components and equipment, using computer-aided design (CAD) technology. Test agricultural machinery and equipment to ensure adequate performance. Design structures for crop storage, animal shelter and loading, and animal and crop processing and supervise their construction. Provide advice on water quality and issues related to pollution management, river control, and groundwater and surface water resources. Conduct educational programs that provide farmers or farm cooperative members with information that can help them improve agricultural productivity. Discuss plans with clients, contractors, consultants, and other engineers so that they can be evaluated and necessary changes made. Supervise food-processing or manufacturing plant operations. Design and supervise environmental and land reclamation projects in agriculture and related industries.

Considerations for Job Outlook: Agricultural engineers are expected to have employment growth of 12 percent from 2008–2018, about as fast as the average for all occupations. Employment growth should result from the need to increase crop yields to feed an expanding population and to produce crops used as renewable energy sources. Moreover, engineers will be needed to develop more efficient agricultural production and to conserve resources. In addition, engineers will be needed to meet the increasing demand for biosensors, used to determine the optimal treatment of crops.

Personality Type: Investigative-Realistic-Enterprising. **Skills:** Technology Design; Science; Mathematics; Management of Material Resources; Complex Problem Solving; Systems Evaluation; Systems Analysis; Writing. **Education and Training Program:** Agricultural Engineering. **Work Environment:** More often indoors than outdoors; sitting.

OTHER FEDERAL JOB FACTS

RELATED GS SERIES: 0890 AGRICULTURAL ENGINEERING

TITLE ON USAJOBS: ENGINEER, AGRICULTURAL

❋ U.S. Federal Workforce: 404

❋ Average Length of Service: 13.4 years

❋ Percent Part-Time: 2.0%

❋ Percent Women: 19.6%

❋ Largest Age Bracket: 50–54 (17.8%)

❋ GS Level with Most Workers: 12

❋ Agency with Most Workers: Agriculture

❋ State with Most Workers: California

Manage, supervise, lead, and/or perform professional engineering and scientific work resolving agricultural issues, problems, and conditions arising from the production and processing of food and fiber materials and management of natural resources in rural locales.

Requirements: Professional knowledge of and skills in agricultural engineering.

Agricultural Inspectors

❋ Education/Training Required: Work experience in a related occupation

❋ Annual Earnings (Federal): $44,460

* Annual Earnings (All Industries): $41,500

* Earnings Growth Potential (Federal): 28.5% (low)

* Earnings Growth Potential (All Industries): 40.6% (medium)

* Job Growth (Federal): 19.7%

* Job Growth (All Industries): 12.8%

* Annual Job Openings (Federal): 140

* Annual Job Openings (All Industries): 550

Inspect agricultural commodities, processing equipment, and facilities and fish and logging operations to ensure compliance with regulations and laws governing health, quality, and safety. Set standards for the production of meat and poultry products and for food ingredients, additives, and compounds used to prepare and package products. Direct and monitor the quarantine and treatment or destruction of plants and plant products. Monitor the operations and sanitary conditions of slaughtering and meat processing plants. Verify that transportation and handling procedures meet regulatory requirements. Take emergency actions such as closing production facilities if product safety is compromised. Set labeling standards and approve labels for meat and poultry products. Review and monitor foreign product inspection systems in countries of origin to ensure equivalence to the U.S. system. Inspect the cleanliness and practices of establishment employees. Advise farmers and growers of development programs or new equipment and techniques to aid in quality production. Inspect livestock to determine effectiveness of medication and feeding programs. Provide consultative services in areas such as equipment and product evaluation, plant construction and layout, and food safety systems. Monitor the grading performed by company employees to verify conformance to standards. Write reports of findings and recommendations and advise farmers, growers, or processors of corrective action to

be taken. Inspect and test horticultural products or livestock to detect harmful diseases, chemical residues, and infestations and to determine the quality of products or animals.

Considerations for Job Outlook: Federal and state governments, the largest employers of these workers, are not expected to hire a significant number of new inspectors. Job prospects should be good to replace the many agricultural inspectors expected to leave the occupation permanently.

Personality Type: Realistic-Conventional-Investigative. **Skills:** Quality Control Analysis; Science; Operation Monitoring; Monitoring; Systems Evaluation; Systems Analysis; Speaking; Troubleshooting. **Education and Training Program:** Agricultural and Food Products Processing. **Work Environment:** More often indoors than outdoors; contaminants; very hot or cold temperatures; sounds, noisy; standing.

OTHER FEDERAL JOB FACTS

RELATED GS SERIES: 1850 AGRICULTURAL WAREHOUSE INSPECTION

* U.S. Federal Workforce: 56

* Average Length of Service: 18.1 years

* Percent Part-Time: 0.0%

* Percent Women: 14.3%

* Largest Age Bracket: 55–59 (30.4%)

* GS Level with Most Workers: 11

* Agency with Most Workers: Agriculture

* State with Most Workers: Missouri

Inspect storage facilities licensed or in the process of being licensed under federal laws; inspect facilities storing products under a government contract or agreement; inspect the condition, quality, and amount of commodity stored in facilities; and conduct and monitor quality audits and warehouse examining projects.

Requirements: Knowledge of applicable laws and regulatory guidance, construction, equipment, and operation of warehouses and facilities in the agricultural industries, inspecting and examining techniques, business, bookkeeping, and business accounting practices, and audit methods to ensure products are safeguarded and available.

RELATED GS SERIES: 1863 FOOD INSPECTION

TITLE ON USAJOBS: FOOD INSPECTOR

- U.S. Federal Workforce: 3,283
- Average Length of Service: 8.1 years
- Percent Part-Time: 17.5%
- Percent Women: 57.5%
- Largest Age Bracket: 45–49 (17.0%)
- GS Level with Most Workers: 7
- Agency with Most Workers: Agriculture
- States with Most Workers: Texas, Georgia

Inspect the slaughter, processing, packaging, shipping, and storing of meat and meat products, poultry and poultry products, fish and fish products, meat products derived from equines, and food establishments engaged in these activities; determine compliance with laws and regulations that establish standards for the protection of the consumer by assuring that products are wholesome, not adulterated, and properly marked, labeled, and packaged.

Requirements: Knowledge of normal conditions in live and slaughtered meat, poultry, and fish; of standards of wholesomeness and sanitation of meat, poultry, and fish products; and of the processing and sanitation practices of the food production industry or industries inspected.

Air Traffic Controllers

- Education/Training Required: Long-term on-the-job training
- Annual Earnings (Federal): $113,840
- Annual Earnings (All Industries): $109,850
- Earnings Growth Potential (Federal): 59.0% (very high)
- Earnings Growth Potential (All Industries): 57.6% (very high)
- Job Growth (Federal): 10.7%
- Job Growth (All Industries): 13.1%
- Annual Job Openings (Federal): 1,230
- Annual Job Openings (All Industries): 1,230

Control air traffic on and within vicinity of airport and movement of air traffic between altitude sectors and control centers according to established procedures and policies. Authorize, regulate, and control commercial airline flights according to government or company regulations to expedite and ensure flight safety. Issue landing and take-off authorizations and instructions. Monitor and direct the movement of aircraft within an assigned air space and on the ground at airports to minimize delays and maximize safety. Monitor aircraft within a specific airspace, using radar, computer equipment, and visual references. Inform pilots about nearby planes as well as potentially hazardous conditions such as weather, speed and direction of wind, and visibility problems. Provide flight path changes or directions to emergency landing fields for pilots traveling in bad weather or in emergency situations. Alert airport emergency services in cases of emergency and when aircraft are experiencing difficulties. Direct pilots to runways when space is available, or direct them to maintain a traffic pattern until there is space for them to land. Transfer control of departing flights to traffic control centers and accept control of arriving flights. Direct ground traffic, including taxiing aircraft, maintenance and baggage vehicles, and airport workers. Determine the timing and procedures for flight vector changes. Maintain radio and telephone contact with adjacent control towers, terminal control units, and other area control centers in order to coordinate aircraft movement. Contact pilots by radio to provide meteorological, navigational, and other information. Initiate and coordinate searches for missing aircraft.

Considerations for Job Outlook: More controllers are expected to be needed to handle increasing air traffic. Competition for admission to the FAA Academy—the usual first step in employment as an air traffic controller—is expected to remain keen.

Personality Type: Enterprising-Conventional. **Skills:** Complex Problem Solving; Operation Monitoring; Judgment and Decision Making; Operations Analysis; Monitoring; Coordination; Systems Analysis; Systems Evaluation. **Education and Training Program:** Air Traffic Controller. **Work Environment:** Indoors; sitting; sounds, noisy; using your hands to handle, control, or feel objects, tools, or controls; making repetitive motions.

OTHER FEDERAL JOB FACTS

RELATED GS SERIES: 2152 AIR TRAFFIC CONTROL

TITLE ON USAJOBS: AIR TRAFFIC CONTROLLER

- U.S. Federal Workforce: 22,157
- Average Length of Service: 15.4 years
- Percent Part-Time: 0.2%
- Percent Women: 16.1%
- Largest Age Bracket: 45–49 (23.3%)
- GS Level with Most Workers: 11
- Agency with Most Workers: Transportation
- State with Most Workers: California

Control air traffic to ensure the safe, orderly, and expeditious movement along air routes and at airports; provide preflight and in-flight assistance to aircraft; or develop, coordinate, and manage air traffic control programs.

Requirements: Extensive knowledge of the laws, rules, regulations, and procedures governing the movement of air traffic; knowledge of aircraft separation standards and control techniques, and the ability to apply them properly, often under conditions of great stress; knowledge of the information pilots need to conduct safe flights; the ability to present that information clearly and concisely.

Aircraft Mechanics and Service Technicians

- Education/Training Required: Postsecondary vocational training
- Annual Earnings (Federal): $53,750
- Annual Earnings (All Industries): $52,810
- Earnings Growth Potential (Federal): 16.1% (very low)
- Earnings Growth Potential (All Industries): 36.8% (medium)
- Job Growth (Federal): 7.6%
- Job Growth (All Industries): 6.4%
- Annual Job Openings (Federal): 330
- Annual Job Openings (All Industries): 3,140

Diagnose, adjust, repair, or overhaul aircraft engines and assemblies such as hydraulic and pneumatic systems. Read and interpret maintenance manuals, service bulletins, and other specifications to determine the feasibility and method of repairing or replacing malfunctioning or damaged components. Inspect completed work to certify that maintenance meets standards and that aircraft are ready for operation. Maintain repair logs, documenting all preventive and corrective aircraft maintenance. Conduct routine and special inspections as required by regulations. Examine and inspect aircraft components, including landing gear, hydraulic systems, and de-icers, to locate cracks, breaks, leaks, or other problems. Inspect airframes for wear or other defects. Maintain, repair, and rebuild aircraft structures; functional components; and parts such as wings and fuselage, rigging, hydraulic units, oxygen systems, fuel systems, electrical systems, gaskets, and seals. Measure the tension of control cables. Replace or repair worn, defective, or damaged components, using hand tools, gauges, and testing equipment. Measure parts for wear, using precision instruments. Assemble and install electrical, plumbing, mechanical, hydraulic, and structural components and accessories, using hand tools and power tools. Test operation of engines and other systems, using test equipment such as ignition analyzers, compression checkers, distributor timers, and ammeters. Obtain fuel and oil samples and check them for contamination. Reassemble engines following repair or inspection and re-install engines in aircraft.

Considerations for Job Outlook: Air traffic is expected to increase due to an expanding economy and a growing population, leading to employment growth for aircraft mechanics and service technicians. Prospects should be best for job seekers who have experience and professional certification.

Personality Type: Realistic-Conventional-Investigative. **Skills:** Equipment Maintenance; Repairing; Troubleshooting; Equipment Selection; Quality Control Analysis; Operation Monitoring; Operation and Control; Science. **Education and Training Program:** Agricultural Mechanics and Equipment/Machine Technology; Aircraft Powerplant Technology/Technician; Airframe Mechanics and Aircraft Maintenance Technology/Technician. **Work Environment:** Using your hands to handle, control, or feel objects, tools, or controls; sounds, noisy; contaminants; standing; bending or twisting the body; cramped work space, awkward positions.

OTHER FEDERAL JOB FACTS

RELATED GS SERIES: 8602 AIRCRAFT ENGINE MECHANIC

- ✴ U.S. Federal Workforce: 3,159
- ✴ Average Length of Service: 12.2 years
- ✴ Percent Part-Time: 0.0%

- ✴ Percent Women: 6.5%
- ✴ Largest Age Bracket: 45–49 (18.7%)
- ✴ GS Level with Most Workers: Not a GS occupation
- ✴ Agency with Most Workers: Defense
- ✴ State with Most Workers: Oklahoma

Perform maintenance, troubleshooting, repair, overhaul, modification, and testing of conventional, modified, and experimental aircraft engines, their components, assemblies, and subassemblies. Also perform work involving engine accessories such as starters, generators, anti-icers, and fuel control devices when such assignments are incidental to work on the completed engine.

Requirements: Skill and knowledge of a variety of conventional or modified aircraft engines and their accessory systems; also skill and knowledge of mechanical systems and methods of scraping and grinding in order to assemble parts to critical tolerances; adjusting and synchronizing complex gear trains and control mechanisms; using standard measuring and testing instruments; reading and interpreting blueprints and specification sheets

RELATED GS SERIES: 8852 AIRCRAFT MECHANIC

- ✴ U.S. Federal Workforce: 10,361
- ✴ Average Length of Service: 10.7 years
- ✴ Percent Part-Time: 0.0%
- ✴ Percent Women: 3.3%
- ✴ Largest Age Bracket: 45–49 (16.6%)
- ✴ GS Level with Most Workers: Not a GS occupation
- ✴ Agency with Most Workers: Defense
- ✴ State with Most Workers: Oklahoma

Maintain, troubleshoot, repair, overhaul, and modify fixed- and rotary-wing aircraft systems, airframes, components, and assemblies.

Requirements: Substantive knowledge of airframe and aircraft mechanical, pneudraulic, and/or electrical systems and their interrelationships; may require some knowledge of electronics.

Related GS Series: 8840 Aircraft Mechanical Parts Repairing

- ❀ U.S. Federal Workforce: 727
- ❀ Average Length of Service: 14.3 years
- ❀ Percent Part-Time: 0.0%
- ❀ Percent Women: 8.1%
- ❀ Largest Age Bracket: 50–54 (15.3%)
- ❀ GS Level with Most Workers: Not a GS occupation
- ❀ Agency with Most Workers: Defense
- ❀ State with Most Workers: Texas

Repair, modify, overhaul, recondition, and test mechanical parts and components removed from fixed- and rotary-wing aircraft, such as control columns, transmissions, gear boxes, landing gear components, clutch assemblies, rotor-head assemblies and blades, constant-speed drives, mechanical actuators, wheel and rotor brake assemblies, cargo hooks, engine controls, cable-tension regulators, accessory-drive gear boxes, cargo winches, turbine blades, and compressor vanes.

Requirements: Knowledge of the mechanical relationships and operational characteristics of mechanical parts and components being repaired or reworked. Does not require a substantive knowledge of aircraft systems and their interrelationships.

Related GS Series: 6652 Aircraft Ordnance Systems Mechanic

- ❀ U.S. Federal Workforce: 1,205
- ❀ Average Length of Service: 11.1 years
- ❀ Percent Part-Time: 0.0%
- ❀ Percent Women: 3.9%

- ❀ Largest Age Bracket: 45–49 (20.7%)
- ❀ GS Level with Most Workers: Not a GS occupation
- ❀ Agency with Most Workers: Defense
- ❀ State with Most Workers: Arizona

Troubleshooting, repair, install, modify, and perform operational and functional testing and adjustment of aircraft ordnance systems, equipment, and components.

Requirements: Knowledge of aircraft ordnance systems, the ability to recognize and determine the best method to correct malfunctions, and the ability to use test equipment and measuring devices common to the occupation.

Related GS Series: 8810 Aircraft Propeller Mechanic

- ❀ U.S. Federal Workforce: 150
- ❀ Average Length of Service: 11.5 years
- ❀ Percent Part-Time: 0.0%
- ❀ Percent Women: 4.0%
- ❀ Largest Age Bracket: 25–29 (16.7%)
- ❀ GS Level with Most Workers: Not a GS occupation
- ❀ Agency with Most Workers: Defense
- ❀ State with Most Workers: Georgia

Perform troubleshooting, repairing, adjusting, overhauling, modifying, testing, and servicing of aircraft propeller assemblies and their components; straighten propeller blades.

Requirements: Overall knowledge of hydraulic, electric, and mechanical controls; drive mechanisms and their subassemblies; and of the interrelationships of the mechanisms, valves, synchrophasers, and other components of the complete propeller assembly.

Airline Pilots, Copilots, and Flight Engineers

⚘ Education/Training Required: Bachelor's degree

⚘ Annual Earnings (Federal): $97,290

⚘ Annual Earnings (All Industries): $106,240

⚘ Earnings Growth Potential (Federal): 24.4% (very low)

⚘ Earnings Growth Potential (All Industries): 46.7% (high)

⚘ Job Growth (Federal): 7.5%

⚘ Job Growth (All Industries): 8.4%

⚘ Annual Job Openings (Federal): 90

⚘ Annual Job Openings (All Industries): 3,250

Pilot and navigate the flight of multi-engine aircraft in regularly scheduled service for the transport of passengers and cargo. Requires Federal Air Transport rating and certification in specific aircraft type used. Use instrumentation to guide flights when visibility is poor. Respond to and report in-flight emergencies and malfunctions. Work as part of a flight team with other crew members, especially during takeoffs and landings. Contact control towers for takeoff clearances, arrival instructions, and other information, using radio equipment. Steer aircraft along planned routes with the assistance of autopilot and flight management computers. Monitor gauges, warning devices, and control panels to verify aircraft performance and to regulate engine speed. Start engines, operate controls, and pilot airplanes to transport passengers, mail, or freight while adhering to flight plans, regulations, and procedures. Inspect aircraft for defects and malfunctions according to pre-flight checklists. Check passenger and cargo distributions and fuel amounts to ensure that weight and balance specifications are met. Monitor engine operation, fuel consumption, and functioning of aircraft systems during flights. Confer with flight dispatchers and weather forecasters to keep abreast of flight conditions. Coordinate flight activities with ground crews and air-traffic control and inform crew members of flight and test procedures. Order changes in fuel supplies, loads, routes, or schedules to ensure safety of flights. Choose routes, altitudes, and speeds that will provide the fastest, safest, and smoothest flights. Direct activities of aircraft crews during flights.

Considerations for Job Outlook: Population growth and economic expansion are expected to boost demand for air travel. Regional airlines and low-cost carriers should have the best opportunities; pilots vying for jobs with major airlines face strong competition.

Personality Type: Realistic-Conventional-Investigative. **Skills:** Operation and Control; Operation Monitoring; Science; Troubleshooting; Instructing; Judgment and Decision Making; Quality Control Analysis; Mathematics. **Education and Training Program:** Airline/Commercial/Professional Pilot and Flight Crew; Flight Instructor. **Work Environment:** Indoors; sitting; using your hands to handle, control, or feel objects, tools, or controls; sounds, noisy; radiation; contaminants.

OTHER FEDERAL JOB FACTS

RELATED GS SERIES: 2183 AIR NAVIGATION

TITLE ON USAJOBS: AIR NAVIGATION SPECIALIST

⚘ U.S. Federal Workforce: 161

⚘ Average Length of Service: 9.1 years

⚘ Percent Part-Time: 0.0%

⚘ Percent Women: 3.7%

⚘ Largest Age Bracket: 45–49 (28.6%)

⚘ GS Level with Most Workers: 12

⚘ Agency with Most Workers: Defense

⚘ State with Most Workers: Georgia

Assist the pilot in aircraft operations by determining, planning, and performing the navigational aspects of the flight. May provide ground and flight instruction in air navigation.

Requirements: Knowledge of the various methods of air navigation; skill in using navigational instruments, equipment, and systems in conjunction with flight instruments to direct the movement and positioning of the aircraft; may require knowledge of the use and deployment of fighter aircraft ordnance; skill to conduct preflight checks, recognize malfunctions, and coordinate delivery with the pilot; and knowledge of weapon ballistics and skill to operate related avionics systems for fighter aircraft.

RELATED GS SERIES: 2181 AIRCRAFT OPERATION

* U.S. Federal Workforce: 2,868
* Average Length of Service: 9.5 years
* Percent Part-Time: 0.3%
* Percent Women: 2.2%
* Largest Age Bracket: 45–49 (22.4%)
* GS Level with Most Workers: 13
* Agency with Most Workers: Defense
* State with Most Workers: Alabama

Pilot or copilot aircraft to carry out various programs and functions of federal agencies; provide ground and flight instruction and in-flight evaluation in the piloting of aircraft; perform flight testing of developmental and modified aircraft and components; perform in-flight inspection and evaluation of air navigation facilities and the environmental conditions affecting instrument flight procedures; and plan, analyze, or administer agency aviation programs.

Requirements: Knowledge and skills appropriate for pilots.

Animal Scientists

* Education/Training Required: Doctoral degree
* Annual Earnings (Federal): $101,350
* Annual Earnings (All Industries): $56,960
* Earnings Growth Potential (Federal): 33.8% (low)
* Earnings Growth Potential (All Industries): 44.3% (high)
* Job Growth (Federal): 10.0%
* Job Growth (All Industries): 13.2%
* Annual Job Openings (Federal): 10
* Annual Job Openings (All Industries): 180

Conduct research in the genetics, nutrition, reproduction, growth, and development of domestic farm animals. Conduct research concerning animal nutrition, breeding, or management to improve products or processes. Advise producers about improved products and techniques that could enhance their animal production efforts. Study nutritional requirements of animals and nutritive values of animal feed materials. Study effects of management practices, processing methods, feed, or environmental conditions on quality and quantity of animal products, such as eggs and milk. Develop improved practices in feeding, housing, sanitation, or parasite and disease control of animals. Research and control animal selection and breeding practices to increase production efficiency and improve animal quality. Determine genetic composition of animal populations and heritability of traits, utilizing principles of genetics. Crossbreed animals with existing strains or cross strains to obtain new combinations of desirable characteristics.

Considerations for Job Outlook: Job growth is expected to stem primarily from efforts to increase the quantity and quality of food for a growing population and to balance output with protection and preservation of soil, water, and ecosystems. Opportunities should be good for agricultural and food scientists in almost all fields.

Personality Type: Investigative-Realistic. **Skills:** Science; Systems Evaluation; Judgment and Decision Making; Writing; Mathematics; Complex Problem Solving; Active Learning; Systems Analysis. **Education and Training Program:** Agricultural Animal Breeding; Agriculture, General; Animal Health; Animal Nutrition; Animal Sciences, Other; Dairy Science; Poultry Science; Range Science and Management. **Work Environment:** More often outdoors than indoors; sitting; contaminants.

OTHER FEDERAL JOB FACTS

Related GS Series: 0487 Animal Science

- ✳ U.S. Federal Workforce: 104
- ✳ Average Length of Service: 14.9 years
- ✳ Percent Part-Time: 1.9%
- ✳ Percent Women: 28.8%
- ✳ Largest Age Bracket: 55–59 (20.2%)
- ✳ GS Levels with Most Workers: 11, 14
- ✳ Agency with Most Workers: Agriculture
- ✳ State with Most Workers: Maryland

Do research or other professional and scientific work in the field of animal science, including nutritional, biophysical, biochemical, and physiological relationships.

Requirements: Full professional education and training in the biological and agricultural sciences and a fundamental knowledge of the principles, methods, techniques, and relationships in the field of animal science and the application of this knowledge in the investigation, analysis, and solution of animal science problems.

Anthropologists and Archeologists

- ✳ Education/Training Required: Master's degree
- ✳ Annual Earnings (Federal): $70,400
- ✳ Annual Earnings (All Industries): $53,460
- ✳ Earnings Growth Potential (Federal): 31.5% (low)
- ✳ Earnings Growth Potential (All Industries): 41.0% (high)
- ✳ Job Growth (Federal): 19.9%
- ✳ Job Growth (All Industries): 28.0%
- ✳ Annual Job Openings (Federal): 70
- ✳ Annual Job Openings (All Industries): 450

Study the origin, development, and behavior of humans. May study the way of life, language, or physical characteristics of existing people in various parts of the world. May engage in systematic recovery and examination of material evidence, such as tools or pottery remaining from past human cultures, to determine the history, customs, and living habits of earlier civilizations.

Considerations for Job Outlook: Anthropologists are projected to have significant employment growth in the management, scientific, and technical consulting industry. Expected job growth for archaeologists is associated with large-scale construction projects that must comply with federal laws to preserve archaeological sites. Job competition is expected, especially for historians.

Job Specialization: Anthropologists

Research, evaluate, and establish public policy concerning the origins of humans; their physical, social, linguistic, and cultural development; and their behavior, as well as the cultures, organizations, and institutions they have

created. Collect information and make judgments through observation, interviews, and the review of documents. Plan and direct research to characterize and compare the economic, demographic, health-care, social, political, linguistic, and religious institutions of distinct cultural groups, communities, and organizations. Write about and present research findings for a variety of specialized and general audiences. Advise government agencies, private organizations, and communities regarding proposed programs, plans, and policies and their potential impacts on cultural institutions, organizations, and communities. Identify culturally specific beliefs and practices affecting health status and access to services for distinct populations and communities in collaboration with medical and public health officials. Build and use text-based database management systems to support the analysis of detailed first-hand observational records, or "field notes." Develop intervention procedures, utilizing techniques such as individual and focus group interviews, consultations, and participant observation of social interaction. Construct and test data collection methods. Explain the origins and physical, social, or cultural development of humans, including physical attributes, cultural traditions, beliefs, languages, resource management practices, and settlement patterns.

Personality Type: Investigative-Artistic. **Skills:** Science; Operations Analysis; Systems Analysis; Writing; Systems Evaluation; Speaking; Social Perceptiveness; Reading Comprehension. **Education and Training Program:** Anthropology; Archeology; Classics and Classical Languages, Literatures, and Linguistics, General; Physical and Biological Anthropology. **Work Environment:** Indoors; sitting.

JOB SPECIALIZATION: ARCHEOLOGISTS

Conduct research to reconstruct record of past human life and culture from human remains, artifacts, architectural features, and structures recovered through excavation, underwater recovery, or other means of discovery. Write, present, and publish reports that record site history, methodology, and artifact analysis results, along with recommendations for conserving and interpreting findings. Compare findings from one site with archeological data from other sites to find similarities or differences. Research, survey, or assess sites of past societies and cultures in search of answers to specific research questions. Study objects and structures recovered by excavation to identify, date, and authenticate them and to interpret their significance. Develop and test theories concerning the origin and development of past cultures. Consult site reports, existing artifacts, and topographic maps to identify archeological sites. Create a grid of each site and draw and update maps of unit profiles, stratum surfaces, features, and findings. Record the exact locations and conditions of artifacts uncovered in diggings or surveys, using drawings and photographs as necessary. Assess archeological sites for resource management, development, or conservation purposes and recommend methods for site protection. Describe artifacts' physical properties or attributes, such as the materials from which artifacts are made and their size, shape, function, and decoration. Teach archeology at colleges and universities. Collect artifacts made of stone, bone, metal, and other materials, placing them in bags and marking them to show where they were found.

Personality Type: Investigative-Realistic-Artistic. **Skills:** Science; Reading Comprehension; Writing; Management of Personnel Resources; Learning Strategies; Mathematics; Active Learning; Critical Thinking. **Education and Training Program:** Anthropology; Archeology; Classics and Classical Languages, Literatures, and Linguistics, General; Physical and Biological Anthropology. **Work Environment:** More often indoors than outdoors; sitting; using your hands to handle, control, or feel objects, tools, or controls.

OTHER FEDERAL JOB FACTS

RELATED GS SERIES: 0193 ARCHEOLOGY

TITLE ON USAJOBS: ARCHEOLOGIST

* U.S. Federal Workforce: 1,233
* Average Length of Service: 13.4 years
* Percent Part-Time: 2.2%
* Percent Women: 44.2%
* Largest Age Bracket: 55–59 (20.8%)
* GS Level with Most Workers: 11
* Agencies with Most Workers: Interior, Agriculture
* State with Most Workers: California

Perform research, field investigations, laboratory analysis, library research, interpretation or consultative work, preparation of reports for publication, curation and exhibition of collections, or development and implementation of programs and projects that carry out such work.

Requirements: Professional knowledge of archeological principles, theories, concepts, methods, and techniques.

RELATED GS SERIES: 0190 GENERAL ANTHROPOLOGY

TITLE ON USAJOBS: ANTHROPOLOGIST

* U.S. Federal Workforce: 183
* Average Length of Service: 9.8 years
* Percent Part-Time: 38.8%
* Percent Women: 56.8%
* Largest Age Bracket: 55–59 (16.9%)
* GS Level with Most Workers: 13
* Agency with Most Workers: Health and Human Services
* State with Most Workers: Hawaii

Advise on, supervise, or perform research or other professional and scientific work in the anthropological sciences except archeology.

Requirements: Professional knowledge of anthropology or one or several of the branches of the scientific field that includes ethnology, physical anthropology, and scientific linguistics.

Arbitrators, Mediators, and Conciliators

* Education/Training Required: Bachelor's or higher degree, plus work experience
* Annual Earnings (Federal): $119,740
* Annual Earnings (All Industries): $52,770
* Earnings Growth Potential (Federal): 15.4% (very low)
* Earnings Growth Potential (All Industries): 41.5% (high)
* Job Growth (Federal): 9.5%
* Job Growth (All Industries): 13.9%
* Annual Job Openings (Federal): 10
* Annual Job Openings (All Industries): 320

Facilitate negotiation and conflict resolution through dialogue. Resolve conflicts outside of the court system by mutual consent of parties involved. Conduct studies of appeals procedures in order to ensure adherence to legal requirements and to facilitate disposition of cases. Rule on exceptions, motions, and admissibility of evidence. Review and evaluate information from documents such as claim applications, birth or death certificates, and physician or employer records. Organize and deliver public presentations about mediation to organizations such as community agencies and schools. Prepare written opinions and decisions regarding cases. Prepare settlement agreements for disputants to sign. Use mediation techniques to facilitate communication between disputants, to further parties' understanding of different perspectives, and to guide parties toward mutual agreement. Notify claimants of denied claims and appeal rights. Analyze evidence and apply relevant laws, regulations, policies, and precedents in order to reach conclusions. Conduct initial meetings with disputants to outline the arbitration process, settle procedural matters such as fees, and determine details such as witness numbers and time requirements. Confer with disputants to clarify issues, identify underlying concerns, and develop an understanding of their respective needs and interests. Participate in court proceedings. Arrange and conduct hearings to obtain information and evidence relative to disposition of claims. Recommend acceptance or rejection of compromise settlement offers.

Considerations for Job Outlook: Budget pressures are expected to limit the hiring of new judges, particularly in federal courts. Alternatives to litigation are usually faster and less expensive, spurring employment growth for other judicial workers, such as arbitrators, mediators, and conciliators.

Personality Type: Social-Enterprising. **Skills:** Negotiation; Persuasion; Active Listening; Speaking; Critical Thinking; Operations Analysis; Social Perceptiveness; Reading Comprehension. **Education and Training Program:** Law (LL.B., J.D.); Legal Professions and Studies, Other; Legal Studies, General. **Work Environment:** Indoors; sitting.

OTHER FEDERAL JOB FACTS

RELATED GS SERIES: 0241 MEDIATION

TITLE ON USAJOBS: MEDIATOR

- U.S. Federal Workforce: 192
- Average Length of Service: 14.7 years
- Percent Part-Time: 0.0%
- Percent Women: 22.9%
- Largest Age Bracket: 60–64 (32.3%)
- GS Level with Most Workers: 14

- Agency with Most Workers: No data available
- State with Most Workers: District of Columbia

Provide mediation assistance to labor and management in the settlement or prevention of industrial labor disputes connected with the formulation, revision, termination, or renewal of collective-bargaining agreements.

Requirements: Ability and skill in applying the techniques of mediation in dealing with the parties to a dispute; knowledge of the field of labor-management relations, particularly of collective bargaining principles, practices, and processes; understanding of economic, industrial, and labor trends, and of current developments and problems in the field of labor relations; and knowledge of applicable labor laws and precedent decisions.

Architects, Except Landscape and Naval

- Education/Training Required: Bachelor's degree
- Annual Earnings (Federal): $89,070
- Annual Earnings (All Industries): $72,700
- Earnings Growth Potential (Federal): 24.8% (very low)
- Earnings Growth Potential (All Industries): 41.8% (high)
- Job Growth (Federal): 5.7%
- Job Growth (All Industries): 16.2%
- Annual Job Openings (Federal): 50
- Annual Job Openings (All Industries): 4,680

Plan and design structures such as private residences, office buildings, theaters, factories, and other structural property. Consult with client to determine functional and spatial requirements of structure. Prepare scale drawings. Plan layout of project. Prepare information regarding design, structure specifications, materials, color, equipment, estimated costs, or construction time. Prepare contract documents for building contractors. Integrate engineering elements into unified design. Direct activities of workers engaged in preparing drawings and specification documents. Conduct periodic on-site observation of work during construction to monitor compliance with plans. Seek new work opportunities through marketing, writing proposals, or giving presentations. Administer construction contracts. Represent client in obtaining bids and awarding construction contracts. Prepare operating and maintenance manuals, studies, and reports.

Considerations for Job Outlook: Changing demographics, such as the population's aging and shifting to warmer states, should lead to employment growth for architects to design new buildings to accommodate these changes. Job competition should be keen.

Personality Type: Artistic-Investigative. **Skills:** Operations Analysis; Management of Financial Resources; Management of Material Resources; Mathematics; Science; Judgment and Decision Making; Quality Control Analysis; Negotiation. **Education and Training Program:** Architectural History and Criticism, General; Architecture (BArch, BA/BS, MArch, MA/MS, PhD); Architecture and Related Services, Other; Environmental Design/Architecture. **Work Environment:** Indoors; sitting; using your hands to handle, control, or feel objects, tools, or controls; making repetitive motions.

OTHER FEDERAL JOB FACTS

RELATED GS SERIES: 0808 ARCHITECTURE

TITLE ON USAJOBS: ARCHITECT

- U.S. Federal Workforce: 1,968
- Average Length of Service: 13.0 years

- Percent Part-Time: 1.5%
- Percent Women: 21.7%
- Largest Age Bracket: 55–59 (19.0%)
- GS Level with Most Workers: 12
- Agency with Most Workers: Defense
- State with Most Workers: District of Columbia

Manage, supervise, lead, and/or perform professional architecture work involving the art and science of conceptualizing, planning, developing, and implementing designs of buildings and structures.

Requirements: Professional knowledge of and skills in architecture.

Artists and Related Workers, All Other

- Education/Training Required: Long-term on-the-job training
- Annual Earnings (Federal): $70,520
- Annual Earnings (All Industries): $53,110
- Earnings Growth Potential (Federal): 54.9% (very high)
- Earnings Growth Potential (All Industries): 53.7% (very high)
- Job Growth (Federal): 7.6%
- Job Growth (All Industries): 7.8%
- Annual Job Openings (Federal): 200
- Annual Job Openings (All Industries): 650

Considerations for Job Outlook: Demand for digital and multimedia artwork is expected to drive growth. Competition should be keen for certain kinds of jobs. Multimedia artists and animators should have better opportunities than other artists.

Personality Type: No data available. **Skills:** No data available. **Education and Training Program:** Fine Arts and Art Studies, Other. **Work Environment:** No data available.

OTHER FEDERAL JOB FACTS

RELATED GS SERIES: 1056 ART SPECIALIST

- ❋ U.S. Federal Workforce: 15
- ❋ Average Length of Service: 24.3 years
- ❋ Percent Part-Time: 0.0%
- ❋ Percent Women: 60.0%
- ❋ Largest Age Bracket: 55–59 (40.0%)
- ❋ GS Level with Most Workers: 9
- ❋ Agency with Most Workers: Defense
- ❋ States with Most Workers: Hawaii, Texas

Plan, supervise, administer, or carry out educational, recreational, cultural, or other programs in art; demonstrate the techniques and instruct in one or more of the arts.

Requirements: Knowledge of the theories and techniques of one or more art forms.

RELATED GS SERIES: 1020 ILLUSTRATING

TITLE ON USAJOBS: ILLUSTRATOR

- ❋ U.S. Federal Workforce: 208
- ❋ Average Length of Service: 18.9 years
- ❋ Percent Part-Time: 2.9%
- ❋ Percent Women: 35.6%
- ❋ Largest Age Bracket: 45–49 (16.8%)
- ❋ GS Level with Most Workers: 11
- ❋ Agency with Most Workers: Defense
- ❋ State with Most Workers: Virginia

Lay out or execute illustrations in black and white or in color; retouch photographs.

Requirements: Artistic ability; the skill to draw freehand or with drawing instruments; the ability to use art media such as pen-and-ink, pencils, tempera, acrylics, oils, wash, watercolor, pastels, air brush, or computer-generated graphics; knowledge of the subject matter being depicted; and knowledge of basic art principles, such as color, line, form, and space.

Astronomers

- ❋ Education/Training Required: Doctoral degree
- ❋ Annual Earnings (Federal): $136,010
- ❋ Annual Earnings (All Industries): $104,720
- ❋ Earnings Growth Potential (Federal): 33.0% (low)
- ❋ Earnings Growth Potential (All Industries): 56.4% (very high)
- ❋ Job Growth (Federal): 10.9%
- ❋ Job Growth (All Industries): 15.6%
- ❋ Annual Job Openings (Federal): 20
- ❋ Annual Job Openings (All Industries): 70

Observe, research, and interpret celestial and astronomical phenomena to increase basic knowledge and apply such information to practical problems. Study celestial phenomena, using a variety of ground-based and space-borne telescopes and scientific instruments. Analyze research data to determine its significance, using computers. Present research findings at scientific conferences and in papers written for scientific journals. Measure radio, infrared, gamma, and X-ray emissions from extraterrestrial sources. Develop theories based on personal observations or on observations and theories of other astronomers. Raise funds for scientific research. Collaborate with other astronomers to carry out research projects. Develop instrumentation and software for astronomical observation and analysis. Teach astronomy or astrophysics. Develop and modify astronomy-related programs for public presentation. Calculate orbits and determine sizes, shapes, brightness, and motions of different celestial bodies. Direct the operations of a planetarium.

Considerations for Job Outlook: An increased focus on basic research, particularly that related to energy, is expected to drive employment growth for these workers. Prospects should be favorable for physicists in applied research, development, and related technical fields and for astronomers in government and academia.

Personality Type: Investigative-Artistic-Realistic. **Skills:** Science; Mathematics; Active Learning; Reading Comprehension; Writing; Operations Analysis; Speaking; Instructing. **Education and Training Program:** Astronomy; Astronomy and Astrophysics, Other; Astrophysics; Planetary Astronomy and Science. **Work Environment:** Indoors; sitting.

OTHER FEDERAL JOB FACTS

RELATED GS SERIES: 1330 ASTRONOMY AND SPACE SCIENCE

TITLE ON USAJOBS: ASTRONOMER/SPACE SCIENTIST

- U.S. Federal Workforce: 459
- Average Length of Service: 16.8 years
- Percent Part-Time: 0.9%
- Percent Women: 19.2%
- Largest Age Bracket: 55–59 (16.3%)
- GS Level with Most Workers: 15
- Agency with Most Workers: Defense
- State with Most Workers: Maryland

Investigate and interpret the physical properties, composition, evolution, position, distance, and motion of extraterrestrial bodies and particles in space.

Requirements: Professional knowledge of the principles and techniques of astronomy and physics.

Avionics Technicians

- Education/Training Required: Postsecondary vocational training
- Annual Earnings (Federal): $51,650
- Annual Earnings (All Industries): $50,570
- Earnings Growth Potential (Federal): 15.5% (very low)
- Earnings Growth Potential (All Industries): 31.5% (low)
- Job Growth (Federal): 7.9%
- Job Growth (All Industries): 10.6%
- Annual Job Openings (Federal): 40
- Annual Job Openings (All Industries): 520

Install, inspect, test, adjust, or repair avionics equipment, such as radar, radio, navigation, and missile control systems in aircraft or space vehicles. Set up and operate ground support and test equipment to perform functional flight tests of electrical and electronic systems. Test and troubleshoot instruments, components, and assemblies, using circuit testers, oscilloscopes, and voltmeters. Keep records of maintenance and repair work. Coordinate work with that of engineers, technicians, and other aircraft maintenance personnel. Interpret flight test data to diagnose malfunctions and systemic performance problems. Install electrical and electronic components, assemblies, and systems in aircraft, using hand tools, power tools, and soldering irons. Adjust, repair, or replace malfunctioning components or assemblies, using hand tools and soldering irons. Connect components to assemblies such as radio systems, instruments, magnetos, inverters, and in-flight refueling systems, using hand tools and soldering irons. Assemble components such as switches, electrical controls, and junction boxes, using hand tools and soldering irons. Fabricate parts and test aids as required. Lay out installation of aircraft assemblies and systems, following documentation such as blueprints, manuals, and wiring diagrams. Assemble prototypes or models of circuits, instruments, and systems so that they can be used for testing. Operate computer-aided drafting and design applications to design avionics system modifications.

Considerations for Job Outlook: Air traffic is expected to increase due to an expanding economy and a growing population, leading to employment growth for aircraft mechanics and service technicians. Prospects should be best for job seekers who have experience and professional certification.

Personality Type: Realistic-Investigative-Conventional. **Skills:** Repairing; Equipment Maintenance; Troubleshooting; Equipment Selection; Installation; Quality Control Analysis; Science; Operation Monitoring. **Education and Training Program:** Airframe Mechanics and Aircraft Maintenance Technology/Technician; Avionics Maintenance Technology/Technician. **Work Environment:** Indoors; sitting; using hands; noise; contaminants; hazardous conditions.

OTHER FEDERAL JOB FACTS

RELATED GS SERIES: 2892 AIRCRAFT ELECTRICIAN

- U.S. Federal Workforce: 2029
- Average Length of Service: 10.9 years
- Percent Part-Time: 0.0%
- Percent Women: 6.9%
- Largest Age Bracket: 45–49 (16.0%)
- GS Level with Most Workers: Not a GS occupation
- Agency with Most Workers: Defense
- State with Most Workers: Oklahoma

Install, troubleshoot, adjust, test, modify, calibrate, and repair aircraft electrical systems and equipment on board conventional and nonconventional aircraft such as electrical power control and distribution systems, lighting systems, refueling and fuel quantity indicating systems, electrical warning, controlling, and actuating circuits; also tie-in power and control circuits for functional systems such as hydraulics, armament, radar, engines, and fire suppression.

Requirements: Understanding of the functional characteristics and relationships of various electrical systems and equipment on aircraft.

Biological Scientists, All Other

- Education/Training Required: Doctoral degree
- Annual Earnings (Federal): $69,860
- Annual Earnings (All Industries): $66,510
- Earnings Growth Potential (Federal): 35.6% (median)
- Earnings Growth Potential (All Industries): 44.7% (high)
- Job Growth (Federal): 19.6%
- Job Growth (All Industries): 18.8%
- Annual Job Openings (Federal): 670
- Annual Job Openings (All Industries): 1,610

Considerations for Job Outlook: Biotechnological research and development should continue to drive job growth. Doctoral degree holders are expected to face competition for research positions in academia.

JOB SPECIALIZATION: BIOINFORMATICS SCIENTISTS

Conduct research using bioinformatics theory and methods in areas such as pharmaceuticals, medical technology, biotechnology,

computational biology, proteomics, computer information science, biology, and medical informatics. May design databases and develop algorithms for processing and analyzing genomic information or other biological information. Recommend new systems and processes to improve operations. Keep abreast of new biochemistries, instrumentation, or software by reading scientific literature and attending professional conferences. Confer with departments such as marketing, business development, and operations to coordinate product development or improvement. Collaborate with software developers in the development and modification of commercial bioinformatics software. Test new and updated bioinformatics tools and software. Provide statistical and computational tools for biologically based activities such as genetic analysis, measurement of gene expression, and gene function determination. Prepare summary statistics of information regarding human genomes. Instruct others in the selection and use of bioinformatics tools. Improve user interfaces to bioinformatics software and databases. Direct the work of technicians and information technology staff applying bioinformatics tools or applications in areas such as proteomics, transcriptomics, metabolomics, and clinical bioinformatics. Develop new software applications or customize existing applications to meet specific scientific project needs. Develop data models and databases. Create or modify web-based bioinformatics tools. Design and apply bioinformatics algorithms including unsupervised and supervised machine learning, dynamic programming, or graphic algorithms. Create novel computational approaches and analytical tools as required by research goals.

Personality Type: Investigative-Conventional-Realistic. **Skills:** No data available. **Education and Training Program:** Bioinformatics. **Work Environment:** No data available.

Job Specialization: Geneticists

Research and study the inheritance of traits at the molecular, organism, or population level. May evaluate or treat patients with genetic disorders. Write grants and papers or attend fundraising events to seek research funds. Verify that cytogenetic, molecular genetic, and related equipment and instrumentation is maintained in working condition to ensure accuracy and quality of experimental results. Maintain laboratory safety programs and train personnel in laboratory safety techniques. Design and maintain genetics computer databases. Confer with information technology specialists to develop computer applications for genetic data analysis. Collaborate with biologists and other professionals to conduct appropriate genetic and biochemical analyses. Attend clinical and research conferences and read scientific literature to keep abreast of technological advances and current genetic research findings. Supervise or direct the work of other geneticists, biologists, technicians, or biometricians working on genetics research projects. Review, approve, or interpret genetic laboratory results.

Personality Type: Investigative-Artistic-Realistic. **Skills:** Science; Mathematics; Writing; Reading Comprehension; Systems Analysis; Learning Strategies; Instructing; Management of Material Resources. **Education and Training Program:** Animal Genetics; Genetics, General; Genetics, Other; Genome Sciences/Genomics; Human/Medical Genetics; Microbial and Eukaryotic Genetics; Molecular Genetics; Plant Genetics. **Work Environment:** Indoors; sitting; using your hands to handle, control, or feel objects, tools, or controls.

Job Specialization: Molecular and Cellular Biologists

Research and study cellular molecules and organelles to understand cell function and organization. Verify all financial, physical, and human resources assigned to research or development projects are used as planned. Develop guidelines for procedures such as the management of viruses. Coordinate molecular or cellular research activities with scientists specializing in other fields. Supervise technical personnel and postdoctoral research fellows. Prepare reports, manuscripts, and meeting presentations. Provide scientific direction for project teams regarding the evaluation or handling of devices, drugs, or cells for in vitro and in vivo disease models. Perform laboratory procedures following protocols including deoxyribonucleic acid (DNA) sequencing, cloning and extraction, ribonucleic acid (RNA) purification, or gel electrophoresis. Monitor or operate specialized equipment such as gas chromatographs and high pressure liquid chromatographs, electrophoresis units, thermocyclers, fluorescence activated cell sorters, and phosphoimagers. Maintain accurate laboratory records and data.

Personality Type: Investigative-Realistic-Artistic. **Skills:** Science; Programming; Reading Comprehension; Active Learning; Mathematics; Management of Financial Resources; Writing; Learning Strategies. **Education and Training Program:** Cell/Cellular Biology and Histology. **Work Environment:** Indoors; sitting; using your hands to handle, control, or feel objects, tools, or controls; hazardous conditions.

OTHER FEDERAL JOB FACTS

Related GS Series: 0401 General Biological Science

Title on USAJobs: Biological and Natural Resources

- ❋ U.S. Federal Workforce: 21,102
- ❋ Average Length of Service: 8 years
- ❋ Percent Part-Time: 4.0%
- ❋ Percent Women: 39.8%
- ❋ Largest Age Bracket: 50–54 (16.6%)
- ❋ GS Levels with Most Workers: 12, 11
- ❋ Agency with Most Workers: Agriculture
- ❋ State with Most Workers: Maryland

Do professional work in biology, agriculture, or related natural resource management when there is no other more specific job title.

Requirements: Degree in biological sciences, agriculture, natural resource management, chemistry, or related disciplines appropriate to the position; or equivalent combination of education and experience.

Related GS Series: 0440 Genetics

Title on USAJobs: Geneticist

- ❋ U.S. Federal Workforce: 462
- ❋ Average Length of Service: 12.8 years
- ❋ Percent Part-Time: 4.1%
- ❋ Percent Women: 31.6%
- ❋ Largest Age Bracket: 55–59 (18.0%)
- ❋ GS Level with Most Workers: 13
- ❋ Agency with Most Workers: Agriculture
- ❋ State with Most Workers: Maryland

Advise on, administer, supervise, or perform professional research in the principles and mechanisms of transmission of characters by inheritance, including in some instances the application of these principles in planning breeding programs.

Requirements: Knowledge of genetic science.

RELATED GS SERIES: 0482 FISHERY BIOLOGY
TITLE ON USAJOBS: BIOLOGIST, FISHERY

- ✹ U.S. Federal Workforce: 2,514
- ✹ Average Length of Service: 14.5 years
- ✹ Percent Part-Time: 2.0%
- ✹ Percent Women: 28.4%
- ✹ Largest Age Bracket: 50–54 (16.5%)
- ✹ GS Level with Most Workers: 11
- ✹ Agencies with Most Workers: Commerce, Interior
- ✹ State with Most Workers: Washington

Develop, conserve, manage, and administer fishery resources; evaluate the impact of construction projects and other socioeconomic activities that present potential or actual adverse effects on fishery resources and their habitat.

Requirements: Professional knowledge and competence in the science of fishery biology; ability to determine, establish, and apply biological facts, principles, methods, techniques, and procedures that are necessary for the production and/or management of aquatic resources in their natural habitat and/or within facilities and systems that have been constructed for their benefit and public use.

Biological Technicians

- ✹ Education/Training Required: Bachelor's degree
- ✹ Annual Earnings (Federal): $32,850
- ✹ Annual Earnings (All Industries): $38,700
- ✹ Earnings Growth Potential (Federal): 26.5% (low)
- ✹ Earnings Growth Potential (All Industries): 36.6% (medium)

- ✹ Job Growth (Federal): 7.6%
- ✹ Job Growth (All Industries): 17.6%
- ✹ Annual Job Openings (Federal): 470
- ✹ Annual Job Openings (All Industries): 4,190

Assist biological and medical scientists in laboratories. Set up, operate, and maintain laboratory instruments and equipment; monitor experiments; make observations; and calculate and record results. May analyze organic substances, such as blood, food, and drugs. Conduct research or assist in the conduct of research, including the collection of information and samples, such as blood, water, soil, plants, and animals. Analyze experimental data and interpret results to write reports and summaries of findings. Keep detailed logs of all work-related activities. Use computers, computer-interfaced equipment, robotics, or high-technology industrial applications to perform work duties. Clean, maintain, and prepare supplies and work areas. Set up, adjust, calibrate, clean, maintain, and troubleshoot laboratory and field equipment. Measure or weigh compounds and solutions for use in testing or animal feed. Isolate, identify, and prepare specimens for examination. Conduct standardized biological, microbiological, or biochemical tests and laboratory analyses to evaluate the quantity or quality of physical or chemical substances in food or other products. Examine animals and specimens to detect the presence of disease or other problems. Participate in the research, development, or manufacturing of medicinal and pharmaceutical preparations. Monitor laboratory work to ensure compliance with set standards. Provide technical support and services for scientists and engineers working in fields such as agriculture, environmental science, resource management, biology, and health sciences. Monitor and observe experiments, recording production and test data for evaluation by research personnel. Feed livestock or laboratory animals.

Considerations for Job Outlook: The continued growth of scientific and medical research and the development and manufacturing of technical products are expected to drive employment growth for these workers. Opportunities are expected to be best for graduates of applied science technology programs who are knowledgeable about equipment used in laboratories or production facilities.

Personality Type: Realistic-Investigative-Conventional. **Skills:** Science; Mathematics; Troubleshooting; Reading Comprehension; Quality Control Analysis; Operation and Control; Operation Monitoring; Judgment and Decision Making. **Education and Training Program:** Biology Technician/Biotechnology Laboratory Technician Training. **Work Environment:** Indoors; using your hands to handle, control, or feel objects, tools, or controls; contaminants; sitting; making repetitive motions.

OTHER FEDERAL JOB FACTS

RELATED GS SERIES: 0404 BIOLOGICAL SCIENCE TECHNICIAN

- ✽ U.S. Federal Workforce: 9,871
- ✽ Average Length of Service: 6.7 years
- ✽ Percent Part-Time: 22.3%
- ✽ Percent Women: 42.4%
- ✽ Largest Age Bracket: 20–24 (19.6%)
- ✽ GS Level with Most Workers: 5
- ✽ Agency with Most Workers: Agriculture
- ✽ State with Most Workers: California

Provide practical technical support to production, research, operations, or program administration efforts in laboratories, field, or other settings including greenhouses, barns, caves, or wildlife refuges.

Requirements: Practical knowledge of the methods and techniques of one or more of the biological or agricultural sciences.

RELATED GS SERIES: 0421 PLANT PROTECTION TECHNICIAN

- ✽ U.S. Federal Workforce: 1,054
- ✽ Average Length of Service: 4.2 years
- ✽ Percent Part-Time: 54.9%
- ✽ Percent Women: 32.4%
- ✽ Largest Age Bracket: 65 or more (17.3%)
- ✽ GS Levels with Most Workers: 3, 7
- ✽ Agency with Most Workers: Agriculture
- ✽ State with Most Workers: Hawaii

Provide technical support in research efforts; in the establishment and enforcement of plant quarantines governing the movement of insects, plant diseases, nematodes, and other plant pests of economic importance; or in the survey, detection, field identification, control, or eradication of plant pests.

Requirements: Practical knowledge of the types and characteristics of plant pests, quarantine procedures, pest control and eradication methods, and plant pest survey techniques.

RELATED GS SERIES: 0455 RANGE TECHNICIAN

- ✽ U.S. Federal Workforce: 2,023
- ✽ Average Length of Service: 6.4 years
- ✽ Percent Part-Time: 4.6%
- ✽ Percent Women: 15.5%
- ✽ Largest Age Bracket: 25–29 (26.1%)
- ✽ GS Level with Most Workers: 7
- ✽ Agency with Most Workers: Interior
- ✽ State with Most Workers: Idaho

Provide practical technical support in range research efforts; in the marketing of the range resource; and in the scientific management, protection, and development of grasslands and other range resources.

Requirements: Practical knowledge of the methods and techniques of range conservation and related resource management fields.

RELATED **GS SERIES:** 0458 SOIL CONSERVATION TECHNICIAN

- ❋ U.S. Federal Workforce: 1,832
- ❋ Average Length of Service: 11.0 years
- ❋ Percent Part-Time: 21.4%
- ❋ Percent Women: 29.7%
- ❋ Largest Age Bracket: 45–49 (14.6%)
- ❋ GS Level with Most Workers: 7
- ❋ Agency with Most Workers: Agriculture
- ❋ State with Most Workers: Iowa

Advise property holders on the effectiveness of applying soil and water conservation practices or assist in research efforts.

Requirements: Practical knowledge of the methods and techniques of soil, water, and environmental conservation as they relate to agricultural operations and land-use measures.

Biomedical Engineers

- ❋ Education/Training Required: Bachelor's degree
- ❋ Annual Earnings (Federal): $87,830
- ❋ Annual Earnings (All Industries): $78,860
- ❋ Earnings Growth Potential (Federal): 39.4% (median)
- ❋ Earnings Growth Potential (All Industries): 37.3% (medium)
- ❋ Job Growth (Federal): 62.8%
- ❋ Job Growth (All Industries): 72.0%
- ❋ Annual Job Openings (Federal): 30
- ❋ Annual Job Openings (All Industries): 1,490

Apply knowledge of engineering, biology, and biomechanical principles to the design, development, and evaluation of biological and health systems and products, such as artificial organs, prostheses, instrumentation, medical information systems, and health management and care delivery systems. Evaluate the safety, efficiency, and effectiveness of biomedical equipment. Advise and assist in the application of instrumentation in clinical environments. Research new materials to be used for products, such as implanted artificial organs. Design and develop medical diagnostic and clinical instrumentation, equipment, and procedures, using the principles of engineering and biobehavioral sciences. Conduct research, along with life scientists, chemists, and medical scientists, on the engineering aspects of the biological systems of humans and animals. Teach biomedical engineering or disseminate knowledge about field through writing or consulting. Design and deliver technology to assist people with disabilities. Analyze new medical procedures to forecast likely outcomes. Develop new applications for energy sources, such as using nuclear power for biomedical implants. Install, adjust, maintain, repair, or provide technical support for biomedical equipment.

Considerations for Job Outlook: Biomedical engineers are expected to have employment growth of 72 percent from 2008–2018, much faster than the average for all occupations. The aging of the population and a growing focus on health issues will drive demand for better medical devices and equipment designed by biomedical engineers. Along with the demand for more sophisticated medical equipment and procedures, an increased concern for cost-effectiveness will boost demand for biomedical engineers, particularly in pharmaceutical manufacturing and related industries. Because of the growing interest in this field, the number of degrees granted in biomedical engineering has increased greatly. Many biomedical engineers, particularly those employed in research laboratories, need a graduate degree.

Personality Type: Investigative-Realistic. **Skills:** Science; Technology Design; Programming; Installation; Operations Analysis; Mathematics;

Troubleshooting; Equipment Selection. **Education and Training Program:** Bioengineering and Biomedical Engineering. **Work Environment:** Indoors; sitting.

OTHER FEDERAL JOB FACTS

RELATED GS SERIES: 0858 BIOENGINEERING AND BIOMEDICAL ENGINEERING

TITLE ON USAJOBS: ENGINEER, BIOMEDICAL

- U.S. Federal Workforce: 596
- Average Length of Service: 9.8 years
- Percent Part-Time: 9.7%
- Percent Women: 35.6%
- Largest Age Bracket: 25–29 (21.0%)
- GS Level with Most Workers: 13
- Agencies with Most Workers: Veterans Affairs, Health and Human Services
- State with Most Workers: Maryland

Manage, supervise, lead, and/or perform professional engineering and scientific work exploring and using biotechnology to enrich practices, techniques, and knowledge in the medical, physiological, and biological sciences; enhance and ensure the health, safety, and welfare of living (i.e., human and animal) systems; and create and improve designs, instrumentation, materials, diagnostic and therapeutic devices, artificial organs, medical systems, and other devices needed in the study and practice of medicine with living systems.

Requirements: Professional knowledge of and skills in bioengineering or biomedical engineering.

Budget Analysts

- Education/Training Required: Bachelor's degree
- Annual Earnings (Federal): $73,120
- Annual Earnings (All Industries): $66,660
- Earnings Growth Potential (Federal): 29.9% (low)
- Earnings Growth Potential (All Industries): 34.6% (low)
- Job Growth (Federal): 19.9%
- Job Growth (All Industries): 15.1%
- Annual Job Openings (Federal): 300
- Annual Job Openings (All Industries): 2,230

Examine budget estimates for completeness, accuracy, and conformance with procedures and regulations. Analyze budgeting and accounting reports for the purpose of maintaining expenditure controls. Direct the preparation of regular and special budget reports. Consult with managers to ensure that budget adjustments are made in accordance with program changes. Match appropriations for specific programs with appropriations for broader programs, including items for emergency funds. Provide advice and technical assistance with cost analysis, fiscal allocation, and budget preparation. Summarize budgets and submit recommendations for the approval or disapproval of funds requests. Seek new ways to improve efficiency and increase profits. Review operating budgets to analyze trends affecting budget needs. Perform cost-benefit analyses to compare operating programs, review financial requests, or explore alternative financing methods. Interpret budget directives and establish policies for carrying out directives. Compile and analyze accounting records and other data to determine the financial resources required to implement a program. Testify before examining and fund-granting authorities, clarifying and promoting the proposed budgets.

Considerations for Job Outlook: Projected employment growth will be driven by the continued demand for financial analysis in both the public and the private sectors. Job seekers with a master's degree should have the best prospects.

Personality Type: Conventional-Enterprising-Investigative. **Skills:** Management of Financial Resources; Operations Analysis; Systems Analysis; Mathematics; Systems Evaluation; Judgment and Decision Making; Active Learning; Critical Thinking. **Education and Training Program:** Accounting; Finance, General. **Work Environment:** Indoors; sitting; making repetitive motions.

OTHER FEDERAL JOB FACTS

RELATED GS SERIES: 0560 BUDGET ANALYSIS

TITLE ON USAJOBS: BUDGET ANALYST

- U.S. Federal Workforce: 13,467
- Average Length of Service: 18.2 years
- Percent Part-Time: 1.0%
- Percent Women: 71.9%
- Largest Age Bracket: 50–54 (20.9%)
- GS Levels with Most Workers: 12, 11
- Agency with Most Workers: Defense
- State with Most Workers: District of Columbia

Perform, advise on, or supervise work in any of the phases of budget administration.

Requirements: Knowledge of and skill in applying budget-related laws, regulations, policies, precedents, methods, and techniques.

Business Operations Specialists, All Other

- Education/Training Required: Bachelor's degree
- Annual Earnings (Federal): $72,120
- Annual Earnings (All Industries): $60,610
- Earnings Growth Potential (Federal): 36.3% (median)
- Earnings Growth Potential (All Industries): 45.9% (high)

- Job Growth (Federal): 7.3%
- Job Growth (All Industries): 11.5%
- Annual Job Openings (Federal): 4,290
- Annual Job Openings (All Industries): 36,830

Considerations for Job Outlook: About average employment growth is projected.

JOB SPECIALIZATION: BUSINESS CONTINUITY PLANNERS

Develop, maintain, and implement business continuity and disaster recovery strategies and solutions. Perform risk analyses. Act as a coordinator for recovery efforts in emergency situations. Write reports to summarize testing activities, including descriptions of goals, planning, scheduling, execution, results, analysis, conclusions, and recommendations. Maintain and update organization information technology applications and network systems blueprints. Interpret government regulations and applicable codes to ensure compliance. Identify individual or transaction targets to direct intelligence collection. Establish, maintain, or test call trees to ensure appropriate communication during disaster. Design or implement products and services to mitigate risk or facilitate use of technology-based tools and methods. Create business continuity and disaster recovery budgets. Create or administer training and awareness presentations or materials. Attend professional meetings, read literature, and participate in training or other educational offerings to keep abreast of new developments and technologies related to disaster recovery and business continuity. Test documented disaster recovery strategies and plans. Review existing disaster recovery, crisis management, or business continuity plans. Recommend or implement methods to monitor, evaluate, or enable resolution of safety, operations, or compliance interruptions. Prepare reports summarizing operational results, financial performance, or accomplishments of specified objectives, goals, or plans.

Personality Type: No data available. **Skills:** No data available. **Education and Training Program:** Business Administration and Management, General. **Work Environment:** No data available.

JOB SPECIALIZATION: CUSTOMS BROKERS

Prepare customs documentation and ensure that shipments meet all applicable laws to facilitate the import and export of goods. Determine and track duties and taxes payable and process payments on behalf of client. Sign documents under a power of attorney. Represent clients in meetings with customs officials and apply for duty refunds and tariff reclassifications. Coordinate transportation and storage of imported goods. Sign documents on behalf of clients, using powers of attorney. Provide advice on transportation options, types of carriers, or shipping routes. Post bonds for the products being imported or assist clients in obtaining bonds. Insure cargo against loss, damage, or pilferage. Obtain line releases for frequent shippers of low-risk commodities, high-volume entries, or multiple-container loads. Contract with freight forwarders for destination services. Arrange for transportation, warehousing, or product distribution of imported or exported products. Suggest best methods of packaging or labeling products. Request or compile necessary import documentation, such as customs invoices, certificates of origin, and cargo-control documents. Stay abreast of changes in import or export laws or regulations by reading current literature, attending meetings or conferences, or conferring with colleagues. Quote duty and tax rates on goods to be imported, based on federal tariffs and excise taxes. Prepare papers for shippers to appeal duty charges. Pay, or arrange for payment of, taxes and duties on shipments. Monitor or trace the location of goods. Maintain relationships with customs brokers in other ports to expedite clearing of cargo. Inform importers and exporters of steps to reduce duties and taxes. Confer with officials in various agencies to facilitate clearance of goods through customs and quarantine. Classify goods according to tariff coding system.

Personality Type: Enterprising-Conventional. **Skills:** No data available. **Education and Training Program:** Traffic, Customs, and Transportation Clerk/Technician Training. **Work Environment:** No data available.

JOB SPECIALIZATION: ENERGY AUDITORS

Conduct energy audits of buildings, building systems, and process systems. May also conduct investment grade audits of buildings or systems. Identify and prioritize energy saving measures. Prepare audit reports containing energy analysis results and recommendations for energy cost savings. Inspect or evaluate building envelopes, mechanical systems, electrical systems, or process systems to determine the energy consumption of each system. Collect and analyze field data related to energy usage. Perform tests such as blower-door tests to locate air leaks. Calculate potential for energy savings. Educate customers on energy efficiency or answer questions on topics such as the costs of running household appliances and the selection of energy efficient appliances. Recommend energy efficient technologies or alternate energy sources. Prepare job specification sheets for home energy improvements such as attic insulation, window retrofits, and heating system upgrades. Quantify energy consumption to establish baselines for energy use and need. Identify opportunities to improve the operation, maintenance, or energy efficiency of building or process systems. Analyze technical feasibility of energy saving measures using knowledge of engineering, energy production, energy use, construction, maintenance, system operation, or process systems. Analyze energy bills including utility rates or tariffs to gather historical energy usage data.

Personality Type: Conventional-Enterprising. **Skills:** Operations Analysis; Science; Systems Evaluation; Systems Analysis; Mathematics; Writing; Operation and Control; Persuasion. **Education and Training Program:** Energy Management and Systems Technology/Technician. **Work Environment:** More often outdoors than indoors; cramped work space, awkward positions; very hot or cold temperatures; extremely bright or inadequate lighting; contaminants.

JOB SPECIALIZATION: SECURITY MANAGEMENT SPECIALISTS

Conduct security assessments for organizations, and design security systems and processes. May specialize in areas such as physical security, personnel security, and information security. May work in fields such as health care, banking, gaming, security engineering, or manufacturing. Prepare documentation for case reports or court proceedings. Review design drawings or technical documents for completeness, correctness, or appropriateness. Monitor tapes or digital recordings to identify the source of losses. Interview witnesses or suspects to identify persons responsible for security breaches, establish losses, pursue prosecutions, or obtain restitution. Budget and schedule security design work. Develop conceptual designs of security systems. Respond to emergency situations on an on-call basis. Train personnel in security procedures or use of security equipment. Prepare, maintain, or update security procedures, security system drawings, or related documentation. Monitor the work of contractors in the design, construction, and startup phases of security systems. Inspect security design features, installations, or programs to ensure compliance with applicable standards or regulations. Inspect fire, intruder detection, or other security systems. Engineer, install, maintain, or repair security systems, programmable logic controls, or other security-related electronic systems. Recommend improvements in security systems or procedures.

Develop or review specifications for design or construction of security systems. Design security policies, programs, or practices to ensure adequate security relating to issues such as protection of assets, alarm response, and access card use.

Personality Type: Realistic-Investigative-Conventional. **Skills:** No data available. **Education and Training Program:** Security and Loss Prevention Services. **Work Environment:** No data available.

JOB SPECIALIZATION: SUSTAINABILITY SPECIALISTS

Address organizational sustainability issues, such as waste stream management, green building practices, and green procurement plans. Review and revise sustainability proposals or policies. Research or review regulatory, technical, or market issues related to sustainability. Identify or investigate violations of natural resources, waste management, recycling, or other environmental policies. Identify or create new sustainability indicators. Write grant applications, rebate applications, or project proposals to secure funding for sustainability projects. Provide technical or administrative support for sustainability programs or issues. Identify or procure needed resources to implement sustainability programs or projects. Create or maintain plans or other documents related to sustainability projects. Develop reports or presentations to communicate the effectiveness of sustainability initiatives. Create marketing or outreach media, such as brochures or websites, to communicate sustainability issues, procedures, or objectives. Collect information about waste stream management or green building practices to inform decision makers. Assess or propose sustainability initiatives, considering factors such as cost effectiveness, technical feasibility, and acceptance. Monitor or track sustainability indicators, such as energy usage, natural resource usage, waste generation, and recycling. Develop sustainability project goals, objectives, initiatives, or strategies in collaboration with other sustainability professionals.

Personality Type: No data available. **Skills:** No data available. **Education and Training Program:** Business Administration and Management, General. **Work Environment:** No data available.

OTHER FEDERAL JOB FACTS

RELATED GS SERIES: 0341 ADMINISTRATIVE OFFICER

- ❋ U.S. Federal Workforce: 8,897
- ❋ Average Length of Service: 19.1 years
- ❋ Percent Part-Time: 6.9%
- ❋ Percent Women: 76.4%
- ❋ Largest Age Bracket: 50–54 (20.5%)
- ❋ GS Levels with Most Workers: 12, 11
- ❋ Agency with Most Workers: Defense
- ❋ States with Most Workers: Maryland, District of Columbia

Provide or obtain a variety of management services essential to the direction and operation of an organization.

Requirements: Extensive knowledge and understanding of management principles, practices, methods and techniques, and skill in integrating management services with the general management of an organization.

RELATED GS SERIES: 1145 AGRICULTURAL PROGRAM SPECIALIST

- ❋ U.S. Federal Workforce: 334
- ❋ Average Length of Service: 22.6 years
- ❋ Percent Part-Time: 0.3%
- ❋ Percent Women: 53.0%
- ❋ Largest Age Bracket: 50–54 (27.2%)
- ❋ GS Level with Most Workers: 12
- ❋ Agency with Most Workers: Agriculture
- ❋ State with Most Workers: District of Columbia

Develop, review, administer, and coordinate programs for direct farmer-producer participation in production adjustment, price support, land conservation, and similar programs.

Requirements: Knowledge of agricultural stabilization, conservation, and related programs; farming customs and practices; crop cultivation; production and marketing methods; and related agricultural activities.

RELATED GS SERIES: 1144 COMMISSARY MANAGEMENT

TITLE ON USAJOBS: COMMISSARY STORE MANAGER

- ❋ U.S. Federal Workforce: 1,242
- ❋ Average Length of Service: 20.0 years
- ❋ Percent Part-Time: 5.2%
- ❋ Percent Women: 51.8%
- ❋ Largest Age Bracket: 50–54 (25.4%)
- ❋ GS Levels with Most Workers: 7, 12
- ❋ Agency with Most Workers: Defense
- ❋ States with Most Workers: Virginia, California

Operate commissary stores, their departments, or overall commissary operations.

Requirements: Knowledge of commercial retail food merchandising and food store management.

RELATED GS SERIES: 0828 CONSTRUCTION ANALYST

- ❋ U.S. Federal Workforce: 528
- ❋ Average Length of Service: 7.8 years
- ❋ Percent Part-Time: 58.7%
- ❋ Percent Women: 10.6%
- ❋ Largest Age Bracket: 55–59 (22.5%)
- ❋ GS Level with Most Workers: 11
- ❋ Agency with Most Workers: Housing and Urban Development
- ❋ State with Most Workers: Texas

B

Examine drawings and specifications for compliance with standards; verify that construction complies with these standards; estimate costs of construction, extension, alteration, remodeling, or repair of housing; and collect, analyze, and develop basic cost information on housing construction.

Requirements: Practical knowledge of both architectural design and construction practices for housing.

Related GS Series: 2030 Distribution Facilities and Storage Management

Title on USAJobs: Distribution Facilities and Storage Management Specialist

- ❋ U.S. Federal Workforce: 522
- ❋ Average Length of Service: 20.8 years
- ❋ Percent Part-Time: 0.2%
- ❋ Percent Women: 25.7%
- ❋ Largest Age Bracket: 55–59 (25.1%)
- ❋ GS Level with Most Workers: 11
- ❋ Agency with Most Workers: Defense
- ❋ States with Most Workers: Pennsylvania, California

Receive, handle, store, maintain while in storage, issue, or physically control items within a storage and distribution system.

Requirements: Knowledge of the principles, practices, and techniques of managing the physical receipt, custody, care, and distribution of material, including the selection of appropriate storage sites, material handling equipment, and facilities.

Related GS Series: 1670 Equipment Services

Title on USAJobs: Equipment Specialist

- ❋ U.S. Federal Workforce: 6,398
- ❋ Average Length of Service: 15.8 years
- ❋ Percent Part-Time: 0.0%
- ❋ Percent Women: 8.1%
- ❋ Largest Age Bracket: 50–54 (23.3%)

- ❋ GS Levels with Most Workers: 11, 12
- ❋ Agency with Most Workers: Defense
- ❋ State with Most Workers: Georgia

Collect, analyze, interpret, and develop specialized information about equipment; provide advisory services to those who design, test, produce, procure, supply, operate, repair, or dispose of equipment; may also develop or revise equipment maintenance programs.

Requirements: Intensive and practical knowledge of the characteristics, properties, and uses of equipment; knowledge is of the type gained from technical training, education, and experience in functions such as repairing, overhauling, maintaining, constructing, or inspecting equipment.

Related GS Series: 1601 Equipment, Facilities, and Services

Title on USAJobs: Equipment and Facilities Specialist

- ❋ U.S. Federal Workforce: 4,178
- ❋ Average Length of Service: 20.6 years
- ❋ Percent Part-Time: 0.2%
- ❋ Percent Women: 10.4%
- ❋ Largest Age Bracket: 50–54 (25.6%)
- ❋ GS Level with Most Workers: 12
- ❋ Agency with Most Workers: Defense
- ❋ State with Most Workers: Virginia

Manage, supervise, lead, or perform administrative work that involves a combination of work characteristics of two or more equipment, facilities, and services occupations or for which no OPM occupation exists.

Requirements: No requirements available.

Related GS Series: 2001 General Supply

Title on USAJobs: Supply Specialist

- ❋ U.S. Federal Workforce: 3,728
- ❋ Average Length of Service: 19.1 years

❋ Percent Part-Time: 1.3%

❋ Percent Women: 44.7%

❋ Largest Age Bracket: 50–54 (21.6%)

❋ GS Level with Most Workers: 9

❋ Agency with Most Workers: Defense

❋ State with Most Workers: Pennsylvania

Supervise, lead, or perform analytical or administrative supply work covered by two or more OPM occupations.

Requirements: No requirements available.

RELATED GS SERIES: 1150 INDUSTRIAL SPECIALIST

❋ U.S. Federal Workforce: 1,112

❋ Average Length of Service: 22.4 years

❋ Percent Part-Time: 0.2%

❋ Percent Women: 29.5%

❋ Largest Age Bracket: 50–54 (24.4%)

❋ GS Level with Most Workers: 11

❋ Agency with Most Workers: Defense

❋ State with Most Workers: California

Develop and carry out plans for the expansion, conversion, integration, or utilization of industrial production facilities, either to meet mobilization or strategic requirements or to strengthen the industrial economy; furnish technical information, assistance, and advice concerning facilities, machinery, methods, materials, and standards for industrial production; develop and/or administer provisions or regulations covering such matters as materials allocation, tariffs, export-import control, etc.; conduct surveys of industrial plants to evaluate capacity and potential for production of specific commodities; or plan, evaluate, and maintain technical surveillance over government production operations.

Requirements: Practical knowledge of the nature and operations of an industry or industries and the materials, facilities, and methods employed by the industry or industries in producing commodities.

RELATED GS SERIES: 2032 PACKAGING

TITLE ON USAJOBS: PACKAGING SPECIALIST

❋ U.S. Federal Workforce: 178

❋ Average Length of Service: 21.4 years

❋ Percent Part-Time: 3.9%

❋ Percent Women: 32.0%

❋ Largest Age Bracket: 50–54 (27.0%)

❋ GS Levels with Most Workers: 11, 12

❋ Agency with Most Workers: Defense

❋ State with Most Workers: Pennsylvania

Plan, design, and develop packaging methods and techniques; direct the use of packages and packaging materials to protect supplies, materials, and equipment between the time of purchase and use.

Requirements: Knowledge of packaging and preservation methods, material, regulations, specifications, and guidelines; also knowledge of methods and techniques to prevent environmental and mechanical damage during handling, shipping, and storage.

RELATED GS SERIES: 1104 PROPERTY DISPOSAL

TITLE ON USAJOBS: PROPERTY DISPOSAL SPECIALIST

❋ U.S. Federal Workforce: 751

❋ Average Length of Service: 21.1 years

❋ Percent Part-Time: 0.3%

❋ Percent Women: 40.9%

❋ Largest Age Bracket: 50–54 (24.4%)

❋ GS Levels with Most Workers: 12, 11

❋ Agency with Most Workers: Defense

❋ State with Most Workers: Michigan

Redistribute, donate, sell, abandon, destroy, and promote the use of excess and surplus personal property.

Requirements: Knowledge of characteristics, proper identities, and uses of property items; merchandising and marketing methods and techniques; and/or property-disposal policies, programs, regulations, and procedures.

RELATED GS SERIES: 1130 PUBLIC UTILITIES SPECIALIST

- U.S. Federal Workforce: 526
- Average Length of Service: 17.3 years
- Percent Part-Time: 1.7%
- Percent Women: 53.4%
- Largest Age Bracket: 55–59 (18.4%)
- GS Level with Most Workers: 13
- Agency with Most Workers: Energy
- State with Most Workers: Oregon

Analyze utility rate schedules to determine their reasonableness and applicability; investigate and analyze the business management organization and financial structure of public utilities; prepare and present testimony before regulatory bodies; and purchase or sell utility resources and services.

Requirements: Practical knowledge of the business practices, rate structures, and operating characteristics of public utilities: telecommunications, electric and gas power, water, steam, and sewage disposal.

RELATED GS SERIES: 1910 QUALITY ASSURANCE

TITLE ON USAJOBS: QUALITY ASSURANCE SPECIALIST

- U.S. Federal Workforce: 8,833
- Average Length of Service: 19.1 years
- Percent Part-Time: 0.4%
- Percent Women: 14.5%
- Largest Age Bracket: 50–54 (23.0%)
- GS Level with Most Workers: 11

- Agency with Most Workers: Defense
- States with Most Workers: California, Virginia

Assure the quality of products acquired and used by the federal government; develop plans and programs for achieving and maintaining product quality throughout the item's life cycle; monitor operations to prevent the production of defects and to verify adherence to quality plans and requirements; and analyze and investigate adverse quality trends or conditions and initiation of corrective action.

Requirements: Analytical ability combined with knowledge and application of assurance principles and techniques; knowledge of pertinent product characteristics and the associated manufacturing processes and techniques.

RELATED GS SERIES: 0080 SECURITY ADMINISTRATION

TITLE ON USAJOBS: SECURITY ADMINISTRATOR

- U.S. Federal Workforce: 12,549
- Average Length of Service: 13.2 years
- Percent Part-Time: 2.5%
- Percent Women: 34.7%
- Largest Age Bracket: 45–49 (22.0%)
- GS Level with Most Workers: 12
- Agency with Most Workers: Defense
- State with Most Workers: District of Columbia

Develop and implement policies, procedures, standards, training, and methods for identifying and protecting information, personnel, property, facilities, operations, or material from unauthorized disclosure, misuse, theft, assault, vandalism, espionage, sabotage, or loss.

Requirements: Knowledge of the basic principles, concepts, policies, practices, and methods of security administration.

RELATED GS SERIES: 1140 TRADE SPECIALIST

- ❋ U.S. Federal Workforce: 807
- ❋ Average Length of Service: 14.1 years
- ❋ Percent Part-Time: 3.2%
- ❋ Percent Women: 48.0%
- ❋ Largest Age Bracket: 40–44 (17.0%)
- ❋ GS Level with Most Workers: 13
- ❋ Agency with Most Workers: Commerce
- ❋ State with Most Workers: District of Columbia

Administer, supervise, or perform promotional, advisory, or analytical functions pertaining to the commercial distribution of goods and services.

Requirements: Practical knowledge of market structure and trends, competitive relationships, retail and wholesale trade practices, distribution channels and costs, business financing and credit practices, trade restrictions and controls, and principles of advertising and consumer motivation.

RELATED GS SERIES: 2130 TRAFFIC MANAGEMENT

TITLE ON USAJOBS: TRAFFIC MANAGEMENT SPECIALIST

- ❋ U.S. Federal Workforce: 1,573
- ❋ Average Length of Service: 18.8 years
- ❋ Percent Part-Time: 0.0%
- ❋ Percent Women: 44.4%
- ❋ Largest Age Bracket: 50–54 (23.8%)
- ❋ GS Level with Most Workers: 11
- ❋ Agency with Most Workers: Defense
- ❋ State with Most Workers: Virginia

Perform, administer, or supervise technical and analytical work concerned with planning, development, and execution of traffic policies and programs; or direct and manage programs to obtain the economical and efficient transportation of freight, personal property, and/or passengers.

Requirements: Knowledge of federal traffic management principles and policies; of transportation industry operations, practices, and capabilities; of special handling or movement requirements associated with freight, passengers, or other transportation operations; and of the relationship of traffic management to other agency or organizational programs and functions.

RELATED GS SERIES: 2101 TRANSPORTATION SPECIALIST

- ❋ U.S. Federal Workforce: 8,510
- ❋ Average Length of Service: 16.7 years
- ❋ Percent Part-Time: 0.2%
- ❋ Percent Women: 15.4%
- ❋ Largest Age Bracket: 45–49 (23.4%)
- ❋ GS Levels with Most Workers: 9, 13
- ❋ Agency with Most Workers: Transportation
- ❋ State with Most Workers: California

Advise on, supervise, or perform work that involves two or more specialized transportation functions or other transportation work not specifically included in other OPM occupations.

Requirements: Degree in accounting, business administration, business or commercial law, commerce, economics, engineering, finance, industrial management, statistics, traffic management, transportation, motor mechanics, or another field related to the position; or relevant work experience that provides a general knowledge and understanding of traffic or transportation programs or operations.

RELATED GS SERIES: 0106 UNEMPLOYMENT INSURANCE

- ❋ U.S. Federal Workforce: 79
- ❋ Average Length of Service: 14.6 years
- ❋ Percent Part-Time: 3.8%
- ❋ Percent Women: 54.4%
- ❋ Largest Age Bracket: 60–64 (25.3%)

* GS Level with Most Workers: 13
* Agency with Most Workers: Labor
* State with Most Workers: District of Columbia

Develop, promote, and evaluate unemployment insurance programs administered under federal-state joint arrangement.

Requirements: Knowledge of the history, concepts, methods, and techniques of social insurance and of the social and economic conditions under which such programs operate.

Captains, Mates, and Pilots of Water Vessels

* Education/Training Required: Work experience in a related occupation
* Annual Earnings (Federal): $63,620
* Annual Earnings (All Industries): $64,240
* Earnings Growth Potential (Federal): 38.3% (median)
* Earnings Growth Potential (All Industries): 52.1% (very high)
* Job Growth (Federal): 28.8%
* Job Growth (All Industries): 17.3%
* Annual Job Openings (Federal): 50
* Annual Job Openings (All Industries): 1,950

Command or supervise operations of ships and water vessels, such as tugboats and ferryboats, that travel into and out of harbors, estuaries, straits, and sounds and on rivers, lakes, bays, and oceans. Required to hold license issued by U.S. Coast Guard. No task data available.

Considerations for Job Outlook: Job growth is expected to stem from increasing tourism and from growth in offshore oil and gas production. Employment is also projected to increase in and around major port cities due to growing international trade. Opportunities should be excellent as the need to replace workers, particularly officers, generates many job openings.

JOB SPECIALIZATION: MATES—SHIP, BOAT, AND BARGE

Supervise and coordinate activities of crew aboard ships, boats, barges, or dredges. Determine geographical position of ship, using lorans, azimuths of celestial bodies, or computers, and use this information to determine the course and speed of the ship. Observe water from ship's masthead to advise on navigational direction. Supervise crews in cleaning and maintaining decks, superstructures, and bridges. Supervise crew members in the repair or replacement of defective gear and equipment. Steer vessels, using navigational devices such as compasses and sextants and navigational aids such as lighthouses and buoys. Inspect equipment such as cargo-handling gear, lifesaving equipment, visual-signaling equipment, and fishing, towing, or dredging gear to detect problems. Arrange for ships to be stocked, fueled, and repaired. Assume command of vessel in the event that ship's master becomes incapacitated. Participate in activities related to maintenance of vessel security. Stand watch on vessel during specified periods while vessel is under way. Observe loading and unloading of cargo and equipment to ensure that handling and storage are performed according to specifications.

Personality Type: Enterprising-Realistic-Conventional. **Skills:** Repairing; Equipment Maintenance; Operation and Control; Troubleshooting; Operation Monitoring; Equipment Selection; Quality Control Analysis; Management of Personnel Resources. **Education and Training Program:** Commercial Fishing; Marine Science/Merchant Marine Officer; Marine Transportation, Other. **Work Environment:** Outdoors; sounds; noisy; contaminants; very hot or cold temperatures; hazardous equipment; extremely bright or inadequate lighting.

Job Specialization: Pilots, Ship

Command ships to steer them into and out of harbors, estuaries, straits, and sounds and on rivers, lakes, and bays. Must be licensed by U.S. Coast Guard with limitations indicating class and tonnage of vessels for which licenses are valid and routes and waters that may be piloted. Maintain and repair boats and equipment. Give directions to crew members who are steering ships. Make nautical maps. Set ships' courses to avoid reefs, outlying shoals, and other hazards, using navigational aids such as lighthouses and buoys. Report to appropriate authorities any violations of federal or state pilotage laws. Relieve crew members on tugs and launches. Provide assistance to vessels approaching or leaving seacoasts, navigating harbors, and docking and undocking. Provide assistance in maritime rescue operations. Prevent ships under their navigational control from engaging in unsafe operations. Operate amphibious craft during troop landings. Maintain ships' logs. Learn to operate new technology systems and procedures, through the use of instruction, simulators, and models. Advise ships' masters on harbor rules and customs procedures. Steer ships into and out of berths or signal tugboat captains to berth and unberth ships. Serve as vessels' docking masters upon arrival at a port and when at a berth. Operate ship-to-shore radios to exchange information needed for ship operations. Consult maps, charts, weather reports, and navigation equipment to determine and direct ship movements. Direct courses and speeds of ships, based on specialized knowledge of local winds, weather, water depths, tides, currents, and hazards. Oversee cargo storage on or below decks.

Personality Type: Realistic-Conventional-Investigative. **Skills:** Operation and Control; Operation Monitoring; Troubleshooting; Management of Personnel Resources; Quality Control Analysis; Complex Problem Solving; Coordination; Monitoring. **Education and Training Program:**

Commercial Fishing; Marine Science/Merchant Marine Officer; Marine Transportation, Other. **Work Environment:** Outdoors; sounds, noisy; contaminants; using your hands to handle, control, or feel objects, tools, or controls; extremely bright or inadequate lighting; very hot or cold temperatures.

Job Specialization: Ship and Boat Captains

Command vessels in oceans, bays, lakes, rivers, and coastal waters. Assign watches and living quarters to crew members. Sort logs, form log booms, and salvage lost logs. Perform various marine duties such as checking for oil spills or other pollutants around ports and harbors and patrolling beaches. Contact buyers to sell cargo such as fish. Tow and maneuver barges, or signal for tugboats to tow barges to destinations. Signal passing vessels, using whistles, flashing lights, flags, and radios. Resolve questions or problems with customs officials. Read gauges to verify sufficient levels of hydraulic fluid, air pressure, and oxygen. Purchase supplies and equipment. Measure depths of water, using depth-measuring equipment. Maintain boats and equipment on board, such as engines, winches, navigational systems, fire extinguishers, and life preservers. Collect fares from customers, or signal ferryboat helpers to collect fares. Arrange for ships to be fueled, restocked with supplies, and/or repaired. Signal crew members or deckhands to rig tow lines, open or close gates and ramps, and pull guard chains across entries. Maintain records of daily activities, personnel reports, ship positions and movements, ports of call, weather and sea conditions, pollution control efforts, and/or cargo and passenger statuses. Inspect vessels to ensure efficient and safe operation of vessels and equipment and conformance to regulations.

Personality Type: Enterprising-Realistic. **Skills:** Operation and Control; Repairing; Management of Material Resources; Management of Financial Resources; Equipment Maintenance;

Troubleshooting; Operation Monitoring; Equipment Selection. **Education and Training Program:** Commercial Fishing; Marine Science/Merchant Marine Officer; Marine Transportation, Other. **Work Environment:** More often outdoors than indoors; sounds, noisy; extremely bright or inadequate lighting; contaminants; using your hands to handle, control, or feel objects, tools, or controls.

OTHER FEDERAL JOB FACTS

RELATED GS SERIES: 5784 RIVERBOAT OPERATING

TITLE ON USAJOBS: RIVERBOAT OPERATOR

- ❈ U.S. Federal Workforce: 121
- ❈ Average Length of Service: 16.6 years
- ❈ Percent Part-Time: 0.8%
- ❈ Percent Women: 1.7%
- ❈ Largest Age Bracket: 50–54 (25.6%)
- ❈ GS Level with Most Workers: Not a GS occupation
- ❈ Agency with Most Workers: Defense
- ❈ States with Most Workers: Mississippi, Tennessee

Operate riverboats, towboats with tows, self-propelled dredges, and other similar craft often larger than 55 meters (180 feet) in length engaged in transporting passengers and freight, moving non-self-propelled vessels and floating plants, making hydrographic surveys, dredging and maintaining waterways, and so forth; steer the boat, stand watch, set and maintain speed and course, determine position using navigational aids, and coordinate activities of members of the crew.

Requirements: Knowledge of river currents, stages, obstructions, navigation locks and dams, and the handling and operation of large vessels or tows on rivers.

RELATED GS SERIES: 5782 SHIP OPERATING

TITLE ON USAJOBS: SHIP OPERATOR

- ❈ U.S. Federal Workforce: 114
- ❈ Average Length of Service: 17.8 years
- ❈ Percent Part-Time: 0.9%
- ❈ Percent Women: 3.5%
- ❈ Largest Age Bracket: 50–54 (29.8%)
- ❈ GS Level with Most Workers: Not a GS occupation
- ❈ Agency with Most Workers: Defense
- ❈ State with Most Workers: Oregon

Operate ships, tugboats, seagoing dredges, fishing vessels, or other similar vessels, often greater than 55 meters (180 feet) in length, engaged in transporting passengers and freight, towing or assisting the maneuvering of large vessels, making hydrographic and oceanographic surveys, drilling or probing subaqueous holes, conducting fishing operations, and so forth; navigate the ship, stand watch, set and maintain speed and course, use navigational aids and devices to compute position, and coordinate the activities of members of the crew.

Requirements: Knowledge of the handling and operation of large vessels offshore or in the Great Lakes and/or large vessels under tow.

Chemical Engineers

- ❈ Education/Training Required: Bachelor's degree
- ❈ Annual Earnings (Federal): $97,350
- ❈ Annual Earnings (All Industries): $88,280
- ❈ Earnings Growth Potential (Federal): 34.9% (low)
- ❈ Earnings Growth Potential (All Industries): 36.5% (medium)
- ❈ Job Growth (Federal): 7.8%
- ❈ Job Growth (All Industries): –2.0%

- ❋ Annual Job Openings (Federal): 20
- ❋ Annual Job Openings (All Industries): 780

Design chemical plant equipment and devise processes for manufacturing chemicals and products such as gasoline, synthetic rubber, plastics, detergents, cement, paper, and pulp by applying principles and technology of chemistry, physics, and engineering. Develop safety procedures to be employed by workers operating equipment or working in close proximity to ongoing chemical reactions. Troubleshoot problems with chemical manufacturing processes. Evaluate chemical equipment and processes to identify ways to optimize performance or to ensure compliance with safety and environmental regulations. Conduct research to develop new and improved chemical manufacturing processes. Determine most effective arrangement of operations such as mixing, crushing, heat transfer, distillation, and drying. Perform tests and monitor performance of processes throughout stages of production to determine degree of control over variables such as temperature, density, specific gravity, and pressure. Design and plan layout of equipment. Prepare estimate of production costs and production progress reports for management. Design measurement and control systems for chemical plants based on data collected in laboratory experiments and in pilot plant operations. Develop processes to separate components of liquids or gases or generate electrical currents using controlled chemical processes. Perform laboratory studies of steps in manufacture of new product and test proposed process in small scale operation such as a pilot plant. Direct activities of workers who operate or who are engaged in constructing and improving absorption, evaporation, or electromagnetic equipment.

Considerations for Job Outlook: Chemical engineers are expected to have an employment decline of 2 percent from 2008–2018. Overall employment in the chemical manufacturing industry is expected to continue to decline, although chemical companies will continue to employ chemical engineers to research and develop new chemicals and more efficient processes to increase output of existing chemicals. However, there will be employment growth for chemical engineers in service-providing industries, such as professional, scientific, and technical services, particularly for research in energy and the developing fields of biotechnology and nanotechnology.

Personality Type: Investigative-Realistic. **Skills:** Science; Operations Analysis; Technology Design; Mathematics; Troubleshooting; Systems Evaluation; Management of Financial Resources; Systems Analysis. **Education and Training Program:** Chemical Engineering. **Work Environment:** Indoors; sitting.

OTHER FEDERAL JOB FACTS

RELATED GS SERIES: 0893 CHEMICAL ENGINEERING
TITLE ON USAJOBS: ENGINEER, CHEMICAL

- ❋ U.S. Federal Workforce: 1,199
- ❋ Average Length of Service: 13.7 years
- ❋ Percent Part-Time: 4.4%
- ❋ Percent Women: 30.4%
- ❋ Largest Age Bracket: 50–54 (15.9%)
- ❋ GS Level with Most Workers: 13
- ❋ Agency with Most Workers: Defense
- ❋ State with Most Workers: Maryland

Manage, supervise, lead, and/or perform professional engineering and scientific work involving chemical processes utilized by industries and scientific technologies to produce useful products and systems and exploring, extending, improving, and providing for chemical and biochemical conversion processes.

Requirements: Professional knowledge of and skills in chemical engineering.

Chemists

- ❋ Education/Training Required: Bachelor's degree
- ❋ Annual Earnings (Federal): $98,860
- ❋ Annual Earnings (All Industries): $68,220
- ❋ Earnings Growth Potential (Federal): 31.6% (low)
- ❋ Earnings Growth Potential (All Industries): 43.0% (high)
- ❋ Job Growth (Federal): 7.7%
- ❋ Job Growth (All Industries): 2.5%
- ❋ Annual Job Openings (Federal): 150
- ❋ Annual Job Openings (All Industries): 3,000

Conduct qualitative and quantitative chemical analyses or chemical experiments in laboratories for quality or process control or to develop new products or knowledge. Analyze organic and inorganic compounds to determine chemical and physical properties, composition, structure, relationships, and reactions, utilizing chromatography, spectroscopy, and spectrophotometry techniques. Maintain laboratory instruments to ensure proper working order and troubleshoot malfunctions when needed. Develop, improve, and customize products, equipment, formulas, processes, and analytical methods. Conduct quality control tests. Direct, coordinate, and advise personnel in test procedures for analyzing components and physical properties of materials. Prepare test solutions, compounds, and reagents for laboratory personnel to conduct test. Compile and analyze test information to determine process or equipment operating efficiency and to diagnose malfunctions. Confer with scientists and engineers to conduct analyses of research projects, interpret test results, or develop nonstandard tests. Write technical papers and reports and prepare standards and specifications for processes, facilities, products, or tests. Induce changes in composition of substances by introducing heat, light, energy, and chemical catalysts for quantitative and qualitative analysis. Study effects of various methods of processing, preserving, and packaging on composition and properties of foods.

Considerations for Job Outlook: Manufacturing companies' outsourcing of research and development and testing operations is expected to limit employment growth for these scientists. Most entry-level chemists should expect competition for jobs, particularly in declining chemical manufacturing industries.

Personality Type: Investigative-Realistic-Conventional. **Skills:** Science; Repairing; Equipment Maintenance; Mathematics; Reading Comprehension; Writing; Operations Analysis; Quality Control Analysis. **Education and Training Program:** Analytical Chemistry; Chemical Physics; Chemistry, General; Chemistry, Other; Inorganic Chemistry; Organic Chemistry; Physical Chemistry; Polymer Chemistry. **Work Environment:** Indoors; contaminants; hazardous conditions; sitting.

OTHER FEDERAL JOB FACTS

RELATED GS SERIES: 1320 CHEMISTRY

TITLE ON USAJOBS: CHEMIST

- ❋ U.S. Federal Workforce: 5,839
- ❋ Average Length of Service: 15.3 years
- ❋ Percent Part-Time: 4.0%
- ❋ Percent Women: 35.3%
- ❋ Largest Age Bracket: 50–54 (16.0%)
- ❋ GS Level with Most Workers: 13
- ❋ Agency with Most Workers: Health and Human Services
- ❋ State with Most Workers: Maryland

Investigate, analyze, and interpret the composition, molecular structure, and properties of substances, the transformations which they undergo, and the amounts of matter and energy included in these transformations; investigate, analyze, and interpret the composition, physical and chemical properties, molecular structure, and chemical reactions of substances; predict transformations they undergo; and predict the amount of matter and energy included in these transformations.

Requirements: Full professional education and training in the field of chemistry.

Civil Engineers

- ❋ Education/Training Required: Bachelor's degree
- ❋ Annual Earnings (Federal): $87,900
- ❋ Annual Earnings (All Industries): $76,590
- ❋ Earnings Growth Potential (Federal): 31.5% (low)
- ❋ Earnings Growth Potential (All Industries): 35.2% (low)
- ❋ Job Growth (Federal): 7.6%
- ❋ Job Growth (All Industries): 24.3%
- ❋ Annual Job Openings (Federal): 320
- ❋ Annual Job Openings (All Industries): 11,460

Perform engineering duties in planning, designing, and overseeing construction and maintenance of building structures and facilities such as roads, railroads, airports, bridges, harbors, channels, dams, irrigation projects, pipelines, power plants, water and sewage systems, and waste disposal units. Includes architectural, structural, traffic, ocean, and geo-technical engineers. Manage and direct staff members and construction, operations, or maintenance activities at project site. Provide technical advice regarding design, construction, or program modifications and structural repairs to industrial and managerial personnel. Inspect project sites to monitor progress and ensure conformance to design specifications and safety or sanitation standards. Estimate quantities and cost of materials, equipment, or labor to determine project feasibility. Test soils and materials to determine the adequacy and strength of foundations, concrete, asphalt, or steel. Compute load and grade requirements, water flow rates, and material stress factors to determine design specifications. Plan and design transportation or hydraulic systems and structures, following construction and government standards and using design software and drawing tools. Analyze survey reports, maps, drawings, blueprints, aerial photography, and other topographical or geologic data to plan projects. Prepare or present public reports on topics such as bid proposals, deeds, environmental impact statements, or property and right-of-way descriptions. Direct or participate in surveying to lay out installations and establish reference points, grades, and elevations to guide construction. Conduct studies of traffic patterns or environmental conditions to identify engineering problems and assess the potential impact of projects.

Considerations for Job Outlook: Civil engineers (including water/wastewater engineers) are expected to have employment growth of 24 percent from 2008–2018, much faster than the average for all occupations. Spurred by general population growth and the related need to improve the nation's infrastructure, more civil engineers will be needed to design and construct or expand transportation, water supply, and pollution control systems and buildings and building complexes. They also will be needed to repair or replace existing roads, bridges, and other public structures. Because construction industries and architectural, engineering, and related services employ many civil engineers, employment opportunities will vary by geographic area and may decrease during economic slowdowns, when construction is often curtailed.

Personality Type: Realistic-Investigative-Conventional. **Skills:** Operations Analysis; Mathematics; Science; Management of Financial Resources; Management of Material Resources; Systems Evaluation; Systems Analysis; Quality Control Analysis. **Education and Training Program:** Civil Engineering, General; Civil Engineering, Other; Transportation and Highway Engineering; Water Resources Engineering. **Work Environment:** Indoors; sitting.

JOB SPECIALIZATION: TRANSPORTATION ENGINEERS

Develop plans for surface transportation projects according to established engineering standards and state or federal construction policy. Prepare plans, estimates, or specifications to design transportation facilities. Plan alterations and modifications of existing streets, highways, or freeways to improve traffic flow. Prepare data, maps, or other information at construction-related public hearings and meetings. Review development plans to determine potential traffic impact. Prepare administrative, technical, or statistical reports on traffic-operation matters, such as accidents, safety measures, and pedestrian volume and practices. Evaluate transportation systems or traffic control devices and lighting systems to determine need for modification or expansion. Evaluate traffic control devices or lighting systems to determine need for modification or expansion. Develop, or assist in the development of, transportation-related computer software or computer processes. Prepare project budgets, schedules, or specifications for labor and materials. Prepare final project layout drawings that include details such as stress calculations. Plan alteration and modification of existing transportation structures to improve safety or function. Participate in contract bidding, negotiation, or administration. Model transportation scenarios to evaluate the impacts of activities such as new development or to identify possible solutions to transportation problems.

Investigate traffic problems and recommend methods to improve traffic flow and safety. Investigate or test specific construction project materials to determine compliance to specifications or standards. Inspect completed transportation projects to ensure safety or compliance with applicable standards or regulations.

Personality Type: Realistic-Investigative. **Skills:** No data available. **Education and Training Program:** Civil Engineering, General; Civil Engineering, Other; Transportation and Highway Engineering; Water Resources Engineering. **Work Environment:** No data available.

JOB SPECIALIZATION: WATER/WASTEWATER ENGINEERS

Design or oversee projects involving provision of fresh water, disposal of wastewater and sewage, or prevention of flood-related damage. Prepare environmental documentation for water resources, regulatory program compliance, data management and analysis, and fieldwork. Perform hydraulic modeling and pipeline design. Write technical reports or publications related to water resources development or water use efficiency. Review and critique proposals, plans, or designs related to water and wastewater treatment systems. Provide technical support on water resource or treatment issues to government agencies. Provide technical direction or supervision to junior engineers, engineering or computer-aided design (CAD) technicians, or other technical personnel. Identify design alternatives for the development of new water resources. Develop plans for new water resources or water efficiency programs. Design or select equipment for use in wastewater processing to ensure compliance with government standards. Conduct water quality studies to identify and characterize water pollutant sources. Perform mathematical modeling of underground or surface water resources, such as floodplains, ocean coastlines, streams, rivers, and wetlands.

Perform hydrological analyses, using three-dimensional simulation software, to model the movement of water or forecast the dispersion of chemical pollutants in the water supply. Perform hydraulic analyses of water supply systems or water distribution networks to model flow characteristics, test for pressure losses, or to identify opportunities to mitigate risks and improve operational efficiency. Oversee the construction of decentralized and on-site wastewater treatment systems, including reclaimed water facilities. Gather and analyze water use data to forecast water demand.

Personality Type: No data available. **Skills:** No data available. **Education and Training Program:** Civil Engineering, General; Civil Engineering, Other; Transportation and Highway Engineering; Water Resources Engineering. **Work Environment:** No data available.

OTHER FEDERAL JOB FACTS

RELATED GS SERIES: 0810 CIVIL ENGINEERING

TITLE ON USAJOBS: ENGINEER, CIVIL

- ❋ U.S. Federal Workforce: 12,243
- ❋ Average Length of Service: 16.0 years
- ❋ Percent Part-Time: 3.8%
- ❋ Percent Women: 17.4%
- ❋ Largest Age Bracket: 50–54 (17.3%)
- ❋ GS Level with Most Workers: 12
- ❋ Agency with Most Workers: Defense
- ❋ State with Most Workers: California

Manage, supervise, lead, and/or perform professional engineering and scientific work involving construction, renovation, inspection, decommissioning, and/or demolition of structures, infrastructures, and their environmental systems above or under Earth's surface; investigate and evaluate Earth's physical, natural, and man-made features.

Requirements: Professional knowledge of and skills in civil engineering.

Claims Adjusters, Examiners, and Investigators

- ❋ Education/Training Required: Long-term on-the-job training
- ❋ Annual Earnings (Federal): $66,580
- ❋ Annual Earnings (All Industries): $57,130
- ❋ Earnings Growth Potential (Federal): 39.9% (median)
- ❋ Earnings Growth Potential (All Industries): 39.1% (medium)
- ❋ Job Growth (Federal): 19.5%
- ❋ Job Growth (All Industries): 7.1%
- ❋ Annual Job Openings (Federal): 1,050
- ❋ Annual Job Openings (All Industries): 9,560

Review settled claims to determine that payments and settlements have been made in accordance with company practices and procedures, ensuring that proper methods have been followed. Report overpayments, underpayments, and other irregularities. Confer with legal counsel on claims requiring litigation. No task data available.

Considerations for Job Outlook: Job growth for adjusters and claims examiners should grow along with the growth of the health-care industry. Employment growth for insurance investigators should be tempered by productivity increases associated with the Internet. Keen competition is expected for investigator jobs.

JOB SPECIALIZATION: CLAIMS EXAMINERS, PROPERTY AND CASUALTY INSURANCE

Review settled insurance claims to determine that payments and settlements have been made in accordance with company practices and procedures. Report overpayments, underpayments,

and other irregularities. Confer with legal counsel on claims requiring litigation. Investigate, evaluate, and settle claims, applying technical knowledge and human relations skills to effect fair and prompt disposal of cases and to contribute to a reduced loss ratio. Pay and process claims within designated authority level. Adjust reserves or provide reserve recommendations to ensure that reserve activities are consistent with corporate policies. Enter claim payments, reserves, and new claims on computer system, inputting concise yet sufficient file documentation. Resolve complex, severe exposure claims, using high service-oriented file handling. Maintain claim files such as records of settled claims and an inventory of claims requiring detailed analysis. Verify and analyze data used in settling claims to ensure that claims are valid and that settlements are made according to company practices and procedures. Examine claims investigated by insurance adjusters, further investigating questionable claims to determine whether to authorize payments.

Personality Type: Conventional-Enterprising. **Skills:** Negotiation; Persuasion; Reading Comprehension; Service Orientation; Writing; Critical Thinking; Mathematics; Active Listening. **Education and Training Program:** Health/Medical Claims Examiner; Insurance. **Work Environment:** Indoors; sitting; making repetitive motions; sounds, noisy.

Job Specialization: Insurance Adjusters, Examiners, and Investigators

Investigate, analyze, and determine the extent of insurance company's liability concerning personal, casualty, or property loss or damages and attempt to effect settlement with claimants. Correspond with or interview medical specialists, agents, witnesses, or claimants to compile information. Calculate benefit payments and approve payment of claims within a certain monetary limit. Examine claims forms and other records to determine insurance coverage. Investigate and assess damage to property and create or review property damage estimates. Interview or correspond with claimants, witnesses, police, physicians, or other relevant parties to determine claim settlement, denial, or review. Review police reports, medical treatment records, medical bills, or physical property damage to determine the extent of liability. Negotiate claim settlements and recommend litigation when settlement cannot be negotiated. Analyze information gathered by investigation, and report findings and recommendations. Interview or correspond with agents and claimants to correct errors or omissions and to investigate questionable claims. Prepare report of findings of investigation. Refer questionable claims to investigator or claims adjuster for investigation or settlement. Collect evidence to support contested claims in court. Obtain credit information from banks and other credit services. Examine titles to property to determine validity and act as company agent in transactions with property owners. Communicate with former associates to verify employment record and to obtain background information regarding persons or businesses applying for credit.

Personality Type: Conventional-Enterprising. **Skills:** Management of Financial Resources; Negotiation; Mathematics; Critical Thinking; Active Listening; Speaking; Reading Comprehension; Writing. **Education and Training Program:** Health/Medical Claims Examiner; Insurance. **Work Environment:** Indoors; sitting; making repetitive motions.

OTHER FEDERAL JOB FACTS

Related GS Series: 0105 Social Insurance Administration

Title on USAJobs: Social Insurance Specialist

- ✳ U.S. Federal Workforce: 29,204
- ✳ Average Length of Service: 17.8 years

- Percent Part-Time: 2.7%
- Percent Women: 70.6%
- Largest Age Bracket: 55–59 (15.9%)
- GS Level with Most Workers: 11
- Agency with Most Workers: Interior
- State with Most Workers: California

Administer, plan, manage, and conduct the federal Social Security old age, survivors, disability, and/or health insurance programs. Includes those positions concerned with the development, preparation, issuance, and interpretation of policies, methods, and procedures for the conduct of such programs; and also those positions that involve representing the programs before the general public and determining eligibility for benefits when the work requires the ability to deal effectively with the general public.

Requirements: Knowledge of the broad concepts and technical provisions of the old age, survivors, disability insurance, and/or health insurance programs established by the Social Security Act, as amended.

Clergy

- Education/Training Required: Master's degree
- Annual Earnings (Federal): $74,360
- Annual Earnings (All Industries): $42,950
- Earnings Growth Potential (Federal): 24.1% (very low)
- Earnings Growth Potential (All Industries): 46.6% (high)
- Job Growth (Federal): 10.2%
- Job Growth (All Industries): 12.7%
- Annual Job Openings (Federal): 310
- Annual Job Openings (All Industries): 21,770

Conduct religious worship and perform other spiritual functions associated with beliefs and practices of religious faith or denomination. Provide spiritual and moral guidance and assistance to members. Pray and promote spirituality. Read from sacred texts such as the Bible, Torah, or Koran. Prepare and deliver sermons and other talks. Organize and lead regular religious services. Share information about religious issues by writing articles, giving speeches, or teaching. Instruct people who seek conversion to a particular faith. Visit people in homes, hospitals, and prisons to provide them with comfort and support. Counsel individuals and groups concerning their spiritual, emotional, and personal needs. Train leaders of church, community, and youth groups. Administer religious rites or ordinances. Study and interpret religious laws, doctrines, and/or traditions. Conduct special ceremonies such as weddings, funerals, and confirmations. Plan and lead religious education programs for their congregations. Respond to requests for assistance during emergencies or crises. Devise ways in which congregation membership can be expanded. Collaborate with committees and individuals to address financial and administrative issues pertaining to congregations. Prepare people for participation in religious ceremonies. Perform administrative duties such as overseeing building management, ordering supplies, contracting for services and repairs, and supervising the work of staff members and volunteers. Refer people to community support services, psychologists, and/or doctors as necessary. Participate in fundraising activities to support congregation activities and facilities.

Considerations for Job Outlook: About average employment growth is projected.

Personality Type: Social-Enterprising-Artistic. **Skills:** Management of Financial Resources; Social Perceptiveness; Persuasion; Negotiation; Learning Strategies; Management of Material Resources; Service Orientation; Systems Evaluation. **Education and Training Program:** Clinical

Pastoral Counseling/Patient Counseling; Divinity/Ministry (BD, MDiv); Pastoral Counseling and Specialized Ministries, Other; Pastoral Studies/Counseling; Philosophy; Pre-Theology/Pre-Ministerial Studies; Rabbinical Studies (M.H.L./Rav); Religion/Religious Studies; Theological and Ministerial Studies, Other; Theology and Religious Vocations, Other; Theology/Theological Studies; Youth Ministry. **Work Environment:** Indoors; sitting.

OTHER FEDERAL JOB FACTS

RELATED GS SERIES: 0060 CHAPLAIN

- ⚘ U.S. Federal Workforce: 1,157
- ⚘ Average Length of Service: 9.6 years
- ⚘ Percent Part-Time: 24.9%
- ⚘ Percent Women: 13.7%
- ⚘ Largest Age Bracket: 65 or more (20.7%)
- ⚘ GS Level with Most Workers: 12
- ⚘ Agency with Most Workers: Veterans Affairs
- ⚘ States with Most Workers: California, Texas

Advise on, administer, supervise, or perform professional work involved in a program of spiritual welfare and religious guidance for patients of government hospitals and homes, for inmates of government correctional and penal or other institutions, or for persons in other government activities where civilian chaplain service is needed.

Requirements: Ordination by a recognized ecclesiastical body.

Coaches and Scouts

- ⚘ Education/Training Required: Long-term on-the-job training
- ⚘ Annual Earnings (Federal): $56,190
- ⚘ Annual Earnings (All Industries): $28,380
- ⚘ Earnings Growth Potential (Federal): 20.9% (very low)

- ⚘ Earnings Growth Potential (All Industries): 43.9% (high)
- ⚘ Job Growth (Federal): 17.9%
- ⚘ Job Growth (All Industries): 24.8%
- ⚘ Annual Job Openings (Federal): 10
- ⚘ Annual Job Openings (All Industries): 9,920

Instruct or coach groups or individuals in the fundamentals of sports. Demonstrate techniques and methods of participation. May evaluate athletes' strengths and weaknesses as possible recruits or to improve the athletes' technique to prepare them for competition. Plan, organize, and conduct practice sessions. Provide training direction, encouragement, and motivation to prepare athletes for games, competitive events, or tours. Identify and recruit potential athletes, arranging and offering incentives such as athletic scholarships. Plan strategies and choose team members for individual games or sports seasons. Plan and direct physical conditioning programs that will enable athletes to achieve maximum performance. Adjust coaching techniques based on the strengths and weaknesses of athletes. File scouting reports that detail player assessments, provide recommendations on athlete recruitment, and identify locations and individuals to be targeted for future recruitment efforts. Keep records of athlete, team, and opposing team performance. Instruct individuals or groups in sports rules, game strategies, and performance principles such as specific ways of moving the body, hands, and feet in order to achieve desired results. Analyze the strengths and weaknesses of opposing teams to develop game strategies. Evaluate athletes' skills and review performance records to determine their fitness and potential in a particular area of athletics. Keep abreast of changing rules, techniques, technologies, and philosophies relevant to their sport. Monitor athletes' use of equipment to ensure safe and proper use. Explain and enforce safety rules and regulations. Develop and arrange competition schedules and programs.

Considerations for Job Outlook: Employment is expected to grow as more people participate in organized sports. Keen competition is expected for many jobs, such as professional athletes. Opportunities should be best for part-time umpires, referees, and other sports officials at the high school level.

Personality Type: Social-Realistic-Enterprising. **Skills:** Management of Personnel Resources; Systems Evaluation; Monitoring; Instructing; Management of Material Resources; Learning Strategies; Negotiation; Social Perceptiveness. **Education and Training Program:** Health and Physical Education, General; Physical Education Teaching and Coaching; Sport and Fitness Administration/Management. **Work Environment:** More often indoors than outdoors; standing; sounds, noisy; walking and running.

OTHER FEDERAL JOB FACTS

RELATED GS SERIES: 0030 SPORTS SPECIALIST

- ❂ U.S. Federal Workforce: 426
- ❂ Average Length of Service: 14.4 years
- ❂ Percent Part-Time: 0.0%
- ❂ Percent Women: 17.1%
- ❂ Largest Age Bracket: 45–49 (17.6%)
- ❂ GS Level with Most Workers: 9
- ❂ Agencies with Most Workers: Justice, Defense
- ❂ State with Most Workers: California

Plan, supervise, administer, or carry out sports programs; conduct clinics or seminars to train coaches or officials; train and develop athletes in individual or team sports; plan, organize, or conduct tournaments or competitions from the intramural to the international levels; or perform other functions requiring knowledge or skill in sports.

Requirements: Knowledge of the physical and psychological factors in individual and team sports, and of the nature, purpose, and organization of recreational or competitive individual and team sports activities.

Combined Food Preparation and Serving Workers, Including Fast Food

- ❂ Education/Training Required: Short-term on-the-job training
- ❂ Annual Earnings (Federal): $29,720
- ❂ Annual Earnings (All Industries): $17,220
- ❂ Earnings Growth Potential (Federal): 32.9% (low)
- ❂ Earnings Growth Potential (All Industries): 13.9% (very low)
- ❂ Job Growth (Federal): 8.1%
- ❂ Job Growth (All Industries): 14.6%
- ❂ Annual Job Openings (Federal): 210
- ❂ Annual Job Openings (All Industries): 96,720

Perform duties that combine food preparation and food service. Accept payment from customers, and make change as necessary. Request and record customer orders, and compute bills using cash registers, multicounting machines, or pencil and paper. Serve customers in eating places that specialize in fast service and inexpensive carry-out food. Prepare and serve cold drinks, or frozen milk drinks or desserts, using drink-dispensing, milkshake, or frozen custard machines. Select food items from serving or storage areas and place them in dishes, on serving trays, or in takeout bags. Notify kitchen personnel of shortages or special orders. Cook or re-heat food items such as french fries. Wash dishes, glassware, and silverware after meals. Collect and return dirty dishes to the kitchen for washing. Relay food orders to cooks. Clean and organize eating, service, and kitchen areas. Communicate with customers regarding orders, comments, and complaints.

Considerations for Job Outlook: Job growth is projected due to an expanding population and the continued popularity of dining out. Opportunities should be excellent.

Personality Type: Conventional-Realistic-Enterprising. **Skills:** None met the criteria. **Education and Training Program:** Food Preparation/Professional Cooking/Kitchen Assistant Training; Institutional Food Workers. **Work Environment:** Indoors; standing; making repetitive motions; using your hands to handle, control, or feel objects, tools, or controls; walking and running; minor burns, cuts, bites, or stings.

OTHER FEDERAL JOB FACTS
Related GS Series: 1667 Food Services
Title on USAJobs: Food Services Specialist

* U.S. Federal Workforce: 325
* Average Length of Service: 15.1 years
* Percent Part-Time: 0.0%
* Percent Women: 22.5%
* Largest Age Bracket: 45–49 (28.6%)
* GS Level with Most Workers: 11
* Agency with Most Workers: Justice
* State with Most Workers: Texas

Operate food services of federal government institutions, including storeroom, kitchen, dining room, and meat and bakery operations.

Requirements: Practical knowledge of menu planning and food service operations.

Compliance Officers, Except Agriculture, Construction, Health and Safety, and Transportation

* Education/Training Required: Long-term on-the-job training
* Annual Earnings (Federal): $45,720
* Annual Earnings (All Industries): $49,750
* Earnings Growth Potential (Federal): 32.3% (low)
* Earnings Growth Potential (All Industries): 37.3% (medium)
* Job Growth (Federal): 29.8%
* Job Growth (All Industries): 31.0%
* Annual Job Openings (Federal): 3,080
* Annual Job Openings (All Industries): 10,850

Examine, evaluate, and investigate eligibility for or conformity with laws and regulations governing contract compliance of licenses and permits and other compliance and enforcement inspection activities not classified elsewhere. No task data available.

Considerations for Job Outlook: Much faster than average employment growth is projected.

Job Specialization: Coroners

Direct activities such as autopsies, pathological and toxicological analyses, and inquests relating to the investigation of deaths occurring within a legal jurisdiction to determine cause of death or to fix responsibility for accidental, violent, or unexplained deaths. Perform medico-legal examinations and autopsies, conducting preliminary examinations of the body in order to identify victims, to locate signs of trauma, and to identify factors that would indicate time of death. Inquire into the cause, manner, and circumstances of human deaths and establish the identities of deceased persons. Direct activities of workers who conduct autopsies, perform pathological and toxicological analyses, and prepare documents for permanent records. Complete death certificates, including the assignment of a cause and manner of death. Observe and record the positions and conditions of bodies and of related evidence. Collect and document any pertinent medical history information. Observe, record, and preserve any objects or personal property related to deaths, including objects such as medication containers and suicide notes. Complete reports and forms required to finalize cases. Remove or supervise removal of bodies from death scenes, using the proper equipment and supplies, and arrange for transportation to morgues. Testify at inquests, hearings, and court trials. Interview persons present at death scenes to obtain information useful in determining the manner of death. Provide information concerning the circumstances of death to relatives of the deceased. Locate and document information regarding the next of kin, including their relationship to the deceased and the status of notification attempts.

Personality Type: Investigative-Realistic-Conventional. **Skills:** Science; Social Perceptiveness; Speaking; Critical Thinking; Writing; Management of Personnel Resources; Learning Strategies; Instructing. **Education and Training Program:** Public Administration. **Work Environment:** More often indoors than outdoors; disease or infections; contaminants; using your hands to handle, control, or feel objects, tools, or controls; hazardous equipment.

JOB SPECIALIZATION: ENVIRONMENTAL COMPLIANCE INSPECTORS

Inspect and investigate sources of pollution to protect the public and environment and ensure conformance with federal, state, and local regulations and ordinances. Determine the nature of code violations and actions to be taken and issue written notices of violation; participate in enforcement hearings as necessary. Examine permits, licenses, applications, and records to ensure compliance with licensing requirements. Prepare, organize, and maintain inspection records. Interview individuals to determine the nature of suspected violations and to obtain evidence of violations. Prepare written, oral, tabular, and graphic reports summarizing requirements and regulations, including enforcement and chain of custody documentation. Monitor follow-up actions in cases where violations were found and review compliance monitoring reports. Investigate complaints and suspected violations regarding illegal dumping, pollution, pesticides, product quality, or labeling laws. Inspect waste pretreatment, treatment, and disposal facilities and systems for conformance to federal, state, or local regulations. Inform individuals and groups of pollution control regulations and inspection findings and explain how problems can be corrected. Determine sampling locations and methods and collect water or wastewater samples for analysis, preserving samples with appropriate containers and preservation methods. Verify that hazardous chemicals are handled, stored, and disposed of in accordance with regulations. Research and keep informed of pertinent information and developments in areas such as EPA laws and regulations.

Personality Type: Conventional-Investigative-Realistic. **Skills:** Quality Control Analysis; Science; Troubleshooting; Mathematics; Reading Comprehension; Writing; Systems Evaluation; Active Learning. **Education and Training Program:** Natural Resources Management and Policy, Other. **Work Environment:** More often indoors than outdoors; sitting; contaminants.

JOB SPECIALIZATION: EQUAL OPPORTUNITY REPRESENTATIVES AND OFFICERS

Monitor and evaluate compliance with equal opportunity laws, guidelines, and policies to ensure that employment practices and contracting arrangements give equal opportunity without regard to race, religion, color, national origin, sex, age, or disability. Investigate employment practices and alleged violations of laws to document and correct discriminatory factors. Interpret civil rights laws and equal opportunity regulations for individuals and employers. Study equal opportunity complaints to clarify issues. Meet with persons involved in equal opportunity complaints to verify case information and to arbitrate and settle disputes. Coordinate, monitor, and revise complaint procedures to ensure timely processing and review of complaints. Prepare reports of selection, survey, and other statistics and recommendations for corrective action. Conduct surveys and evaluate findings to determine whether systematic discrimination exists. Develop guidelines for nondiscriminatory employment practices and monitor their implementation and impact. Review company contracts to determine actions required to meet governmental equal opportunity provisions. Counsel newly hired members of minority and disadvantaged groups, informing them about details of civil rights laws. Provide information, technical assistance, and training to supervisors, managers, and employees on topics such as employee supervision, hiring, grievance procedures, and staff development. Verify that all job descriptions are submitted for review and approval and that descriptions meet regulatory standards. Act as liaisons between minority placement agencies and employers or between job search committees and other equal opportunity administrators.

Personality Type: Social-Enterprising-Conventional. **Skills:** Persuasion; Reading Comprehension; Active Listening; Active Learning; Negotiation; Writing; Systems Evaluation; Speaking. **Education and Training Program:** Public Administration and Social Service Professions, Other. **Work Environment:** Indoors; sitting; making repetitive motions.

JOB SPECIALIZATION: GOVERNMENT PROPERTY INSPECTORS AND INVESTIGATORS

Investigate or inspect government property to ensure compliance with contract agreements and government regulations. Prepare correspondence, reports of inspections or investigations, and recommendations for action. Inspect government-owned equipment and materials in the possession of private contractors to ensure compliance with contracts and regulations and to prevent misuse. Examine records, reports, and documents to establish facts and detect discrepancies. Inspect manufactured or processed products to ensure compliance with contract specifications and legal requirements. Locate and interview plaintiffs, witnesses, or representatives of business or government to gather facts relevant to inspections or alleged violations. Recommend legal or administrative action to protect government property. Submit samples of products to government laboratories for testing as required. Coordinate with and assist law enforcement agencies in matters of mutual concern. Testify in court or at administrative proceedings concerning findings of investigations. Collect, identify, evaluate, and preserve case evidence. Monitor investigations of suspected offenders to ensure that they are conducted in accordance with constitutional requirements. Investigate applications for special licenses or permits, as well as alleged violations of licenses or permits.

Personality Type: Conventional-Enterprising-Realistic. **Skills:** Quality Control Analysis; Persuasion; Systems Evaluation; Writing; Operation and Control; Speaking; Judgment and Decision Making; Operation Monitoring. **Education and Training Program:** Building/Home/ConstructionInspection/Inspector. **Work Environment:** More often outdoors than indoors; sounds, noisy; contaminants; very hot or cold temperatures; sitting.

Job Specialization: Licensing Examiners and Inspectors

Examine, evaluate, and investigate eligibility for, conformity with, or liability under licenses or permits. Issue licenses to individuals meeting standards. Evaluate applications, records, and documents in order to gather information about eligibility or liability issues. Administer oral, written, road, or flight tests to license applicants. Score tests and observe equipment operation and control in order to rate ability of applicants. Advise licensees and other individuals or groups concerning licensing, permit, or passport regulations. Warn violators of infractions or penalties. Prepare reports of activities, evaluations, recommendations, and decisions. Prepare correspondence to inform concerned parties of licensing decisions and of appeals processes. Confer with and interview officials, technical or professional specialists, and applicants in order to obtain information or to clarify facts relevant to licensing decisions. Report law or regulation violations to appropriate boards and agencies. Visit establishments to verify that valid licenses and permits are displayed and that licensing standards are being upheld.

Personality Type: Conventional-Enterprising. **Skills:** Quality Control Analysis; Judgment and Decision Making; Social Perceptiveness; Speaking; Operation Monitoring; Service Orientation; Systems Evaluation; Reading Comprehension. **Education and Training Program:** Public Administration and Social Service Professions, Other. **Work Environment:** More often indoors than outdoors; making repetitive motions; contaminants; using your hands to handle, control, or feel objects, tools, or controls; sitting.

Job Specialization: Regulatory Affairs Specialists

Coordinate and document internal regulatory processes, such as internal audits, inspections, license renewals, or registrations. May compile and prepare materials for submission to regulatory agencies. Coordinate, prepare, or review regulatory submissions for domestic or international projects. Provide technical review of data or reports that will be incorporated into regulatory submissions to assure scientific rigor, accuracy, and clarity of presentation. Review product promotional materials, labeling, batch records, specification sheets, or test methods for compliance with applicable regulations and policies. Maintain current knowledge base of existing and emerging regulations, standards, or guidance documents. Interpret regulatory rules or rule changes and ensure that they are communicated through corporate policies and procedures. Advise project teams on subjects such as premarket regulatory requirements, export and labeling requirements, and clinical study compliance issues. Determine the types of regulatory submissions or internal documentation that are required in situations such as proposed device changes and labeling changes. Prepare or maintain technical files as necessary to obtain and sustain product approval. Coordinate efforts associated with the preparation of regulatory documents or submissions. Prepare or direct the preparation of additional information or responses as requested by regulatory agencies. Analyze product complaints and make recommendations regarding their reportability. Escort government inspectors during inspections and provide post-inspection follow-up information as requested.

Personality Type: Conventional-Enterprising. **Skills:** Systems Analysis; Systems Evaluation; Judgment and Decision Making; Persuasion; Writing; Speaking; Coordination; Reading Comprehension. **Education and Training Program:** Business Administration and Management, General. **Work Environment:** Indoors; sitting.

OTHER FEDERAL JOB FACTS

RELATED GS SERIES: 1815 AIR SAFETY INVESTIGATING

- U.S. Federal Workforce: 77
- Average Length of Service: 16.7 years
- Percent Part-Time: 0.0%
- Percent Women: 14.3%
- Largest Age Bracket: 50–54 (23.4%)
- GS Levels with Most Workers: 14, 13
- Agencies with Most Workers: Transportation, Defense
- State with Most Workers: District of Columbia

Investigate and prevent accidents and incidents involving United States aircraft anywhere in the world; establish programs and procedures to provide for the notification and reporting of accidents; report the facts, conditions, and circumstances relating to each accident; determine the probable cause of the accident, along with recommendations for remedial action designed to prevent similar accidents in the future; conduct special studies and investigations on matters pertaining to safety in air navigation and the prevention of accidents.

Requirements: Broad technical knowledge in the field of aviation, and experience or training that provides a knowledge of investigative techniques and/or legal procedures and practices.

RELATED GS SERIES: 1895 CUSTOMS AND BORDER PROTECTION

TITLE ON USAJOBS: CUSTOMS AND BORDER PROTECTION OFFICER

- U.S. Federal Workforce: 19,449
- Average Length of Service: 10.4 years
- Percent Part-Time: 0.1%
- Percent Women: 18.5%
- Largest Age Bracket: 30–34 (17.3%)
- GS Level with Most Workers: 12
- Agency with Most Workers: Homeland Security
- States with Most Workers: Texas, California

Detect and prevent terrorists and instruments of terror from entering the United States; enforce and administer laws relating to the right of persons to enter, reside in, or depart from the United States, Puerto Rico, Guam, and the U.S. Virgin Islands, and the importation/exportation of merchandise.

Requirements: Knowledge of federal immigration, customs, agriculture, or other laws.

RELATED GS SERIES: 0260 EQUAL EMPLOYMENT OPPORTUNITY

TITLE ON USAJOBS: EQUAL EMPLOYMENT OPPORTUNITY SPECIALIST

- U.S. Federal Workforce: 2,659
- Average Length of Service: 20.4 years
- Percent Part-Time: 0.6%
- Percent Women: 69.3%
- Largest Age Bracket: 50–54 (21.8%)
- GS Level with Most Workers: 13
- Agency with Most Workers: Defense
- State with Most Workers: District of Columbia

Develop, administer, evaluate, or advise on the federal government's internal equal employment opportunity program within various federal agencies; solve the specialized employment problems of women, minorities, veterans, the handicapped, persons over age forty, and others as they relate to federal employment.

Requirements: Knowledge of federal equal employment opportunity regulations and principles; compliance and enforcement skills; administrative, management, and consulting skills; and knowledge of federal personnel administration.

RELATED GS SERIES: 0360 EQUAL OPPORTUNITY COMPLIANCE

TITLE ON USAJOBS: EQUAL OPPORTUNITY COMPLIANCE SPECIALIST

- ❋ U.S. Federal Workforce: 1,713
- ❋ Average Length of Service: 16.9 years
- ❋ Percent Part-Time: 1.9%
- ❋ Percent Women: 62.5%
- ❋ Largest Age Bracket: 55–59 (18.7%)
- ❋ GS Level with Most Workers: 12
- ❋ Agency with Most Workers: Labor
- ❋ State with Most Workers: District of Columbia

Analyze, evaluate, and interpret compliance with equal opportunity and civil rights laws; apply civil rights and equal opportunity laws, regulations, and precedent decisions to eliminate illegal discrimination and to remove barriers to equal opportunity; analyze and solve equal opportunity and civil rights problems through fact finding, problem analysis, negotiation, and voluntary compliance programs.

Requirements: Judgment in applying equal opportunity principles to solve problems or recommend action. May require specialized knowledge and skill in investigating and resolving allegations of discrimination.

RELATED GS SERIES: 1801 GENERAL INSPECTION, INVESTIGATION, ENFORCEMENT, AND COMPLIANCE

- ❋ U.S. Federal Workforce: 32,643
- ❋ Average Length of Service: 9.7 years
- ❋ Percent Part-Time: 0.2%
- ❋ Percent Women: 30.0%
- ❋ Largest Age Bracket: 40–44 (17.5%)
- ❋ GS Levels with Most Workers: 12, 9

- ❋ Agency with Most Workers: Homeland Security
- ❋ State with Most Workers: California

Supervise, lead, or perform inspection, investigation, enforcement, or compliance work. The work is not covered by another administrative occupation in this group or is covered equally by two or more administrative occupations in this group.

Requirements: No requirements available.

RELATED GS SERIES: 1889 IMPORT COMPLIANCE

- ❋ U.S. Federal Workforce: 1,048
- ❋ Average Length of Service: 17.3 years
- ❋ Percent Part-Time: 1.3%
- ❋ Percent Women: 59.4%
- ❋ Largest Age Bracket: 40–44 (16.3%)
- ❋ GS Level with Most Workers: 11
- ❋ Agency with Most Workers: Homeland Security
- ❋ State with Most Workers: New York

Assess customs duties and associated taxes to be paid on imported merchandise and ensure compliance with related laws and regulations.

Requirements: Knowledge of tariff and other import-related laws, regulations, policies, procedures, and administrative and judicial rulings; of technical or physical characteristics, commercial uses, and trade practices associated with imported merchandise; and of import admissibility, classification and valuation of merchandise, final settlement of duties and taxes due, and related matters.

RELATED GS SERIES: 0244 LABOR-MANAGEMENT RELATIONS EXAMINING

- ❋ U.S. Federal Workforce: 330
- ❋ Average Length of Service: 19.7 years
- ❋ Percent Part-Time: 6.7%
- ❋ Percent Women: 55.5%

* Largest Age Bracket: 55–59 (17.6%)
* GS Level with Most Workers: 13
* Agency with Most Workers: No data available
* State with Most Workers: California

Investigate, evaluate, and resolve cases involving charges of unfair labor practices or collective bargaining representation issues or disputes that arise under the National Labor Relations Act.

Requirements: Knowledge of the field of labor-management relations, of collective bargaining processes, of applicable labor laws and precedent decisions, and of the regulations, policies and practices of the National Labor Relations Board; also the ability to apply investigative techniques and to negotiate constructively and persuasively.

RELATED GS SERIES: 0967 PASSPORT AND VISA EXAMINING

TITLE ON USAJOBS: PASSPORT AND VISA EXAMINER

* U.S. Federal Workforce: 1,462
* Average Length of Service: 10.0 years
* Percent Part-Time: 0.8%
* Percent Women: 64.4%
* Largest Age Bracket: 30–34 (14.7%)
* GS Level with Most Workers: 11
* Agency with Most Workers: State
* State with Most Workers: New Hampshire

Manage, supervise, or perform administrative work concerned with adjudicating applications for United States passports or visas, including related work involving determining citizenship or fitness of noncitizens for admission to the United States.

Requirements: Knowledge of legal and regulatory provisions governing U.S. citizenship, nationality, and/or visas; knowledge of principles, systems, and operations related to the issuance of passports or other citizenship registration, certificates, or visas.

RELATED GS SERIES: 1849 WAGE AND HOUR INVESTIGATION

* U.S. Federal Workforce: 1,214
* Average Length of Service: 13.9 years
* Percent Part-Time: 1.3%
* Percent Women: 48.8%
* Largest Age Bracket: 45–49 (14.7%)
* GS Levels with Most Workers: 12, 9
* Agency with Most Workers: Labor
* State with Most Workers: California

Conduct on-site investigations to obtain compliance by employers with wage and hour and related laws; establish, revise, and interpret wage and hour program policies and guidelines; and/or evaluate enforcement operations.

Requirements: Knowledge of related laws; understanding of business organizations, records systems, and practices related to the laws administered; and skill to apply varied investigative techniques to obtain compliance, including on-site questioning of employees and employers, negotiation and conciliation, instruction, persuasion, and litigation.

Computer and Information Research Scientists

* Education/Training Required: Doctoral degree
* Annual Earnings (Federal): $99,730
* Annual Earnings (All Industries): $101,570
* Earnings Growth Potential (Federal): 32.2% (low)
* Earnings Growth Potential (All Industries): 39.5% (medium)
* Job Growth (Federal): 19.5%
* Job Growth (All Industries): 24.2%
* Annual Job Openings (Federal): 200
* Annual Job Openings (All Industries): 1,320

Conduct research into fundamental computer and information science as theorists, designers, or inventors. Develop solutions to problems in the field of computer hardware and software. Analyze problems to develop solutions involving computer hardware and software. Assign or schedule tasks in order to meet work priorities and goals. Evaluate project plans and proposals to assess feasibility issues. Apply theoretical expertise and innovation to create or apply new technology, such as adapting principles for applying computers to new uses. Consult with users, management, vendors, and technicians to determine computing needs and system requirements. Meet with managers, vendors, and others to solicit cooperation and resolve problems. Conduct logical analyses of business, scientific, engineering, and other technical problems, formulating mathematical models of problems for solution by computers. Develop and interpret organizational goals, policies, and procedures. Participate in staffing decisions and direct training of subordinates. Develop performance standards, and evaluate work in light of established standards. Design computers and the software that runs them. Maintain network hardware and software, direct network security measures, and monitor networks to ensure availability to system users. Participate in multidisciplinary projects in areas such as virtual reality, human-computer interaction, or robotics. Approve, prepare, monitor, and adjust operational budgets. Direct daily operations of departments, coordinating project activities with other departments.

Considerations for Job Outlook: Employment is expected to increase because of high demand for sophisticated technological research. Job prospects should be excellent.

Personality Type: Investigative-Realistic-Conventional. **Skills:** Programming; Technology Design; Systems Evaluation; Management of Financial Resources; Mathematics; Systems Analysis; Operations Analysis; Science. **Education and Training Program:** Artificial Intelligence; Computer and Information Sciences and Support Services, Other; Computer and Information Sciences, General; Computer Science; Computer Systems Analysis/Analyst; Information Science/Studies; Medical Informatics. **Work Environment:** Indoors; sitting; using hands; repetitive motions.

OTHER FEDERAL JOB FACTS
Related GS Series: 1550 Computer Science
Title on USAJobs: Computer Scientist

- U.S. Federal Workforce: 6,251
- Average Length of Service: 12.1 years
- Percent Part-Time: 2.0%
- Percent Women: 26.5%
- Largest Age Bracket: 45–49 (18.6%)
- GS Level with Most Workers: 13
- Agency with Most Workers: Defense
- State with Most Workers: Virginia

Apply research computer science methods and techniques to store, manipulate, transform, or present information by means of computer systems.

Requirements: Professional competence in applying the theoretical foundations of computer science, including computer system architecture and system software organization, the representation and transformation of information structures, and the theoretical models for such representations and transformations; specialized knowledge of the design characteristics, limitations, and potential applications of systems having the ability to transform information, and of broad areas of applications of computing which have common structures, processes, and techniques; and knowledge of relevant mathematical and statistical sciences.

C

Computer and Information Systems Managers

- ❋ Education/Training Required: Bachelor's or higher degree, plus work experience
- ❋ Annual Earnings (Federal): $133,440
- ❋ Annual Earnings (All Industries): $113,720
- ❋ Earnings Growth Potential (Federal): 31.9% (low)
- ❋ Earnings Growth Potential (All Industries): 38.5% (medium)
- ❋ Job Growth (Federal): 8.3%
- ❋ Job Growth (All Industries): 16.9%
- ❋ Annual Job Openings (Federal): 100
- ❋ Annual Job Openings (All Industries): 9,710

Plan, direct, or coordinate activities in such fields as electronic data processing, information systems, systems analysis, and computer programming. Review project plans to plan and coordinate project activity. Manage backup, security, and user help systems. Develop and interpret organizational goals, policies, and procedures. Develop computer information resources, providing for data security and control, strategic computing, and disaster recovery. Consult with users, management, vendors, and technicians to assess computing needs and system requirements. Stay abreast of advances in technology. Meet with department heads, managers, supervisors, vendors, and others to solicit cooperation and resolve problems. Provide users with technical support for computer problems. Recruit, hire, train, and supervise staff or participate in staffing decisions. Evaluate data processing proposals to assess project feasibility and requirements. Review and approve all systems charts and programs prior to their implementation. Control operational budget and expenditures. Direct daily operations of department, analyzing workflow, establishing priorities, developing standards, and setting deadlines. Assign and review the work of systems analysts, programmers, and other computer-related workers. Evaluate the organization's technology use and needs and recommend improvements such as hardware and software upgrades. Prepare and review operational reports or project progress reports. Purchase necessary equipment.

Considerations for Job Outlook: New applications of technology in the workplace should continue to drive demand for IT services, fueling employment growth of these managers. Job prospects are expected to be excellent.

Personality Type: Enterprising-Conventional-Investigative. **Skills:** Management of Financial Resources; Management of Material Resources; Programming; Systems Evaluation; Equipment Selection; Troubleshooting; Repairing; Technology Design. **Education and Training Program:** Computer and Information Sciences, General; Computer Science; Information Resources Management/CIO Training; Information Science/Studies; Knowledge Management; Management Information Systems, General; Network and System Administration/Administrator; Operations Management and Supervision. **Work Environment:** Indoors; sitting; using your hands to handle, control, or feel objects, tools, or controls.

OTHER FEDERAL JOB FACTS

RELATED GS SERIES: 1550 COMPUTER SCIENCE

TITLE ON USAJOBS: COMPUTER SCIENTIST

- ❋ U.S. Federal Workforce: 6,251
- ❋ Average Length of Service: 12.1 years
- ❋ Percent Part-Time: 2.0%
- ❋ Percent Women: 26.5%
- ❋ Largest Age Bracket: 45–49 (18.6%)
- ❋ GS Level with Most Workers: 13

* Agency with Most Workers: Defense
* State with Most Workers: Virginia

Apply research computer science methods and techniques to store, manipulate, transform, or present information by means of computer systems.

Requirements: Professional competence in applying the theoretical foundations of computer science, including computer system architecture and system software organization, the representation and transformation of information structures, and the theoretical models for such representations and transformations; specialized knowledge of the design characteristics, limitations, and potential applications of systems having the ability to transform information, and of broad areas of applications of computing which have common structures, processes, and techniques; and knowledge of relevant mathematical and statistical sciences.

Computer Hardware Engineers

* Education/Training Required: Bachelor's degree
* Annual Earnings (Federal): $100,560
* Annual Earnings (All Industries): $98,820
* Earnings Growth Potential (Federal): 31.9% (low)
* Earnings Growth Potential (All Industries): 38.6% (medium)
* Job Growth (Federal): 7.6%
* Job Growth (All Industries): 3.8%
* Annual Job Openings (Federal): 110
* Annual Job Openings (All Industries): 2,350

Research, design, develop, and test computer or computer-related equipment for commercial, industrial, military, or scientific use. May supervise the manufacturing and installation of computer or computer-related equipment and components. Update knowledge and skills to keep up with rapid advancements in computer technology. Provide technical support to designers, marketing and sales departments, suppliers, engineers, and other team members throughout the product development and implementation process. Test and verify hardware and support peripherals to ensure that they meet specifications and requirements, analyzing and recording test data. Monitor functioning of equipment and make necessary modifications to ensure system operates in conformance with specifications. Analyze information to determine, recommend, and plan layout, including type of computers and peripheral equipment modifications. Build, test, and modify product prototypes, using working models or theoretical models constructed using computer simulation. Analyze user needs and recommend appropriate hardware. Direct technicians, engineering designers, or other technical support personnel as needed. Confer with engineering staff and consult specifications to evaluate interface between hardware and software and operational and performance requirements of overall system. Select hardware and material, assuring compliance with specifications and product requirements. Store, retrieve, and manipulate data for analysis of system capabilities and requirements. Write detailed functional specifications that document the hardware development process and support hardware introduction.

Considerations for Job Outlook: Computer hardware engineers are expected to have employment growth of 4 percent from 2008–2018, slower than the average for all occupations. Although the use of information technology continues to expand rapidly, the manufacture of computer hardware is expected to be adversely affected by intense foreign competition. As computer and semiconductor manufacturers contract out more of their engineering needs to both domestic and foreign design firms, much of the growth in employment of hardware engineers is expected to take place in the computer systems design and related services industry.

Personality Type: Investigative-Realistic-Conventional. **Skills:** Troubleshooting; Science; Programming; Operations Analysis; Systems Evaluation; Quality Control Analysis; Complex Problem Solving; Systems Analysis. **Education and Training Program:** Computer Engineering, General; Computer Hardware Engineering. **Work Environment:** Indoors; sitting.

OTHER FEDERAL JOB FACTS

RELATED **GS** SERIES: 0854 COMPUTER ENGINEERING

TITLE ON **USAJOBS:** ENGINEER, COMPUTERS

- ❋ U.S. Federal Workforce: 4,512
- ❋ Average Length of Service: 13.5 years
- ❋ Percent Part-Time: 0.8%
- ❋ Percent Women: 17.9%
- ❋ Largest Age Bracket: 45–49 (20.4%)
- ❋ GS Level with Most Workers: 13
- ❋ Agency with Most Workers: Defense
- ❋ State with Most Workers: Maryland

Manage, supervise, lead, and/or perform professional engineering and scientific work involving the design, construction, and operation of computer systems, including hardware and software and their integration.

Requirements: Professional knowledge of and skills in computer engineering.

Conservation Scientists

- ❋ Education/Training Required: Bachelor's degree
- ❋ Annual Earnings (Federal): $69,580
- ❋ Annual Earnings (All Industries): $60,160
- ❋ Earnings Growth Potential (Federal): 30.7% (low)
- ❋ Earnings Growth Potential (All Industries): 40.9% (medium)

- ❋ Job Growth (Federal): 8.0%
- ❋ Job Growth (All Industries): 11.9%
- ❋ Annual Job Openings (Federal): 110
- ❋ Annual Job Openings (All Industries): 410

Manage, improve, and protect natural resources to maximize their use without damaging the environment. May conduct soil surveys and develop plans to eliminate soil erosion or to protect rangelands from fire and rodent damage. May instruct farmers, agricultural production managers, or ranchers in best ways to use crop rotation, contour plowing, or terracing to conserve soil and water; in the number and kind of livestock and forage plants best suited to particular ranges; and in range and farm improvements, such as fencing and reservoirs for stock watering. No task data available.

Considerations for Job Outlook: Increased conservation efforts and continued pressure to maximize efficient use of natural resources are expected to lead to more jobs for conservation scientists. Job seekers with a bachelor's degree should have the best prospects.

JOB SPECIALIZATION: PARK NATURALISTS

Plan, develop, and conduct programs to inform public of historical, natural, and scientific features of national, state, or local park. Provide visitor services by explaining regulations; answering visitor requests, needs, and complaints; and providing information about the park and surrounding areas. Conduct field trips to point out scientific, historic, and natural features of parks, forests, historic sites, or other attractions. Prepare and present illustrated lectures and interpretive talks about park features. Perform emergency duties to protect human life, government property, and natural features of park. Confer with park staff to determine subjects and schedules for park programs. Assist with operations of general facilities, such as visitor centers. Plan, organize, and direct activities of seasonal staff members. Perform routine maintenance on park structures. Prepare brochures and write newspaper articles. Construct historical, scientific, and nature visitor-center displays. Research stories regarding the area's natural history or environment. Interview specialists in desired fields to obtain and develop data for park information programs. Compile and maintain official park photographic and information files. Take photographs and motion pictures for use in lectures and publications and to develop displays. Survey park to determine forest conditions and distribution and abundance of fauna and flora. Plan and develop audiovisual devices for public programs.

Personality Type: Social-Realistic-Artistic. **Skills:** Operations Analysis; Equipment Maintenance; Science; Writing; Learning Strategies; Speaking; Management of Personnel Resources; Critical Thinking. **Education and Training Program:** Forest Management/Forest Resources Management; Forest Sciences and Biology; Forestry, General; Forestry, Other; Land Use Planning and Management/Development; Natural Resources and Conservation, Other; Natural Resources Management and Policy; Natural Resources Management and Policy, Other; Natural Resources/Conservation, General; Water, Wetlands, and Marine Resources Management; Wildlife, Fish and Wildlands Science and Management. **Work Environment:** More often indoors than outdoors; very hot or cold temperatures; minor burns, cuts, bites, or stings; using your hands to handle, control, or feel objects, tools, or controls; sitting.

Job Specialization: Range Managers

Research or study range land management practices to provide sustained production of forage, livestock, and wildlife. Regulate grazing and help ranchers plan and organize grazing systems to manage, improve, and protect rangelands and maximize their use. Measure and assess vegetation resources for biological assessment

companies, environmental impact statements, and rangeland monitoring programs. Maintain soil stability and vegetation for non-grazing uses, such as wildlife habitats and outdoor recreation. Mediate agreements among rangeland users and preservationists as to appropriate land use and management. Study rangeland management practices and research range problems to provide sustained production of forage, livestock, and wildlife. Manage forage resources through fire, herbicide use, or revegetation to maintain a sustainable yield from the land. Offer advice to rangeland users on water management, forage production methods, and control of brush. Plan and direct construction and maintenance of range improvements such as fencing, corrals, stock-watering reservoirs, and soil-erosion control structures. Tailor conservation plans to landowners' goals, such as livestock support, wildlife, or recreation. Develop technical standards and specifications used to manage, protect, and improve the natural resources of rangelands and related grazing lands. Study grazing patterns to determine number and kind of livestock that can be most profitably grazed and to determine the best grazing seasons. Plan and implement revegetation of disturbed sites.

Personality Type: Realistic-Investigative-Enterprising. **Skills:** Science; Operations Analysis; Systems Analysis; Negotiation; Mathematics; Complex Problem Solving; Management of Material Resources; Operation and Control. **Education and Training Program:** Forest Management/Forest Resources Management; Forest Sciences and Biology; Forestry, General; Forestry, Other; Land Use Planning and Management/Development; Natural Resources and Conservation, Other; Natural Resources Management and Policy; Natural Resources Management and Policy, Other; Natural Resources/Conservation, General; Water, Wetlands, and Marine Resources Management; Wildlife, Fish and Wildlands Science and Management. **Work Environment:** More often outdoors than indoors; sitting; sounds, noisy; very hot or cold temperatures; minor burns, cuts, bites, or stings.

JOB SPECIALIZATION: SOIL AND WATER CONSERVATIONISTS

Plan and develop coordinated practices for soil erosion control, soil and water conservation, and sound land use. Develop and maintain working relationships with local government staff and board members. Advise land users such as farmers and ranchers on conservation plans, problems, and alternative solutions and provide technical and planning assistance. Apply principles of specialized fields of science, such as agronomy, soil science, forestry, or agriculture, to achieve conservation objectives. Plan soil management and conservation practices, such as crop rotation, reforestation, permanent vegetation, contour plowing, or terracing, to maintain soil and conserve water. Visit areas affected by erosion problems to seek sources and solutions. Monitor projects during and after construction to ensure projects conform to design specifications. Compute design specifications for implementation of conservation practices, using survey and field information technical guides, engineering manuals, and calculator. Revisit land users to view implemented land use practices and plans. Coordinate and implement technical, financial, and administrative assistance programs for local government units to ensure efficient program implementation and timely responses to requests for assistance. Analyze results of investigations to determine measures needed to maintain or restore proper soil management. Participate on work teams to plan, develop, and implement water and land management programs and policies.

Personality Type: Investigative-Realistic-Enterprising. **Skills:** Science; Operations Analysis; Mathematics; Management of Financial Resources; Systems Evaluation; Persuasion; Systems Analysis; Quality Control Analysis. **Education and Training Program:** Forest Management/Forest Resources Management; Forest Sciences and Biology; Forestry, General; Forestry, Other; Land Use Planning and Management/Development; Natural Resources and Conservation, Other; Natural Resources Management and Policy; Natural Resources Management and Policy, Other; Natural Resources/Conservation, General; Water, Wetlands, and Marine Resources Management; Wildlife, Fish and Wildlands Science and Management. **Work Environment:** More often outdoors than indoors; sitting; contaminants.

OTHER FEDERAL JOB FACTS
RELATED GS SERIES: 0408 ECOLOGY
TITLE ON USAJOBS: ECOLOGIST

- ✹ U.S. Federal Workforce: 1,401
- ✹ Average Length of Service: 12.2 years
- ✹ Percent Part-Time: 6.9%
- ✹ Percent Women: 38.8%
- ✹ Largest Age Bracket: 35–39 (17.3%)
- ✹ GS Level with Most Workers: 12
- ✹ Agency with Most Workers: Interior
- ✹ State with Most Workers: California

Perform advisory, research, analytical, or other professional work in the science of ecology; analyze biological components and processes in the context of ecosystems including environmental factors, physical-chemical relationships, and social relationships; use quantitative and systems analysis techniques to predict effects of planned or natural changes in ecosystems and to develop understanding of and solutions to ecological problems.

Requirements: Professional knowledge of ecology.

RELATED GS SERIES: 0454 RANGELAND MANAGEMENT

- ✹ U.S. Federal Workforce: 1,063
- ✹ Average Length of Service: 14.0 years
- ✹ Percent Part-Time: 0.9%

- Percent Women: 29.3%
- Largest Age Bracket: 25–29 (17.9%)
- GS Level with Most Workers: 11
- Agency with Most Workers: Agriculture
- States with Most Workers: New Mexico, Colorado

Analyze and protect natural resources, develop programs and standards for rangeland use and conservation, and advise state officials and private and Indian landowners in rangeland management practices.

Requirements: Professional knowledge and competence in rangeland management to perform work involving the preservation, development, and management of rangelands.

Related GS Series: 0457 Soil Conservation

Title on USAJobs: Soil Conservationist

- U.S. Federal Workforce: 4,245
- Average Length of Service: 17.1 years
- Percent Part-Time: 0.9%
- Percent Women: 29.3%
- Largest Age Bracket: 50–54 (19.8%)
- GS Levels with Most Workers: 11, 12
- Agency with Most Workers: Agriculture
- State with Most Workers: Texas

Perform professional work in the conservation of soil, water, and related environmental resources to achieve sound land use.

Requirements: Knowledge of soils and crops; knowledge of the pertinent elements of agronomy, engineering, hydrology, range conservation, biology, and forestry; and skill in oral and written communication methods and techniques sufficient to impart knowledge to selected client groups.

Construction and Building Inspectors

- Education/Training Required: Work experience in a related occupation
- Annual Earnings (Federal): $63,330
- Annual Earnings (All Industries): $51,530
- Earnings Growth Potential (Federal): 26.4% (low)
- Earnings Growth Potential (All Industries): 37.8% (medium)
- Job Growth (Federal): 7.8%
- Job Growth (All Industries): 16.8%
- Annual Job Openings (Federal): 80
- Annual Job Openings (All Industries): 3,970

Inspect structures using engineering skills to determine structural soundness and compliance with specifications, building codes, and other regulations. Inspections may be general in nature or may be limited to a specific area, such as electrical systems or plumbing. Issue violation notices and stop-work orders, conferring with owners, violators, and authorities to explain regulations and recommend rectifications. Inspect bridges, dams, highways, buildings, wiring, plumbing, electrical circuits, sewers, heating systems, and foundations during and after construction for structural quality, general safety, and conformance to specifications and codes. Approve and sign plans that meet required specifications. Review and interpret plans, blueprints, site layouts, specifications, and construction methods to ensure compliance to legal requirements and safety regulations. Monitor installation of plumbing, wiring, equipment, and appliances to ensure that installation is performed properly and is in compliance with applicable regulations. Inspect and monitor construction sites to ensure adherence to safety standards, building codes, and specifications.

Measure dimensions and verify level, alignment, and elevation of structures and fixtures to ensure compliance to building plans and codes. Maintain daily logs and supplement inspection records with photographs. Use survey instruments, metering devices, tape measures, and test equipment such as concrete strength measurers to perform inspections. Train, direct, and supervise other construction inspectors. Issue permits for construction, relocation, demolition, and occupancy.

Considerations for Job Outlook: Employment growth is expected to be driven by desires for safety and improved quality of construction. Prospects should be best for workers who have some college education, certification, and construction experience.

Personality Type: Realistic-Conventional-Investigative. **Skills:** Science; Quality Control Analysis; Operation and Control; Systems Evaluation; Mathematics; Systems Analysis; Operation Monitoring; Persuasion. **Education and Training Program:** Building/Home/Construction Inspection/Inspector. **Work Environment:** More often outdoors than indoors; very hot or cold temperatures; contaminants; extremely bright or inadequate lighting; cramped work space, awkward positions.

OTHER FEDERAL JOB FACTS

RELATED GS SERIES: 0809 CONSTRUCTION CONTROL TECHNICAL

TITLE ON USAJOBS: CONSTRUCTION INSPECTOR

- ❋ U.S. Federal Workforce: 2,257
- ❋ Average Length of Service: 17.0 years
- ❋ Percent Part-Time: 3.6%
- ❋ Percent Women: 5.4%
- ❋ Largest Age Bracket: 55–59 (21.1%)
- ❋ GS Level with Most Workers: 11
- ❋ Agency with Most Workers: Defense
- ❋ State with Most Workers: Texas

Conduct on-site inspection of construction or monitor and control construction operations.

Requirements: Practical knowledge of engineering methods and techniques; knowledge of construction practices, methods, techniques, costs, materials, and equipment; and ability to read and interpret engineering and architectural plans and specifications.

Correctional Officers and Jailers

- ❋ Education/Training Required: Moderate-term on-the-job training
- ❋ Annual Earnings (Federal): $53,360
- ❋ Annual Earnings (All Industries): $39,050
- ❋ Earnings Growth Potential (Federal): 22.9% (very low)
- ❋ Earnings Growth Potential (All Industries): 33.5% (low)
- ❋ Job Growth (Federal): 7.6%
- ❋ Job Growth (All Industries): 9.4%
- ❋ Annual Job Openings (Federal): 350
- ❋ Annual Job Openings (All Industries): 14,360

Guard inmates in penal or rehabilitative institution in accordance with established regulations and procedures. May guard prisoners in transit between jail, courtroom, prison, or other point. Includes deputy sheriffs and police who spend the majority of their time guarding prisoners in correctional institutions. Conduct head counts to ensure that each prisoner is present. Monitor conduct of prisoners in housing unit or during work or recreational activities according to established policies, regulations, and procedures to prevent escape or violence. Inspect conditions of locks, window bars, grills, doors, and gates at correctional facilities to ensure security and help prevent escapes. Record information such as prisoner identification, charges, and incidences of inmate disturbance and keep daily logs of prisoner activities. Search prisoners and vehicles and conduct shakedowns of cells for valuables and contraband, such as weapons or drugs. Use weapons, handcuffs, and physical force to maintain discipline and order among prisoners. Guard facility entrances to screen visitors. Inspect mail for the presence of contraband. Maintain records of prisoners' identification and charges. Process or book convicted individuals into prison. Settle disputes between inmates. Conduct fire, safety, and sanitation inspections. Provide to supervisors oral and written reports of the quality and quantity of work performed by inmates, inmate disturbances and rule violations, and unusual occurrences. Participate in required job training. Take prisoners into custody and escort to locations within and outside of facility, such as visiting room, courtroom, or airport. Serve meals, distribute commissary items, and dispense prescribed medication to prisoners.

Considerations for Job Outlook: Employment growth is expected to stem from population increases and a corresponding rise in the prison population. Favorable job opportunities are expected.

Personality Type: Realistic-Enterprising-Conventional. **Skills:** Negotiation; Persuasion; Social Perceptiveness; Service Orientation; Monitoring; Instructing; Coordination; Operation Monitoring. **Education and Training Program:** Corrections; Corrections and Criminal Justice, Other; Juvenile Corrections. **Work Environment:** Indoors; disease or infections; sounds, noisy; standing; using your hands to handle, control, or feel objects, tools, or controls; walking and running.

OTHER FEDERAL JOB FACTS

Related GS Series: 0007 Correctional Officer

- U.S. Federal Workforce: 17,716
- Average Length of Service: 10.1 years
- Percent Part-Time: 0.0%
- Percent Women: 14.1%

- Largest Age Bracket: 35–39 (21.2%)
- GS Levels with Most Workers: 7, 8
- Agency with Most Workers: Justice
- States with Most Workers: Texas, California

Conduct the correctional treatment, custody, and supervision of criminal offenders in correctional institutions or community-based correctional treatment or rehabilitation facilities.

Requirements: Knowledge and application of correctional skills and techniques.

Dentists

- Education/Training Required: First professional degree
- Annual Earnings (Federal): $137,950
- Annual Earnings (All Industries): $142,090
- Earnings Growth Potential (Federal): 62.2% (very high)
- Earnings Growth Potential (All Industries): 64.0% (very high)
- Job Growth (Federal): 9.9%
- Job Growth (All Industries): 15.6%
- Annual Job Openings (Federal): 80
- Annual Job Openings (All Industries): 6,150

Examine, diagnose, and treat diseases, injuries, and malformations of teeth and gums. May treat diseases of nerve, pulp, and other dental tissues affecting oral hygiene and retention of teeth. May fit dental appliances or provide preventive care. Use masks, gloves, and safety glasses to protect themselves and their patients from infectious diseases. Administer anesthetics to limit the amount of pain experienced by patients during procedures. Examine teeth, gums, and related tissues, using dental instruments, X-rays, and other diagnostic equipment, to evaluate dental health, diagnose diseases or abnormalities, and plan appropriate treatments. Formulate plan of treatment for patient's teeth and mouth tissue. Use air turbine and hand instruments, dental appliances, and surgical implements. Advise and instruct patients regarding preventive dental care, the causes and treatment of dental problems, and oral health-care services. Design, make, and fit prosthodontic appliances such as space maintainers, bridges, and dentures or write fabrication instructions or prescriptions for denturists and dental technicians. Diagnose and treat diseases, injuries, and malformations of teeth, gums, and related oral structures and provide preventive and corrective services. Fill pulp chamber and canal with endodontic materials. Write prescriptions for antibiotics and other medications. Analyze and evaluate dental needs to determine changes and trends in patterns of dental disease.

Considerations for Job Outlook: An increase in the elderly population—who often need complicated dental work—and expanded insurance coverage for dental procedures are expected to create job growth. Good prospects are expected from the need to replace the large number of dentists who are retiring.

Personality Type: Investigative-Realistic Social. **Skills:** Science; Management of Financial Resources; Management of Material Resources; Active Learning; Reading Comprehension; Operation and Control; Judgment and Decision Making; Complex Problem Solving. **Education and Training Program:** Advanced General Dentistry (Cert., MS, PhD); Dental Public Health and Education (Cert., MS/MPH, PhD/DPH); Dental Public Health Specialty; Dentistry (DDS, DMD); Pediatric Dentistry Residency Program; Pediatric Dentistry/Pedodontics (Cert., MS, PhD). **Work Environment:** Indoors; sitting; using hands; bending or twisting the body; repetitive motions; noise; contaminants; exposed to disease or infections.

OTHER FEDERAL JOB FACTS
RELATED GS SERIES: 0680 DENTAL OFFICER

- U.S. Federal Workforce: 2,065
- Average Length of Service: 8.5 years
- Percent Part-Time: 32.5%
- Percent Women: 27.4%
- Largest Age Bracket: 55–59 (20.0%)
- GS Level with Most Workers: 13
- Agency with Most Workers: Veterans Affairs
- State with Most Workers: California

Advise on, administer, supervise, or perform professional and scientific work in the field of dentistry; prevent, diagnose, and treat diseases, injuries, and deformities of the teeth, the jaws, organs of the mouth, and other structures and connective tissues associated with the oral cavity and the masticatory system.

Requirements: Degree of Doctor of Dental Surgery or Doctor of Dental Medicine.

Detectives and Criminal Investigators

- Education/Training Required: Work experience in a related occupation
- Annual Earnings (Federal): $73,320
- Annual Earnings (All Industries): $62,110
- Earnings Growth Potential (Federal): 41.1% (high)
- Earnings Growth Potential (All Industries): 38.9% (medium)
- Job Growth (Federal): 29.8%
- Job Growth (All Industries): 16.6%
- Annual Job Openings (Federal): 1,160
- Annual Job Openings (All Industries): 4,160

Conduct investigations related to suspected violations of federal, state, or local laws to prevent or solve crimes. No task data available.

Considerations for Job Outlook: Population growth is the main source of demand for police services. Overall, opportunities in local police departments should be favorable for qualified applicants.

Job Specialization: Criminal Investigators and Special Agents

Investigate alleged or suspected criminal violations of federal, state, or local laws to determine if evidence is sufficient to recommend prosecution. Record evidence and documents, using equipment such as cameras and photocopy machines. Obtain and verify evidence by interviewing and observing suspects and witnesses or by analyzing records. Examine records to locate links in chains of evidence or information. Prepare reports that detail investigation findings. Determine scope, timing, and direction of investigations. Collaborate with other offices and agencies to exchange information and coordinate activities. Testify before grand juries concerning criminal activity investigations. Analyze evidence in laboratories or in the field. Investigate organized crime, public corruption, financial crime, copyright infringement, civil rights violations, bank robbery, extortion, kidnapping, and other violations of federal or state statutes. Identify case issues and evidence needed, based on analysis of charges, complaints, or allegations of law violations. Obtain and use search and arrest warrants. Serve subpoenas or other official papers. Collaborate with other authorities on activities such as surveillance, transcription, and research. Develop relationships with informants to obtain information related to cases. Search for and collect evidence such as fingerprints, using investigative equipment. Collect and record physical information about arrested suspects, including fingerprints, height and weight measurements, and photographs.

Personality Type: Enterprising-Investigative. **Skills:** Science; Persuasion; Negotiation; Active Listening; Speaking; Critical Thinking; Writing; Operation and Control. **Education and Training Program:** Criminal Justice/Police Science; Criminalistics and Criminal Science. **Work Environment:** More often outdoors than indoors; very hot or cold temperatures; sounds, noisy; standing.

Job Specialization: Immigration and Customs Inspectors

Investigate and inspect persons, common carriers, goods, and merchandise arriving in or departing from the United States or moving between states to detect violations of immigration and customs laws and regulations. Examine immigration applications, visas, and passports and interview persons to determine eligibility for admission, residence, and travel in U.S. Detain persons found to be in violation of customs or immigration laws and arrange for legal action such as deportation. Locate and seize contraband or undeclared merchandise and vehicles, aircraft, or boats that contain such merchandise. Interpret and explain laws and regulations to travelers, prospective immigrants, shippers, and manufacturers. Inspect cargo, baggage, and personal articles entering or leaving U.S. for compliance with revenue laws and U.S. Customs Service regulations. Record and report job-related activities, findings, transactions, violations, discrepancies, and decisions. Institute civil and criminal prosecutions and cooperate with other law enforcement agencies in the investigation and prosecution of those in violation of immigration or customs laws. Testify regarding decisions at immigration appeals or in federal court. Determine duty and taxes to be paid on goods. Collect samples of merchandise for examination, appraisal, or testing. Investigate applications for duty refunds and petition for remission or mitigation of penalties when warranted.

Personality Type: Conventional-Enterprising-Realistic. **Skills:** Active Listening; Persuasion; Negotiation; Operation and Control; Speaking; Social Perceptiveness; Time Management; Judgment and Decision Making. **Education and Training Program:** Criminal Justice/Police Science; Criminalistics and Criminal Science. **Work Environment:** More often outdoors than indoors; contaminants; sounds, noisy; hazardous equipment; radiation.

JOB SPECIALIZATION: INTELLIGENCE ANALYSTS

Gather, analyze, and evaluate information from a variety of sources, such as law enforcement databases, surveillance, intelligence networks and geographic information systems. Use data to anticipate and prevent organized crime activities, such as terrorism. Predict future gang, organized crime, or terrorist activity, using analyses of intelligence data. Study activities relating to narcotics, money laundering, gangs, auto theft rings, terrorism, or other national security threats. Design, use, or maintain databases and software applications, such as geographic information systems (GIS) mapping and artificial intelligence tools. Establish criminal profiles to aid in connecting criminal organizations with their members. Evaluate records of communications, such as telephone calls, to plot activity and determine the size and location of criminal groups and members. Gather and evaluate information, using tools such as aerial photographs, radar equipment, or sensitive radio equipment. Gather intelligence information by field observation, confidential information sources, or public records. Gather, analyze, correlate, or evaluate information from a variety of resources, such as law enforcement databases. Link or chart suspects to criminal organizations or events to determine activities and interrelationships. Operate cameras, radios, or other surveillance equipment to intercept communications or document activities. Prepare comprehensive written reports, presentations, maps, or charts based on research, collection, and analysis of intelligence data. Prepare plans to intercept foreign communications transmissions. Study the assets of criminal suspects to determine the flow of money from or to targeted groups.

Personality Type: No data available. **Skills:** No data available. **Education and Training Program:** Criminalistics and Criminal Science. **Work Environment:** No data available.

JOB SPECIALIZATION: POLICE DETECTIVES

Conduct investigations to prevent crimes or solve criminal cases. Provide testimony as witnesses in court. Secure deceased bodies and obtain evidence from them, preventing bystanders from tampering with bodies prior to medical examiners' arrival. Examine crime scenes to obtain clues and evidence such as loose hairs, fibers, clothing, or weapons. Obtain evidence from suspects. Record progress of investigations, maintain informational files on suspects, and submit reports to commanding officers or magistrates to authorize warrants. Check victims for signs of life such as breathing and pulse. Prepare charges or responses to charges, or information for court cases, according to formalized procedures. Obtain facts or statements from complainants, witnesses, and accused persons and record interviews, using recording devices. Prepare and serve search and arrest warrants. Note, mark, and photograph locations of objects found such as footprints, tire tracks, bullets, and bloodstains, and take measurements of each scene. Question individuals or observe persons and establishments to confirm information given to patrol officers. Preserve, process, and analyze items of evidence obtained from crime scenes and suspects, placing them in proper containers and destroying evidence no longer needed. Secure persons at scenes, keeping witnesses from conversing or leaving scenes before investigators arrive. Take photographs from all angles of relevant parts of crime scenes, including entrance and exit routes and streets and intersections.

Personality Type: Enterprising-Investigative. **Skills:** Science; Negotiation; Operation and Control; Social Perceptiveness; Operation Monitoring; Service Orientation; Active Learning; Systems Analysis. **Education and Training Program:** Criminal Justice/Police Science; Criminalistics and Criminal Science. **Work Environment:** More often outdoors than indoors; very hot or cold temperatures; sitting; sounds, noisy; contaminants.

Job Specialization: Police Identification and Records Officers

Collect evidence at crime scene, classify and identify fingerprints, and photograph evidence for use in criminal and civil cases. Photograph crime or accident scenes for evidence records. Testify in court and present evidence. Dust selected areas of crime scene and lift latent fingerprints, adhering to proper preservation procedures. Look for trace evidence, such as fingerprints, hairs, fibers, or shoe impressions, using alternative light sources when necessary. Analyze and process evidence at crime scenes and in the laboratory, wearing protective equipment and using powders and chemicals. Package, store, and retrieve evidence. Maintain records of evidence and write and review reports. Submit evidence to supervisors, crime labs, or court officials for legal proceedings. Identify, compare, classify, and file fingerprints using systems such as Automated Fingerprint Identification System (AFIS) or the Henry Classification System. Serve as technical advisor and coordinate with other law enforcement workers or legal personnel to exchange information on crime scene collection activities.

Personality Type: Conventional-Realistic-Investigative. **Skills:** Operation and Control; Speaking; Operation Monitoring; Negotiation; Critical Thinking; Active Listening; Persuasion; Reading Comprehension. **Education and Training Program:** Criminal Justice/Police Science; Criminalistics and Criminal Science. **Work Environment:** Indoors; contaminants; sounds, noisy; hazardous conditions; using your hands to handle, control, or feel objects, tools, or controls; sitting.

OTHER FEDERAL JOB FACTS
Related GS Series: 1896 Border Patrol Enforcement

- ✺ U.S. Federal Workforce: 20,261
- ✺ Average Length of Service: 7.3 years
- ✺ Percent Part-Time: 0.0%
- ✺ Percent Women: 5.1%
- ✺ Largest Age Bracket: 25–29 (23.7%)
- ✺ GS Level with Most Workers: 12
- ✺ Agency with Most Workers: Homeland Security
- ✺ State with Most Workers: Texas

Enforce the laws that protect the nation's homeland by the detection, interdiction, and apprehension of those who attempt to illegally enter or smuggle any person or contraband across the nation's borders.

Requirements: Knowledge of statutes, regulations, instructions, and precedent-setting decisions pertaining to enforcement of immigration and naturalization laws and regulations; knowledge of standard investigative techniques and law enforcement procedures to enforce immigration and naturalization laws and related federal statutes; skill in evaluating information rapidly, making timely decisions, and taking prompt and appropriate actions under less than optimal conditions; proficiency in a foreign language; and understanding of foreign cultures and customs.

D

Related GS Series: 1811 Criminal Investigation

Title on USAJobs: Criminal Investigator

- ❋ U.S. Federal Workforce: 43,965
- ❋ Average Length of Service: 13.7 years
- ❋ Percent Part-Time: 0.2%
- ❋ Percent Women: 16.9%
- ❋ Largest Age Bracket: 40–44 (22.9%)
- ❋ GS Level with Most Workers: 13
- ❋ Agency with Most Workers: Justice
- ❋ State with Most Workers: District of Columbia

Plan, conduct, or manage investigations related to alleged or suspected criminal violations of Federal laws; recognize, develop, and present evidence to reconstruct events, sequences, time elements, relationships, responsibilities, legal liabilities, and conflicts of interest; conduct investigations in a manner meeting legal and procedural requirements; and provide advice and assistance both in and out of court to the U.S. Attorney's Office during investigations and prosecutions.

Requirements: Knowledge of criminal investigative techniques, rules of criminal procedures, laws, and precedent court decisions concerning the admissibility of evidence, constitutional rights, search and seizure, and related issues in the conduct of investigations.

Related GS Series: 1810 General Investigation

Title on USAJobs: General Investigator

- ❋ U.S. Federal Workforce: 3,360
- ❋ Average Length of Service: 15.9 years
- ❋ Percent Part-Time: 0.7%
- ❋ Percent Women: 50.7%
- ❋ Largest Age Bracket: 50–54 (15.8%)
- ❋ GS Level with Most Workers: 12

- ❋ Agency with Most Workers: Agriculture
- ❋ State with Most Workers: Maryland

Plan, conduct, or manage investigations not involving criminal violations of Federal laws; use the results of general investigations to make or invoke administrative judgments, sanctions, or penalties.

Requirements: Knowledge of investigative techniques and the laws, rules, regulations, and objectives of the employing agency; and skill in interviewing, following leads, researching records, reconstructing events, and preparing reports.

Related GS Series: 0082 United States Marshal

- ❋ U.S. Federal Workforce: 900
- ❋ Average Length of Service: 3.5 years
- ❋ Percent Part-Time: 0.4%
- ❋ Percent Women: 9.9%
- ❋ Largest Age Bracket: 25–29 (30.1%)
- ❋ GS Level with Most Workers: 7
- ❋ Agency with Most Workers: Justice
- ❋ State with Most Workers: Texas

Handle a range of law enforcement responsibilities including serving of civil writs and criminal warrants issued by federal courts; tracing and arresting people wanted under court warrants; seizing and disposing of property under court orders; safeguarding and transporting prisoners; providing for the physical security of court facilities and personnel; providing for the physical security of jurors and key government witnesses and their families; preventing civil disturbances or restoring order in riot and mob violence situations; and performing other special law enforcement duties as directed by a court order or by the Department of Justice.

Requirements: Ability to locate and identify wanted persons or property, knowledge of court procedure, basic knowledge of business records and practices, knowledge of federal and state laws that deputies must enforce, knowledge of relevant court decisions, and ability to deal with people from all levels of society.

Directors, Religious Activities and Education

- ❋ Education/Training Required: Bachelor's degree
- ❋ Annual Earnings (Federal): $89,210
- ❋ Annual Earnings (All Industries): $36,190
- ❋ Earnings Growth Potential (Federal): 21.7% (very low)
- ❋ Earnings Growth Potential (All Industries): 48.4% (high)
- ❋ Job Growth (Federal): 10.5%
- ❋ Job Growth (All Industries): 12.6%
- ❋ Annual Job Openings (Federal): 20
- ❋ Annual Job Openings (All Industries): 2,640

Direct and coordinate activities of their chosen denominational groups to meet religious needs of students. Plan, direct, or coordinate church school programs designed to promote religious education among church membership. May provide counseling and guidance relative to marital, health, financial, and religious problems. Analyze member participation and changes in congregation emphasis to determine needs for religious education. Collaborate with other ministry members to establish goals and objectives for religious education programs and to develop ways to encourage program participation. Interpret religious education activities to the public through speaking, leading discussions, and writing articles for local and national publications. Implement program plans by ordering needed materials, scheduling speakers, reserving spaces, and handling other administrative details. Confer with clergy members, congregation officials, and congregation organizations to encourage support of and participation in religious education activities. Develop and direct study courses and religious education programs within congregations. Locate and distribute resources such as periodicals and curricula in order to enhance the effectiveness of educational programs. Visit congregation members' homes, or arrange for pastoral visits, in order to provide information and resources regarding religious education programs. Identify and recruit potential volunteer workers. Participate in denominational activities aimed at goals such as promoting interfaith understanding or providing aid to new or small congregations. Publicize programs through sources such as newsletters, bulletins, and mailings. Counsel individuals regarding interpersonal, health, financial, and religious problems.

Considerations for Job Outlook: About average employment growth is projected.

Personality Type: Enterprising-Social-Conventional. **Skills:** Management of Financial Resources; Social Perceptiveness; Management of Material Resources; Management of Personnel Resources; Learning Strategies; Persuasion; Systems Evaluation; Operations Analysis. **Education and Training Program:** Bible/Biblical Studies; Missions/Missionary Studies and Missiology; Philosophy; Religious Education; Youth Ministry. **Work Environment:** Indoors; standing.

OTHER FEDERAL JOB FACTS

RELATED GS SERIES: 0060 CHAPLAIN

- ❋ U.S. Federal Workforce: 1,157
- ❋ Average Length of Service: 9.6 years
- ❋ Percent Part-Time: 24.9%
- ❋ Percent Women: 13.7%
- ❋ Largest Age Bracket: 65 or more (20.7%)
- ❋ GS Level with Most Workers: 12
- ❋ Agency with Most Workers: Veterans Affairs
- ❋ States with Most Workers: California, Texas

D

Advise on, administer, supervise, or perform professional work involved in a program of spiritual welfare and religious guidance for patients of government hospitals and homes, for inmates of government correctional and penal or other institutions, or for persons in other government activities where civilian chaplain service is needed.

Requirements: Ordination by a recognized ecclesiastical body.

Economists

- ❋ Education/Training Required: Master's degree
- ❋ Annual Earnings (Federal): $104,530
- ❋ Annual Earnings (All Industries): $86,930
- ❋ Earnings Growth Potential (Federal): 39.4% (median)
- ❋ Earnings Growth Potential (All Industries): 48.6% (high)
- ❋ Job Growth (Federal): –1.5%
- ❋ Job Growth (All Industries): 5.8%
- ❋ Annual Job Openings (Federal): 110
- ❋ Annual Job Openings (All Industries): 500

Conduct research, prepare reports, or formulate plans to aid in solution of economic problems arising from production and distribution of goods and services. May collect and process economic and statistical data, using econometric and sampling techniques. Study economic and statistical data in area of specialization, such as finance, labor, or agriculture. Provide advice and consultation on economic relationships to businesses, public and private agencies, and other employers. Compile, analyze, and report data to explain economic phenomena and forecast market trends, applying mathematical models and statistical techniques. Formulate recommendations, policies, or plans to solve economic problems or

to interpret markets. Develop economic guidelines and standards and prepare points of view used in forecasting trends and formulating economic policy. Testify at regulatory or legislative hearings concerning the estimated effects of changes in legislation or public policy and present recommendations based on cost-benefit analyses. Supervise research projects and students' study projects. Forecast production and consumption of renewable resources and supply, consumption, and depletion of non-renewable resources. Teach theories, principles, and methods of economics.

Considerations for Job Outlook: Although demand for economic analysis will grow, projected employment declines for economists in government sectors will temper overall growth. Job seekers who have a graduate degree in economics should have the best prospects.

Personality Type: Investigative-Conventional-Enterprising. **Skills:** Mathematics; Systems Analysis; Operations Analysis; Complex Problem Solving; Systems Evaluation; Writing; Speaking; Critical Thinking. **Education and Training Program:** Agricultural Economics; Applied Economics; Business/Managerial Economics; Development Economics and International Development; Econometrics and Quantitative Economics; Economics, General; Economics, Other; International Economics. **Work Environment:** Indoors; sitting.

JOB SPECIALIZATION: ENVIRONMENTAL ECONOMISTS

Assess and quantify the benefits of environmental alternatives, such as use of renewable energy resources. Prepare and deliver presentations to communicate economic and environmental study results, to present policy recommendations, or to raise awareness of environmental consequences. Monitor or analyze market and environmental trends. Interpret indicators to ascertain the overall health of an environment. Identify and recommend environmentally friendly business practices.

Demonstrate or promote the economic benefits of sound environmental regulations. Write technical documents or academic articles to communicate study results or economic forecasts. Write social, legal, or economic impact statements to inform decision makers for natural resource policies, standards, or programs. Write research proposals and grant applications to obtain private or public funding for environmental and economic studies. Examine the exhaustibility of natural resources or the long-term costs of environmental rehabilitation. Develop systems for collecting, analyzing, and interpreting environmental and economic data. Develop programs or policy recommendations to achieve economic and environmental sustainability. Develop environmental research project plans, including information on budgets, goals, deliverables, timelines, and resource requirements. Develop economic models, forecasts, or scenarios to predict future economic and environmental outcomes. Collect and analyze data to compare the environmental implications of economic policy or practice alternatives.

Personality Type: No data available. **Skills:** No data available. **Education and Training Program:** Agricultural Economics; Applied Economics; Business/Managerial Economics; Development Economics and International Development; Econometrics and Quantitative Economics; Economics, General; Economics, Other; International Economics. **Work Environment:** No data available.

OTHER FEDERAL JOB FACTS

Related GS Series: 0110 Economist

- ❋ U.S. Federal Workforce: 4,520
- ❋ Average Length of Service: 14.1 years
- ❋ Percent Part-Time: 4.2%
- ❋ Percent Women: 32.8%
- ❋ Largest Age Bracket: 55–59 (12.5%)
- ❋ GS Levels with Most Workers: 13, 12

- ❋ Agency with Most Workers: Labor
- ❋ State with Most Workers: District of Columbia

Research economic phenomena, analyze economic data, and prepare interpretive reports; advise and consult on economic matters to governmental officials and private organizations or citizens; and perform other professional work in economics, including supervision and direction of economists engaged in the various economics programs of the federal government.

Requirements: Professional knowledge of economics.

Education, Training, and Library Workers, All Other

- ❋ Education/Training Required: Bachelor's degree
- ❋ Annual Earnings (Federal): $38,860
- ❋ Annual Earnings (All Industries): $36,300
- ❋ Earnings Growth Potential (Federal): 22.3% (very low)
- ❋ Earnings Growth Potential (All Industries): 47.2% (high)
- ❋ Job Growth (Federal): 7.6%
- ❋ Job Growth (All Industries): 15.8%
- ❋ Annual Job Openings (Federal): 210
- ❋ Annual Job Openings (All Industries): 4,290

Considerations for Job Outlook: Faster than average employment growth is projected.

Personality Type: No data available. **Skills:** No data available. **Education and Training Program:** Education, Other. **Work Environment:** No data available.

E

OTHER FEDERAL JOB FACTS

RELATED GS SERIES: 1702 EDUCATION AND TRAINING

TITLE ON USAJOBS: TRAINING AND EDUCATION TECHNICIAN

- U.S. Federal Workforce: 7,180
- Average Length of Service: 12.9 years
- Percent Part-Time: 14.2%
- Percent Women: 73.0%
- Largest Age Bracket: 45–49 (19.4%)
- GS Level with Most Workers: 5
- Agency with Most Workers: Defense
- State with Most Workers: California

Nonprofessional work of a technical, specialized, or support nature in the field of education and training that is not covered by another OPM occupation.

Requirements: Knowledge of program objectives, policies, procedures, or pertinent regulatory requirements affecting the particular education or training activity; practical understanding or specialized skills and knowledge of the particular education or training activities involved. Does not require full professional knowledge of education concepts, principles, techniques, and practices.

RELATED GS SERIES: 1720 EDUCATION PROGRAM

TITLE ON USAJOBS: EDUCATION PROGRAM SPECIALIST

- U.S. Federal Workforce: 736
- Average Length of Service: 13.9 years
- Percent Part-Time: 3.4%
- Percent Women: 65.5%
- Largest Age Bracket: 55–59 (21.6%)
- GS Level with Most Workers: 13

- Agency with Most Workers: Education
- State with Most Workers: District of Columbia

Promote, coordinate, and improve education policies, programs, standards, activities, and opportunities in accordance with national policies and objectives; perform, supervise, or formulate and implement policy concerning education problems and issues.

Requirements: Professional knowledge of education theories, principles, processes, and practices at early childhood, elementary, secondary, or postsecondary levels, or in adult or continuing education; also knowledge of the federal government's interrelationships with state and local educational agencies or with public and private postsecondary institutions.

RELATED GS SERIES: 1740 EDUCATION SERVICES

TITLE ON USAJOBS: EDUCATION SERVICES SPECIALIST

- U.S. Federal Workforce: 904
- Average Length of Service: 15.1 years
- Percent Part-Time: 0.2%
- Percent Women: 51.8%
- Largest Age Bracket: 55–59 (19.4%)
- GS Level with Most Workers: 11
- Agency with Most Workers: Defense
- States with Most Workers: Texas, Virginia

Administer, supervise, promote, conduct, or evaluate programs and activities designed to provide individualized career-related or self-development education plans.

Requirements: Requires knowledge of education theories, principles, procedures, and practices of secondary, adult, or continuing education. Some positions require skill in counseling students or enrollees to establish educational and occupational objectives.

RELATED GS SERIES: 0090 GUIDE

- ❋ U.S. Federal Workforce: 1,433
- ❋ Average Length of Service: 3.7 years
- ❋ Percent Part-Time: 46.7%
- ❋ Percent Women: 47.9%
- ❋ Largest Age Bracket: 20–24 (28.2%)
- ❋ GS Level with Most Workers: 4
- ❋ Agency with Most Workers: Interior
- ❋ State with Most Workers: New York

Provide or supervise nonprofessional interpretive and guide services to visitors to parks, dams, and other sites of public interest; give formal talks, interpret natural and historic features, explain engineering structures and related water resource developments, answer questions, guide tours, and provide miscellaneous services to visitors. May be responsible for visitor safety and protection of historic and scientific objects and natural or engineering features.

Requirements: Skill in preparing oral presentations, a good speaking voice, a fluent command of English, and other traits common to good public speaking; ability to think quickly, answer questions courteously, and exercise judgment in how much detail to supply; ability to acquire and apply knowledge of facts, events, personalities, and their influence that contributed to the importance of the area to be interpreted; skill in dealing with diverse types of visitors under a variety of circumstances; maturity and leadership ability for dealing with a large group of people who are in unfamiliar surroundings, where there is a serious potential for accident and injury.

RELATED GS SERIES: 1750 INSTRUCTIONAL SYSTEMS
TITLE ON USAJOBS: INSTRUCTIONAL SYSTEMS SPECIALIST

- ❋ U.S. Federal Workforce: 1,983
- ❋ Average Length of Service: 13.1 years
- ❋ Percent Part-Time: 0.2%
- ❋ Percent Women: 42.8%
- ❋ Largest Age Bracket: 55–59 (21.6%)
- ❋ GS Level with Most Workers: 12
- ❋ Agency with Most Workers: Defense
- ❋ State with Most Workers: Texas

Administer, supervise, advise on, design, develop, or provide educational or training services in formal education or training programs.

Requirements: Knowledge of learning theory and the principles, methods, practices, and techniques of one or more specialties of the instructional systems field; may require knowledge of one or more subjects or occupations in which educational or training instruction is provided.

Electrical and Electronic Engineering Technicians

- ❋ Education/Training Required: Associate degree
- ❋ Annual Earnings (Federal): $61,500
- ❋ Annual Earnings (All Industries): $54,820
- ❋ Earnings Growth Potential (Federal): 8.3% (very low)
- ❋ Earnings Growth Potential (All Industries): 39.1% (medium)
- ❋ Job Growth (Federal): –2.9%
- ❋ Job Growth (All Industries): –2.2%

- Annual Job Openings (Federal): 220
- Annual Job Openings (All Industries): 3,100

Apply electrical and electronic theory and related knowledge, usually under the direction of engineering staff, to design, build, repair, calibrate, and modify electrical components, circuitry, controls, and machinery for subsequent evaluation and use by engineering staff in making engineering design decisions. No task data available.

Considerations for Job Outlook: Labor-saving efficiencies and the automation of many engineering support activities will limit the need for new engineering technicians. In general, opportunities should be best for job seekers who have an associate degree or other postsecondary training in engineering technology.

Personality Type: No data available. **Skills:** No data available. **Education and Training Program:** Computer Engineering Technology/Technician; Computer Technology/Computer Systems Technology; Electrical and Electronic Engineering Technologies/Technicians, Other; Electrical, Electronic and Communications Engineering Technology/Technician; Telecommunications Technology/Technician. **Work Environment:** No data available.

OTHER FEDERAL JOB FACTS

RELATED GS SERIES: 3314 INSTRUMENT MAKING

- U.S. Federal Workforce: 18
- Average Length of Service: 26.3 years
- Percent Part-Time: 5.6%
- Percent Women: 0.0%
- Largest Age Bracket: No data available.
- GS Level with Most Workers: Not a GS occupation
- Agency with Most Workers: Commerce
- State with Most Workers: Maryland

Plan and fabricate complex research and prototype instruments that are made from a variety of materials and are used to detect, measure, record, and regulate heat, pressure, speed, vibration, sound, illumination, biomedical phenomena, and other areas of interest to scientific, engineering, or medical personnel.

Requirements: Skill and knowledge of more than one specific trade, such as machining, welding, metal surface treating, metal working, or electronics.

RELATED GS SERIES: 0856 ELECTRONICS TECHNICAL

- U.S. Federal Workforce: 8,398
- Average Length of Service: 17.5 years
- Percent Part-Time: 0.2%
- Percent Women: 5.3%
- Largest Age Bracket: 50–54 (22.1%)
- GS Levels with Most Workers: 11, 12
- Agency with Most Workers: Defense
- State with Most Workers: California

Develop, test, or perform other work on electronic equipment: maintenance, installation, fabrication, testing and evaluation, research and development, and troubleshooting.

Requirements: At a level less than that of a professional engineer, knowledge of the techniques and theories characteristic of electronics, such as a knowledge of basic electricity and electronic theory, algebra, and elementary physics; ability to apply that knowledge to duties involved in engineering functions, such as design, development, evaluation, testing, installation, and maintenance of electronic equipment; and knowledge of the capabilities, limitations, operations, design characteristics, and functional use of a variety of types and models of electronic equipment and systems.

Electrical and Electronics Repairers, Commercial and Industrial Equipment

⚜ Education/Training Required:
Postsecondary vocational training

⚜ Annual Earnings (Federal): $53,870

⚜ Annual Earnings (All Industries):
$50,730

⚜ Earnings Growth Potential (Federal):
16.8% (very low)

⚜ Earnings Growth Potential (All
Industries): 38.0% (medium)

⚜ Job Growth (Federal): 12.0%

⚜ Job Growth (All Industries): 3.8%

⚜ Annual Job Openings (Federal): 160

⚜ Annual Job Openings (All Industries):
1,640

Repair, test, adjust, or install electronic equipment, such as industrial controls, transmitters, and antennas. Test faulty equipment to diagnose malfunctions, using test equipment and software, and applying knowledge of the functional operation of electronic units and systems. Inspect components of industrial equipment for accurate assembly and installation and for defects such as loose connections and frayed wires. Install repaired equipment in various settings, such as industrial or military establishments. Examine work orders and converse with equipment operators to detect equipment problems and to ascertain whether mechanical or human errors contributed to the problems. Perform scheduled preventive maintenance tasks, such as checking, cleaning, and repairing equipment, to detect and prevent problems. Set up and test industrial equipment to ensure that it functions properly. Study blueprints, schematics, manuals, and other specifications to determine installation procedures. Repair and adjust equipment, machines, and defective components, replacing worn parts such as gaskets and seals in watertight electrical equipment. Calibrate testing instruments and installed or repaired equipment to prescribed specifications. Maintain equipment logs that record performance problems, repairs, calibrations, and tests. Develop or modify industrial electronic devices, circuits, and equipment according to available specifications. Coordinate efforts with other workers involved in installing and maintaining equipment or components.

Considerations for Job Outlook: Employment growth for these workers is expected to be limited as improvements in the quality of electrical and electronic equipment result in less need for repairs. The best prospects are expected for job seekers who have certification, an associate degree, and relevant experience.

Personality Type: Realistic-Investigative-Conventional. **Skills:** Installation; Repairing; Equipment Maintenance; Equipment Selection; Troubleshooting; Quality Control Analysis; Technology Design; Operation Monitoring. **Education and Training Program:** Computer Installation and Repair Technology/Technician; Industrial Electronics Technology/Technician. **Work Environment:** Indoors; sounds, noisy; contaminants; hazardous equipment; hazardous conditions; using your hands to handle, control, or feel objects, tools, or controls.

JOB SPECIALIZATION: ELECTRONICS ENGINEERING TECHNICIANS

Lay out, build, test, troubleshoot, repair, and modify developmental and production electronic components, parts, equipment, and systems, such as computer equipment, missile control instrumentation, electron tubes, test equipment, and machine tool numerical controls, applying principles and theories of electronics, electrical circuitry, engineering mathematics, electronic and electrical testing, and physics. Usually work under direction of engineering staff. Read blueprints, wiring diagrams, schematic drawings, and engineering instructions for assembling electronics units, applying knowledge of electronic theory and components. Test electronics units, using standard test equipment, and analyze results to evaluate performance and determine need for adjustment. Perform preventative maintenance and calibration of equipment and systems. Assemble, test, and maintain circuitry or electronic components according to engineering instructions, technical manuals, and knowledge of electronics, using hand and power tools. Adjust and replace defective or improperly functioning circuitry and electronics components, using hand tools and soldering iron. Write reports and record data on testing techniques, laboratory equipment, and specifications to assist engineers. Identify and resolve equipment malfunctions, working with manufacturers and field representatives as necessary to procure replacement parts. Provide user applications and engineering support and recommendations for new and existing equipment with regard to installation, upgrades, and enhancement. Maintain system logs and manuals to document testing and operation of equipment.

Personality Type: Realistic-Investigative. **Skills:** Repairing; Equipment Maintenance; Troubleshooting; Equipment Selection; Operations Analysis; Science; Programming; Quality Control Analysis. **Education and Training Program:** Computer Engineering Technology/Technician; Computer Technology/Computer Systems Technology; Electrical and Electronic Engineering Technologies/Technicians, Other; Electrical, Electronic and Communications Engineering Technology/Technician; Telecommunications Technology/Technician. **Work Environment:** Indoors; sitting; using hands; noise.

JOB SPECIALIZATION: ELECTRICAL ENGINEERING TECHNICIANS

Test or modify developmental or operational electrical machinery or electrical control equipment and circuitry in industrial or commercial plants or laboratories. Usually work under direction of engineers or technologists. Assemble electrical and electronic systems and prototypes according to engineering data and knowledge of electrical principles, using hand tools and measuring instruments. Provide technical assistance and resolution when electrical or engineering problems are encountered before, during, and after construction. Install and maintain electrical control systems and solid state equipment. Modify electrical prototypes, parts, assemblies, and systems to correct functional deviations. Set up and operate test equipment to evaluate performance of developmental parts, assemblies, or systems under simulated operating conditions and record results. Collaborate with electrical engineers and other personnel to identify, define, and solve developmental problems. Build, calibrate, maintain, troubleshoot, and repair electrical instruments or testing equipment. Analyze and interpret test information to resolve design-related problems. Write commissioning procedures for electrical installations. Prepare project cost and work-time estimates. Evaluate engineering proposals, shop drawings, and design comments for sound electrical engineering practice and conformance with established safety and design criteria and recommend approval or disapproval.

Personality Type: Realistic-Investigative-Conventional. **Skills:** Installation; Technology Design; Repairing; Equipment Maintenance; Equipment Selection; Troubleshooting; Quality Control Analysis; Operation Monitoring. **Education and Training Program:** Computer Engineering Technology/Technician; Computer Technology/Computer Systems Technology; Electrical and Electronic Engineering Technologies/Technicians, Other; Electrical, Electronic and Communications Engineering Technology/Technician; Telecommunications Technology/Technician. **Work Environment:** Indoors; sitting; using hands; noise.

OTHER FEDERAL JOB FACTS

RELATED GS SERIES: 2606 ELECTRONIC INDUSTRIAL CONTROLS MECHANIC

- ❋ U.S. Federal Workforce: 974
- ❋ Average Length of Service: 16.5 years

⊛ Percent Part-Time: 0.0%

⊛ Percent Women: 1.8%

⊛ Largest Age Bracket: 50–54 (21.5%)

⊛ GS Level with Most Workers: Not a GS occupation

⊛ Agency with Most Workers: Defense

⊛ State with Most Workers: Texas

Install, maintain, troubleshoot, repair, and calibrate electronic controls and indicating and recording systems used on industrial machinery or engines, in automated materials-storage and materials-handling systems, in aircraft engine and similar test facilities, or in energy monitoring and control systems.

Requirements: Knowledge of the practical application of electronics theories and circuits that are applicable to power, timing, motion control, indicating devices, and pulse and counting mechanisms, including special-purpose digital computers (microprocessors) dedicated to control functions, as well as a knowledge of industrial equipment operation and processes.

RELATED GS SERIES: 2604 ELECTRONICS MECHANIC

⊛ U.S. Federal Workforce: 5,664

⊛ Average Length of Service: 13.2 years

⊛ Percent Part-Time: 0.2%

⊛ Percent Women: 1.2%

⊛ Largest Age Bracket: 50–54 (15.0%)

⊛ GS Level with Most Workers: Not a GS occupation

⊛ Agency with Most Workers: Defense

⊛ State with Most Workers: Pennsylvania

Fabricate, overhaul, modify, install, troubleshoot, repair, and maintain ground, airborne, and marine electronic equipment; use both manual and automated test equipment; may use a personal computer and numerous software packages to program or realign various components or systems, download information, and detect equipment deficiencies.

Requirements: Knowledge of electronic principles; the ability to recognize improper operation, locate the cause, and determine the best method to correct the defect; and the skill to disassemble, assemble, and adjust electronic equipment.

Electrical Engineers

⊛ Education/Training Required: Bachelor's degree

⊛ Annual Earnings (Federal): $89,130

⊛ Annual Earnings (All Industries): $83,110

⊛ Earnings Growth Potential (Federal): 33.5% (low)

⊛ Earnings Growth Potential (All Industries): 35.6% (low)

⊛ Job Growth (Federal): 7.7%

⊛ Job Growth (All Industries): 1.7%

⊛ Annual Job Openings (Federal): 70

⊛ Annual Job Openings (All Industries): 3,890

Design, develop, test, or supervise the manufacturing and installation of electrical equipment, components, or systems for commercial, industrial, military, or scientific use. Prepare and study technical drawings, specifications of electrical systems, and topographical maps to ensure that installation and operations conform to standards and customer requirements. Operate computer-assisted engineering and design software and equipment to perform engineering tasks. Confer with engineers, customers, and others to discuss existing or potential engineering projects and products. Direct and coordinate manufacturing, construction, installation, maintenance, support, documentation, and testing activities to ensure compliance with specifications, codes, and customer requirements. Design, implement,

E

maintain, and improve electrical instruments, equipment, facilities, components, products, and systems for commercial, industrial, and domestic purposes. Prepare specifications for purchase of materials and equipment. Perform detailed calculations to compute and establish manufacturing, construction, and installation standards and specifications. Investigate customer or public complaints, determine nature and extent of problem, and recommend remedial measures. Oversee project production efforts to assure projects are completed satisfactorily, on time, and within budget. Plan and implement research methodology and procedures to apply principles of electrical theory to engineering projects. Develop budgets, estimating labor, material, and construction costs. Compile data and write reports regarding existing and potential engineering studies and projects.

Considerations for Job Outlook: Electrical engineers are expected to have employment growth of 2 percent from 2008–2018. Although strong demand for electrical devices—including electric power generators, wireless phone transmitters, high-density batteries, and navigation systems—should spur job growth, international competition and the use of engineering services performed in other countries will limit employment growth. Electrical engineers working in firms providing engineering expertise and design services to manufacturers should have better job prospects.

Personality Type: Investigative-Realistic. **Skills:** Science; Troubleshooting; Operations Analysis; Mathematics; Operation Monitoring; Quality Control Analysis; Systems Evaluation; Writing. **Education and Training Program:** Electrical and Electronics Engineering. **Work Environment:** Indoors; sitting; sounds, noisy.

OTHER FEDERAL JOB FACTS

RELATED GS SERIES: 0850 ELECTRICAL ENGINEERING

TITLE ON USAJOBS: ENGINEER, ELECTRICAL

- ❈ U.S. Federal Workforce: 4,713
- ❈ Average Length of Service: 12.9 years
- ❈ Percent Part-Time: 1.7%
- ❈ Percent Women: 12.8%
- ❈ Largest Age Bracket: 45–49 (16.4%)
- ❈ GS Level with Most Workers: 12
- ❈ Agency with Most Workers: Defense
- ❈ State with Most Workers: Virginia

Manage, supervise, lead, and/or perform professional engineering and scientific work concerned with utilizing and exploring electrical and electronic phenomena and the motion, emissions, conduction, and behavior of electrical energy currents; designing electrical equipment, components, or systems; and generating and transmitting electrical energy in an efficient manner.

Requirements: Professional knowledge of and skills in electrical engineering.

Electronics Engineers, Except Computer

- ❈ Education/Training Required: Bachelor's degree
- ❈ Annual Earnings (Federal): $102,730
- ❈ Annual Earnings (All Industries): $89,310
- ❈ Earnings Growth Potential (Federal): 31.3% (low)
- ❈ Earnings Growth Potential (All Industries): 36.3% (medium)
- ❈ Job Growth (Federal): 7.5%
- ❈ Job Growth (All Industries): 0.3%

⊛ Annual Job Openings (Federal): 300

⊛ Annual Job Openings (All Industries): 3,340

Research, design, develop, and test electronic components and systems for commercial, industrial, military, or scientific use, utilizing knowledge of electronic theory and materials properties. Design electronic circuits and components for use in fields such as telecommunications, aerospace guidance and propulsion control, acoustics, or instruments and controls. Design electronic components, software, products, or systems for commercial, industrial, medical, military, or scientific applications. Provide technical support and instruction to staff or customers regarding equipment standards, assisting with specific, difficult in-service engineering. Operate computer-assisted engineering and design software and equipment to perform engineering tasks. Analyze system requirements, capacity, cost, and customer needs to determine feasibility of project and develop system plan. Confer with engineers, customers, vendors or others to discuss existing and potential engineering projects or products. Review and evaluate work of others, inside and outside the organization, to ensure effectiveness, technical adequacy, and compatibility in the resolution of complex engineering problems. Determine material and equipment needs and order supplies.

Considerations for Job Outlook: Electronics engineers, except computer (including radio frequency identification device specialists), are expected to experience little to no employment change from 2008–2018. Although rising demand for electronic goods—including communications equipment, defense-related equipment, medical electronics, and consumer products—should continue to increase demand for electronics engineers, foreign competition in electronic products development and the use of engineering services performed in other countries will limit employment

growth. Growth is expected to be fastest in service-providing industries—particularly in firms that provide engineering and design services.

Personality Type: Investigative-Realistic. **Skills:** Programming; Repairing; Technology Design; Equipment Selection; Equipment Maintenance; Troubleshooting; Operation and Control; Quality Control Analysis. **Education and Training Program:** Electrical and Electronics Engineering. **Work Environment:** Indoors; sitting; using your hands to handle, control, or feel objects, tools, or controls.

JOB SPECIALIZATION: RADIO FREQUENCY IDENTIFICATION DEVICE SPECIALISTS

Design and implement radio frequency identification device (RFID) systems used to track shipments or goods. Verify compliance of developed applications with architectural standards and established practices. Read current literature, attend meetings or conferences, or talk with colleagues to stay abreast of industry research about new technologies. Provide technical support for RFID technology. Perform systems analysis or programming of RFID technology. Document equipment or process details of RFID technology. Train users in details of system operation. Analyze RFID-related supply chain data. Test tags or labels to ensure readability. Test RFID software to ensure proper functioning. Select appropriate RFID tags and determine placement locations. Perform site analyses to determine system configurations, processes to be impacted, or on-site obstacles to technology implementation. Perform acceptance testing on newly installed or updated systems. Identify operational requirements for new systems to inform selection of technological solutions. Determine usefulness of new RFID technologies. Develop process flows, work instructions, or standard operating procedures for RFID systems.

E

Personality Type: Realistic-Investigative-Conventional. **Skills:** No data available. **Education and Training Program:** Electrical and Electronics Engineering. **Work Environment:** No data available.

OTHER FEDERAL JOB FACTS

RELATED **GS** SERIES: 0855 ELECTRONICS ENGINEERING

TITLE ON **USAJOBS:** ENGINEER, ELECTRONIC

- U.S. Federal Workforce: 20,169
- Average Length of Service: 16.9 years
- Percent Part-Time: 0.8%
- Percent Women: 10.9%
- Largest Age Bracket: 45–49 (22.5%)
- GS Levels with Most Workers: 12, 13
- Agency with Most Workers: Defense
- State with Most Workers: California

Manage, supervise, lead, and/or perform professional engineering and scientific work involving electronic circuits, circuit elements, equipment, systems, and associated phenomena concerned with electromagnetic or acoustical wave energy or electrical information for purposes such as communication, computation, sensing, control, measurement, and navigation.

Requirements: Knowledge of theories, principles, practical concepts, processes, and systems related to the science of electronics engineering and the traditional engineering science disciplines (e.g., mechanical and chemical); physical science disciplines (e.g., chemistry and physics); and advanced mathematics, computer science, and economics.

Eligibility Interviewers, Government Programs

- Education/Training Required: Moderate-term on-the-job training
- Annual Earnings (Federal): $46,430
- Annual Earnings (All Industries): $40,180
- Earnings Growth Potential (Federal): 29.4% (low)
- Earnings Growth Potential (All Industries): 31.5% (low)
- Job Growth (Federal): 8.6%
- Job Growth (All Industries): 9.2%
- Annual Job Openings (Federal): 670
- Annual Job Openings (All Industries): 3,880

Determine eligibility of persons applying to receive assistance from government programs and agency resources, such as welfare, unemployment benefits, Social Security, and public housing. Answer applicants' questions about benefits and claim procedures. Interview benefits recipients at specified intervals to certify their eligibility for continuing benefits. Interpret and explain information such as eligibility requirements, application details, payment methods, and applicants' legal rights. Initiate procedures to grant, modify, deny, or terminate assistance or refer applicants to other agencies for assistance. Compile, record, and evaluate personal and financial data to verify completeness and accuracy and to determine eligibility status. Interview and investigate applicants for public assistance to gather information pertinent to their applications. Check with employers or other references to verify answers and obtain further information. Keep records of assigned cases and prepare required reports. Schedule benefits claimants for adjudication interviews to address questions of eligibility. Prepare applications and forms for applicants for such purposes as school enrollment, employment, and medical services. Refer applicants to job openings or to interviews with other staff in accordance with administrative guidelines or office procedures. Provide social workers with pertinent information gathered during applicant interviews. Compute and authorize amounts of assistance for programs such as grants, monetary payments, and food stamps. Monitor the payments of benefits throughout the duration of a claim.

Considerations for Job Outlook: As the population ages, retires, and becomes eligible for benefits and programs, employment in this occupation is expected to increase. But employment growth may be tempered by a trend toward automated services, such as online application. Job opportunities are expected to be favorable.

Answer applicants' questions about benefits and claim procedures. Interview benefits recipients at specified intervals to certify their eligibility for continuing benefits. Interpret and explain information such as eligibility requirements, application details, payment methods, and applicants' legal rights. Initiate procedures to grant, modify, deny, or terminate assistance or refer applicants to other agencies for assistance. Compile, record, and evaluate personal and financial data to verify completeness and accuracy and to determine eligibility status. Interview and investigate applicants for public assistance to gather information pertinent to their applications. Check with employers or other references to verify answers and obtain further information. Keep records of assigned cases and prepare required reports. Schedule benefits claimants for adjudication interviews to address questions of eligibility. Prepare applications and forms for applicants for such purposes as school enrollment, employment, and medical services. Refer applicants to job openings or to interviews with other staff in accordance with administrative guidelines or office procedures. Provide social workers with pertinent information gathered during applicant interviews. Compute and authorize amounts of assistance for programs such as grants, monetary payments, and food stamps. Monitor the payments of benefits throughout the duration of a claim.

Personality Type: Social-Conventional-Enterprising. **Skills:** Service Orientation; Speaking; Active Listening; Social Perceptiveness; Reading Comprehension; Negotiation; Writing; Critical Thinking. **Education and Training Program:** Community Organization and Advocacy. **Work Environment:** Indoors; sitting; making repetitive motions; using your hands to handle, control, or feel objects, tools, or controls; contaminants.

OTHER FEDERAL JOB FACTS

RELATED GS SERIES: 0962 CONTACT REPRESENTATIVE

- ❈ U.S. Federal Workforce: 27,234
- ❈ Average Length of Service: 10.8 years
- ❈ Percent Part-Time: 3.0%
- ❈ Percent Women: 71.8%
- ❈ Largest Age Bracket: 50–54 (14.2%)
- ❈ GS Level with Most Workers: 8
- ❈ Agency with Most Workers: Treasury
- ❈ State with Most Workers: California

Supervise, lead, or perform support and related work in connection with dispersing information to the public on rights, benefits, privileges, or obligations under a body of law; explaining pertinent legal provisions, regulations, and related administrative practices and their application to specific cases; and assisting individuals in developing needed evidence and preparing required documents.

Requirements: Specialized (but not professional) knowledge of laws, precedent decisions, regulations, agency policies and practices, and judicial or administrative proceedings. May require practical knowledge of subject-matter areas related to the agency's substantive programs.

E

RELATED **GS** SERIES: 0187 SOCIAL SERVICES
TITLE ON **USAJOBS**: SOCIAL SERVICE
REPRESENTATIVE

- ⁑ U.S. Federal Workforce: 285
- ⁑ Average Length of Service: 14.0 years
- ⁑ Percent Part-Time: 3.5%
- ⁑ Percent Women: 69.1%
- ⁑ Largest Age Bracket: 55–59 (21.8%)
- ⁑ GS Levels with Most Workers: 8, 9
- ⁑ Agency with Most Workers: Veterans Affairs
- ⁑ States with Most Workers: California, Texas

Provide assistance to individuals and families served by social welfare programs; may obtain selected background information through interviews and home visits, establish eligibility to make use of agency resources, help individuals identify needs that are related to services the agency can provide, explain and encourage the use of agency and community resources as means of dealing with identified problems, or make appropriate referrals to sources of additional help.

Requirements: Specialized knowledge of the social service program. Does not require a broad theoretical approach to social problems acquired through professional education in social work or in other recognized disciplines in the social sciences.

Engineering Managers

- ⁑ Education/Training Required: Bachelor's or higher degree, plus work experience
- ⁑ Annual Earnings (Federal): $125,730
- ⁑ Annual Earnings (All Industries): $117,000
- ⁑ Earnings Growth Potential (Federal): 18.2% (very low)
- ⁑ Earnings Growth Potential (All Industries): 35.6% (low)
- ⁑ Job Growth (Federal): 7.6%

- ⁑ Job Growth (All Industries): 6.2%
- ⁑ Annual Job Openings (Federal): 110
- ⁑ Annual Job Openings (All Industries): 4,870

Plan, direct, or coordinate activities or research and development in such fields as architecture and engineering. Confer with management, production, and marketing staff to discuss project specifications and procedures. Coordinate and direct projects, making detailed plans to accomplish goals and directing the integration of technical activities. Analyze technology, resource needs, and market demand, to plan and assess the feasibility of projects. Plan and direct the installation, testing, operation, maintenance, and repair of facilities and equipment. Direct, review, and approve product design and changes. Recruit employees, assign, direct, and evaluate their work, and oversee the development and maintenance of staff competence. Prepare budgets, bids, and contracts, and direct the negotiation of research contracts. Develop and implement policies, standards, and procedures for the engineering and technical work performed in the department, service, laboratory, or firm. Review and recommend or approve contracts and cost estimates. Perform administrative functions such as reviewing and writing reports, approving expenditures, enforcing rules, and making decisions about the purchase of materials or services. Present and explain proposals, reports, and findings to clients. Consult or negotiate with clients to prepare project specifications. Set scientific and technical goals within broad outlines provided by top management. Administer highway planning, construction, and maintenance. Direct the engineering of water control, treatment, and distribution projects.

Considerations for Job Outlook: Employment is expected to grow along with that of the scientists and engineers these workers supervise. Prospects should be better in the rapidly growing areas of environmental and biomedical engineering and medical and environmental sciences.

Personality Type: Enterprising-Realistic-Investigative. **Skills:** Operations Analysis; Management of Financial Resources; Management of Material Resources; Science; Mathematics; Systems Evaluation; Management of Personnel Resources; Systems Analysis. **Education and Training Program:** Aerospace, Aeronautical, and Astronautical/Space Engineering; Agricultural Engineering; Architectural Engineering; Architecture (BArch, BA/BS, MArch, MA/MS, PhD); Bioengineering and Biomedical Engineering; Ceramic Sciences and Engineering; Chemical Engineering; City/Urban, Community and Regional Planning; Civil Engineering, General; Civil Engineering, Other; Computer Engineering, General; Computer Engineering, Other; Computer Hardware Engineering; Computer Software Engineering; others. **Work Environment:** Indoors; sitting; sounds, noisy.

JOB SPECIALIZATION: BIOFUELS/BIODIESEL TECHNOLOGY AND PRODUCT DEVELOPMENT MANAGERS

Define, plan, or execute biofuel/biodiesel research programs that evaluate alternative feedstock and process technologies with near-term commercial potential. Develop lab scale models of industrial scale processes, such as fermentation. Develop computational tools or approaches to improve biofuels research and development activities. Develop carbohydrates arrays and associated methods for screening enzymes involved in biomass conversion. Provide technical or scientific guidance to technical staff in the conduct of biofuels research or development. Prepare, or oversee the preparation of, experimental plans for biofuels research or development. Prepare biofuels research and development reports for senior management or technical professionals. Perform protein functional analysis and engineering for processing of feedstock and creation of biofuels. Develop separation

processes to recover biofuels. Develop methods to recover ethanol or other fuels from complex bioreactor liquid and gas streams. Develop methods to estimate the efficiency of biomass pretreatments. Design or execute solvent or product recovery experiments in laboratory or field settings. Design or conduct applied biodiesel or biofuels research projects on topics such as transport, thermodynamics, mixing, filtration, distillation, fermentation, extraction, and separation. Design chemical conversion processes, such as etherification, esterification, interesterification, transesterification, distillation, hydrogenation, oxidation or reduction of fats and oils, and vegetable oil refining. Conduct experiments on biomass or pretreatment technologies.

Personality Type: No data available. **Skills:** No data available. **Education and Training Program:** Agricultural Engineering; Bioengineering and Biomedical Engineering; Chemical Engineering; Engineering, Other; Manufacturing Engineering. **Work Environment:** No data available.

OTHER FEDERAL JOB FACTS

RELATED GS SERIES: 0801 GENERAL ENGINEERING
TITLE ON USAJOBS: ENGINEER, GENERAL

- ✿ U.S. Federal Workforce: 24,247
- ✿ Average Length of Service: 17.4 years
- ✿ Percent Part-Time: 1.2%
- ✿ Percent Women: 16.1%
- ✿ Largest Age Bracket: 45–49 (22.4%)
- ✿ GS Level with Most Workers: 13
- ✿ Agency with Most Workers: Defense
- ✿ States with Most Workers: Maryland, Alabama

Manage, supervise, lead, and/or perform professional engineering and scientific work not covered by another OPM occupation.

Requirements: Professional knowledge of and skills in two or more professional engineering specializations.

Engineering Technicians, Except Drafters, All Other

* Education/Training Required: Associate degree
* Annual Earnings (Federal): $67,080
* Annual Earnings (All Industries): $57,530
* Earnings Growth Potential (Federal): 56.9% (very high)
* Earnings Growth Potential (All Industries): 46.3% (high)
* Job Growth (Federal): 7.6%
* Job Growth (All Industries): 5.2%
* Annual Job Openings (Federal): 340
* Annual Job Openings (All Industries): 1,850

Considerations for Job Outlook: Labor-saving efficiencies and the automation of many engineering support activities will limit the need for new engineering technicians. In general, opportunities should be best for job seekers who have an associate degree or other postsecondary training in engineering technology.

JOB SPECIALIZATION: ELECTRICAL ENGINEERING TECHNOLOGISTS

Apply engineering theory and technical skills to support electrical engineering activities such as process control, electrical power distribution, and instrumentation design. Prepare layouts of machinery and equipment, plan the flow of work, conduct statistical studies, and analyze production costs. Participate in training and continuing education activities to stay abreast of engineering and industry advances. Assist engineers and scientists in conducting applied research in electrical engineering. Diagnose, test, or analyze the performance of electrical components, assemblies, and systems. Set up and operate standard and specialized testing equipment. Review installation and quality assurance documentation. Review, develop, and prepare maintenance standards. Compile and maintain records documenting engineering schematics, installed equipment, installation and operational problems, resources used, and repairs or corrective action performed. Supervise the construction and testing of electrical prototypes according to general instructions and established standards. Review electrical engineering plans to ensure adherence to design specifications and compliance with applicable electrical codes and standards. Install or maintain electrical control systems, industrial automation systems, and electrical equipment including control circuits, variable speed drives, or programmable logic controllers. Design or modify engineering schematics for electrical transmission and distribution systems or for electrical installation in residential, commercial, or industrial buildings, using computer-aided design (CAD) software. Calculate design specifications or cost, material, and resource estimates, and prepare project schedules and budgets.

Personality Type: Realistic-Investigative-Conventional. **Skills:** No data available. **Education and Training Program:** Electrical, Electronic, and Communications Engineering Technology/Technician. **Work Environment:** No data available.

JOB SPECIALIZATION: ELECTROMECHANICAL ENGINEERING TECHNOLOGISTS

Apply engineering theory and technical skills to support electromechanical engineering activities such as computer-based process control,

instrumentation, and machine design. Prepare layouts of machinery and equipment, plan the flow of work, conduct statistical studies, and analyze production costs. Modify, maintain, or repair electrical, electronic, and mechanical components, equipment, and systems to ensure proper functioning. Specify, coordinate, and conduct quality-control and quality-assurance programs and procedures. Establish and maintain inventory, records, and documentation systems. Fabricate or assemble mechanical, electrical, and electronic components and assemblies. Select electromechanical equipment, materials, components, and systems to meet functional specifications. Select and use laboratory, operational, and diagnostic techniques and test equipment to assess electromechanical circuits, equipment, processes, systems, and subsystems. Produce electrical, electronic, and mechanical drawings and other related documents or graphics necessary for electromechanical design using computer-aided design (CAD) software. Install and program computer hardware and machine and instrumentation software in microprocessor-based systems. Consult with machinists and technicians to ensure that electromechanical equipment and systems meet design specifications. Translate electromechanical drawings into design specifications, applying principles of engineering, thermal and fluid sciences, mathematics, and statistics. Collaborate with engineers to implement electromechanical designs in industrial or other settings.

Personality Type: Realistic-Investigative-Conventional. **Skills:** No data available. **Education and Training Program:** Electrical, Electronic, and Communications Engineering Technology/Technician. **Work Environment:** No data available.

JOB SPECIALIZATION: ELECTRONICS ENGINEERING TECHNOLOGISTS

Apply engineering theory and technical skills to support electronics engineering activities such as electronics systems and instrumentation design and digital signal processing. Provide support to technical sales staff regarding product characteristics. Educate equipment operators on the proper use of equipment. Modify, maintain, and repair electronics equipment and systems to ensure that they function properly. Assemble circuitry for electronic systems according to engineering instructions, production specifications, and technical manuals. Specify, coordinate, or conduct quality control and quality assurance programs and procedures. Prepare and maintain design, testing, or operational records and documentation. Troubleshoot microprocessors and electronic instruments, equipment, and systems using electronic test equipment such as logic analyzers. Set up and operate specialized and standard test equipment to diagnose, test, and analyze the performance of electronic components, assemblies, and systems. Select electronics equipment, components, and systems to meet functional specifications.

Personality Type: Realistic-Investigative-Conventional. **Skills:** Repairing; Equipment Maintenance; Equipment Selection; Troubleshooting; Technology Design; Installation; Programming; Science. **Education and Training Program:** Electrical, Electronic, and Communications Engineering Technology/Technician. **Work Environment:** Indoors; using your hands to handle, control, or feel objects, tools, or controls; sitting; hazardous conditions; sounds, noisy.

JOB SPECIALIZATION: FUEL CELL TECHNICIANS

Install, operate, and maintain integrated fuel cell systems in transportation, stationary, or portable applications. Troubleshoot test equipment. Recommend improvements to fuel cell design and performance. Perform routine vehicle maintenance procedures, such as part replacements and tune-ups. Build or test power plant systems, including pumps, blowers, heat exchangers, or sensors. Order testing materials. Build or test electrical systems, making electrical calculations as needed. Report results of fuel cell test results. Perform routine and preventive maintenance on test equipment. Document or analyze fuel cell test data using spreadsheets or other computer software. Collect and maintain fuel cell test data. Calibrate equipment used for fuel cell testing. Build prototypes, following engineering specifications. Test fuel cells or fuel cell stacks, using complex electronic equipment. Assemble fuel cells or fuel cell stacks according to mechanical or electrical assembly documents or schematics.

Personality Type: No data available. **Skills:** No data available. **Education and Training Program:** Manufacturing Engineering Technology/Technician. **Work Environment:** No data available.

JOB SPECIALIZATION: INDUSTRIAL ENGINEERING TECHNOLOGISTS

Apply engineering theory and technical skills to support industrial engineering activities such as quality control, inventory control, and material flow methods. May conduct statistical studies and analyze production costs. Interpret engineering drawings, sketches, or diagrams. Prepare schedules for equipment use or routine maintenance. Request equipment upgrades or purchases. Supervise production workers. Create computer applications for manufacturing processes or operations using computer-aided design (CAD) or computer-assisted manufacturing (CAM) tools. Oversee and inspect production processes. Prepare reports regarding inventories of raw materials and finished products. Modify equipment or processes to improve resource or cost efficiency. Develop and conduct quality control tests to ensure consistent production quality. Compile operational data to develop cost or time estimates, schedules, or specifications. Collect and analyze data related to quality or industrial health and safety programs. Analyze operational, production, economic, or

other data using statistical procedures. Prepare layouts of machinery and equipment using drafting equipment or computer-aided design (CAD) software. Plan the flow of work or materials to maximize efficiency. Monitor and control inventory. Conduct time and motion studies to identify opportunities to improve worker efficiency. Design plant or production facility layouts. Develop and implement programs to address problems related to production, materials, safety, or quality. Analyze, estimate, or report production costs.

Personality Type: Investigative-Realistic-Conventional. **Skills:** No data available. **Education and Training Program:** Quality Control Technology/Technician. **Work Environment:** No data available.

JOB SPECIALIZATION: MANUFACTURING ENGINEERING TECHNOLOGISTS

Apply engineering theory and technical skills to support manufacturing engineering activities. Develop tools, implement designs, and integrate machinery, equipment, and computer technologies to ensure effective manufacturing processes. Recommend corrective or preventive actions to assure or improve product quality or reliability. Prepare layouts, drawings, or sketches of machinery and equipment such as shop tooling, scale layouts, and new equipment design using drafting equipment or computer-aided design software. Identify and implement new manufacturing technologies, processes, or equipment. Identify opportunities for improvements in quality, cost, or efficiency of automation equipment. Monitor or measure manufacturing processes to identify ways to reduce losses, decrease time requirements, or improve quality. Ensure adherence to safety rules and practices. Coordinate equipment purchases, installations, or transfers. Plan, estimate, or schedule production work. Select material quantities and processing methods needed to achieve efficient production. Develop or maintain programs associated with automated production equipment. Estimate manufacturing costs. Install and evaluate manufacturing equipment, materials, or components. Oversee equipment start-up, characterization, qualification, or release. Develop production, inventory, or quality assurance programs. Create computer applications for manufacturing processes or operations using computer-aided design (CAD) or computer-assisted manufacturing (CAM) tools. Develop manufacturing infrastructure to integrate or deploy new manufacturing processes. Verify weights, measurements, counts, or calculations and record results on batch records.

Personality Type: Realistic-Investigative-Conventional. **Skills:** Equipment Selection; Installation; Technology Design; Equipment Maintenance; Programming; Management of Financial Resources; Mathematics; Troubleshooting. **Education and Training Program:** Manufacturing Engineering Technology/Technician. **Work Environment:** Indoors; sounds, noisy; sitting; contaminants.

JOB SPECIALIZATION: MANUFACTURING PRODUCTION TECHNICIANS

Apply knowledge of manufacturing engineering systems and tools to set up, test, and adjust manufacturing machinery and equipment, using any combination of electrical, electronic, mechanical, hydraulic, pneumatic, and computer technologies. Adhere to all applicable regulations, policies, and procedures for health, safety, and environmental compliance. Inspect finished products for quality and adherence to customer specifications. Set up and operate production equipment in accordance with current good manufacturing practices and standard operating procedures. Calibrate or adjust equipment to ensure quality production using tools such as calipers, micrometers, height gauges, protractors, and ring gauges. Set up and verify the functionality of safety equipment. Troubleshoot problems

with equipment, devices, or products. Monitor and adjust production processes or equipment for quality and productivity. Test products or subassemblies for functionality or quality. Plan and lay out work to meet production and schedule requirements. Start up and shut down processing equipment. Prepare and assemble materials. Provide advice or training to other technicians. Measure and record data associated with operating equipment. Assist engineers in developing, building, or testing prototypes and new products, processes, or procedures. Prepare production documents such as standard operating procedures, manufacturing batch records, inventory reports, and productivity reports. Install new equipment. Keep production logs. Clean production equipment and work areas. Provide production, progress, or changeover reports to shift supervisors.

Personality Type: Realistic-Investigative. **Skills:** Equipment Maintenance; Repairing; Troubleshooting; Operation and Control; Quality Control Analysis; Operation Monitoring; Equipment Selection; Science. **Education and Training Program:** Manufacturing Engineering Technology/Technician. **Work Environment:** Indoors; sounds, noisy; hazardous equipment; standing; using your hands to handle, control, or feel objects, tools, or controls; contaminants.

JOB SPECIALIZATION: MECHANICAL ENGINEERING TECHNOLOGISTS

Apply engineering theory and technical skills to support mechanical engineering activities such as generation, transmission, and use of mechanical and fluid energy. Prepare layouts of machinery and equipment and plan the flow of work. May conduct statistical studies and analyze production costs. Prepare equipment inspection schedules, reliability schedules, work plans, and other records. Prepare cost and materials estimates and project schedules. Provide technical support to other employees regarding mechanical design, fabrication, testing, or documentation. Interpret engineering sketches, specifications, and drawings. Perform routine maintenance on equipment such as leak detectors, glove boxes, and mechanical pumps. Design specialized or customized equipment, machines, or structures. Design molds, tools, dies, jigs, or fixtures for use in manufacturing processes. Conduct failure analyses, document results, and recommend corrective actions. Assist engineers to design, develop, test, or manufacture industrial machinery, consumer products, or other equipment. Analyze or estimate production costs such as labor, equipment, and plant space. Apply testing or monitoring apparatus to operating equipment. Test machines, components, materials, or products to determine characteristics such as performance, strength, and response to stress. Prepare specifications, designs, or sketches for machines, components, and systems related to the generation, transmission, or use of mechanical and fluid energy. Prepare layouts of machinery, tools, plants, and equipment. Inspect and test mechanical equipment. Oversee, monitor, or inspect mechanical installations or construction projects.

Personality Type: Realistic-Investigative-Conventional. **Skills:** No data available. **Education and Training Program:** Mechanical Engineering/Mechanical Technology/Technician. **Work Environment:** No data available.

JOB SPECIALIZATION: NANOTECHNOLOGY ENGINEERING TECHNICIANS

Operate commercial-scale production equipment to produce, test, and modify materials, devices, and systems of molecular or macromolecular composition. Work under the supervision of engineering staff. Track inventory and order new supplies, as needed. Repair nanotechnology processing or testing equipment, or submit work orders for equipment repair. Maintain work area according to clean-room and other processing

standards. Set up and execute experiments according to detailed instructions. Compile information and prepare reports. Record test results in logs, laboratory notebooks, or spreadsheet software. Produce detailed images and measurement of objects, using tools such as scanning tunneling microscopes and oscilloscopes. Perform functional tests of nano-enhanced assemblies, components, or systems, using equipment such as torque gauges and conductivity meters. Operate computer-controlled machine tools. Monitor equipment during operation to ensure adherence to specifications for characteristics such as pressure, temperature, and flow. Measure or mix chemicals or compounds in accordance with detailed instructions or formulas. Calibrate nanotechnology equipment, such as weighing, testing, and production equipment. Inspect work products to ensure quality and adherence to specifications. Maintain accurate production record or batch record documentation. Assist scientists, engineers, or technologists in writing process specifications or documentation. Assist scientists, engineers, or technologists in processing or characterizing materials according to physical and chemical properties.

Personality Type: No data available. **Skills:** No data available. **Education and Training Program:** Nanotechnology. **Work Environment:** No data available.

JOB SPECIALIZATION: NANOTECHNOLOGY ENGINEERING TECHNOLOGISTS

Implement production processes for nanoscale designs to produce and modify materials, devices, and systems of unique molecular or macromolecular composition. Operate advanced microscopy equipment to manipulate nanoscale objects. Work under the supervision of engineering staff. Supervise or provide technical direction to technicians engaged in nanotechnology research or production. Install nanotechnology production equipment at customer or manufacturing sites. Contribute written material or data for grant or patent applications. Produce images and measurements, using tools and techniques such as atomic force microscopy, scanning electron microscopy, optical microscopy, particle size analysis, and zeta potential analysis. Prepare detailed verbal or written presentations for scientists, engineers, project managers, or upper management. Prepare capability data, training materials, or other documentation for transfer of processes to production. Develop or modify wet chemical or industrial laboratory experimental techniques for nanoscale use. Collect and compile nanotechnology research and engineering data. Inspect or measure thin films of carbon nanotubes, polymers, or inorganic coatings, using a variety of techniques and analytical tools. Implement new or enhanced methods and processes for the processing, testing, or manufacture of nanotechnology materials or products. Design or conduct experiments in collaboration with scientists or engineers supportive of the development of nanotechnology materials, components, devices, or systems.

Personality Type: No data available. **Skills:** No data available. **Education and Training Program:** Nanotechnology. **Work Environment:** No data available.

JOB SPECIALIZATION: NON-DESTRUCTIVE TESTING SPECIALISTS

Test the safety of structures, vehicles, or vessels using X-ray, ultrasound, fiber optic, or related equipment. Supervise or direct the work of non-destructive testing (NDT) trainees or staff. Produce images of objects on film using radiographic techniques. Evaluate material properties using radio astronomy, voltage and amperage measurement, or rheometric flow measurement. Develop or use new non-destructive testing (NDT) methods such as acoustic emission testing, leak testing, and thermal or infrared testing. Document non-destructive testing (NDT) methods, processes, or results. Map the presence of imperfections within

objects using sonic measurements. Make radiographic images to detect flaws in objects while leaving objects intact. Visually examine materials, structures, or components using tools and equipment such as endoscopes, closed circuit television systems, and fiber optics for signs of corrosion, metal fatigue, cracks, or other flaws. Interpret or evaluate test results in accordance with applicable codes, standards, specifications, or procedures. Identify defects in concrete or other building materials using thermal or infrared testing. Identify defects in solid materials using ultrasonic testing techniques. Select, calibrate, or operate equipment used in the non-destructive testing (NDT) of products or materials. Conduct liquid penetrant tests to locate surface cracks by coating objects with fluorescent dyes, cleaning excess penetrant, and applying developer. Prepare reports on non-destructive testing (NDT) results.

Personality Type: Realistic-Investigative-Conventional. **Skills:** No data available. **Education and Training Program:** Industrial Radiologic Technology/Technician. **Work Environment:** No data available.

JOB SPECIALIZATION: PHOTONICS TECHNICIANS

Build, install, test, and maintain optical and fiber optic equipment such as lasers, lenses, and mirrors using spectrometers, interferometers, or related equipment. Recommend design or material changes to reduce costs or processing times. Monitor inventory levels and order supplies as necessary. Maintain clean working environments according to clean room standards. Document procedures such as calibration. Maintain activity logs. Record test results and compute test data. Test and perform failure analysis for optomechanical or optoelectrical products according to test plans. Assist scientists or engineers in the conduct of photonic experiments. Perform diagnostic analyses of processing steps using analytical or metrological tools such as microscopy, profilometry, and ellipsometry devices. Optimize process parameters by making prototype and production devices. Mix, pour, and use processing chemicals or gases according to safety standards and established operating procedures. Design, build, or modify fixtures used to assemble parts. Lay out cutting lines for machining using drafting tools. Assist engineers in the development of new products, fixtures, tools, or processes. Assemble and adjust parts or related electrical units of prototypes to prepare for testing. Splice fibers using fusion splicing or other techniques. Terminate, cure, polish, or test fiber cables with mechanical connectors. Set up or operate prototype or test apparatus such as control consoles, collimators, recording equipment, and cables.

Personality Type: Realistic-Investigative-Conventional. **Skills:** No data available. **Education and Training Program:** Engineering-Related Technologies, Other. **Work Environment:** No data available.

OTHER FEDERAL JOB FACTS

RELATED GS SERIES: 0802 ENGINEERING TECHNICAL

TITLE ON USAJOBS: ENGINEERING TECHNICIAN

- ❀ U.S. Federal Workforce: 16,630
- ❀ Average Length of Service: 18.4 years
- ❀ Percent Part-Time: 3.6%
- ❀ Percent Women: 11.4%
- ❀ Largest Age Bracket: 50–54 (21.4%)
- ❀ GS Level with Most Workers: 11
- ❀ Agency with Most Workers: Defense
- ❀ State with Most Workers: Virginia

Perform engineering or architectural work at a level below professional and of a kind not covered by another OPM occupation.

Requirements: Practical knowledge of the methods and techniques of engineering or architecture

and of the construction, application, properties, operations, and limitations of engineering systems, processes, structures, machinery, devices, and materials. Does not require a bachelor's degree in engineering or architecture.

Engineers, All Other

- ❀ Education/Training Required: Bachelor's degree
- ❀ Annual Earnings (Federal): $110,860
- ❀ Annual Earnings (All Industries): $89,560
- ❀ Earnings Growth Potential (Federal): 48.3% (high)
- ❀ Earnings Growth Potential (All Industries): 44.9% (high)
- ❀ Job Growth (Federal): 7.6%
- ❀ Job Growth (All Industries): 6.7%
- ❀ Annual Job Openings (Federal): 520
- ❀ Annual Job Openings (All Industries): 5,020

Considerations for Job Outlook: Competitive pressures and advancing technology are expected to result in businesses hiring more engineers. Overall, job opportunities are expected to be good. Professional, scientific, and technical services industries should generate most of the employment growth.

JOB SPECIALIZATION: BIOCHEMICAL ENGINEERS

Apply knowledge of biology, chemistry, and engineering to develop usable, tangible products. Solve problems related to materials, systems, and processes that interact with humans, plants, animals, microorganisms, and biological materials. Read current scientific and trade literature to stay abreast of scientific, industrial, or technological advances. Prepare technical reports, data summary documents, or research articles for scientific publication, regulatory submissions, or patent applications. Prepare project plans for equipment or facility improvements, including time lines, budgetary estimates, or capital spending requests. Participate in equipment or process validation activities. Communicate with suppliers regarding the design and specifications of production equipment, instrumentation, or materials. Communicate with regulatory authorities regarding licensing or compliance responsibilities, such as good manufacturing practices. Collaborate in the development or delivery of biochemical manufacturing training materials. Prepare piping and instrumentation diagrams or other schematics for proposed process improvements, using computer-aided design software. Modify and control biological systems to replace, augment, or sustain chemical and mechanical processes. Maintain databases of experiment characteristics and results. Lead studies to examine or recommend changes in process sequences, operation protocols. Direct experimental or developmental activities at contracted laboratories. Develop statistical models or simulations of biochemical production, using statistical or modeling software. Consult with chemists and biologists to develop or evaluate novel technologies.

Personality Type: Investigative-Realistic. **Skills:** No data available. **Education and Training Program:** Biochemical Engineering. **Work Environment:** No data available.

JOB SPECIALIZATION: ENERGY ENGINEERS

Design, develop, and evaluate energy-related projects and programs to reduce energy costs or improve energy efficiency during the designing, building, or remodeling stages of construction. May specialize in electrical systems; heating, ventilation, and air-conditioning (HVAC) systems; green buildings; lighting; air quality; or energy procurement. Identify energy savings opportunities and make recommendations to achieve more energy efficient operation. Manage the development, design, or construction of energy conservation projects to ensure acceptability of budgets and time lines, conformance to federal and state laws, or adherence to approved specifications. Conduct energy audits to evaluate energy use, costs, or conservation measures. Monitor and analyze energy consumption. Perform energy modeling, measurement, verification, commissioning, or retro-commissioning. Oversee design or construction aspects related to energy such as energy engineering, energy management, and sustainable design. Conduct jobsite observations, field inspections, or sub-metering to collect data for energy conservation analyses. Review architectural, mechanical, or electrical plans and specifications to evaluate energy efficiency or determine economic, service, or engineering feasibility. Inspect or monitor energy systems including heating, ventilation, and air conditioning (HVAC) or daylighting systems to determine energy use or potential energy savings. Evaluate construction design information such as detail and assembly drawings, design calculations, system layouts and sketches, or specifications. Direct the work of contractors or staff in the implementation of energy management projects. Prepare project reports and other program or technical documentation. Make recommendations regarding energy fuel selection.

Personality Type: Investigative-Realistic. **Skills:** Science; Operations Analysis; Systems Analysis; Mathematics; Reading Comprehension; Complex Problem Solving; Writing; Systems Evaluation. **Education and Training Program:** Engineering, Other. **Work Environment:** Indoors; sitting.

JOB SPECIALIZATION: MANUFACTURING ENGINEERS

Apply knowledge of materials and engineering theory and methods to design, integrate, and

improve manufacturing systems or related processes. May work with commercial or industrial designers to refine product designs to increase producibility and decrease costs. Identify opportunities or implement changes to improve products or reduce costs using knowledge of fabrication processes, tooling and production equipment, assembly methods, quality control standards, or product design, materials, and parts. Provide technical expertise or support related to manufacturing. Determine root causes of failures using statistical methods and recommend changes in designs, tolerances, or processing methods. Incorporate new methods and processes to improve existing operations. Supervise technicians, technologists, analysts, administrative staff, or other engineers. Troubleshoot new and existing product problems involving designs, materials, or processes. Review product designs for manufacturability and completeness. Train production personnel in new or existing methods. Communicate manufacturing capabilities, production schedules, or other information to facilitate production processes. Design, install, or troubleshoot manufacturing equipment. Prepare documentation for new manufacturing processes or engineering procedures. Apply continuous improvement methods such as lean manufacturing to enhance manufacturing quality, reliability, or cost-effectiveness. Investigate or resolve operational problems such as material use variances and bottlenecks. Estimate costs, production times, or staffing requirements for new designs. Evaluate manufactured products according to specifications and quality standards. Purchase equipment, materials, or parts.

Personality Type: Realistic-Investigative. **Skills:** Technology Design; Equipment Selection; Installation; Troubleshooting; Management of Financial Resources; Equipment Maintenance; Mathematics; Management of Material Resources. **Education and Training Program:** Manufacturing Engineering. **Work Environment:** Indoors; sounds, noisy; contaminants; sitting; hazardous equipment.

JOB SPECIALIZATION: MECHATRONICS ENGINEERS

Apply knowledge of mechanical, electrical, and computer engineering theory and methods to the design of automation, intelligent systems, smart devices, or industrial systems control. Publish engineering reports documenting design details and qualification test results. Provide consultation or training on topics such as mechatronics and automated control. Oversee the work of contractors in accordance with project requirements. Create mechanical design documents for parts, assemblies, or finished products. Maintain technical project files. Analyze existing development or manufacturing procedures and suggest improvements. Implement and test design solutions. Research, select, and apply sensors, communication technologies, or control devices for motion control, position sensing, pressure sensing, or electronic communication. Identify and select materials appropriate for mechatronic system designs. Design, develop, or implement control circuits and algorithms for electromechanical and pneumatic devices or systems. Design engineering systems for the automation of industrial tasks. Design advanced electronic control systems for mechanical systems. Create embedded software design programs. Create mechanical models and tolerance analyses to simulate mechatronic design concepts. Conduct studies to determine the feasibility, costs, or performance benefits of new mechatronic equipment. Upgrade the design of existing devices by adding mechatronic elements. Develop electronic, mechanical, or computerized processes to perform tasks in dangerous situations such as underwater exploration and extraterrestrial mining.

Personality Type: Investigative-Realistic-Conventional. **Skills:** No data available. **Education and Training Program:** Mechatronics, Robotics, and Automation Engineering. **Work Environment:** No data available.

JOB SPECIALIZATION: MICROSYSTEMS ENGINEERS

Apply knowledge of electronic and mechanical engineering theory and methods, as well as specialized manufacturing technologies, to design and develop microelectromechanical systems (MEMS) devices. Manage new product introduction projects to ensure effective deployment of microelectromechanical systems (MEMS) devices and applications. Plan or schedule engineering research or development projects involving microelectromechanical systems (MEMS) technology. Develop or implement microelectromechanical systems (MEMS) processing tools, fixtures, gages, dies, molds, and trays. Identify, procure, or develop test equipment, instrumentation, and facilities for characterization of microelectromechanical systems (MEMS) applications. Develop and verify customer documentation, such as performance specifications, training manuals, and operating instructions. Develop and file intellectual property and patent disclosure or application documents related to microelectromechanical systems (MEMS) devices, products, and systems. Develop and communicate operating characteristics or performance experience to other engineers and designers for training or new product development purposes. Demonstrate miniaturized systems that contain components such as microsensors, microactuators, or integrated electronic circuits fabricated on silicon or silicon carbide wafers. Create or maintain formal engineering documents, such as schematics, bill of materials, components and materials specifications, and packaging requirements.

Personality Type: Investigative-Realistic-Conventional. **Skills:** No data available. **Education and Training Program:** Nanotechnology. **Work Environment:** No data available.

JOB SPECIALIZATION: NANOSYSTEMS ENGINEERS

Design, develop, and supervise the production of materials, devices, and systems of unique molecular or macromolecular composition, applying principles of nanoscale physics and electrical, chemical, and biological engineering. Write proposals to secure external funding or to partner with other companies. Supervise technologists or technicians engaged in nanotechnology research or production. Synthesize, process, or characterize nanomaterials, using advanced tools and techniques. Identify new applications for existing nanotechnologies. Provide technical guidance and support to customers on topics such as nanosystem start-up, maintenance, or use. Generate high-resolution images or measure force-distance curves, using techniques such as atomic force microscopy. Prepare reports, deliver presentations, or participate in program review activities to communicate engineering results and recommendations. Prepare nanotechnology-related invention disclosures or patent applications. Develop processes or identify equipment needed for pilot or commercial nanoscale production. Provide scientific or technical guidance and expertise to scientists, engineers, technologists, technicians, or others using knowledge of chemical, analytical, or biological processes as applied to micro and nanoscale systems. Engineer production processes for specific nanotechnology applications, such as electroplating, nanofabrication, or epoxy. Design or conduct tests of new nanotechnology products, processes, or systems. Coordinate or supervise the work of suppliers or vendors in the designing, building, or testing of nanosystem devices, such as lenses or probes.

Personality Type: No data available. **Skills:** No data available. **Education and Training Program:** Nanotechnology. **Work Environment:** No data available.

JOB SPECIALIZATION: PHOTONICS ENGINEERS

Apply knowledge of engineering and mathematical theory and methods to design technologies specializing in light information and light energy. Design, integrate, or test photonics systems and components. Develop optical or imaging systems such as optical imaging products, optical components, image processes, signal process technologies, and optical systems. Analyze system performance or operational requirements. Write reports or research proposals. Assist in the transition of photonic prototypes to production. Develop and test photonic prototypes or models. Conduct testing to determine functionality and optimization or to establish limits of photonics systems or components. Design electro-optical sensing or imaging systems. Read current literature, talk with colleagues, continue education, or participate in professional organizations or conferences to keep abreast of developments in the field. Conduct research on new photonics technologies. Determine applications of photonics appropriate to meet product objectives and features. Document design processes including objectives, issues, and outcomes. Oversee or provide expertise on manufacturing, assembly, or fabrication processes. Train operators, engineers, or other personnel. Determine commercial, industrial, scientific, or other uses for electro-optical applications or devices. Design gas lasers, solid state lasers, infrared, or other light emitting or light sensitive devices. Analyze, fabricate, or test fiber-optic links. Create or maintain photonic design histories. Develop laser-processed designs such as laser-cut medical devices.

Personality Type: Investigative-Realistic-Conventional. **Skills:** Technology Design; Equipment Selection; Mathematics; Science; Programming; Repairing; Quality Control Analysis; Troubleshooting. **Education and Training Program:** Engineering, Other. **Work Environment:** Indoors; sitting.

JOB SPECIALIZATION: ROBOTICS ENGINEERS

Research, design, develop, and test robotic applications. Supervise technicians, technologists, or other engineers. Integrate robotics with peripherals such as welders, controllers, or other equipment. Provide technical support for robotic systems. Review or approve designs, calculations, or cost estimates. Make system device lists and event timing charts. Document robotic application development, maintenance, or changes. Write algorithms and programming code for ad hoc robotic applications. Create back-ups of robot programs or parameters. Process and interpret signals or sensor data. Plan mobile robot paths and teach path plans to robots. Investigate mechanical failures or unexpected maintenance problems. Install, calibrate, operate, or maintain robots. Debug robotics programs. Design end-of-arm tooling. Conduct research on robotic technology to create new robotic systems or system capabilities.

Personality Type: Investigative-Realistic-Conventional. **Skills:** Programming; Equipment Selection; Installation; Technology Design; Equipment Maintenance; Repairing; Mathematics; Troubleshooting. **Education and Training Program:** Mechatronics, Robotics, and Automation Engineering. **Work Environment:** Indoors; sounds, noisy; using your hands to handle, control, or feel objects, tools, or controls; sitting; hazardous equipment.

JOB SPECIALIZATION: SOLAR ENERGY SYSTEMS ENGINEERS

Perform site-specific engineering analysis or evaluation of energy efficiency and solar projects involving residential, commercial, or industrial customers. Design solar domestic hot water and space heating systems for new and existing structures, applying knowledge of structural energy requirements, local climates, solar technology, and thermodynamics. Test or evaluate photovoltaic (PV) cells or modules. Review specifications and recommend engineering or manufacturing changes to achieve solar design objectives. Perform thermal, stress, or cost reduction analyses for solar systems. Develop standard operation procedures and quality or safety standards for solar installation work. Design or develop vacuum tube collector systems for solar applications. Provide technical direction or support to installation teams during installation, start-up, testing, system commissioning, or performance monitoring. Perform computer simulation of solar photovoltaic (PV) generation system performance or energy production to optimize efficiency. Develop design specifications and functional requirements for residential, commercial, or industrial solar energy systems or components. Create plans for solar energy system development, monitoring, and evaluation activities. Create electrical single-line diagrams, panel schedules, or connection diagrams for solar electric systems using computer-aided design (CAD) software. Create checklists for review or inspection of completed solar installation projects. Design or coordinate design of photovoltaic (PV) or solar thermal systems, including system components, for residential and commercial buildings. Conduct engineering site audits to collect structural, electrical, and related site information for use in the design of residential or commercial solar power systems.

Personality Type: No data available. **Skills:** No data available. **Education and Training Program:** Engineering, Other. **Work Environment:** No data available.

Job Specialization: Validation Engineers

Design and plan protocols for equipment and processes to produce products meeting internal and external purity, safety, and quality requirements. Analyze validation test data to determine whether systems or processes have met validation criteria and to identify root causes of production problems. Prepare validation and performance qualification protocols for new or modified manufacturing processes, systems, or equipment for pharmaceutical, electronics, and other types of production. Coordinate the implementation or scheduling of validation testing with affected departments and personnel. Study product characteristics or customer requirements and confer with management to determine validation objectives and standards. Prepare, maintain, or review validation and compliance documentation such as engineering change notices, schematics, and protocols. Resolve testing problems by modifying testing methods or revising test objectives and standards. Create, populate, or maintain databases for tracking validation activities, test results, or validated systems. Prepare detailed reports and design statements based on results of validation and qualification tests or reviews of procedures and protocols. Identify deviations from established product or process standards and provide recommendations for resolving deviations. Direct validation activities such as protocol creation or testing. Develop validation master plans, process flow diagrams, test cases, or standard operating procedures. Communicate with regulatory agencies regarding compliance documentation or validation results.

Personality Type: Investigative-Realistic-Conventional. **Skills:** Science; Operations Analysis; Mathematics; Systems Analysis; Operation Monitoring; Systems Evaluation; Reading Comprehension; Writing. **Education and Training Program:** Engineering, Other. **Work Environment:** Indoors; sitting.

Job Specialization: Wind Energy Engineers

Design underground or overhead wind farm collector systems and prepare and develop site specifications. Write reports to document wind farm collector system test results. Oversee the work activities of wind farm consultants or subcontractors. Recommend process or infrastructure changes to improve wind turbine performance, reduce operational costs, or comply with regulations. Investigate experimental wind turbines or wind turbine technologies for properties such as aerodynamics, production, noise, and load. Test wind turbine equipment to determine effects of stress or fatigue. Test wind turbine components, using mechanical or electronic testing equipment. Provide engineering technical support to designers of prototype wind turbines. Perform root cause analysis on wind turbine tower component failures. Monitor wind farm construction to ensure compliance with regulatory standards or environmental requirements. Direct balance of plant (BOP) construction, generator installation, testing, commissioning, or supervisory control and data acquisition (SCADA) to ensure compliance with specifications. Develop specifications for wind technology components, such as gearboxes, blades, generators, frequency converters, and pad transformers. Develop active control algorithms, electronics, software, electromechanical, or electrohydraulic systems for wind turbines. Create or maintain wind farm layouts, schematics, or other visual documentation for wind farms.

Personality Type: No data available. **Skills:** No data available. **Education and Training Program:** Engineering, Other. **Work Environment:** No data available.

OTHER FEDERAL JOB FACTS

Related GS Series: 0804 Fire Protection Engineering

Title on USAJobs: Engineer, Fire Prevention

- ❁ U.S. Federal Workforce: 231
- ❁ Average Length of Service: 11.8 years
- ❁ Percent Part-Time: 1.3%
- ❁ Percent Women: 9.5%

- ❁ Largest Age Bracket: 50–54 (17.3%)
- ❁ GS Level with Most Workers: 13
- ❁ Agency with Most Workers: Defense
- ❁ State with Most Workers: District of Columbia

Manage, supervise, lead, and/or perform professional engineering and scientific work to protect life and property from destructive fire; assess and predict fire hazards or risks; mitigate fire damage by proper design, construction, and arrangement of facilities; research, develop, and test fire protection technologies (e.g., halon and water mist applicators); design, construct, inspect, test, and operate fire detection and fire suppression apparatus, appliances, devices, and systems; and assess fire protection requirements.

Requirements: No requirements available.

Related GS Series: 1380 Forest Products Technology

- ❁ U.S. Federal Workforce: 24
- ❁ Average Length of Service: 17.6 years
- ❁ Percent Part-Time: 4.2%
- ❁ Percent Women: 16.7%
- ❁ Largest Age Bracket: 50–54 (29.2%)
- ❁ GS Level with Most Workers: 13
- ❁ Agency with Most Workers: Agriculture
- ❁ State with Most Workers: Wisconsin

Develop, improve, and use wood or wood products; study preservation and treatment methods, the processing and production of wood products, the properties and structure of wood, and the production of lumber.

Requirements: Degree in wood technology, wood utilization, forestry, biological science, chemistry, physics, mathematics, engineering, or a related discipline; or a combination of relevant courses and work experience.

Environmental Engineers

- ❋ Education/Training Required: Bachelor's degree
- ❋ Annual Earnings (Federal): $98,760
- ❋ Annual Earnings (All Industries): $77,040
- ❋ Earnings Growth Potential (Federal): 29.0% (low)
- ❋ Earnings Growth Potential (All Industries): 38.1% (medium)
- ❋ Job Growth (Federal): 7.5%
- ❋ Job Growth (All Industries): 30.6%
- ❋ Annual Job Openings (Federal): 150
- ❋ Annual Job Openings (All Industries): 2,790

Design, plan, or perform engineering duties in the prevention, control, and remediation of environmental health hazards, using various engineering disciplines. Work may include waste treatment, site remediation, or pollution control technology. Collaborate with environmental scientists, planners, hazardous waste technicians, engineers, and other specialists and experts in law and business to address environmental problems. Inspect industrial and municipal facilities and programs to evaluate operational effectiveness and ensure compliance with environmental regulations. Prepare, review, and update environmental investigation and recommendation reports. Design and supervise the development of systems processes or equipment for control, management, or remediation of water, air, or soil quality. Provide environmental engineering assistance in network analysis, regulatory analysis, and planning or reviewing database development. Obtain, update, and maintain plans, permits, and standard operating procedures. Provide technical-level support for environmental remediation and litigation projects, including remediation system design and determination of regulatory applicability. Monitor progress of environmental improvement programs. Inform company employees and other interested parties of environmental issues. Advise corporations and government agencies of procedures to follow in cleaning up contaminated sites to protect people and the environment. Develop proposed project objectives and targets and report to management on progress in attaining them. Request bids from suppliers or consultants. Advise industries and government agencies about environmental policies and standards.

Considerations for Job Outlook: Environmental engineers are expected to have employment growth of 31 percent from 2008–2018, much faster than the average for all occupations. More environmental engineers will be needed to help companies comply with environmental regulations and to develop methods of cleaning up environmental hazards. A shift in emphasis toward preventing problems rather than controlling those which already exist, as well as increasing public health concerns resulting from population growth, also are expected to spur demand for environmental engineers. Because of this employment growth, job opportunities should be favorable.

Personality Type: Investigative-Realistic-Conventional. **Skills:** Mathematics; Science; Systems Analysis; Management of Financial Resources; Operations Analysis; Quality Control Analysis; Systems Evaluation; Complex Problem Solving. **Education and Training Program:** Environmental/Environmental Health Engineering. **Work Environment:** More often indoors than outdoors; sitting; sounds, noisy; using your hands to handle, control, or feel objects, tools, or controls; contaminants.

E

OTHER FEDERAL JOB FACTS

RELATED GS SERIES: 0819 ENVIRONMENTAL ENGINEERING

TITLE ON USAJOBS: ENGINEER, ENVIRONMENTAL

- ❋ U.S. Federal Workforce: 4,382
- ❋ Average Length of Service: 17.3 years
- ❋ Percent Part-Time: 5.4%
- ❋ Percent Women: 29.6%
- ❋ Largest Age Bracket: 50–54 (20.2%)
- ❋ GS Level with Most Workers: 13
- ❋ Agency with Most Workers: Defense
- ❋ State with Most Workers: California

Manage, supervise, lead, and/or perform professional engineering and scientific work involving environmental programs and projects in the areas of environmental planning; environmental compliance; identification and cleanup of contamination; and restoring and sustaining environmental conservation.

Requirements: Professional knowledge of and skills in environmental engineering.

Environmental Scientists and Specialists, Including Health

- ❋ Education/Training Required: Master's degree
- ❋ Annual Earnings (Federal): $91,550
- ❋ Annual Earnings (All Industries): $61,010
- ❋ Earnings Growth Potential (Federal): 34.3% (low)
- ❋ Earnings Growth Potential (All Industries): 39.2% (medium)
- ❋ Job Growth (Federal): 7.6%
- ❋ Job Growth (All Industries): 27.9%
- ❋ Annual Job Openings (Federal): 230
- ❋ Annual Job Openings (All Industries): 4,840

Conduct research or perform investigation for the purpose of identifying, abating, or eliminating sources of pollutants or hazards that affect either the environment or the health of the population. Using knowledge of various scientific disciplines, may collect, synthesize, study, report, and take action based on data derived from measurements or observations of air, food, soil, water, and other sources. Collect, synthesize, analyze, manage, and report environmental data such as pollution emission measurements, atmospheric monitoring measurements, meteorological and mineralogical information, and soil or water samples. Analyze data to determine validity, quality, and scientific significance, and to interpret correlations between human activities and environmental effects. Communicate scientific and technical information to the public, organizations, or internal audiences through oral briefings, written documents, workshops, conferences, training sessions, or public hearings. Provide scientific and technical guidance, support, coordination, and oversight to governmental agencies, environmental programs, industry, or the public. Process and review environmental permits, licenses, and related materials. Review and implement environmental technical standards, guidelines, policies, and formal regulations that meet all appropriate requirements. Prepare charts or graphs from data samples, providing summary information on the environmental relevance of the data. Determine data collection methods to be employed in research projects and surveys. Investigate and report on accidents affecting the environment. Research sources of pollution to determine their effects on the environment and to develop theories or methods of pollution abatement or control.

Considerations for Job Outlook: A growing population and increased awareness of environmental concerns are expected to increase employment of environmental scientists. These workers should have good job prospects, particularly in state and local governments.

Personality Type: Investigative-Realistic-Conventional.

JOB SPECIALIZATION: CLIMATE CHANGE ANALYSTS

Research and analyze policy developments related to climate change. Make climate-related recommendations for actions such as legislation, awareness campaigns, or fundraising approaches. Write reports or academic papers to communicate findings of climate-related studies. Promote initiatives to mitigate climate change with government or environmental groups. Present climate-related information at public interest, governmental, or other meetings. Present and defend proposals for climate change research projects. Prepare grant applications to obtain funding for programs related to climate change, environmental management, or sustainability. Gather and review climate-related studies from government agencies, research laboratories, and other organizations. Develop, or contribute to the development of, educational or outreach programs on the environment or climate change. Review existing policies or legislation to identify environmental impacts. Provide analytical support for policy briefs related to renewable energy, energy efficiency, or climate change. Prepare study reports, memoranda, briefs, testimonies, or other written materials to inform government or environmental groups on environmental issues such as climate change. Make legislative recommendations related to climate change or environmental management, based on climate change policies, principles, programs, practices, and processes. Research policies, practices, or procedures for climate or environmental management. Propose new or modified policies involving use of traditional and alternative fuels, transportation of goods, and other factors relating to climate and climate change.

Personality Type: No data available. **Skills:** No data available. **Education and Training Program:**

Environmental Science; Environmental Studies. **Work Environment:** No data available.

JOB SPECIALIZATION: ENVIRONMENTAL RESTORATION PLANNERS

Collaborate with field and biology staff to oversee the implementation of restoration projects and to develop new products. Process and synthesize complex scientific data into practical strategies for restoration, monitoring, or management. Notify regulatory or permitting agencies of deviations from implemented remediation plans. Develop environmental restoration project schedules and budgets. Develop and communicate recommendations for landowners to maintain or restore environmental conditions. Create diagrams to communicate environmental remediation planning using geographic information systems (GIS), computer-aided design (CAD), or other mapping or diagramming software. Apply for permits required for the implementation of environmental remediation projects. Review existing environmental remediation designs. Supervise and provide technical guidance, training, or assistance to employees working in the field to restore habitats. Provide technical direction on environmental planning to energy engineers, biologists, geologists, or other professionals working to develop restoration plans or strategies. Plan or supervise environmental studies to achieve compliance with environmental regulations in construction, modification, operation, acquisition, or divestiture of facilities such as power plants. Inspect active remediation sites to ensure compliance with environmental or safety policies, standards, or regulations. Plan environmental restoration projects, using biological databases, environmental strategies, and planning software. Identify short- and long-term impacts of environmental remediation activities.

Personality Type: No data available. **Skills:** No data available. **Education and Training Program:** Environmental Science; Environmental Studies. **Work Environment:** No data available.

Job Specialization: Industrial Ecologists

Study or investigate industrial production and natural ecosystems to achieve high production, sustainable resources, and environmental safety or protection. May apply principles and activities of natural ecosystems to develop models for industrial systems. Write ecological reports and other technical documents for publication in the research literature or in industrial or government reports. Recommend methods to protect the environment or minimize environmental damage. Investigate accidents affecting the environment to assess ecological impact. Investigate the adaptability of various animal and plant species to changed environmental conditions. Review industrial practices, such as the methods and materials used in construction or production, to identify potential liabilities and environmental hazards. Research sources of pollution to determine environmental impact or to develop methods of pollution abatement or control. Provide industrial managers with technical materials on environmental issues, regulatory guidelines, or compliance actions. Plan or conduct studies of the ecological implications of historic or projected changes in industrial processes or development. Plan or conduct field research on topics such as industrial production, industrial ecology, population ecology, and environmental production or sustainability. Monitor the environmental impact of development activities, pollution, or land degradation. Model alternative energy investment scenarios to compare economic and environmental costs and benefits. Identify or develop strategies or methods to minimize the environmental impact of industrial production processes. Investigate the impact of changed land management or land use practices on ecosystems.

Personality Type: No data available. **Skills:** No data available. **Education and Training Program:** Environmental Science; Environmental Studies. **Work Environment:** No data available.

OTHER FEDERAL JOB FACTS
Related GS Series: 0028 Environmental Protection Specialist

- ❋ U.S. Federal Workforce: 5,873
- ❋ Average Length of Service: 18.4 years
- ❋ Percent Part-Time: 3.4%
- ❋ Percent Women: 46.0%
- ❋ Largest Age Bracket: 45–49 (19.1%)
- ❋ GS Level with Most Workers: 13
- ❋ Agency with Most Workers: Defense
- ❋ State with Most Workers: District of Columbia

Advise on, manage, supervise, or perform administrative or program work relating to programs to protect or improve environmental quality, control pollution, remedy environmental damage, or ensure compliance with environmental laws and regulations.

Requirements: Specialized knowledge of the principles and methods of administering environmental protection programs and the laws and regulations related to environmental protection activities.

Related GS Series: 1313 Geophysics
Title on USAJobs: Geophysicist

- ❋ U.S. Federal Workforce: 450
- ❋ Average Length of Service: 18.3 years
- ❋ Percent Part-Time: 3.6%
- ❋ Percent Women: 22.7%
- ❋ Largest Age Bracket: 55–59 (22.0%)
- ❋ GS Level with Most Workers: 13
- ❋ Agency with Most Workers: Interior
- ❋ States with Most Workers: Colorado, California

Investigate, measure, analyze, evaluate, and interpret geophysical phenomena and artificially applied forces and fields related to the structure, composition, and physical properties of the earth and its atmosphere.

Requirements: Knowledge of the principles and techniques of geophysics and related sciences.

Financial Examiners

* Education/Training Required: Bachelor's degree
* Annual Earnings (Federal): $101,770
* Annual Earnings (All Industries): $71,750
* Earnings Growth Potential (Federal): 48.5% (high)
* Earnings Growth Potential (All Industries): 43.3% (high)
* Job Growth (Federal): 41.5%
* Job Growth (All Industries): 41.2%
* Annual Job Openings (Federal): 260
* Annual Job Openings (All Industries): 1,600

Enforce or ensure compliance with laws and regulations governing financial and securities institutions and financial and real estate transactions. May examine, verify correctness of, or establish authenticity of records. Investigate activities of institutions in order to enforce laws and regulations and to ensure legality of transactions and operations or financial solvency. Review and analyze new, proposed, or revised laws, regulations, policies, and procedures in order to interpret their meaning and determine their impact. Plan, supervise, and review work of assigned subordinates. Recommend actions to ensure compliance with laws and regulations or to protect solvency of institutions. Examine the minutes of meetings of directors, stockholders, and committees in order to investigate the specific authority extended at various levels of management. Prepare reports, exhibits, and other supporting schedules that detail an institution's safety and soundness, compliance with laws and regulations, and recommended solutions to questionable financial conditions. Review balance sheets, operating income and expense accounts, and loan documentation in order to confirm institution assets and liabilities. Review audit reports of internal and external auditors in order to monitor adequacy of scope of reports or to discover specific weaknesses in internal routines. Train other examiners in the financial examination process. Establish guidelines for procedures and policies that comply with new and revised regulations and direct their implementation.

Considerations for Job Outlook: Much faster than average employment growth is projected.

Personality Type: Enterprising-Conventional. **Skills:** Management of Personnel Resources; Systems Evaluation; Active Learning; Systems Analysis; Learning Strategies; Mathematics; Writing; Judgment and Decision Making. **Education and Training Program:** Accounting; Taxation. **Work Environment:** Indoors; sitting.

OTHER FEDERAL JOB FACTS

RELATED GS SERIES: 0570 FINANCIAL INSTITUTION EXAMINING

TITLE ON USAJOBS: FINANCIAL INSTITUTION EXAMINER

* U.S. Federal Workforce: 5,564
* Average Length of Service: 15.2 years
* Percent Part-Time: 3.9%
* Percent Women: 36.1%
* Largest Age Bracket: 45–49 (3.9%)
* GS Levels with Most Workers: 15, 14
* Agency with Most Workers: Treasury
* State with Most Workers: Texas

Direct, supervise, advise on, or perform examinations of financial institutions such as banks, savings or building and loan associations, cooperative banks, home financing institutions, cooperative savings and lending organizations, and similar institutions for such purposes as determining financial condition; quality of assets; extent of liabilities; operating results, trends, and policies; extent of compliance with provisions of charters, by-laws, and regulatory laws and regulations; accuracy of financial records; and whether irregularities have occurred.

Requirements: Some, but less than full, professional knowledge of accounting and auditing principles, procedures, and techniques; and knowledge of the laws and regulations controlling the organization and operation of such institutions and the operating methods, procedures, and practices of financial institutions.

Financial Managers

- ❀ Education/Training Required: Bachelor's or higher degree, plus work experience
- ❀ Annual Earnings (Federal): $117,190
- ❀ Annual Earnings (All Industries): $101,190
- ❀ Earnings Growth Potential (Federal): 22.2% (very low)
- ❀ Earnings Growth Potential (All Industries): 45.9% (high)
- ❀ Job Growth (Federal): 7.0%
- ❀ Job Growth (All Industries): 7.6%
- ❀ Annual Job Openings (Federal): 210
- ❀ Annual Job Openings (All Industries): 13,820

Plan, direct, and coordinate accounting, investing, banking, insurance, securities, and other financial activities of a branch, office, or department of an establishment. No task data available.

Considerations for Job Outlook: Business expansion and globalization will require financial expertise, which is expected to drive employment growth for these managers. Job growth, however, is expected to be tempered by mergers and downsizing. Keen competition is expected.

JOB SPECIALIZATION: TREASURERS AND CONTROLLERS

Direct financial activities, such as planning, procurement, and investments, for all or part of an organization. Prepare and file annual tax returns or prepare financial information so that outside accountants can complete tax returns. Prepare or direct preparation of financial statements, business activity reports, financial position forecasts, annual budgets, and/or reports required by regulatory agencies. Supervise employees performing financial reporting, accounting, billing, collections, payroll, and budgeting duties. Delegate authority for the receipt, disbursement, banking, protection, and custody of funds, securities, and financial instruments. Maintain current knowledge of organizational policies and procedures, federal and state policies and directives, and current accounting standards. Conduct or coordinate audits of company accounts and financial transactions to ensure compliance with state and federal requirements and statutes. Receive and record requests for disbursements; authorize disbursements in accordance with policies and procedures. Monitor financial activities and details such as reserve levels to ensure that all legal and regulatory requirements are met. Monitor and evaluate the performance of accounting and other financial staff; recommend and implement personnel actions such as promotions and dismissals. Develop and maintain relationships with banking, insurance, and non-organizational accounting personnel in order to facilitate financial activities.

Personality Type: Conventional-Enterprising. **Skills:** Management of Financial Resources; Management of Material Resources; Systems Analysis; Operations Analysis; Judgment and Decision Making; Systems Evaluation; Management of Personnel Resources; Mathematics. **Education and**

Training Program: Accounting and Business/Management; Accounting and Finance; Credit Management; Finance and Financial Management Services, Other; Finance, General; International Finance; Public Finance. **Work Environment:** Indoors; sitting.

JOB SPECIALIZATION: FINANCIAL MANAGERS, BRANCH OR DEPARTMENT

Direct and coordinate financial activities of workers in a branch, office, or department of an establishment, such as branch bank, brokerage firm, risk and insurance department, or credit department. Establish and maintain relationships with individual and business customers and provide assistance with problems these customers may encounter. Examine, evaluate, and process loan applications. Plan, direct, and coordinate the activities of workers in branches, offices, or departments of such establishments as branch banks, brokerage firms, risk and insurance departments, or credit departments. Oversee the flow of cash and financial instruments. Recruit staff members and oversee training programs. Network within communities to find and attract new business. Approve or reject, or coordinate the approval and rejection of, lines of credit and commercial, real estate, and personal loans. Prepare financial and regulatory reports required by laws, regulations, and boards of directors. Establish procedures for custody and control of assets, records, loan collateral, and securities in order to ensure safekeeping. Review collection reports to determine the status of collections and the amounts of outstanding balances. Prepare operational and risk reports for management analysis. Evaluate financial reporting systems, accounting and collection procedures, and investment activities and make recommendations for changes to procedures, operating systems, budgets, and other financial control functions. Plan, direct, and coordinate risk and insurance programs of establishments to control risks and losses.

Submit delinquent accounts to attorneys or outside agencies for collection.

Personality Type: Enterprising-Conventional. **Skills:** Management of Financial Resources; Management of Personnel Resources; Persuasion; Service Orientation; Systems Evaluation; Learning Strategies; Time Management; Monitoring. **Education and Training Program:** Accounting and Business/Management; Accounting and Finance; Credit Management; Finance and Financial Management Services, Other; Finance, General; International Finance; Public Finance. **Work Environment:** Indoors; sitting.

OTHER FEDERAL JOB FACTS

RELATED GS SERIES: 0505 FINANCIAL MANAGEMENT

TITLE ON USAJOBS: FINANCIAL PROGRAM SPECIALIST

- U.S. Federal Workforce: 1,274
- Average Length of Service: 20.9 years
- Percent Part-Time: 0.9%
- Percent Women: 45.1%
- Largest Age Bracket: 50–54 (25.4%)
- GS Levels with Most Workers: 13, 14
- Agency with Most Workers: Defense
- State with Most Workers: District of Columbia

Manage or direct a program for the management of the financial resources of an organizational segment, field establishment, bureau, department, independent agency, or other organizational entity of the federal government.

Requirements: Broad knowledge of and ability to utilize principles, methods, techniques, and systems of financial management; ability to plan, direct, and coordinate difficult and complex programs; ability to develop, apply, and adjust financial plans and policies to attain agency objectives;

ability to select, develop, and supervise a subordinate staff; ability to establish and maintain effective working relationships, not only with subordinate staff, but with all levels of key management officials, the latter particularly requiring the exercise of tact, ingenuity, and resourcefulness; ability to make oral and written presentations in a clear and concise manner; ability to apply a high level of sound, independent judgment in the solution of financial problems and in the administration of a financial management program; broad knowledge of agency operating programs.

Fire Fighters

- ❋ Education/Training Required: Long-term on-the-job training
- ❋ Annual Earnings (Federal): $46,630
- ❋ Annual Earnings (All Industries): $45,050
- ❋ Earnings Growth Potential (Federal): 19.6% (very low)
- ❋ Earnings Growth Potential (All Industries): 49.0% (high)
- ❋ Job Growth (Federal): 19.1%
- ❋ Job Growth (All Industries): 18.5%
- ❋ Annual Job Openings (Federal): 310
- ❋ Annual Job Openings (All Industries): 15,280

Control and extinguish fires or respond to emergency situations where life, property, or the environment is at risk. Duties may include fire prevention, emergency medical service, hazardous material response, search and rescue, and disaster management. No task data available.

Considerations for Job Outlook: Most job growth will stem from the conversion of volunteer fire fighting positions into paid positions. Job seekers are expected to face keen competition. Those who have completed some fire fighter education at

a community college and have EMT or paramedic certification should have the best prospects.

JOB SPECIALIZATION: FOREST FIRE FIGHTERS

Control and suppress fires in forests or vacant public land. Maintain contact with fire dispatchers at all times to notify them of the need for additional firefighters and supplies or to detail any difficulties encountered. Rescue fire victims and administer emergency medical aid. Collaborate with other firefighters as a member of a firefighting crew. Patrol burned areas after fires to locate and eliminate hot spots that may restart fires. Extinguish flames and embers to suppress fires, using shovels or engine- or hand-driven water or chemical pumps. Fell trees, cut and clear brush, and dig trenches to create firelines, using axes, chainsaws, or shovels. Maintain knowledge of current firefighting practices by participating in drills and by attending seminars, conventions, and conferences. Operate pumps connected to high-pressure hoses. Participate in physical training to maintain high levels of physical fitness. Establish water supplies, connect hoses, and direct water onto fires. Maintain fire equipment and firehouse living quarters.

Personality Type: Realistic-Social. **Skills:** Repairing; Equipment Maintenance; Equipment Selection; Operation and Control; Troubleshooting; Quality Control Analysis; Operation Monitoring; Coordination. **Education and Training Program:** Fire Protection, Other; Fire Science/Fire-fighting. **Work Environment:** Outdoors; contaminants; hazardous conditions; very hot or cold temperatures; hazardous equipment; minor burns, cuts, bites, or stings.

JOB SPECIALIZATION: MUNICIPAL FIRE FIGHTERS

Control and extinguish municipal fires, protect life and property, and conduct rescue efforts. Rescue victims from burning buildings and accident sites. Search burning buildings to locate fire victims. Administer first aid and cardio-pulmonary resuscitation to injured persons. Dress with equipment such as fire resistant clothing and breathing apparatus. Drive and operate fire fighting vehicles and equipment. Move toward the source of a fire using knowledge of types of fires, construction design, building materials, and physical layout of properties. Respond to fire alarms and other calls for assistance, such as automobile and industrial accidents. Assess fires and situations and report conditions to superiors to receive instructions, using two-way radios. Position and climb ladders to gain access to upper levels of buildings or to rescue individuals from burning structures. Create openings in buildings for ventilation or entrance, using axes, chisels, crowbars, electric saws, or core cutters. Lay hose lines and connect them to water supplies. Operate pumps connected to high-pressure hoses. Collaborate with police to respond to accidents, disasters, and arson investigation calls. Take action to contain hazardous chemicals that might catch fire, leak, or spill. Select and attach hose nozzles, depending on fire type, and direct streams of water or chemicals onto fires. Participate in fire drills and demonstrations of fire fighting techniques. Prepare written reports that detail specifics of fire incidents.

Personality Type: Realistic-Social-Enterprising. **Skills:** Equipment Maintenance; Repairing; Troubleshooting; Operation and Control; Equipment Selection; Science; Operation Monitoring; Quality Control Analysis. **Education and Training Program:** Fire Protection, Other; Fire Science/Fire-fighting. **Work Environment:** Outdoors; sounds, noisy; hazardous equipment; hazardous conditions; very hot or cold temperatures; contaminants.

OTHER FEDERAL JOB FACTS

RELATED GS SERIES: 0081 FIRE PROTECTION AND PREVENTION

TITLE ON USAJOBS: FIRE PROTECTION AND PREVENTION SPECIALIST

- U.S. Federal Workforce: 9,126
- Average Length of Service: 13.6 years
- Percent Part-Time: 0.1%
- Percent Women: 2.6%
- Largest Age Bracket: 30–34 (19.2%)
- GS Level with Most Workers: 7
- Agency with Most Workers: Defense
- State with Most Workers: California

Control and extinguish fires, rescue persons endangered by fire, and reduce or eliminate potential fire hazards; control hazardous materials incidents; train personnel in fire protection and prevention; operate fire communications equipment; develop and implement fire protection and prevention plans, procedures, and standards; and advise on improvements to structures for better fire prevention.

Requirements: Knowledge of firefighting and fire prevention theory and techniques, knowledge of fixed and mobile firefighting equipment operation; and/or the ability to plan, direct, or carry out fire protection and prevention programs and operations.

First-Line Supervisors/Managers of Correctional Officers

- Education/Training Required: Work experience in a related occupation
- Annual Earnings (Federal): $69,570
- Annual Earnings (All Industries): $57,690
- Earnings Growth Potential (Federal): 12.9% (very low)

- Earnings Growth Potential (All Industries): 40.0% (medium)
- Job Growth (Federal): 7.5%
- Job Growth (All Industries): 8.5%
- Annual Job Openings (Federal): 40
- Annual Job Openings (All Industries): 1,940

Directly supervise and coordinate activities of correctional officers and jailers. Take, receive, and check periodic inmate counts. Maintain order, discipline, and security within assigned areas in accordance with relevant rules, regulations, policies, and laws. Respond to emergencies such as escapes. Maintain knowledge of, comply with, and enforce all institutional policies, rules, procedures, and regulations. Supervise and direct the work of correctional officers to ensure the safe custody, discipline, and welfare of inmates. Restrain, secure, and control offenders, using chemical agents, firearms, and other weapons of force as necessary. Supervise and perform searches of inmates and their quarters to locate contraband items. Monitor behavior of subordinates to ensure alert, courteous, and professional behavior toward inmates, parolees, fellow employees, visitors, and the public. Complete administrative paperwork and supervise the preparation and maintenance of records, forms, and reports. Instruct employees and provide on-the-job training. Conduct roll calls of correctional officers. Supervise activities such as searches, shakedowns, riot control, and institutional tours. Carry injured offenders or employees to safety and provide emergency first aid when necessary.

Considerations for Job Outlook: Employment growth is expected to stem from population increases and a corresponding rise in the prison population. Favorable job opportunities are expected.

Personality Type: Enterprising-Conventional-Realistic. **Skills:** Management of Personnel Resources; Negotiation; Persuasion; Time Management; Social Perceptiveness; Coordination;

Systems Evaluation; Learning Strategies. **Education and Training Program:** Corrections; Corrections Administration. **Work Environment:** More often indoors than outdoors; more often sitting than standing; walking and running; using hands; noise; very hot or cold; bright or inadequate lighting; contaminants; exposed to disease or infections.

OTHER FEDERAL JOB FACTS

RELATED GS SERIES: 0006 CORRECTIONAL INSTITUTION ADMINISTRATION

TITLE ON USAJOBS: CORRECTIONAL INSTITUTION ADMINISTRATOR

- U.S. Federal Workforce: 1731
- Average Length of Service: 20.4 years
- Percent Part-Time: 0.1%
- Percent Women: 33.7%
- Largest Age Bracket: 45–49 (39.2%)
- GS Levels with Most Workers: 12, 14
- Agency with Most Workers: Justice
- State with Most Workers: Texas

Manage or participate in the overall management of correctional institutions, correctional systems, or correctional programs.

Requirements: Knowledge of penological theories, principles, and techniques, and the problems, methods, and techniques of institutional management.

First-Line Supervisors/Managers of Police and Detectives

- Education/Training Required: Work experience in a related occupation
- Annual Earnings (Federal): $93,390
- Annual Earnings (All Industries): $76,500
- Earnings Growth Potential (Federal): 27.6% (low)

❊ Earnings Growth Potential (All Industries): 38.8% (medium)

❊ Job Growth (Federal): 6.8%

❊ Job Growth (All Industries): 8.1%

❊ Annual Job Openings (Federal): 240

❊ Annual Job Openings (All Industries): 5,050

Supervise and coordinate activities of members of police force. Supervise and coordinate the investigation of criminal cases, offering guidance and expertise to investigators, and ensuring that procedures are conducted in accordance with laws and regulations. Maintain logs, prepare reports, and direct the preparation, handling, and maintenance of departmental records. Explain police operations to subordinates to assist them in performing their job duties. Cooperate with court personnel and officials from other law enforcement agencies and testify in court as necessary. Review contents of written orders to ensure adherence to legal requirements. Investigate and resolve personnel problems within organization and charges of misconduct against staff. Direct collection, preparation, and handling of evidence and personal property of prisoners. Inform personnel of changes in regulations and policies, implications of new or amended laws, and new techniques of police work. Train staff in proper police work procedures. Monitor and evaluate the job performance of subordinates, and authorize promotions and transfers. Prepare work schedules and assign duties to subordinates. Conduct raids and order detention of witnesses and suspects for questioning. Discipline staff for violation of departmental rules and regulations. Develop, implement, and revise departmental policies and procedures. Inspect facilities, supplies, vehicles, and equipment to ensure conformance to standards. Requisition and issue equipment and supplies.

Considerations for Job Outlook: Population growth is the main source of demand for police services. Overall, opportunities in local police departments should be favorable for qualified applicants.

Personality Type: Enterprising-Social-Conventional. **Skills:** Management of Financial Resources; Management of Personnel Resources; Persuasion; Management of Material Resources; Monitoring; Learning Strategies; Time Management; Instructing. **Education and Training Program:** Corrections; Criminal Justice/Law Enforcement Administration; Criminal Justice/Safety Studies. **Work Environment:** More often indoors than outdoors; sitting; sounds, noisy; contaminants; very hot or cold temperatures.

OTHER FEDERAL JOB FACTS
RELATED GS SERIES: 0083 POLICE
TITLE ON USAJOBS: POLICE OFFICER/FEDERAL PROTECTIVE OFFICER

❊ U.S. Federal Workforce: 14,356

❊ Average Length of Service: 9.9 years

❊ Percent Part-Time: 0.0%

❊ Percent Women: 8.7%

❊ Largest Age Bracket: 40–44 (16.7%)

❊ GS Level with Most Workers: 6

❊ Agency with Most Workers: Defense

❊ State with Most Workers: District of Columbia

Perform or supervise law enforcement work in the preservation of the peace; prevent, detect, and investigate crimes; arrest or apprehend violators; and provide assistance to citizens in emergency situations, including the protection of civil rights.

Requirements: Knowledge of federal, state, county, and municipal laws and ordinances and agency rules and regulations pertaining to law enforcement work.

Forensic Science Technicians

- ✷ Education/Training Required: Bachelor's degree
- ✷ Annual Earnings (Federal): $95,620
- ✷ Annual Earnings (All Industries): $51,480
- ✷ Earnings Growth Potential (Federal): 41.0% (high)
- ✷ Earnings Growth Potential (All Industries): 37.0% (medium)
- ✷ Job Growth (Federal): 16.7%
- ✷ Job Growth (All Industries): 19.6%
- ✷ Annual Job Openings (Federal): 10
- ✷ Annual Job Openings (All Industries): 800

Collect, identify, classify, and analyze physical evidence related to criminal investigations. Perform tests on weapons or substances such as fiber, hair, and tissue to determine significance to investigation. May testify as expert witnesses on evidence or crime laboratory techniques. May serve as specialists in area of expertise, such as ballistics, fingerprinting, handwriting, or biochemistry. Collect evidence from crime scenes, storing it in conditions that preserve its integrity. Keep records and prepare reports detailing findings, investigative methods, and laboratory techniques. Use chemicals and other substances to examine latent fingerprint evidence and compare developed prints to those of known persons in databases. Testify in court about investigative and analytical methods and findings. Visit morgues, examine scenes of crimes, or contact other sources to obtain evidence or information to be used in investigations. Take photographs of evidence. Collect impressions of dust from surfaces to obtain and identify fingerprints. Reconstruct crime scenes to determine relationships among pieces of evidence. Operate and maintain laboratory equipment and apparatus. Train new technicians and other personnel on forensic science techniques. Examine and analyze blood stain patterns at crime scenes. Prepare solutions, reagents, and sample formulations needed for laboratory work. Confer with ballistics, fingerprinting, handwriting, documents, electronics, medical, chemical, or metallurgical experts concerning evidence and its interpretation. Interpret laboratory findings and test results to identify and classify substances, materials, and other evidence collected at crime scenes. Examine physical evidence such as hair, fiber, wood, or soil residues to obtain information about its source and composition.

Considerations for Job Outlook: The continued growth of scientific and medical research and the development and manufacturing of technical products are expected to drive employment growth for these workers. Opportunities are expected to be best for graduates of applied science technology programs who are knowledgeable about equipment used in laboratories or production facilities.

Personality Type: Investigative-Realistic-Conventional. **Skills:** Science; Instructing; Speaking; Writing; Critical Thinking; Mathematics; Reading Comprehension; Active Learning. **Education and Training Program:** Forensic Science and Technology. **Work Environment:** More often indoors than outdoors; contaminants; sitting; using your hands to handle, control, or feel objects, tools, or controls; hazardous conditions.

OTHER FEDERAL JOB FACTS

RELATED GS SERIES: 0072 FINGERPRINT IDENTIFICATION

TITLE ON USAJOBS: FINGERPRINT IDENTIFICATION TECHNICIAN

- ✷ U.S. Federal Workforce: 577
- ✷ Average Length of Service: 10.6 years
- ✷ Percent Part-Time: 4.9%

- Percent Women: 57.5%
- Largest Age Bracket: 35–39 (20.8%)
- GS Level with Most Workers: 8
- Agency with Most Workers: Justice
- State with Most Workers: District of Columbia

Classify, search, verify, and file fingerprints and other vestigial prints (such as footprints or palm prints) for identifying persons.

Requirements: Knowledge of the methods used in fingerprint classification and identification.

Forest and Conservation Technicians

- Education/Training Required: Associate degree
- Annual Earnings (Federal): $31,390
- Annual Earnings (All Industries): $32,860
- Earnings Growth Potential (Federal): 22.0% (very low)
- Earnings Growth Potential (All Industries): 25.5% (low)
- Job Growth (Federal): 7.5%
- Job Growth (All Industries): 8.6%
- Annual Job Openings (Federal): 1,750
- Annual Job Openings (All Industries): 1,750

Compile data pertaining to size, content, condition, and other characteristics of forest tracts under direction of foresters; train and lead forest workers in forest propagation and fire prevention and suppression. May assist conservation scientists in managing, improving, and protecting rangelands and wildlife habitats and help provide technical assistance regarding the conservation of soil, water, and related natural resources. Train and lead forest and conservation workers in seasonal activities, such as planting tree seedlings, putting out forest fires, and maintaining recreational facilities. Monitor activities of logging companies and contractors. Select and mark trees for thinning or logging, drawing detailed plans that include access roads. Thin and space trees and control weeds and undergrowth, using manual tools and chemicals, or supervise workers performing these tasks. Manage forest protection activities, including fire control, fire crew training, and coordination of fire detection and public education programs. Survey, measure, and map access roads and forest areas such as burns, cut-over areas, experimental plots, and timber sales sections. Patrol park or forest areas to protect resources and prevent damage. Provide information about, and enforce, regulations such as those concerning environmental protection, resource utilization, fire safety, and accident prevention.

Considerations for Job Outlook: The continued growth of scientific and medical research and the development and manufacturing of technical products are expected to drive employment growth for these workers. Opportunities are expected to be best for graduates of applied science technology programs who are knowledgeable about equipment used in laboratories or production facilities.

Personality Type: Realistic-Investigative-Enterprising. **Skills:** Mathematics; Operation and Control; Management of Personnel Resources; Quality Control Analysis; Learning Strategies; Science; Judgment and Decision Making; Coordination. **Education and Training Program:** Forest Management/Forest Resources Management; Forest Resources Production and Management; Forest Sciences and Biology; Forest Technology/Technician; Forestry, General; Forestry, Other; Land Use Planning and Management/Development; Natural Resources and Conservation, Other; Natural Resources Management and Policy, Other; Natural Resources/Conservation, General; Urban Forestry; Water, Wetlands, and Marine Resources Management. **Work**

Environment: Outdoors; very hot or cold temperatures; minor burns, cuts, bites, or stings; walking and running; using your hands to handle, control, or feel objects, tools, or controls; sounds, noisy.

OTHER FEDERAL JOB FACTS

RELATED GS SERIES: 0462 FORESTRY TECHNICIAN

- ❀ U.S. Federal Workforce: 18,142
- ❀ Average Length of Service: 7.2 years
- ❀ Percent Part-Time: 3.7%
- ❀ Percent Women: 18.2%
- ❀ Largest Age Bracket: 25–29 (22.2%)
- ❀ GS Levels with Most Workers: 4, 5
- ❀ Agency with Most Workers: Agriculture
- ❀ State with Most Workers: California

Provide practical technical support in forestry research efforts; in the marketing of forest resources; or in the scientific management, protection, and development of forest resources.

Requirements: Practical knowledge of the methods and techniques of forestry and other biologically based resource management fields.

Foresters

- ❀ Education/Training Required: Bachelor's degree
- ❀ Annual Earnings (Federal): $60,630
- ❀ Annual Earnings (All Industries): $53,840
- ❀ Earnings Growth Potential (Federal): 23.1% (very low)
- ❀ Earnings Growth Potential (All Industries): 34.5% (low)
- ❀ Job Growth (Federal): 10.8%
- ❀ Job Growth (All Industries): 12.2%
- ❀ Annual Job Openings (Federal): 30
- ❀ Annual Job Openings (All Industries): 260

Manage forested lands for economic, recreational, and conservation purposes. May inventory the type, amount, and location of standing timber; appraise the timber's worth; negotiate the purchase; and draw up contracts for procurement. May determine how to conserve wildlife habitats, creek beds, water quality, and soil stability and how best to comply with environmental regulations. May devise plans for planting and growing new trees, monitor trees for healthy growth, and determine the best time for harvesting. Develop forest management plans for public and privately owned forested lands. Monitor contract compliance and results of forestry activities to assure adherence to government regulations. Establish short- and long-term plans for management of forest lands and forest resources. Supervise activities of other forestry workers. Choose and prepare sites for new trees, using controlled burning, bulldozers, or herbicides to clear weeds, brush, and logging debris. Plan and supervise forestry projects, such as determining the type, number, and placement of trees to be planted; managing tree nurseries; thinning forest; and monitoring growth of new seedlings. Negotiate terms and conditions of agreements and contracts for forest harvesting, forest management, and leasing of forest lands. Direct and participate in forest-fire suppression. Determine methods of cutting and removing timber with minimum waste and environmental damage. Analyze effect of forest conditions on tree growth rates and tree species prevalence and the yield, duration, seed production, growth viability, and germination of different species. Monitor forest-cleared lands to ensure that they are reclaimed to their most suitable end use. Plan and implement projects for conservation of wildlife habitats and soil and water quality. Plan and direct forest surveys and related studies and prepare reports and recommendations. Perform inspections of forests or forest nurseries. Map forest area soils and vegetation to estimate the amount of standing timber and future value and growth.

Considerations for Job Outlook: Increased conservation efforts and continued pressure to maximize efficient use of natural resources are expected to lead to more jobs for conservation scientists. Job seekers with a bachelor's degree should have the best prospects.

Personality Type: Realistic-Investigative-Enterprising. **Skills:** Systems Analysis; Science; Systems Evaluation; Coordination; Monitoring; Management of Financial Resources; Judgment and Decision Making; Management of Material Resources. **Education and Training Program:** Forest Management/Forest Resources Management; Forest Resources Production and Management; Forest Sciences and Biology; Forestry, General; Forestry, Other; Natural Resources and Conservation, Other; Natural Resources Management and Policy; Natural Resources Management and Policy, Other; Natural Resources/Conservation, General; Urban Forestry; Wood Science and Wood Products/Pulp and Paper Technology. **Work Environment:** More often indoors than outdoors; sitting; sounds, noisy.

OTHER FEDERAL JOB FACTS

RELATED GS SERIES: 0460 FORESTRY

TITLE ON USAJOBS: FORESTER

- U.S. Federal Workforce: 2,333
- Average Length of Service: 19.1 years
- Percent Part-Time: 1.3%
- Percent Women: 23.8%
- Largest Age Bracket: 55–59 (21.4%)
- GS Level with Most Workers: 11
- Agency with Most Workers: Agriculture
- State with Most Workers: Oregon

Develop, produce, conserve, and utilize the natural resources of forests and associated lands; inventory, plan, evaluate, and manage forest resources; protect resources against fire, insects, disease, floods, erosion, and other depredations; evaluate, manage, and protect forest lands and properties; interpret and communicate principles, facts, and legislation upon which the management of forest land rests; and develop new, improved, or more economic scientific methods, practices, or techniques necessary to perform such work.

Requirements: Professional knowledge and competence in forestry science.

Funeral Directors

- Education/Training Required: Associate degree
- Annual Earnings (Federal): $67,620
- Annual Earnings (All Industries): $54,370
- Earnings Growth Potential (Federal): 0.0% (very low)
- Earnings Growth Potential (All Industries): 43.5% (high)
- Job Growth (Federal): 22.5%
- Job Growth (All Industries): 11.9%
- Annual Job Openings (Federal): 10
- Annual Job Openings (All Industries): 960

Perform various tasks to arrange and direct funeral services, such as coordinating transportation of bodies to mortuaries for embalming, interviewing families or other authorized people to arrange details, selecting pallbearers, procuring officials for religious rites, and providing transportation for mourners. Consult with families or friends of the deceased to arrange funeral details such as obituary notice wording, casket selection, and plans for services. Plan, schedule, and coordinate funerals, burials, and cremations, arranging such details as the time and place of services. Obtain information needed to complete legal documents such as death certificates and burial permits. Oversee the preparation and care of the remains of people who have died. Contact cemeteries to schedule the opening and closing of graves. Provide information on funeral service options, products, and merchandise and maintain a casket display area. Manage funeral home operations, including hiring and supervising embalmers, funeral attendants, and other staff. Offer counsel and comfort to bereaved families and friends. Close caskets and lead funeral corteges to churches or burial sites. Arrange for clergy members to perform needed services. Provide or arrange transportation between sites for the remains, mourners, pallbearers, clergy, and flowers. Perform embalming duties as necessary. Direct preparations and shipment of bodies for out-of-state burial. Discuss and negotiate prearranged funerals with clients. Maintain financial records, order merchandise, and prepare accounts. Inform survivors of benefits for which they may be eligible. Plan placement of caskets at funeral sites, and place and adjust lights, fixtures, and floral displays.

Considerations for Job Outlook: Projected employment growth reflects overall expansion of the death care services industry, due to the aging of the population. Job opportunities are expected to be good.

Personality Type: Enterprising-Social-Conventional. **Skills:** Management of Financial Resources; Social Perceptiveness; Management of Material Resources; Service Orientation; Management of Personnel Resources; Persuasion; Negotiation; Speaking. **Education and Training Program:** Funeral Direction/Service; Funeral Service and Mortuary Science, General. **Work Environment:** More often indoors than outdoors; disease or infections; contaminants; using your hands to handle, control, or feel objects, tools, or controls; standing.

OTHER FEDERAL JOB FACTS

RELATED GS SERIES: 0050 FUNERAL DIRECTING

- U.S. Federal Workforce: 368
- Average Length of Service: 5.9 years

- Percent Part-Time: 93.2%
- Percent Women: 16.0%
- Largest Age Bracket: 45–49 (19.0%)
- GS Level with Most Workers: 12
- Agency with Most Workers: Health and Human Services
- State with Most Workers: New York

Supervise or perform work at a hospital or other station involved in planning and directing details relating to funeral and burial services of deceased persons, including responsibility for the embalming and preparation of decedents; or administer the mortuary program of a federal agency.

Requirements: Knowledge of relevant policies, procedures, and public health regulations.

Geographers

- Education/Training Required: Master's degree
- Annual Earnings (Federal): $74,890
- Annual Earnings (All Industries): $71,470
- Earnings Growth Potential (Federal): 32.7% (low)
- Earnings Growth Potential (All Industries): 41.3% (high)
- Job Growth (Federal): 17.8%
- Job Growth (All Industries): 26.0%
- Annual Job Openings (Federal): 40
- Annual Job Openings (All Industries): 100

Study nature and use of areas of Earth's surface, relating and interpreting interactions of physical and cultural phenomena. Conduct research on physical aspects of a region, including land forms, climates, soils, plants, and animals, and conduct research on the spatial implications of human activities within a given area, including

social characteristics, economic activities, and political organization, as well as researching interdependence between regions at scales ranging from local to global. Create and modify maps, graphs, or diagrams, using geographical information software and related equipment and principles of cartography such as coordinate systems, longitude, latitude, elevation, topography, and map scales. Write and present reports of research findings. Develop, operate, and maintain geographical information (GIS) computer systems, including hardware, software, plotters, digitizers, printers, and video cameras. Locate and obtain existing geographic information databases. Analyze geographic distributions of physical and cultural phenomena on local, regional, continental, or global scales. Teach geography. Gather and compile geographic data from sources including censuses, field observations, satellite imagery, aerial photographs, and existing maps. Conduct fieldwork at outdoor sites. Study the economic, political, and cultural characteristics of a specific region's population. Provide consulting services in fields including resource development and management, business location and market area analysis, environmental hazards, regional cultural history, and urban social planning. Collect data on physical characteristics of specified areas, such as geological formations, climates, and vegetation, using surveying or meteorological equipment. Provide geographical information systems support to the private and public sectors.

Considerations for Job Outlook: Anthropologists are projected to have significant employment growth in the management, scientific, and technical consulting industry. Expected job growth for archaeologists is associated with large-scale construction projects that must comply with federal laws to preserve archaeological sites. Job competition is expected, especially for historians.

Personality Type: Investigative-Realistic-Artistic.
Skills: Science; Writing; Systems Analysis; Systems Evaluation; Operations Analysis; Reading Comprehension; Active Learning; Instructing.
Education and Training Program: Geography.
Work Environment: Indoors; sitting.

OTHER FEDERAL JOB FACTS
RELATED GS SERIES: 0150 GEOGRAPHY
TITLE ON USAJOBS: GEOGRAPHER

- U.S. Federal Workforce: 839
- Average Length of Service: 10.5 years
- Percent Part-Time: 4.5%
- Percent Women: 34.1%
- Largest Age Bracket: 40–44 (15.3%)
- GS Level with Most Workers: 13
- Agency with Most Workers: Interior
- State with Most Workers: Maryland

Compile, synthesize, analyze, interpret, and presentat information regarding the location, distribution, and interrelationships of and processes of change affecting such natural and human phenomena as the physical features of the Earth, climate, plant and animal life, and human settlements and institutions.

Requirements: Basic knowledge of the principles of geography and the general worldwide complexion of physical and human geography, plus familiarity with graphic representation of geographic facts. Intensive knowledge of specific geographic features and events; the ability to read and interpret photographs (especially aerial) and maps and charts of different scales and projections; taxonomic and bibliographic skills; skill in terrain analysis and in making analyses based upon location and distribution theory; the ability to present and illustrate geographic information in written and graphic form; the ability to integrate geographic information for presentation from an area or regional viewpoint, or from the viewpoint of an area of geographic emphasis; the ability to use statistics and statistical methods; and the ability to use geographic field methods.

Geoscientists, Except Hydrologists and Geographers

* Education/Training Required: Master's degree
* Annual Earnings (Federal): $92,410
* Annual Earnings (All Industries): $81,220
* Earnings Growth Potential (Federal): 34.0% (low)
* Earnings Growth Potential (All Industries): 46.9% (high)
* Job Growth (Federal): 7.4%
* Job Growth (All Industries): 17.5%
* Annual Job Openings (Federal): 80
* Annual Job Openings (All Industries): 1,540

Study the composition, structure, and other physical aspects of Earth. May use knowledge of geology, physics, and mathematics in exploration for oil, gas, minerals, or underground water or in waste disposal, land reclamation, or other environmental problems. May study Earth's internal composition, atmospheres, and oceans and its magnetic, electrical, and gravitational forces. Includes mineralogists, crystallographers, paleontologists, stratigraphers, geodesists, and seismologists. Analyze and interpret geological, geochemical, and geophysical information from sources such as survey data, well logs, bore holes, and aerial photos. Locate and estimate probable natural gas, oil, and mineral ore deposits and underground water resources, using aerial photographs, charts, or research and survey results. Plan and conduct geological, geochemical, and geophysical field studies and surveys, sample collection, or drilling and testing programs used to collect data for research or application. Analyze and interpret geological data, using computer software. Search for and review research articles or environmental, historical, and technical reports.

Assess ground and surface water movement to provide advice regarding issues such as waste management, route and site selection, and the restoration of contaminated sites. Prepare geological maps, cross-sectional diagrams, charts, and reports concerning mineral extraction, land use, and resource management, using results of field work and laboratory research. Investigate the composition, structure, and history of the Earth's crust through the collection, examination, measurement, and classification of soils, minerals, rocks, or fossil remains. Conduct geological and geophysical studies to provide information for use in regional development, site selection, and development of public works projects.

Considerations for Job Outlook: The need for energy services, environmental protection services, and responsible land and water management is expected to spur employment growth for these workers. Job seekers who have a master's degree in geoscience should have excellent opportunities.

Personality Type: Investigative-Realistic. **Skills:** Science; Reading Comprehension; Operations Analysis; Mathematics; Writing; Systems Evaluation; Systems Analysis; Active Listening. **Education and Training Program:** Geochemistry; Geochemistry and Petrology; Geological and Earth Sciences/Geosciences, Other; Geology/Earth Science, General; Geophysics and Seismology; Oceanography, Chemical and Physical; Paleontology. **Work Environment:** Indoors; sitting.

OTHER FEDERAL JOB FACTS

RELATED GS SERIES: 1313 GEOPHYSICS

TITLE ON USAJOBS: GEOPHYSICIST

* U.S. Federal Workforce: 450
* Average Length of Service: 18.3 years
* Percent Part-Time: 3.6%
* Percent Women: 22.7%
* Largest Age Bracket: 55–59 (22.0%)
* GS Level with Most Workers: 13

- ❊ Agency with Most Workers: Interior
- ❊ States with Most Workers: Colorado, California

Investigate, measure, analyze, evaluate, and interpret geophysical phenomena and artificially applied forces and fields related to the structure, composition, and physical properties of the earth and its atmosphere.

Requirements: Knowledge of the principles and techniques of geophysics and related sciences.

RELATED GS SERIES: 1360 OCEANOGRAPHY
TITLE ON USAJOBS: OCEANOGRAPHER

- ❊ U.S. Federal Workforce: 661
- ❊ Average Length of Service: 16.4 years
- ❊ Percent Part-Time: 7.6%
- ❊ Percent Women: 28.6%
- ❊ Largest Age Bracket: 50–54 (17.9%)
- ❊ GS Level with Most Workers: 13
- ❊ Agency with Most Workers: Defense
- ❊ State with Most Workers: Mississippi

Plan, organize, conduct, and administer seagoing and land-based study and research of ocean phenomena for the purpose of interpreting, predicting, utilizing, and controlling ocean forces and events.

Requirements: A fundamental background in chemistry, physics, and mathematics and appropriate knowledge in the field of oceanography.

Graphic Designers

- ❊ Education/Training Required: Bachelor's degree
- ❊ Annual Earnings (Federal): $73,130
- ❊ Annual Earnings (All Industries): $43,180
- ❊ Earnings Growth Potential (Federal): 31.1% (low)
- ❊ Earnings Growth Potential (All Industries): 38.8% (medium)
- ❊ Job Growth (Federal): 7.4%
- ❊ Job Growth (All Industries): 12.9%
- ❊ Annual Job Openings (Federal): 70
- ❊ Annual Job Openings (All Industries): 12,480

Design or create graphics to meet specific commercial or promotional needs such as packaging, displays, or logos. May use a variety of media to achieve artistic or decorative effects. Create designs, concepts, and sample layouts based on knowledge of layout principles and esthetic design concepts. Determine size and arrangement of illustrative material and copy; and select style and size of type. Confer with clients to discuss and determine layout designs. Develop graphics and layouts for product illustrations, company logos, and Internet websites. Review final layouts and suggest improvements as needed. Prepare illustrations or rough sketches of material, discussing them with clients or supervisors and making necessary changes. Use computer software to generate new images. Key information into computer equipment to create layouts for client or supervisor. Maintain archive of images, photos, or previous work products. Prepare notes and instructions for workers who assemble and prepare final layouts for printing. Draw and print charts, graphs, illustrations, and other artwork, using computer. Study illustrations and photographs to plan presentations of materials, products, or services. Research new software or design concepts. Mark up, paste, and assemble final layouts to prepare layouts for printer. Produce still and animated graphics for on-air and taped portions of television news broadcasts, using electronic video equipment. Photograph layouts, using cameras, to make layout prints for supervisors or clients. Develop negatives and prints to produce layout photographs, using negative and print developing equipment and tools.

Considerations for Job Outlook: Advertising firms that specialize in digital and interactive designs are expected to drive growth, but declines in print publishing will temper this growth. Competition is expected to be keen.

Personality Type: Artistic-Realistic-Enterprising. **Skills:** Operations Analysis; Negotiation; Time Management; Complex Problem Solving; Operation and Control; Equipment Selection; Installation; Programming. **Education and Training Program:** Agricultural Communication/Journalism; Commercial and Advertising Art; Computer Graphics; Design and Visual Communications, General; Graphic Design; Industrial and Product Design; Web Page, Digital/Multimedia and Information Resources Design. **Work Environment:** Indoors; sitting; making repetitive motions; using your hands to handle, control, or feel objects, tools, or controls.

OTHER FEDERAL JOB FACTS

RELATED GS SERIES: 1084 VISUAL INFORMATION

TITLE ON USAJOBS: VISUAL INFORMATION SPECIALIST

- ❀ U.S. Federal Workforce: 1,794
- ❀ Average Length of Service: 17.3 years
- ❀ Percent Part-Time: 2.1%
- ❀ Percent Women: 46.1%
- ❀ Largest Age Bracket: 55–59 (18.8%)
- ❀ GS Levels with Most Workers: 11, 12
- ❀ Agency with Most Workers: Defense
- ❀ State with Most Workers: District of Columbia

Communicate information through visual means; design and display visual materials, such as photographs, illustrations, diagrams, graphs, objects, models, slides, and charts.

Requirements: Knowledge of and ability to apply the principles of visual design; knowledge of the technical characteristics associated with various methods of visual display; and the ability to present subject-matter information in an effective visual form.

Health Diagnosing and Treating Practitioners, All Other

- ❀ Education/Training Required: Bachelor's degree
- ❀ Annual Earnings (Federal): $85,610
- ❀ Annual Earnings (All Industries): $65,220
- ❀ Earnings Growth Potential (Federal): 39.1% (median)
- ❀ Earnings Growth Potential (All Industries): 44.8% (high)
- ❀ Job Growth (Federal): 7.6%
- ❀ Job Growth (All Industries): 13.0%
- ❀ Annual Job Openings (Federal): 340
- ❀ Annual Job Openings (All Industries): 1,530

Considerations for Job Outlook: About average employment growth is projected.

JOB SPECIALIZATION: ACUPUNCTURISTS

Provide treatment of symptoms and disorders using needles and small electrical currents. May provide massage treatment. May also provide preventive treatments. Formulate herbal preparations to treat conditions considering herbal properties such as taste, toxicity, effects of preparation, contraindications, and incompatibilities. Maintain and follow standard quality, safety, environmental, and infection control policies and procedures. Maintain detailed and complete records of health care plans and prognoses. Dispense herbal formulas and inform patients of dosages and frequencies, treatment duration, possible side effects, and drug interactions. Consider Western medical procedures in health assessment, health care team communication, and care referrals. Adhere to local, state, and federal laws, regulations, and statutes. Treat patients, using tools such as needles, cups, ear balls, seeds, pellets, and nutritional supplements. Educate patients on topics such as meditation, ergonomics, stretching, exercise, nutrition, the healing process, breathing, and relaxation techniques. Evaluate treatment outcomes and recommend new or altered treatments as necessary to further promote, restore, or maintain health. Assess patients' general physical appearance to make diagnoses. Collect medical histories and general health and life style information from patients. Apply moxibustion directly or indirectly to patients, using Chinese, non-scarring, stick, or pole moxa. Apply heat or cold therapy to patients, using materials such as heat pads, hydrocollator packs, warm compresses, cold compresses, heat lamps, and vapor coolants.

Personality Type: Social-Realistic-Investigative. **Skills:** No data available. **Education and Training Program:** Acupuncture and Oriental Medicine. **Work Environment:** No data available.

JOB SPECIALIZATION: NURSE ANESTHETISTS

Administer anesthetics to induce total or partial loss of sensation or consciousness in patients during surgeries, births, or other medical and dental procedures. Manage patients' airway or pulmonary status using techniques such as endotracheal intubation, mechanical ventilation, pharmacological support, respiratory therapy, and extubation. Assess patients' medical histories to predict anesthesia response. Select, order, or administer anesthetics, adjuvant drugs, accessory drugs, fluids, or blood products as necessary. Prepare prescribed solutions and administer local, intravenous, spinal, or other anesthetics following specified methods and procedures. Develop anesthesia care plans. Monitor patients' responses, including skin color, pupil dilation, pulse, heart rate, blood pressure, respiration, ventilation, or urine output, using invasive and noninvasive techniques. Select, prepare, or use equipment, monitors, supplies, or drugs for the administration of anesthetics. Obtain informed consent from patients for anesthesia procedures. Respond to emergency situations by providing airway management, administering emergency fluids or drugs, or using basic or advanced cardiac life support techniques. Perform or manage regional anesthetic techniques such as local, spinal, epidural, caudal, nerve blocks, and intravenous blocks. Evaluate patients' post-surgical or post-anesthesia responses, taking appropriate corrective actions or requesting consultation if complications occur. Administer post-anesthesia medications or fluids to support patients' cardiovascular systems. Calibrate and test anesthesia equipment.

Personality Type: Investigative-Realistic-Social. **Skills:** Science; Equipment Maintenance; Equipment Selection; Operations Analysis; Operation and Control; Troubleshooting; Social Perceptiveness; Service Orientation. **Education and Training Program:** Nurse Anesthetist Training. **Work Environment:** Indoors; disease or infections; contaminants; using your hands to handle, control, or feel objects, tools, or controls; radiation; sounds, noisy.

JOB SPECIALIZATION: NURSE PRACTITIONERS

Provide advanced nursing care and treatment to patients. Perform physical examinations, order diagnostic tests, develop treatment plans, and prescribe drugs or other therapies. Order, perform, or interpret the results of diagnostic tests such as complete blood counts (CBCs), electrocardiograms (EKGs), and radiographs (X-rays). Analyze and interpret patients' histories, symptoms, physical findings, or diagnostic information to develop appropriate diagnoses. Prescribe medication dosages, routes, and frequencies based on patients' characteristics such as age and gender. Develop treatment plans based on scientific rationale, standards of care, and professional practice guidelines. Diagnose or treat acute health care problems such as illnesses, infections, and injuries. Prescribe medications based on efficacy, safety, and cost as legally authorized. Counsel patients about drug regimens and possible side effects or interactions with other substances such as food supplements, over-the-counter (OTC) medications, and herbal remedies. Recommend interventions to modify behavior associated with health risks. Educate patients about self-management of acute or chronic illnesses, tailoring instructions to patients' individual circumstances. Detect and respond to adverse drug reactions, with special attention to vulnerable populations such as infants, children, pregnant and lactating women, and older adults. Diagnose or treat chronic health-care problems such as high blood pressure and diabetes. Provide patients with information needed to promote health, reduce risk factors, or prevent disease or disability.

Personality Type: Social-Investigative-Realistic. **Skills:** Science; Operations Analysis; Service Orientation; Social Perceptiveness; Instructing; Reading Comprehension; Active Listening; Systems Analysis. **Education and Training Program:** Nursing Practice. **Work Environment:** Indoors; disease or infections; contaminants; using your hands to handle, control, or feel objects, tools, or controls; standing.

JOB SPECIALIZATION: NATUROPATHIC PHYSICIANS

Diagnose, treat, and help prevent diseases using a system of practice that is based on the natural healing capacity of individuals. May use physiological, psychological, or mechanical methods. May also use natural medicines, prescription or legend drugs, foods, herbs, or other natural remedies. Interview patients to document symptoms and health histories. Advise patients about therapeutic exercise and nutritional medicine regimens. Administer, dispense, or prescribe natural medicines such as food or botanical extracts, herbs, dietary supplements, vitamins, nutraceuticals, and amino acids. Document patients' histories, including identifying data, chief complaints, illnesses, previous medical or family histories, or psychosocial characteristics. Educate patients about health care management. Diagnose health conditions based on patients' symptoms and health histories, laboratory and diagnostic radiology test results, or other physiological measurements, such as electrocardiograms and electroencephalographs. Conduct physical examinations and physiological function tests for diagnostic purposes. Maintain professional development through activities such as post-graduate education, continuing education, preceptorships, and residency programs. Order diagnostic imaging procedures such as radiographs (X-rays), ultrasounds, mammograms, and bone densitometry tests, or refer patients to other health professionals for these procedures. Administer treatments or therapies, such as homeopathy, hydrotherapy, Oriental or Ayurvedic medicine, electrotherapy, and diathermy, using physical agents including air, heat, cold, water, sound, or ultraviolet light to catalyze the body to heal itself.

Personality Type: Investigative-Social. **Skills:** Science; Social Perceptiveness; Operations Analysis; Reading Comprehension; Judgment and Decision Making; Service Orientation; Systems Evaluation; Active Learning. **Education and Training Program:** Naturopathic Medicine/Naturopathy (ND). **Work Environment:** Indoors; disease or infections; sitting.

JOB SPECIALIZATION: ORTHOPTISTS

Diagnose and treat visual system disorders such as binocular vision and eye movement impairments. Perform diagnostic tests or measurements such as motor testing, visual acuity testing, lensometry, retinoscopy, and color vision testing. Examine patients with problems related to ocular motility, binocular vision, amblyopia, or strabismus. Evaluate, diagnose, or treat disorders of the visual system with an emphasis on binocular vision or abnormal eye movements. Develop non-surgical treatment plans for patients with conditions such as strabismus, nystagmus, and other visual disorders. Provide instructions to patients or family members concerning diagnoses or treatment plans. Provide non-surgical interventions, including corrective lenses, patches, drops, fusion exercises, or stereograms, to treat conditions such as strabismus, heterophoria, and convergence insufficiency. Develop or use special test and communication techniques to facilitate diagnosis and treatment of children or disabled patients. Interpret clinical or diagnostic test results. Refer patients to ophthalmic surgeons or other physicians. Provide training related to clinical methods or orthoptics to students, resident physicians, or other health professionals. Prepare diagnostic or treatment reports for other medical practitioners or therapists. Collaborate with ophthalmologists, optometrists, or other specialists in the diagnosis, treatment, or management of conditions such as glaucoma, cataracts, and retinal diseases.

Personality Type: Investigative-Social-Realistic. **Skills:** Science; Operations Analysis; Reading Comprehension; Service Orientation; Instructing; Systems Evaluation; Active Learning; Learning Strategies. **Education and Training Program:** Orthoptics/Orthoptist. **Work Environment:** Indoors; using your hands to handle, control, or feel objects, tools, or controls; sitting; disease or infections; making repetitive motions.

OTHER FEDERAL JOB FACTS

RELATED GS SERIES: 0601 GENERAL HEALTH SCIENCE

TITLE ON USAJOBS: HEALTH SCIENTIST

* U.S. Federal Workforce: 11,282
* Average Length of Service: 9.5 years

* Percent Part-Time: 14.4%
* Percent Women: 57.2%
* Largest Age Bracket: 55–59 (16.0%)
* GS Level with Most Workers: 14
* Agencies with Most Workers: Veterans Affairs, Health and Human Services
* State with Most Workers: Maryland

Perform research or other professional and scientific work that is specifically health-oriented in character, when the work is of such generalized or miscellaneous specialized nature that the positions are not more appropriately classifiable elsewhere.

Requirements: A background of knowledge, skills, and techniques gained from professional training in a health science or allied scientific field.

Health Technologists and Technicians, All Other

* Education/Training Required: Postsecondary vocational training
* Annual Earnings (Federal): $52,080
* Annual Earnings (All Industries): $38,490
* Earnings Growth Potential (Federal): 22.0% (very low)
* Earnings Growth Potential (All Industries): 34.1% (low)
* Job Growth (Federal): 7.6%
* Job Growth (All Industries): 18.7%
* Annual Job Openings (Federal): 80
* Annual Job Openings (All Industries): 3,200

Considerations for Job Outlook: Faster than average employment growth is projected.

JOB SPECIALIZATION:
ELECTRONEURODIAGNOSTIC TECHNOLOGISTS

Conduct electroneurodiagnostic (END) tests such as electroencephalograms, evoked potentials, polysomnograms, or electronystagmograms. May perform nerve conduction studies. Attach electrodes to patients using adhesives. Summarize technical data to assist physicians to diagnose brain, sleep, or nervous system disorders. Conduct tests or studies such as electroencephalography (EEG), polysomnography (PSG), nerve conduction studies (NCS), electromyography (EMG), and intraoperative monitoring (IOM). Calibrate, troubleshoot, or repair equipment and correct malfunctions as needed. Conduct tests to determine cerebral death, the absence of brain activity, or the probability of recovery from a coma. Measure visual, auditory, or somatosensory evoked potentials (EPs) to determine responses to stimuli. Indicate artifacts or interferences derived from sources outside of the brain, such as poor electrode contact or patient movement, on electroneurodiagnostic recordings. Measure patients' body parts and mark locations where electrodes are to be placed.

Personality Type: Realistic-Investigative. **Skills:** Repairing; Troubleshooting; Equipment Maintenance; Operation and Control; Quality Control Analysis; Operation Monitoring; Science; Learning Strategies. **Education and Training Program:** Electroneurodiagnostic/Electroencephalographic Technology/Technologist. **Work Environment:** Indoors; disease or infections; using your hands to handle, control, or feel objects, tools, or controls; sitting; contaminants.

JOB SPECIALIZATION: HEARING AID SPECIALISTS

Select and fit hearing aids for customers. Administer and interpret tests of hearing. Assess hearing instrument efficacy. Take ear impressions and prepare, design, and modify ear molds. Select and administer tests to evaluate hearing or related disabilities. Administer basic hearing tests including air conduction, bone conduction, or speech audiometry tests. Train clients to use hearing aids or other augmentative communication devices. Create or modify impressions for earmolds and hearing aid shells. Maintain or repair hearing aids or other communication devices. Demonstrate assistive listening devices (ALDs) to clients. Diagnose and treat hearing or related disabilities under the direction of an audiologist. Perform basic screening procedures such as pure tone screening, otoacoustic screening, immittance screening, and screening of ear canal status using otoscope. Assist audiologists in performing aural procedures such as real ear measurements, speech audiometry, auditory brainstem responses, electronystagmography, and cochlear implant mapping. Read current literature, talk with colleagues, and participate in professional organizations or conferences to keep abreast of developments in audiology.

Personality Type: Social-Investigative-Realistic. **Skills:** No data available. **Education and Training Program:** Hearing Instrument Specialist. **Work Environment:** No data available.

JOB SPECIALIZATION: OPHTHALMIC MEDICAL TECHNOLOGISTS AND TECHNICIANS

Conduct diagnostic tests such as central and peripheral visual field, ocular motility, color vision, or pharmacological pupil tests; or tonometry, tonography and tensilon tonography tests to determine intraocular pressure and pupil testing for size, equality, and reaction prior to dilation. Administer diagnostic tests such as central and peripheral visual field tests, ocular motility tests, color vision tests, and pharmacological pupil tests. Conduct tonometry or tonography tests to determine intraocular pressure. Administer topical ophthalmic or oral medications. Assist physicians in performing ophthalmic procedures. Maintain ophthalmic instruments or equipment. Measure and record lens power, using lensometers. Measure distance and near visual acuity, using appropriate tests. Operate ophthalmic equipment such as autorefractors, phoropters, tomographs, and retinoscopes. Perform refractometric procedures to determine subjective refractive errors or vertex distances. Collect ophthalmic information, using ultrasound equipment. Document patients' medical histories.

Personality Type: Realistic-Social-Investigative. **Skills:** Equipment Maintenance; Operation Monitoring; Service Orientation; Negotiation; Operation and Control; Instructing; Persuasion; Social Perceptiveness. **Education and Training Program:** Ophthalmic Technician/Technologist Training. **Work Environment:** Indoors; disease or infections; making repetitive motions; using your hands to handle, control, or feel objects, tools, or controls; standing; walking and running.

JOB SPECIALIZATION: NURSE MIDWIVES

Provide advanced nursing care and education to obstetrical and gynecological patients. Provide prenatal, intrapartum, postpartum, or newborn care to patients. Document findings of physical examinations. Write information in medical records or provide narrative summaries to communicate patient information to other health care providers. Consult with or refer patients to appropriate specialists when conditions exceed the scope of practice or expertise. Perform physical examinations by taking vital signs, checking neurological reflexes, examining breasts, or performing pelvic examinations. Document patients' health histories, symptoms, physical conditions, or other diagnostic information. Order and interpret diagnostic or laboratory tests. Initiate emergency interventions to stabilize patients. Monitor fetal development by listening to fetal heartbeat, taking external uterine measurements, identifying fetal position, or estimating fetal size and weight. Provide primary health care, including pregnancy and childbirth, to women. Prescribe medications as permitted by state regulations. Educate patients

and family members regarding prenatal, intrapartum, postpartum, newborn, or interconceptional care. Provide patients with direct family planning services such as inserting intrauterine devices, dispensing oral contraceptives, and fitting cervical barriers including cervical caps or diaphragms. Explain procedures to patients, family members, staff members, or others. Develop and implement individualized plans for health care management.

Personality Type: Social-Investigative. **Skills:** Science; Service Orientation; Social Perceptiveness; Persuasion; Operations Analysis; Systems Evaluation; Instructing; Judgment and Decision Making. **Education and Training Program:** Nurse Midwife/Nursing Midwifery. **Work Environment:** Indoors; disease or infections; using your hands to handle, control, or feel objects, tools, or controls; standing.

OTHER FEDERAL JOB FACTS

RELATED GS SERIES: 0698 ENVIRONMENTAL HEALTH TECHNICIAN

* U.S. Federal Workforce: 126
* Average Length of Service: 11.0 years
* Percent Part-Time: 7.9%
* Percent Women: 34.9%
* Largest Age Bracket: 50–54 (18.3%)
* GS Levels with Most Workers: 9, 7
* Agency with Most Workers: Defense
* State with Most Workers: California

Investigate, evaluate, and provide information on sanitation practices, techniques, and methods for the purpose of identifying, preventing, and eliminating environmental health hazards.

Requirements: Practical knowledge of basic environmental health concepts, principles, methods, and techniques, including survey techniques, inspection techniques, and control and eradication methods.

RELATED GS SERIES: 0649 MEDICAL INSTRUMENT TECHNICIAN

- ❋ U.S. Federal Workforce: 2,772
- ❋ Average Length of Service: 11.8 years
- ❋ Percent Part-Time: 3.5%
- ❋ Percent Women: 61.6%
- ❋ Largest Age Bracket: 55–59 (17.6%)
- ❋ GS Level with Most Workers: 8
- ❋ Agency with Most Workers: Veterans Affairs
- ❋ State with Most Workers: Texas

Perform diagnostic examinations or medical treatment procedures as part of the diagnostic or treatment plan for patients; operate or monitor diagnostic and therapeutic medical instruments and equipment associated with cardiac catheterization, pulmonary examinations and evaluations, heart bypass surgery, electrocardiography, electroencephalography, hemodialysis, and ultrasonography.

Requirements: Knowledge of the capabilities and operating characteristics of one or more kinds of instruments and a practical knowledge of human anatomy and physiology; also practical understanding of medical data generated by patient/equipment connections.

RELATED GS SERIES: 0648 THERAPEUTIC RADIOLOGIC TECHNOLOGIST

TITLE ON USAJOBS: RADIOLOGIC TECHNOLOGIST, THERAPEUTIC

- ❋ U.S. Federal Workforce: 196
- ❋ Average Length of Service: 9.5 years
- ❋ Percent Part-Time: 2.0%
- ❋ Percent Women: 55.6%
- ❋ Largest Age Bracket: 45–49 (23.0%)
- ❋ GS Level with Most Workers: 10
- ❋ Agency with Most Workers: Veterans Affairs
- ❋ States with Most Workers: Texas, Florida

Supervise or perform technical work that is subordinate to the work of radiotherapists or other professional or scientific personnel and that involves the operation of ionizing radiation equipment and sealed radiation sources as part of a therapeutic treatment plan for patients.

Requirements: Knowledge of radiation protection standards and techniques; the function of skeletal components and major organs; the properties of X-rays, electric power, and electric circuits; basic radiotherapeutic procedures and technical factors (control settings); how to position patients; basic medical terminology; first aid; skill to apply such knowledge to perform routine radiotherapeutic procedures; to understand and comply with X-ray requests; and to assist as a team member in radiotherapeutic treatments.

Healthcare Support Workers, All Other

- ❋ Education/Training Required: Short-term on-the-job training
- ❋ Annual Earnings (Federal): $40,020
- ❋ Annual Earnings (All Industries): $29,930
- ❋ Earnings Growth Potential (Federal): 22.1% (very low)
- ❋ Earnings Growth Potential (All Industries): 31.8% (low)
- ❋ Job Growth (Federal): 7.6%
- ❋ Job Growth (All Industries): 17.1%
- ❋ Annual Job Openings (Federal): 280
- ❋ Annual Job Openings (All Industries): 5,670

Considerations for Job Outlook: Faster than average employment growth is projected.

JOB SPECIALIZATION: SPEECH-LANGUAGE PATHOLOGY ASSISTANTS

Assist speech-language pathologists in the assessment and treatment of speech, language, voice, and fluency disorders. Implement speech and language programs or activities as planned and directed by speech-language pathologists. Monitor the use of alternative communication devices and systems. Collect and compile data to document clients' performance or assess program quality. Document clients' progress toward meeting established treatment objectives. Test or maintain equipment to ensure correct performance. Assist speech-language pathologists in the conduct of speech-language research projects. Conduct in-service training sessions, or family and community education programs. Perform support duties such as preparing materials, keeping records, maintaining supplies, and scheduling activities. Prepare charts, graphs, or other visual displays to communicate clients' performance information. Select or prepare speech-language instructional materials.

Personality Type: Social-Conventional. **Skills:** No data available. **Education and Training Program:** Speech-Language Pathology Assistant Training. **Work Environment:** No data available.

OTHER FEDERAL JOB FACTS

RELATED GS SERIES: 0625 AUTOPSY ASSISTANT

- ❀ U.S. Federal Workforce: 16
- ❀ Average Length of Service: 12.7 years
- ❀ Percent Part-Time: 25.0%
- ❀ Percent Women: 37.5%
- ❀ Largest Age Bracket: 40–44 (25.0%)
- ❀ GS Level with Most Workers: 5
- ❀ Agency with Most Workers: Veterans Affairs
- ❀ State with Most Workers: Texas

Provide technical assistance and related services to pathologists or physicians during autopsies and/or inquests.

Requirements: Knowledge of human anatomy and of embalming processes, plus skill in dissecting procedures.

RELATED GS SERIES: 0640 HEALTH AID AND TECHNICIAN

- ❀ U.S. Federal Workforce: 13,148
- ❀ Average Length of Service: 9.6 years
- ❀ Percent Part-Time: 19.3%
- ❀ Percent Women: 55.0%
- ❀ Largest Age Bracket: 45–49 (15.4%)
- ❀ GS Levels with Most Workers: 7, 6
- ❀ Agency with Most Workers: Veterans Affairs
- ❀ State with Most Workers: California

Do nonprofessional work of technical, specialized, or support nature in the field of health or medicine when the work is of such generalized, specialized, or miscellaneous nature that it is not covered by a more appropriate job title.

Requirements: No requirements available.

RELATED GS SERIES: 0636 REHABILITATION THERAPY ASSISTANT

- ❀ U.S. Federal Workforce: 956
- ❀ Average Length of Service: 12.2 years
- ❀ Percent Part-Time: 3.8%
- ❀ Percent Women: 63.6%
- ❀ Largest Age Bracket: 50–54 (18.2%)
- ❀ GS Level with Most Workers: 7
- ❀ Agency with Most Workers: Veterans Affairs
- ❀ State with Most Workers: Texas

Treat, instruct, or work with patients in carrying out therapeutic activities prescribed for their physical or mental rehabilitation; work in such fields of therapy as occupational, physical, corrective, manual arts, and educational.

H

Requirements: Ability to apply a practical knowledge of therapeutic methods and techniques; does not require a full professional knowledge of the concepts, principles, and practices of the specialized field of therapy.

Hydrologists

- ⊛ Education/Training Required: Master's degree
- ⊛ Annual Earnings (Federal): $83,370
- ⊛ Annual Earnings (All Industries): $73,670
- ⊛ Earnings Growth Potential (Federal): 32.3% (low)
- ⊛ Earnings Growth Potential (All Industries): 37.2% (medium)
- ⊛ Job Growth (Federal): 5.4%
- ⊛ Job Growth (All Industries): 18.2%
- ⊛ Annual Job Openings (Federal): 80
- ⊛ Annual Job Openings (All Industries): 380

Research the distribution, circulation, and physical properties of underground and surface waters; study the form and intensity of precipitation and its rate of infiltration into the soil, its movement through the earth, and its return to the ocean and atmosphere. Study and document quantities, distribution, disposition, and development of underground and surface waters. Prepare hydrogeologic evaluations of known or suspected hazardous waste sites and land treatment and feedlot facilities. Design and conduct scientific hydrogeological investigations to ensure that accurate and appropriate information is available for use in water resource management decisions. Collect and analyze water samples as part of field investigations or to validate data from automatic monitors. Apply research findings to help minimize the environmental impacts of pollution, waterborne diseases, erosion, and sedimentation. Measure and graph phenomena such as lake levels, stream flows,

and changes in water volumes. Investigate complaints or conflicts related to the alteration of public waters, gathering information, recommending alternatives, informing participants of progress, and preparing draft orders.

Considerations for Job Outlook: The need for energy services, environmental protection services, and responsible land and water management is expected to spur employment growth for these workers. Job seekers who have a master's degree in geoscience should have excellent opportunities.

Personality Type: Investigative-Realistic. **Skills:** Science; Programming; Mathematics; Systems Analysis; Writing; Systems Evaluation; Active Learning; Reading Comprehension. **Education and Training Program:** Geology/Earth Science, General; Hydrology and Water Resources Science; Oceanography, Chemical and Physical. **Work Environment:** More often indoors than outdoors; sitting.

OTHER FEDERAL JOB FACTS

RELATED GS SERIES: 1315 HYDROLOGY

TITLE ON USAJOBS: HYDROLOGIST

- ⊛ U.S. Federal Workforce: 2,419
- ⊛ Average Length of Service: 18.6 years
- ⊛ Percent Part-Time: 5.4%
- ⊛ Percent Women: 25.6%
- ⊛ Largest Age Bracket: 50–54 (20.4%)
- ⊛ GS Level with Most Workers: 12
- ⊛ Agency with Most Workers: Interior
- ⊛ State with Most Workers: California

Perform basic and applied research on water and water resources; collect, measure, analyze, and interpret information on water resources; forecast water supply and water flows; and develop new, improved, or more economical methods, techniques, and instruments.

Requirements: Professional knowledge of hydrology, the science concerned with the study of water in the hydrologic cycle.

Industrial Engineering Technicians

- ❋ Education/Training Required: Associate degree
- ❋ Annual Earnings (Federal): $64,910
- ❋ Annual Earnings (All Industries): $46,760
- ❋ Earnings Growth Potential (Federal): 17.6% (very low)
- ❋ Earnings Growth Potential (All Industries): 34.1% (low)
- ❋ Job Growth (Federal): 18.1%
- ❋ Job Growth (All Industries): 6.6%
- ❋ Annual Job Openings (Federal): 20
- ❋ Annual Job Openings (All Industries): 1,850

Apply engineering theory and principles to problems of industrial layout or manufacturing production, usually under the direction of engineering staff. May study and record time, motion, method, and speed involved in performance of production, maintenance, clerical, and other worker operations for such purposes as establishing standard production rates or improving efficiency. Recommend revision to methods of operation, material handling, equipment layout, or other changes to increase production or improve standards. Study time, motion, methods, and speed involved in maintenance, production, and other operations to establish standard production rate and improve efficiency. Interpret engineering drawings, schematic diagrams, or formulas and confer with management or engineering staff to determine quality and reliability standards. Recommend modifications to existing quality or production standards to achieve optimum quality within limits of equipment capability. Aid in planning work assignments in accordance with worker performance, machine capacity, production schedules, and anticipated delays. Observe workers using equipment to verify that equipment is being operated and maintained according to quality assurance standards. Observe workers operating equipment or performing tasks to determine time involved and fatigue rate, using timing devices. Prepare charts, graphs, and diagrams to illustrate workflow, routing, floor layouts, material handling, and machine utilization. Evaluate data and write reports to validate or indicate deviations from existing standards. Read worker logs, product processing sheets, and specification sheets to verify that records adhere to quality assurance specifications. Prepare graphs or charts of data or enter data into computer for analysis. Record test data, applying statistical quality control procedures.

Considerations for Job Outlook: Labor-saving efficiencies and the automation of many engineering support activities will limit the need for new engineering technicians. In general, opportunities should be best for job seekers who have an associate degree or other postsecondary training in engineering technology.

Personality Type: Investigative-Realistic-Conventional. **Skills:** Technology Design; Mathematics; Systems Evaluation; Monitoring; Systems Analysis; Quality Control Analysis; Judgment and Decision Making; Active Learning. **Education and Training Program:** Engineering/Industrial Management; Industrial Production Technologies/Technicians, Other; Industrial Technology/Technician; Manufacturing Engineering Technology/Technician. **Work Environment:** Indoors; contaminants; sounds, noisy; standing; hazardous equipment; walking and running.

OTHER FEDERAL JOB FACTS

RELATED GS SERIES: 0802 ENGINEERING TECHNICAL

TITLE ON USAJOBS: ENGINEERING TECHNICIAN

- ❋ U.S. Federal Workforce: 16,630
- ❋ Average Length of Service: 18.4 years
- ❋ Percent Part-Time: 3.6%
- ❋ Percent Women: 11.4%
- ❋ Largest Age Bracket: 50–54 (21.4%)
- ❋ GS Level with Most Workers: 11
- ❋ Agency with Most Workers: Defense
- ❋ State with Most Workers: Virginia

Perform engineering or architectural work at a level below professional and of a kind not covered by another OPM occupation.

Requirements: Practical knowledge of the methods and techniques of engineering or architecture and of the construction, application, properties, operations, and limitations of engineering systems, processes, structures, machinery, devices, and materials. Does not require a bachelor's degree in engineering or architecture.

Industrial Engineers

- ❋ Education/Training Required: Bachelor's degree
- ❋ Annual Earnings (Federal): $86,260
- ❋ Annual Earnings (All Industries): $75,110
- ❋ Earnings Growth Potential (Federal): 29.9% (low)
- ❋ Earnings Growth Potential (All Industries): 35.0% (low)
- ❋ Job Growth (Federal): 18.9%
- ❋ Job Growth (All Industries): 14.2%
- ❋ Annual Job Openings (Federal): 40
- ❋ Annual Job Openings (All Industries): 8,540

Design, develop, test, and evaluate integrated systems for managing industrial production processes, including human work factors, quality control, inventory control, logistics and material flow, cost analysis, and production coordination. Analyze statistical data and product specifications to determine standards and establish quality and reliability objectives of finished product. Develop manufacturing methods, labor utilization standards, and cost analysis systems to promote efficient staff and facility utilization. Recommend methods for improving utilization of personnel, material, and utilities. Plan and establish sequence of operations to fabricate and assemble parts or products and to promote efficient utilization. Apply statistical methods and perform mathematical calculations to determine manufacturing processes, staff requirements, and production standards. Coordinate quality control objectives and activities to resolve production problems, maximize product reliability, and minimize cost. Confer with vendors, staff, and management personnel regarding purchases, procedures, product specifications, manufacturing capabilities, and project status. Draft and design layout of equipment, materials, and workspace to illustrate maximum efficiency, using drafting tools and computer. Review production schedules, engineering specifications, orders, and related information to obtain knowledge of manufacturing methods, procedures, and activities. Communicate with management and user personnel to develop production and design standards. Estimate production cost and effect of product design changes for management review, action, and control.

Considerations for Job Outlook: Industrial engineers are expected to have employment growth of 14 percent from 2008–2018, faster than the average for all occupations. As firms look for new ways to reduce costs and raise productivity, they increasingly will turn to industrial engineers to develop more efficient processes and reduce costs, delays, and waste. This focus should lead to job growth for these engineers, even in some manufacturing industries with declining employment overall. Because their work is similar to that done in management occupations, many industrial engineers leave the occupation to become managers. Numerous openings will be created by the need to replace industrial engineers who transfer to other occupations or leave the labor force.

Personality Type: Investigative-Conventional-Enterprising. **Skills:** Management of Material Resources; Management of Financial Resources; Mathematics; Systems Evaluation; Systems Analysis; Reading Comprehension; Complex Problem Solving; Writing. **Education and Training Program:** Industrial Engineering. **Work Environment:** Indoors; sounds, noisy; contaminants; sitting; hazardous equipment.

JOB SPECIALIZATION: HUMAN FACTORS ENGINEERS AND ERGONOMISTS

Design objects, facilities, and environments to optimize human well-being and overall system performance, applying theory, principles, and data regarding the relationship between humans and respective technology. Investigate and analyze characteristics of human behavior and performance as it relates to the use of technology. Write, review, or comment on documents such as proposals, test plans, and procedures. Train users in task techniques or ergonomic principles. Review health, safety, accident, or worker compensation records to evaluate safety program effectiveness or to identify jobs with high incidents of injury. Provide human factors technical expertise on topics such as advanced user-interface technology development and the role of human users in automated or autonomous sub-systems in advanced vehicle systems. Investigate theoretical or conceptual issues, such as the human design considerations of lunar landers or habitats. Estimate time and resource requirements for ergonomic or human factors research or development projects.

Conduct interviews or surveys of users or customers to collect information on topics such as requirements, needs, fatigue, ergonomics, and interface. Recommend workplace changes to improve health and safety, using knowledge of potentially harmful factors, such as heavy loads and repetitive motions. Provide technical support to clients through activities such as rearranging workplace fixtures to reduce physical hazards or discomfort and modifying task sequences to reduce cycle time. Prepare reports or presentations summarizing results or conclusions of human factors engineering or ergonomics activities, such as testing, investigation, and validation.

Personality Type: No data available. **Skills:** No data available. **Education and Training Program:** Industrial Engineering. **Work Environment:** No data available.

OTHER FEDERAL JOB FACTS

RELATED GS SERIES: 0896 INDUSTRIAL ENGINEERING

TITLE ON USAJOBS: ENGINEER, INDUSTRIAL

- U.S. Federal Workforce: 1,244
- Average Length of Service: 12.8 years
- Percent Part-Time: 1.2%
- Percent Women: 26.4%
- Largest Age Bracket: 45–49 (17.4%)
- GS Level with Most Workers: 12
- Agency with Most Workers: Defense
- State with Most Workers: Maryland

Manage, supervise, lead, and/or perform professional engineering and scientific work to determine, evaluate, predict, and advise on effective ways for an organization to use its production factors (i.e., people, equipment, materials, information, and energy) to make or process a product or provide a service.

Requirements: Professional knowledge of and skills in industrial engineering.

RELATED GS SERIES: 0803 SAFETY ENGINEERING
TITLE ON USAJOBS: ENGINEER, SAFETY

* U.S. Federal Workforce: 532
* Average Length of Service: 17.0 years
* Percent Part-Time: 0.9%
* Percent Women: 20.1%
* Largest Age Bracket: 45–49 (21.2%)
* GS Level with Most Workers: 13
* Agency with Most Workers: Defense
* States with Most Workers: Florida, Alabama

Manage, supervise, lead, and/or perform professional engineering and scientific work involving safety, health, and environmental issues anticipating, dealing with, eliminating, or controlling hazardous conditions, exposures, and practices.

Requirements: Professional knowledge of and skills in safety engineering.

Industrial Machinery Mechanics

* Education/Training Required: Long-term on-the-job training
* Annual Earnings (Federal): $54,090
* Annual Earnings (All Industries): $44,470
* Earnings Growth Potential (Federal): 19.7% (very low)
* Earnings Growth Potential (All Industries): 34.4% (low)
* Job Growth (Federal): 24.7%
* Job Growth (All Industries): 7.3%
* Annual Job Openings (Federal): 70
* Annual Job Openings (All Industries): 6,240

Repair, install, adjust, or maintain industrial production and processing machinery or refinery and pipeline distribution systems.

Disassemble machinery and equipment to remove parts and make repairs. Repair and replace broken or malfunctioning components of machinery and equipment. Repair and maintain the operating condition of industrial production and processing machinery and equipment. Examine parts for defects such as breakage and excessive wear. Reassemble equipment after completion of inspections, testing, or repairs. Observe and test the operation of machinery and equipment in order to diagnose malfunctions, using voltmeters and other testing devices. Operate newly repaired machinery and equipment to verify the adequacy of repairs. Clean, lubricate, and adjust parts, equipment, and machinery. Analyze test results, machine error messages, and information obtained from operators in order to diagnose equipment problems. Record repairs and maintenance performed. Record parts and materials used and order or requisition new parts and materials as necessary. Study blueprints and manufacturers' manuals to determine correct installation and operation of machinery. Cut and weld metal to repair broken metal parts, fabricate new parts, and assemble new equipment. Demonstrate equipment functions and features to machine operators. Enter codes and instructions to program computer-controlled machinery.

Considerations for Job Outlook: The increasing reliance on machinery in manufacturing is expected to lead to employment growth for these maintenance and installation workers. Favorable job prospects are expected.

Personality Type: Realistic-Investigative-Conventional. **Skills:** Repairing; Equipment Maintenance; Troubleshooting; Installation; Operation Monitoring; Equipment Selection; Operation and Control; Quality Control Analysis. **Education and Training Program:** Heavy/Industrial Equipment Maintenance Technologies, Other; Industrial Mechanics and Maintenance Technology. **Work Environment:** Hazardous equipment;

contaminants; sounds, noisy; using your hands to handle, control, or feel objects, tools, or controls; standing; hazardous conditions.

OTHER FEDERAL JOB FACTS

RELATED GS SERIES: 4255 FUEL DISTRIBUTION SYSTEM MECHANIC

TITLE ON USAJOBS: FUEL DISTRIBUTION SYSTEMS MECHANIC

- ❋ U.S. Federal Workforce: 145
- ❋ Average Length of Service: 14.1 years
- ❋ Percent Part-Time: 0.0%
- ❋ Percent Women: 2.8%
- ❋ Largest Age Bracket: 45–49 (0.7%)
- ❋ GS Level with Most Workers: Not a GS occupation
- ❋ Agency with Most Workers: Defense
- ❋ States with Most Workers: Maryland, Texas

Maintain and overhaul pumps, control valves and meters, gauges, filters, separators, tanks, pipelines, and other equipment of one or more mechanical, aqua, or high-speed hydrant fueling and defueling systems.

Requirements: No requirements available.

RELATED GS SERIES: 4737 GENERAL EQUIPMENT MECHANIC

- ❋ U.S. Federal Workforce: 442
- ❋ Average Length of Service: 11.5 years
- ❋ Percent Part-Time: 0.0%
- ❋ Percent Women: 16.5%
- ❋ Largest Age Bracket: 50–54 (17.0%)
- ❋ GS Level with Most Workers: Not a GS occupation
- ❋ Agency with Most Workers: Defense
- ❋ State with Most Workers: Alabama

Install, maintain, and repair two or more different kinds of machinery or equipment, such as optical instruments, electronic controls, industrial machinery, electrical equipment, hydraulic systems, electromechanical devices, heavy mobile or automotive equipment, artillery systems and components, communications equipment.

Requirements: Knowledge of various trade practices associated with occupations in more than one job group and ability to perform the highest level of work in at least two of the trades involved.

RELATED GS SERIES: 5352 INDUSTRIAL EQUIPMENT MECHANIC

- ❋ U.S. Federal Workforce: 1,217
- ❋ Average Length of Service: 17.2 years
- ❋ Percent Part-Time: 0.4%
- ❋ Percent Women: 1.0%
- ❋ Largest Age Bracket: 50–54 (20.4%)
- ❋ GS Level with Most Workers: Not a GS occupation
- ❋ Agency with Most Workers: Defense
- ❋ State with Most Workers: Washington

Dismantle, repair, relocate, modify, maintain, align, and install general nonproduction industrial plant machinery, equipment, and systems such as bridge cranes, towveyor/conveyor and pneumatic tube systems, sandblasting machines, and other industrial plant support machinery and equipment; service, industrial waste, and flood control equipment such as compressors, pumps, and valves; and engraving machines, aircraft test block equipment, and fire extinguishing systems.

Requirements: Practical knowledge of the mechanical, hydraulic, and pneumatic systems and components of diverse industrial plant support machinery and equipment and other equipment that control industrial waste and provide service to establishments such as industrial plants, machine tool repair shops, and hospitals.

RELATED GS SERIES: 5317 LAUNDRY AND DRY CLEANING EQUIPMENT REPAIRING

TITLE ON USAJOBS: LAUNDRY & DRY CLEANING EQUIPMENT MECHANIC

- ❋ U.S. Federal Workforce: 30
- ❋ Average Length of Service: 20.8 years
- ❋ Percent Part-Time: 0.0%
- ❋ Percent Women: 0.0%
- ❋ Largest Age Bracket: 45–49 (26.7%)
- ❋ GS Level with Most Workers: Not a GS occupation
- ❋ Agency with Most Workers: Veterans Affairs
- ❋ States with Most Workers: Arkansas, New York

Perform repair work on laundry, dry cleaning, and related equipment.

Requirements: No requirements available.

RELATED GS SERIES: 5334 MARINE MACHINERY MECHANIC

TITLE ON USAJOBS: MARINE MACHINERY REPAIRER

- ❋ U.S. Federal Workforce: 2,084
- ❋ Average Length of Service: 13.5 years
- ❋ Percent Part-Time: 0.1%
- ❋ Percent Women: 5.4%
- ❋ Largest Age Bracket: 50–54 (16.8%)
- ❋ GS Level with Most Workers: Not a GS occupation
- ❋ Agency with Most Workers: Defense
- ❋ States with Most Workers: Washington, Virginia

Dismantle, repair, relocate, modify, maintain, align, and install a wide variety of marine machinery, equipment, and systems, such as propulsion machinery, propellers, rudders, cargo handling machinery, lifeboat davits, anchor handling gear, and missile tube equipment that are located aboard submarines, ships, and other floating craft.

Requirements: Practical knowledge of the mechanical, hydraulic, and pneumatic systems and components of diverse marine machinery and their attachments.

RELATED GS SERIES: 5350 PRODUCTION MACHINERY MECHANIC

- ❋ U.S. Federal Workforce: 539
- ❋ Average Length of Service: 16.5 years
- ❋ Percent Part-Time: 0.0%
- ❋ Percent Women: 2.4%
- ❋ Largest Age Bracket: 50–54 (19.9%)
- ❋ GS Level with Most Workers: Not a GS occupation
- ❋ Agency with Most Workers: Defense
- ❋ State with Most Workers: Oklahoma

Dismantle, repair, relocate, modify, maintain, align, and install fixed and semi-fixed production machinery, equipment, and systems, such as various standard and numerically controlled (N/C) machine tools, woodworking, and metalworking machines used in the production of goods.

Requirements: Practical knowledge of the mechanical, hydraulic, and pneumatic systems and components of diverse industrial production machinery and their attachments.

Installation, Maintenance, and Repair Workers, All Other

- ❋ Education/Training Required: Moderate-term on-the-job training
- ❋ Annual Earnings (Federal): $49,640
- ❋ Annual Earnings (All Industries): $35,520
- ❋ Earnings Growth Potential (Federal): 20.4% (very low)

- ❋ Earnings Growth Potential (All Industries): 43.0% (high)
- ❋ Job Growth (Federal): 7.8%
- ❋ Job Growth (All Industries): 9.2%
- ❋ Annual Job Openings (Federal): 270
- ❋ Annual Job Openings (All Industries): 4,180

Considerations for Job Outlook: About average employment growth is projected.

JOB SPECIALIZATION: GEOTHERMAL TECHNICIANS

Perform technical activities at power plants or individual installations necessary for the generation of power from geothermal energy sources. Monitor and control operating activities at geothermal power generation facilities and perform maintenance and repairs as necessary. Install, test, and maintain residential and commercial geothermal heat pumps. Identify and correct malfunctions of geothermal plant equipment, electrical systems, instrumentation, or controls. Install, maintain, or repair ground or water source-coupled heat pumps to heat and cool residential or commercial building air or water. Monitor and adjust operations of geothermal power plant equipment or systems. Adjust power production systems to meet load and distribution demands. Backfill piping trenches to protect pipes from damage. Calculate heat loss and heat gain factors for residential properties to determine heating and cooling required by installed geothermal systems. Design and lay out geothermal heat systems according to property characteristics, heating and cooling requirements, piping and equipment requirements, applicable regulations, or other factors. Determine the type of geothermal loop system most suitable to a specific property and its heating and cooling needs. Dig trenches for system piping to appropriate depths and lay piping in trenches. Prepare newly installed geothermal heat systems for operation by flushing, purging, or other actions. Identify equipment options, such as compressors, and make appropriate selections. Install and maintain geothermal system instrumentation or controls.

Personality Type: No data available. **Skills:** No data available. **Education and Training Program:** No data available. **Work Environment:** No data available.

OTHER FEDERAL JOB FACTS

RELATED GS SERIES: 4361 RUBBER EQUIPMENT REPAIRING

- ❋ U.S. Federal Workforce: 38
- ❋ Average Length of Service: 11.4 years
- ❋ Percent Part-Time: 0.0%
- ❋ Percent Women: 18.7%
- ❋ Largest Age Bracket: 35–39 (23.7%)
- ❋ GS Level with Most Workers: Not a GS occupation
- ❋ Agency with Most Workers: Defense
- ❋ State with Most Workers: Oklahoma

Repair, modify, test, and install synthetic and natural rubber equipment such as oil, water, and alcohol cells and tanks, life rafts, weather and pressure seals, and tires and tubes, using cold patching and vulcanizing repair procedures; check items for damage, select materials and prepare surface for repair, and operate low-pressure forming and curing equipment.

Requirements: No requirements available.

RELATED GS SERIES: 4717 BOAT BUILDING AND REPAIRING

TITLE ON USAJOBS: BOAT BUILDER AND REPAIRER

- ❋ U.S. Federal Workforce: 49
- ❋ Average Length of Service: 15.2 years
- ❋ Percent Part-Time: 0.0%

- ❋ Percent Women: 4.2%
- ❋ Largest Age Bracket: 55–59 (18.4%)
- ❋ GS Level with Most Workers: Not a GS occupation
- ❋ Agency with Most Workers: Homeland Security
- ❋ State with Most Workers: Maryland

Construct and repair aluminum, fiberglass, and plywood hulls of small craft and vessels; fit replacement planks, ribs, keelson, deadwood, and keel; caulk seams; repair decks and topsides; replace canvas and molding; install deadlights, metal or wood coatings, and marine hardware; and bore shaft logs and construct cradles to fit hulls.

Requirements: Skill and knowledge of more than one specific trade.

Related GS Series: 4807 Chemical Equipment Repairing

- ❋ U.S. Federal Workforce: 39
- ❋ Average Length of Service: 10.9 years
- ❋ Percent Part-Time: 0.0%
- ❋ Percent Women: 0.0%
- ❋ Largest Age Bracket: 55–59 (28.2%)
- ❋ GS Level with Most Workers: Not a GS occupation
- ❋ Agency with Most Workers: Defense
- ❋ State with Most Workers: Arkansas

Fabricate component parts, modify, overhaul, and repair chemical equipment, such as flame throwers, smoke generators, air compressors, and hand- and power-driven decontaminating devices, impregnating plants, and collective protectors.

Requirements: No requirements available.

Related GS Series: 4816 Protective and Safety Equipment Fabricating and Repairing

Title on USAJobs: Protective and Safety Equipment Maker and Repairer

- ❋ U.S. Federal Workforce: 99
- ❋ Average Length of Service: 16.5 years
- ❋ Percent Part-Time: 0.0%
- ❋ Percent Women: 2.9%
- ❋ Largest Age Bracket: 50–54 (25.3%)
- ❋ GS Level with Most Workers: Not a GS occupation
- ❋ Agency with Most Workers: Defense
- ❋ State with Most Workers: Alabama

Assemble, fabricate, modify, and/or repair a variety of protective and safety equipment, including but not limited to gas masks, hoods, respirators, filters, canisters, collective protectors, boots, detection kits, manually operated decontaminating equipment, safety glasses, and goggles.

Requirements: No requirements available.

Related GS Series: 6656 Special Weapons Systems Mechanic

- ❋ U.S. Federal Workforce: 45
- ❋ Average Length of Service: 12.3 years
- ❋ Percent Part-Time: 0.0%
- ❋ Percent Women: 2.2%
- ❋ Largest Age Bracket: 50–54 (31.1%)
- ❋ GS Level with Most Workers: Not a GS occupation
- ❋ Agency with Most Workers: Defense
- ❋ State with Most Workers: Utah

Examine, disassemble, repair, modify, assemble, calibrate, and test various types of advanced weapons systems and components; recondition and repair weapon skin sections, such as airframes and fins; and maintain special handling equipment and containers. Weapon components include such items as motor generators, hydrostats, differential switches, accelerometer gauges, control boxes, fusing components, batteries, radar, and so forth.

Requirements: Knowledge of pneumatic, hydraulic, mechanical, electrical, and electronic systems and circuitry, and of radioactive, explosive, electrical, and other hazards unique to advanced weapons.

RELATED GS SERIES: 5806 MOBILE EQUIPMENT SERVICING

TITLE ON USAJOBS: MOBILE EQUIPMENT SERVICER

- ❋ U.S. Federal Workforce: 361
- ❋ Average Length of Service: 8.5 years
- ❋ Percent Part-Time: 2.2%
- ❋ Percent Women: 3.0%
- ❋ Largest Age Bracket: 50–54 (16.6%)
- ❋ GS Level with Most Workers: Not a GS occupation
- ❋ Agency with Most Workers: Defense
- ❋ State with Most Workers: Missouri

Service automotive and mobile equipment such as automobiles, trucks, buses, ambulances, forklifts, and bulldozers; includes dispensing gasoline, checking fluid levels and tire pressures, inflating tires, washing cars, lubricating vehicles, installing simple accessory items, and changing and repairing tires and tubes.

Requirements: No requirements available.

RELATED GS SERIES: 6610 SMALL ARMS REPAIRING

TITLE ON USAJOBS: SMALL ARMS REPAIRER

- ❋ U.S. Federal Workforce: 588
- ❋ Average Length of Service: 9.5 years
- ❋ Percent Part-Time: 0.2%
- ❋ Percent Women: 6.6%

- ❋ Largest Age Bracket: 25–29 (14.5%)
- ❋ GS Level with Most Workers: Not a GS occupation
- ❋ Agency with Most Workers: Defense
- ❋ State with Most Workers: Alabama

Repair, rebuild, and modify small arms, which includes such weapons as machine guns, mortars, rocket launchers, recoilless rifles, and portable flame throwers.

Requirements: Knowledge of weapons' mechanical systems, the ability to recognize and determine the best method to correct malfunctions, and the skill to fit and adjust mechanical parts and assemblies.

RELATED GS SERIES: 4819 BOWLING EQUIPMENT REPAIRING

TITLE ON USAJOBS: BOWLING EQUIPMENT REPAIRER

- ❋ U.S. Federal Workforce: 14
- ❋ Average Length of Service: 18.1 years
- ❋ Percent Part-Time: 0.0%
- ❋ Percent Women: 0.0%
- ❋ Largest Age Bracket: 50–54 (28.6%)
- ❋ GS Level with Most Workers: Not a GS occupation
- ❋ Agency with Most Workers: Defense
- ❋ State with Most Workers: California

Maintain and repair bowling equipment; make operational and test equipment checks, diagnose malfunctions, disassemble, repair, and replace parts, reassemble and adjust equipment, and make final operational tests; also condition and make minor repairs to bowling lane approaches and pins.

Requirements: Knowledge and application of mechanical and electrical operating principles of the equipment, the ability to determine malfunctions, and the skill to repair and maintain a variety of bowling equipment.

Instructional Coordinators

- ❋ Education/Training Required: Master's degree
- ❋ Annual Earnings (Federal): $83,910
- ❋ Annual Earnings (All Industries): $58,780
- ❋ Earnings Growth Potential (Federal): 26.8% (low)
- ❋ Earnings Growth Potential (All Industries): 43.0% (high)
- ❋ Job Growth (Federal): 7.6%
- ❋ Job Growth (All Industries): 23.2%
- ❋ Annual Job Openings (Federal): 80
- ❋ Annual Job Openings (All Industries): 6,060

Develop instructional material, coordinate educational content, and incorporate current technology in specialized fields that provide guidelines to educators and instructors for developing curricula and conducting courses. Conduct or participate in workshops, committees, and conferences designed to promote the intellectual, social, and physical welfare of students. Plan and conduct teacher training programs and conferences dealing with new classroom procedures, instructional materials and equipment, and teaching aids. Advise teaching and administrative staff in curriculum development, use of materials and equipment, and implementation of state and federal programs and procedures. Recommend, order, or authorize purchase of instructional materials, supplies, equipment, and visual aids designed to meet student educational needs and district standards. Interpret and enforce provisions of state education codes and rules and regulations of state education boards. Confer with members of educational committees and advisory groups to obtain knowledge of subject areas and to relate curriculum materials to specific subjects, individual student needs, and occupational areas.

Considerations for Job Outlook: Continued efforts to improve educational standards are expected to result in more new jobs for these workers. Opportunities should be best for job seekers who train teachers to use classroom technology and who have experience in reading, mathematics, and science.

Personality Type: Social-Investigative-Enterprising. **Skills:** Learning Strategies; Systems Evaluation; Instructing; Management of Material Resources; Negotiation; Writing; Management of Personnel Resources; Systems Analysis. **Education and Training Program:** Curriculum and Instruction; Educational/Instructional Technology. **Work Environment:** Indoors; standing.

JOB SPECIALIZATION: INSTRUCTIONAL DESIGNERS AND TECHNOLOGISTS

Develop instructional materials and products and assist in the technology-based redesign of courses. Assist faculty in learning about, becoming proficient in, and applying instructional technology. Observe and provide feedback on instructional techniques, presentation methods, or instructional aids. Edit instructional materials, such as books, simulation exercises, lesson plans, instructor guides, and tests. Develop measurement tools to evaluate the effectiveness of instruction or training interventions. Develop instructional materials, such as lesson plans, handouts, or examinations. Define instructional, learning, or performance objectives. Assess effectiveness and efficiency of instruction according to ease of instructional technology use and student learning, knowledge transfer, and satisfaction. Analyze performance data to determine effectiveness of instructional systems, courses, or instructional materials. Research and evaluate emerging instructional technologies or methods. Recommend instructional methods, such as individual or group instruction, self-study, lectures, demonstrations, simulation exercises, and role-playing, appropriate for content and learner characteristics. Recommend changes to curricula or delivery methods, based on information such as instructional effectiveness data, current or future performance requirements, feasibility, and costs. Provide technical support to clients in the implementation of designed instruction or in task analyses and instructional systems design.

Personality Type: No data available. **Skills:** No data available. **Education and Training Program:** Curriculum and Instruction; Educational/Instructional Technology. **Work Environment:** No data available.

OTHER FEDERAL JOB FACTS

RELATED GS SERIES: 1750 INSTRUCTIONAL SYSTEMS

TITLE ON USAJOBS: INSTRUCTIONAL SYSTEMS SPECIALIST

* U.S. Federal Workforce: 1,983
* Average Length of Service: 13.1 years
* Percent Part-Time: 0.2%
* Percent Women: 42.8%
* Largest Age Bracket: 55–59 (21.6%)
* GS Level with Most Workers: 12
* Agency with Most Workers: Defense
* State with Most Workers: Texas

Administer, supervise, advise on, design, develop, or provide educational or training services in formal education or training programs.

Requirements: Knowledge of learning theory and the principles, methods, practices, and techniques of one or more specialties of the instructional systems field; may require knowledge of one or more subjects or occupations in which educational or training instruction is provided.

Interpreters and Translators

* Education/Training Required: Long-term on-the-job training
* Annual Earnings (Federal): $67,600
* Annual Earnings (All Industries): $40,860
* Earnings Growth Potential (Federal): 22.5% (very low)
* Earnings Growth Potential (All Industries): 44.2% (high)
* Job Growth (Federal): 18.4%
* Job Growth (All Industries): 22.2%
* Annual Job Openings (Federal): 20
* Annual Job Openings (All Industries): 2,340

Translate or interpret written, oral, or sign language text into another language for others. Follow ethical codes that protect the confidentiality of information. Identify and resolve conflicts related to the meanings of words, concepts, practices, or behaviors. Proofread, edit, and revise translated materials. Translate messages simultaneously or consecutively into specified languages orally or by using hand signs, maintaining message content, context, and style as much as possible. Check translations of technical terms and terminology to ensure that they are accurate and remain consistent throughout translation revisions. Read written materials such as legal documents, scientific works, or news reports and rewrite material into specified languages. Refer to reference materials such as dictionaries, lexicons, encyclopedias, and computerized terminology banks as needed to ensure translation accuracy. Compile terminology and information to be used in translations, including technical terms such as those for legal or medical material. Adapt translations to students' cognitive and grade levels, collaborating with educational team members as necessary. Listen to speakers' statements to determine meanings and to prepare translations, using electronic listening systems as necessary. Check original texts or confer with authors to ensure that translations retain the content, meaning, and feeling of the original material.

Considerations for Job Outlook: Globalization and large increases in the number of nonnative English speakers in the United States are expected to lead to employment increases for these workers. Job prospects vary by specialty and language.

Personality Type: Artistic-Social. **Skills:** Writing; Reading Comprehension; Active Listening; Speaking; Social Perceptiveness; Service Orientation; Learning Strategies; Monitoring. **Education and Training Program:** African Languages, Literatures, and Linguistics; Albanian Language and Literature; American Indian/Native American Languages, Literatures, and Linguistics; American Sign Language (ASL); Ancient Near Eastern and Biblical Languages, Literatures, and Linguistics; Ancient/Classical Greek Language and Literature; Arabic Language and Literature; Australian/Oceanic/Pacific Languages, Literatures, and Linguistics; Baltic Languages, Literatures, and Linguistics; Bengali Language and Literature; others. **Work Environment:** Indoors; sitting; making repetitive motions.

OTHER FEDERAL JOB FACTS
RELATED GS SERIES: 1040 LANGUAGE SPECIALIST

- U.S. Federal Workforce: 1,030
- Average Length of Service: 10.1 years
- Percent Part-Time: 15.0%
- Percent Women: 56.9%
- Largest Age Bracket: 50–54 (17.7%)
- GS Level with Most Workers: 12
- Agency with Most Workers: Justice
- States with Most Workers: New York, District of Columbia

Objectively and accurately render from a foreign language into English or from English into a foreign language the spoken or written word.

Requirements: Knowledge of English and of one or more other languages. Depending on level of position, varies from knowledge of vocabulary, grammar, syntax, and pronunciation necessary to convey facts and simple ideas to a highly developed native knowledge of the language and culture necessary for accurately understanding complex facts and abstractions and clearly expressing them in another language. Also varies from the literal rendering of words, phrases, and sentences from one language to another to skill in instantly interpreting or translating concrete factual information and abstract ideas between two languages with such accuracy that the product can be used with confidence in making policy decisions, legal determinations, or the like. Subject-matter knowledge varies from knowledge of common subjects in everyday conversation and the popular press to broad knowledge of the vocabularies, concepts, principles, and theories of fields such as international law, physical science, medicine, technology, and politics. For additional information, see www.usajobs.gov/EI/linguists.asp.

Lawyers

- Education/Training Required: First professional degree
- Annual Earnings (Federal): $131,410
- Annual Earnings (All Industries): $113,240
- Earnings Growth Potential (Federal): 33.8% (low)
- Earnings Growth Potential (All Industries): 51.2% (very high)
- Job Growth (Federal): 8.4%
- Job Growth (All Industries): 13.0%
- Annual Job Openings (Federal): 960
- Annual Job Openings (All Industries): 24,040

Represent clients in criminal and civil litigation and other legal proceedings, draw up legal documents, and manage or advise clients on legal transactions. May specialize in a single area or may practice broadly in many areas of law. Advise clients concerning business transactions, claim liability, advisability of prosecuting or defending lawsuits, or legal rights and obligations. Interpret laws, rulings, and regulations for individuals and businesses. Analyze the probable outcomes of cases, using knowledge of legal precedents. Present and summarize cases to judges and juries. Gather evidence to formulate defense or to initiate legal actions by such means as interviewing clients and witnesses to ascertain the facts of a case. Evaluate findings and develop strategies and arguments in preparation for presentation of cases. Represent clients in court or before government agencies. Examine legal data to determine advisability of defending or prosecuting lawsuit. Select jurors, argue motions, meet with judges, and question witnesses during the course of a trial. Present evidence to defend clients or prosecute defendants in criminal or civil litigation. Study Constitution, statutes, decisions, regulations, and ordinances of quasi-judicial bodies to determine ramifications for cases. Prepare and draft legal documents, such as wills, deeds, patent applications, mortgages, leases, and contracts. Prepare legal briefs and opinions and file appeals in state and federal courts of appeal. Negotiate settlements of civil disputes. Confer with colleagues with specialties in appropriate areas of legal issue to establish and verify bases for legal proceedings.

Considerations for Job Outlook: Growth in both population and business activity is expected to result in more civil disputes and criminal cases and, thus, employment growth for lawyers. This growth is expected to be constrained, however, as paralegals and other workers perform some of the tasks previously done by lawyers. Keen competition is expected.

Personality Type: Enterprising-Investigative. **Skills:** Persuasion; Negotiation; Speaking; Writing; Critical Thinking; Judgment and Decision Making; Active Learning; Active Listening. **Education and Training Program:** Advanced Legal Research/Studies, General (LL.M., M.C.L., M.L.I., M.S.L., J.S.D./S.J.D.); American/U.S. Law/Legal Studies/Jurisprudence (LL.M., M.C.J., J.S.D./S.J.D.); Banking, Corporate, Finance, and Securities Law (LL.M., J.S.D./S.J.D.); Canadian Law/Legal Studies/Jurisprudence (LL.M., M.C.J., J.S.D./S.J.D.); Comparative Law (LL.M., M.C.L., J.S.D./S.J.D.); Energy, Environment, and Natural Resources Law (LL.M., M.S., J.S.D./S.J.D.); Health Law (LL.M., M.J., J.S.D./S.J.D.); others. **Work Environment:** Indoors; sitting.

OTHER FEDERAL JOB FACTS

RELATED GS SERIES: 0905 GENERAL ATTORNEY

TITLE ON USAJOBS: ATTORNEY

- U.S. Federal Workforce: 34,510
- Average Length of Service: 13.1 years
- Percent Part-Time: 3.2%
- Percent Women: 46.1%
- Largest Age Bracket: 35–39 (15.1%)
- GS Level with Most Workers: 15
- Agency with Most Workers: Justice
- State with Most Workers: District of Columbia

Prepare cases for trial; try cases before a court or an administrative body or persons having quasi-judicial power; render legal advice and services with respect to questions, regulations, practices, or other matters falling within the purview of a federal government agency; prepare interpretative and administrative orders, rules, or regulations to give effect to the provisions of governing statutes or other requirements of law; draft, negotiate, or examine contracts or other legal documents required by an agency's activities; draft, prepare formal comments, or otherwise make substantive recommendations with respect to proposed legislation; edit and prepare for publication statutes enacted by Congress, opinions, or discussions of a court, commission, or board; draft and review decisions for consideration and adoption by agency officials.

Requirements: Admission to the bar. For additional information, see www.usajobs.gov/EI/attorneys.asp.

Related GS Series: 0904 Law Clerk

- ❋ U.S. Federal Workforce: 377
- ❋ Average Length of Service: 0.3 years
- ❋ Percent Part-Time: 2.7%
- ❋ Percent Women: 58.4%
- ❋ Largest Age Bracket: 25–29 (71.4%)
- ❋ GS Level with Most Workers: 11
- ❋ Agency with Most Workers: Justice
- ❋ State with Most Workers: District of Columbia

Perform professional legal work as law clerk trainees.

Requirements: Graduation from a recognized law school or equivalent experience, pending admission to the bar. For additional information, see www.usajobs.gov/EI/attorneys.asp.

Related GS Series: 1222 Patent Attorney

- ❋ U.S. Federal Workforce: 303
- ❋ Average Length of Service: 14.8 years
- ❋ Percent Part-Time: 1.3%
- ❋ Percent Women: 23.4%
- ❋ Largest Age Bracket: 45–49 (24.1%)
- ❋ GS Level with Most Workers: 15
- ❋ Agency with Most Workers: Commerce
- ❋ State with Most Workers: Virginia

Render opinions on validity and infringement of patents; negotiate patent licenses; settle patent claims; negotiate patent clauses in contracts; provide professional legal advice to contracting officers and other procurement personnel on patent matters; and prepare and/or present briefs and arguments before the Patent Office or before the federal courts. May perform similar professional legal functions regarding trademark.

Requirements: A degree in one of the scientific or engineering disciplines, plus a law degree and admission to the bar. For additional information, see www.usajobs.gov/EI/attorneys.asp.

Librarians

- ❋ Education/Training Required: Master's degree
- ❋ Annual Earnings (Federal): $77,970
- ❋ Annual Earnings (All Industries): $53,710
- ❋ Earnings Growth Potential (Federal): 26.7% (low)
- ❋ Earnings Growth Potential (All Industries): 37.7% (medium)
- ❋ Job Growth (Federal): 7.8%
- ❋ Job Growth (All Industries): 7.8%
- ❋ Annual Job Openings (Federal): 40
- ❋ Annual Job Openings (All Industries): 5,450

Administer libraries and perform related library services. Work in a variety of settings, including public libraries, schools, colleges and universities, museums, corporations, government agencies, law firms, non-profit organizations, and health-care providers. Tasks may include selecting, acquiring, cataloguing, classifying, circulating, and maintaining library materials and furnishing reference, bibliographical, and readers' advisory services. May perform in-depth,

strategic research and synthesize, analyze, edit, and filter information. May set up or work with databases and information systems to catalogue and access information. Analyze patrons' requests to determine needed information, and assist in furnishing or locating that information. Search standard reference materials, including online sources and the Internet, to answer patrons' reference questions. Teach library patrons basic computer skills, such as searching computerized databases. Plan and teach classes on topics such as information literacy, library instruction, and technology use. Review and evaluate materials, using book reviews, catalogs, faculty recommendations, and current holdings, to select and order print, audiovisual, and electronic resources. Locate unusual or unique information in response to specific requests. Explain use of library facilities, resources, equipment, and services, and provide information about library policies. Plan and deliver client-centered programs and services such as special services for corporate clients, storytelling for children, newsletters, or programs for special groups. Respond to customer complaints, taking action as necessary. Organize collections of books, publications, documents, audiovisual aids, and other reference materials for convenient access. Develop library policies and procedures. Confer with colleagues, faculty, and community members and organizations to conduct informational programs, make collection decisions, and determine library services to offer.

Considerations for Job Outlook: Growth in the number of librarians is expected to be limited by government budget constraints and the increasing use of electronic resources. Although many openings are expected, there will be competition for jobs in some regions.

Personality Type: Conventional-Social-Enterprising. **Skills:** Management of Material Resources; Service Orientation; Instructing; Operations Analysis; Negotiation; Writing; Systems Evaluation;

Systems Analysis. **Education and Training Program:** Library and Information Science; Library Science, Other; School Librarian/School Library Media Specialist. **Work Environment:** Indoors; sitting; making repetitive motions.

OTHER FEDERAL JOB FACTS

Related GS Series: 1410 Librarian

- ❋ U.S. Federal Workforce: 1,232
- ❋ Average Length of Service: 16.9 years
- ❋ Percent Part-Time: 4.7%
- ❋ Percent Women: 74.4%
- ❋ Largest Age Bracket: 55–59 (25.0%)
- ❋ GS Levels with Most Workers: 11, 12
- ❋ Agency with Most Workers: Defense
- ❋ States with Most Workers: District of Columbia, Maryland

Select, organize, preserve, access, and disseminate information; determine the most cost-effective way to provide information that will best meet user needs; perform collection development, acquisition, cataloging and classification, reference, circulation, computer system and database management, and preservation.

Requirements: Professional knowledge of the theories, objectives, principles, and techniques of librarianship. May also require knowledge of one or more subject-matter specializations or foreign languages.

Licensed Practical and Licensed Vocational Nurses

- ❋ Education/Training Required: Postsecondary vocational training
- ❋ Annual Earnings (Federal): $43,160
- ❋ Annual Earnings (All Industries): $39,820
- ❋ Earnings Growth Potential (Federal): 20.5% (very low)

- ❋ Earnings Growth Potential (All Industries): 27.4% (low)
- ❋ Job Growth (Federal): 7.6%
- ❋ Job Growth (All Industries): 20.6%
- ❋ Annual Job Openings (Federal): 590
- ❋ Annual Job Openings (All Industries): 39,130

Care for ill, injured, convalescent, or disabled persons in hospitals, nursing homes, clinics, private homes, group homes, and similar institutions. May work under the supervision of a registered nurse. Licensing required. Administer prescribed medications or start intravenous fluids, recording times and amounts on patients' charts. Observe patients, charting and reporting changes in patients' conditions, such as adverse reactions to medication or treatment, and taking any necessary actions. Provide basic patient care and treatments such as taking temperatures or blood pressures, dressing wounds, treating bedsores, giving enemas or douches, rubbing with alcohol, massaging, or performing catheterizations. Sterilize equipment and supplies, using germicides, sterilizer, or autoclave. Answer patients' calls and determine how to assist them. Work as part of a health-care team to assess patient needs, plan and modify care, and implement interventions. Measure and record patients' vital signs, such as height, weight, temperature, blood pressure, pulse, and respiration. Collect samples such as blood, urine, and sputum from patients and perform routine laboratory tests on samples. Prepare patients for examinations, tests, or treatments and explain procedures. Assemble and use equipment such as catheters, tracheotomy tubes, and oxygen suppliers. Evaluate nursing intervention outcomes, conferring with other health-care team members as necessary. Record food and fluid intake and output. Help patients with bathing, dressing, maintaining personal hygiene, moving in bed, or standing and walking. Apply compresses, ice bags, and hot water bottles. Inventory and requisition supplies and instruments.

Considerations for Job Outlook: An aging population is expected to boost demand for nursing services. Job prospects are expected to be very good, especially in employment settings that serve older populations.

Personality Type: Social-Realistic. **Skills:** Science; Social Perceptiveness; Service Orientation; Operation and Control; Persuasion; Negotiation; Speaking; Time Management. **Education and Training Program:** Licensed Practical/Vocational Nurse Training. **Work Environment:** Indoors; disease or infections; standing; walking and running; contaminants; using your hands to handle, control, or feel objects, tools, or controls.

OTHER FEDERAL JOB FACTS

RELATED GS SERIES: 0620 PRACTICAL NURSE

TITLE ON USAJOBS: NURSE, PRACTICAL

- ❋ U.S. Federal Workforce: 16,156
- ❋ Average Length of Service: 9.4 years
- ❋ Percent Part-Time: 4.8%
- ❋ Percent Women: 84.1%
- ❋ Largest Age Bracket: 50–54 (17.1%)
- ❋ GS Level with Most Workers: 6
- ❋ Agency with Most Workers: Veterans Affairs
- ❋ State with Most Workers: Texas

Perform a variety of nursing care and practices that do not require full professional nurse education.

Requirements: Licensure as a practical or vocational nurses by a state, territory, or the District of Columbia.

Life, Physical, and Social Science Technicians, All Other

- ❋ Education/Training Required: Associate degree
- ❋ Annual Earnings (Federal): $48,280
- ❋ Annual Earnings (All Industries): $42,110

⊛ Earnings Growth Potential (Federal): 38.4% (median)

⊛ Earnings Growth Potential (All Industries): 41.8% (high)

⊛ Job Growth (Federal): 7.7%

⊛ Job Growth (All Industries): 13.3%

⊛ Annual Job Openings (Federal): 310

⊛ Annual Job Openings (All Industries): 3,640

Considerations for Job Outlook: About average employment growth is projected.

JOB SPECIALIZATION: PRECISION AGRICULTURE TECHNICIANS

Apply geospatial technologies, including geographic information systems (GIS) and Global Positioning System (GPS), to agricultural production and management activities, such as pest scouting, site-specific pesticide application, yield mapping, and variable-rate irrigation. May use computers to develop and analyze maps and remote sensing images to compare physical topography with data on soils, fertilizer, pests, or weather. Collect information about soil and field attributes, yield data, or field boundaries, using field data recorders and basic geographic information systems (GIS). Create, layer, and analyze maps showing precision agricultural data such as crop yields, soil characteristics, input applications, terrain, drainage patterns, and field management history. Document and maintain records of precision agriculture information. Compile and analyze geospatial data to determine agricultural implications of factors such as soil quality, terrain, field productivity, fertilizers, and weather conditions. Divide agricultural fields into georeferenced zones based on soil characteristics and production potentials. Develop soil sampling grids or identify sampling sites, using geospatial technology, for soil testing on characteristics such as nitrogen, phosphorus, and potassium content, pH, and micronutrients. Compare crop yield maps with maps of soil test data, chemical application patterns, or other information to develop site-specific crop management plans. Apply knowledge of government regulations when making agricultural recommendations. Recommend best crop varieties and seeding rates for specific field areas, based on analysis of geospatial data. Draw and read maps such as soil, contour, and plat maps. Process and analyze data from harvester monitors to develop yield maps.

Personality Type: Realistic-Investigative-Conventional. **Skills:** Equipment Maintenance; Repairing; Science; Troubleshooting; Equipment Selection; Operations Analysis; Quality Control Analysis; Operation and Control. **Education and Training Program:** Agricultural Mechanics and Equipment/Machine Technology. **Work Environment:** Outdoors; very hot or cold temperatures.

JOB SPECIALIZATION: QUALITY CONTROL ANALYSTS

Conduct tests to determine quality of raw materials, bulk intermediate and finished products. May conduct stability sample tests. Train other analysts to perform laboratory procedures and assays. Perform visual inspections of finished products. Serve as a technical liaison between quality control and other departments, vendors, or contractors. Participate in internal assessments and audits as required. Identify and troubleshoot equipment problems. Evaluate new technologies and methods to make recommendations regarding their use. Ensure that lab cleanliness and safety standards are maintained. Develop and qualify new testing methods. Coordinate testing with contract laboratories and vendors. Write technical reports or documentation such as deviation reports, testing protocols, and trend analyses.

Write or revise standard quality control operating procedures. Supply quality control data necessary for regulatory submissions. Receive and inspect raw materials. Review data from contract laboratories to ensure accuracy and regulatory compliance. Prepare or review required method transfer documentation including technical transfer protocols or reports. Perform validations or transfers of analytical methods in accordance with applicable policies or guidelines. Participate in out-of-specification and failure investigations and recommend corrective actions. Monitor testing procedures to ensure that all tests are performed according to established item specifications, standard test methods, or protocols. Investigate or report questionable test results.

Personality Type: Conventional-Investigative-Realistic. **Skills:** No data available. **Education and Training Program:** Quality Control Technology/Technician. **Work Environment:** No data available.

JOB SPECIALIZATION: REMOTE SENSING TECHNICIANS

Apply remote sensing technologies to assist scientists in areas such as natural resources, urban planning, and homeland security. May prepare flight plans and sensor configurations for flight trips. Participate in the planning and development of mapping projects. Maintain records of survey data. Document methods used and write technical reports containing information collected. Develop specialized computer software routines to customize and integrate image analysis. Collect verification data on the ground using equipment such as global positioning receivers, digital cameras, and notebook computers. Verify integrity and accuracy of data contained in remote sensing image analysis systems. Prepare documentation and presentations including charts, photos, or graphs. Operate airborne remote sensing equipment such as survey cameras, sensors, and scanners. Monitor raw data quality during collection and make equipment

corrections as necessary. Merge scanned images or build photo mosaics of large areas using image processing software. Integrate remotely sensed data with other geospatial data. Evaluate remote sensing project requirements to determine the types of equipment or computer software necessary to meet project requirements such as specific image types and output resolutions. Develop and maintain geospatial information databases. Correct raw data for errors due to factors such as skew and atmospheric variation. Calibrate data collection equipment. Consult with remote sensing scientists, surveyors, cartographers, or engineers to determine project needs.

Personality Type: Realistic-Investigative-Conventional. **Skills:** No data available. **Education and Training Program:** Geographic Information Science and Cartography; Signal/Geospatial Intelligence. **Work Environment:** No data available.

OTHER FEDERAL JOB FACTS
RELATED GS SERIES: 0021 COMMUNITY PLANNING TECHNICIAN

- ❈ U.S. Federal Workforce: 52
- ❈ Average Length of Service: 13.7 years
- ❈ Percent Part-Time: 1.9%
- ❈ Percent Women: 46.2%
- ❈ Largest Age Bracket: 55–59 (26.9%)
- ❈ GS Level with Most Workers: 11
- ❈ Agency with Most Workers: Defense
- ❈ State with Most Workers: California

Collect, select, compute, adjust, and process data; prepare charts, exhibits, and reports; and perform related duties supporting professional planning work.

Requirements: Practical knowledge of community planning methods and techniques. Does not require education and training equivalent in scope and nature to that required for professional positions in community planning.

RELATED GS SERIES: 1397 DOCUMENT ANALYSIS

- ❊ U.S. Federal Workforce: 102
- ❊ Average Length of Service: 13.8 years
- ❊ Percent Part-Time: 5.9%
- ❊ Percent Women: 45.1%
- ❊ Largest Age Bracket: 50–54 (16.7%)
- ❊ GS Level with Most Workers: 14
- ❊ Agency with Most Workers: Justice
- ❊ State with Most Workers: District of Columbia

Direct, administer, supervise, advise on, or perform technical work in examining and identifying questioned documents; conduct examinations to determine the genuineness or spuriousness of a document or any of its parts; decipher or restore eradicated or obliterated writings and markings; detect alterations, additions, interlineations, or other tampering with the original document; determine authorship of a signature or other writing; determine the validity of a date or the alleged age of a document or a particular entry; identify the particular machine used to produce a document; or identify the source of a document.

Requirements: Knowledge of the properties, characteristics, and techniques of analysis of handwriting, typewriting, printing, and duplicating, and of inks, papers, and other writing, printing, and recording instruments and materials; knowledge and skill in the use of photographic and laboratory equipment and techniques; and ability to develop evidence and to present it convincingly in written reports or orally.

RELATED GS SERIES: 0119 ECONOMICS ASSISTANT

- ❊ U.S. Federal Workforce: 434
- ❊ Average Length of Service: 9.5 years
- ❊ Percent Part-Time: 91.5%
- ❊ Percent Women: 64.7%
- ❊ Largest Age Bracket: 60–64 (20.0%)
- ❊ GS Level with Most Workers: 7
- ❊ Agency with Most Workers: Labor
- ❊ States with Most Workers: California, District of Columbia

Supervise or perform subordinate research and related work involved in the collecting, compiling, verifying, analyzing, or reporting data.

Requirements: Specialized or technical knowledge or skills in one or more fields of economics. Does not require full professional competence in economic theories, principles, and concepts.

RELATED GS SERIES: 1316 HYDROLOGIC TECHNICIAN

- ❊ U.S. Federal Workforce: 1,702
- ❊ Average Length of Service: 12.7 years
- ❊ Percent Part-Time: 11.6%
- ❊ Percent Women: 21.7%
- ❊ Largest Age Bracket: 25–29 (13.5%)
- ❊ GS Level with Most Workers: 9
- ❊ Agency with Most Workers: Interior
- ❊ State with Most Workers: California

Gather information on the quantity, quality, availability, movement, and distribution of ground water and surface water; evaluate water samples and data, prepare reports, and carry out related duties that support professional work in hydrology.

Requirements: Knowledge of hydrology less than that represented by completion of a bachelor's degree.

RELATED GS SERIES: 1341 METEOROLOGICAL TECHNICIAN

- ❊ U.S. Federal Workforce: 635
- ❊ Average Length of Service: 17.3 years

- Percent Part-Time: 1.4%
- Percent Women: 12.8%
- Largest Age Bracket: 50–54 (23.1%)
- GS Level with Most Workers: 11
- Agency with Most Workers: Commerce
- State with Most Workers: Alaska

Observe and analyze weather elements or predict the effects of weather in the atmosphere and on the earth's surface.

Requirements: Practical knowledge of meteorological equipment, principles, and methods, as well as skill in collecting data, making observations, forecasting weather, and verifying data. Does not require a bachelor's degree in meteorology.

Related GS Series: 1311 Physical Science Technician

- U.S. Federal Workforce: 2,284
- Average Length of Service: 13.2 years
- Percent Part-Time: 9.1%
- Percent Women: 29.9%
- Largest Age Bracket: 50–54 (14.4%)
- GS Levels with Most Workers: 9, 10
- Agency with Most Workers: Defense
- State with Most Workers: Virginia

Perform technical work in such fields as astronomy, chemistry, geology, physics, geophysics, health physics, metallurgy, and oceanography for which a specific technician series has not been established.

Requirements: Knowledge of physical science less than that represented by completion of a bachelor's degree.

Related GS Series: 0181 Psychology Aid and Technician

- U.S. Federal Workforce: 806
- Average Length of Service: 10.4 years
- Percent Part-Time: 8.4%

- Percent Women: 61.4%
- Largest Age Bracket: 55–59 (13.4%)
- GS Level with Most Workers: 7
- Agency with Most Workers: Veterans Affairs
- State with Most Workers: California

Perform nonprofessional technical work in connection with a program of research or direct services in psychology.

Requirements: Practical understanding of some of the principles, methods, and techniques of psychology, but does not require formal education in psychology.

Related GS Series: 0102 Social Science Aid and Technician

Title on USAJobs: Social Science Aid/ Technician

- U.S. Federal Workforce: 1,071
- Average Length of Service: 6.5 years
- Percent Part-Time: 9.6%
- Percent Women: 46.0%
- Largest Age Bracket: 25–29 (19.9%)
- GS Level with Most Workers: 7
- Agencies with Most Workers: Veterans Affairs, Agriculture
- State with Most Workers: California

Do nonprofessional work of a technical, specialized, or support nature in one or more of the social science or other occupational fields.

Requirements: Practical understanding of the objectives, policies, procedures, or regulatory requirements pertaining to the work and the ability to apply skills or knowledge of the occupation involved. Does not require full professional competence (or equivalent professional-level preparation) in the theories, principles, and concepts of the field.

Loan Officers

- ❋ Education/Training Required: Moderate-term on-the-job training
- ❋ Annual Earnings (Federal): $69,920
- ❋ Annual Earnings (All Industries): $54,880
- ❋ Earnings Growth Potential (Federal): 28.9% (low)
- ❋ Earnings Growth Potential (All Industries): 43.5% (high)
- ❋ Job Growth (Federal): 14.0%
- ❋ Job Growth (All Industries): 10.1%
- ❋ Annual Job Openings (Federal): 70
- ❋ Annual Job Openings (All Industries): 6,880

Evaluate, authorize, or recommend approval of commercial, real estate, or credit loans. Advise borrowers on financial status and methods of payments. Includes mortgage loan officers and agents, collection analysts, loan servicing officers, and loan underwriters. Meet with applicants to obtain information for loan applications and to answer questions about the process. Approve loans within specified limits and refer loan applications outside those limits to management for approval. Analyze applicants' financial status, credit, and property evaluations to determine feasibility of granting loans. Explain to customers the different types of loans and credit options that are available, as well as the terms of those services. Obtain and compile copies of loan applicants' credit histories, corporate financial statements, and other financial information. Review and update credit and loan files. Review loan agreements to ensure that they are complete and accurate according to policy. Compute payment schedules. Stay abreast of new types of loans and other financial services and products to better meet customers' needs. Submit applications to credit analysts for verification and recommendation. Handle customer complaints and take appropriate action to resolve them. Work with clients to identify their financial goals and to find ways of reaching those goals. Confer with underwriters to aid in resolving mortgage application problems. Negotiate payment arrangements with customers who have delinquent loans. Market bank products to individuals and firms, promoting bank services that may meet customers' needs. Supervise loan personnel. Set credit policies, credit lines, procedures, and standards in conjunction with senior managers.

Considerations for Job Outlook: Overall economic expansion and population growth are expected to increase employment of these workers. However, increased automation through the use of the Internet loan application will temper employment growth. Good job opportunities are expected.

Personality Type: Conventional-Enterprising-Social. **Skills:** Mathematics; Service Orientation; Speaking; Operations Analysis; Writing; Judgment and Decision Making; Reading Comprehension; Active Listening. **Education and Training Program:** Credit Management; Finance, General. **Work Environment:** Indoors; sitting; making repetitive motions.

OTHER FEDERAL JOB FACTS

RELATED GS SERIES: 1165 LOAN SPECIALIST

- ❋ U.S. Federal Workforce: 5,034
- ❋ Average Length of Service: 18.0 years
- ❋ Percent Part-Time: 0.7%
- ❋ Percent Women: 50.3%
- ❋ Largest Age Bracket: 50–54 (21.7%)
- ❋ GS Level with Most Workers: 12
- ❋ Agency with Most Workers: Agriculture
- ❋ State with Most Workers: Texas

Direct or perform analytical and evaluative work related to loans granted, insured, or guaranteed by the federal government.

Requirements: Knowledge of credit risk factors and lending principles involved in loans of specialized types granted, insured, or guaranteed by the federal government; financial structures and practices of business organizations concerned with such loans; and pertinent statutory, regulatory, and administrative provisions.

Logisticians

- ✲ Education/Training Required: Bachelor's degree
- ✲ Annual Earnings (Federal): $76,000
- ✲ Annual Earnings (All Industries): $67,960
- ✲ Earnings Growth Potential (Federal): 32.5% (low)
- ✲ Earnings Growth Potential (All Industries): 40.4% (medium)
- ✲ Job Growth (Federal): 17.8%
- ✲ Job Growth (All Industries): 19.5%
- ✲ Annual Job Openings (Federal): 730
- ✲ Annual Job Openings (All Industries): 4,190

Analyze and coordinate the logistical functions of a firm or organization. Responsible for the entire life cycle of a product, including acquisition, distribution, internal allocation, delivery, and final disposal of resources. Maintain and develop positive business relationships with a customer's key personnel involved in or directly relevant to a logistics activity. Develop an understanding of customers' needs and take actions to ensure that such needs are met. Direct availability and allocation of materials, supplies, and finished products. Collaborate with other departments as necessary to meet customer requirements, to take advantage of sales opportunities, or, in the case of shortages, to minimize negative impacts on a business. Protect and control proprietary materials. Review logistics performance with customers against targets, benchmarks, and service

agreements. Develop and implement technical project management tools such as plans, schedules, and responsibility and compliance matrices. Direct team activities, establishing task priorities, scheduling and tracking work assignments, providing guidance, and ensuring the availability of resources. Report project plans, progress, and results. Direct and support the compilation and analysis of technical source data necessary for product development. Explain proposed solutions to customers, management, or other interested parties through written proposals and oral presentations. Provide project management services, including the provision and analysis of technical data. Develop proposals that include documentation for estimates.

Considerations for Job Outlook: Faster than average employment growth is projected.

Personality Type: Enterprising-Conventional. **Skills:** Operations Analysis; Management of Personnel Resources; Coordination; Monitoring; Systems Evaluation; Systems Analysis; Persuasion; Service Orientation. **Education and Training Program:** Logistics, Materials, and Supply Chain Management; Operations Management and Supervision; Transportation/Mobility Management. **Work Environment:** Indoors; sitting.

JOB SPECIALIZATION: LOGISTICS ANALYSTS

Design and analyze operational solutions for projects such as transportation optimization, network modeling, process and methods analysis, cost containment, capacity enhancement, routing and shipment optimization, and information management. Propose logistics solutions for customers. Prepare production strategies and conceptual designs for production facilities. Interview key staff or tour facilities to identify efficiency-improvement, cost-reduction, or service-delivery opportunities. Direct the work of logistics analysts. Design plant distribution centers. Develop specifications for equipment, tools, facility layouts, or material-handling systems. Review contractual commitments, customer specifications, or related information to determine logistics and support requirements. Prepare or validate documentation on automated logistics or maintenance-data reporting and management information systems. Identify cost-reduction and process-improvement opportunities. Identify or develop business rules and standard operating procedures to streamline operating processes. Develop metrics, internal analysis tools, or key performance indicators for business units within logistics. Develop and maintain cost estimates, forecasts, or cost models. Determine feasibility of designing new facilities or modifying existing facilities, based on such factors as cost, available space, schedule, technical requirements, and ergonomics. Determine logistics support requirements, such as facility details, staffing needs, and safety or maintenance plans. Conduct logistics studies and analyses, such as time studies, zero-base analyses, rate analyses, network analyses, flow-path analyses, and supply chain analyses.

Personality Type: Investigative-Conventional-Realistic. **Skills:** No data available. **Education and Training Program:** Logistics, Materials, and Supply Chain Management; Operations Management and Supervision; Transportation/Mobility Management. **Work Environment:** No data available.

JOB SPECIALIZATION: LOGISTICS ENGINEERS

Analyze product delivery or supply chain processes to identify or recommend changes. May manage route activity including invoicing, electronic bills, and shipment tracing. Identify opportunities for inventory reductions. Monitor industry standards, trends, or practices to identify developments in logistics planning or execution. Enter logistics-related data into databases. Develop and maintain payment systems to ensure accuracy of vendor payments. Determine packaging requirements. Develop and maintain freight rate databases for use by supply chain departments to determine the most economical modes of transportation. Contact potential vendors to determine material availability. Contact carriers for rates or schedules. Communicate with and monitor service providers, such as ocean carriers, air freight forwarders, global consolidators, customs brokers, and trucking companies. Track product flow from origin to final delivery. Write or revise standard operating procedures for logistics processes. Review procedures such as distribution and inventory management to ensure maximum efficiency and minimum cost. Recommend improvements to existing or planned logistics processes. Provide ongoing analyses in areas such as transportation costs, parts procurement, back orders, and delivery processes. Prepare reports on logistics performance measures. Manage systems to ensure that pricing structures adequately reflect logistics costing. Monitor inventory transactions at warehouse facilities to assess receiving, storage, shipping, or inventory integrity. Maintain databases of logistics information. Maintain logistics records in accordance with corporate policies.

Personality Type: Conventional-Enterprising-Investigative. **Skills:** No data available. **Education and Training Program:** Logistics, Materials, and Supply Chain Management; Operations Management and Supervision; Transportation/Mobility Management. **Work Environment:** No data available.

OTHER FEDERAL JOB FACTS

RELATED GS SERIES: 2010 INVENTORY MANAGEMENT

TITLE ON USAJOBS: INVENTORY MANAGEMENT SPECIALIST

- ✱ U.S. Federal Workforce: 5,076
- ✱ Average Length of Service: 17.1 years
- ✱ Percent Part-Time: 0.2%

❋ Percent Women: 51.3%

❋ Largest Age Bracket: 50–54 (20.2%)

❋ GS Levels with Most Workers: 11, 9

❋ Agency with Most Workers: Defense

❋ State with Most Workers: Georgia

Manage, regulate, coordinate, or otherwise exercise control over supplies, equipment, or other material.

Requirements: Knowledge of acquisition processes, automated records and control systems, material substitution criteria, and storage, issue, and disposal processes.

RELATED GS SERIES: 0346 LOGISTICS MANAGEMENT

TITLE ON USAJOBS: LOGISTICS MANAGEMENT SPECIALIST

❋ U.S. Federal Workforce: 18,364

❋ Average Length of Service: 15.0 years

❋ Percent Part-Time: 0.3%

❋ Percent Women: 31.9%

❋ Largest Age Bracket: 45–49 (6.0%)

❋ GS Level with Most Workers: 12

❋ Agency with Most Workers: Defense

❋ States with Most Workers: Alabama, Virginia

Plan, coordinate, or evaluate logistical actions required to support a specified mission, weapons system, or other designated program; identify the specific requirements for money, manpower, materiel, facilities, and services needed to support the program; and correlate those requirements with program plans to assure that the needed support is provided at the right time and place.

Requirements: Knowledge of agency program planning, funding, and management information systems; broad knowledge of the organization and functions of activities involved in providing logistical support; and ability to coordinate and evaluate the efforts of functional specialists to identify specific requirements and to develop and adjust plans and schedules for the actions needed to meet each requirement on time.

RELATED GS SERIES: 2003 SUPPLY PROGRAM MANAGEMENT

TITLE ON USAJOBS: SUPPLY MANAGEMENT SPECIALIST

❋ U.S. Federal Workforce: 3,990

❋ Average Length of Service: 18.1 years

❋ Percent Part-Time: 5.7%

❋ Percent Women: 40.9%

❋ Largest Age Bracket: 50–54 (23.7%)

❋ GS Levels with Most Workers: 11, 12

❋ Agency with Most Workers: Defense

❋ States with Most Workers: Virginia, Pennsylvania

Manage, direct, or administer a supply program that includes a mixture of technical supply functions; or analyze, develop, evaluate, or promote improvements in the policies, plans, methods, procedures, systems, or techniques of a supply program.

Requirements: Broad understanding of the interrelated chain of activities involving the process of supply, from the conception or acquisition of a new item through storage, distribution, property utilization, consumption, or disposal.

Maintenance and Repair Workers, General

❋ Education/Training Required: Moderate-term on-the-job training

❋ Annual Earnings (Federal): $52,920

❋ Annual Earnings (All Industries): $34,620

❋ Earnings Growth Potential (Federal): 27.8% (low)

- ✺ Earnings Growth Potential (All Industries): 39.9% (medium)
- ✺ Job Growth (Federal): –0.1%
- ✺ Job Growth (All Industries): 10.9%
- ✺ Annual Job Openings (Federal): 420
- ✺ Annual Job Openings (All Industries): 35,750

Perform work involving the skills of two or more maintenance or craft occupations to keep machines, mechanical equipment, or the structure of an establishment in repair. Duties may involve pipe fitting; boiler making; insulating; welding; machining; carpentry; repairing electrical or mechanical equipment; installing, aligning, and balancing new equipment; and repairing buildings, floors, or stairs. Repair or replace defective equipment parts, using hand tools and power tools, and reassemble equipment. Perform routine preventive maintenance to ensure that machines continue to run smoothly, building systems operate efficiently, or the physical condition of buildings does not deteriorate. Inspect drives, motors, and belts, check fluid levels, replace filters, or perform other maintenance actions, following checklists. Use tools ranging from common hand and power tools, such as hammers, hoists, saws, drills, and wrenches, to precision measuring instruments and electrical and electronic testing devices. Assemble, install or repair wiring, electrical and electronic components, pipe systems and plumbing, machinery, and equipment. Diagnose mechanical problems and determine how to correct them, checking blueprints, repair manuals, and parts catalogs as necessary. Inspect, operate, and test machinery and equipment to diagnose machine malfunctions. Record type and cost of maintenance or repair work. Clean and lubricate shafts, bearings, gears, and other parts of machinery. Dismantle devices to access and remove defective parts, using hoists, cranes, hand tools, and power tools. Plan and lay out repair work, using diagrams, drawings, blueprints, maintenance manuals, and schematic diagrams.

Considerations for Job Outlook: Employment is related to the extent of building stock and the amount of equipment needing maintenance and repair. Opportunities should be excellent, especially for job seekers with experience or certification.

Personality Type: Realistic-Conventional-Investigative. **Skills:** Repairing; Equipment Maintenance; Installation; Equipment Selection; Troubleshooting; Quality Control Analysis; Operation and Control; Technology Design. **Education and Training Program:** Building/Construction Site Management/Manager. **Work Environment:** Indoors; using your hands to handle, control, or feel objects, tools, or controls; standing; minor burns, cuts, bites, or stings; sounds, noisy; walking and running.

OTHER FEDERAL JOB FACTS

Related GS Series: 3725 Battery Repairing

- ✺ U.S. Federal Workforce: 30
- ✺ Average Length of Service: 18.5 years
- ✺ Percent Part-Time: 0.0%
- ✺ Percent Women: 0.0%
- ✺ Largest Age Bracket: 55–59 (23.3%)
- ✺ GS Level with Most Workers: Not a GS occupation
- ✺ Agency with Most Workers: Defense
- ✺ State with Most Workers: District of Columbia

Disassemble, repair, reassemble, and charge batteries used in aircraft, electric trucks, motor vehicles, and other types of equipment; break down batteries, wash down and diagnose extent of repairs needed, and repair and/or rebuild batteries according to diagnosis requirements.

Requirements: Knowledge of maintenance, installation and construction of storage batteries; uses of lead molds, burning torches and battery servicing equipment and tools; installation of conduit and connectors as part of a battery control system; methods, materials, tools, and equipment used in electroplating work; principles, practices, and materials relating to the manufacture and use of storage batteries; practices and equipment used in inspecting, testing, and charging of battery components; safety precautions observed when working with acids, hot lead, and electricity as they apply to battery repair and electroplating work; chemical and electrical principles involved in building and maintaining storage batteries.

RELATED GS SERIES: 5310 KITCHEN/BAKERY EQUIPMENT REPAIRING

- U.S. Federal Workforce: 14
- Average Length of Service: 21.2 years
- Percent Part-Time: 0.0%
- Percent Women: 0.0%
- Largest Age Bracket: 45–49 (21.4%)
- GS Level with Most Workers: Not a GS occupation
- Agency with Most Workers: Defense
- States with Most Workers: Kansas, New York

Install, repair, overhaul, alter, rebuild, adjust, and replace parts of commercial kitchen and/or bakery equipment, such as electric and gas ranges, fryers, steam tables, disposers, dishwashers, meat and bread slicers, bone and meat cutters, potato peelers, bread and dough mixers, doughnut machines, dividers and dough hoppers, dough rounders, flour handling machines, proofers, and other food equipment.

Requirements: No requirements available.

RELATED GS SERIES: 5318 LOCK AND DAM REPAIRING

TITLE ON USAJOBS: LOCK AND DAM EQUIPMENT MECHANIC

- U.S. Federal Workforce: 483
- Average Length of Service: 18.4 years
- Percent Part-Time: 0.6%
- Percent Women: 2.9%
- Largest Age Bracket: 55–59 (19.3%)
- GS Level with Most Workers: Not a GS occupation
- Agency with Most Workers: Defense
- State with Most Workers: Illinois

Repair flood control or navigation lock and dam equipment and machinery; maintain and repair buildings, grounds, and structures peculiar to operation of locks and dams.

Requirements: No requirements available.

RELATED GS SERIES: 4749 MAINTENANCE MECHANIC

- U.S. Federal Workforce: 11,844
- Average Length of Service: 13.8 years
- Percent Part-Time: 3.5%
- Percent Women: 3.6%
- Largest Age Bracket: 55–59 (18.6%)
- GS Level with Most Workers: Not a GS occupation
- Agencies with Most Workers: Interior, Defense
- State with Most Workers: California

Maintain and repair grounds, exterior structures, buildings, and related fixtures and utilities.

Requirements: Knowledge of various trade practices associated with occupations such as carpentry, masonry, plumbing, electrical, air conditioning, cement work, painting, and other related trades.

Management Analysts

- ❋ Education/Training Required: Bachelor's or higher degree, plus work experience
- ❋ Annual Earnings (Federal): $83,140
- ❋ Annual Earnings (All Industries): $75,250
- ❋ Earnings Growth Potential (Federal): 32.7% (low)
- ❋ Earnings Growth Potential (All Industries): 43.5% (high)
- ❋ Job Growth (Federal): 8.4%
- ❋ Job Growth (All Industries): 23.9%
- ❋ Annual Job Openings (Federal): 1,970
- ❋ Annual Job Openings (All Industries): 30,650

Conduct organizational studies and evaluations, design systems and procedures, conduct work simplifications and measurement studies, and prepare operations and procedures manuals to assist management in operating more efficiently and effectively. Includes program analysts and management consultants. Gather and organize information on problems or procedures. Analyze data gathered and develop solutions or alternative methods of proceeding. Confer with personnel concerned to ensure successful functioning of newly implemented systems or procedures. Develop and implement records management program for filing, protection, and retrieval of records and assure compliance with program. Review forms and reports and confer with management and users about format, distribution, and purpose and to identify problems and improvements. Document findings of study and prepare recommendations for implementation of new systems, procedures, or organizational changes. Interview personnel and conduct on-site observation to ascertain unit functions; work performed; and methods, equipment, and personnel used. Prepare manuals and train workers in use of new forms, reports, procedures, or equipment according to organizational policy. Design, evaluate, recommend, and approve changes of forms and reports. Plan study of work problems and procedures, such as organizational change, communications, information flow, integrated production methods, inventory control, or cost analysis. Recommend purchase of storage equipment and design area layout to locate equipment in space available.

Considerations for Job Outlook: Organizations are expected to rely increasingly on outside expertise in an effort to maintain competitiveness and improve performance. Keen competition is expected. Opportunities are expected to be best for those who have a graduate degree, specialized expertise, and ability in salesmanship and public relations.

Personality Type: Investigative-Enterprising-Conventional. **Skills:** Operations Analysis; Systems Evaluation; Systems Analysis; Judgment and Decision Making; Writing; Management of Personnel Resources; Instructing; Persuasion. **Education and Training Program:** Business Administration and Management, General; Business/Commerce, General. **Work Environment:** Indoors; sitting.

OTHER FEDERAL JOB FACTS

RELATED GS SERIES: 0341 ADMINISTRATIVE OFFICER

- ❋ U.S. Federal Workforce: 8,897
- ❋ Average Length of Service: 19.1 years
- ❋ Percent Part-Time: 6.9%
- ❋ Percent Women: 76.4%
- ❋ Largest Age Bracket: 50–54 (20.5%)
- ❋ GS Levels with Most Workers: 12, 11
- ❋ Agency with Most Workers: Defense
- ❋ States with Most Workers: Maryland, District of Columbia

Provide or obtain a variety of management services essential to the direction and operation of an organization.

Requirements: Extensive knowledge and understanding of management principles, practices, methods and techniques, and skill in integrating management services with the general management of an organization.

RELATED GS SERIES: 0107 HEALTH INSURANCE ADMINISTRATION

TITLE ON USAJOBS: HEALTH INSURANCE SPECIALIST

- ❋ U.S. Federal Workforce: 2,495
- ❋ Average Length of Service: 14.3 years
- ❋ Percent Part-Time: 2.1%
- ❋ Percent Women: 72.5%
- ❋ Largest Age Bracket: 55–59 (15.0%)
- ❋ GS Level with Most Workers: 13
- ❋ Agency with Most Workers: Health and Human Services
- ❋ State with Most Workers: Maryland

Administer and operate national health insurance programs such as Medicare and Medicaid; interpret program requirements; formulate policies, methods, and procedures; monitor, review, evaluate, and assess the integrity and quality of program operations; prepare and analyze health-care data related to the programs; and perform other related activities.

Requirements: Knowledge of the laws, regulations, principles, and operational requirements of national health insurance programs; knowledge of the interrelationships among these programs and other related federal and state programs; and analytical skills and abilities used in planning, developing, and evaluating the operation and delivery of these programs to the public.

RELATED GS SERIES: 0343 MANAGEMENT AND PROGRAM ANALYSIS

TITLE ON USAJOBS: MANAGEMENT AND PROGRAM ANALYST

- ❋ U.S. Federal Workforce: 66,508
- ❋ Average Length of Service: 16.7 years
- ❋ Percent Part-Time: 0.9%
- ❋ Percent Women: 62.2%
- ❋ Largest Age Bracket: 50–54 (19.7%)
- ❋ GS Level with Most Workers: 13
- ❋ Agency with Most Workers: Defense
- ❋ State with Most Workers: District of Columbia

Serve as analyst or advisor to management on the evaluation of the effectiveness of government programs and operations or the productivity and efficiency of the management of federal agencies or both.

Requirements: Knowledge of the substantive nature of agency programs and activities; agency missions, policies, and objectives; management principles and processes; and the analytical and evaluative methods and techniques for assessing program development or execution and improving organizational effectiveness and efficiency. Also requires skill in application of fact-finding and investigative techniques; oral and written communications; and development of presentations and reports. May also require an understanding of basic budgetary and financial management principles and techniques as they relate to long range planning of programs and objectives.

RELATED GS SERIES: 0301 MISCELLANEOUS ADMINISTRATION AND PROGRAM

- ❋ U.S. Federal Workforce: 102,890
- ❋ Average Length of Service: 13.4 years
- ❋ Percent Part-Time: 13.7%
- ❋ Percent Women: 51.7%

❋ Largest Age Bracket: 50–54 (18.7%)

❋ GS Levels with Most Workers: 12, 11

❋ Agency with Most Workers: Defense

❋ State with Most Workers: District of Columbia

Perform, supervise, or manage administrative or program work for which no other job title is appropriate.

Requirements: Analytical ability, judgment, discretion, and knowledge of a substantial body of administrative or program principles, concepts, policies, and objectives.

RELATED GS SERIES: 0340 PROGRAM MANAGEMENT

TITLE ON USAJOBS: PROGRAM MANAGER

❋ U.S. Federal Workforce: 13,917

❋ Average Length of Service: 20.5 years

❋ Percent Part-Time: 0.9%

❋ Percent Women: 34.9%

❋ Largest Age Bracket: 50–54 (26.3%)

❋ GS Level with Most Workers: 15

❋ Agency with Most Workers: Defense

❋ State with Most Workers: District of Columbia

Manage, direct, or assist in a line capacity in managing or directing one or more programs, including appropriate supporting service organizations.

Requirements: Management and executive knowledge and ability; does not require competence in a specialized subject-matter or functional area.

RELATED GS SERIES: 2110 TRANSPORTATION INDUSTRY ANALYSIS

TITLE ON USAJOBS: TRANSPORTATION INDUSTRY ANALYST

❋ U.S. Federal Workforce: 144

❋ Average Length of Service: 13.8 years

❋ Percent Part-Time: 1.4%

❋ Percent Women: 35.4%

❋ Largest Age Bracket: 55–59 (18.8%)

❋ GS Level with Most Workers: 14

❋ Agency with Most Workers: Transportation

❋ State with Most Workers: District of Columbia

Perform work pertaining to regulation of the transportation industry with regard to operations, economics, equity in industry practices, and protection of the public interest.

Requirements: Knowledge of transportation industry regulatory controls, of the customs and competitive practices of carriers, and of carrier operations, services, and facilities; also general knowledge of economics, statistics, law, business management, and related subject-matter areas. Does not require full training and professional competence in any of those fields.

Marine Engineers and Naval Architects

❋ Education/Training Required: Bachelor's degree

❋ Annual Earnings (Federal): $100,920

❋ Annual Earnings (All Industries): $74,330

❋ Earnings Growth Potential (Federal): 37.1% (median)

❋ Earnings Growth Potential (All Industries): 44.7% (high)

❋ Job Growth (Federal): 8.9%

❋ Job Growth (All Industries): 5.8%

❋ Annual Job Openings (Federal): 30

❋ Annual Job Openings (All Industries): 230

Design, develop, and evaluate the operation of marine vessels; ship machinery; and related

equipment, such as power supply and propulsion systems. No task data available.

Considerations for Job Outlook: Marine engineers and naval architects are expected to have employment growth of 6 percent from 2008–2018, slower than the average for all occupations. Continued demand for naval vessels and recreational small craft should more than offset the long-term decline in the domestic design and construction of large oceangoing vessels. Good prospects are expected for marine engineers and naval architects because of growth in employment, the need to replace workers who retire or take other jobs, and the limited number of students pursuing careers in this occupation.

Job Specialization: Marine Engineers

Design, develop, and take responsibility for the installation of ship machinery and related equipment, including propulsion machines and power supply systems. Prepare, or direct the preparation of, product or system layouts and detailed drawings and schematics. Inspect marine equipment and machinery in order to draw up work requests and job specifications. Conduct analytical, environmental, operational, or performance studies in order to develop designs for products such as marine engines, equipment, and structures. Design and oversee testing, installation, and repair of marine apparatus and equipment. Prepare plans, estimates, design and construction schedules, and contract specifications, including any special provisions. Investigate and observe tests on machinery and equipment for compliance with standards. Coordinate activities with regulatory bodies in order to ensure repairs and alterations are at minimum cost consistent with safety. Prepare technical reports for use by engineering, management, or sales personnel. Conduct environmental, operational, or performance tests on marine machinery and equipment. Maintain contact with, and formulate reports for, contractors and clients to ensure completion of work at minimum cost. Evaluate operation of marine equipment during acceptance testing and shakedown cruises. Analyze data in order to determine feasibility of product proposals. Determine conditions under which tests are to be conducted, as well as sequences and phases of test operations. Procure materials needed to repair marine equipment and machinery.

Personality Type: Investigative-Realistic. **Skills:** Science; Operations Analysis; Mathematics; Technology Design; Management of Financial Resources; Troubleshooting; Quality Control Analysis; Active Learning. **Education and Training Program:** Naval Architecture and Marine Engineering. **Work Environment:** Outdoors; sitting; sounds, noisy.

Job Specialization: Marine Architects

Design and oversee construction and repair of marine craft and floating structures such as ships, barges, tugs, dredges, submarines, torpedoes, floats, and buoys. May confer with marine engineers. Design complete hull and superstructure according to specifications and test data and in conformity with standards of safety, efficiency, and economy. Design layout of craft interior, including cargo space, passenger compartments, ladder wells, and elevators. Study design proposals and specifications to establish basic characteristics of craft, such as size, weight, speed, propulsion, displacement, and draft. Confer with marine engineering personnel to establish arrangement of boiler room equipment and propulsion machinery, heating and ventilating systems, refrigeration equipment, piping, and other functional equipment. Evaluate performance of craft during dock and sea trials to determine design changes and conformance with national and international standards. Oversee construction and testing of prototype in model basin and develop sectional and waterline curves of hull to establish center of gravity, ideal hull form, and buoyancy and stability data.

Personality Type: Investigative-Realistic-Artistic. **Skills:** Operations Analysis; Technology Design; Mathematics; Science; Reading Comprehension; Management of Material Resources; Quality Control Analysis; Active Learning. **Education and Training Program:** Naval Architecture and Marine Engineering. **Work Environment:** Indoors; sitting.

OTHER FEDERAL JOB FACTS

RELATED GS SERIES: 0871 NAVAL ARCHITECTURE

TITLE ON USAJOBS: ARCHITECT, NAVAL

- U.S. Federal Workforce: 856
- Average Length of Service: 15.9 years
- Percent Part-Time: 0.8%
- Percent Women: 13.4%
- Largest Age Bracket: 50–54 (20.0%)
- GS Level with Most Workers: 12
- Agency with Most Workers: Defense
- States with Most Workers: Maryland, District of Columbia

Manage, supervise, lead, and/or perform professional, architectural, engineering, and scientific work relating to the form, strength, stability, performance, and operational characteristics of marine structures and waterborne vessels.

Requirements: Professional knowledge of and skills in naval architecture.

Market Research Analysts and Marketing Specialists

- Education/Training Required: Bachelor's degree
- Annual Earnings (Federal): $87,720
- Annual Earnings (All Industries): $61,580
- Earnings Growth Potential (Federal): 31.5% (low)

- Earnings Growth Potential (All Industries): 44.4% (high)
- Job Growth (Federal): 13.5%
- Job Growth (All Industries): 28.1%
- Annual Job Openings (Federal): 30
- Annual Job Openings (All Industries): 13,730

Research market conditions in local, regional, or national areas, or gather information to determine potential sales of a product or service, or create a marketing campaign. May gather information on competitors, prices, sales, and methods of marketing and distribution. Collect and analyze data on customer demographics, preferences, needs, and buying habits to identify potential markets and factors affecting product demand. Prepare reports of findings, illustrating data graphically and translating complex findings into written text. Measure and assess customer and employee satisfaction. Forecast and track marketing and sales trends, analyzing collected data. Seek and provide information to help companies determine their position in the marketplace. Measure the effectiveness of marketing, advertising, and communications programs and strategies. Conduct research on consumer opinions and marketing strategies, collaborating with marketing professionals, statisticians, pollsters, and other professionals. Attend staff conferences to provide management with information and proposals concerning the promotion, distribution, design, and pricing of company products or services. Gather data on competitors and analyze their prices, sales, and method of marketing and distribution. Monitor industry statistics and follow trends in trade literature. Devise and evaluate methods and procedures for collecting data, such as surveys, opinion polls, or questionnaires, or arrange to obtain existing data. Develop and implement procedures for identifying advertising needs. Direct trained survey interviewers.

Considerations for Job Outlook: Demand for market research is expected as businesses strive to increase sales and as governments rely on survey research to form public policy. Opportunities should be best for job seekers who have a doctoral degree and strong quantitative skills.

Personality Type: Investigative-Enterprising-Conventional. **Skills:** Programming; Systems Analysis; Operations Analysis; Systems Evaluation; Reading Comprehension; Management of Financial Resources; Mathematics; Writing. **Education and Training Program:** Applied Economics; Business/Managerial Economics; Econometrics and Quantitative Economics; Economics, General; International Economics; Marketing Research. **Work Environment:** Indoors; sitting.

OTHER FEDERAL JOB FACTS

RELATED GS SERIES: 1147 AGRICULTURAL MARKET REPORTING

TITLE ON USAJOBS: AGRICULTURAL MARKET REPORTER

- U.S. Federal Workforce: 160
- Average Length of Service: 18.0 years
- Percent Part-Time: 5.0%
- Percent Women: 35.0%
- Largest Age Bracket: 55–59 (26.3%)
- GS Level with Most Workers: 11
- Agency with Most Workers: Agriculture
- State with Most Workers: Iowa

Collect, analyze, and disseminate current information on available supplies, movement, demand, prices, marketing trends, and other facts relating to the marketing of agricultural products.

Requirements: Knowledge of the methods and practices characteristic of markets in the assigned commodity area; ability to establish and maintain sound working relationships with the industry; and knowledge of the physical characteristics, production factors, and quality-grading or inspection criteria of the assigned group of commodities.

RELATED GS SERIES: 1146 AGRICULTURAL MARKETING

TITLE ON USAJOBS: AGRICULTURAL MARKETING SPECIALIST

- U.S. Federal Workforce: 482
- Average Length of Service: 17.9 years
- Percent Part-Time: 1.5%
- Percent Women: 47.9%
- Largest Age Bracket: 50–54 (21.0%)
- GS Level with Most Workers: 12
- Agency with Most Workers: Agriculture
- State with Most Workers: District of Columbia

Perform managerial, research, analytical, regulatory, or other specialized work concerned with the marketing of one or more agricultural commodities or products.

Requirements: Practical knowledge of marketing functions and practices, such as in commodity exchanges and markets, agricultural trade, or agricultural marketing or agribusiness operations.

RELATED GS SERIES: 0135 FOREIGN AGRICULTURAL AFFAIRS

TITLE ON USAJOBS: FOREIGN AGRICULTURAL AFFAIRS SPECIALIST

- U.S. Federal Workforce: 59
- Average Length of Service: 23.3 years
- Percent Part-Time: 0.0%
- Percent Women: 32.2%
- Largest Age Bracket: 55–59 (28.8%)
- GS Level with Most Workers: No data available
- Agency with Most Workers: Agriculture
- State with Most Workers: District of Columbia

Advise on, administer, supervise, or perform professional work in market and economic analysis and interpretation, as well as foreign reporting, in connection with the development of foreign markets for United States agricultural commodities; in analysis of the agricultural economy, developments, trends, and conditions in foreign countries; and in representing the government in matters affecting foreign agricultural affairs.

Requirements: No requirements available.

Materials Engineers

- ✳ Education/Training Required: Bachelor's degree
- ✳ Annual Earnings (Federal): $108,670
- ✳ Annual Earnings (All Industries): $83,190
- ✳ Earnings Growth Potential (Federal): 34.3% (low)
- ✳ Earnings Growth Potential (All Industries): 36.7% (medium)
- ✳ Job Growth (Federal): 19.4%
- ✳ Job Growth (All Industries): 9.3%
- ✳ Annual Job Openings (Federal): 30
- ✳ Annual Job Openings (All Industries): 810

Evaluate materials and develop machinery and processes to manufacture materials for use in products that must meet specialized design and performance specifications. Develop new uses for known materials. Includes those working with composite materials or specializing in one type of material, such as graphite, metal and metal alloys, ceramics and glass, plastics and polymers, and naturally occurring materials. Analyze product failure data and laboratory test results in order to determine causes of problems and develop solutions. Monitor material performance and evaluate material deterioration. Supervise the work of technologists, technicians, and other engineers and scientists. Design and direct the testing and/or control of processing procedures. Evaluate technical specifications and economic factors relating to process or product design objectives. Conduct or supervise tests on raw materials or finished products in order to ensure their quality. Perform managerial functions such as preparing proposals and budgets, analyzing labor costs, and writing reports. Solve problems in a number of engineering fields, such as mechanical, chemical, electrical, civil, nuclear, and aerospace. Plan and evaluate new projects, consulting with other engineers and corporate executives as necessary. Review new product plans and make recommendations for material selection based on design objectives, such as strength, weight, heat resistance, electrical conductivity, and cost. Design processing plants and equipment. Modify properties of metal alloys, using thermal and mechanical treatments. Guide technical staff engaged in developing materials for specific uses in projected products or devices. Plan and implement laboratory operations for the purpose of developing material and fabrication procedures that meet cost, product specification, and performance standards.

Considerations for Job Outlook: Materials engineers are expected to have employment growth of 9 percent from 2008–2018, about as fast as the average for all occupations. Growth should result from increased use of composite and other nontraditional materials developed through biotechnology and nanotechnology research. As manufacturing firms contract for their materials engineering needs, most employment growth is expected in professional, scientific, and technical services industries.

Personality Type: Investigative-Realistic-Enterprising. **Skills:** Science; Operations Analysis; Mathematics; Active Learning; Systems Analysis; Systems Evaluation; Quality Control Analysis; Reading Comprehension. **Education and Training Program:** Ceramic Sciences and Engineering; Materials Engineering; Metallurgical

Engineering. **Work Environment:** Indoors; sitting; sounds, noisy; contaminants.

OTHER FEDERAL JOB FACTS

RELATED GS SERIES: 1380 FOREST PRODUCTS TECHNOLOGY

- U.S. Federal Workforce: 24
- Average Length of Service: 17.6 years
- Percent Part-Time: 4.2%
- Percent Women: 16.7%
- Largest Age Bracket: 50–54 (29.2%)
- GS Level with Most Workers: 13
- Agency with Most Workers: Agriculture
- State with Most Workers: Wisconsin

Develop, improve, and use wood or wood products; study preservation and treatment methods, the processing and production of wood products, the properties and structure of wood, and the production of lumber.

Requirements: Degree in wood technology, wood utilization, forestry, biological science, chemistry, physics, mathematics, engineering, or a related discipline or a combination of relevant courses and work experience.

RELATED GS SERIES: 0806 MATERIALS ENGINEERING

TITLE ON USAJOBS: ENGINEER, MATERIALS

- U.S. Federal Workforce: 1,263
- Average Length of Service: 15.7 years
- Percent Part-Time: 1.5%
- Percent Women: 17.7%
- Largest Age Bracket: 45–49 (19.4%)
- GS Level with Most Workers: 13
- Agency with Most Workers: Defense
- States with Most Workers: Maryland, Ohio

Manage, supervise, lead, and/or perform professional engineering and scientific work to determine and advise on a material's essential composition, atomic and molecular configuration, and processing; relate the material's essential composition to its properties, end use, and performance; examine the interaction of materials in their processes and applications; develop, maintain, and apply materials and material solutions to meet certain mechanical, electrical, environmental, and chemical requirements; and/or test and evaluate substances for new applications.

Requirements: Professional knowledge of and skills in materials engineering.

Mathematicians

- Education/Training Required: Doctoral degree
- Annual Earnings (Federal): $104,540
- Annual Earnings (All Industries): $93,580
- Earnings Growth Potential (Federal): 35.1% (median)
- Earnings Growth Potential (All Industries): 45.5% (high)
- Job Growth (Federal): 6.6%
- Job Growth (All Industries): 22.4%
- Annual Job Openings (Federal): 40
- Annual Job Openings (All Industries): 150

Conduct research in fundamental mathematics or in application of mathematical techniques to science, management, and other fields. Solve or direct solutions to problems in various fields by mathematical methods. Apply mathematical theories and techniques to the solution of practical problems in business, engineering, the sciences, or other fields. Develop computational methods for solving problems that occur in areas of science and engineering or that come from applications in business or industry. Maintain knowledge in the field by reading professional journals, talking with other mathematicians, and attending professional conferences. Perform computations and apply methods of numerical analysis to data. Develop mathematical or statistical models of phenomena to be used for analysis or for computational simulation. Assemble sets of assumptions and explore the consequences of each set. Address the relationships of quantities, magnitudes, and forms through the use of numbers and symbols. Develop new principles and new relationships between existing mathematical principles to advance mathematical science. Design, analyze, and decipher encryption systems designed to transmit military, political, financial, or law-enforcement-related information in code. Conduct research to extend mathematical knowledge in traditional areas, such as algebra, geometry, probability, and logic.

Considerations for Job Outlook: Technological advances are expected to expand applications of mathematics, leading to employment growth of mathematicians. Competition is expected to be keen. Job seekers with a strong background in math and a related discipline should have the best prospects.

Personality Type: Investigative-Conventional-Artistic. **Skills:** Mathematics; Science; Active Learning; Programming; Reading Comprehension; Complex Problem Solving; Critical Thinking; Systems Analysis. **Education and Training Program:** Algebra and Number Theory; Analysis and Functional Analysis; Applied Mathematics, General; Applied Mathematics, Other; Computational Mathematics; Geometry/Geometric Analysis; Logic; Mathematical Statistics and Probability; Mathematics and Statistics, Other; Mathematics, General; Mathematics, Other; Topology and Foundations. **Work Environment:** Indoors; sitting.

OTHER FEDERAL JOB FACTS
RELATED GS SERIES: 1520 MATHEMATICS
TITLE ON USAJOBS: MATHEMATICIAN

- ❋ U.S. Federal Workforce: 1,031
- ❋ Average Length of Service: 16.0 years
- ❋ Percent Part-Time: 5.1%
- ❋ Percent Women: 36.7%
- ❋ Largest Age Bracket: 45–49 (15.1%)
- ❋ GS Level with Most Workers: 13
- ❋ Agency with Most Workers: Defense
- ❋ State with Most Workers: Virginia

Conduct research on basic mathematical principles, methods, procedures, techniques, or relationships; or develop mathematical methods to solve a variety of scientific, engineering, economic, and/or military problems, where precise specification of the relationships, rigor, and economy of mathematical operations and logical deduction are the controlling considerations.

Requirements: Degree in mathematics or in a related major or a combination of course work and relevant work experience; courses must have included differential and integral calculus plus four advanced mathematics courses requiring calculus or equivalent mathematics courses as a prerequisite.

Mechanical Engineers

- ❋ Education/Training Required: Bachelor's degree
- ❋ Annual Earnings (Federal): $91,520
- ❋ Annual Earnings (All Industries): $77,020
- ❋ Earnings Growth Potential (Federal): 35.2% (low)
- ❋ Earnings Growth Potential (All Industries): 35.4% (low)
- ❋ Job Growth (Federal): 8.5%

- Job Growth (All Industries): 6.0%
- Annual Job Openings (Federal): 240
- Annual Job Openings (All Industries): 7,570

Perform engineering duties in planning and designing tools, engines, machines, and other mechanically functioning equipment. Oversee installation, operation, maintenance, and repair of such equipment as centralized heat, gas, water, and steam systems. Read and interpret blueprints, technical drawings, schematics, and computer-generated reports. Assist drafters in developing the structural design of products using drafting tools or computer-assisted design (CAD) or drafting equipment and software. Research, design, evaluate, install, operate, and maintain mechanical products, equipment, systems, and processes to meet requirements, applying knowledge of engineering principles. Confer with engineers and other personnel to implement operating procedures, resolve system malfunctions, and provide technical information. Recommend design modifications to eliminate machine or system malfunctions. Conduct research that tests and analyzes the feasibility, design, operation, and performance of equipment, components, and systems. Investigate equipment failures and difficulties to diagnose faulty operation and to make recommendations to maintenance crew. Develop and test models of alternate designs and processing methods to assess feasibility, operating condition effects, possible new applications, and necessity of modification. Develop, coordinate, and monitor all aspects of production, including selection of manufacturing methods, fabrication, and operation of product designs. Specify system components or direct modification of products to ensure conformance with engineering design and performance specifications.

Considerations for Job Outlook: Mechanical engineers are expected to have employment growth of 6 percent from 2008–2018, slower than the average for all occupations. Mechanical engineers are involved in the production of a wide range of products, and continued efforts to improve those products will create continued demand for their services. In addition, some new job opportunities will be created through the effects of emerging technologies in biotechnology, materials science, and nanotechnology. Additional opportunities outside of mechanical engineering will exist because the skills acquired through earning a degree in mechanical engineering often can be applied in other engineering specialties.

Personality Type: Investigative-Realistic-Conventional. **Skills:** Technology Design; Science; Mathematics; Operations Analysis; Programming; Quality Control Analysis; Troubleshooting; Systems Evaluation. **Education and Training Program:** Mechanical Engineering. **Work Environment:** Indoors; sitting; sounds, noisy.

JOB SPECIALIZATION: AUTOMOTIVE ENGINEERS

Develop new or improved designs for vehicle structural members, engines, transmissions, and other vehicle systems, using computer-assisted design technology. Direct building, modification, and testing of vehicle and components. Read current literature, attend meetings or conferences, and talk with colleagues to stay abreast of new technology and competitive products. Establish production or quality control standards. Prepare and present technical or project status reports. Develop or implement operating methods and procedures. Write, review, or maintain engineering documentation. Conduct research studies to develop new concepts in the field of automotive engineering. Coordinate production activities with other functional units such as procurement, maintenance, and quality control. Provide technical direction to other engineers or engineering support personnel. Perform failure, variation, or root cause analyses. Develop or integrate control feature requirements. Develop engineering specifications and cost estimates for automotive design concepts. Develop calibration methodologies, test methodologies, or tools. Conduct automotive design reviews. Calibrate vehicle systems, including control algorithms and other software systems. Build models for algorithm and control feature verification testing. Alter or modify designs to obtain specified functional and operational performance. Design or analyze automobile systems in areas such as aerodynamics, alternate fuels, ergonomics, hybrid power, brakes, transmissions, steering, calibration, safety, and diagnostics. Conduct or direct system-level automotive testing.

Personality Type: No data available. **Skills:** No data available. **Education and Training Program:** Mechanical Engineering. **Work Environment:** No data available.

JOB SPECIALIZATION: FUEL CELL ENGINEERS

Design, evaluate, modify, and construct fuel cell components and systems for transportation, stationary, or portable applications. Write technical reports or proposals related to engineering projects. Read current literature, attend meetings or conferences, and talk with colleagues to stay abreast of new technology and competitive products. Prepare test stations, instrumentation, or data acquisition systems for use in specific tests. Plan or implement cost reduction or product improvement projects in collaboration with other engineers, suppliers, support personnel, or customers. Coordinate engineering or test schedules with departments outside engineering, such as manufacturing. Validate design of fuel cells, fuel cell components, or fuel cell systems. Authorize the release of parts or subsystems for production. Simulate or model fuel cell, motor, or other system information using simulation software programs. Recommend or implement changes to fuel cell system design. Provide technical consultation or direction related to the development or production of fuel cell systems.

Plan or conduct experiments to validate new materials, optimize startup protocols, reduce conditioning time, or examine contaminant tolerance. Manage hybrid system architecture, including sizing of components such as fuel cells, energy storage units, and electric drives, for fuel cell battery hybrids. Integrate electric drive subsystems with other vehicle systems to optimize performance or mitigate faults. Identify and define the vehicle and system integration challenges for fuel cell vehicles.

Personality Type: No data available. **Skills:** No data available. **Education and Training Program:** Mechanical Engineering. **Work Environment:** No data available.

OTHER FEDERAL JOB FACTS

RELATED GS SERIES: 0830 MECHANICAL ENGINEERING

TITLE ON USAJOBS: ENGINEER, MECHANICAL

- ❀ U.S. Federal Workforce: 12,016
- ❀ Average Length of Service: 13.2 years
- ❀ Percent Part-Time: 1.3%
- ❀ Percent Women: 10.1%
- ❀ Largest Age Bracket: 25–29 (17.2%)
- ❀ GS Level with Most Workers: 12
- ❀ Agency with Most Workers: Defense
- ❀ State with Most Workers: Maryland

Manage, supervise, lead, and/or perform professional engineering and scientific work involving the design, development, commission, manufacture, operation, maintenance, and disposal of mechanical devices and systems and their equipment and/or components; ensure mechanical devices and systems and their equipment and/or components function safely, reliably, efficiently, and economically.

Requirements: Professional knowledge of and skills in mechanical engineering.

Media and Communication Equipment Workers, All Other

- ❋ Education/Training Required: Moderate-term on-the-job training
- ❋ Annual Earnings (Federal): $77,920
- ❋ Annual Earnings (All Industries): $57,490
- ❋ Earnings Growth Potential (Federal): 28.2% (low)
- ❋ Earnings Growth Potential (All Industries): 56.3% (very high)
- ❋ Job Growth (Federal): 7.6%
- ❋ Job Growth (All Industries): 12.5%
- ❋ Annual Job Openings (Federal): 150
- ❋ Annual Job Openings (All Industries): 760

Considerations for Job Outlook: About average employment growth is projected.

Personality Type: No data available. **Skills:** No data available. **Education and Training Program:** Audiovisual Communications Technologies/Technicians, Other. **Work Environment:** No data available.

OTHER FEDERAL JOB FACTS

RELATED GS SERIES: 0391 TELECOMMUNICATIONS

TITLE ON USAJOBS: TELECOMMUNICATIONS SPECIALIST

- ❋ U.S. Federal Workforce: 5,923
- ❋ Average Length of Service: 14.4 years
- ❋ Percent Part-Time: 6.1%
- ❋ Percent Women: 18.3%
- ❋ Largest Age Bracket: 50–54 (21.2%)
- ❋ GS Level with Most Workers: 12

- ❋ Agency with Most Workers: Defense
- ❋ State with Most Workers: Virginia

Plan, develop, acquire, test, integrate, install, utilize, or modify telecommunications systems, facilities, services, and procedures; perform managerial and staff work in the planning, implementation, or program management of telecommunications programs, systems, and services; or supervise communications operations, when such work includes responsibility for management functions such as planning, recommending changes and determining organizational structure, staffing, training, and budgetary requirements.

Requirements: Knowledge of telecommunications techniques to facilitate the flow of messages.

Medical and Clinical Laboratory Technologists

- ❋ Education/Training Required: Bachelor's degree
- ❋ Annual Earnings (Federal): $61,630
- ❋ Annual Earnings (All Industries): $55,140
- ❋ Earnings Growth Potential (Federal): 16.8% (very low)
- ❋ Earnings Growth Potential (All Industries): 31.9% (low)
- ❋ Job Growth (Federal): 7.7%
- ❋ Job Growth (All Industries): 11.9%
- ❋ Annual Job Openings (Federal): 120
- ❋ Annual Job Openings (All Industries): 5,330

Perform complex medical laboratory tests for diagnosis, treatment, and prevention of disease. May train or supervise staff. Conduct chemical analysis of bodily fluids, including blood, urine, and spinal fluid, to determine presence of normal and abnormal components. Analyze laboratory findings to check the accuracy of the results. Enter data from analysis of medical tests and clinical results into computer for storage. Operate, calibrate, and maintain equipment used in quantitative and qualitative analysis, such as spectrophotometers, calorimeters, flame photometers, and computer-controlled analyzers. Establish and monitor quality assurance programs and activities to ensure the accuracy of laboratory results. Set up, clean, and maintain laboratory equipment. Provide technical information about test results to physicians, family members, and researchers. Supervise, train, and direct lab assistants, medical and clinical laboratory technicians and technologists, and other medical laboratory workers engaged in laboratory testing. Collect and study blood samples to determine the number of cells, their morphology, or their blood group, blood type, and compatibility for transfusion purposes, using microscopic techniques. Analyze samples of biological material for chemical content or reaction. Cultivate, isolate, and assist in identifying microbial organisms, and perform various tests on these microorganisms. Obtain, cut, stain, and mount biological material on slides for microscopic study and diagnosis, following standard laboratory procedures.

Considerations for Job Outlook: Employment of these workers is expected to rise as the volume of laboratory tests continues to increase with population growth and the development of new tests. Excellent opportunities are expected.

Personality Type: Investigative-Realistic-Conventional. **Skills:** Science; Equipment Selection; Equipment Maintenance; Quality Control Analysis; Operation Monitoring; Troubleshooting; Operation and Control; Management of Personnel Resources. **Education and Training Program:** Clinical Laboratory Science/Medical Technology/Technologist; Clinical/Medical Laboratory Science and Allied Professions, Other; Cytogenetics/Genetics/Clinical Genetics Technology/Technologist; Cytotechnology/Cytotechnologist;

Histologic Technology/Histotechnologist; Renal/Dialysis Technologist/Technician. **Work Environment:** Indoors; disease or infections; contaminants; using your hands to handle, control, or feel objects, tools, or controls; sounds, noisy; standing.

JOB SPECIALIZATION: CYTOGENETIC TECHNOLOGISTS

Analyze chromosomes found in biological specimens such as amniotic fluids, bone marrow, and blood to aid in the study, diagnosis, or treatment of genetic diseases. Develop and implement training programs for trainees, medical students, resident physicians or post-doctoral fellows. Stain slides to make chromosomes visible for microscopy. Summarize test results and report to appropriate authorities. Select or prepare specimens and media for cell cultures using aseptic techniques, knowledge of medium components, or cell nutritional requirements. Select banding methods to permit identification of chromosome pairs. Identify appropriate methods of specimen collection, preservation, or transport. Prepare slides of cell cultures following standard procedures. Select appropriate methods of preparation and storage of media to maintain potential of hydrogen (pH), sterility, or ability to support growth. Harvest cell cultures using substances such as mitotic arrestants, cell releasing agents, and cell fixatives. Create chromosome images using computer imaging systems. Determine optimal time sequences and methods for manual or robotic cell harvests.

Personality Type: Investigative-Realistic-Conventional. **Skills:** Science; Reading Comprehension; Writing; Active Learning; Speaking; Mathematics; Instructing; Active Listening. **Education and Training Program:** Clinical Laboratory Science/Medical Technology/Technologist; Cytogenetics/Genetics/Clinical Genetics Technology/Technologist. **Work Environment:** Indoors; disease or infections; sitting; using your hands to handle, control, or feel objects, tools, or controls; making repetitive motions; hazardous conditions.

JOB SPECIALIZATION: CYTOTECHNOLOGISTS

Stain, mount, and study cells to detect evidence of cancer, hormonal abnormalities, and other pathological conditions following established standards and practices. Examine cell samples to detect abnormalities in the color, shape, or size of cellular components and patterns. Examine specimens using microscopes to evaluate specimen quality. Prepare and analyze samples, such as Papanicolaou (PAP) smear body fluids and fine needle aspirations (FNAs), to detect abnormal conditions. Provide patient clinical data or microscopic findings to assist pathologists in the preparation of pathology reports. Assist pathologists or other physicians to collect cell samples such as by fine needle aspiration (FNA) biopsies. Document specimens by verifying patients' and specimens' information. Maintain effective laboratory operations by adhering to standards of specimen collection, preparation, or laboratory safety. Submit slides with abnormal cell structures to pathologists for further examination. Adjust, maintain, or repair laboratory equipment such as microscopes. Assign tasks or coordinate task assignments to ensure adequate performance of laboratory activities.

Personality Type: Investigative-Realistic. **Skills:** Science; Mathematics; Reading Comprehension; Writing; Operation Monitoring; Judgment and Decision Making; Learning Strategies; Instructing. **Education and Training Program:** Clinical Laboratory Science/Medical Technology/ Technologist; Cytotechnology/Cytotechnologist. **Work Environment:** Indoors; making repetitive motions; sitting; using your hands to handle, control, or feel objects, tools, or controls; disease or infections; hazardous conditions.

JOB SPECIALIZATION: HISTOTECHNOLOGISTS AND HISTOLOGIC TECHNICIANS

Prepare histologic slides from tissue sections for microscopic examination and diagnosis by pathologists. May assist in research studies. Cut sections of body tissues for microscopic examination using microtomes. Embed tissue specimens into paraffin wax blocks or infiltrate tissue specimens with wax. Freeze tissue specimens. Mount tissue specimens on glass slides. Stain tissue specimens with dyes or other chemicals to make cell details visible under microscopes. Examine slides under microscopes to ensure tissue preparation meets laboratory requirements. Identify tissue structures or cell components to be used in the diagnosis, prevention, or treatment of diseases. Operate computerized laboratory equipment to dehydrate, decalcify, or microincinerate tissue samples. Perform procedures associated with histochemistry to prepare specimens for immunofluorescence or microscopy. Maintain laboratory equipment such as microscopes, mass spectrometers, microtomes, immunostainers, tissue processors, embedding centers, and water baths. Prepare or use prepared tissue specimens for teaching, research, or diagnostic purposes.

Personality Type: Realistic-Investigative-Conventional. **Skills:** Science; Equipment Maintenance; Equipment Selection; Repairing; Operation and Control; Troubleshooting; Mathematics; Quality Control Analysis. **Education and Training Program:** Clinical Laboratory Science/Medical Technology/Technologist; Histologic Technology/ Histotechnologist. **Work Environment:** Indoors; hazardous conditions; contaminants; using your hands to handle, control, or feel objects, tools, or controls; making repetitive motions; disease or infections.

OTHER FEDERAL JOB FACTS

RELATED GS SERIES: 0644 MEDICAL TECHNOLOGIST

- ❋ U.S. Federal Workforce: 5,990
- ❋ Average Length of Service: 14.5 years
- ❋ Percent Part-Time: 5.2%
- ❋ Percent Women: 71.2%
- ❋ Largest Age Bracket: 55–59 (19.1%)

⊛ GS Level with Most Workers: 9

⊛ Agency with Most Workers: Veterans Affairs

⊛ State with Most Workers: Texas

Perform, advise on, or supervise clinical laboratory testing of human blood, urine, and other body fluids or tissues, using manual or automated techniques; confirm test results and develop data that may be used by physicians in determining the presence and extent of disease or in support of medical research; modify or design laboratory procedures; establish and monitor quality control systems and measures; and provide instruction in the basic theory, technical skills, and application of laboratory test procedures.

Requirements: Professional knowledge and competence in the field of medical technology, specifically in such areas as hematology, bacteriology, mycology, virology, parasitology, immunology, serology, immunohematology (blood banking), clinical chemistry (including endocrinology and toxicology), and urinalysis as they relate to clinical laboratory practice.

Medical and Health Services Managers

⊛ Education/Training Required: Bachelor's or higher degree, plus work experience

⊛ Annual Earnings (Federal): $104,530

⊛ Annual Earnings (All Industries): $81,850

⊛ Earnings Growth Potential (Federal): 23.1% (very low)

⊛ Earnings Growth Potential (All Industries): 39.2% (medium)

⊛ Job Growth (Federal): 7.6%

⊛ Job Growth (All Industries): 16.0%

⊛ Annual Job Openings (Federal): 190

⊛ Annual Job Openings (All Industries): 9,940

Plan, direct, or coordinate medicine and health services in hospitals, clinics, managed care organizations, public health agencies, or similar organizations. Conduct and administer fiscal operations, including accounting, planning budgets, authorizing expenditures, establishing rates for services, and coordinating financial reporting. Direct, supervise, and evaluate work activities of medical, nursing, technical, clerical, service, maintenance, and other personnel. Maintain communication between governing boards, medical staff, and department heads by attending board meetings and coordinating interdepartmental functioning. Review and analyze facility activities and data to aid planning and cash and risk management and to improve service utilization. Plan, implement, and administer programs and services in a health-care or medical facility, including personnel administration, training, and coordination of medical, nursing, and physical plant staff. Direct or conduct recruitment, hiring, and training of personnel. Establish work schedules and assignments for staff, according to workload, space, and equipment availability. Maintain awareness of advances in medicine, computerized diagnostic and treatment equipment, data processing technology, government regulations, health insurance changes, and financing options. Monitor the use of diagnostic services, inpatient beds, facilities, and staff to ensure effective use of resources and assess the need for additional staff, equipment, and services.

Considerations for Job Outlook: The health-care industry is expected to continue growing and diversifying, requiring managers increasingly to run business operations. Opportunities should be good, especially for job seekers who have work experience in health care and strong business management skills.

Personality Type: Enterprising-Conventional-Social. **Skills:** Management of Financial Resources; Operations Analysis; Management of Material Resources; Science; Management of Personnel Resources; Systems Evaluation; Coordination;

Time Management. **Education and Training Program:** Community Health and Preventive Medicine; Health and Medical Administrative Services, Other; Health Information/Medical Records Administration/Administrator; Health Services Administration; Health Unit Manager/Ward Supervisor; Health/Health Care Administration/Management; Hospital and Health Care Facilities Administration/Management; Public Health, General. **Work Environment:** Indoors; sitting; disease or infections.

Job Specialization: Clinical Nurse Specialists

Plan, direct, or coordinate daily patient care activities in a clinical practice. Ensure adherence to established clinical policies, protocols, regulations, and standards. Collaborate with other health care professionals and service providers to ensure optimal patient care. Provide specialized direct and indirect care to inpatients and outpatients within a designated specialty such as obstetrics, neurology, oncology, or neonatal care. Observe, interview, and assess patients to identify care needs. Read current literature, talk with colleagues, or participate in professional organizations or conferences to keep abreast of developments in nursing. Monitor or evaluate medical conditions of patients in collaboration with other health care professionals. Develop or assist others in development of care and treatment plans. Develop, implement, or evaluate standards of nursing practice in specialty areas such as pediatrics, acute care, and geriatrics. Plan, evaluate, or modify treatment programs based on information gathered by observing and interviewing patients or by analyzing patient records. Make clinical recommendations to physicians, other health care providers, insurance companies, patients, or health care organizations. Identify training needs or conduct training sessions for nursing students or medical staff. Maintain departmental policies, procedures, objectives,

or infection control standards. Evaluate the quality and effectiveness of nursing practice or organizational systems. Present clients with information required to make informed health care and treatment decisions.

Personality Type: Enterprising-Social-Conventional. **Skills:** Science; Operations Analysis; Instructing; Service Orientation; Negotiation; Persuasion; Judgment and Decision Making; Systems Evaluation. **Education and Training Program:** Community Health and Preventive Medicine; Health and Medical Administrative Services, Other; Health Information/Medical Records Administration/Administrator; Health Services Administration; Health Unit Manager/Ward Supervisor; Health/Health Care Administration/Management; Hospital and Health Care Facilities Administration/Management; Public Health, General. **Work Environment:** Indoors; disease or infections; sounds, noisy; contaminants; standing; radiation.

OTHER FEDERAL JOB FACTS
Related GS Series: 0670 Health System Administration
Title on USAJobs: Health System Administrator

- U.S. Federal Workforce: 713
- Average Length of Service: 19.0 years
- Percent Part-Time: 2.5%
- Percent Women: 44.0%
- Largest Age Bracket: 50–54 (23.6%)
- GS Levels with Most Workers: 15, 14
- Agency with Most Workers: Veterans Affairs
- State with Most Workers: Texas

Manage a health-care delivery system that may range from a nationwide network including many hospitals to a major subdivision of an individual hospital; effectively use all available resources to provide the best possible patient care.

Requirements: Understanding of the critical balance between the administrative and clinical functions in the health-care delivery system and ability to coordinate and control programs and resources to achieve this balance; also the ability to apply the specialized principles and practices of health-care management in directing a health care delivery system. Does not require a physician's education or license.

Medical Records and Health Information Technicians

* Education/Training Required: Associate degree
* Annual Earnings (Federal): $44,460
* Annual Earnings (All Industries): $31,290
* Earnings Growth Potential (Federal): 26.1% (low)
* Earnings Growth Potential (All Industries): 33.4% (low)
* Job Growth (Federal): 7.6%
* Job Growth (All Industries): 20.3%
* Annual Job Openings (Federal): 150
* Annual Job Openings (All Industries): 7,030

Compile, process, and maintain medical records of hospital and clinic patients in a manner consistent with medical, administrative, ethical, legal, and regulatory requirements of the health-care system. Protect the security of medical records to ensure that confidentiality is maintained. Review records for completeness, accuracy, and compliance with regulations. Retrieve patient medical records for physicians, technicians, or other medical personnel. Release information to persons and agencies according to regulations. Plan, develop, maintain, and operate a variety of health record indexes and storage and retrieval systems to collect, classify, store, and analyze information. Enter data such as demographic characteristics, history and extent of disease, diagnostic procedures, and treatment into computer. Process and prepare business and government forms. Compile and maintain patients' medical records to document condition and treatment and to provide data for research or cost control and care improvement efforts. Process patient admission and discharge documents. Assign the patient to diagnosis-related groups (DRGs), using appropriate computer software. Transcribe medical reports. Identify, compile, abstract, and code patient data, using standard classification systems. Resolve or clarify codes and diagnoses with conflicting, missing, or unclear information by consulting with doctors or others or by participating in the coding team's regular meetings. Compile medical care and census data for statistical reports on diseases treated, surgeries performed, or use of hospital beds. Post medical insurance billings. Train medical records staff.

Considerations for Job Outlook: Employment of these workers is expected to grow as the number of elderly—a demographic group with a higher incidence of injury and illness—increases. Job prospects should be best for technicians who have strong skills in technology and computer software.

Personality Type: Conventional-Enterprising. **Skills:** None met the criteria. **Education and Training Program:** Health Information/Medical Records Technology/Technician; Medical Insurance Coding Specialist/Coder. **Work Environment:** Indoors; sitting; using your hands to handle, control, or feel objects, tools, or controls; making repetitive motions; disease or infections.

OTHER FEDERAL JOB FACTS

RELATED GS SERIES: 0669 MEDICAL RECORDS ADMINISTRATION

TITLE ON USAJOBS: MEDICAL RECORDS ADMINISTRATOR

- ❋ U.S. Federal Workforce: 779
- ❋ Average Length of Service: 14.2 years
- ❋ Percent Part-Time: 0.9%
- ❋ Percent Women: 88.4%
- ❋ Largest Age Bracket: 45–49 (18.4%)
- ❋ GS Levels with Most Workers: 11, 9
- ❋ Agency with Most Workers: Veterans Affairs
- ❋ State with Most Workers: California

Manage, advise on, preserve, analyze, and supervise the use of diagnostic and therapeutic medical records; develop medical records policies and procedures; and provide advice on the use of medical records.

Requirements: Knowledge of medical records administration and management skills and abilities.

RELATED GS SERIES: 0675 MEDICAL RECORDS TECHNICIAN

- ❋ U.S. Federal Workforce: 4,909
- ❋ Average Length of Service: 12.8 years
- ❋ Percent Part-Time: 0.9%
- ❋ Percent Women: 85.8%
- ❋ Largest Age Bracket: 50–54 (19.3%)
- ❋ GS Levels with Most Workers: 8, 7
- ❋ Agency with Most Workers: Veterans Affairs
- ❋ States with Most Workers: Texas, Arizona

Supervise, lead, or perform support work in connection with processing and maintaining medical records for compliance with regulatory requirements; review, analyze, code, abstract, and compile or extract medical records data.

Requirements: Practical knowledge of medical record procedures and references and the organization and consistency of medical records; also a basic knowledge of human anatomy, physiology, and medical terminology.

Medical Scientists, Except Epidemiologists

- ❋ Education/Training Required: Doctoral degree
- ❋ Annual Earnings (Federal): $110,260
- ❋ Annual Earnings (All Industries): $74,590
- ❋ Earnings Growth Potential (Federal): 28.8% (low)
- ❋ Earnings Growth Potential (All Industries): 44.6% (high)
- ❋ Job Growth (Federal): 29.0%
- ❋ Job Growth (All Industries): 40.4%
- ❋ Annual Job Openings (Federal): 50
- ❋ Annual Job Openings (All Industries): 6,620

Conduct research dealing with the understanding of human diseases and the improvement of human health. Engage in clinical investigation or other research, production, technical writing, or related activities. Conduct research to develop methodologies, instrumentation, and procedures for medical application, analyzing data, and presenting findings. Plan and direct studies to investigate human or animal disease, preventive methods, and treatments for disease. Follow strict safety procedures when handling toxic materials to avoid contamination. Evaluate effects of drugs, gases, pesticides, parasites, and microorganisms at various levels. Teach principles of medicine and medical and laboratory procedures to physicians, residents, students, and technicians. Prepare and analyze organ, tissue, and cell samples to identify toxicity, bacteria, or microorganisms or to study cell structure. Standardize drug dosages, methods of immunization, and procedures for manufacture of drugs and medicinal compounds. Investigate cause, progress, life cycle, or mode of transmission of diseases or parasites. Confer with health department, industry personnel, physicians, and others to develop health safety standards and public health improvement programs. Study animal and human health and physiological processes. Consult with and advise physicians, educators, researchers, and others regarding medical applications of physics, biology, and chemistry. Use equipment such as atomic absorption spectrometers, electron microscopes, flow cytometers, and chromatography systems.

Considerations for Job Outlook: New discoveries in biological and medical science are expected to create strong employment growth for these workers. Medical scientists with both doctoral and medical degrees should have the best opportunities.

Personality Type: Investigative-Realistic-Artistic. **Skills:** Science; Operations Analysis; Reading Comprehension; Mathematics; Systems Evaluation; Instructing; Complex Problem Solving; Systems Analysis. **Education and Training Program:** Anatomy; Biochemistry; Biomedical Sciences, General; Biophysics; Biostatistics; Cardiovascular Science; Cell Physiology; Cell/Cellular Biology and Histology; Endocrinology; Environmental Toxicology; Epidemiology; Exercise Physiology; Human/Medical Genetics; Immunology; Medical Microbiology and Bacteriology; Medical Scientist; Molecular Biology; Molecular Pharmacology; Molecular Physiology; Molecular Toxicology; Neuropharmacology; Oncology and Cancer Biology; Pathology/Experimental Pathology; others. **Work Environment:** Indoors; sitting; using your hands to handle, control, or feel objects, tools, or controls.

OTHER FEDERAL JOB FACTS
RELATED GS SERIES: 0405 PHARMACOLOGY
TITLE ON USAJOBS: PHARMACOLOGIST

- U.S. Federal Workforce: 619
- Average Length of Service: 10.7 years
- Percent Part-Time: 14.4%
- Percent Women: 41.4%
- Largest Age Bracket: 55–59 (16.3%)
- GS Level with Most Workers: 14
- Agency with Most Workers: Health and Human Services
- State with Most Workers: Maryland

Administer, advise on, supervise, or perform research, analytical, advisory, or other professional and scientific work in the discipline of pharmacology.

Requirements: Knowledge of the history, sources, physical and chemical properties, biochemical, toxic, and physiological effects, mechanisms of action, absorption, distribution, metabolism, biotransformation and excretion, and therapeutic and other uses of drugs. Does not require full professional training in medicine or veterinary medicine.

OTHER FEDERAL JOB FACTS
RELATED GS SERIES: 0415 TOXICOLOGY
TITLE ON USAJOBS: TOXICOLOGIST

- U.S. Federal Workforce: 504
- Average Length of Service: 11.7 years
- Percent Part-Time: 20.6%
- Percent Women: 36.9%
- Largest Age Bracket: 60–64 (16.3%)
- GS Levels with Most Workers: 14, 13
- Agency with Most Workers: Health and Human Services
- States with Most Workers: Maryland, District of Columbia

Administer, advise on, supervise, or perform research, analytical, advisory, or other professional and scientific work in the discipline of toxicology; study the adverse effects of chemical substances or similar agents on living organisms and/or the environment; assess the probability of their occurrence under specified conditions of use or exposure.

Requirements: Knowledge including, but not limited to, pathology, anatomy, chemistry, biochemistry, microbiology, physiology, pharmacology, toxicology, and materials sciences. Does not require full preparation for practice in any one of those disciplines or full professional training in medicine or veterinary medicine.

Microbiologists

- ❋ Education/Training Required: Doctoral degree
- ❋ Annual Earnings (Federal): $92,580
- ❋ Annual Earnings (All Industries): $66,580
- ❋ Earnings Growth Potential (Federal): 33.0% (low)
- ❋ Earnings Growth Potential (All Industries): 41.2% (high)
- ❋ Job Growth (Federal): 7.4%
- ❋ Job Growth (All Industries): 12.2%
- ❋ Annual Job Openings (Federal): 80
- ❋ Annual Job Openings (All Industries): 750

Investigate the growth, structure, development, and other characteristics of microscopic organisms, such as bacteria, algae, or fungi. Includes medical microbiologists who study the relationship between organisms and disease or the effects of antibiotics on microorganisms. Investigate the relationship between organisms and disease including the control of epidemics and the effects of antibiotics on microorganisms. Prepare technical reports and recommendations based upon research outcomes. Supervise biological technologists and technicians and other scientists. Provide laboratory services for health departments, for community environmental health programs, and for physicians needing information for diagnosis and treatment. Use a variety of specialized equipment such as electron microscopes, gas chromatographs, and high pressure liquid chromatographs, electrophoresis units, thermocyclers, fluorescence activated cell sorters, and phosphoimagers. Examine physiological, morphological, and cultural characteristics, using microscopes, to identify and classify microorganisms in human, water, and food specimens. Study growth, structure, development, and general characteristics of bacteria and other microorganisms to understand their relationships to human, plant, and animal health. Isolate and maintain cultures of bacteria or other microorganisms in prescribed or developed media, controlling moisture, aeration, temperature, and nutrition. Observe action of microorganisms upon living tissues of plants, higher animals, and other microorganisms, and on dead organic matter. Study the structure and function of human, animal, and plant tissues, cells, pathogens, and toxins. Conduct chemical analyses of substances such as acids, alcohols, and enzymes.

Considerations for Job Outlook: Biotechnological research and development should continue to drive job growth. Doctoral degree holders are expected to face competition for research positions in academia.

Personality Type: Investigative-Realistic. **Skills:** Science; Active Learning; Mathematics; Reading Comprehension; Learning Strategies; Operations Analysis; Writing; Systems Analysis. **Education and Training Program:** Biochemistry and Molecular Biology; Cell/Cellular Biology and Anatomical Sciences, Other; Microbiology, General; Soil Microbiology; Structural Biology. **Work Environment:** Indoors; disease or infections; using your hands to handle, control, or feel objects, tools, or controls; hazardous conditions; sitting.

OTHER FEDERAL JOB FACTS

RELATED GS SERIES: 0403 MICROBIOLOGY

TITLE ON USAJOBS: MICROBIOLOGIST

* U.S. Federal Workforce: 2,613
* Average Length of Service: 12.9 years
* Percent Part-Time: 3.2%
* Percent Women: 48.8%
* Largest Age Bracket: 55–59 (16.9%)
* GS Levels with Most Workers: 13, 12
* Agency with Most Workers: Health and Human Services
* State with Most Workers: Maryland

Perform scientific and professional work in the field of microbiology.

Requirements: Professional knowledge of microbiology.

Motor Vehicle Operators, All Other

* Education/Training Required: Short-term on-the-job training
* Annual Earnings (Federal): $44,020
* Annual Earnings (All Industries): $26,130
* Earnings Growth Potential (Federal): 20.0% (very low)
* Earnings Growth Potential (All Industries): 37.4% (medium)
* Job Growth (Federal): 7.7%
* Job Growth (All Industries): 8.4%
* Annual Job Openings (Federal): 110
* Annual Job Openings (All Industries): 2,060

Considerations for Job Outlook: About average employment growth is projected.

Personality Type: No data available. **Skills:** No data available. **Education and Training Program:** No related CIP programs; this job is learned through informal short-term on-the-job training. **Work Environment:** No data available.

OTHER FEDERAL JOB FACTS

RELATED GS SERIES: 5703 MOTOR VEHICLE OPERATING

TITLE ON USAJOBS: MOTOR VEHICLE OPERATOR

* U.S. Federal Workforce: 5,594
* Average Length of Service: 14.4 years
* Percent Part-Time: 6.0%
* Percent Women: 7.8%
* Largest Age Bracket: 55–59 (21.6%)
* GS Level with Most Workers: Not a GS occupation
* Agency with Most Workers: Defense
* State with Most Workers: California

Operate gasoline, diesel, or electric-powered wheeled vehicles to haul cargo and fuel, transport passengers, or to tow or recover equipment; drive the vehicles in restricted traffic environments on government installations, over public roads and highways, or under cross-country conditions.

Requirements: Knowledge and skill required to operate the vehicle safely.

Museum Technicians and Conservators

* Education/Training Required: Bachelor's degree
* Annual Earnings (Federal): $38,450
* Annual Earnings (All Industries): $37,120

- Earnings Growth Potential (Federal): 35.4% (median)
- Earnings Growth Potential (All Industries): 36.6% (medium)
- Job Growth (Federal): 18.1%
- Job Growth (All Industries): 25.6%
- Annual Job Openings (Federal): 120
- Annual Job Openings (All Industries): 610

Prepare specimens, such as fossils, skeletal parts, lace, and textiles, for museum collection and exhibits. May restore documents or install, arrange, and exhibit materials. Install, arrange, assemble, and prepare artifacts for exhibition, ensuring the artifacts' safety, reporting their status and condition, and identifying and correcting any problems with the set-up. Coordinate exhibit installations, assisting with design, constructing displays, dioramas, display cases, and models, and ensuring the availability of necessary materials. Determine whether objects need repair and choose the safest and most effective method of repair. Clean objects, such as paper, textiles, wood, metal, glass, rock, pottery, and furniture, using cleansers, solvents, soap solutions, and polishes. Prepare artifacts for storage and shipping. Supervise and work with volunteers. Perform tests and examinations to establish storage and conservation requirements, policies, and procedures. Notify superior when restoration of artifacts requires outside experts. Direct and supervise curatorial, technical, and student staff in the handling, mounting, care, and storage of art objects.

Considerations for Job Outlook: Employment for archivists is expected to increase as public and private organizations need categorization of and access to increasing volumes of records and information. Employment growth for curators and museum technicians should be strong as museum attendance levels remain high. Keen competition is expected.

Personality Type: Realistic-Artistic. **Skills:** Writing; Quality Control Analysis; Systems Evaluation; Systems Analysis; Management of Material Resources; Installation; Programming; Operation Monitoring. **Education and Training Program:** Art History, Criticism and Conservation; Museology/Museum Studies; Public/Applied History. **Work Environment:** Indoors; using your hands to handle, control, or feel objects, tools, or controls; sitting; contaminants; sounds, noisy.

OTHER FEDERAL JOB FACTS

RELATED GS SERIES: 1016 MUSEUM SPECIALIST AND TECHNICIAN

TITLE ON USAJOBS: MUSEUM SPECIALIST / TECHNICIAN

- U.S. Federal Workforce: 882
- Average Length of Service: 13.2 years
- Percent Part-Time: 12.0%
- Percent Women: 54.3%
- Largest Age Bracket: 55–59 (16.7%)
- GS Levels with Most Workers: 9, 11
- Agency with Most Workers: Interior
- State with Most Workers: District of Columbia

Perform technical and specialized work in connection with the operation of public museums or the management of museum collections.

Requirements: Varies with level of responsibility. May require ability to do repetitive and manual work, follow simple oral direction, work with others in a crew; familiarity with routine procedures and practices of museums; knowledge of procedures for handling museum collection material and records; knowledge of one or more general areas of information such as geography, general science or biology, chemistry or physics, American or European history, archeology, art, and so forth; knowledge of research methods and conservation techniques related to the collection; knowledge of procedures and methods used in management; ability in writing, speaking, or design work.

Natural Sciences Managers

- ✱ Education/Training Required: Bachelor's or higher degree, plus work experience
- ✱ Annual Earnings (Federal): $106,160
- ✱ Annual Earnings (All Industries): $114,560
- ✱ Earnings Growth Potential (Federal): 21.7% (very low)
- ✱ Earnings Growth Potential (All Industries): 40.1% (medium)
- ✱ Job Growth (Federal): 7.7%
- ✱ Job Growth (All Industries): 15.5%
- ✱ Annual Job Openings (Federal): 290
- ✱ Annual Job Openings (All Industries): 2,010

Plan, direct, or coordinate activities in such fields as life sciences, physical sciences, mathematics, and statistics and research and development in these fields. Confer with scientists, engineers, regulators, and others to plan and review projects and to provide technical assistance. Develop client relationships and communicate with clients to explain proposals, present research findings, establish specifications, or discuss project status. Plan and direct research, development, and production activities. Prepare project proposals. Design and coordinate successive phases of problem analysis, solution proposals, and testing. Review project activities and prepare and review research, testing, and operational reports. Hire, supervise, and evaluate engineers, technicians, researchers, and other staff. Determine scientific and technical goals within broad outlines provided by top management and make detailed plans to accomplish these goals. Develop and implement policies, standards, and procedures for the architectural, scientific, and technical work performed

to ensure regulatory compliance and operations enhancement. Develop innovative technology and train staff for its implementation. Provide for stewardship of plant and animal resources and habitats, studying land use; monitoring animal populations; and providing shelter, resources, and medical treatment for animals. Conduct own research in field of expertise. Recruit personnel and oversee the development and maintenance of staff competence. Advise and assist in obtaining patents or meeting other legal requirements.

Considerations for Job Outlook: Employment is expected to grow along with that of the scientists and engineers these workers supervise. Prospects should be better in the rapidly growing areas of environmental and biomedical engineering and medical and environmental sciences.

Personality Type: Enterprising-Investigative. **Skills:** Science; Operations Analysis; Management of Financial Resources; Technology Design; Management of Personnel Resources; Mathematics; Time Management; Reading Comprehension. **Education and Training Program:** Acoustics; Algebra and Number Theory; Analysis and Functional Analysis; Analytical Chemistry; Anatomy; Animal Genetics; Animal Physiology; Applied Mathematics, General; Applied Mathematics, Other; Astronomy; Astrophysics; Atmospheric Chemistry and Climatology; Atmospheric Physics and Dynamics; Atmospheric Sciences and Meteorology, General; Atmospheric Sciences and Meteorology, Other; Atomic/Molecular Physics; Biochemistry; Biological and Biomedical Sciences, Other; others. **Work Environment:** Indoors; sitting; sounds, noisy.

JOB SPECIALIZATION: CLINICAL RESEARCH COORDINATORS

Plan, direct, or coordinate clinical research projects. Direct the activities of workers engaged in clinical research projects to ensure compliance with protocols and overall clinical objectives.

May evaluate and analyze clinical data. Solicit industry-sponsored trials through contacts and professional organizations. Review scientific literature, participate in continuing education activities, or attend conferences and seminars to maintain current knowledge of clinical studies affairs and issues. Register protocol patients with appropriate statistical centers as required. Prepare for or participate in quality assurance audits conducted by study sponsors, federal agencies, or specially designated review groups. Participate in preparation and management of research budgets and monetary disbursements. Perform specific protocol procedures such as interviewing subjects, taking vital signs, and performing electrocardiograms. Interpret protocols and advise treating physicians on appropriate dosage modifications or treatment calculations based on patient characteristics. Develop advertising and other informational materials to be used in subject recruitment. Contact industry representatives to ensure equipment and software specifications necessary for successful study completion. Confer with health care professionals to determine the best recruitment practices for studies. Track enrollment status of subjects and document dropout information such as dropout causes and subject contact efforts. Review proposed study protocols to evaluate factors such as sample collection processes, data management plans, and potential subject risks.

Personality Type: Enterprising-Investigative-Conventional. **Skills:** No data available. **Education and Training Program:** Biometry/Biometrics; Biostatistics; Biotechnology; Cell/Cellular Biology and Anatomical Sciences, Other; Immunology; Medical Microbiology and Bacteriology; Microbiology, General; Nutrition Sciences; Parasitology; Pathology/Experimental Pathology; Pharmacology; Statistics, General; Toxicology; Virology. **Work Environment:** No data available.

Job Specialization: Water Resource Specialists

Design or implement programs and strategies related to water resource issues, such as supply, quality, and regulatory compliance issues. Supervise teams of workers who capture water from wells and rivers. Review or evaluate designs for water detention facilities, storm drains, flood control facilities, or other hydraulic structures. Negotiate for water rights with communities or water facilities to meet water supply demands. Perform hydrologic, hydraulic, or water quality modeling. Compile water resource data, using geographic information systems (GIS) or global position systems (GPS) software. Compile and maintain documentation on the health of a body of water. Write proposals, project reports, informational brochures, or other documents on wastewater purification, water supply and demand, or other water resource subjects. Recommend new or revised policies, procedures, or regulations to support water resource or conservation goals. Provide technical expertise to assist communities in the development or implementation of storm water monitoring or other water programs. Present water resource proposals to government, public interest groups, or community groups. Identify methods for distributing purified wastewater into rivers, streams, or oceans. Monitor water use, demand, or quality in a particular geographic area. Identify and characterize specific causes or sources of water pollution. Develop plans to protect watershed health or rehabilitate watersheds. Develop or implement standardized water monitoring and assessment methods.

Personality Type: No data available. **Skills:** No data available. **Education and Training Program:** Geology/Earth Science, General; Geochemistry; Geological and Earth Sciences/Geosciences, Other; Hydrology and Water Resources Science; Oceanography, Chemical and Physical. **Work Environment:** No data available.

OTHER FEDERAL JOB FACTS

RELATED GS SERIES: 1301 GENERAL PHYSICAL SCIENCE

TITLE ON USAJOBS: PHYSICAL SCIENTIST, GENERAL

- ❂ U.S. Federal Workforce: 8,394
- ❂ Average Length of Service: 15.6 years
- ❂ Percent Part-Time: 4.5%
- ❂ Percent Women: 33.3%
- ❂ Largest Age Bracket: 50–54 (19.5%)
- ❂ GS Level with Most Workers: 13
- ❂ Agency with Most Workers: Defense
- ❂ State with Most Workers: Maryland

Perform professional work in the physical sciences that is not covered by another OPD occupation, or work that is a combination of physical science fields, with no one predominant.

Requirements: Professional knowledge of one or more physical science fields.

Nuclear Engineers

- ❂ Education/Training Required: Bachelor's degree
- ❂ Annual Earnings (Federal): $91,050
- ❂ Annual Earnings (All Industries): $96,910
- ❂ Earnings Growth Potential (Federal): 38.5% (median)
- ❂ Earnings Growth Potential (All Industries): 31.3% (low)
- ❂ Job Growth (Federal): 11.6%
- ❂ Job Growth (All Industries): 11.0%
- ❂ Annual Job Openings (Federal): 50
- ❂ Annual Job Openings (All Industries): 540

Conduct research on nuclear engineering problems or apply principles and theory of nuclear science to problems concerned with release, control, and utilization of nuclear energy and nuclear waste disposal. Examine accidents to obtain data that can be used to design preventive measures. Monitor nuclear facility operations to identify any design, construction, or operation practices that violate safety regulations and laws or that could jeopardize the safety of operations. Keep abreast of developments and changes in the nuclear field by reading technical journals and by independent study and research. Perform experiments that will provide information about acceptable methods of nuclear material usage, nuclear fuel reclamation, and waste disposal. Design and oversee construction and operation of nuclear reactors and power plants and nuclear fuels reprocessing and reclamation systems. Design and develop nuclear equipment such as reactor cores, radiation shielding, and associated instrumentation and control mechanisms. Initiate corrective actions or order plant shutdowns in emergency situations.

Considerations for Job Outlook: Nuclear engineers are expected to have employment growth of 11 percent from 2008–2018, about as fast as the average for all occupations. Most job growth will be in research and development and engineering services. Although no commercial nuclear power plants have been built in the United States for many years, increased interest in nuclear power as an energy source will spur demand for nuclear engineers to research and develop new designs for reactors. They also will be needed to work in defense-related areas, to develop nuclear medical technology, and to improve and enforce waste management and safety standards. Nuclear engineers are expected to have good employment opportunities because the small number of nuclear engineering graduates is likely to be in rough balance with the number of job openings.

Personality Type: Investigative-Realistic-Conventional. **Skills:** Operations Analysis; Science; Technology Design; Mathematics; Operation Monitoring; Troubleshooting; Quality Control

Analysis; Systems Evaluation. **Education and Training Program:** Nuclear Engineering. **Work Environment:** Indoors; sitting; radiation.

OTHER FEDERAL JOB FACTS

RELATED GS SERIES: 0840 NUCLEAR ENGINEERING

TITLE ON USAJOBS: ENGINEER, NUCLEAR

- ✳ U.S. Federal Workforce: 2,717
- ✳ Average Length of Service: 14.5 years
- ✳ Percent Part-Time: 1.6%
- ✳ Percent Women: 11.8%
- ✳ Largest Age Bracket: 30–34 (15.6%)
- ✳ GS Level with Most Workers: 12
- ✳ Agency with Most Workers: Defense
- ✳ State with Most Workers: Washington

Manage, supervise, lead, and/or perform professional engineering and scientific work involving processes, instruments, and systems used to generate and/or control nuclear energy and radiation.

Requirements: Professional knowledge of and skills in nuclear engineering.

Occupational Health and Safety Specialists

- ✳ Education/Training Required: Bachelor's degree
- ✳ Annual Earnings (Federal): $74,370
- ✳ Annual Earnings (All Industries): $63,230
- ✳ Earnings Growth Potential (Federal): 24.3% (very low)
- ✳ Earnings Growth Potential (All Industries): 40.0% (medium)
- ✳ Job Growth (Federal): 6.5%
- ✳ Job Growth (All Industries): 11.2%
- ✳ Annual Job Openings (Federal): 260
- ✳ Annual Job Openings (All Industries): 2,490

Review, evaluate, and analyze work environments, and design programs and procedures to control, eliminate, and prevent diseases or injuries caused by chemical, physical, and biological agents or ergonomic factors. Order suspension of activities that pose threats to workers' health and safety. Recommend measures to help protect workers from potentially hazardous work methods, processes, or materials. Investigate accidents to identify causes and to determine how such accidents might be prevented in the future. Investigate the adequacy of ventilation, exhaust equipment, lighting, and other conditions that could affect employee health, comfort, or performance. Develop and maintain hygiene programs such as noise surveys, continuous atmosphere monitoring, ventilation surveys, and asbestos management plans. Inspect and evaluate workplace environments, equipment, and practices in order to ensure compliance with safety standards and government regulations. Collaborate with engineers and physicians to institute control and remedial measures for hazardous and potentially hazardous conditions or equipment. Conduct safety training and education programs and demonstrate the use of safety equipment. Provide new-employee health and safety orientations and develop materials for these presentations. Collect samples of dust, gases, vapors, and other potentially toxic materials for analysis. Investigate health-related complaints and inspect facilities to ensure that they comply with public health legislation and regulations. Coordinate "right-to-know" programs regarding hazardous chemicals and other substances. Maintain and update emergency response plans and procedures.

Considerations for Job Outlook: These workers will be needed to ensure workplace safety in response to changing hazards, regulations, public expectations, and technology.

Personality Type: Investigative-Conventional. **Skills:** Science; Operations Analysis; Quality Control Analysis; Operation Monitoring; Persuasion; Troubleshooting; Systems Evaluation; Systems Analysis. **Education and Training Program:** Environmental Health; Industrial Safety Technology/Technician; Occupational Health and Industrial Hygiene; Occupational Safety and Health Technology/Technician; Quality Control and Safety Technologies/Technicians, Other. **Work Environment:** More often indoors than outdoors; sounds, noisy; sitting; contaminants.

OTHER FEDERAL JOB FACTS

RELATED GS SERIES: 0696 CONSUMER SAFETY

TITLE ON USAJOBS: CONSUMER SAFETY OFFICER

- U.S. Federal Workforce: 3,255
- Average Length of Service: 13.1 years
- Percent Part-Time: 0.7%
- Percent Women: 53.4%
- Largest Age Bracket: 45–49 (15.1%)
- GS Level with Most Workers: 13
- Agency with Most Workers: Health and Human Services
- State with Most Workers: Maryland

Enforce the laws and regulations protecting consumers from foods, drugs, cosmetics, fabrics, toys, household products, and equipment that are impure, unwholesome, ineffective, improperly or deceptively labeled or packaged, or in some other way dangerous or defective; identify substances and sources of adulteration and contamination; evaluate manufacturing practices, production processes, quality control systems, laboratory analyses, and clinical investigation programs.

Requirements: Knowledge of various scientific fields, such as chemistry, biology, pharmacology, and food technology.

Operations Research Analysts

- Education/Training Required: Master's degree
- Annual Earnings (Federal): $103,780
- Annual Earnings (All Industries): $70,070
- Earnings Growth Potential (Federal): 37.2% (median)
- Earnings Growth Potential (All Industries): 42.9% (high)
- Job Growth (Federal): 15.4%
- Job Growth (All Industries): 22.0%
- Annual Job Openings (Federal): 160
- Annual Job Openings (All Industries): 3,220

Formulate and apply mathematical modeling and other optimizing methods, using a computer to develop and interpret information that assists management with decision making, policy formulation, or other managerial functions. May develop related software, service, or products. Frequently concentrates on collecting and analyzing data and developing decision support software. May develop and supply optimal time, cost, or logistics networks for program evaluation, review, or implementation. Formulate mathematical or simulation models of problems, relating constants and variables, restrictions, alternatives, and conflicting objectives and their numerical parameters. Collaborate with others in the organization to ensure successful implementation of chosen problem solutions. Analyze information obtained from management in order to conceptualize and define operational problems. Perform validation and testing of models to ensure adequacy; reformulate models as necessary. Collaborate with senior managers and decision makers to identify and solve a variety of problems and to clarify management objectives. Define data requirements; then gather and validate information, applying judgment and statistical tests. Study and analyze information about alternative courses of action in order to determine which plan will offer the best outcomes. Prepare management reports defining and evaluating problems and recommending solutions. Break systems into their component parts, assign numerical values to each component, and examine the mathematical relationships between them. Specify manipulative or computational methods to be applied to models. Observe the current system in operation and gather and analyze information about each of the parts of component problems, using a variety of sources. Design, conduct, and evaluate experimental operational models in cases where models cannot be developed from existing data.

Considerations for Job Outlook: As technology advances and companies further emphasize efficiency, demand for operations research analysis should continue to grow. Excellent opportunities are expected, especially for those who have an advanced degree.

Personality Type: Investigative-Conventional-Enterprising. **Skills:** Operations Analysis; Science; Mathematics; Systems Evaluation; Systems Analysis; Programming; Complex Problem Solving; Active Learning. **Education and Training Program:** Management Science; Management Sciences and Quantitative Methods, Other; Operations Research. **Work Environment:** Indoors; sitting.

OTHER FEDERAL JOB FACTS

RELATED GS SERIES: 1515 OPERATIONS RESEARCH
TITLE ON USAJOBS: OPERATIONS RESEARCH ANALYST

* U.S. Federal Workforce: 4,440
* Average Length of Service: 13.6 years
* Percent Part-Time: 1.0%
* Percent Women: 29.2%
* Largest Age Bracket: 50–54 (18.1%)
* GS Level with Most Workers: 13

* Agency with Most Workers: Defense
* State with Most Workers: Virginia

Design, develop, and adapt mathematical, statistical, econometric, and other scientific methods and techniques; analyze management problems and provide advice and insight about the probable effects of alternative solutions to these problems.

Requirements: Competence in the rigorous methods of scientific inquiry and analysis.

Optometrists

* Education/Training Required: First professional degree
* Annual Earnings (Federal): $76,720
* Annual Earnings (All Industries): $96,140
* Earnings Growth Potential (Federal): 60.8% (very high)
* Earnings Growth Potential (All Industries): 49.8% (high)
* Job Growth (Federal): 9.1%
* Job Growth (All Industries): 24.4%
* Annual Job Openings (Federal): 20
* Annual Job Openings (All Industries): 2,010

Diagnose, manage, and treat conditions and diseases of the human eye and visual system. Examine eyes and visual systems, diagnose problems or impairments, prescribe corrective lenses, and provide treatment. May prescribe therapeutic drugs to treat specific eye conditions. Examine eyes, using observation, instruments, and pharmaceutical agents, to determine visual acuity and perception, focus, and coordination and to diagnose diseases and other abnormalities such as glaucoma or color blindness. Prescribe medications to treat eye diseases if state laws permit. Analyze test results and develop treatment plans. Prescribe, supply, fit, and adjust eyeglasses, contact lenses, and other vision aids. Educate and counsel patients on contact lens care, visual hygiene, lighting arrangements, and safety factors. Remove foreign bodies from eyes. Consult with and refer patients to ophthalmologist or other health care practitioners if additional medical treatment is determined necessary. Provide patients undergoing eye surgeries such as cataract and laser vision correction, with pre- and post-operative care. Prescribe therapeutic procedures to correct or conserve vision. Provide vision therapy and low vision rehabilitation.

Considerations for Job Outlook: An aging population and increasing insurance coverage for vision care are expected to lead to employment growth for optometrists. Excellent opportunities are expected.

Personality Type: Investigative-Social-Realistic. **Skills:** Science; Reading Comprehension; Operations Analysis; Quality Control Analysis; Operation and Control; Service Orientation; Active Learning; Critical Thinking. **Education and Training Program:** Optometry (OD). **Work Environment:** Indoors; using your hands to handle, control, or feel objects, tools, or controls; disease or infections; sitting.

OTHER FEDERAL JOB FACTS

RELATED GS SERIES: 0662 OPTOMETRIST

* U.S. Federal Workforce: 977
* Average Length of Service: 7.1 years
* Percent Part-Time: 19.4%
* Percent Women: 51.6%
* Largest Age Bracket: 25–29 (20.7%)
* GS Level with Most Workers: 12
* Agency with Most Workers: Veterans Affairs
* States with Most Workers: California, Ohio

Examine and analyze the eye for diseases and defects; prescribe correctional lenses or exercises.

Requirements: Professional optometric knowledge and skills. Except for positions not involving patient care responsibility (e.g., research optometrist), requires a current license to practice optometry in a state or territory of the United States or in the District of Columbia.

Orthotists and Prosthetists

* Education/Training Required: Bachelor's degree
* Annual Earnings (Federal): $65,800
* Annual Earnings (All Industries): $62,070
* Earnings Growth Potential (Federal): 34.8% (low)
* Earnings Growth Potential (All Industries): 45.2% (high)
* Job Growth (Federal): 10.2%
* Job Growth (All Industries): 15.4%
* Annual Job Openings (Federal): 10
* Annual Job Openings (All Industries): 210

Assist patients with disabling conditions of limbs and spine or with partial or total absence of limb by fitting and preparing orthopedic braces or prostheses. Examine, interview, and measure patients in order to determine their appliance needs and to identify factors that could affect appliance fit. Fit, test, and evaluate devices on patients and make adjustments for proper fit, function, and comfort. Instruct patients in the use and care of orthoses and prostheses. Design orthopedic and prosthetic devices based on physicians' prescriptions and examination and measurement of patients. Maintain patients' records. Make and modify plaster casts of areas that will be fitted with prostheses or orthoses for use in the device construction process. Select materials and components to be used, based on device design. Confer with physicians to formulate specifications and prescriptions for orthopedic or prosthetic devices. Repair, rebuild, and modify prosthetic and orthopedic appliances. Construct and fabricate appliances or supervise others who are constructing the appliances. Train and supervise orthopedic and prosthetic assistants and technicians and other support staff. Update skills and knowledge by attending conferences and seminars. Show and explain orthopedic and prosthetic appliances to healthcare workers. Research new ways to construct and use orthopedic and prosthetic devices. Publish research findings and present them at conferences and seminars.

Considerations for Job Outlook: Faster than average employment growth is projected.

Personality Type: Social-Realistic-Investigative. **Skills:** Operations Analysis; Technology Design; Science; Instructing; Service Orientation; Writing; Active Listening; Systems Evaluation. **Education and Training Program:** Assistive/Augmentative Technology and Rehabilitation Engineering; Orthotist/Prosthetist. **Work Environment:** Indoors; contaminants; hazardous equipment; using your hands to handle, control, or feel objects, tools, or controls; disease or infections; sounds, noisy.

OTHER FEDERAL JOB FACTS

RELATED GS SERIES: 0667 ORTHOTIST AND PROSTHETIST

TITLE ON USAJOBS: ORTHOTIST/PROSTHETIST

- U.S. Federal Workforce: 290
- Average Length of Service: 11.9 years
- Percent Part-Time: 0.3%
- Percent Women: 14.5%
- Largest Age Bracket: 55–59 (19.7%)
- GS Level with Most Workers: 11
- Agency with Most Workers: Veterans Affairs
- States with Most Workers: New York, Texas

Design, fabricate, or fit orthotic or prosthetic devices to preserve or restore function to patients with disabling conditions of the limbs and spine or with partial or total absence of limbs.

Requirements: Knowledge of anatomy, physiology, body mechanics, the application and function of orthoses (braces and orthopedic shoes) and prostheses (artificial limbs), and of the materials available for the fabrication of such devices; skill in the use of tools and specialized equipment; and the ability to deal effectively with patients and their problems and to work with other members of the medical team.

Painters, Construction and Maintenance

- Education/Training Required: Moderate-term on-the-job training
- Annual Earnings (Federal): $47,470
- Annual Earnings (All Industries): $33,720
- Earnings Growth Potential (Federal): 16.3% (very low)
- Earnings Growth Potential (All Industries): 32.8% (low)
- Job Growth (Federal): 7.9%
- Job Growth (All Industries): 7.0%
- Annual Job Openings (Federal): 140
- Annual Job Openings (All Industries): 10,650

Paint walls, equipment, buildings, bridges, and other structural surfaces with brushes, rollers, and spray guns. May remove old paint to prepare surfaces before painting. May mix colors or oils to obtain desired color or consistencies. Cover surfaces with dropcloths or masking tape and paper to protect surfaces during painting. Fill cracks, holes, and joints with caulk, putty, plaster, or other fillers, using caulking guns or putty knives. Apply primers or sealers to prepare new surfaces, such as bare wood or metal, for finish coats. Apply paint, stain, varnish, enamel, and other finishes to equipment, buildings, bridges, and/or other structures, using brushes, spray guns, or rollers. Calculate amounts of required materials and estimate costs, based on surface measurements and/or work orders. Read work orders or receive instructions from supervisors or homeowners in order to determine work requirements. Erect scaffolding and swing gates, or set up ladders, to work above ground level. Remove fixtures such as pictures, door knobs, lamps, and electric switch covers prior to painting. Wash and treat surfaces with oil, turpentine, mildew remover, or other preparations, and sand rough spots to ensure that finishes will adhere properly. Mix and match colors of paint, stain, or varnish with oil and thinning and drying additives in order to obtain desired colors and consistencies. Remove old finishes by stripping, sanding, wire brushing, burning, or using water and/or abrasive blasting. Select and purchase tools and finishes for surfaces to be covered, considering durability, ease of handling, methods of application, and customers' wishes.

Considerations for Job Outlook: Construction, remodeling, and maintenance of existing buildings and infrastructure will drive employment growth for these workers. Job prospects should be good because of the need to replace workers who leave these occupations permanently.

Personality Type: Realistic-Conventional. **Skills:** None met the criteria. **Education and Training Program:** Painting/Painter and Wall Coverer. **Work Environment:** Standing; making repetitive motions; using your hands to handle, control, or feel objects, tools, or controls; contaminants; climbing ladders, scaffolds, or poles; bending or twisting the body.

OTHER FEDERAL JOB FACTS
RELATED GS SERIES: 4102 PAINTING
TITLE ON USAJOBS: PAINTER

* U.S. Federal Workforce: 4,218
* Average Length of Service: 12.9 years
* Percent Part-Time: 0.7%
* Percent Women: 7.5%
* Largest Age Bracket: 50–54 (16.0%)
* GS Level with Most Workers: Not a GS occupation
* Agency with Most Workers: Defense
* State with Most Workers: Georgia

Apply coating materials (for example, paint, varnish, lacquer, shellac, epoxy resin, and teflon) on wood, metal, glass, synthetic, concrete, and other surfaces; use brushes, rollers, spray guns, and other related methods and techniques; coat the insides and outsides of buildings, aircraft, vessels, mobile equipment, fittings, furnishings, machinery, and other surfaces.

Requirements: Knowledge of standard surface preparation and coating methods and techniques and how they are used to get a variety of finish results on various kinds of surfaces.

Paralegals and Legal Assistants

* Education/Training Required: Associate degree
* Annual Earnings (Federal): $60,500
* Annual Earnings (All Industries): $46,980
* Earnings Growth Potential (Federal): 31.9% (low)
* Earnings Growth Potential (All Industries): 36.6% (medium)
* Job Growth (Federal): 18.2%
* Job Growth (All Industries): 28.1%

⊛ Annual Job Openings (Federal): 420

⊛ Annual Job Openings (All Industries): 10,400

Assist lawyers by researching legal precedent, investigating facts, or preparing legal documents. Conduct research to support a legal proceeding, to formulate a defense, or to initiate legal action. Prepare legal documents, including briefs, pleadings, appeals, wills, contracts, and real estate closing statements. Prepare affidavits or other documents, maintain document file, and file pleadings with court clerk. Gather and analyze research data, such as statutes; decisions; and legal articles, codes, and documents. Investigate facts and law of cases to determine causes of action and to prepare cases. Call upon witnesses to testify at hearing. Direct and coordinate law office activity, including delivery of subpoenas. Arbitrate disputes between parties and assist in real estate closing process. Keep and monitor legal volumes to ensure that law library is up to date. Appraise and inventory real and personal property for estate planning.

Considerations for Job Outlook: Increased demand for accessible, cost-efficient legal services is expected to increase employment for paralegals, who may perform more tasks previously done by lawyers. Keen competition is expected. Experienced, formally trained paralegals should have the best job prospects.

Personality Type: Conventional-Investigative-Enterprising. **Skills:** Writing; Active Listening; Speaking; Quality Control Analysis; Operation and Control; Equipment Maintenance; Troubleshooting; Repairing. **Education and Training Program:** Legal Assistant/Paralegal Training. **Work Environment:** Indoors; sitting; making repetitive motions.

OTHER FEDERAL JOB FACTS

RELATED GS SERIES: 0950 PARALEGAL SPECIALIST

⊛ U.S. Federal Workforce: 7,129

⊛ Average Length of Service: 17.8 years

⊛ Percent Part-Time: 1.3%

⊛ Percent Women: 78.7%

⊛ Largest Age Bracket: 50–54 (18.2%)

⊛ GS Level with Most Workers: 11

⊛ Agency with Most Workers: Justice

⊛ State with Most Workers: District of Columbia

Analyze the legal impact of legislative developments and administrative and judicial decisions, opinions, determinations, and rulings on agency programs; conduct research for the preparation of legal opinions on matters of interest to the agency; perform substantive legal analysis of requests for information under the provisions of various acts; or perform other similar legal support functions that require discretion and independent judgment.

Requirements: Specialized (but not professional) knowledge of laws, precedent decisions, regulations, agency policies and practices, and judicial or administrative proceedings. May require practical knowledge of subject-matter areas related to the agency's substantive programs.

RELATED GS SERIES: 0987 TAX LAW SPECIALIST

⊛ U.S. Federal Workforce: 596

⊛ Average Length of Service: 16.8 years

⊛ Percent Part-Time: 2.0%

⊛ Percent Women: 51.7%

⊛ Largest Age Bracket: 55–59 (21.5%)

⊛ GS Levels with Most Workers: 9, 14

⊛ Agency with Most Workers: Treasury

⊛ State with Most Workers: District of Columbia

Administer, supervise, or perform quasi-legal technical tax work requiring analysis and application of tax principles; interpret the Internal Revenue Code, related laws, regulations, rulings, and precedents; prepare regulations, rulings, and technical guides; and make or review determinations and decisions in such matters.

Requirements: Specialized (but not professional) knowledge of tax laws.

Petroleum Engineers

- ❀ Education/Training Required: Bachelor's degree
- ❀ Annual Earnings (Federal): $96,480
- ❀ Annual Earnings (All Industries): $108,910
- ❀ Earnings Growth Potential (Federal): 33.7% (low)
- ❀ Earnings Growth Potential (All Industries): 46.2% (high)
- ❀ Job Growth (Federal): 30.0%
- ❀ Job Growth (All Industries): 18.4%
- ❀ Annual Job Openings (Federal): 10
- ❀ Annual Job Openings (All Industries): 860

Devise methods to improve oil and gas well production and determine the need for new or modified tool designs. Oversee drilling and offer technical advice to achieve economical and satisfactory progress. Assess costs and estimate the production capabilities and economic value of oil and gas wells to evaluate the economic viability of potential drilling sites. Monitor production rates, and plan rework processes to improve production. Analyze data to recommend placement of wells and supplementary processes to enhance production. Specify and supervise well modification and stimulation programs to maximize oil and gas recovery. Direct and monitor the completion and evaluation of wells, well testing, or well surveys.

Assist engineering and other personnel to solve operating problems. Develop plans for oil and gas field drilling and for product recovery and treatment. Maintain records of drilling and production operations. Confer with scientific, engineering, and technical personnel to resolve design, research, and testing problems. Write technical reports for engineering and management personnel. Evaluate findings to develop, design, or test equipment or processes.

Considerations for Job Outlook: Petroleum engineers are expected to have employment growth of 18 percent from 2008–2018, faster than the average for all occupations. Petroleum engineers increasingly will be needed to develop new resources as well as new methods of extracting more from existing sources. Excellent opportunities are expected for petroleum engineers because the number of job openings is likely to exceed the relatively small number of graduates. Petroleum engineers work around the world, and, in fact, the best employment opportunities may include some work in other countries.

Personality Type: Investigative-Realistic-Conventional. **Skills:** Science; Systems Evaluation; Management of Financial Resources; Mathematics; Management of Material Resources; Technology Design; Operation Monitoring; Systems Analysis. **Education and Training Program:** Petroleum Engineering. **Work Environment:** Indoors; sitting.

OTHER FEDERAL JOB FACTS
RELATED GS SERIES: 0881 PETROLEUM ENGINEERING

- ❀ U.S. Federal Workforce: 300
- ❀ Average Length of Service: 17.2 years
- ❀ Percent Part-Time: 0.3%
- ❀ Percent Women: 14.0%
- ❀ Largest Age Bracket: 50–54 (24.7%)
- ❀ GS Level with Most Workers: 13

❊ Agency with Most Workers: Interior

❊ State with Most Workers: Louisiana

Manage, supervise, lead, and/or perform professional engineering and scientific work involved in the discovery and recovery of oil, natural gas (e.g., methane, ethane, propane, and butane), and helium.

Requirements: Professional knowledge of and skills in petroleum engineering.

Pharmacists

❊ Education/Training Required: First professional degree

❊ Annual Earnings (Federal): $107,330

❊ Annual Earnings (All Industries): $109,180

❊ Earnings Growth Potential (Federal): 40.9% (high)

❊ Earnings Growth Potential (All Industries): 27.4% (low)

❊ Job Growth (Federal): 7.7%

❊ Job Growth (All Industries): 17.0%

❊ Annual Job Openings (Federal): 190

❊ Annual Job Openings (All Industries): 10,580

Compound and dispense medications, following prescriptions issued by physicians, dentists, or other authorized medical practitioners. Review prescriptions to assure accuracy, to ascertain the needed ingredients, and to evaluate their suitability. Provide information and advice regarding drug interactions, side effects, dosage, and proper medication storage. Assess the identity, strength, and purity of medications. Maintain records, such as pharmacy files, patient profiles, charge system files, inventories, control records for radioactive nuclei, and registries of poisons, narcotics, and controlled drugs. Compound and dispense medications as prescribed by doctors and dentists, by calculating, weighing, measuring, and mixing ingredients, or oversee these activities. Plan, implement, and maintain procedures for mixing, packaging, and labeling pharmaceuticals, according to policy and legal requirements, to ensure quality, security, and proper disposal. Teach pharmacy students serving as interns in preparation for their graduation or licensure. Advise customers on the selection of medication brands, medical equipment, and health-care supplies. Provide specialized services to help patients manage conditions such as diabetes, asthma, smoking cessation, or high blood pressure. Collaborate with other health care professionals to plan, monitor, review, and evaluate the quality and effectiveness of drugs and drug regimens, providing advice on drug applications and characteristics. Analyze prescribing trends to monitor patient compliance and to prevent excessive usage or harmful interactions.

Considerations for Job Outlook: The increasing numbers of middle-aged and elderly people—who use more prescription drugs than younger people—should continue to spur employment growth for pharmacists. Job prospects are expected to be excellent.

Personality Type: Investigative-Conventional-Social. **Skills:** Science; Operations Analysis; Reading Comprehension; Management of Material Resources; Active Listening; Writing; Instructing; Management of Financial Resources. **Education and Training Program:** Clinical, Hospital, and Managed Care Pharmacy (MS, PhD); Industrial and Physical Pharmacy and Cosmetic Sciences (MS, PhD); Medicinal and Pharmaceutical Chemistry (MS, PhD); Natural Products Chemistry and Pharmacognosy (MS, PhD); Pharmaceutics and Drug Design (MS, PhD); Pharmacoeconomics/ Pharmaceutical Economics (MS, PhD); Pharmacy (PharmD [USA], PharmD or BS/BPharm [Canada]); Pharmacy Administration and Pharmacy Policy and Regulatory Affairs (MS, PhD); others. **Work Environment:** Indoors; using your hands to handle, control, or feel objects, tools, or controls; standing; disease or infections; making repetitive motions.

OTHER FEDERAL JOB FACTS
RELATED GS SERIES: 0660 PHARMACIST

- U.S. Federal Workforce: 8,610
- Average Length of Service: 9.5 years
- Percent Part-Time: 16.1%
- Percent Women: 60.5%
- Largest Age Bracket: 25–29 (14.4%)
- GS Level with Most Workers: 12
- Agency with Most Workers: Veterans Affairs
- States with Most Workers: Florida, California

Compound prescriptions of physicians, dentists, and other licensed practitioners; formulate, prepare, compound, select, dispense, and preserve drugs, medicines, and chemicals; and research and investigate special vehicles or variations of standard formulas to meet the needs of individual patients.

Requirements: This series covers all positions that involve professional and scientific work in the field of pharmacy.

Pharmacy Technicians

- Education/Training Required: Moderate-term on-the-job training
- Annual Earnings (Federal): $38,870
- Annual Earnings (All Industries): $28,070
- Earnings Growth Potential (Federal): 18.2% (very low)
- Earnings Growth Potential (All Industries): 30.6% (low)
- Job Growth (Federal): 18.5%
- Job Growth (All Industries): 30.6%
- Annual Job Openings (Federal): 210
- Annual Job Openings (All Industries): 18,200

Prepare medications under the direction of a pharmacist. May measure, mix, count out, label, and record amounts and dosages of medications. Receive written prescription or refill requests and verify that information is complete and accurate. Establish and maintain patient profiles, including lists of medications taken by individual patients. Maintain proper storage and security conditions for drugs. Prepack bulk medicines, fill bottles with prescribed medications, and type and affix labels. Answer telephones, responding to questions or requests. Mix pharmaceutical preparations according to written prescriptions. Clean, and help maintain, equipment and work areas, and sterilize glassware according to prescribed methods. Price and file prescriptions that have been filled. Receive and store incoming supplies, verify quantities against invoices, check for outdated medications in current inventory, and inform supervisors of stock needs and shortages. Assist customers by answering simple questions, locating items or referring them to the pharmacist for medication information. Order, label, and count stock of medications, chemicals, and supplies, and enter inventory data into computer. Operate cash registers to accept payment from customers. Transfer medication from vials to the appropriate number of sterile, disposable syringes, using aseptic techniques. Supply and monitor robotic machines that dispense medicine into containers, and label the containers. Prepare and process medical insurance claim forms and records. Deliver medications and pharmaceutical supplies to patients, nursing stations, or surgery.

Considerations for Job Outlook: Growth in the population of middle-aged and elderly people—who use more prescription drugs than younger people—should spur employment increases for these workers. Job prospects are expected to be good.

Personality Type: Conventional-Realistic. **Skills:** Service Orientation; Mathematics; Active Listening; Quality Control Analysis; Installation; Operation Monitoring; Operation and Control; Troubleshooting. **Education and Training Program:** Pharmacy Technician/Assistant Training. **Work Environment:** Indoors; standing; using your hands to handle, control, or feel objects, tools, or controls; walking and running; making repetitive motions; disease or infections.

OTHER FEDERAL JOB FACTS

RELATED GS SERIES: 0661 PHARMACY TECHNICIAN

- ❋ U.S. Federal Workforce: 5,676
- ❋ Average Length of Service: 9.4 years
- ❋ Percent Part-Time: 8.1%
- ❋ Percent Women: 72.9%
- ❋ Largest Age Bracket: 50–54 (14.6%)
- ❋ GS Level with Most Workers: 6
- ❋ Agency with Most Workers: Veterans Affairs
- ❋ State with Most Workers: Texas

Perform technical support work in a pharmacy under the supervision of a registered pharmacist.

Requirements: Practical knowledge of pharmaceutical nomenclature; characteristics, strengths, and dosage forms of pharmaceuticals; pharmaceutical systems of weights and measures; operation and care of pharmacy equipment; and pharmaceutical procedures and techniques.

Physical Scientists, All Other

- ❋ Education/Training Required: Bachelor's degree
- ❋ Annual Earnings (Federal): $104,480
- ❋ Annual Earnings (All Industries): $93,950
- ❋ Earnings Growth Potential (Federal): 45.1% (high)
- ❋ Earnings Growth Potential (All Industries): 48.6% (high)
- ❋ Job Growth (Federal): 7.6%
- ❋ Job Growth (All Industries): 11.1%
- ❋ Annual Job Openings (Federal): 230
- ❋ Annual Job Openings (All Industries): 1,010

Considerations for Job Outlook: About average employment growth is projected.

JOB SPECIALIZATION: REMOTE SENSING SCIENTISTS AND TECHNOLOGISTS

Apply remote sensing principles and methods to analyze data and solve problems in areas such as natural resource management, urban planning, and homeland security. May develop new analytical techniques and sensor systems or develop new applications for existing systems. Analyze data acquired from aircraft, satellites, or ground-based platforms using statistical analysis software, image analysis software, or Geographic Information Systems (GIS). Manage or analyze data obtained from remote sensing systems to obtain meaningful results. Process aerial and satellite imagery to create products such as landcover maps. Develop and build databases for remote sensing and related geospatial project information. Monitor quality of remote sensing data collection operations to determine if procedural or equipment changes are necessary. Attend meetings or seminars and read current literature to maintain knowledge of developments in the field of remote sensing. Prepare and deliver reports and presentations of geospatial project information. Conduct research into the application and enhancement of remote sensing technology. Discuss project goals, equipment requirements, and methodologies with colleagues and team members. Integrate other geospatial data sources into projects. Organize and maintain geospatial data and associated documentation. Participate in fieldwork as required. Design and implement strategies for collection, analysis, or display of geographic data. Collect supporting data such as climatic and field survey data to corroborate remote sensing data analyses. Develop new analytical techniques or sensor systems. Train technicians in the use of remote sensing technology.

Personality Type: Realistic-Investigative. **Skills:** Science; Operations Analysis; Mathematics; Writing; Systems Evaluation; Systems Analysis; Reading Comprehension; Complex Problem Solving. **Education and Training Program:** Geographic Information Science and Cartography; Signal/Geospatial Intelligence. **Work Environment:** Indoors; sitting.

OTHER FEDERAL JOB FACTS

RELATED GS SERIES: 1301 GENERAL PHYSICAL SCIENCE

TITLE ON USAJOBS: PHYSICAL SCIENTIST, GENERAL

- ❋ U.S. Federal Workforce: 8,394
- ❋ Average Length of Service: 15.6 years
- ❋ Percent Part-Time: 4.5%
- ❋ Percent Women: 33.3%
- ❋ Largest Age Bracket: 50–54 (19.5%)
- ❋ GS Level with Most Workers: 13
- ❋ Agency with Most Workers: Defense
- ❋ State with Most Workers: Maryland

Perform professional work in the physical sciences that is not covered by another OPD occupation, or work that is a combination of physical science fields, with no one predominant.

Requirements: Professional knowledge of one or more physical science fields.

RELATED GS SERIES: 1386 PHOTOGRAPHIC TECHNOLOGY

- ❋ U.S. Federal Workforce: 19
- ❋ Average Length of Service: 16.8 years
- ❋ Percent Part-Time: 0.0%
- ❋ Percent Women: 5.3%
- ❋ Largest Age Bracket: 45–49 (26.3%)
- ❋ GS Level with Most Workers: 14
- ❋ Agency with Most Workers: Justice
- ❋ State with Most Workers: District of Columbia

Plan, research, design, develop, modify, test, and evaluate photographic equipment and techniques.

Requirements: Professional interdisciplinary knowledge and skills in the scientific and engineering fields that comprise photographic technology.

RELATED GS SERIES: 1384 TEXTILE TECHNOLOGY

- ❋ U.S. Federal Workforce: 71
- ❋ Average Length of Service: 16.2 years
- ❋ Percent Part-Time: 1.4%
- ❋ Percent Women: 66.2%
- ❋ Largest Age Bracket: 50–54 (25.4%)
- ❋ GS Level with Most Workers: 12
- ❋ Agency with Most Workers: Defense
- ❋ State with Most Workers: Massachusetts

Perform scientific and technological work with textile or fibers, including investigation, development, production, processing, evaluation, and application.

Requirements: Degree in cotton, fiber, or textile technology; or in a related subject such as physics, chemistry, or mechanical or electrical engineering with significant course work in cotton, fiber, or textile technology; or a combination of relevant courses and work experience.

Physical Therapists

- ❋ Education/Training Required: Master's degree
- ❋ Annual Earnings (Federal): $75,960
- ❋ Annual Earnings (All Industries): $74,480
- ❋ Earnings Growth Potential (Federal): 14.6% (very low)
- ❋ Earnings Growth Potential (All Industries): 30.0% (low)
- ❋ Job Growth (Federal): 9.7%
- ❋ Job Growth (All Industries): 30.3%
- ❋ Annual Job Openings (Federal): 50
- ❋ Annual Job Openings (All Industries): 7,860

Assess, plan, organize, and participate in rehabilitative programs that improve mobility, relieve pain, increase strength, and decrease or prevent deformity of patients suffering from disease or injury. Perform and document initial exams, evaluating data to identify problems and determine diagnoses prior to interventions. Plan, prepare, and carry out individually designed programs of physical treatment to maintain, improve, or restore physical functioning; alleviate pain; and prevent physical dysfunction in patients. Record prognoses, treatments, responses, and progresses in patients' charts or enter information into computers. Identify and document goals, anticipated progresses, and plans for reevaluation. Evaluate effects of treatments at various stages and adjust treatments to achieve maximum benefits. Administer manual exercises, massages, or traction to help relieve pain, increase patient strength, or decrease or prevent deformity or crippling. Test and measure patients' strength, motor development and function, sensory perception, functional capacity, and respiratory and circulatory efficiency and record data. Instruct patients and families in treatment procedures to be continued at home. Confer with patients, medical practitioners, and appropriate others to plan, implement, and assess intervention programs. Review physicians' referrals and patients' medical records to help determine diagnoses and physical therapy treatments required. Obtain patients' informed consent to proposed interventions. Discharge patients from physical therapy when goals or projected outcomes have been attained and provide for appropriate follow-up care or referrals.

Considerations for Job Outlook: Employment of physical therapists is expected to increase as the population ages and as better medical technology increases survival rates of people who become injured or ill. Job opportunities should be good in settings that treat primarily the elderly.

Personality Type: Social-Investigative-Realistic. **Skills:** Science; Operations Analysis; Service Orientation; Instructing; Persuasion; Time Management; Social Perceptiveness; Reading Comprehension. **Education and Training Program:** Kinesiotherapy/Kinesiotherapist; Physical Therapy/Therapist. **Work Environment:** Indoors; disease or infections; standing.

OTHER FEDERAL JOB FACTS
RELATED GS SERIES: 0633 PHYSICAL THERAPIST

- ❋ U.S. Federal Workforce: 1,680
- ❋ Average Length of Service: 8.0 years
- ❋ Percent Part-Time: 11.3%
- ❋ Percent Women: 61.7%
- ❋ Largest Age Bracket: 35–39 (16.7%)
- ❋ GS Level with Most Workers: 11
- ❋ Agency with Most Workers: Veterans Affairs
- ❋ State with Most Workers: California

Plan and carry out treatment utilizing therapeutic exercise, massage, and physical agents such as air, water, electricity, sound, and radiant energy; perform tests and measurements involving manual or electrical means; and interpret results; also devise adaptations of equipment to meet the specific needs of patients.

Requirements: Knowledge of the concepts, principles, and practices of physical therapy for the treatment or prevention of physical disability or disease.

Physician Assistants

- ❋ Education/Training Required: Master's degree
- ❋ Annual Earnings (Federal): $83,370
- ❋ Annual Earnings (All Industries): $84,420
- ❋ Earnings Growth Potential (Federal): 25.7% (low)
- ❋ Earnings Growth Potential (All Industries): 33.8% (low)
- ❋ Job Growth (Federal): 18.3%
- ❋ Job Growth (All Industries): 39.0%
- ❋ Annual Job Openings (Federal): 90
- ❋ Annual Job Openings (All Industries): 4,280

Under the supervision of physicians, provide health-care services typically performed by a physician. Conduct complete physicals, provide treatment, and counsel patients. May, in some cases, prescribe medication. Must graduate from an accredited educational program for physician assistants. Examine patients to obtain information about their physical conditions. Obtain, compile, and record patient medical data, including health history, progress notes, and results of physical examinations. Interpret diagnostic test results for deviations from normal. Make tentative diagnoses and decisions about management and treatment of patients. Prescribe therapy or medication with physician approval. Administer or order diagnostic tests, such as X-ray, electrocardiogram, and laboratory tests. Instruct and counsel patients about prescribed therapeutic

regimens, normal growth and development, family planning, emotional problems of daily living, and health maintenance. Perform therapeutic procedures such as injections, immunizations, suturing and wound care, and infection management. Provide physicians with assistance during surgery or complicated medical procedures. Visit and observe patients on hospital rounds or house calls, updating charts, ordering therapy, and reporting back to physicians. Supervise and coordinate activities of technicians and technical assistants. Order medical and laboratory supplies and equipment.

Considerations for Job Outlook: Employment growth for these workers should be driven by an aging population and by health-care providers' increasing use of physician assistants to contain costs. Opportunities should be good, particularly in underserved areas.

Personality Type: Social-Investigative-Realistic. **Skills:** Science; Instructing; Service Orientation; Judgment and Decision Making; Social Perceptiveness; Reading Comprehension; Operations Analysis; Systems Evaluation. **Education and Training Program:** Physician Assistant Training. **Work Environment:** Indoors; disease or infections; standing; using your hands to handle, control, or feel objects, tools, or controls.

JOB SPECIALIZATION: ANESTHESIOLOGIST ASSISTANTS

Assist anesthesiologists in the administration of anesthesia for surgical and non-surgical procedures. Monitor patient status and provide patient care during surgical treatment. Verify availability of operating room supplies, medications, and gases. Provide clinical instruction, supervision, or training to staff in areas such as anesthesia practices. Collect samples or specimens for diagnostic testing. Participate in seminars, workshops, or other professional activities to keep abreast of developments in anesthesiology. Collect and document patients' pre-anesthetic health

P

histories. Provide airway management interventions, including tracheal intubation, fiber optics, or ventilary support. Respond to emergency situations by providing cardiopulmonary resuscitation (CPR), basic cardiac life support (BLS), advanced cardiac life support (ACLS), or pediatric advanced life support (PALS). Monitor and document patients' progress during post-anesthesia period. Pretest and calibrate anesthesia delivery systems and monitors. Assist anesthesiologists in monitoring of patients, including electrocardiogram (EKG), direct arterial pressure, central venous pressure, arterial blood gas, hematocrit, or routine measurement of temperature, respiration, blood pressure, and heart rate. Assist in the provision of advanced life support techniques including those procedures using high frequency ventilation or intra-arterial cardiovascular assistance devices. Assist anesthesiologists in performing anesthetic procedures such as epidural and spinal injections.

Personality Type: Realistic-Social-Investigative. **Skills:** No data available. **Education and Training Program:** Physician Assistant Training. **Work Environment:** No data available.

OTHER FEDERAL JOB FACTS

RELATED GS SERIES: 0603 PHYSICIAN ASSISTANT

TITLE ON USAJOBS: PHYSICIAN'S ASSISTANT

- U.S. Federal Workforce: 3,169
- Average Length of Service: 9.7 years
- Percent Part-Time: 12.4%
- Percent Women: 45.4%
- Largest Age Bracket: 55–59 (17.9%)
- GS Level with Most Workers: 11
- Agency with Most Workers: Veterans Affairs
- State with Most Workers: Texas

Assist a physician by providing diagnostic and therapeutic medical care and services under the guidance of the physician; take case histories, conduct physical examinations, and order laboratory studies during hospital rounds and clinic visits; as directed by a physician, carry out special procedures.

Requirements: Knowledge of specific observation and examination procedures; and ability to perform diagnostic and therapeutic tasks. Does no require the full professional background of the licensed physician.

Physicists

- Education/Training Required: Doctoral degree
- Annual Earnings (Federal): $111,370
- Annual Earnings (All Industries): $106,390
- Earnings Growth Potential (Federal): 35.4% (median)
- Earnings Growth Potential (All Industries): 47.2% (high)
- Job Growth (Federal): 7.5%
- Job Growth (All Industries): 15.9%
- Annual Job Openings (Federal): 110
- Annual Job Openings (All Industries): 690

Conduct research into phases of physical phenomena, develop theories and laws on basis of observation and experiments, and devise methods to apply laws and theories to industry and other fields. Perform complex calculations as part of the analysis and evaluation of data, using computers. Describe and express observations and conclusions in mathematical terms. Analyze data from research conducted to detect and measure physical phenomena. Report experimental results by writing papers for scientific journals or by presenting information at scientific conferences. Design computer simulations to model physical data so that it can be better understood. Collaborate with other scientists in the design, development, and testing of experimental, industrial, or medical equipment, instrumentation, and procedures. Direct testing and monitoring of contamination of radioactive equipment, and recording of personnel and plant area radiation exposure data. Observe the structure and properties of matter, and the transformation and propagation of energy, using equipment such as masers, lasers, and telescopes, in order to explore and identify the basic principles governing these phenomena. Develop theories and laws on the basis of observation and experiments, and apply these theories and laws to problems in areas such as nuclear energy, optics, and aerospace technology. Teach physics to students. Develop manufacturing, assembly, and fabrication processes of lasers, masers, infrared, and other light-emitting and light-sensitive devices.

Considerations for Job Outlook: An increased focus on basic research, particularly that related to energy, is expected to drive employment growth for these workers. Prospects should be favorable for physicists in applied research, development, and related technical fields and for astronomers in government and academia.

Personality Type: Investigative-Realistic. **Skills:** Science; Programming; Mathematics; Technology Design; Active Learning; Reading Comprehension; Learning Strategies; Writing. **Education and Training Program:** Acoustics; Astrophysics; Atomic/Molecular Physics; Condensed Matter and Materials Physics; Elementary Particle Physics; Health/Medical Physics; Nuclear Physics; Optics/Optical Sciences; Physics, General; Physics, Other; Plasma and High-Temperature Physics; Theoretical and Mathematical Physics. **Work Environment:** Indoors; sitting.

OTHER FEDERAL JOB FACTS

RELATED GS SERIES: 1310 PHYSICS

TITLE ON USAJOBS: PHYSICIST

- ❋ U.S. Federal Workforce: 2,547
- ❋ Average Length of Service: 15.7 years

- ❋ Percent Part-Time: 3.3%
- ❋ Percent Women: 11.7%
- ❋ Largest Age Bracket: 45–49 (15.5%)
- ❋ GS Level with Most Workers: 15
- ❋ Agency with Most Workers: Defense
- ❋ State with Most Workers: Maryland

Advise, administer, supervise, or perform research or other professional and scientific work in the investigation and application of the relations between space, time, matter, and energy in the areas of mechanics, sound, optics, heat, electricity, magnetism, radiation, or atomic and nuclear phenomena.

Requirements: Professional knowledge of physics.

Plant and System Operators, All Other

- ❋ Education/Training Required: Long-term on-the-job training
- ❋ Annual Earnings (Federal): $56,520
- ❋ Annual Earnings (All Industries): $49,760
- ❋ Earnings Growth Potential (Federal): 18.1% (very low)
- ❋ Earnings Growth Potential (All Industries): 41.6% (high)
- ❋ Job Growth (Federal): 7.9%
- ❋ Job Growth (All Industries): –4.7%
- ❋ Annual Job Openings (Federal): 30
- ❋ Annual Job Openings (All Industries): 290

Considerations for Job Outlook: Slow decline in employment is projected.

JOB SPECIALIZATION: BIOFUELS PROCESSING TECHNICIANS

Calculate, measure, load, mix, and process refined feedstock with additives in fermentation or reaction process vessels and monitor production process. Perform, and keep records of, plant maintenance, repairs, and safety inspections. Calculate, measure, load, or mix refined feedstock used in biofuels production. Operate chemical processing equipment for the production of biofuels. Operate equipment, such as a centrifuge, to extract biofuels products and secondary by-products or reusable fractions. Operate valves, pumps, engines, or generators to control and adjust biofuels production. Process refined feedstock with additives in fermentation or reaction process vessels. Assess the quality of biofuels additives for reprocessing. Calibrate liquid flow devices and meters including fuel, chemical, and water meters. Collect biofuels samples and perform routine laboratory tests or analyses to assess biofuels quality. Inspect biofuels plant or processing equipment regularly, recording or reporting damage and mechanical problems. Measure and monitor raw biofuels feedstock. Monitor and record biofuels processing data. Monitor and record flow meter performance. Monitor batch, continuous flow, or hybrid biofuels production processes. Monitor stored biofuels products or secondary by-products until reused or transferred to users. Preprocess feedstock in preparation for physical, chemical, or biological fuel production processes. Clean biofuels processing work area, ensuring compliance with safety regulations. Coordinate raw product sourcing or collection. Perform routine maintenance on mechanical, electrical, or electronic equipment or instruments used in the processing of biofuels.

Personality Type: No data available. **Skills:** No data available. **Education and Training Program:** Chemical Engineering Technology/Technician. **Work Environment:** No data available.

JOB SPECIALIZATION: BIOMASS PLANT TECHNICIANS

Control and monitor biomass plant activities and perform maintenance as needed. Measure and monitor raw biomass feedstock, including wood, waste, or refuse materials. Operate valves, pumps, engines, or generators to control and adjust production of biofuels or biomass-fueled power. Perform routine maintenance or make minor repairs to mechanical, electrical, or electronic equipment in biomass plants. Assess quality of biomass feedstock. Calculate, measure, load, or mix biomass feedstock for power generation. Calibrate liquid flow devices or meters, including fuel, chemical, and water meters. Inspect biomass power plant or processing equipment, recording or reporting damage and mechanical problems. Operate biomass fuel-burning boiler or biomass fuel gasification system equipment in accordance with specifications or instructions. Operate equipment to heat biomass, using knowledge of controls, combustion, and firing mechanisms. Operate equipment to start, stop, or regulate biomass-fueled generators, generator units, boilers, engines, or auxiliary systems. Operate high-pressure steam boiler or water chiller equipment for electrical cogeneration operations. Preprocess feedstock to prepare for biochemical or thermochemical production processes. Record or report operational data such as readings on meters, instruments, and gauges. Clean work areas to ensure compliance with safety regulations. Manage parts and supply inventories for biomass plants.

Personality Type: No data available. **Skills:** No data available. **Education and Training Program:** Industrial Mechanics and Maintenance Technology. **Work Environment:** No data available.

JOB SPECIALIZATION: HYDROELECTRIC PLANT TECHNICIANS

Monitor and control activities associated with hydropower generation. Operate plant

equipment, such as turbines, pumps, valves, gates, fans, electric control boards, and battery banks. Monitor equipment operation and performance and make necessary adjustments to ensure optimal performance. Perform equipment maintenance and repair as necessary. Identify and address malfunctions of hydroelectric plant operational equipment, such as generators, transformers, and turbines. Monitor hydroelectric power plant equipment operation and performance, adjusting to performance specifications, as necessary. Start, adjust, and stop generating units, operating valves, gates, or auxiliary equipment in hydroelectric power generating plants. Communicate status of hydroelectric operating equipment to dispatchers or supervisors. Implement load and switching orders in hydroelectric plants in accordance with specifications or instructions. Inspect water-powered electric generators and auxiliary equipment in hydroelectric plants to verify proper operation and to determine maintenance or repair needs. Install and calibrate electrical and mechanical equipment, such as motors, engines, switchboards, relays, switch gears, meters, pumps, hydraulics, and flood channels. Maintain logs, reports, work requests, and other records of work performed in hydroelectric plants. Maintain or repair hydroelectric plant electrical, mechanical, and electronic equipment, such as motors, transformers, voltage regulators, generators, relays, battery systems, air compressors, sump pumps, gates, and valves. Operate high voltage switches and related devices in hydropower stations. Operate hydroelectric plant equipment, such as turbines, pumps, valves, gates, fans, electric control boards, and battery banks.

Personality Type: No data available. **Skills:** No data available. **Education and Training Program:** Industrial Mechanics and Maintenance Technology. **Work Environment:** No data available.

JOB SPECIALIZATION: METHANE/LANDFILL GAS GENERATION SYSTEM TECHNICIANS

Monitor, operate, and maintain landfill gas collection system components and environmental monitoring and control systems. Operate landfill gas, methane, or natural gas fueled electrical generation systems. Perform routine maintenance or minor repairs to landfill gas collection and power generation systems, including equipment such as pneumatic pumps, blower or flare systems, and condensate management systems. Balance individual gas extraction wells at landfill gas facilities. Diagnose or troubleshoot problems with methane or landfill gas collection systems. Download landfill gas well field monitoring data. Measure landfill gas vegetative covering, installing additional covering as required. Measure liquid levels in landfill gas extraction wells. Monitor landfill well fields periodically to ensure proper functioning and performance. Prepare and submit compliance, operational, and safety forms or reports. Read, interpret, and adjust monitoring equipment, such as flow meters and pressure or vacuum gauges. Record and maintain log of well-head gauge pressure readings. Verify that well field monitoring data conforms to applicable regulations. Analyze the layout, instrumentation, or function of electrical generation or transmission facilities. Monitor landfill gas perimeter probes to identify landfill gas migration. Perform landfill surface scans to determine overall effectiveness of the landfill gas site. Repair or replace landfill gas piping. Trace electrical circuitry for landfill gas buildings to ensure compliance of electrical systems with applicable codes or laws.

Personality Type: No data available. **Skills:** No data available. **Education and Training Program:** Chemical Engineering Technology/Technician. **Work Environment:** No data available.

OTHER FEDERAL JOB FACTS

RELATED GS SERIES: 5427 CHEMICAL PLANT OPERATING

- ❋ U.S. Federal Workforce: 27
- ❋ Average Length of Service: 19.5 years
- ❋ Percent Part-Time: 0.0%
- ❋ Percent Women: 3.7%
- ❋ Largest Age Bracket: 55–59 (33.3%)
- ❋ GS Level with Most Workers: Not a GS occupation
- ❋ Agency with Most Workers: Defense
- ❋ State with Most Workers: Maryland

Operate and maintain chemical plant equipment utilized in the development, manufacture, and processing of chemicals and chemical products or the development of chemical and related processes; control temperatures, pressures, flows, and reaction time by reading and recording data, adjusting temperature, flow rate, pressure, and similar gauges and instruments; perform routine chemical analyses and calculations.

Requirements: No requirements available.

RELATED GS SERIES: 5413 FUEL DISTRIBUTION SYSTEM OPERATING

TITLE ON USAJOBS: FUEL DISTRIBUTION SYSTEM WORKER

- ❋ U.S. Federal Workforce: 882
- ❋ Average Length of Service: 12.1 years
- ❋ Percent Part-Time: 0.1%
- ❋ Percent Women: 4.1%
- ❋ Largest Age Bracket: 45–49 (16.2%)
- ❋ GS Level with Most Workers: Not a GS occupation
- ❋ Agency with Most Workers: Defense
- ❋ State with Most Workers: California

Work at one or several work stations of a fuel distribution system or operate a complete system to receive, store, transfer, and issue petroleum and other products such as liquid oxygen, liquid nitrogen, and anhydrous ammonia.

Requirements: Practical knowledge of the entire fuel distribution system and user requirements in order to locate problems and initiate immediate corrective action to maintain adequate fuel distribution.

RELATED GS SERIES: 1658 LAUNDRY OPERATIONS SERVICES

- ❋ U.S. Federal Workforce: 108
- ❋ Average Length of Service: 21.5 years
- ❋ Percent Part-Time: 0.0%
- ❋ Percent Women: 13.9%
- ❋ Largest Age Bracket: 50–54 (29.6%)
- ❋ GS Level with Most Workers: 9
- ❋ Agency with Most Workers: Justice
- ❋ State with Most Workers: California

Operate a laundry and/or dry cleaning facility.

Requirements: Practical knowledge of laundry and dry cleaning equipment and processing operations.

Podiatrists

- ❋ Education/Training Required: First professional degree
- ❋ Annual Earnings (Federal): $110,850
- ❋ Annual Earnings (All Industries): $116,250
- ❋ Earnings Growth Potential (Federal): 63.9% (very high)
- ❋ Earnings Growth Potential (All Industries): 58.0% (very high)
- ❋ Job Growth (Federal): 9.4%
- ❋ Job Growth (All Industries): 9.0%
- ❋ Annual Job Openings (Federal): 10
- ❋ Annual Job Openings (All Industries): 320

Diagnose and treat diseases and deformities of the human foot. Treat bone, muscle, and joint disorders affecting the feet. Diagnose diseases and deformities of the foot, using medical histories, physical examinations, X-rays, and laboratory test results. Prescribe medications, corrective devices, physical therapy, or surgery. Treat conditions such as corns, calluses, ingrown nails, tumors, shortened tendons, bunions, cysts, and abscesses by surgical methods. Advise patients about treatments and foot care techniques necessary for prevention of future problems. Refer patients to physicians when symptoms indicative of systemic disorders, such as arthritis or diabetes, are observed in feet and legs. Correct deformities by means of plaster casts and strapping. Make and fit prosthetic appliances. Perform administrative duties such as hiring employees, ordering supplies, and keeping records. Educate the public about the benefits of foot care through techniques such as speaking engagements, advertising, and other forums. Treat deformities, using mechanical methods, such as whirlpool or paraffin baths, and electrical methods, such as shortwave and low-voltage currents.

Considerations for Job Outlook: Projected employment growth reflects a more active, older population that is sustaining a rising number of foot injuries. Opportunities for entry-level job seekers should be good for qualified applicants.

Personality Type: Investigative-Social-Realistic. **Skills:** Science; Management of Financial Resources; Active Learning; Technology Design; Management of Material Resources; Reading Comprehension; Service Orientation; Instructing. **Education and Training Program:** Podiatric Medicine/Podiatry (DPM). **Work Environment:** Indoors; disease or infections; using your hands to handle, control, or feel objects, tools, or controls; contaminants; sitting; making repetitive motions.

OTHER FEDERAL JOB FACTS
RELATED GS SERIES: 0668 PODIATRIST

- U.S. Federal Workforce: 663
- Average Length of Service: 7.5 years
- Percent Part-Time: 23.1%
- Percent Women: 34.2%
- Largest Age Bracket: 25–29 (17.6%)
- GS Level with Most Workers: 14
- Agency with Most Workers: Veterans Affairs
- State with Most Workers: California

Perform professional work involved in the care and treatment of the feet, including work in the prevention, diagnosis, and treatment of foot diseases and disorders by physical, medical, and/or surgical methods; the writing of prescriptions for topical medications, corrective exercises, corrective footwear and other purposes; and/or investigative research for analytical evaluations and experimental purposes.

Requirements: Professional podiatry knowledge and skills.

Political Scientists

- Education/Training Required: Master's degree
- Annual Earnings (Federal): $113,050
- Annual Earnings (All Industries): $104,090
- Earnings Growth Potential (Federal): 35.3% (median)
- Earnings Growth Potential (All Industries): 55.3% (very high)
- Job Growth (Federal): 18.4%
- Job Growth (All Industries): 19.4%
- Annual Job Openings (Federal): 120
- Annual Job Openings (All Industries): 280

P

Study the origin, development, and operation of political systems. Research a wide range of subjects, such as relations between the United States and foreign countries, the beliefs and institutions of foreign nations, or the politics of small towns or a major metropolis. May study topics such as public opinion, political decision making, and ideology. May analyze the structure and operation of governments, as well as various political entities. May conduct public opinion surveys, analyze election results, or analyze public documents. Teach political science. Disseminate research results through academic publications, written reports, or public presentations. Identify issues for research and analysis. Develop and test theories, using information from interviews, newspapers, periodicals, case law, historical papers, polls, and/or statistical sources. Maintain current knowledge of government policy decisions. Collect, analyze, and interpret data such as election results and public opinion surveys; report on findings, recommendations, and conclusions. Interpret and analyze policies; public issues; legislation; and the operations of governments, businesses, and organizations. Evaluate programs and policies and make related recommendations to institutions and organizations. Write drafts of legislative proposals and prepare speeches, correspondence, and policy papers for governmental use. Forecast political, economic, and social trends. Consult with and advise government officials, civic bodies, research agencies, the media, political parties, and others concerned with political issues. Provide media commentary and/or criticism related to public policy and political issues and events.

Considerations for Job Outlook: Employment growth of sociologists in a variety of fields is tied to expected demand for their research and analytical skills. Political scientists are expected to experience employment growth especially in nonprofit, political lobbying, and civic organizations.

Opportunities should be best for job seekers who have an advanced degree.

Personality Type: Investigative-Artistic-Social. **Skills:** Science; Speaking; Writing; Critical Thinking; Active Listening; Active Learning; Systems Analysis; Reading Comprehension. **Education and Training Program:** American Government and Politics (United States); Canadian Government and Politics; International Relations and Affairs; International/Global Studies; Political Science and Government, General; Political Science and Government, Other. **Work Environment:** Indoors; sitting.

OTHER FEDERAL JOB FACTS

RELATED GS SERIES: 0130 FOREIGN AFFAIRS

TITLE ON USAJOBS: FOREIGN AFFAIRS SPECIALIST

- ✸ U.S. Federal Workforce: 2,703
- ✸ Average Length of Service: 14.3 years
- ✸ Percent Part-Time: 24.0%
- ✸ Percent Women: 42.0%
- ✸ Largest Age Bracket: 65 or more (15.8%)
- ✸ GS Level with Most Workers: 14
- ✸ Agency with Most Workers: State
- ✸ State with Most Workers: District of Columbia

Formulate and direct the foreign affairs of the government or study and disseminate information bearing on international relations.

Requirements: Degree or substantial course work in international law and international relations, political science, economics, history, sociology, geography, social or cultural anthropology, law, statistics, or in the humanities; or a combination of course work in one of these majors and in statistics or quantitative methods; or several years of relevant work experience.

RELATED GS SERIES: 0132 INTELLIGENCE

TITLE ON USAJOBS: INTELLIGENCE ANALYST/SPECIALIST

- U.S. Federal Workforce: 10,485
- Average Length of Service: 10.7 years
- Percent Part-Time: 0.6%
- Percent Women: 34.1%
- Largest Age Bracket: 45–49 (15.7%)
- GS Level with Most Workers: 13
- Agency with Most Workers: Defense
- State with Most Workers: District of Columbia

Collect, analyze, evaluate, interpret, and disseminate information on political, economic, social, cultural, physical, geographic, scientific, or military conditions, trends, and forces in foreign and domestic areas that directly or indirectly affect national security.

Requirements: Basic knowledge and understanding of one or more of the natural or social sciences, engineering, or military science; does not demand, as a primary qualification requirement, full knowledge of the current state of the art.

RELATED GS SERIES: 0136 INTERNATIONAL COOPERATION

- U.S. Federal Workforce: 14
- Average Length of Service: 20.7 years
- Percent Part-Time: 0.0%
- Percent Women: 71.4%
- Largest Age Bracket: 35–39 (21.4%)
- GS Levels with Most Workers: 14, 15
- Agency with Most Workers: No data available
- State with Most Workers: District of Columbia

Plan, develop, and implement foreign economic assistance programs undertaken by the United States.

Requirements: Knowledge of economic, social, cultural, and political conditions in the country of assignment and of United States foreign policy.

RELATED GS SERIES: 0131 INTERNATIONAL RELATIONS

TITLE ON USAJOBS: INTERNATIONAL RELATIONS SPECIALIST

- U.S. Federal Workforce: 243
- Average Length of Service: 10.8 years
- Percent Part-Time: 2.1%
- Percent Women: 47.3%
- Largest Age Bracket: 30–34 (18.9%)
- GS Level with Most Workers: 13
- Agency with Most Workers: Defense
- State with Most Workers: District of Columbia

Formulate and implement political or politico-economic policy for the conduct of relations of the United States with other governments.

Requirements: Degree or substantial course work in international law and international relations, political science, economics, history, sociology, geography, social or cultural anthropology, law, statistics, or in the humanities; or a combination of course work in one of these majors and in statistics or quantitative methods; or several years of relevant work experience.

Postal Service Clerks

- Education/Training Required: Short-term on-the-job training
- Annual Earnings (Federal): $52,530
- Annual Earnings (All Industries): $52,530

P

- Earnings Growth Potential (Federal): 11.7% (very low)
- Earnings Growth Potential (All Industries): 11.7% (very low)
- Job Growth (Federal): –18.0%
- Job Growth (All Industries): –18.0%
- Annual Job Openings (Federal): 1,610
- Annual Job Openings (All Industries): 1,610

Perform any combination of tasks in a post office, such as receive letters and parcels; sell postage and revenue stamps, postal cards, and stamped envelopes; fill out and sell money orders; place mail in pigeon holes of mail rack or in bags; and examine mail for correct postage. Keep money drawers in order, and record and balance daily transactions. Weigh letters and parcels; compute mailing costs based on type, weight, and destination; and affix correct postage. Obtain signatures from recipients of registered or special delivery mail. Register, certify, and insure letters and parcels. Sell and collect payment for products such as stamps, prepaid mail envelopes, and money orders. Check mail in order to ensure correct postage and that packages and letters are in proper condition for mailing. Answer questions regarding mail regulations and procedures, postage rates, and post office boxes. Complete forms regarding changes of address, or theft or loss of mail, or for special services such as registered or priority mail. Provide assistance to the public in complying with federal regulations of Postal Service and other federal agencies. Sort incoming and outgoing mail, according to type and destination, by hand or by operating electronic mail-sorting and scanning devices. Cash money orders. Rent post office boxes to customers. Put undelivered parcels away, retrieve them when customers come to claim them, and complete any related documentation.

Considerations for Job Outlook: Postal Service clerks will be adversely affected by continued declines in the volume of first-class mail. Keen competition is expected because this occupation has relatively few entry requirements and attractive wages and benefits.

Personality Type: Conventional-Realistic. **Skills:** Management of Financial Resources; Service Orientation; Quality Control Analysis; Mathematics; Troubleshooting; Programming. **Education and Training Program:** General Office Occupations and Clerical Services. **Work Environment:** Indoors; standing; using hands; bending or twisting the body; repetitive motions; noise; contaminants.

RELATED GS SERIES: NOT IN OPM DATABASE

- U.S. Federal Workforce: 75,780
- Average Length of Service: No data available
- Percent Part-Time: No data available
- Percent Women: 41.7%
- Largest Age Bracket: No data available
- GS Level with Most Workers: Not a GS occupation
- State with Most Workers: California

Postal Service Mail Carriers

- Education/Training Required: Short-term on-the-job training
- Annual Earnings (Federal): $52,200
- Annual Earnings (All Industries): $52,200
- Earnings Growth Potential (Federal): 27.3% (low)
- Earnings Growth Potential (All Industries): 27.3% (low)
- Job Growth (Federal): –1.1%
- Job Growth (All Industries): –1.1%

- ❀ Annual Job Openings (Federal): 10,720
- ❀ Annual Job Openings (All Industries): 10,720

Sort mail for delivery. Deliver mail on established routes by vehicle or on foot. Obtain signed receipts for registered, certified, and insured mail; collect associated charges; and complete any necessary paperwork. Sort mail for delivery, arranging it in delivery sequence. Deliver mail to residences and business establishments along specified routes by walking and/or driving, using a combination of satchels, carts, cars, and small trucks. Return to the post office with mail collected from homes, businesses, and public mailboxes. Turn in money and receipts collected along mail routes. Sign for cash-on-delivery and registered mail before leaving the post office. Record address changes and redirect mail for those addresses. Hold mail for customers who are away from delivery locations. Bundle mail in preparation for delivery or transportation to relay boxes. Leave notices telling patrons where to collect mail that could not be delivered. Meet schedules for the collection and return of mail. Return incorrectly addressed mail to senders. Maintain accurate records of deliveries. Answer customers' questions about postal services and regulations. Provide customers with change of address cards and other forms. Report any unusual circumstances concerning mail delivery, including the condition of street letter boxes. Register, certify, and insure parcels and letters. Travel to post offices to pick up the mail for routes and/or pick up mail from postal relay boxes. Enter change of address orders into computers that process forwarding address stickers.

Considerations for Job Outlook: Declining mail volume, along with automation, is expected to offset employment growth driven by the need to provide mail-delivery services to a growing population. Keen competition is expected. Opportunities are expected to be best in areas experiencing population growth.

Personality Type: Conventional-Realistic. **Skills:** Operation and Control; Troubleshooting; Equipment Maintenance; Operation Monitoring; Repairing; Installation; Management of Financial Resources; Programming. **Education and Training Program:** General Office Occupations and Clerical Services. **Work Environment:** Outdoors; making repetitive motions; using your hands to handle, control, or feel objects, tools, or controls; contaminants; very hot or cold temperatures; standing.

RELATED GS SERIES: NOT IN OPM DATABASE

- ❀ U.S. Federal Workforce: 343,340
- ❀ Average Length of Service: No data available
- ❀ Percent Part-Time: No data available
- ❀ Percent Women: 39.1%
- ❀ Largest Age Bracket: No data available
- ❀ GS Level with Most Workers: Not a GS occupation
- ❀ State with Most Workers: California

Postal Service Mail Sorters, Processors, and Processing Machine Operators

- ❀ Education/Training Required: Short-term on-the-job training
- ❀ Annual Earnings (Federal): $52,520
- ❀ Annual Earnings (All Industries): $52,520
- ❀ Earnings Growth Potential (Federal): 34.3% (low)
- ❀ Earnings Growth Potential (All Industries): 34.3% (low)
- ❀ Job Growth (Federal): –30.4%
- ❀ Job Growth (All Industries): –30.4%
- ❀ Annual Job Openings (Federal): 1,170
- ❀ Annual Job Openings (All Industries): 1,170

Prepare incoming and outgoing mail for distribution. Examine, sort, and route mail. Load, operate, and occasionally adjust and repair mail processing, sorting, and canceling machinery. Keep records of shipments, pouches, and sacks; and perform other duties related to mail handling within the postal service. Direct items according to established routing schemes, using computer-controlled keyboards or voice recognition equipment. Bundle, label, and route sorted mail to designated areas depending on destinations and according to established procedures and deadlines. Serve the public at counters or windows, such as by selling stamps and weighing parcels. Supervise other mail sorters. Train new workers. Distribute incoming mail into the correct boxes or pigeonholes. Operate various types of equipment, such as computer scanning equipment, addressographs, mimeographs, optical character readers, and bar-code sorters. Search directories to find correct addresses for redirected mail. Clear jams in sorting equipment. Open and label mail containers. Check items to ensure that addresses are legible and correct, that sufficient postage has been paid or the appropriate documentation is attached, and that items are in a suitable condition for processing. Rewrap soiled or broken parcels. Weigh articles to determine required postage. Move containers of mail, using equipment such as forklifts and automated "trains."

Considerations for Job Outlook: Increased automation is expected to decrease employment of these workers. Keen competition is expected to continue because this occupation has relatively few entry requirements and attractive wages and benefits.

Personality Type: Conventional-Realistic. **Skills:** Operation and Control; Troubleshooting; Operation Monitoring; Programming. **Education and Training Program:** General Office Occupations and Clerical Services. **Work Environment:** Indoors; standing; using hands; bending or twisting the body; repetitive motions; noise; contaminants.

OTHER FEDERAL JOB FACTS
RELATED GS SERIES: NOT IN OPM DATABASE

- ❋ U.S. Federal Workforce: 179,890
- ❋ Average Length of Service: No data available
- ❋ Percent Part-Time: 3.8%
- ❋ Percent Women: 41.7%
- ❋ Largest Age Bracket: No data available
- ❋ GS Level with Most Workers: Not a GS occupation
- ❋ State with Most Workers: California

Postmasters and Mail Superintendents

- ❋ Education/Training Required: Work experience in a related occupation
- ❋ Annual Earnings (Federal): $58,780
- ❋ Annual Earnings (All Industries): $58,770
- ❋ Earnings Growth Potential (Federal): 38.4% (median)
- ❋ Earnings Growth Potential (All Industries): 38.4% (medium)
- ❋ Job Growth (Federal): –15.1%
- ❋ Job Growth (All Industries): –15.1%
- ❋ Annual Job Openings (Federal): 520
- ❋ Annual Job Openings (All Industries): 520

Direct and coordinate operational, administrative, management, and supportive services of a U.S. post office or coordinate activities of workers engaged in postal and related work in assigned post office. Organize and supervise activities such as the processing of incoming and outgoing mail. Direct and coordinate operational, management, and supportive services of one or a number of postal facilities. Resolve customer complaints. Hire and train employees and evaluate their performance. Prepare employee work schedules. Negotiate labor disputes. Prepare and submit detailed and summary reports of post office activities to designated supervisors. Collect rents for post office boxes. Issue and cash money orders. Inform the public of available services and of postal laws and regulations. Select and train postmasters and managers of associate postal units. Confer with suppliers to obtain bids for proposed purchases and to requisition supplies; disburse funds according to federal regulations.

Considerations for Job Outlook: Employment is projected to decline rapidly.

Personality Type: Enterprising-Conventional-Social. **Skills:** Management of Financial Resources; Management of Material Resources; Management of Personnel Resources; Persuasion; Time Management; Negotiation; Learning Strategies; Systems Evaluation. **Education and Training Program:** Public Administration. **Work Environment:** Indoors; contaminants; standing.

OTHER FEDERAL JOB FACTS
RELATED GS SERIES: NOT IN OPM DATABASE

* U.S. Federal Workforce: 25,570
* Average Length of Service: No data available
* Percent Part-Time: No data available
* Percent Women: 33.0%
* Largest Age Bracket: No data available
* GS Level with Most Workers: Not a GS occupation
* State with Most Workers: California

Precision Instrument and Equipment Repairers, All Other

* Education/Training Required: Moderate-term on-the-job training
* Annual Earnings (Federal): $54,550
* Annual Earnings (All Industries): $50,140
* Earnings Growth Potential (Federal): 19.2% (very low)

* Earnings Growth Potential (All Industries): 37.5% (medium)
* Job Growth (Federal): 7.6%
* Job Growth (All Industries): 2.5%
* Annual Job Openings (Federal): 60
* Annual Job Openings (All Industries): 500

Considerations for Job Outlook: Slower than average employment growth is projected.

Personality Type: No data available. **Skills:** No data available. **Education and Training Program:** Precision Systems Maintenance and Repair Technologies, Other. **Work Environment:** No data available.

OTHER FEDERAL JOB FACTS
RELATED GS SERIES: 4818 AIRCRAFT SURVIVAL FLIGHT EQUIPMENT REPAIRING

TITLE ON USAJOBS: AIRCRAFT SURVIVAL & FLIGHT EQUIPMENT REPAIRER

* U.S. Federal Workforce: 785
* Average Length of Service: 9.7 years
* Percent Part-Time: 0.4%
* Percent Women: 13.6%
* Largest Age Bracket: 45–49 (17.7%)
* GS Level with Most Workers: Not a GS occupation
* Agency with Most Workers: Defense
* State with Most Workers: Texas

Disassemble, repair, test, troubleshoot, examine, fit, modify, maintain, install, and determine serviceability of aircraft survival and flight equipment, such as helmets, torso harness assemblies, preservers, parachutes, life rafts, chemical and biological protective devices, survival kits, oxygen masks, and anti-G-suits; perform operational and circuit checks of emergency signaling and communication devices, such as survival radios and beacons.

Requirements: Knowledge of mechanical and electrical repair and maintenance procedures, pyrotechnic and explosive devices, and aircraft egress systems; familiarity with aircraft assigned to the unit; detailed knowledge of the operation and characteristics of aircraft survival and flight equipment; and the ability to demonstrate and explain proper usage and operation of the equipment.

RELATED GS SERIES: 2602 ELECTRONIC MEASUREMENT EQUIPMENT MECHANIC

* U.S. Federal Workforce: 986
* Average Length of Service: 15.4 years
* Percent Part-Time: 0.2%
* Percent Women: 6.8%
* Largest Age Bracket: 50–54 (19.9%)
* GS Level with Most Workers: Not a GS occupation
* Agency with Most Workers: Defense
* States with Most Workers: Oklahoma, Georgia

Perform nonsupervisory work involved in maintenance, repair, calibration, and certification of electronic test, measurement, and reference equipment used for precise measurement of a variety of electrical and electronic values, quantities, and relationships such as voltage, resistance, capacitance, frequency, and inductance.

Requirements: Working knowledge and practical application of electronic principles and the ability to perform precise measurement of electrical and electronic values, quantities, and relationships; also skill in performing such processes as troubleshooting, repairing, modifying, overhauling, testing, installing, and calibrating a variety of measurement equipment, instruments, and consoles.

RELATED GS SERIES: 3306 OPTICAL INSTRUMENT REPAIRING

* U.S. Federal Workforce: 126
* Average Length of Service: 15.3 years
* Percent Part-Time: 0.0%
* Percent Women: 6.3%
* Largest Age Bracket: 50–54 (18.9%)
* GS Level with Most Workers: Not a GS occupation
* Agency with Most Workers: Defense
* State with Most Workers: California

Troubleshoot, overhaul, modify, maintain, and test optical instruments such as binoculars, telescopes, cameras, sextants, gun sights, periscopes, and cinetheodolites.

Requirements: Knowledge and application of optical principles, procedures, and materials; knowledge of mechanical and electrical methods of mounting and controlling optical systems.

RELATED GS SERIES: 4745 RESEARCH LABORATORY MECHANIC

* U.S. Federal Workforce: 32
* Average Length of Service: 17.0 years
* Percent Part-Time: 0.0%
* Percent Women: 0.0%
* Largest Age Bracket: 45–49 (31.3%)
* GS Level with Most Workers: Not a GS occupation
* Agency with Most Workers: Defense
* State with Most Workers: California

Fabricate, install, maintain, operate, modify, and repair research laboratory facilities or unique types of experimental equipment used in research and development programs.

Requirements: Skill and knowledge of more than one specific trade, such as fabrication and modification of test stands and rigs for supporting engines or structures during ultrahigh-velocity wind tunnel studies; finishing of surfaces to microspecifications for air-flow effect studies; and maintaining, modifying, and operating test facilities and related equipment such as altitude simulators to achieve and hold prescribed environments for particular research studies.

Procurement Clerks

- ❁ Education/Training Required: Moderate-term on-the-job training
- ❁ Annual Earnings (Federal): $41,920
- ❁ Annual Earnings (All Industries): $36,110
- ❁ Earnings Growth Potential (Federal): 21.7% (very low)
- ❁ Earnings Growth Potential (All Industries): 35.3% (low)
- ❁ Job Growth (Federal): 7.6%
- ❁ Job Growth (All Industries): 5.8%
- ❁ Annual Job Openings (Federal): 380
- ❁ Annual Job Openings (All Industries): 2,970

Compile information and records to draw up purchase orders for procurement of materials and services. Prepare purchase orders and send copies to suppliers and to departments originating requests. Determine if inventory quantities are sufficient for needs, ordering more materials when necessary. Respond to customer and supplier inquiries about order status, changes, or cancellations. Perform buying duties when necessary. Contact suppliers to schedule or expedite deliveries and to resolve shortages, missed or late deliveries, and other problems. Review requisition orders to verify accuracy, terminology, and specifications. Prepare, maintain, and review purchasing files, reports, and price lists. Compare prices, specifications, and delivery dates to determine the best bid among potential suppliers. Track the status of requisitions, contracts, and orders. Calculate costs of orders and charge or forward invoices to appropriate accounts. Check shipments when they arrive to ensure that orders have been filled correctly and that goods meet specifications. Compare suppliers' bills with bids and purchase orders to verify accuracy. Approve bills for payment. Locate suppliers, using sources such as catalogs and the Internet, and interview them to gather information about products to be ordered. Maintain knowledge of all organizational and governmental rules affecting purchases and provide information about these rules to organization staff members and to vendors. Monitor in-house inventory movement and complete inventory transfer forms for bookkeeping purposes.

Considerations for Job Outlook: Employment of procurement clerks should diminish as computers are increasingly used by suppliers to place direct orders and by consumers to place Internet orders. Job prospects are expected to be favorable.

Personality Type: Conventional-Enterprising. **Skills:** Negotiation; Management of Financial Resources; Active Learning; Reading Comprehension; Active Listening; Service Orientation; Critical Thinking; Judgment and Decision Making. **Education and Training Program:** General Office Occupations and Clerical Services. **Work Environment:** Indoors; sitting; making repetitive motions; sounds, noisy.

OTHER FEDERAL JOB FACTS

RELATED GS SERIES: 1106 PROCUREMENT CLERICAL AND TECHNICIAN

TITLE ON USAJOBS: PROCUREMENT CLERK/ TECHNICIAN

- ❁ U.S. Federal Workforce: 1,664
- ❁ Average Length of Service: 19.4 years
- ❁ Percent Part-Time: 2.5%
- ❁ Percent Women: 79.3%
- ❁ Largest Age Bracket: 55–59 (18.3%)

❋ GS Level with Most Workers: 7

❋ Agency with Most Workers: Defense

❋ State with Most Workers: California

Prepare, control, and review procurement documents and reports; verify or abstract information contained in documents and reports; contact vendors to get status of orders and expedite delivery; maintain various procurement files; resolve a variety of shipment, payment, or other discrepancies; or perform other similar work in support of procurement programs and operations.

Requirements: Practical knowledge of procurement procedures, operations, regulations, and programs.

RELATED **GS** SERIES: 2005 SUPPLY CLERICAL AND TECHNICIAN

TITLE ON **USAJOBS:** SUPPLY CLERK/TECHNICIAN

❋ U.S. Federal Workforce: 11,955

❋ Average Length of Service: 13.7 years

❋ Percent Part-Time: 0.6%

❋ Percent Women: 41.7%

❋ Largest Age Bracket: 50–54 (17.7%)

❋ GS Level with Most Workers: 7

❋ Agency with Most Workers: Defense

❋ States with Most Workers: Texas, California

Supervise or perform clerical or technical supply support work necessary to ensure the effective operation of ongoing supply activities.

Requirements: Knowledge of supply operations and program requirements; the ability to apply established supply policies, day-to-day servicing techniques, regulations, or procedures.

Producers and Directors

❋ Education/Training Required: Bachelor's or higher degree, plus work experience

❋ Annual Earnings (Federal): $77,300

❋ Annual Earnings (All Industries): $66,720

❋ Earnings Growth Potential (Federal): 31.6% (low)

❋ Earnings Growth Potential (All Industries): 54.2% (very high)

❋ Job Growth (Federal): 7.3%

❋ Job Growth (All Industries): 9.8%

❋ Annual Job Openings (Federal): 40

❋ Annual Job Openings (All Industries): 4,040

Produce or direct stage, television, radio, video, or motion picture productions for entertainment, information, or instruction. Responsible for creative decisions, such as interpretation of script, choice of guests, set design, sound, special effects, and choreography. No task data available.

Considerations for Job Outlook: Employment growth is expected to be driven by expanding film and television operations and an increase in production of online and mobile video content. Keen competition is expected.

Personality Type: No data available. **Skills:** Management of Financial Resources; Management of Material Resources; Operations Analysis; Management of Personnel Resources; Systems Evaluation; Systems Analysis; Instructing; Time Management. **Education and Training Program:** Cinematography and Film/Video Production; Directing and Theatrical Production; Drama and Dramatics/Theatre Arts, General; Dramatic/Theatre Arts and Stagecraft, Other; Film/Cinema/Video Studies; Radio and Television. **Work Environment:** Indoors; sitting; sounds, noisy.

JOB SPECIALIZATION: DIRECTORS—STAGE, MOTION PICTURES, TELEVISION, AND RADIO

Interpret script, conduct rehearsals, and direct activities of cast and technical crew for stage,

motion pictures, television, or radio programs. Direct live broadcasts, films and recordings, or nonbroadcast programming for public entertainment or education. Supervise and coordinate the work of camera, lighting, design, and sound crewmembers. Confer with technical directors, managers, crew members, and writers to discuss details of production, such as photography, script, music, sets, and costumes. Plan details such as framing, composition, camera movement, sound, and actor movement for each shot or scene. Establish pace of programs and sequences of scenes according to time requirements and cast and set accessibility. Identify and approve equipment and elements required for productions, such as scenery, lights, props, costumes, choreography, and music. Select plays or scripts for production, and determine how material should be interpreted and performed. Compile cue words and phrases, and cue announcers, cast members, and technicians during performances.

Personality Type: Enterprising-Artistic. **Skills:** Management of Personnel Resources; Negotiation; Persuasion; Coordination; Speaking; Instructing; Time Management; Active Listening. **Education and Training Program:** Cinematography and Film/Video Production; Directing and Theatrical Production; Drama and Dramatics/Theatre Arts, General; Dramatic/Theatre Arts and Stagecraft, Other; Film/Cinema/Video Studies; Radio and Television. **Work Environment:** Indoors; sitting; making repetitive motions; using your hands to handle, control, or feel objects, tools, or controls; sounds, noisy.

JOB SPECIALIZATION: PRODUCERS

Plan and coordinate various aspects of radio, television, stage, or motion picture production, such as selecting script; coordinating writing, directing, and editing; and arranging financing. Coordinate the activities of writers, directors, managers, and other personnel throughout the production process. Monitor post-production processes to ensure accurate completion of all details. Perform management activities such as budgeting, scheduling, planning, and marketing. Determine production size, content, and budget, establishing details such as production schedules and management policies. Compose and edit scripts or provide screenwriters with story outlines from which scripts can be written. Conduct meetings with staff to discuss production progress and to ensure production objectives are attained. Resolve personnel problems that arise during the production process by acting as liaisons between dissenting parties when necessary. Produce shows for special occasions, such as holidays or testimonials. Edit and write news stories from information collected by reporters. Write and submit proposals to bid on contracts for projects. Hire directors, principal cast members, and key production staff members. Arrange financing for productions. Select plays, scripts, books, or ideas to be produced. Review film, recordings, or rehearsals to ensure conformance to production and broadcast standards. Perform administrative duties such as preparing operational reports, distributing rehearsal call sheets and script copies, and arranging for rehearsal quarters. Obtain and distribute costumes, props, music, and studio equipment needed to complete productions.

Personality Type: Enterprising-Artistic. **Skills:** Management of Financial Resources; Management of Material Resources; Coordination; Monitoring; Management of Personnel Resources; Time Management; Negotiation; Writing. **Education and Training Program:** Cinematography and Film/Video Production; Directing and Theatrical Production; Drama and Dramatics/Theatre Arts, General; Dramatic/Theatre Arts and Stagecraft, Other; Film/Cinema/Video Studies; Radio and Television. **Work Environment:** Indoors; sitting.

Job Specialization: Program Directors

Direct and coordinate activities of personnel engaged in preparation of radio or television station program schedules and programs such as sports or news. Plan and schedule programming and event coverage based on broadcast length; time availability; and other factors such as community needs, ratings data, and viewer demographics. Monitor and review programming to ensure that schedules are met, guidelines are adhered to, and performances are of adequate quality. Direct and coordinate activities of personnel engaged in broadcast news, sports, or programming. Check completed program logs for accuracy and conformance with FCC rules and regulations and resolve program log inaccuracies. Establish work schedules and assign work to staff members. Coordinate activities between departments such as news and programming. Perform personnel duties such as hiring staff and evaluating work performance. Evaluate new and existing programming for suitability and to assess the need for changes, using information such as audience surveys and feedback. Develop budgets for programming and broadcasting activities and monitor expenditures to ensure that they remain within budgetary limits. Confer with directors and production staff to discuss issues such as production and casting problems, budgets, policies, and news coverage. Select, acquire, and maintain programs, music, films, and other needed materials and obtain legal clearances for their use as necessary. Monitor network transmissions for advisories concerning daily program schedules, program content, special feeds, or program changes. Develop promotions for current programs and specials.

Personality Type: Enterprising-Conventional-Artistic. **Skills:** Management of Financial Resources; Management of Material Resources; Operations Analysis; Management of Personnel Resources; Systems Evaluation; Systems Analysis; Instructing; Time Management. **Education and**

Training Program: Cinematography and Film/Video Production; Directing and Theatrical Production; Drama and Dramatics/Theatre Arts, General; Dramatic/Theatre Arts and Stagecraft, Other; Film/Cinema/Video Studies; Radio and Television. **Work Environment:** Indoors; sitting; sounds, noisy.

Job Specialization: Talent Directors

Audition and interview performers to select most appropriate talent for parts in stage, television, radio, or motion picture productions. Review performer information such as photos, resumes, voice tapes, videos, and union membership, in order to decide whom to audition for parts. Read scripts and confer with producers in order to determine the types and numbers of performers required for a given production. Select performers for roles or submit lists of suitable performers to producers or directors for final selection. Audition and interview performers in order to match their attributes to specific roles or to increase the pool of available acting talent. Maintain talent files that include information such as performers' specialties, past performances, and availability. Prepare actors for auditions by providing scripts and information about roles and casting requirements. Serve as liaisons between directors, actors, and agents. Attend or view productions in order to maintain knowledge of available actors. Negotiate contract agreements with performers, with agents, or between performers and agents or production companies. Contact agents and actors in order to provide notification of audition and performance opportunities and to set up audition times. Hire and supervise workers who help locate people with specified attributes and talents. Arrange for and/or design screen tests or auditions for prospective performers. Locate performers or extras for crowd and background scenes, and stand-ins or photo doubles for actors, by direct contact or through agents.

Personality Type: Enterprising-Artistic. **Skills:** Negotiation; Persuasion; Management of Personnel

Resources; Speaking; Social Perceptiveness; Reading Comprehension; Monitoring; Coordination. **Education and Training Program:** Cinematography and Film/Video Production; Directing and Theatrical Production; Drama and Dramatics/Theatre Arts, General; Dramatic/Theatre Arts and Stagecraft, Other; Film/Cinema/Video Studies; Radio and Television. **Work Environment:** Indoors; sitting; sounds, noisy.

JOB SPECIALIZATION: TECHNICAL DIRECTORS/MANAGERS

Coordinate activities of technical departments, such as taping, editing, engineering, and maintenance, to produce radio or television programs. Test equipment to ensure proper operation. Monitor broadcasts to ensure that programs conform to station or network policies and regulations. Observe pictures through monitors, and direct camera and video staff concerning shading and composition. Act as liaisons between engineering and production departments. Supervise and assign duties to workers engaged in technical control and production of radio and television programs. Schedule use of studio and editing facilities for producers and engineering and maintenance staff. Confer with operations directors to formulate and maintain fair and attainable technical policies for programs. Train workers in use of equipment such as switchers, cameras, monitors, microphones, and lights. Discuss filter options, lens choices, and the visual effects of objects being filmed with photography directors and video operators.

Personality Type: Enterprising-Realistic-Conventional. **Skills:** Monitoring; Management of Personnel Resources; Coordination; Systems Analysis; Operation and Control; Instructing; Operation Monitoring; Systems Evaluation. **Education and Training Program:** Cinematography and Film/Video Production; Directing and Theatrical Production; Drama and Dramatics/Theatre Arts, General; Dramatic/Theatre Arts and Stagecraft,

Other; Film/Cinema/Video Studies; Radio and Television. **Work Environment:** Indoors; sitting; using your hands to handle, control, or feel objects, tools, or controls.

OTHER FEDERAL JOB FACTS

RELATED GS SERIES: 1071 AUDIOVISUAL PRODUCTION

TITLE ON USAJOBS: AUDIO-VISUAL PRODUCTION SPECIALIST

- U.S. Federal Workforce: 1,166
- Average Length of Service: 15.3 years
- Percent Part-Time: 0.4%
- Percent Women: 24.0%
- Largest Age Bracket: 45–49 (18.2%)
- GS Level with Most Workers: 12
- Agency with Most Workers: Defense
- State with Most Workers: District of Columbia

Supervise or perform work in the production of videotaped and live television programs; live and prerecorded radio broadcasts; motion picture films; broadcast type closed circuit teleconferences; and other similar productions, such as slide shows with sound accompaniments.

Requirements: Ability to plan, organize, and direct the work of writers, editors, actors, narrators, musicians, set designers, audio and lighting technicians, camera operators, and other associated technical personnel to produce, select, and arrange the actions, sounds, and visual effects required for the finished production.

RELATED GS SERIES: 1054 THEATER SPECIALIST

- U.S. Federal Workforce: 15
- Average Length of Service: 12.7 years
- Percent Part-Time: 26.7%
- Percent Women: 13.3%

P

- ✳ Largest Age Bracket: 50–54 (26.7%)
- ✳ GS Level with Most Workers: 7
- ✳ Agency with Most Workers: Interior
- ✳ States with Most Workers: District of Columbia, Virginia

Plan, supervise, administer, or carry out educational, recreational, cultural, or other programs in theater, such as children's theater or creative dramatics; produce, stage, or direct theatrical productions; instruct or serve as a specialist in direction; technical production; dance production; performance techniques; playwriting; play or music theater production; or theater administration, management or promotion; or perform other functions requiring knowledge and skill in the theater arts.

Requirements: Knowledge of the techniques of producing, staging, rehearsing, or performing in theatrical productions; of technical production; or of theatrical history and literature.

Psychologists, All Other

- ✳ Education/Training Required: Master's degree
- ✳ Annual Earnings (Federal): $91,110
- ✳ Annual Earnings (All Industries): $86,540
- ✳ Earnings Growth Potential (Federal): 54.0% (very high)
- ✳ Earnings Growth Potential (All Industries): 52.5% (very high)
- ✳ Job Growth (Federal): 7.8%
- ✳ Job Growth (All Industries): 14.4%
- ✳ Annual Job Openings (Federal): 240
- ✳ Annual Job Openings (All Industries): 680

Considerations for Job Outlook: Employment growth is expected due to increased emphasis on mental health in a variety of specializations, including school counseling, depression, and substance abuse. Job seekers with a doctoral degree should have the best opportunities.

JOB SPECIALIZATION: NEUROPSYCHOLOGISTS AND CLINICAL NEUROPSYCHOLOGISTS

Apply theories and principles of neuropsychology to diagnose and treat disorders of higher cerebral functioning. Write or prepare detailed clinical neuropsychological reports using data from psychological or neuropsychological tests, self-report measures, rating scales, direct observations, or interviews. Provide psychotherapy, behavior therapy, or other counseling interventions to patients with neurological disorders. Provide education or counseling to individuals and families. Participate in educational programs, in-service training, or workshops to remain current in methods and techniques. Read current literature, talk with colleagues, and participate in professional organizations or conferences to keep abreast of developments in neuropsychology. Interview patients to obtain comprehensive medical histories. Identify and communicate risks associated with specific neurological surgical procedures such as epilepsy surgery. Educate and supervise practicum students, psychology interns, or hospital staff.

Personality Type: Investigative-Social-Artistic. **Skills:** Science; Social Perceptiveness; Reading Comprehension; Active Learning; Writing; Learning Strategies; Systems Evaluation; Instructing. **Education and Training Program:** Physiological Psychology/Psychobiology. **Work Environment:** Indoors; sitting; disease or infections; using your hands to handle, control, or feel objects, tools, or controls.

OTHER FEDERAL JOB FACTS

RELATED GS SERIES: 0180 PSYCHOLOGY

TITLE ON USAJOBS: PSYCHOLOGIST

- ❋ U.S. Federal Workforce: 6,824
- ❋ Average Length of Service: 8.6 years
- ❋ Percent Part-Time: 6.6%
- ❋ Percent Women: 57.2%
- ❋ Largest Age Bracket: 30–34 (17.0%)
- ❋ GS Level with Most Workers: 13
- ❋ Agency with Most Workers: Veterans Affairs
- ❋ State with Most Workers: California

Perform professional work relating to the behavior, capacities, traits, interests, and activities of human and animal organisms. This work may involve experimentation; applying professional knowledge to practical situations and problems; or providing consultative services or training.

Requirements: Degree in psychology plus doctorate in clinical psychology or master's or two years of graduate study in counseling psychology.

Public Relations Managers

- ❋ Education/Training Required: Bachelor's or higher degree, plus work experience
- ❋ Annual Earnings (Federal): $140,970
- ❋ Annual Earnings (All Industries): $89,690
- ❋ Earnings Growth Potential (Federal): 14.6% (very low)
- ❋ Earnings Growth Potential (All Industries): 46.7% (high)
- ❋ Job Growth (Federal): 5.9%
- ❋ Job Growth (All Industries): 12.9%
- ❋ Annual Job Openings (Federal): 10
- ❋ Annual Job Openings (All Industries): 2,060

Plan and direct public relations programs designed to create and maintain a favorable public image for employer or client or, if engaged in fundraising, plan and direct activities to solicit and maintain funds for special projects and nonprofit organizations. Identify main client groups and audiences and determine the best way to communicate publicity information to them. Write interesting and effective press releases, prepare information for media kits, and develop and maintain company Internet or intranet webpages. Develop and maintain the company's corporate image and identity, which includes the use of logos and signage. Manage communications budgets. Manage special events such as sponsorship of races, parties introducing new products, or other activities the firm supports to gain public attention through the media without advertising directly. Draft speeches for company executives and arrange interviews and other forms of contact for them. Assign, supervise, and review the activities of public relations staff. Evaluate advertising and promotion programs for compatibility with public relations efforts. Establish and maintain effective working relationships with local and municipal government officials and media representatives. Confer with labor relations managers to develop internal communications that keep employees informed of company activities. Direct activities of external agencies, establishments, and departments that develop and implement communication strategies and information programs. Formulate policies and procedures related to public information programs, working with public relations executives. Respond to requests for information about employers' activities or status.

Considerations for Job Outlook: Job growth is expected to result from companies' need to distinguish their products and services in an increasingly competitive marketplace. Keen competition is expected.

Personality Type: Enterprising-Artistic. **Skills:** Management of Financial Resources; Persuasion;

Management of Material Resources; Negotiation; Management of Personnel Resources; Systems Evaluation; Systems Analysis; Coordination. **Education and Training Program:** Public Relations/Image Management. **Work Environment:** Indoors; sitting.

OTHER FEDERAL JOB FACTS

RELATED GS SERIES: 1035 PUBLIC AFFAIRS

TITLE ON USAJOBS: PUBLIC AFFAIRS SPECIALIST

- ⊛ U.S. Federal Workforce: 5,393
- ⊛ Average Length of Service: 14.9 years
- ⊛ Percent Part-Time: 1.9%
- ⊛ Percent Women: 54.7%
- ⊛ Largest Age Bracket: 55–59 (16.7%)
- ⊛ GS Levels with Most Workers: 12, 13
- ⊛ Agency with Most Workers: Defense
- ⊛ State with Most Workers: District of Columbia

Establish and maintain mutual communication between federal agencies and the general public and various other pertinent publics, including internal or external, foreign or domestic audiences; advise agency management on policy formulation and the potential public reaction to proposed policy; identify communication needs; develop informational materials.

Requirements: Skills in written and oral communication, analysis, and interpersonal relations.

Public Relations Specialists

- ⊛ Education/Training Required: Bachelor's degree
- ⊛ Annual Earnings (Federal): $83,440
- ⊛ Annual Earnings (All Industries): $51,960
- ⊛ Earnings Growth Potential (Federal): 35.2% (median)
- ⊛ Earnings Growth Potential (All Industries): 41.3% (high)
- ⊛ Job Growth (Federal): 18.0%
- ⊛ Job Growth (All Industries): 24.0%
- ⊛ Annual Job Openings (Federal): 180
- ⊛ Annual Job Openings (All Industries): 13,130

Engage in promoting or creating goodwill for individuals, groups, or organizations by writing or selecting favorable publicity material and releasing it through various communications media. May prepare and arrange displays and make speeches. Prepare or edit organizational publications for internal and external audiences, including employee newsletters and stockholders' reports. Respond to requests for information from the media or designate another appropriate spokesperson or information source. Establish and maintain cooperative relationships with representatives of community, consumer, employee, and public interest groups. Plan and direct development and communication of informational programs to maintain favorable public and stockholder perceptions of an organization's accomplishments and agenda. Confer with production and support personnel to produce or coordinate production of advertisements and promotions. Arrange public appearances, lectures, contests, or exhibits for clients to increase product and service awareness and to promote goodwill. Study the objectives, promotional policies, and needs of organizations to develop public relations strategies that will influence public opinion or promote ideas, products, and services. Consult with advertising agencies or staff to arrange promotional campaigns in all types of media for products, organizations, or individuals. Confer with other managers to identify trends and key group interests and concerns or to provide advice on business decisions. Coach client representatives in effective communication with the public and with employees. Prepare and deliver speeches to further public relations objectives.

Considerations for Job Outlook: As the business environment becomes increasingly globalized, the need for good public relations and communications is growing rapidly. Opportunities should be best for workers with knowledge of more than one language.

Personality Type: Enterprising-Artistic-Social. **Skills:** Operations Analysis; Social Perceptiveness; Negotiation; Writing; Systems Evaluation; Speaking; Persuasion; Time Management. **Education and Training Program:** Family and Consumer Sciences/Human Sciences Communication; Health Communication; Political Communication; Public Relations/Image Management; Speech Communication and Rhetoric. **Work Environment:** Indoors; sitting.

OTHER FEDERAL JOB FACTS

RELATED GS SERIES: 1035 PUBLIC AFFAIRS

TITLE ON USAJOBS: PUBLIC AFFAIRS SPECIALIST

- U.S. Federal Workforce: 5,393
- Average Length of Service: 14.9 years
- Percent Part-Time: 1.9%
- Percent Women: 54.7%
- Largest Age Bracket: 55–59 (16.7%)
- GS Levels with Most Workers: 12, 13
- Agency with Most Workers: Defense
- State with Most Workers: District of Columbia

Establish and maintain mutual communication between federal agencies and the general public and various other pertinent publics, including internal or external, foreign or domestic audiences; advise agency management on policy formulation and the potential public reaction to proposed policy; identify communication needs; develop informational materials.

Requirements: Skills in written and oral communication, analysis, and interpersonal relations.

Purchasing Agents, Except Wholesale, Retail, and Farm Products

- Education/Training Required: Long-term on-the-job training
- Annual Earnings (Federal): $75,050
- Annual Earnings (All Industries): $54,810
- Earnings Growth Potential (Federal): 40.6% (high)
- Earnings Growth Potential (All Industries): 37.7% (medium)
- Job Growth (Federal): 17.8%
- Job Growth (All Industries): 13.9%
- Annual Job Openings (Federal): 950
- Annual Job Openings (All Industries): 11,860

Purchase machinery, equipment, tools, parts, supplies, or services necessary for the operation of an establishment. Purchase raw or semi-finished materials for manufacturing. Purchase the highest-quality merchandise at the lowest possible price and in correct amounts. Prepare purchase orders, solicit bid proposals, and review requisitions for goods and services. Research and evaluate suppliers based on price, quality, selection, service, support, availability, reliability, production and distribution capabilities, and the supplier's reputation and history. Analyze price proposals, financial reports, and other data and information to determine reasonable prices. Monitor and follow applicable laws and regulations. Negotiate, or renegotiate, and administer contracts with suppliers, vendors, and other representatives. Monitor shipments to ensure that goods come in on time and trace shipments and follow up on undelivered goods in the event of problems. Confer with staff, users, and vendors to discuss defective or unacceptable goods or services and determine corrective action. Evaluate and monitor contract performance to ensure compliance with contractual obligations and to determine need for changes. Maintain and review computerized or manual records of items purchased, costs, delivery, product performance, and inventories. Review catalogs, industry periodicals, directories, trade journals, and Internet sites and consult with other department personnel to locate necessary goods and services. Study sales records and inventory levels of current stock to develop strategic purchasing programs that facilitate employee access to supplies.

Considerations for Job Outlook: Almost all of the growth is expected to be for purchasing agents, except wholesale, retail, and farm products, as more companies demand a greater number of goods and services.

Personality Type: Conventional-Enterprising. **Skills:** Management of Financial Resources; Negotiation; Monitoring; Persuasion; Judgment and Decision Making; Speaking; Writing; Systems Evaluation. **Education and Training Program:** Insurance; Merchandising and Buying Operations; Sales, Distribution, and Marketing Operations, General. **Work Environment:** Indoors; sitting; using your hands to handle, control, or feel objects, tools, or controls; making repetitive motions.

OTHER FEDERAL JOB FACTS

RELATED GS SERIES: 1102 CONTRACTING

TITLE ON USAJOBS: CONTRACT SPECIALIST

- ❋ U.S. Federal Workforce: 35,116
- ❋ Average Length of Service: 15.5 years
- ❋ Percent Part-Time: 0.9%
- ❋ Percent Women: 57.9%
- ❋ Largest Age Bracket: 50–54 (18.1%)
- ❋ GS Level with Most Workers: 12
- ❋ Agency with Most Workers: Defense
- ❋ State with Most Workers: Virginia

Procure supplies, services, construction, or research and development, using formal advertising or negotiation procedures; evaluate contract price proposals; and administer contracts.

Requirements: Knowledge of the legislation, regulations, and methods used in contracting and knowledge of business and industry practices, sources of supply, cost factors, and requirements.

RELATED GS SERIES: 1105 PURCHASING

TITLE ON USAJOBS: PURCHASING AGENT

- ❋ U.S. Federal Workforce: 3,482
- ❋ Average Length of Service: 16.1 years
- ❋ Percent Part-Time: 0.7%
- ❋ Percent Women: 68.9%
- ❋ Largest Age Bracket: 50–54 (20.1%)
- ❋ GS Level with Most Workers: 7
- ❋ Agencies with Most Workers: Defense, Veterans Affairs
- ❋ State with Most Workers: Maryland

Acquire supplies, services, and construction by purchase, rental, or lease through delivery orders and/or small purchase procedures.

Requirements: Knowledge of policies and procedures for delivery orders and small purchases; also knowledge of commercial supply sources and common business practices related to sales, prices, discounts, units of measurement, deliveries, stocks, and shipments.

Purchasing Managers

- ❋ Education/Training Required: Bachelor's or higher degree, plus work experience
- ❋ Annual Earnings (Federal): $119,840
- ❋ Annual Earnings (All Industries): $91,440
- ❋ Earnings Growth Potential (Federal): 14.3 (very low)%
- ❋ Earnings Growth Potential (All Industries): 42.1% (high)

- Job Growth (Federal): 7.4%
- Job Growth (All Industries): 1.5%
- Annual Job Openings (Federal): 70
- Annual Job Openings (All Industries): 2,110

Plan, direct, or coordinate the activities of buyers, purchasing officers, and related workers involved in purchasing materials, products, and services. Maintain records of goods ordered and received. Locate vendors of materials, equipment, or supplies and interview them to determine product availability and terms of sales. Prepare and process requisitions and purchase orders for supplies and equipment. Control purchasing department budgets. Interview and hire staff and oversee staff training. Review purchase order claims and contracts for conformance to company policy. Analyze market and delivery systems to assess present and future material availability. Develop and implement purchasing and contract management instructions, policies, and procedures. Participate in the development of specifications for equipment, products, or substitute materials. Resolve vendor or contractor grievances and claims against suppliers. Represent companies in negotiating contracts and formulating policies with suppliers. Review, evaluate, and approve specifications for issuing and awarding bids. Direct and coordinate activities of personnel engaged in buying, selling, and distributing materials, equipment, machinery, and supplies. Prepare bid awards requiring board approval. Prepare reports regarding market conditions and merchandise costs. Administer online purchasing systems. Arrange for disposal of surplus materials.

Considerations for Job Outlook: Almost all of the growth is expected to be for purchasing agents, except wholesale, retail, and farm products, as more companies demand a greater number of goods and services.

Personality Type: Enterprising-Conventional. **Skills:** Management of Financial Resources; Management of Material Resources; Negotiation; Management of Personnel Resources; Persuasion; Systems Evaluation; Systems Analysis; Coordination. **Education and Training Program:** Purchasing, Procurement/Acquisitions and Contracts Management. **Work Environment:** Indoors; sitting.

OTHER FEDERAL JOB FACTS

RELATED GS SERIES: 1105 PURCHASING

TITLE ON USAJOBS: PURCHASING AGENT

- U.S. Federal Workforce: 3,482
- Average Length of Service: 16.1 years
- Percent Part-Time: 0.7%
- Percent Women: 68.9%
- Largest Age Bracket: 50–54 (20.1%)
- GS Level with Most Workers: 7
- Agencies with Most Workers: Defense, Veterans Affairs
- State with Most Workers: Maryland

Acquire supplies, services, and construction by purchase, rental, or lease through delivery orders and/or small purchase procedures.

Requirements: Knowledge of policies and procedures for delivery orders and small purchases; also knowledge of commercial supply sources and common business practices related to sales, prices, discounts, units of measurement, deliveries, stocks, and shipments.

Radiologic Technologists and Technicians

- Education/Training Required: Associate degree
- Annual Earnings (Federal): $55,600
- Annual Earnings (All Industries): $53,240
- Earnings Growth Potential (Federal): 24.1% (very low)

R

- ❋ Earnings Growth Potential (All Industries): 32.9% (low)
- ❋ Job Growth (Federal): 7.6%
- ❋ Job Growth (All Industries): 17.2%
- ❋ Annual Job Openings (Federal): 90
- ❋ Annual Job Openings (All Industries): 6,800

Take X-rays and CAT scans or administer non-radioactive materials into patient's bloodstream for diagnostic purposes. Includes technologists who specialize in other modalities, such as computed tomography and magnetic resonance. Includes workers whose primary duties are to demonstrate portions of the human body on X-ray film or fluoroscopic screen. No task data available.

Considerations for Job Outlook: As the population grows and ages, demand for diagnostic imaging is expected to increase. Job seekers who have knowledge of multiple technologies should have the best prospects.

JOB SPECIALIZATION: RADIOLOGIC TECHNOLOGISTS

Take X-rays and Computerized Axial Tomography (CAT or CT) scans or administer nonradioactive materials into patient's bloodstream for diagnostic purposes. Includes technologists who specialize in other modalities such as computed tomography, ultrasound, and magnetic resonance. Use radiation safety measures and protection devices to comply with government regulations and to ensure safety of patients and staff. Review and evaluate developed X-rays, videotape, or computer-generated information to determine if images are satisfactory for diagnostic purposes. Position imaging equipment and adjust controls to set exposure times and distances, according to specification of examinations. Explain procedures and observe patients to ensure safety and comfort during scans. Key commands and data into computers

to document and specify scan sequences, adjust transmitters and receivers, or photograph certain images. Operate or oversee operation of radiologic and magnetic imaging equipment to produce images of the body for diagnostic purposes. Position and immobilize patients on examining tables. Record, process, and maintain patient data and treatment records, and prepare reports. Take thorough and accurate patient medical histories. Remove and process film. Set up examination rooms, ensuring that all necessary equipment is ready. Monitor patients' conditions and reactions, reporting abnormal signs to physicians. Coordinate work with clerical personnel or other technologists. Provide assistance in dressing or changing seriously ill, injured, or disabled patients. Demonstrate new equipment, procedures, and techniques to staff and provide technical assistance.

Personality Type: Realistic-Social. **Skills:** Science; Operation and Control; Service Orientation; Quality Control Analysis; Operation Monitoring; Instructing; Social Perceptiveness; Coordination. **Education and Training Program:** Allied Health Diagnostic, Intervention, and Treatment Professions, Other; Medical Radiologic Technology/Science—Radiation Therapist; Radiologic Technology/Science—Radiographer. **Work Environment:** Indoors; disease or infections; using your hands to handle, control, or feel objects, tools, or controls; radiation; making repetitive motions; standing.

JOB SPECIALIZATION: RADIOLOGIC TECHNICIANS

Maintain and use equipment and supplies necessary to demonstrate portions of the human body on X-ray film or fluoroscopic screen for diagnostic purposes. Use beam-restrictive devices and patient-shielding techniques to minimize radiation exposure to patient and staff. Position X-ray equipment and adjust controls to set exposure factors, such as time and distance. Position patient on examining table and set up and adjust equipment to obtain optimum view of specific body area as requested by physician. Explain procedures to patients to reduce anxieties and obtain cooperation. Determine patients' X-ray needs by reading requests or instructions from physicians. Operate mobile X-ray equipment in operating room, emergency room, or at patient's bedside. Prepare and set up X-ray room for patient. Assure that sterile and non-sterile supplies such as contrast materials, catheters, films, chemicals, or other required equipment are present and in working order or requisition materials. Process exposed radiographs using film processors or computer generated methods. Make exposures necessary for the requested procedures, rejecting and repeating work that does not meet established standards. Operate digital picture archiving communications systems. Collect and maintain records of patients examined, examinations performed, patient medical histories, views taken, and technical factors used. Perform procedures such as linear tomography, mammography, sonograms, joint and cyst aspirations, routine contrast studies, routine fluoroscopy and examinations of the head, trunk, and extremities under supervision of physician.

Personality Type: Realistic-Conventional-Social. **Skills:** Operation and Control; Science; Operation Monitoring; Service Orientation; Coordination; Quality Control Analysis; Social Perceptiveness; Reading Comprehension. **Education and Training Program:** Allied Health Diagnostic, Intervention, and Treatment Professions, Other; Medical Radiologic Technology/Science—Radiation Therapist; Radiologic Technology/Science—Radiographer. **Work Environment:** Indoors; disease or infections; radiation; using your hands to handle, control, or feel objects, tools, or controls; standing; making repetitive motions.

OTHER FEDERAL JOB FACTS

RELATED GS SERIES: 0647 DIAGNOSTIC RADIOLOGIC TECHNOLOGIST

TITLE ON USAJOBS: RADIOLOGIC TECHNOLOGIST, DIAGNOSTIC

- U.S. Federal Workforce: 4,211
- Average Length of Service: 10.8 years
- Percent Part-Time: 6.8%
- Percent Women: 55.1%
- Largest Age Bracket: 45–49 (15.7%)
- GS Level with Most Workers: 8
- Agency with Most Workers: Veterans Affairs
- State with Most Workers: Texas

Perform or supervise technical work in the field of diagnostic radiologic examinations under the direction of a physician; operate radiologic equipment in a hospital or clinic environment as part of the diagnostic plan for patients.

Requirements: Knowledge of radiation protection standards and techniques; the function of skeletal components and major organs; the properties of X-rays, electric power, and electric circuits; basic radiographic procedures and technical factors (control settings); how to position patients; basic medical terminology; and first aid. Skill to apply such knowledge to perform routine diagnostic procedures; to understand and comply with X-ray requests; and to assist as a team member in radiologic examinations.

Real Estate Sales Agents

- Education/Training Required: Postsecondary vocational training
- Annual Earnings (Federal): $73,050
- Annual Earnings (All Industries): $40,100
- Earnings Growth Potential (Federal): 32.8% (low)

R

- Earnings Growth Potential (All Industries): 48.1% (high)
- Job Growth (Federal): 8.5%
- Job Growth (All Industries): 16.2%
- Annual Job Openings (Federal): 170
- Annual Job Openings (All Industries): 12,830

Rent, buy, or sell property for clients. Perform duties such as studying property listings, interviewing prospective clients, accompanying clients to property site, discussing conditions of sale, and drawing up real estate contracts. Includes agents who represent buyer. Present purchase offers to sellers for consideration. Act as an intermediary in negotiations between buyers and sellers, generally representing one or the other. Compare a property with similar properties that have recently sold to determine its competitive market price. Advise clients on market conditions, prices, mortgages, legal requirements and related matters. Promote sales of properties through advertisements, open houses, and participation in multiple listing services. Accompany buyers during visits to and inspections of property, advising them on the suitability and value of the homes they are visiting. Confer with escrow companies, lenders, home inspectors, and pest control operators to ensure that terms and conditions of purchase agreements are met before closing dates. Prepare documents such as representation contracts, purchase agreements, closing statements, deeds, and leases. Interview clients to determine what kinds of properties they are seeking. Coordinate property closings, overseeing signing of documents and disbursement of funds. Generate lists of properties that are compatible with buyers' needs and financial resources. Contact property owners and advertise services to solicit property sales listings. Arrange for title searches to determine whether clients have clear property titles. Display commercial, industrial, agricultural, and residential properties to clients and explain their features.

Considerations for Job Outlook: A growing population is expected to require the services of real estate agents and brokers, creating more jobs for these workers. People who are well-trained, ambitious, and socially and professionally active in their communities should have the best prospects.

Personality Type: Enterprising-Conventional. **Skills:** Negotiation; Persuasion; Service Orientation; Systems Evaluation; Judgment and Decision Making; Mathematics; Speaking; Coordination. **Education and Training Program:** Real Estate. **Work Environment:** More often indoors than outdoors; sitting.

OTHER FEDERAL JOB FACTS

RELATED GS SERIES: 1170 REALTY

TITLE ON USAJOBS: REALTY SPECIALIST

- U.S. Federal Workforce: 3,389
- Average Length of Service: 17.6 years
- Percent Part-Time: 2.8%
- Percent Women: 55.7%
- Largest Age Bracket: 55–59 (18.9%)
- GS Levels with Most Workers: 12, 11
- Agency with Most Workers: Defense
- State with Most Workers: California

Acquire real property; manage federally or Indian-owned, -leased, or -consigned space or property; or dispose of real property.

Requirements: Knowledge of real estate laws, principles, practices, and markets.

Recreational Therapists

- Education/Training Required: Bachelor's degree
- Annual Earnings (Federal): $63,780
- Annual Earnings (All Industries): $39,440
- Earnings Growth Potential (Federal): 19.5% (very low)

- Earnings Growth Potential (All Industries): 37.9% (medium)
- Job Growth (Federal): 11.4%
- Job Growth (All Industries): 14.6%
- Annual Job Openings (Federal): 30
- Annual Job Openings (All Industries): 1,160

Plan, direct, or coordinate medically approved recreation programs for patients in hospitals, nursing homes, or other institutions. Activities include sports, trips, dramatics, social activities, and arts and crafts. May assess a patient condition and recommend appropriate recreational activity. Observe, analyze, and record patients' participation, reactions, and progress during treatment sessions, modifying treatment programs as needed. Develop treatment plan to meet needs of patient, based on needs assessment, patient interests, and objectives of therapy. Encourage clients with special needs and circumstances to acquire new skills and get involved in health-promoting leisure activities, such as sports, games, arts and crafts, and gardening. Counsel and encourage patients to develop leisure activities. Confer with members of treatment team to plan and evaluate therapy programs. Conduct therapy sessions to improve patients' mental and physical well-being. Instruct patient in activities and techniques, such as sports, dance, music, art, or relaxation techniques, designed to meet their specific physical or psychological needs. Obtain information from medical records, medical staff, family members, and the patients themselves to assess patients' capabilities, needs, and interests. Plan, organize, direct, and participate in treatment programs and activities to facilitate patients' rehabilitation, help them integrate into the community, and prevent further medical problems. Prepare and submit reports and charts to treatment team to reflect patients' reactions and evidence of progress or regression.

Considerations for Job Outlook: Employment growth for recreational therapists is expected to continue as the population ages and better medical technology increases the survival rates of people who become injured or ill.

Personality Type: Social-Artistic. **Skills:** Service Orientation; Operations Analysis; Social Perceptiveness; Science; Persuasion; Negotiation; Coordination; Learning Strategies. **Education and Training Program:** Therapeutic Recreation/Recreational Therapy. **Work Environment:** Indoors; disease or infections; standing.

OTHER FEDERAL JOB FACTS

Related GS Series: 0638 Recreation/Creative Arts Therapist

- U.S. Federal Workforce: 884
- Average Length of Service: 13.3 years
- Percent Part-Time: 4.0%
- Percent Women: 70.2%
- Largest Age Bracket: 50–54 (17.9%)
- GS Level with Most Workers: 10
- Agency with Most Workers: Veterans Affairs
- States with Most Workers: California, New York

Evaluate the history, interests, aptitudes, and skills of patients by interviews, inventories, tests, and measurements, and use such findings, along with medical records and the therapy orders of physicians or nurses, to develop and implement therapy activities for individual patients.

Requirements: Knowledge of the concepts, principles, and practices of recreation therapy and the use of recreational modalities; or knowledge of the concepts, principles, and practices of a specialized creative arts therapy field (i.e., art, dance, music, and psychodrama) and the use of appropriate specialized activity modalities.

R

Registered Nurses

- ❋ Education/Training Required: Associate degree
- ❋ Annual Earnings (Federal): $74,790
- ❋ Annual Earnings (All Industries): $63,750
- ❋ Earnings Growth Potential (Federal): 27.0% (low)
- ❋ Earnings Growth Potential (All Industries): 31.0% (low)
- ❋ Job Growth (Federal): 14.0%
- ❋ Job Growth (All Industries): 22.2%
- ❋ Annual Job Openings (Federal): 1,790
- ❋ Annual Job Openings (All Industries): 103,900

Assess patient health problems and needs, develop and implement nursing care plans, and maintain medical records. Administer nursing care to ill, injured, convalescent, or disabled patients. May advise patients on health maintenance and disease prevention or provide case management. Licensing or registration required. Maintain accurate, detailed reports and records. Monitor, record, and report symptoms and changes in patients' conditions. Record patients' medical information and vital signs. Modify patient treatment plans as indicated by patients' responses and conditions. Consult and coordinate with health care team members to assess, plan, implement, and evaluate patient care plans. Order, interpret, and evaluate diagnostic tests to identify and assess patient's condition. Monitor all aspects of patient care, including diet and physical activity. Direct and supervise less skilled nursing or health care personnel or supervise a particular unit. Prepare patients for, and assist with, examinations and treatments. Observe nurses and visit patients to ensure proper nursing care. Assess the needs of individuals, families, or communities, including assessment of individuals' home or work environments to identify potential health or safety problems. Instruct individuals, families, and other groups on topics such as health education, disease prevention, and childbirth and develop health improvement programs. Prepare rooms, sterile instruments, equipment, and supplies and ensure that stock of supplies is maintained. Inform physician of patient's condition during anesthesia. Administer local, inhalation, intravenous, and other anesthetics.

Considerations for Job Outlook: Employment growth for registered nurses will be driven by the medical needs of an aging population. In addition, registered nurses are expected to provide more primary care as a low-cost alternative to physician-provided care. Job opportunities should be excellent.

Personality Type: Social-Investigative-Conventional. **Skills:** Science; Social Perceptiveness; Quality Control Analysis; Service Orientation; Learning Strategies; Management of Material Resources; Coordination; Instructing. **Education and Training Program:** Adult Health Nurse/Nursing; Clinical Nurse Specialist Training; Critical Care Nursing; Family Practice Nurse/Nursing; Maternal/Child Health and Neonatal Nurse/Nursing; Nurse Anesthetist Training; Nurse Midwife/Nursing Midwifery; Nursing Science; Occupational and Environmental Health Nursing; Pediatric Nurse/Nursing; Perioperative/Operating Room and Surgical Nurse/Nursing; Psychiatric/Mental Health Nurse/Nursing; Public Health/Community Nurse/Nursing; Registered Nursing/Registered Nurse Training. **Work Environment:** Indoors; standing; walking and running; using hands; disease or infections.

JOB SPECIALIZATION: ACUTE CARE NURSES

Provide advanced nursing care for patients with acute conditions such as heart attacks, respiratory distress syndrome, or shock. May care for

pre- and post-operative patients or perform advanced, invasive diagnostic or therapeutic procedures. Perform emergency medical procedures, such as basic cardiac life support (BLS), advanced cardiac life support (ACLS), and other condition stabilizing interventions. Document data related to patients' care including assessment results, interventions, medications, patient responses, or treatment changes. Manage patients' pain relief and sedation by providing pharmacologic and non-pharmacologic interventions, monitoring patients' responses, and changing care plans accordingly. Administer blood and blood product transfusions or intravenous infusions, monitoring patients for adverse reactions. Order, perform, or interpret the results of diagnostic tests and screening procedures based on assessment results, differential diagnoses, and knowledge about age, gender, and health status of clients. Assess urgent and emergent health conditions using both physiologically and technologically derived data. Interpret information obtained from electrocardiograms (EKGs) or radiographs (X-rays). Set up, operate, or monitor invasive equipment and devices such as colostomy or tracheotomy equipment, mechanical ventilators, catheters, gastrointestinal tubes, and central lines. Diagnose acute or chronic conditions that could result in rapid physiological deterioration or life-threatening instability. Discuss illnesses and treatments with patients and family members. Collaborate with members of multidisciplinary health care teams to plan, manage, or assess patient treatments.

Personality Type: Social-Investigative-Realistic. **Skills:** Science; Social Perceptiveness; Reading Comprehension; Operation Monitoring; Service Orientation; Systems Evaluation; Operation and Control; Active Learning. **Education and Training Program:** Critical Care Nursing. **Work Environment:** Indoors; disease or infections; standing; contaminants; sounds, noisy; using your hands to handle, control, or feel objects, tools, or controls.

JOB SPECIALIZATION: ADVANCED PRACTICE PSYCHIATRIC NURSES

Provide advanced nursing care for patients with psychiatric disorders. May provide psychotherapy under the direction of a psychiatrist. Teach classes in mental health topics such as stress reduction. Participate in activities aimed at professional growth and development including conferences or continuing education activities. Direct or provide home health services. Monitor the use and status of medical and pharmaceutical supplies. Develop practice protocols for mental health problems based on review and evaluation of published research. Develop, implement, or evaluate programs such as outreach activities, community mental health programs, and crisis situation response activities. Write prescriptions for psychotropic medications as allowed by state regulations and collaborative practice agreements. Refer patients requiring more specialized or complex treatment to psychiatrists, primary care physicians, or other medical specialists. Participate in treatment team conferences regarding diagnosis or treatment of difficult cases.

Personality Type: Social-Investigative. **Skills:** Social Perceptiveness; Science; Negotiation; Service Orientation; Systems Evaluation; Persuasion; Learning Strategies; Reading Comprehension. **Education and Training Program:** Psychiatric/Mental Health Nurse/Nursing. **Work Environment:** Indoors; sitting; disease or infections.

JOB SPECIALIZATION: CRITICAL CARE NURSES

Provide advanced nursing care for patients in critical or coronary care units. Assess patients' pain levels and sedation requirements. Monitor patients for changes in status and indications of conditions such as sepsis or shock and institute appropriate interventions. Set up and monitor medical equipment and devices such as cardiac monitors, mechanical ventilators and alarms, oxygen delivery devices, transducers, and pressure lines. Administer medications intravenously, by

R

injection, orally, through gastric tubes, or by other methods. Evaluate patients' vital signs and laboratory data to determine emergency intervention needs. Prioritize nursing care for assigned critically ill patients based on assessment data and identified needs. Document patients' medical histories and assessment findings. Conduct pulmonary assessments to identify abnormal respiratory patterns or breathing sounds that indicate problems. Advocate for patients' and families' needs, or provide emotional support for patients and their families. Administer blood and blood products, monitoring patients for signs and symptoms related to transfusion reactions. Monitor patients' fluid intake and output to detect emerging problems such as fluid and electrolyte imbalances. Compile and analyze data obtained from monitoring or diagnostic tests. Document patients' treatment plans, interventions, outcomes, or plan revisions. Collaborate with other health care professionals to develop and revise treatment plans based on identified needs and assessment data.

Personality Type: Social-Investigative-Realistic. **Skills:** Science; Social Perceptiveness; Operation and Control; Quality Control Analysis; Operation Monitoring; Service Orientation; Monitoring; Active Learning. **Education and Training Program:** Critical Care Nursing. **Work Environment:** Indoors; disease or infections; standing; contaminants; cramped work space, awkward positions; sounds, noisy.

OTHER FEDERAL JOB FACTS

RELATED GS SERIES: 0610 NURSE

- ❋ U.S. Federal Workforce: 68,021
- ❋ Average Length of Service: 10.4 years
- ❋ Percent Part-Time: 10.8%
- ❋ Percent Women: 84.7%
- ❋ Largest Age Bracket: 55–59 (19.9%)
- ❋ GS Level with Most Workers: 11
- ❋ Agency with Most Workers: Veterans Affairs
- ❋ States with Most Workers: California, Texas

Provide care to patients in hospitals, clinics, occupational health units, homes, schools, and communities; administer anesthetic agents and supportive treatments to patients undergoing surgery or other medical procedures; promote better health practices; teach; perform research in one or more phases of the field of nursing; or consult with and advise nurses who provide direct care to patients.

Requirements: Professional knowledge of nursing.

Sailors and Marine Oilers

- ❋ Education/Training Required: Short-term on-the-job training
- ❋ Annual Earnings (Federal): $37,300
- ❋ Annual Earnings (All Industries): $35,810
- ❋ Earnings Growth Potential (Federal): 13.6 (very low)%
- ❋ Earnings Growth Potential (All Industries): 39.6% (medium)
- ❋ Job Growth (Federal): 19.6%
- ❋ Job Growth (All Industries): 11.7%
- ❋ Annual Job Openings (Federal): 80
- ❋ Annual Job Openings (All Industries): 1,790

Stand watch to look for obstructions in path of vessels; measure water depths; turn wheels on bridges; or use emergency equipment as directed by captains, mates, or pilots. Break out, rig, overhaul, and store cargo-handling gear, stationary rigging, and running gear. Perform a variety of maintenance tasks to preserve the painted surface of ships and to maintain line and ship equipment. Must hold government-issued certification and tankerman certification when working aboard liquid-carrying vessels. Provide engineers with assistance in repairing and adjusting machinery. Attach hoses and operate pumps to transfer substances to and from liquid cargo tanks. Give directions to crew members engaged in cleaning wheelhouses and quarterdecks. Load or unload materials from vessels. Lower and man lifeboats when emergencies occur. Participate in shore patrols. Read pressure and temperature gauges or displays and record data in engineering logs. Record in ships' logs data such as weather conditions and distances traveled. Stand by wheels when ships are on automatic pilot and verify accuracy of courses, using magnetic compasses. Steer ships under the direction of commanders or navigating officers or direct helmsmen to steer, following designated courses. Chip and clean rust spots on decks, superstructures, and sides of ships, using wire brushes and hand or air chipping machines. Relay specified signals to other ships, using visual signaling devices such as blinker lights and semaphores. Splice and repair ropes, wire cables, and cordage, using marlinespikes, wirecutters, twine, and hand tools. Paint or varnish decks, superstructures, lifeboats, or sides of ships. Overhaul lifeboats and lifeboat gear and lower or raise lifeboats with winches or falls. Operate, maintain, and repair ship equipment such as winches, cranes, derricks, and weapons systems. Measure depths of water in shallow or unfamiliar waters, using leadlines, and telephone or shout depth information to vessel bridges.

Considerations for Job Outlook: Job growth is expected to stem from increasing tourism and from growth in offshore oil and gas production. Employment is also projected to increase in and around major port cities due to growing international trade. Opportunities should be excellent as the need to replace workers, particularly officers, generates many job openings.

Personality Type: Realistic-Conventional. **Skills:** Repairing; Equipment Maintenance; Operation and Control; Troubleshooting; Equipment Selection; Operation Monitoring; Quality Control Analysis; Coordination. **Education and Training Program:** Marine Transportation, Other. **Work Environment:** More often outdoors than indoors; contaminants; sounds, noisy; very hot or cold temperatures; standing.

OTHER FEDERAL JOB FACTS
RELATED GS SERIES: 5788 DECKHAND

- U.S. Federal Workforce: 237
- Average Length of Service: 10.6 years
- Percent Part-Time: 2.5%
- Percent Women: 6.3%
- Largest Age Bracket: 50–54 (17.3%)
- GS Level with Most Workers: Not a GS occupation
- Agency with Most Workers: Defense
- State with Most Workers: Mississippi

Do general maintenance work; repair and paint decks, hulls, superstructure and interior spaces of vessels; operate cargo gear and deck machinery; rig booms; handle lines during docking, moving, and towing operations; mend lines and canvas; stand lookout, security and wheel watches; connect and disconnect hoses and pipelines; operate fishing gear; and do similar work.

Requirements: No requirements available.

Security Guards

- Education/Training Required: Short-term on-the-job training
- Annual Earnings (Federal): $35,410
- Annual Earnings (All Industries): $23,820
- Earnings Growth Potential (Federal): 13.1% (very low)
- Earnings Growth Potential (All Industries): 29.3% (low)
- Job Growth (Federal): 8.3%
- Job Growth (All Industries): 14.2%
- Annual Job Openings (Federal): 120
- Annual Job Openings (All Industries): 37,390

Guard, patrol, or monitor premises to prevent theft, violence, or infractions of rules. May operate X-ray and metal detector equipment. Patrol industrial or commercial premises to prevent and detect signs of intrusion and ensure security of doors, windows, and gates. Answer alarms and investigate disturbances. Monitor and authorize entrance and departure of employees, visitors, and other persons to guard against theft and maintain security of premises. Write reports of daily activities and irregularities such as equipment or property damage, theft, presence of unauthorized persons, or unusual occurrences. Call police or fire departments in cases of emergency, such as fire or presence of unauthorized persons. Circulate among visitors, patrons, or employees to preserve order and protect property. Answer telephone calls to take messages, answer questions, and provide information during non-business hours or when switchboard is closed. Warn persons of rule infractions or violations, and apprehend or evict violators from premises, using force when necessary. Operate detecting devices to screen individuals and prevent passage of prohibited articles into restricted areas. Escort or drive motor vehicle to transport individuals to specified locations or to provide personal protection.

Considerations for Job Outlook: Concern about crime, vandalism, and terrorism are expected to result in increased demand for security services. This increased demand, along with the need to replace workers leaving the occupation permanently, should result in favorable job opportunities.

Personality Type: Realistic-Conventional-Enterprising. **Skills:** Operation and Control. **Education and Training Program:** Securities Services Administration/Management; Security and Loss Prevention Services. **Work Environment:** More often indoors than outdoors; standing; walking and running; using hands; noise; contaminants.

OTHER FEDERAL JOB FACTS
RELATED GS SERIES: 0085 SECURITY GUARD

- ❋ U.S. Federal Workforce: 5,767
- ❋ Average Length of Service: 8.1 years
- ❋ Percent Part-Time: 0.9%
- ❋ Percent Women: 87.8%
- ❋ Largest Age Bracket: 25–29 (15.0%)
- ❋ GS Levels with Most Workers: 5, 7
- ❋ Agency with Most Workers: Defense
- ❋ State with Most Workers: District of Columbia

Guard federally owned or leased buildings and property, protect government equipment and material, and control access to federal installations by employees, visitors, residents, and patients; protect and prevent loss of materials or processes important for national defense, for public health or safety, or as national treasures.

Requirements: Knowledge of established rules, regulations, and legal authorities that apply to detention authority and to the use of force (including weapons); knowledge of the rights of individuals.

Set and Exhibit Designers

- ❋ Education/Training Required: Bachelor's degree
- ❋ Annual Earnings (Federal): $67,080
- ❋ Annual Earnings (All Industries): $45,400
- ❋ Earnings Growth Potential (Federal): 29.9% (low)
- ❋ Earnings Growth Potential (All Industries): 43.6% (high)
- ❋ Job Growth (Federal): 7.9%
- ❋ Job Growth (All Industries): 16.6%
- ❋ Annual Job Openings (Federal): 20
- ❋ Annual Job Openings (All Industries): 510

Design special exhibits and movie, television, and theater sets. May study scripts, confer with directors, and conduct research to determine appropriate architectural styles. Examine objects to be included in exhibits to plan where and how to display them. Acquire, or arrange for acquisition of, specimens or graphics required to complete exhibits. Prepare rough drafts and scale working drawings of sets, including floor plans, scenery, and properties to be constructed. Confer with clients and staff to gather information about exhibit space, proposed themes and content, timelines, budgets, materials, and promotion requirements. Estimate set- or exhibit-related costs, including materials, construction, and rental of props or locations. Develop set designs based on evaluation of scripts, budgets, research information, and available locations. Direct and coordinate construction, erection, or decoration activities to ensure that sets or exhibits meet design, budget, and schedule requirements. Inspect installed exhibits for conformance to specifications and satisfactory operation of special effects components. Plan for location-specific issues such as space limitations, traffic flow patterns, and safety concerns. Submit plans for approval and adapt plans to serve intended purposes or to conform to budget or fabrication restrictions. Prepare preliminary renderings of proposed exhibits, including detailed construction, layout, and material specifications and diagrams relating to aspects such as special effects and lighting. Select and purchase lumber and hardware necessary for set construction.

Considerations for Job Outlook: Faster than average employment growth is projected.

Personality Type: Artistic-Realistic. **Skills:** Management of Financial Resources; Operations Analysis; Management of Material Resources; Mathematics; Management of Personnel Resources; Time Management; Coordination; Quality Control Analysis. **Education and Training Program:**

Design and Applied Arts, Other; Design and Visual Communications, General; Illustration; Technical Theatre/Theatre Design and Technology. **Work Environment:** Indoors; sitting; using your hands to handle, control, or feel objects, tools, or controls.

OTHER FEDERAL JOB FACTS

Related GS Series: 1010 Exhibits Specialist

- U.S. Federal Workforce: 368
- Average Length of Service: 17.1 years
- Percent Part-Time: 3.8%
- Percent Women: 17.4%
- Largest Age Bracket: 50–54 (21.5%)
- GS Level with Most Workers: 11
- Agency with Most Workers: Interior
- State with Most Workers: District of Columbia

Plan, construct, install, and operate exhibits, prepare gallery space for exhibits, preserve historic buildings, or prepare items to be exhibited.

Requirements: A combination of artistic abilities, technical knowledge and skills, and ability to understand the subject matter concepts that assigned exhibits projects are intended to convey.

Sheet Metal Workers

- Education/Training Required: Long-term on-the-job training
- Annual Earnings (Federal): $50,890
- Annual Earnings (All Industries): $40,640
- Earnings Growth Potential (Federal): 11.5% (very low)
- Earnings Growth Potential (All Industries): 39.7% (medium)
- Job Growth (Federal): 7.7%
- Job Growth (All Industries): 6.5%

- Annual Job Openings (Federal): 160
- Annual Job Openings (All Industries): 5,170

Fabricate, assemble, install, and repair sheet metal products and equipment, such as ducts, control boxes, drainpipes, and furnace casings. Work may involve any of the following: setting up and operating fabricating machines to cut, bend, and straighten sheet metal; shaping metal over anvils, blocks, or forms, using hammer; operating soldering and welding equipment to join sheet metal parts; and inspecting, assembling, and smoothing seams and joints of burred surfaces. Determine project requirements, including scope, assembly sequences, and required methods and materials, according to blueprints, drawings, and written or verbal instructions. Lay out, measure, and mark dimensions and reference lines on material, such as roofing panels, according to drawings or templates, using calculators, scribes, dividers, squares, and rulers. Maneuver completed units into position for installation, and anchor the units. Convert blueprints into shop drawings to be followed in the construction and assembly of sheet metal products. Install assemblies, such as flashing, pipes, tubes, heating and air conditioning ducts, furnace casings, rain gutters, and down spouts, in supportive frameworks. Select gauges and types of sheet metal or non-metallic material, according to product specifications. Drill and punch holes in metal, for screws, bolts, and rivets.

Considerations for Job Outlook: Employment of sheet metal workers in the construction industry is expected to increase along with building activity. But employment is likely to decline somewhat in manufacturing, due to increased automation and the movement of some work abroad. Opportunities should be particularly good for job seekers who have apprenticeship training or who are certified welders.

Personality Type: Realistic. **Skills:** Repairing; Equipment Maintenance; Equipment Selection; Quality Control Analysis; Mathematics; Troubleshooting; Operation and Control; Operation Monitoring. **Education and Training Program:** Sheet Metal Technology/Sheetworking. **Work Environment:** Sounds, noisy; contaminants; minor burns, cuts, bites, or stings; using your hands to handle, control, or feel objects, tools, or controls; hazardous equipment; standing.

OTHER FEDERAL JOB FACTS
RELATED GS SERIES: 3806 SHEET METAL MECHANIC

- U.S. Federal Workforce: 7,330
- Average Length of Service: 12.1 years
- Percent Part-Time: 0.0%
- Percent Women: 6.9%
- Largest Age Bracket: 50–54 (16.0%)
- GS Level with Most Workers: Not a GS occupation
- Agency with Most Workers: Defense
- States with Most Workers: Oklahoma, Georgia

Repair, fabricate, modify, and install sheet metal parts, items, and assemblies.

Requirements: Skill and knowledge in using shop mathematics to determine curves, angles, and pitch; planning and making pattern and template layouts; using measuring instruments; operating shop tools and equipment to construct manufactured items and systems with various seams; and working with various kinds of metal, including magnesium, honeycomb material, galvanized and black iron, aluminum and aluminum alloys, stainless steel, copper and brass sheets, lead alloys, and bronze.

Ship Engineers

- ❋ Education/Training Required: Work experience in a related occupation
- ❋ Annual Earnings (Federal): $47,570
- ❋ Annual Earnings (All Industries): $63,630
- ❋ Earnings Growth Potential (Federal): 26.9% (low)
- ❋ Earnings Growth Potential (All Industries): 44.9% (high)
- ❋ Job Growth (Federal): 29.8%
- ❋ Job Growth (All Industries): 18.6%
- ❋ Annual Job Openings (Federal): 50
- ❋ Annual Job Openings (All Industries): 700

Supervise and coordinate activities of crew engaged in operating and maintaining engines; boilers; deck machinery; and electrical, sanitary, and refrigeration equipment aboard ship. Record orders for changes in ship speed and direction, and note gauge readings and test data, such as revolutions per minute and voltage output, in engineering logs and bellbooks. Install engine controls, propeller shafts, and propellers. Perform and participate in emergency drills as required. Fabricate engine replacement parts such as valves, stay rods, and bolts, using metalworking machinery. Operate and maintain off-loading liquid pumps and valves. Maintain and repair engines, electric motors, pumps, winches, and other mechanical and electrical equipment, or assist other crew members with maintenance and repair duties. Maintain electrical power, heating, ventilation, refrigeration, water, and sewerage. Monitor and test operations of engines and other equipment so that malfunctions and their causes can be identified. Monitor engine, machinery, and equipment indicators when vessels are underway, and report abnormalities to appropriate shipboard staff. Start engines to propel ships, and regulate engines and power transmissions to control speeds of ships, according to directions from captains or bridge computers. Order and receive engine rooms' stores such as oil and spare parts; maintain inventories and record usage of supplies. Act as liaisons between ships' captains and shore personnel to ensure that schedules and budgets are maintained and that ships are operated safely and efficiently. Clean engine parts, and keep engine rooms clean.

Considerations for Job Outlook: Job growth is expected to stem from increasing tourism and from growth in offshore oil and gas production. Employment is also projected to increase in and around major port cities due to growing international trade. Opportunities should be excellent as the need to replace workers, particularly officers, generates many job openings.

Personality Type: Realistic-Conventional-Enterprising. **Skills:** Repairing; Equipment Maintenance; Troubleshooting; Equipment Selection; Operation and Control; Operation Monitoring; Quality Control Analysis; Science. **Education and Training Program:** Marine Maintenance/Fitter and Ship Repair Technology/Technician. **Work Environment:** Outdoors; sounds, noisy; contaminants; very hot or cold temperatures; hazardous equipment; using your hands to handle, control, or feel objects, tools, or controls.

OTHER FEDERAL JOB FACTS

RELATED GS SERIES: 5782 SHIP OPERATING

TITLE ON USAJOBS: SHIP OPERATOR

- ❋ U.S. Federal Workforce: 114
- ❋ Average Length of Service: 17.8 years
- ❋ Percent Part-Time: 0.9%
- ❋ Percent Women: 3.5%
- ❋ Largest Age Bracket: 50–54 (29.8%)
- ❋ GS Level with Most Workers: Not a GS occupation
- ❋ Agency with Most Workers: Defense
- ❋ State with Most Workers: Oregon

Operate ships, tugboats, seagoing dredges, fishing vessels, or other similar vessels, often greater than 55 meters (180 feet) in length, engaged in transporting passengers and freight, towing or assisting the maneuvering of large vessels, making hydrographic and oceanographic surveys, drilling or probing subaqueous holes, conducting fishing operations, and so forth; navigate the ship, stand watch, set and maintain speed and course, use navigational aids and devices to compute position, and coordinate the activities of members of the crew.

Requirements: Knowledge of the handling and operation of large vessels offshore or in the Great Lakes and/or large vessels under tow.

Social and Community Service Managers

- ❋ Education/Training Required: Bachelor's degree
- ❋ Annual Earnings (Federal): $91,140
- ❋ Annual Earnings (All Industries): $56,600
- ❋ Earnings Growth Potential (Federal): 21.6% (very low)
- ❋ Earnings Growth Potential (All Industries): 40.9% (medium)
- ❋ Job Growth (Federal): 12.2%
- ❋ Job Growth (All Industries): 13.8%
- ❋ Annual Job Openings (Federal): 10
- ❋ Annual Job Openings (All Industries): 4,820

Plan, organize, or coordinate the activities of a social service program or community outreach organization. Oversee the program or organization's budget and policies regarding participant involvement, program requirements, and benefits. Work may involve directing social workers, counselors, or probation officers. Establish and maintain relationships with other agencies and organizations in community to meet community

needs and to ensure that services are not duplicated. Prepare and maintain records and reports, such as budgets, personnel records, or training manuals. Direct activities of professional and technical staff members and volunteers. Evaluate the work of staff and volunteers to ensure that programs are of appropriate quality and that resources are used effectively. Establish and oversee administrative procedures to meet objectives set by boards of directors or senior management. Participate in the determination of organizational policies regarding such issues as participant eligibility, program requirements, and program benefits. Research and analyze member or community needs to determine program directions and goals. Speak to community groups to explain and interpret agency purposes, programs, and policies. Recruit, interview, and hire or sign up volunteers and staff. Represent organizations in relations with governmental and media institutions. Plan and administer budgets for programs, equipment, and support services. Analyze proposed legislation, regulations, or rule changes to determine how agency services could be impacted. Act as consultants to agency staff and other community programs regarding the interpretation of program-related federal, state, and county regulations and policies. Implement and evaluate staff training programs.

Considerations for Job Outlook: Faster than average employment growth is projected.

Personality Type: Enterprising-Social. **Skills:** Management of Financial Resources; Management of Personnel Resources; Management of Material Resources; Systems Evaluation; Operations Analysis; Social Perceptiveness; Systems Analysis; Learning Strategies. **Education and Training Program:** Business Administration and Management, General; Business, Management, Marketing, and Related Support Services, Other; Business/Commerce, General; Community Organization and Advocacy; Entrepreneurship/Entrepreneurial Studies; Human Services, General; Non-Profit/Public/Organizational Management;

Public Administration. **Work Environment:** Indoors; sitting.

OTHER FEDERAL JOB FACTS

RELATED GS SERIES: 0187 SOCIAL SERVICES

TITLE ON USAJOBS: SOCIAL SERVICES REPRESENTATIVE

- ❋ U.S. Federal Workforce: 285
- ❋ Average Length of Service: 14.0 years
- ❋ Percent Part-Time: 3.5%
- ❋ Percent Women: 69.1%
- ❋ Largest Age Bracket: 55–59 (21.8%)
- ❋ GS Levels with Most Workers: 8, 9
- ❋ Agency with Most Workers: Veterans Affairs
- ❋ State with Most Workers: California

Provide assistance to individuals and families served by social welfare programs; obtain selected background information through interviews and home visits, establish eligibility to make use of agency resources, help individuals identify needs that are related to services the agency can provide, explain and encourage the use of agency and community resources as means of dealing with identified problems, and make appropriate referrals to sources of additional help.

Requirements: Specialized knowledge of the social service program, but not a broad theoretical approach to social problems acquired through professional education in social work or in other recognized disciplines in the social sciences.

RELATED GS SERIES: 1630 CEMETERY ADMINISTRATION SERVICES

- ❋ U.S. Federal Workforce: 96
- ❋ Average Length of Service: 17.2 years
- ❋ Percent Part-Time: 0.0%
- ❋ Percent Women: 28.1%
- ❋ Largest Age Bracket: 45–49 (26.0%)
- ❋ GS Level with Most Workers: 13

- ❋ Agency with Most Workers: Veterans Affairs
- ❋ State with Most Workers: Missouri

Manage, supervise, lead, or perform administrative work that involves the operation or maintenance of one or more federal cemeteries.

Requirements: Broad administrative knowledge of the operation and maintenance requirements of cemeteries.

Social and Human Service Assistants

- ❋ Education/Training Required: Moderate-term on-the-job training
- ❋ Annual Earnings (Federal): $42,210
- ❋ Annual Earnings (All Industries): $27,940
- ❋ Earnings Growth Potential (Federal): 27.1% (low)
- ❋ Earnings Growth Potential (All Industries): 34.5% (low)
- ❋ Job Growth (Federal): 11.4%
- ❋ Job Growth (All Industries): 22.6%
- ❋ Annual Job Openings (Federal): 50
- ❋ Annual Job Openings (All Industries): 15,390

Assist professionals from a wide variety of fields such as psychology, rehabilitation, or social work to provide client services, as well as support for families. May assist clients in identifying available benefits and social and community services and help clients obtain them. May assist social workers with developing, organizing, and conducting programs to prevent and resolve problems relevant to substance abuse, human relationships, rehabilitation, or adult daycare. Keep records and prepare reports for owner or management concerning visits with clients. Submit reports and review reports or problems with superior. Interview individuals and family members to compile information on social, educational, criminal, institutional, or drug histories. Provide information and refer individuals to public or private agencies or community services for assistance. Consult with supervisors concerning programs for individual families. Advise clients regarding food stamps, child care, food, money management, sanitation, or housekeeping. Oversee day-to-day group activities of residents in institution. Visit individuals in homes or attend group meetings to provide information on agency services, requirements, and procedures. Monitor free, supplementary meal program to ensure cleanliness of facility and that eligibility guidelines are met for persons receiving meals. Meet with youth groups to acquaint them with consequences of delinquent acts. Assist in planning of food budgets, using charts and sample budgets. Transport and accompany clients to shopping areas or to appointments, using automobiles. Assist in locating housing for displaced individuals. Observe and discuss meal preparation and suggest alternate methods of food preparation. Observe clients' food selections and recommend alternative economical and nutritional food choices. Explain rules established by owner or management, such as sanitation and maintenance requirements or parking regulations.

Considerations for Job Outlook: As the elderly population grows, demand for the services provided by these workers is expected to increase. Opportunities are expected to be excellent, particularly for job seekers with some postsecondary education, such as a certificate or associate degree in a related subject.

Personality Type: Conventional-Social-Enterprising. **Skills:** Social Perceptiveness; Service Orientation; Active Listening; Science; Systems Analysis; Speaking; Learning Strategies; Persuasion. **Education and Training Program:** Mental and Social Health Services and Allied Professions, Other. **Work Environment:** Indoors; sitting.

OTHER FEDERAL JOB FACTS
RELATED GS SERIES: 0186 SOCIAL SERVICES AIDE AND ASSISTANT

TITLE ON USAJOBS: SOCIAL SERVICES AID/ASSISTANT

- U.S. Federal Workforce: 1,161
- Average Length of Service: 9.8 years
- Percent Part-Time: 6.4%
- Percent Women: 55.0%
- Largest Age Bracket: 55–59 (17.0%)
- GS Level with Most Workers: 7
- Agencies with Most Workers: Agriculture, Defense
- State with Most Workers: Texas

Support counseling, guidance, and related social services work in social, employment assistance, or similar programs; persons served may be individuals or families in the community or individuals in an institution, dormitory, or other government facility.

Requirements: Skill to communicate effectively and to work constructively with members of the particular group involved; also practical knowledge of program requirements and procedures, plus practical understanding of some of the more routine methods and techniques of counseling.

Social Scientists and Related Workers, All Other

- Education/Training Required: Master's degree
- Annual Earnings (Federal): $75,540
- Annual Earnings (All Industries): $69,860
- Earnings Growth Potential (Federal): 30.6% (low)

⊛ Earnings Growth Potential (All Industries): 45.0% (high)

⊛ Job Growth (Federal): 19.3%

⊛ Job Growth (All Industries): 22.5%

⊛ Annual Job Openings (Federal): 800

⊛ Annual Job Openings (All Industries): 2,380

Considerations for Job Outlook: Much faster than average employment growth is projected.

JOB SPECIALIZATION: TRANSPORTATION PLANNERS

Prepare studies for proposed transportation projects. Gather, compile, and analyze data. Study the use and operation of transportation systems. Develop transportation models or simulations. Prepare or review engineering studies or specifications. Represent jurisdictions in the legislative and administrative approval of land development projects. Prepare necessary documents to obtain project approvals or permits. Direct urban traffic counting programs. Develop or test new methods and models of transportation analysis. Define or update information such as urban boundaries and classification of roadways. Analyze transportation-related consequences of federal and state legislative proposals. Analyze information from traffic counting programs. Review development plans for transportation system effects, infrastructure requirements, or compliance with applicable transportation regulations. Prepare reports and recommendations on transportation planning. Produce environmental documents, such as environmental assessments and environmental impact statements. Participate in public meetings or hearings to explain planning proposals, to gather feedback from those affected by projects, or to achieve consensus on project designs. Document and evaluate transportation project needs and costs. Develop design ideas for new or improved transport infrastructure, such as junction improvements, pedestrian projects, bus facilities, and car parking areas. Develop computer models to address transportation planning issues. Design transportation surveys to identify areas of public concern.

Personality Type: Investigative-Conventional-Realistic. **Skills:** No data available. **Education and Training Program:** City/Urban, Community and Regional Planning. **Work Environment:** No data available.

OTHER FEDERAL JOB FACTS
RELATED GS SERIES: 0101 SOCIAL SCIENCE
TITLE ON USAJOBS: SOCIAL SCIENCE SPECIALIST

⊛ U.S. Federal Workforce: 9,881

⊛ Average Length of Service: 11.9 years

⊛ Percent Part-Time: 2.8%

⊛ Percent Women: 55.5%

⊛ Largest Age Bracket: 50–54 (15.2%)

⊛ GS Level with Most Workers: 11

⊛ Agency with Most Workers: Defense

⊛ State with Most Workers: District of Columbia

Advise on, administer, supervise, or perform research or other professional and scientific work in one or any combination of the social sciences when such work is not covered by another OPM occupation.

Requirements: Degree in a social or behavioral science or a related discipline; or several years of relevant work experience.

Soil and Plant Scientists

- ✺ Education/Training Required: Bachelor's degree
- ✺ Annual Earnings (Federal): $71,460
- ✺ Annual Earnings (All Industries): $59,180
- ✺ Earnings Growth Potential (Federal): 28.2% (low)
- ✺ Earnings Growth Potential (All Industries): 41.0% (high)
- ✺ Job Growth (Federal): 7.5%
- ✺ Job Growth (All Industries): 15.5%
- ✺ Annual Job Openings (Federal): 70
- ✺ Annual Job Openings (All Industries): 700

Conduct research in breeding, physiology, production, yield, and management of crops and agricultural plants, their growth in soils, and control of pests or study the chemical, physical, biological, and mineralogical composition of soils as they relate to plant or crop growth. May classify and map soils and investigate effects of alternative practices on soil and crop productivity. Communicate research and project results to other professionals and the public or teach related courses, seminars, or workshops. Provide information and recommendations to farmers and other landowners regarding ways in which they can best use land, promote plant growth, and avoid or correct problems such as erosion. Investigate responses of soils to specific management practices to determine the use capabilities of soils and the effects of alternative practices on soil productivity. Develop methods of conserving and managing soil that can be applied by farmers and forestry companies. Conduct experiments to develop new or improved varieties of field crops, focusing on characteristics such as yield, quality, disease resistance, nutritional value, or adaptation to specific soils or climates. Investigate soil problems and poor water quality to determine sources and effects. Study soil characteristics to classify soils on the basis of factors such as geographic location, landscape position, and soil properties. Develop improved measurement techniques, soil conservation methods, soil sampling devices, and related technology. Conduct experiments investigating how soil forms and changes and how it interacts with land-based ecosystems and living organisms. Identify degraded or contaminated soils and develop plans to improve their chemical, biological, and physical characteristics.

Considerations for Job Outlook: Job growth is expected to stem primarily from efforts to increase the quantity and quality of food for a growing population and to balance output with protection and preservation of soil, water, and ecosystems. Opportunities should be good for agricultural and food scientists in almost all fields.

Personality Type: Investigative-Realistic. **Skills:** Science; Operations Analysis; Mathematics; Reading Comprehension; Systems Analysis; Writing; Systems Evaluation; Speaking. **Education and Training Program:** Agricultural and Horticultural Plant Breeding; Agriculture, General; Horticultural Science; Plant Protection and Integrated Pest Management; Plant Sciences, General; Plant Sciences, Other; Range Science and Management; Soil Chemistry and Physics; Soil Microbiology; Soil Science and Agronomy, General. **Work Environment:** More often indoors than outdoors; sitting.

OTHER FEDERAL JOB FACTS

RELATED GS SERIES: 0471 AGRONOMY

TITLE ON USAJOBS: AGRONOMIST

- ✺ U.S. Federal Workforce: 256
- ✺ Average Length of Service: 18.8 years
- ✺ Percent Part-Time: 1.6%
- ✺ Percent Women: 13.7%
- ✺ Largest Age Bracket: 55–59 (23.0%)
- ✺ GS Level with Most Workers: 12

❋ Agency with Most Workers: Agriculture

❋ State with Most Workers: Texas

Perform professional and scientific work in the field of agronomy; apply the fundamental principles of plant, soil, and related sciences; improve, produce, manage, and use field crops, pasture crops, cover crops, turf, and related types of vegetation; manage soil; and develop and use weed controls and plant regulators.

Requirements: Professional knowledge and competence in agronomy.

RELATED GS SERIES: 0470 SOIL SCIENCE

TITLE ON USAJOBS: SOIL SCIENTIST

❋ U.S. Federal Workforce: 1,169

❋ Average Length of Service: 18.6 years

❋ Percent Part-Time: 1.5%

❋ Percent Women: 20.4%

❋ Largest Age Bracket: 55–59 (23.4%)

❋ GS Level with Most Workers: 12

❋ Agency with Most Workers: Agriculture

❋ States with Most Workers: California, Texas

Perform professional and scientific work in the investigation of soils, their management, and their adaptation for alternative uses.

Requirements: Knowledge of chemical, physical, mineralogical and biological properties and processes of the soils and their relationships to climatic, physiographic, and biologic influences.

Speech-Language Pathologists

❋ Education/Training Required: Master's degree

❋ Annual Earnings (Federal): $81,130

❋ Annual Earnings (All Industries): $65,090

❋ Earnings Growth Potential (Federal): 30.5% (low)

❋ Earnings Growth Potential (All Industries): 35.0% (low)

❋ Job Growth (Federal): 7.9%

❋ Job Growth (All Industries): 18.5%

❋ Annual Job Openings (Federal): 40

❋ Annual Job Openings (All Industries): 4,380

Assess and treat persons with speech, language, voice, and fluency disorders. May select alternative communication systems and teach their use. May perform research related to speech and language problems. Monitor patients' progress and adjust treatments accordingly. Evaluate hearing or speech and language test results, barium swallow results, and medical or background information to diagnose and plan treatment for speech, language, fluency, voice, and swallowing disorders. Administer hearing or speech and language evaluations, tests, or examinations to patients to collect information on type and degree of impairments, using written and oral tests and special instruments. Write reports and maintain proper documentation of information, such as client Medicaid and billing records and caseload activities, including the initial evaluation, treatment, progress, and discharge of clients. Develop and implement treatment plans for problems such as stuttering, delayed language, swallowing disorders, and inappropriate pitch or harsh voice problems, based on own assessments and recommendations of physicians, psychologists, or social workers. Develop individual or group activities and programs in schools to deal with behavior, speech, language, or swallowing problems. Participate in and write reports for meetings regarding patients' progress, such as individualized educational planning (IEP) meetings, in-service meetings, or intervention assistance team meetings. Complete administrative responsibilities, such as coordinating paperwork, scheduling case management activities, or writing lesson plans.

Considerations for Job Outlook: The aging population, better medical technology that increases the survival rates of people who become injured or ill, and growing enrollments in elementary and secondary schools are expected to increase employment of these workers. Job prospects are expected to be favorable.

Personality Type: Social-Investigative-Artistic. **Skills:** Science; Learning Strategies; Social Perceptiveness; Writing; Monitoring; Systems Evaluation; Active Learning; Operations Analysis. **Education and Training Program:** Audiology/Audiologist and Speech-Language Pathology/Pathologist; Communication Disorders Sciences and Services, Other; Communication Disorders, General; Communication Sciences and Disorders, General; Speech-Language Pathology/Pathologist. **Work Environment:** Indoors; sitting; sounds, noisy; disease or infections.

OTHER FEDERAL JOB FACTS

RELATED GS SERIES: 0665 SPEECH PATHOLOGY AND AUDIOLOGY

TITLE ON USAJOBS: SPEECH PATHOLOGIST/ AUDIOLOGIST

- U.S. Federal Workforce: 1,670
- Average Length of Service: 9.2 years
- Percent Part-Time: 14.9%
- Percent Women: 80.4%
- Largest Age Bracket: 30–34 (16.2%)
- GS Level with Most Workers: 12
- Agency with Most Workers: Veterans Affairs
- State with Most Workers: California

Do professional work in the study and/or treatment of human communications disorders, as reflected in impaired hearing, voice, language, or speech. May provide direct clinical services in the evaluation and resolution of communications disorders; provide graduate level training in communications disorders; plan and administer a comprehensive program for evaluating and treating communications disorders; and/or plan, administer, and perform laboratory and clinical research in communications disorders.

Requirements: Professional knowledge of the nature of human communications disorders, their causes, and methods of therapeutic treatment.

Statisticians

- Education/Training Required: Master's degree
- Annual Earnings (Federal): $92,720
- Annual Earnings (All Industries): $72,820
- Earnings Growth Potential (Federal): 44.5%v
- Earnings Growth Potential (All Industries): 47.2% (high)
- Job Growth (Federal): 6.9%
- Job Growth (All Industries): 13.1%
- Annual Job Openings (Federal): 140
- Annual Job Openings (All Industries): 960

Engage in the development of mathematical theory or apply statistical theory and methods to collect, organize, interpret, and summarize numerical data to provide usable information. May specialize in fields such as bio-statistics, agricultural statistics, business statistics, economic statistics, or other fields. Report results of statistical analyses, including information in the form of graphs, charts, and tables. Process large amounts of data for statistical modeling and graphic analysis, using computers. Identify relationships and trends in data, as well as any factors that could affect the results of research. Analyze and interpret statistical data in order to identify significant differences in relationships among sources of information. Prepare data for processing by organizing information, checking for any inaccuracies, and adjusting and weighting the raw data. Evaluate the statistical methods and procedures used to obtain data in order to ensure validity, applicability, efficiency, and accuracy. Evaluate sources of information in order to determine any limitations in terms of reliability or usability. Plan data collection methods for specific projects and determine the types and sizes of sample groups to be used. Design research projects that apply valid scientific techniques and utilize information obtained from baselines or historical data in order to structure uncompromised and efficient analyses. Develop an understanding of fields to which statistical methods are to be applied in order to determine whether methods and results are appropriate. Supervise and provide instructions for workers collecting and tabulating data. Apply sampling techniques or utilize complete enumeration bases in order to determine and define groups to be surveyed.

Considerations for Job Outlook: As data processing becomes faster and more efficient, employers are expected to need statisticians to analyze data. Projected employment growth for biostatisticians is related to the need for workers who can conduct research and clinical trials.

Personality Type: Conventional-Investigative. **Skills:** Programming; Mathematics; Science; Operations Analysis; Active Learning; Reading Comprehension; Critical Thinking; Learning Strategies. **Education and Training Program:** Applied Mathematics, General; Biostatistics; Business Statistics; Mathematical Statistics and Probability; Mathematics, General; Statistics, General; Statistics, Other. **Work Environment:** Indoors; sitting; using your hands to handle, control, or feel objects, tools, or controls; making repetitive motions.

JOB SPECIALIZATION: BIOSTATISTICIANS

Develop and apply biostatistical theory and methods to the study of life sciences. Write research proposals or grant applications for submission to external bodies. Teach graduate or continuing education courses or seminars in biostatistics. Read current literature, attend meetings or conferences, and talk with colleagues to keep abreast of methodological or conceptual developments in fields such as biostatistics, pharmacology, life sciences, and social sciences. Prepare statistical data for inclusion in reports to data monitoring committees, federal regulatory agencies, managers, or clients. Prepare articles for publication or presentation at professional conferences. Calculate sample size requirements for clinical studies. Determine project plans, timelines, or technical objectives for statistical aspects of biological research studies. Assign work to biostatistical assistants or programmers. Write program code to analyze data using statistical analysis software.

Personality Type: Investigative-Conventional. **Skills:** Programming; Science; Mathematics; Writing; Reading Comprehension; Operations Analysis; Active Learning; Instructing. **Education and Training Program:** Applied Mathematics, General; Biostatistics; Business Statistics; Mathematical Statistics and Probability; Mathematics, General; Statistics, General; Statistics, Other. **Work Environment:** Indoors; sitting.

JOB SPECIALIZATION: CLINICAL DATA MANAGERS

Apply knowledge of health care and database management to analyze clinical data, and to identify and report trends. Provide support and information to functional areas such as marketing, clinical monitoring, and medical affairs. Evaluate processes and technologies, and suggest revisions to increase productivity and efficiency. Develop technical specifications for data management programming and communicate needs to information technology staff. Contribute to the compilation, organization, and production of protocols, clinical study reports, regulatory submissions, or other controlled documentation. Write work instruction manuals, data capture guidelines, or standard operating procedures. Track the flow of work forms including in-house data flow or electronic forms transfer. Train staff on technical procedures or software program usage. Supervise the work of data management project staff. Prepare data analysis listings and activity, performance, or progress reports. Perform quality control audits to ensure accuracy, completeness, or proper usage of clinical systems and data.

Personality Type: Conventional-Investigative. **Skills:** Programming; Mathematics; Operations Analysis; Systems Evaluation; Systems Analysis; Instructing; Writing; Monitoring. **Education and Training Program:** Applied Mathematics, General; Biostatistics; Business Statistics; Mathematical Statistics and Probability; Mathematics, General; Statistics, General; Statistics, Other. **Work Environment:** Indoors; sitting; making repetitive motions.

OTHER FEDERAL JOB FACTS

RELATED GS SERIES: 1529 MATHEMATICAL STATISTICS

TITLE ON USAJOBS: MATHEMATICAL STATISTICIAN

- U.S. Federal Workforce: 1,481
- Average Length of Service: 13.3 years
- Percent Part-Time: 5.1%
- Percent Women: 41.1%
- Largest Age Bracket: 45–49 (13.5%)
- GS Level with Most Workers: 13
- Agency with Most Workers: Health and Human Services
- State with Most Workers: Maryland

Design, develop, and adapt mathematical methods and techniques to statistical processes; or do research that relates to the basic theories and science of statistics.

Requirements: Degree that includes substantial course work in mathematics and statistics, or a combination of relevant courses and experience. Courses must have included at least four of the following: differential calculus, integral calculus, advanced calculus, theory of equations, vector analysis, advanced algebra, linear algebra, mathematical logic, differential equations, or any other advanced course in mathematics for which one of these was a prerequisite.

Surveyors

- Education/Training Required: Bachelor's degree
- Annual Earnings (Federal): $81,140
- Annual Earnings (All Industries): $54,180
- Earnings Growth Potential (Federal): 26.9% (low)
- Earnings Growth Potential (All Industries): 44.4% (high)
- Job Growth (Federal): 8.0%
- Job Growth (All Industries): 14.9%
- Annual Job Openings (Federal): 20
- Annual Job Openings (All Industries): 2,330

Make exact measurements and determine property boundaries. Provide data relevant to the shape, contour, gravitation, location, elevation, or dimension of land or land features on or near Earth's surface for engineering, mapmaking, mining, land evaluation, construction, and other purposes. Verify the accuracy of survey data including measurements and calculations conducted at survey sites. Calculate heights, depths, relative positions, property lines, and other characteristics of terrain. Search legal records, survey records, and land titles to obtain information about property boundaries in areas to be surveyed. Prepare and maintain sketches, maps, reports, and legal descriptions of surveys to describe, certify, and assume liability for work performed. Direct or conduct surveys to establish legal boundaries for properties, based on legal deeds and titles. Prepare or supervise preparation of all data, charts, plots, maps, records, and documents related to surveys. Write descriptions of property boundary surveys for use in deeds, leases, or other legal documents. Compute geodetic measurements and interpret survey data to determine positions, shapes, and elevations of geomorphic and topographic features. Determine longitudes and latitudes of important features and boundaries in survey areas using theodolites, transits, levels, and satellite-based global positioning systems (GPS). Record the results of surveys including the shape, contour, location, elevation, and dimensions of land or land features. Coordinate findings with the work of engineering and architectural personnel, clients, and others concerned with projects. Establish fixed points for use in making maps, using geodetic and engineering instruments.

Considerations for Job Outlook: Increasing demand for geographic information should be the main source of employment growth. Job seekers with a bachelor's degree and strong technical skills should have favorable prospects.

Personality Type: Realistic-Conventional-Investigative. **Skills:** Science; Equipment Selection; Mathematics; Management of Personnel Resources; Quality Control Analysis; Operation Monitoring; Operation and Control; Learning Strategies. **Education and Training Program:** Surveying Technology/Surveying. **Work Environment:** Outdoors; very hot or cold temperatures; using your hands to handle, control, or feel objects, tools, or controls; hazardous equipment; minor burns, cuts, bites, or stings; standing.

JOB SPECIALIZATION: GEODETIC SURVEYORS

Measure large areas of Earth's surface, using satellite observations, global navigation satellite systems (GNSS), light detection and ranging (LIDAR), or related sources. Review existing standards, controls, or equipment used, recommending changes or upgrades as needed. Provide training and interpretation in the use of methods or procedures for observing and checking controls for geodetic and plane coordinates. Plan or direct the work of geodetic surveying staff, providing technical consultation as needed. Distribute compiled geodetic data to government agencies or the general public. Read current literature, talk with colleagues, continue education, or participate in professional organizations or conferences to keep abreast of developments in technology, equipment, or systems. Verify the mathematical correctness of newly collected survey data. Request additional survey data when field collection errors occur or engineering surveying specifications are not maintained. Prepare progress or technical reports. Maintain databases of geodetic and related information including coordinate, descriptive, or quality assurance data.

Personality Type: Investigative-Conventional-Realistic. **Skills:** Mathematics; Programming; Science; Quality Control Analysis; Writing; Operation and Control; Management of Personnel Resources; Reading Comprehension. **Education and Training Program:** Surveying Technology/Surveying. **Work Environment:** More often outdoors than indoors; using your hands to handle, control, or feel objects, tools, or controls; standing; very hot or cold temperatures.

OTHER FEDERAL JOB FACTS
RELATED GS SERIES: 1370 CARTOGRAPHY

- ❋ U.S. Federal Workforce: 698
- ❋ Average Length of Service: 18.2 years
- ❋ Percent Part-Time: 1.6%
- ❋ Percent Women: 26.4%
- ❋ Largest Age Bracket: 50–54 (21.8%)
- ❋ GS Level with Most Workers: 12

❀ Agency with Most Workers: Interior

❀ State with Most Workers: Maryland

Plan, design, research, develop, construct, evaluate, and modify mapping and charting systems, products, and technology.

Requirements: Professional knowledge and skills in mapping and related sciences, relevant mathematics, and statistics.

RELATED GS SERIES: 1372 GEODESY

❀ U.S. Federal Workforce: 80

❀ Average Length of Service: 21.2 years

❀ Percent Part-Time: 0.0%

❀ Percent Women: 17.5%

❀ Largest Age Bracket: 55–59 (30.0%)

❀ GS Levels with Most Workers: 12, 13

❀ Agency with Most Workers: Commerce

❀ State with Most Workers: Maryland

Determine the size and shape of the earth and its gravitational field, measure the intensity and direction of the force of gravity, and determine the horizontal and vertical positions of points on the earth and in space, where consideration of the curvature of the earth is required.

Requirements: Professional knowledge of the principles and techniques of geodesy.

RELATED GS SERIES: 1373 LAND SURVEYING

TITLE ON USAJOBS: LAND SURVEYOR

❀ U.S. Federal Workforce: 427

❀ Average Length of Service: 19.6 years

❀ Percent Part-Time: 1.2%

❀ Percent Women: 8.0%

❀ Largest Age Bracket: 55–59 (27.2%)

❀ GS Level with Most Workers: 12

❀ Agency with Most Workers: Interior

❀ States with Most Workers: Oregon, Alaska

Establish, investigate, and reestablish land and property boundaries, and prepare plats and legal descriptions for tracts of land.

Requirements: Professional knowledge of the concepts, principles, and techniques of surveying, including underlying mathematics and physical science, in combination with a practical knowledge of land ownership laws.

Tax Examiners, Collectors, and Revenue Agents

❀ Education/Training Required: Bachelor's degree

❀ Annual Earnings (Federal): $56,420

❀ Annual Earnings (All Industries): $48,550

❀ Earnings Growth Potential (Federal): 33.8% (low)

❀ Earnings Growth Potential (All Industries): 40.3% (medium)

❀ Job Growth (Federal): 19.5%

❀ Job Growth (All Industries): 13.0%

❀ Annual Job Openings (Federal): 1,060

❀ Annual Job Openings (All Industries): 3,520

Determine tax liability or collect taxes from individuals or business firms according to prescribed laws and regulations. Collect taxes from individuals or businesses according to prescribed laws and regulations. Maintain knowledge of tax code changes and of accounting procedures and theory to properly evaluate financial information. Maintain records for each case, including contacts, telephone numbers, and actions taken. Confer with taxpayers or their representatives to discuss the issues, laws, and regulations involved in returns and to resolve problems with returns. Contact taxpayers by mail or telephone to address discrepancies and to request supporting documentation.

Send notices to taxpayers when accounts are delinquent. Notify taxpayers of any overpayment or underpayment and either issue a refund or request further payment. Conduct independent field audits and investigations of income tax returns to verify information or to amend tax liabilities. Review filed tax returns to determine whether claimed tax credits and deductions are allowed by law. Review selected tax returns to determine the nature and extent of audits to be performed on them. Enter tax return information into computers for processing. Examine accounting systems and records to determine whether accounting methods used were appropriate and in compliance with statutory provisions. Process individual and corporate income tax returns and sales and excise tax returns. Impose payment deadlines on delinquent taxpayers and monitor payments to ensure that deadlines are met.

Considerations for Job Outlook: Employment growth of revenue agents and tax collectors should remain strong. The federal government is expected to increase its tax enforcement efforts, but demand for these workers' services is expected to be adversely affected by the automation of examiners' tasks and outsourcing of collection duties to private agencies.

Personality Type: Conventional-Enterprising. **Skills:** Reading Comprehension; Mathematics; Active Learning; Operations Analysis; Judgment and Decision Making; Negotiation; Active Listening; Writing. **Education and Training Program:** Accounting; Taxation. **Work Environment:** Indoors; sitting; making repetitive motions.

OTHER FEDERAL JOB FACTS

RELATED GS SERIES: 1894 CUSTOMS ENTRY AND LIQUIDATING

TITLE ON USAJOBS: CUSTOMS ENTRY AND LIQUIDATING OFFICER

- ✺ U.S. Federal Workforce: 498
- ✺ Average Length of Service: 20.6 years

- ✺ Percent Part-Time: 0.8%
- ✺ Percent Women: 74.7%
- ✺ Largest Age Bracket: 55–59 (20.1%)
- ✺ GS Level with Most Workers: 11
- ✺ Agency with Most Workers: Homeland Security
- ✺ State with Most Workers: New York

Examine, accept, process, or issue documents required for the entry of imported merchandise into the United States and the initial classification of merchandise covered by the entries; make final determinations of the statutory classification of merchandise covered by the entries; determine customs duties and applicable internal revenue taxes accruing on such merchandise; ascertain drawback to be paid on exported articles manufactured with the use of duty-paid or tax-paid imported merchandise or substituted domestic merchandise; and determine the validity of protests against liquidation decisions on formal entries.

Requirements: Knowledge about imported merchandise—uses, commercial or common designations, manufacturing procedures, component materials, and usual countries of origin; familiarity with Customs procedures; ability to analyze facts and to apply provisions of laws and regulations; ability to verify details accurately and alertness in detecting discrepancies; effectiveness in meeting and dealing with people.

RELATED GS SERIES: 0512 INTERNAL REVENUE AGENT

- ✺ U.S. Federal Workforce: 14,666
- ✺ Average Length of Service: 15.2 years
- ✺ Percent Part-Time: 2.0%
- ✺ Percent Women: 50.1%
- ✺ Largest Age Bracket: 50–54 (17.9%)
- ✺ GS Level with Most Workers: 13
- ✺ Agency with Most Workers: Treasury
- ✺ State with Most Workers: California

Determine or advise on liability for federal taxes.

Requirements: Professional knowledge of accounting theories, concepts, principles, and standards; knowledge of pertinent tax laws, regulations, and related matters.

RELATED GS SERIES: 1169 INTERNAL REVENUE OFFICER

- ⚜ U.S. Federal Workforce: 5,934
- ⚜ Average Length of Service: 17.7 years
- ⚜ Percent Part-Time: 1.2%
- ⚜ Percent Women: 56.6%
- ⚜ Largest Age Bracket: 50–54 (19.6%)
- ⚜ GS Levels with Most Workers: 12, 9
- ⚜ Agency with Most Workers: Treasury
- ⚜ State with Most Workers: California

Collect delinquent taxes, survey for unreported taxes, and secure delinquent returns.

Requirements: Knowledge of general or specialized business practices; pertinent tax laws, regulations, procedures, and precedents; judicial processes, laws of evidence, and the interrelationship between federal and state laws with respect to collection and assessment processes; and investigative techniques and methods.

RELATED GS SERIES: 0592 TAX EXAMINING

- ⚜ U.S. Federal Workforce: 12,209
- ⚜ Average Length of Service: 15.6 years
- ⚜ Percent Part-Time: 2.0%
- ⚜ Percent Women: 76.6%
- ⚜ Largest Age Bracket: 50–54 (17.8%)
- ⚜ GS Level with Most Workers: 7
- ⚜ Agency with Most Workers: Treasury
- ⚜ State with Most Workers: Utah

Perform or supervise work in the Internal Revenue Service involving the processing of original tax returns, establishing tax account records, or changing such records based on later information affecting taxes and refunds; collecting taxes and/or obtaining tax returns; computing or verifying tax, penalty, and interest; and determining proper tax liability.

Requirements: Knowledge of standardized processing and collection procedures to record tax information and knowledge of applicable portions of tax laws and tax rulings to accept, request proof of, or reject a variety of taxpayer claims, credits, and deductions.

RELATED GS SERIES: 0526 TAX SPECIALIST

- ⚜ U.S. Federal Workforce: 1,901
- ⚜ Average Length of Service: 15.2 years
- ⚜ Percent Part-Time: 1.3%
- ⚜ Percent Women: 64.9%
- ⚜ Largest Age Bracket: 50–54 (18.5%)
- ⚜ GS Level with Most Workers: 9
- ⚜ Agency with Most Workers: Treasury
- ⚜ State with Most Workers: California

Determine, supervise, educate, advise, and perform work related to federal tax liability and, as required, duties and tariffs when such work involves contact with taxpayers, manufacturers, producers, importers, third-party organizations, and/or their representatives.

Requirements: Knowledge of financial accounting principles, practices, and methods; knowledge of pertinent laws, regulations, and rulings pertaining to taxes, and/or, as required, duties and tariffs.

Teachers and Instructors, All Other

- ⚜ Education/Training Required: Bachelor's degree
- ⚜ Annual Earnings (Federal): $62,840
- ⚜ Annual Earnings (All Industries): $31,540
- ⚜ Earnings Growth Potential (Federal): 25.8% (low)

- ✺ Earnings Growth Potential (All Industries): 44.5% (high)
- ✺ Job Growth (Federal): 7.4%
- ✺ Job Growth (All Industries): 14.7%
- ✺ Annual Job Openings (Federal): 430
- ✺ Annual Job Openings (All Industries): 22,570

Considerations for Job Outlook: Faster than average employment growth is projected.

JOB SPECIALIZATION: ADAPTIVE PHYSICAL EDUCATION SPECIALISTS

Provide individualized physical education instruction or services to children, youth, or adults with exceptional physical needs, due to gross motor developmental delays or other impairments. Review adaptive physical education programs or practices to ensure compliance with government or other regulations. Request or order physical education equipment, following standard procedures. Write reports to summarize student performance, social growth, or physical development. Attend in-service training, workshops, or meetings to keep abreast of current practices or trends in adapted physical education. Write or modify individualized education plans (IEPs) for students with intellectual or physical disabilities. Provide students positive feedback to encourage them and help them develop an appreciation for physical education. Provide individual or small groups of students with adaptive physical education instruction that meets desired physical needs or goals. Prepare lesson plans in accordance with individualized education plans (IEPs) and the functional abilities or needs of students. Maintain thorough student records to document attendance, participation, or progress, ensuring confidentiality of all records. Maintain inventory of instructional equipment, materials, or aids. Evaluate the motor needs of individual students to determine

their need for adapted physical education services. Establish and maintain standards of behavior to create safe, orderly, and effective environments for learning. Communicate behavioral observations and student progress reports to students, parents, teachers, or administrators.

Personality Type: No data available. **Skills:** No data available. **Education and Training Program:** Kinesiology and Exercise Science. **Work Environment:** No data available.

JOB SPECIALIZATION: TUTORS

Provide non-classroom, academic instruction to students on an individual or small-group basis for proactive or remedial purposes. Travel to students' homes, libraries, or schools to conduct tutoring sessions. Schedule tutoring appointments with students or their parents. Research or recommend textbooks, software, equipment, or other learning materials to complement tutoring. Prepare and facilitate tutoring workshops, collaborative projects, or academic support sessions for small groups of students. Participate in training and development sessions to improve tutoring practices or learn new tutoring techniques. Organize tutoring environment to promote productivity and learning. Monitor student performance or assist students in academic environments, such as classrooms, laboratories, or computing centers. Review class material with students by discussing text, working solutions to problems, or reviewing worksheets or other assignments. Provide feedback to students using positive reinforcement techniques to encourage, motivate, or build confidence in students. Prepare lesson plans or learning modules for tutoring sessions according to students' needs and goals. Maintain records of students' assessment results, progress, feedback, or school performance, ensuring confidentiality of all records. Identify, develop, or implement intervention strategies, tutoring plans, or individualized education plans (IEPs) for students. Develop teaching or training materials, such as handouts, study materials, or quizzes.

Personality Type: No data available. **Skills:** No data available. **Education and Training Program:** Adult Literacy Tutor/Instructor Training; Teaching Assistants/Aides, Other, Training. **Work Environment:** No data available.

OTHER FEDERAL JOB FACTS

RELATED GS SERIES: 1701 GENERAL EDUCATION AND TRAINING

TITLE ON USAJOBS: EDUCATIONAL AND TRAINING PROGRAM SPECIALIST

* U.S. Federal Workforce: 6,824
* Average Length of Service: 10.5 years
* Percent Part-Time: 3.5%
* Percent Women: 48.4%
* Largest Age Bracket: 55–59 (17.0%)
* GS Level with Most Workers: 9
* Agency with Most Workers: Defense
* State with Most Workers: California

Perform professional work in the field of education and training not covered by another OPM occupation.

Requirements: Degree in education or in a subject-matter field appropriate to the position, or some relevant education plus work experience in a setting such as a preschool, early elementary school, church school, or day care center. For information about teaching overseas, see www.usajobs.gov/EI/overseasemploymentforteachers.asp.

Technical Writers

* Education/Training Required: Bachelor's degree
* Annual Earnings (Federal): $73,340
* Annual Earnings (All Industries): $62,730
* Earnings Growth Potential (Federal): 31.3% (low)
* Earnings Growth Potential (All Industries): 40.9% (medium)
* Job Growth (Federal): 10.0%
* Job Growth (All Industries): 18.2%
* Annual Job Openings (Federal): 30
* Annual Job Openings (All Industries): 1,680

Write technical materials, such as equipment manuals, appendices, or operating and maintenance instructions. May assist in layout work. Organize material and complete writing assignment according to set standards regarding order, clarity, conciseness, style, and terminology. Maintain records and files of work and revisions. Edit, standardize, or make changes to material prepared by other writers or establishment personnel. Confer with customer representatives, vendors, plant executives, or publisher to establish technical specifications and to determine subject material to be developed for publication. Review published materials and recommend revisions or changes in scope, format, content, and methods of reproduction and binding. Select photographs, drawings, sketches, diagrams, and charts to illustrate material. Study drawings, specifications, mockups, and product samples to integrate and delineate technology, operating procedure, and production sequence and detail. Interview production and engineering personnel and read journals and other material to become familiar with product technologies and production methods. Observe production, developmental, and experimental activities to determine operating procedure and detail. Arrange for typing, duplication, and distribution of material. Assist in laying out material for publication. Analyze developments in specific field to determine need for revisions in previously published materials and development of new material. Review manufacturer's and trade catalogs, drawings, and other data relative to operation, maintenance, and service of equipment.

Considerations for Job Outlook: Fast growth is expected because of the need for technical writers to explain an increasing number of scientific and technical products. Prospects should be good, especially for workers with strong technical and communication skills. Competition will be keen for some jobs.

Personality Type: Artistic-Investigative-Conventional. **Skills:** Writing; Reading Comprehension; Active Learning; Speaking; Critical Thinking; Complex Problem Solving; Active Listening; Quality Control Analysis. **Education and Training Program:** Business/Corporate Communications; Speech Communication and Rhetoric. **Work Environment:** Indoors; sitting; making repetitive motions; using your hands to handle, control, or feel objects, tools, or controls.

OTHER FEDERAL JOB FACTS

RELATED GS SERIES: 1083 TECHNICAL WRITING AND EDITING

TITLE ON USAJOBS: TECHNICAL WRITER/EDITOR

- U.S. Federal Workforce: 1,215
- Average Length of Service: 14.0 years
- Percent Part-Time: 1.6%
- Percent Women: 59.9%
- Largest Age Bracket: 55–59 (17.9%)
- GS Level with Most Workers: 12
- Agency with Most Workers: Defense
- State with Most Workers: Maryland

Write or edit technical materials; select, analyze, and present information on a specialized subject in a form and at a level suitable for the intended audience.

Requirements: Substantial knowledge of a particular subject-matter area, such as the natural or social sciences, engineering, law, or other fields.

Transportation Inspectors

- Education/Training Required: Work experience in a related occupation
- Annual Earnings (Federal): $100,100
- Annual Earnings (All Industries): $56,290
- Earnings Growth Potential (Federal): 26.3% (low)
- Earnings Growth Potential (All Industries): 49.2% (high)
- Job Growth (Federal): 18.3%
- Job Growth (All Industries): 18.4%
- Annual Job Openings (Federal): 150
- Annual Job Openings (All Industries): 1,130

Inspect equipment or goods in connection with the safe transport of cargo or people. Includes rail transport inspectors, such as freight inspectors, car inspectors, rail inspectors, and other nonprecision inspectors of other types of transportation vehicles. No task data available.

Considerations for Job Outlook: Faster than average employment growth is projected.

JOB SPECIALIZATION: AVIATION INSPECTORS

Inspect aircraft, maintenance procedures, air navigational aids, air traffic controls, and communications equipment to ensure conformance with federal safety regulations. Inspect work of aircraft mechanics performing maintenance, modification, or repair and overhaul of aircraft and aircraft mechanical systems to ensure adherence to standards and procedures. Start aircraft and observe gauges, meters, and other instruments to detect evidence of malfunctions. Examine aircraft access plates and doors for security. Examine landing gear, tires, and exteriors of fuselage, wings, and engines for evidence of damage or corrosion and to determine whether repairs are needed. Prepare and maintain detailed repair, inspection, investigation, and certification records and reports. Inspect new, repaired, or modified aircraft to identify damage or defects and to assess airworthiness and conformance to standards, using checklists, hand tools, and test instruments. Examine maintenance records and flight logs to determine if service and maintenance checks and overhauls were performed at prescribed intervals. Recommend replacement, repair, or modification of aircraft equipment. Recommend changes in rules, policies, standards, and regulations based on knowledge of operating conditions, aircraft improvements, and other factors. Issue pilots' licenses to individuals meeting standards. Investigate air accidents and complaints to determine causes. Observe flight activities of pilots to assess flying skills and to ensure conformance to flight and safety regulations.

Personality Type: Realistic-Conventional-Investigative. **Skills:** Science; Equipment Maintenance; Troubleshooting; Repairing; Operation and Control; Equipment Selection; Quality Control Analysis; Operation Monitoring. **Education and Training Program:** Aircraft Powerplant Technology/Technician. **Work Environment:** More often indoors than outdoors; sounds, noisy; sitting.

JOB SPECIALIZATION: TRANSPORTATION VEHICLE, EQUIPMENT, AND SYSTEMS INSPECTORS, EXCEPT AVIATION

Inspect and monitor transportation equipment, vehicles, or systems to ensure compliance with regulations and safety standards. Conduct vehicle or transportation equipment tests, using diagnostic equipment. Investigate and make recommendations on carrier requests for waiver of federal standards. Prepare reports on investigations or inspections and actions taken. Issue notices and recommend corrective actions when infractions or problems are found. Investigate incidents or violations such as delays, accidents, and equipment failures. Investigate complaints regarding safety

violations. Inspect repairs to transportation vehicles and equipment to ensure that repair work was performed properly. Examine transportation vehicles, equipment, or systems to detect damage, wear, or malfunction. Inspect vehicles and other equipment for evidence of abuse, damage, or mechanical malfunction. Examine carrier operating rules, employee qualification guidelines, and carrier training and testing programs for compliance with regulations or safety standards. Inspect vehicles or equipment to ensure compliance with rules, standards, or regulations.

Personality Type: Realistic-Conventional-Investigative. **Skills:** Equipment Maintenance; Repairing; Troubleshooting; Science; Operation and Control; Quality Control Analysis; Operation Monitoring; Equipment Selection. **Education and Training Program:** No related CIP programs; this job is learned through work experience in a related occupation. **Work Environment:** Contaminants; using your hands to handle, control, or feel objects, tools, or controls; sounds, noisy; very hot or cold temperatures; cramped work space, awkward positions; hazardous equipment.

JOB SPECIALIZATION: FREIGHT AND CARGO INSPECTORS

Inspect the handling, storage, and stowing of freight and cargoes. Prepare and submit reports after completion of freight shipments. Inspect shipments to ensure that freight is securely braced and blocked. Record details about freight conditions, handling of freight, and any problems encountered. Advise crews in techniques of stowing dangerous and heavy cargo. Observe loading of freight to ensure that crews comply with procedures. Recommend remedial procedures to correct any violations found during inspections. Inspect loaded cargo, cargo lashed to decks or in storage facilities, and cargo handling devices to determine compliance with health and safety regulations and need for maintenance. Measure ships' holds and depths of fuel and water in tanks, using sounding lines and tape measures. Notify workers of any special treatment required for shipments. Direct crews to reload freight or to insert additional bracing or packing as necessary. Check temperatures and humidities of shipping and storage areas to ensure that they are at appropriate levels to protect cargo. Determine cargo transportation capabilities by reading documents that set forth cargo loading and securing procedures, capacities, and stability factors. Read draft markings to determine depths of vessels in water. Issue certificates of compliance for vessels without violations. Write certificates of admeasurement that list details such as designs, lengths, depths, and breadths of vessels and methods of propulsion.

Personality Type: Realistic-Conventional. **Skills:** Operation and Control; Quality Control Analysis; Operation Monitoring; Management of Personnel Resources; Writing; Troubleshooting; Equipment Maintenance; Installation. **Education and Training Program:** No related CIP programs; this job is learned through work experience in a related occupation. **Work Environment:** More often outdoors than indoors; sounds, noisy; contaminants; very hot or cold temperatures; extremely bright or inadequate lighting.

OTHER FEDERAL JOB FACTS

RELATED GS SERIES: 1825 AVIATION SAFETY

TITLE ON USAJOBS: AVIATION SAFETY INSPECTOR

- ❀ U.S. Federal Workforce: 4,289
- ❀ Average Length of Service: 13.2 years
- ❀ Percent Part-Time: 0.0%
- ❀ Percent Women: 7.6%
- ❀ Largest Age Bracket: 60–64 (18.9%)
- ❀ GS Level with Most Workers: 12

- ❀ Agency with Most Workers: Transportation
- ❀ State with Most Workers: Texas

Develop, administer, or enforce regulations and standards concerning civil aviation safety, including the airworthiness of aircraft and aircraft systems; the competence of pilots, mechanics, and other airmen; and safety aspects of aviation facilities, equipment, and procedures.

Requirements: Knowledge and skill in the operation, maintenance, or manufacture of aircraft and aircraft systems.

RELATED GS SERIES: 0873 MARINE SURVEY TECHNICAL

- ❀ U.S. Federal Workforce: 86
- ❀ Average Length of Service: 15.9 years
- ❀ Percent Part-Time: 0.0%
- ❀ Percent Women: 1.2%
- ❀ Largest Age Bracket: 50–54 (27.9%)
- ❀ GS Level with Most Workers: 13
- ❀ Agency with Most Workers: Defense
- ❀ State with Most Workers: Virginia

Supervise, lead, or perform work involving surveying government-owned and/or operated vessels, or privately owned and operated merchant vessels, to determine their condition and the extent of work necessary for the vessels and their components to meet specified requirements.

Requirements: Practical knowledge of preparing specifications, including estimates of labor and material costs, to cover work determined to be necessary as a result of surveys; and inspecting and accepting the work accomplished to place the vessel in the condition specified.

Transportation, Storage, and Distribution Managers

- ❋ Education/Training Required: Work experience in a related occupation
- ❋ Annual Earnings (Federal): $94,890
- ❋ Annual Earnings (All Industries): $79,490
- ❋ Earnings Growth Potential (Federal): 35.6% (median)
- ❋ Earnings Growth Potential (All Industries): 42.5% (high)
- ❋ Job Growth (Federal): –5.7%
- ❋ Job Growth (All Industries): –5.3%
- ❋ Annual Job Openings (Federal): 160
- ❋ Annual Job Openings (All Industries): 2,740

Plan, direct, or coordinate transportation, storage, or distribution activities in accordance with governmental policies and regulations. No task data available.

Considerations for Job Outlook: Employment is projected to decline slowly.

JOB SPECIALIZATION: STORAGE AND DISTRIBUTION MANAGERS

Plan, direct, and coordinate the storage and distribution operations within organizations or the activities of organizations that are engaged in storing and distributing materials and products. Supervise the activities of workers engaged in receiving, storing, testing, and shipping products or materials. Plan, develop, and implement warehouse safety and security programs and activities. Review invoices, work orders, consumption reports, and demand forecasts to estimate peak delivery periods and to issue work assignments. Schedule and monitor air or surface pickup, delivery, or distribution of products or materials. Interview, select, and train warehouse and supervisory personnel. Confer with department heads to coordinate warehouse activities, such as production, sales, records control, and purchasing. Respond to customers' or shippers' questions and complaints regarding storage and distribution services. Inspect physical conditions of warehouses, vehicle fleets, and equipment and order testing, maintenance, repair, or replacement as necessary. Develop and document standard and emergency operating procedures for receiving, handling, storing, shipping, or salvaging products or materials. Examine products or materials to estimate quantities or weight and type of container required for storage or transport. Issue shipping instructions and provide routing information to ensure that delivery times and locations are coordinated. Negotiate with carriers, warehouse operators, and insurance company representatives for services and preferential rates. Examine invoices and shipping manifests for conformity to tariff and customs regulations.

Personality Type: Enterprising-Conventional. **Skills:** Management of Financial Resources; Management of Material Resources; Operations Analysis; Management of Personnel Resources; Negotiation; Coordination; Operation and Control; Systems Evaluation. **Education and Training Program:** Aeronautics/Aviation/Aerospace Science and Technology, General; Aviation/Airway Management and Operations; Business Administration and Management, General; Business/Commerce, General; Logistics, Materials, and Supply Chain Management; Public Administration; Transportation/Mobility Management. **Work Environment:** Indoors; standing.

JOB SPECIALIZATION: TRANSPORTATION MANAGERS

Plan, direct, and coordinate the transportation operations within an organization or the activities of organizations that provide transportation services. Analyze expenditures and other financial information to develop plans, policies, and budgets for increasing profits and improving services. Set operations policies and standards, including determination of safety procedures for the handling of dangerous goods. Plan, organize, and manage the work of subordinate staff to ensure that the work is accomplished in a manner consistent with organizational requirements. Negotiate and authorize contracts with equipment and materials suppliers, and monitor contract fulfillment. Collaborate with other managers and staff members to formulate and implement policies, procedures, goals, and objectives. Monitor spending to ensure that expenses are consistent with approved budgets. Supervise workers assigning tariff classifications and preparing billing. Promote safe work activities by conducting safety audits, attending company safety meetings, and meeting with individual staff members. Direct investigations to verify and resolve customer or shipper complaints. Direct procurement processes including equipment research and testing, vendor contracts, and requisitions approval. Recommend or authorize capital expenditures for acquisition of new equipment or property to increase efficiency and services of operations department. Monitor operations to ensure that staff members comply with administrative policies and procedures, safety rules, union contracts, and government regulations.

Personality Type: Enterprising-Conventional. **Skills:** Management of Financial Resources; Systems Evaluation; Negotiation; Systems Analysis; Management of Material Resources; Social Perceptiveness; Management of Personnel Resources; Time Management. **Education and Training Program:** Aeronautics/Aviation/Aerospace Science and Technology, General; Aviation/Airway Management and Operations; Business Administration and Management, General; Business/Commerce, General; Logistics, Materials, and Supply Chain Management; Public Administration; Transportation/Mobility Management. **Work Environment:** Indoors; sitting.

OTHER FEDERAL JOB FACTS

RELATED GS SERIES: 2030 DISTRIBUTION FACILITIES AND STORAGE MANAGEMENT

TITLE ON USAJOBS: DISTRIBUTION FACILITIES AND STORAGE MANAGEMENT SPECIALIST

- ❋ U.S. Federal Workforce: 522
- ❋ Average Length of Service: 20.8 years
- ❋ Percent Part-Time: 0.2%
- ❋ Percent Women: 25.7%
- ❋ Largest Age Bracket: 55–59 (25.1%)
- ❋ GS Levels with Most Workers: 11, 9
- ❋ Agency with Most Workers: Defense
- ❋ State with Most Workers: Pennsylvania

Do analytical or managerial work concerned with receiving, handling, storing, maintaining while in storage, issuing, or physically controlling items within a storage and distribution system.

Requirements: Knowledge of the principles, practices, and techniques of managing the physical receipt, custody, care, and distribution of material, including the selection of appropriate storage sites, material handling equipment, and facilities.

Veterinarians

- ❋ Education/Training Required: First professional degree
- ❋ Annual Earnings (Federal): $81,130
- ❋ Annual Earnings (All Industries): $80,510
- ❋ Earnings Growth Potential (Federal): 14.3% (very low)
- ❋ Earnings Growth Potential (All Industries): 40.8% (medium)
- ❋ Job Growth (Federal): 7.6%
- ❋ Job Growth (All Industries): 32.9%
- ❋ Annual Job Openings (Federal): 50
- ❋ Annual Job Openings (All Industries): 3,020

Diagnose and treat diseases and dysfunctions of animals. May engage in a particular function, such as research and development, consultation, administration, technical writing, sale or production of commercial products, or rendering of technical services to commercial firms or other organizations. Includes veterinarians who inspect livestock. Treat sick or injured animals by prescribing medication, setting bones, dressing wounds, or performing surgery. Examine animals to detect and determine the nature of diseases or injuries. Provide care to a wide range of animals or specialize in a particular species, such as horses or exotic birds. Inoculate animals against various diseases such as rabies and distemper. Advise animal owners regarding sanitary measures, feeding, general care, medical conditions, and treatment options. Operate diagnostic equipment such as radiographic and ultrasound equipment, and interpret the resulting images. Educate the public about diseases that can be spread from animals to humans. Collect body tissue, feces, blood, urine, or other body fluids for examination and analysis. Attend lectures, conferences, and continuing education courses. Euthanize animals. Train and supervise workers who handle and care for animals. Conduct postmortem studies and analyses to determine the causes of animals' deaths. Specialize in a particular type of treatment such as dentistry, pathology, nutrition, surgery, microbiology, or internal medicine. Direct the overall operations of animal hospitals, clinics, or mobile services to farms. Drive mobile clinic vans to farms so that health problems can be treated or prevented. Establish and conduct quarantine and testing procedures that prevent the spread of diseases to other animals or to humans and that comply with applicable government regulations.

Considerations for Job Outlook: Growth in the pet population and pet owners' increased willingness to pay for intensive veterinary care and treatment are projected to create significantly more jobs for veterinarians. Excellent job opportunities are expected.

Personality Type: Investigative-Realistic. **Skills:** Science; Operations Analysis; Reading Comprehension; Active Learning; Instructing; Service Orientation; Writing; Judgment and Decision Making. **Education and Training Program:** Comparative and Laboratory Animal Medicine (Cert., MS, PhD); Laboratory Animal Medicine; Large Animal/Food Animal and Equine Surgery and Medicine (Cert., MS, PhD); Small/Companion Animal Surgery and Medicine (Cert., MS, PhD); Theriogenology; Veterinary Anatomy (Cert., MS, PhD); Veterinary Anesthesiology; Veterinary Biomedical and Clinical Sciences, Other (Cert., MS, PhD); Veterinary Dentistry; Veterinary Dermatology; Veterinary Emergency and Critical Care Medicine; others. **Work Environment:** Indoors; using your hands to handle, control, or feel objects, tools, or controls; standing; disease or infections; contaminants; minor burns, cuts, bites, or stings.

OTHER FEDERAL JOB FACTS

RELATED GS SERIES: 0701 VETERINARY MEDICAL SCIENCE

TITLE ON USAJOBS: VETERINARY MEDICAL OFFICER

- ❀ U.S. Federal Workforce: 2,204
- ❀ Average Length of Service: 11.9 years
- ❀ Percent Part-Time: 11.0%
- ❀ Percent Women: 38.3%
- ❀ Largest Age Bracket: 55–59 (19.6%)
- ❀ GS Level with Most Workers: 13
- ❀ Agency with Most Workers: Agriculture
- ❀ State with Most Workers: Maryland

Investigate, inspect, and deal with animal diseases, animal pollution, contamination of food of animal origin, health and safety of imported animals and animal products, safety and efficacy of many animals, as well as human, drugs, and biological products, and cooperative enforcement activities involving both the public and private sectors.

Requirements: Degree of Doctor of Veterinary Medicine or an equivalent degree; a knowledge of current, advanced, or specialized veterinary medical arts and science principles and practices of the profession; and the ability to apply that knowledge in programs established to protect and improve the health, products, and environment of or for the nation's livestock, poultry, or other species.

Veterinary Technologists and Technicians

- ❋ Education/Training Required: Associate degree
- ❋ Annual Earnings (Federal): $46,440
- ❋ Annual Earnings (All Industries): $29,280
- ❋ Earnings Growth Potential (Federal): 25.3% (low)
- ❋ Earnings Growth Potential (All Industries): 31.1% (low)
- ❋ Job Growth (Federal): 12.5%
- ❋ Job Growth (All Industries): 35.8%
- ❋ Annual Job Openings (Federal): 30
- ❋ Annual Job Openings (All Industries): 4,850

Perform medical tests in a laboratory environment for use in the treatment and diagnosis of diseases in animals. Prepare vaccines and serums for prevention of diseases. Prepare tissue samples; take blood samples; and execute laboratory tests such as urinalysis and blood counts. Clean and sterilize instruments and materials and maintain equipment and machines. Observe the behavior and condition of animals, and monitor their clinical symptoms. Maintain controlled drug inventory and related log books. Administer anesthesia to animals, under the direction of a veterinarian, and monitor animals' responses to anesthetics so that dosages can be adjusted. Care for and monitor the condition of animals recovering from surgery. Perform laboratory tests on blood, urine, and feces, such as urinalyses and blood counts, to assist in the diagnosis and treatment of animal health problems. Administer emergency first aid, such as performing emergency resuscitation or other life saving procedures. Prepare and administer medications, vaccines, serums, and treatments, as prescribed by veterinarians. Fill prescriptions, measuring medications and labeling containers. Collect, prepare, and label samples for laboratory testing, culture, or microscopic examination. Prepare treatment rooms for surgery. Take and develop diagnostic radiographs, using X-ray equipment. Clean kennels, animal holding areas, surgery suites, examination rooms, and animal loading/unloading facilities to control the spread of disease. Take animals into treatment areas, and assist with physical examinations by performing such duties as obtaining temperature, pulse, and respiration data. Provide veterinarians with the correct equipment and instruments, as needed. Clean and sterilize instruments, equipment, and materials.

Considerations for Job Outlook: Increases in the pet population and in advanced veterinary care are expected to create employment growth for these workers. Excellent job opportunities are expected.

Personality Type: Realistic-Investigative. **Skills:** Science; Equipment Maintenance; Operation and Control; Quality Control Analysis; Service Orientation; Troubleshooting; Critical Thinking; Management of Material Resources. **Education and Training Program:** Veterinary/Animal Health Technology/Technician and Veterinary Assistant. **Work Environment:** Indoors; contaminants; disease or infections; radiation; standing; using your hands to handle, control, or feel objects, tools, or controls.

OTHER FEDERAL JOB FACTS

Related GS Series: 0704 Animal Health Technician

- ❀ U.S. Federal Workforce: 631
- ❀ Average Length of Service: 11.2 years
- ❀ Percent Part-Time: 23.3%
- ❀ Percent Women: 42.9%
- ❀ Largest Age Bracket: 50–54 (15.7%)
- ❀ GS Level with Most Workers: 8
- ❀ Agency with Most Workers: Agriculture
- ❀ State with Most Workers: Texas

Perform technical work concerned with animal health in support of veterinarians or veterinary medical programs; includes inspection, quarantine, identification, collection of specimens, vaccination, appraisal and disposal of diseased animals, and disinfection for the control and eradication of infectious and communicable animal diseases.

Requirements: Practical knowledge of normal and certain abnormal animal health conditions, agency policy and guidelines applicable to the work, and related animal health laws and regulations.

Writers and Authors

- ❀ Education/Training Required: Bachelor's degree
- ❀ Annual Earnings (Federal): $80,410
- ❀ Annual Earnings (All Industries): $53,900
- ❀ Earnings Growth Potential (Federal): 34.3% (low)
- ❀ Earnings Growth Potential (All Industries): 47.9% (high)
- ❀ Job Growth (Federal): 9.7%
- ❀ Job Growth (All Industries): 14.8%
- ❀ Annual Job Openings (Federal): 110
- ❀ Annual Job Openings (All Industries): 5,420

Originate and prepare written material, such as scripts, stories, advertisements, and other material. No task data available.

Considerations for Job Outlook: Projected job growth for these workers stems from increased use of online media and growing demand for Web-based information. But print publishing is expected to continue weakening. Job competition should be keen.

Job Specialization: Copy Writers

Write advertising copy for use by publication or broadcast media to promote sale of goods and services. Write advertising copy for use by publication, broadcast, or Internet media to promote the sale of goods and services. Present drafts and ideas to clients. Discuss the product, advertising themes and methods, and any changes that should be made in advertising copy with the client. Consult with sales, media, and marketing representatives to obtain information on product or service and discuss style and length of advertising copy. Vary language and tone of messages based on product and medium. Edit or rewrite existing copy as necessary and submit copy for approval by supervisor. Write to customers in their terms and on their level so that the advertiser's sales message is more readily received. Write articles; bulletins; sales letters; speeches; and other related informative, marketing, and promotional material. Invent names for products and write the slogans that appear on packaging, brochures, and other promotional material. Review advertising trends, consumer surveys, and other data regarding marketing of goods and services to determine the best way to promote products. Develop advertising campaigns for a wide range of clients, working with an advertising agency's creative director and art director to determine the best way to present advertising information. Conduct research and interviews to determine which of a product's selling features should be promoted.

Personality Type: Enterprising-Artistic. **Skills:** Writing; Persuasion; Reading Comprehension; Negotiation; Active Listening; Management of Personnel Resources; Speaking; Critical Thinking. **Education and Training Program:** Broadcast Journalism; Business/Corporate Communications; Communication, Journalism, and Related Programs, Other; Family and Consumer Sciences/Human Sciences Communication; Journalism; Mass Communication/Media Studies; Playwriting and Screenwriting; Speech Communication and Rhetoric. **Work Environment:** Indoors; sitting.

JOB SPECIALIZATION: POETS, LYRICISTS, AND CREATIVE WRITERS

Create original written works, such as scripts, essays, prose, poetry, or song lyrics, for publication or performance. Revise written material to meet personal standards and to satisfy needs of clients, publishers, directors, or producers. Choose subject matter and suitable form to express personal feelings and experiences or ideas or to narrate stories or events. Plan project arrangements or outlines and organize material accordingly. Prepare works in appropriate format for publication and send them to publishers or producers. Follow appropriate procedures to get copyrights for completed work. Write fiction or nonfiction prose such as short stories, novels, biographies, articles, descriptive or critical analyses, and essays. Develop factors such as themes, plots, characterizations, psychological analyses, historical environments, action, and dialogue to create material. Confer with clients, editors, publishers, or producers to discuss changes or revisions to written material. Conduct research to obtain factual information and authentic detail, using sources such as newspaper accounts, diaries, and interviews. Write narrative, dramatic, lyric, or other types of poetry for publication. Attend book launches and publicity events or conduct public readings. Write words to fit musical compositions, including lyrics for operas, musical plays, and choral works. Adapt text to accommodate musical requirements of composers and singers. Teach writing classes. Write humorous material for publication or for performances such as comedy routines, gags, and comedy shows.

Personality Type: Artistic-Investigative. **Skills:** Writing; Reading Comprehension; Active Learning; Persuasion; Active Listening; Social Perceptiveness; Negotiation; Complex Problem Solving. **Education and Training Program:** Broadcast Journalism; Business/Corporate Communications; Communication, Journalism, and Related Programs, Other; Family and Consumer Sciences/Human Sciences Communication; Journalism; Mass Communication/Media Studies; Playwriting and Screenwriting; Speech Communication and Rhetoric. **Work Environment:** Indoors; sitting; making repetitive motions; using your hands to handle, control, or feel objects, tools, or controls.

OTHER FEDERAL JOB FACTS

RELATED GS SERIES: 1082 WRITING AND EDITING

TITLE ON USAJOBS: WRITER/EDITOR

- U.S. Federal Workforce: 1,368
- Average Length of Service: 14.5 years
- Percent Part-Time: 2.9%
- Percent Women: 67.0%
- Largest Age Bracket: 55–59 (17.4%)
- GS Levels with Most Workers: 13, 12
- Agency with Most Workers: Defense
- State with Most Workers: District of Columbia

Write and edit materials such as reports, regulations, articles, newsletters, magazines, news releases, training materials, brochures, interpretive handbooks, pamphlets, guidebooks, scholarly works, reference works, speeches, or scripts; acquire information on a variety of subjects in the course of completing assignments; develop, analyze, and select appropriate information; present the information in a form and at a level suitable for the intended audience.

Requirements: Knowledge of grammar, writing and editing practices, and the style requirements of the media and the publications used; knowledge of readily available sources of information on the appropriate subjects, including library resources and subject-matter experts; may require ability to use desktop publishing technology to develop manuscripts into camera-ready copy.

Zoologists and Wildlife Biologists

- ✸ Education/Training Required: Bachelor's degree
- ✸ Annual Earnings (Federal): $70,190
- ✸ Annual Earnings (All Industries): $56,500
- ✸ Earnings Growth Potential (Federal): 29.1% (low)
- ✸ Earnings Growth Potential (All Industries): 37.6% (medium)
- ✸ Job Growth (Federal): 7.4%
- ✸ Job Growth (All Industries): 12.8%
- ✸ Annual Job Openings (Federal): 160
- ✸ Annual Job Openings (All Industries): 880

Study the origins, behavior, diseases, genetics, and life processes of animals and wildlife. May specialize in wildlife research and management, including the collection and analysis of biological data to determine the environmental effects of present and potential use of land and water areas. Study animals in their natural habitats, assessing effects of environment and industry on animals, interpreting findings, and recommending alternative operating conditions for industry. Inventory or estimate plant and wildlife populations. Make recommendations on management systems and planning for wildlife populations and habitat, consulting with stakeholders and the public at large to explore options. Disseminate information by writing reports and scientific papers or journal articles and by making presentations and giving talks for schools, clubs, interest groups, and park interpretive programs. Study characteristics of animals such as origin, interrelationships, classification, life histories and diseases, development, genetics, and distribution. Organize and conduct experimental studies with live animals in controlled or natural surroundings.

Considerations for Job Outlook: Biotechnological research and development should continue to drive job growth. Doctoral degree holders are expected to face competition for research positions in academia.

Personality Type: Investigative-Realistic. **Skills:** Science; Writing; Reading Comprehension; Systems Evaluation; Systems Analysis; Time Management; Mathematics; Operation and Control. **Education and Training Program:** Animal Behavior and Ethology; Animal Physiology; Cell/Cellular Biology and Anatomical Sciences, Other; Ecology; Entomology; Wildlife Biology; Wildlife, Fish and Wildlands Science and Management; Zoology/Animal Biology; Zoology/Animal Biology, Other. **Work Environment:** More often indoors than outdoors; sitting.

OTHER FEDERAL JOB FACTS

RELATED GS SERIES: 0480 FISH AND WILDLIFE ADMINISTRATION

TITLE ON USAJOBS: FISH AND WILDLIFE ADMINISTRATOR

- ✸ U.S. Federal Workforce: 324
- ✸ Average Length of Service: 21.0 years
- ✸ Percent Part-Time: 0.6%
- ✸ Percent Women: 29.9%
- ✸ Largest Age Bracket: 55–59 (29.0%)
- ✸ GS Level with Most Workers: 14

❋ Agency with Most Workers: Interior

❋ States with Most Workers: California, Oregon

Perform professional and scientific work in administering, directing, or exercising administrative and technical control over programs, regulatory activities, projects, or operations that are concerned with the conservation and management of fishery resources, wildlife resources, or fish and wildlife resources.

Requirements: Degree in biological sciences, agriculture, natural resource management, chemistry, or related disciplines; or several years of appropriate experience. Some positions with the Interior Department require a pilot license, flight experience, and a Class II Medical Certificate.

Related GS Series: 0482 Fish Biology

Title on USAJobs: Biologist, Fishery

❋ U.S. Federal Workforce: 2,514

❋ Average Length of Service: 14.5 years

❋ Percent Part-Time: 2.0%

❋ Percent Women: 28.4%

❋ Largest Age Bracket: 50–54 (16.5%)

❋ GS Level with Most Workers: 11

❋ Agencies with Most Workers: Commerce, Interior

❋ State with Most Workers: Washington

Develop, conserve, manage, and administer fishery resources; evaluate the impact of construction projects and other socioeconomic activities that present potential or actual adverse effects on fishery resources and their habitat.

Requirements: Professional knowledge and competence in the science of fishery biology; also an ability to determine, establish, and apply biological facts, principles, methods, techniques, and procedures.

Related GS Series: 0486 Wildlife Biology

Title on USAJobs: Biologist, Wildlife

❋ U.S. Federal Workforce: 2,477

❋ Average Length of Service: 15.0 years

❋ Percent Part-Time: 1.8%

❋ Percent Women: 32.5%

❋ Largest Age Bracket: 40–44 (16.4%)

❋ GS Level with Most Workers: 11

❋ Agencies with Most Workers: Agriculture, Interior

❋ State with Most Workers: California

Conserve, propagate, manage, and protect wildlife species; or determine, establish, and apply biological facts, principles, methods, techniques, and procedures necessary for the conservation and management of wildlife resources and habitats.

Requirements: Professional knowledge of the distribution, habits, life histories, and classification of birds, mammals, and other forms of wildlife.

Related GS Series: 0485 Wildlife Refuge Management

Title on USAJobs: Wildlife Refuge Manager

❋ U.S. Federal Workforce: 631

❋ Average Length of Service: 19.6 years

❋ Percent Part-Time: 0.8%

❋ Percent Women: 23.8%

❋ Largest Age Bracket: 45–49 (21.7%)

❋ GS Levels with Most Workers: 12, 13

❋ Agency with Most Workers: Interior

❋ State with Most Workers: California

Perform biological analyses, planning, and evaluation to conserve, protect, and propagate wildlife species and manipulate and utilize their required habitats.

Requirements: Professional knowledge and competence in the management, administration, and scientific operation of public lands and waters designated as national wildlife refuges.

N

Appendix A: Definitions of Skills Referenced in This Book

Definitions of Skills	
Skill Name	**Definition**
Active Learning	Working with new material or information to grasp its implications.
Active Listening	Listening to what other people are saying and asking questions as appropriate.
Complex Problem Solving	Identifying complex problems, reviewing the options, and implementing solutions.
Coordination	Adjusting actions in relation to others' actions.
Critical Thinking	Using logic and analysis to identify the strengths and weaknesses of different approaches.
Equipment Maintenance	Performing routine maintenance and determining when and what kind of maintenance is needed.
Equipment Selection	Determining the kind of tools and equipment needed to do a job.
Installation	Installing equipment, machines, wiring, or programs to meet specifications.
Instructing	Teaching others how to do something.

(continued)

(continued)

Definitions of Skills

Skill Name	Definition
Judgment and Decision Making	Weighing the relative costs and benefits of a potential action.
Learning Strategies	Using multiple approaches when learning or teaching new things.
Management of Financial Resources	Determining how money will be spent to get the work done and accounting for these expenditures.
Management of Material Resources	Obtaining and seeing to the appropriate use of equipment, facilities, and materials needed to do certain work.
Management of Personnel Resources	Motivating, developing, and directing people as they work; identifying the best people for the job.
Mathematics	Using mathematics to solve problems.
Monitoring	Assessing how well one is doing when learning or doing something.
Negotiation	Bringing others together and trying to reconcile differences.
Operation and Control	Controlling operations of equipment or systems.
Operation Monitoring	Watching gauges, dials, or other indicators to make sure a machine is working properly.
Operations Analysis	Analyzing needs and product requirements to create a design.
Persuasion	Persuading others to approach things differently.
Programming	Writing computer programs for various purposes.
Quality Control Analysis	Evaluating the quality or performance of products, services, or processes.
Reading Comprehension	Understanding written sentences and paragraphs in work-related documents.
Repairing	Repairing machines or systems, using the needed tools.
Science	Using scientific methods to solve problems.
Service Orientation	Actively looking for ways to help people.
Social Perceptiveness	Being aware of others' reactions and understanding why they react the way they do.
Speaking	Talking to others to effectively convey information.
Systems Analysis	Determining how a system should work and how changes will affect outcomes.
Systems Evaluation	Looking at many indicators of system performance and taking into account their accuracy.

Definitions of Skills

Skill Name	Definition
Technology Design	Generating or adapting equipment and technology to serve user needs.
Time Management	Managing one's own time and the time of others.
Troubleshooting	Determining what is causing an operating error and deciding what to do about it.
Writing	Communicating effectively with others in writing as indicated by the needs of the audience.

Appendix B: Categories of GS Series

You may notice that every specific federal job (GS series) listed in Part III has a four-digit number. If you're wondering what this number means, the following table should be helpful. It shows the 59 categories of GS series. Most of these are called "families," but a few are called "groups."

Note that in the Advanced Search on the USAJobs site, you can search for jobs within an entire category by specifying just the first two digits. So, for example, you could search for all legal occupations by entering "09."

GS Series Categories	
Code Number	**Title**
0000	Miscellaneous Occupations Group
0100	Social Science, Psychology, and Welfare Group
0200	Human Resources Management Group
0300	General Administrative, Clerical, and Office Services Group
0400	Natural Resources Management and Biological Sciences Group
0500	Accounting and Budget Group
0600	Medical, Hospital, Dental, and Public Health Group
0700	Veterinary Medical Science Group
0800	Engineering and Architecture Group
0900	Legal and Kindred Group
1000	Information and Arts Group
1100	Business and Industry Group
1200	Copyright, Patent, and Trademark Group
1300	Physical Sciences Group
1400	Library and Archives Group

(continued)

(continued)

GS Series Categories

Code Number	Title
1500	Mathematical Sciences Group
1600	Equipment, Facilities, and Services Group
1700	Education Group
1800	Inspection, Investigation, Enforcement, and Compliance Group
1900	Quality Assurance, Inspection, and Grading Group
2000	Supply Group
2100	Transportation Group
2200	Information Technology Group
2500	Wire Communications Equipment Installation and Maintenance Family
2600	Electronic Equipment Installation and Maintenance Family
2800	Electrical Installation and Maintenance Family
3100	Fabric and Leather Work Family
3300	Instrument Work Family
3400	Machine Tool Work Family
3500	General Services and Support Work Family
3600	Structural and Finishing Work Family
3700	Metal Processing Family
3800	Metal Work Family
3900	Motion Picture, Radio, Television, and Sound Equipment Operation Family
4000	Lens and Crystal Work Family
4100	Painting and Paperhanging Family
4200	Plumbing and Pipefitting Family
4300	Pliable Materials Work Family
4400	Printing Family
4600	Wood Work Family
4700	General Maintenance and Operations Work Family
4800	General Equipment Maintenance Family
5000	Plant and Animal Work Family
5200	Miscellaneous Occupations Family
5300	Industrial Equipment Maintenance Family
5400	Industrial Equipment Operation Family

GS Series Categories

Code Number	Title
5700	Transportation/Mobile Equipment Operation Family
5800	Transportation/Mobile Equipment Maintenance Family
6500	Ammunition, Explosives, and Toxic Materials Work Family
6600	Armament Work Family
6900	Warehousing and Stock Handling Family
7000	Packing and Processing Family
7300	Laundry, Dry Cleaning, and Pressing Family
7400	Food Preparation and Serving Family
7600	Personal Services Family
8200	Fluid Systems Maintenance Family
8600	Engine Overhaul Family
8800	Aircraft Overhaul Family
9000	Film Processing Family

Appendix C: Best Jobs with Largest Work-forces, by State

If you want to get a federal job without relocating to some distant state, you may find the following lists helpful. For each state, plus the District of Columbia, I show the 20 best federal jobs that have the largest number of workers.

Alabama	
Job	**Federal Workers**
1. Business Operations Specialists, All Other	5,793
2. Postal Service Mail Carriers	5,300
3. Management Analysts	3,797
4. Engineering Managers	2,537
5. Logisticians	2,093
6. Postal Service Mail Sorters, Processors, and Processing Machine Operators	1,700
7. Purchasing Agents, Except Wholesale, Retail, and Farm Products	1,536
8. Aerospace Engineers	1,414
9. Claims Adjusters, Examiners, and Investigators	1,042
10. Postal Service Clerks	980
11. Registered Nurses	972
12. Eligibility Interviewers, Government Programs	788
13. Teachers and Instructors, All Other	747
14. Electrical Engineers	726
15. Electronics Engineers, Except Computer	578

(continued)

(continued)

Alabama

Job	Federal Workers
16. Maintenance and Repair Workers, General	528
17. Computer Hardware Engineers	493
18. Postmasters and Mail Superintendents	480
19. Compliance Officers, Except Agriculture, Construction, Health and Safety, and Transportation	472
20. Engineering Technicians, Except Drafters, All Other	467

Alaska

Job	Federal Workers
1. Business Operations Specialists, All Other	1,879
2. Management Analysts	985
3. Biological Scientists, All Other	536
4. Postal Service Mail Sorters, Processors, and Processing Machine Operators	520
5. Air Traffic Controllers	496
6. Postal Service Mail Carriers	430
7. Zoologists and Wildlife Biologists	405
8. Microbiologists	359
9. Forest and Conservation Technicians	331
10. Compliance Officers, Except Agriculture, Construction, Health and Safety, and Transportation	297
11. Registered Nurses	287
12. Maintenance and Repair Workers, General	274
13. Industrial Machinery Mechanics	271
14. Postal Service Clerks	270
15. Biological Technicians	265
16. Fire Fighters	207
17. Civil Engineers	197
18. Aircraft Mechanics and Service Technicians	192
19. Purchasing Agents, Except Wholesale, Retail, and Farm Products	188
20. Social Scientists and Related Workers, All Other	187

Arizona

Job	Federal Workers
1. Postal Service Mail Carriers	5,300
2. Detectives and Criminal Investigators	4,883
3. Business Operations Specialists, All Other	3,438
4. Postal Service Mail Sorters, Processors, and Processing Machine Operators	2,320
5. Registered Nurses	2,058
6. Management Analysts	2,020
7. Compliance Officers, Except Agriculture, Construction, Health and Safety, and Transportation	1,705
8. Forest and Conservation Technicians	1,200
9. Postal Service Clerks	1,110
10. Teachers and Instructors, All Other	943
11. Aircraft Mechanics and Service Technicians	652
12. Maintenance and Repair Workers, General	602
13. Industrial Machinery Mechanics	596
14. Claims Adjusters, Examiners, and Investigators	584
15. Purchasing Agents, Except Wholesale, Retail, and Farm Products	561
16. Correctional Officers and Jailers	554
17. Biological Scientists, All Other	458
18. Tax Examiners, Collectors, and Revenue Agents	424
19. Microbiologists	422
20. Social Scientists and Related Workers, All Other	420

Arkansas

Job	Federal Workers
1. Postal Service Mail Carriers	3,140
2. Business Operations Specialists, All Other	1,302
3. Postal Service Mail Sorters, Processors, and Processing Machine Operators	1,100
4. Registered Nurses	1,037
5. Postal Service Clerks	800
6. Management Analysts	743
7. Postmasters and Mail Superintendents	570
8. Claims Adjusters, Examiners, and Investigators	440
9. Compliance Officers, Except Agriculture, Construction, Health and Safety, and Transportation	374

(continued)

(continued)

Arkansas

Job	Federal Workers
10. Microbiologists	336
11. Biological Scientists, All Other	300
12. Correctional Officers and Jailers	284
13. Forest and Conservation Technicians	243
14. Agricultural Inspectors	214
15. Licensed Practical and Licensed Vocational Nurses	210
16. Maintenance and Repair Workers, General	209
17. Electrical and Electronic Engineering Technicians	196
18. Engineering Technicians, Except Drafters, All Other	196
19. Industrial Machinery Mechanics	176
20. Healthcare Support Workers, All Other	172

California

Job	Federal Workers
1. Postal Service Mail Carriers	37,100
2. Postal Service Mail Sorters, Processors, and Processing Machine Operators	17,830
3. Business Operations Specialists, All Other	17,609
4. Management Analysts	10,354
5. Compliance Officers, Except Agriculture, Construction, Health and Safety, and Transportation	8,431
6. Postal Service Clerks	8,180
7. Detectives and Criminal Investigators	6,590
8. Forest and Conservation Technicians	5,680
9. Registered Nurses	5,530
10. Tax Examiners, Collectors, and Revenue Agents	4,955
11. Claims Adjusters, Examiners, and Investigators	4,160
12. Electrical Engineers	3,772
13. Electronics Engineers, Except Computer	3,423
14. Eligibility Interviewers, Government Programs	3,193
15. Engineering Technicians, Except Drafters, All Other	3,114
16. Electrical and Electronic Engineering Technicians	3,098
17. Teachers and Instructors, All Other	3,057
18. Purchasing Agents, Except Wholesale, Retail, and Farm Products	2,440
19. Lawyers	2,348
20. Air Traffic Controllers	2,253

Colorado

	Job	Federal Workers
1.	Business Operations Specialists, All Other	6,047
2.	Postal Service Mail Carriers	5,150
3.	Management Analysts	3,924
4.	Postal Service Mail Sorters, Processors, and Processing Machine Operators	3,080
5.	Postal Service Clerks	1,300
6.	Registered Nurses	1,108
7.	Forest and Conservation Technicians	983
8.	Purchasing Agents, Except Wholesale, Retail, and Farm Products	923
9.	Accountants and Auditors	777
10.	Compliance Officers, Except Agriculture, Construction, Health and Safety, and Transportation	761
11.	Correctional Officers and Jailers	758
12.	Microbiologists	730
13.	Biological Scientists, All Other	722
14.	Air Traffic Controllers	718
15.	Eligibility Interviewers, Government Programs	679
16.	Claims Adjusters, Examiners, and Investigators	630
17.	Civil Engineers	589
18.	Lawyers	578
19.	Biological Technicians	574
20.	Hydrologists	573

Connecticut

	Job	Federal Workers
1.	Postal Service Mail Carriers	4,880
2.	Postal Service Mail Sorters, Processors, and Processing Machine Operators	2,030
3.	Postal Service Clerks	1,170
4.	Business Operations Specialists, All Other	1,041
5.	Registered Nurses	565
6.	Management Analysts	518
7.	Tax Examiners, Collectors, and Revenue Agents	327
8.	Claims Adjusters, Examiners, and Investigators	305
9.	Postmasters and Mail Superintendents	210
10.	Healthcare Support Workers, All Other	204

(continued)

(continued)

Connecticut

Job	Federal Workers
11. Compliance Officers, Except Agriculture, Construction, Health and Safety, and Transportation	199
12. Purchasing Agents, Except Wholesale, Retail, and Farm Products	179
13. Teachers and Instructors, All Other	144
14. Detectives and Criminal Investigators	136
15. Lawyers	133
16. Accountants and Auditors	131
17. Aircraft Mechanics and Service Technicians	110
18. Correctional Officers and Jailers	105
19. Electrical and Electronic Engineering Technicians	94
20. Engineering Technicians, Except Drafters, All Other	94

Delaware

Job	Federal Workers
1. Postal Service Mail Carriers	1,070
2. Postal Service Mail Sorters, Processors, and Processing Machine Operators	480
3. Business Operations Specialists, All Other	346
4. Postal Service Clerks	230
5. Registered Nurses	195
6. Management Analysts	185
7. Aircraft Mechanics and Service Technicians	141
8. Agricultural Inspectors	91
9. Compliance Officers, Except Agriculture, Construction, Health and Safety, and Transportation	82
10. Claims Adjusters, Examiners, and Investigators	81
11. Tax Examiners, Collectors, and Revenue Agents	71
12. Licensed Practical and Licensed Vocational Nurses	53
13. Postmasters and Mail Superintendents	50
14. Procurement Clerks	48
15. Healthcare Support Workers, All Other	47
16. Maintenance and Repair Workers, General	45
17. Industrial Machinery Mechanics	43
18. Motor Vehicle Operators, All Other	42

Delaware

Job	Federal Workers
19. Education, Training, and Library Workers, All Other	41
20. Logisticians	40

District of Columbia

Job	Federal Workers
1. Business Operations Specialists, All Other	50,886
2. Management Analysts	42,849
3. Lawyers	13,530
4. Economists	7,992
5. Social Scientists and Related Workers, All Other	6,939
6. Detectives and Criminal Investigators	6,837
7. Political Scientists	5,061
8. Accountants and Auditors	4,218
9. Purchasing Agents, Except Wholesale, Retail, and Farm Products	3,364
10. Compliance Officers, Except Agriculture, Construction, Health and Safety, and Transportation	3,235
11. First-Line Supervisors/Managers of Police and Detectives	2,441
12. Engineering Managers	2,376
13. Budget Analysts	2,270
14. Paralegals and Legal Assistants	1,622
15. Artists and Related Workers, All Other	1,410
16. Electrical Engineers	1,232
17. Registered Nurses	1,161
18. Public Relations Managers	1,101
19. Public Relations Specialists	1,101
20. Hydrologists	1,061

Florida

Job	Federal Workers
1. Postal Service Mail Carriers	19,570
2. Business Operations Specialists, All Other	10,553
3. Postal Service Mail Sorters, Processors, and Processing Machine Operators	8,610

(continued)

(continued)

Florida

Job	Federal Workers
4. Management Analysts	6,601
5. Registered Nurses	4,771
6. Compliance Officers, Except Agriculture, Construction, Health and Safety, and Transportation	4,277
7. Postal Service Clerks	4,140
8. Claims Adjusters, Examiners, and Investigators	2,294
9. Air Traffic Controllers	1,800
10. Detectives and Criminal Investigators	1,678
11. Engineering Managers	1,586
12. Purchasing Agents, Except Wholesale, Retail, and Farm Products	1,571
13. Tax Examiners, Collectors, and Revenue Agents	1,505
14. Eligibility Interviewers, Government Programs	1,361
15. Correctional Officers and Jailers	1,353
16. Electrical Engineers	1,303
17. Electronics Engineers, Except Computer	1,176
18. Biological Scientists, All Other	1,121
19. Lawyers	1,054
20. Healthcare Support Workers, All Other	1,008

Georgia

Job	Federal Workers
1. Business Operations Specialists, All Other	12,130
2. Postal Service Mail Carriers	10,210
3. Management Analysts	7,701
4. Postal Service Mail Sorters, Processors, and Processing Machine Operators	4,240
5. Compliance Officers, Except Agriculture, Construction, Health and Safety, and Transportation	2,422
6. Postal Service Clerks	2,270
7. Logisticians	1,969
8. Registered Nurses	1,923
9. Health Diagnosing and Treating Practitioners, All Other	1,686
10. Occupational Health and Safety Specialists	1,618
11. Sheet Metal Workers	1,552

Georgia

Job	Federal Workers
12. Tax Examiners, Collectors, and Revenue Agents	1,437
13. Microbiologists	1,387
14. Claims Adjusters, Examiners, and Investigators	1,364
15. Teachers and Instructors, All Other	1,349
16. Electrical Engineers	1,347
17. Purchasing Agents, Except Wholesale, Retail, and Farm Products	1,249
18. Electronics Engineers, Except Computer	1,236
19. Eligibility Interviewers, Government Programs	1,113
20. Air Traffic Controllers	1,029

Hawaii

Job	Federal Workers
1. Business Operations Specialists, All Other	3,276
2. Management Analysts	1,745
3. Industrial Machinery Mechanics	683
4. Registered Nurses	629
5. Engineering Technicians, Except Drafters, All Other	510
6. Electrical and Electronic Engineering Technicians	497
7. Biological Technicians	486
8. Compliance Officers, Except Agriculture, Construction, Health and Safety, and Transportation	460
9. First-Line Supervisors/Managers of Police and Detectives	420
10. Purchasing Agents, Except Wholesale, Retail, and Farm Products	408
11. Electrical Engineers	406
12. Engineering Managers	389
13. Biological Scientists, All Other	362
14. Industrial Engineering Technicians	357
15. Maintenance and Repair Workers, General	345
16. Social Scientists and Related Workers, All Other	345
17. Microbiologists	326
18. Forest and Conservation Technicians	320
19. Logisticians	311
20. Fire Fighters	290

Idaho

Job	Federal Workers
1. Forest and Conservation Technicians	2,132
2. Postal Service Mail Carriers	1,480
3. Business Operations Specialists, All Other	983
4. Biological Technicians	767
5. Management Analysts	606
6. Postal Service Mail Sorters, Processors, and Processing Machine Operators	520
7. Biological Scientists, All Other	484
8. Microbiologists	382
9. Postal Service Clerks	370
10. Registered Nurses	256
11. Postmasters and Mail Superintendents	210
12. Zoologists and Wildlife Biologists	192
13. Compliance Officers, Except Agriculture, Construction, Health and Safety, and Transportation	189
14. Conservation Scientists	172
15. Electrical and Electronic Engineering Technicians	156
16. Engineering Technicians, Except Drafters, All Other	156
17. Claims Adjusters, Examiners, and Investigators	139
18. Maintenance and Repair Workers, General	138
19. Purchasing Agents, Except Wholesale, Retail, and Farm Products	138
20. Foresters	137

Illinois

Job	Federal Workers
1. Postal Service Mail Carriers	16,180
2. Postal Service Mail Sorters, Processors, and Processing Machine Operators	9,310
3. Business Operations Specialists, All Other	7,058
4. Management Analysts	4,321
5. Postal Service Clerks	2,920
6. Registered Nurses	2,075
7. Claims Adjusters, Examiners, and Investigators	1,914
8. Compliance Officers, Except Agriculture, Construction, Health and Safety, and Transportation	1,739
9. Purchasing Agents, Except Wholesale, Retail, and Farm Products	1,411

Illinois

Job	Federal Workers
10. Tax Examiners, Collectors, and Revenue Agents	1,181
11. Logisticians	1,157
12. Lawyers	1,155
13. Postmasters and Mail Superintendents	1,140
14. Air Traffic Controllers	1,039
15. Detectives and Criminal Investigators	819
16. Accountants and Auditors	710
17. Eligibility Interviewers, Government Programs	655
18. Correctional Officers and Jailers	539
19. Healthcare Support Workers, All Other	492
20. Engineering Managers	476

Indiana

Job	Federal Workers
1. Postal Service Mail Carriers	7,340
2. Postal Service Mail Sorters, Processors, and Processing Machine Operators	2,850
3. Business Operations Specialists, All Other	1,955
4. Postal Service Clerks	1,430
5. Management Analysts	1,302
6. Accountants and Auditors	1,162
7. Registered Nurses	1,005
8. Engineering Technicians, Except Drafters, All Other	797
9. Electrical and Electronic Engineering Technicians	792
10. Air Traffic Controllers	725
11. Electrical Engineers	701
12. Electronics Engineers, Except Computer	698
13. Postmasters and Mail Superintendents	640
14. Claims Adjusters, Examiners, and Investigators	626
15. Eligibility Interviewers, Government Programs	399
16. Correctional Officers and Jailers	390
17. Logisticians	320
18. Purchasing Agents, Except Wholesale, Retail, and Farm Products	318
19. Industrial Engineering Technicians	305
20. Tax Examiners, Collectors, and Revenue Agents	303

Iowa

Job	Federal Workers
1. Postal Service Mail Carriers	3,960
2. Postal Service Mail Sorters, Processors, and Processing Machine Operators	2,000
3. Business Operations Specialists, All Other	877
4. Postmasters and Mail Superintendents	850
5. Postal Service Clerks	760
6. Registered Nurses	614
7. Management Analysts	526
8. Biological Technicians	502
9. Claims Adjusters, Examiners, and Investigators	292
10. Eligibility Interviewers, Government Programs	214
11. Microbiologists	208
12. Compliance Officers, Except Agriculture, Construction, Health and Safety, and Transportation	191
13. Forest and Conservation Technicians	180
14. Conservation Scientists	177
15. Agricultural Inspectors	167
16. Licensed Practical and Licensed Vocational Nurses	157
17. Tax Examiners, Collectors, and Revenue Agents	143
18. Aircraft Mechanics and Service Technicians	141
19. Healthcare Support Workers, All Other	136
20. Loan Officers	136

Kansas

Job	Federal Workers
1. Postal Service Mail Carriers	3,540
2. Business Operations Specialists, All Other	2,144
3. Postal Service Mail Sorters, Processors, and Processing Machine Operators	1,310
4. Management Analysts	1,296
5. Registered Nurses	839
6. Postal Service Clerks	680
7. Postmasters and Mail Superintendents	550
8. Eligibility Interviewers, Government Programs	533
9. Teachers and Instructors, All Other	509
10. Air Traffic Controllers	468

Kansas

Job	Federal Workers
11. Social Scientists and Related Workers, All Other	446
12. Licensed Practical and Licensed Vocational Nurses	262
13. Claims Adjusters, Examiners, and Investigators	259
14. Compliance Officers, Except Agriculture, Construction, Health and Safety, and Transportation	214
15. Correctional Officers and Jailers	188
16. Biological Technicians	181
17. Maintenance and Repair Workers, General	180
18. Purchasing Agents, Except Wholesale, Retail, and Farm Products	180
19. Industrial Machinery Mechanics	168
20. Healthcare Support Workers, All Other	167

Kentucky

Job	Federal Workers
1. Postal Service Mail Carriers	4,720
2. Business Operations Specialists, All Other	2,253
3. Postal Service Mail Sorters, Processors, and Processing Machine Operators	1,810
4. Tax Examiners, Collectors, and Revenue Agents	1,608
5. Management Analysts	1,392
6. Registered Nurses	1,304
7. Postal Service Clerks	920
8. Correctional Officers and Jailers	898
9. Eligibility Interviewers, Government Programs	849
10. Postmasters and Mail Superintendents	650
11. Claims Adjusters, Examiners, and Investigators	600
12. Teachers and Instructors, All Other	567
13. Compliance Officers, Except Agriculture, Construction, Health and Safety, and Transportation	509
14. Licensed Practical and Licensed Vocational Nurses	417
15. Education, Training, and Library Workers, All Other	412
16. Healthcare Support Workers, All Other	348
17. Maintenance and Repair Workers, General	348
18. Security Guards	328
19. Procurement Clerks	306
20. Civil Engineers	251

Louisiana

Job	Federal Workers
1. Postal Service Mail Carriers	4,450
2. Business Operations Specialists, All Other	2,829
3. Management Analysts	1,859
4. Postal Service Mail Sorters, Processors, and Processing Machine Operators	1,820
5. Postal Service Clerks	1,090
6. Registered Nurses	846
7. Compliance Officers, Except Agriculture, Construction, Health and Safety, and Transportation	663
8. Correctional Officers and Jailers	586
9. Claims Adjusters, Examiners, and Investigators	557
10. Civil Engineers	500
11. Postmasters and Mail Superintendents	420
12. Detectives and Criminal Investigators	371
13. Aircraft Mechanics and Service Technicians	301
14. Accountants and Auditors	282
15. Lawyers	268
16. Biological Scientists, All Other	263
17. Licensed Practical and Licensed Vocational Nurses	253
18. Air Traffic Controllers	251
19. Microbiologists	248
20. Engineering Technicians, Except Drafters, All Other	236

Maine

Job	Federal Workers
1. Postal Service Mail Carriers	1,710
2. Business Operations Specialists, All Other	1,113
3. Postal Service Mail Sorters, Processors, and Processing Machine Operators	830
4. Engineering Technicians, Except Drafters, All Other	596
5. Electrical and Electronic Engineering Technicians	584
6. Industrial Engineering Technicians	538
7. Postal Service Clerks	530
8. Compliance Officers, Except Agriculture, Construction, Health and Safety, and Transportation	464
9. Management Analysts	426

Maine

	Job	Federal Workers
10.	Postmasters and Mail Superintendents	390
11.	Registered Nurses	334
12.	Industrial Machinery Mechanics	329
13.	Nuclear Engineers	293
14.	Claims Adjusters, Examiners, and Investigators	274
15.	Engineering Managers	266
16.	Detectives and Criminal Investigators	258
17.	Painters, Construction and Maintenance	240
18.	Mechanical Engineers	187
19.	Electrical and Electronics Repairers, Commercial and Industrial Equipment	126
20.	Maintenance and Repair Workers, General	109

Maryland

	Job	Federal Workers
1.	Business Operations Specialists, All Other	20,465
2.	Management Analysts	17,991
3.	Postal Service Mail Carriers	6,630
4.	Microbiologists	4,600
5.	Postal Service Mail Sorters, Processors, and Processing Machine Operators	3,900
6.	Biological Scientists, All Other	3,888
7.	Health Diagnosing and Treating Practitioners, All Other	3,403
8.	Purchasing Agents, Except Wholesale, Retail, and Farm Products	3,394
9.	Mathematicians	2,731
10.	Engineering Managers	2,629
11.	Claims Adjusters, Examiners, and Investigators	2,602
12.	Statisticians	2,553
13.	Electrical Engineers	2,529
14.	Occupational Health and Safety Specialists	2,493
15.	Registered Nurses	2,405
16.	Engineering Technicians, Except Drafters, All Other	2,114
17.	Electrical and Electronic Engineering Technicians	2,112
18.	Electronics Engineers, Except Computer	2,054
19.	Chemists	1,919
20.	Logisticians	1,823

Massachusetts

Job	Federal Workers
1. Postal Service Mail Carriers	8,960
2. Postal Service Mail Sorters, Processors, and Processing Machine Operators	4,500
3. Business Operations Specialists, All Other	3,627
4. Postal Service Clerks	2,340
5. Management Analysts	2,332
6. Registered Nurses	1,366
7. Tax Examiners, Collectors, and Revenue Agents	1,357
8. Compliance Officers, Except Agriculture, Construction, Health and Safety, and Transportation	972
9. Claims Adjusters, Examiners, and Investigators	816
10. Purchasing Agents, Except Wholesale, Retail, and Farm Products	703
11. Eligibility Interviewers, Government Programs	701
12. Lawyers	590
13. Accountants and Auditors	487
14. Detectives and Criminal Investigators	408
15. Postmasters and Mail Superintendents	360
16. Biological Scientists, All Other	354
17. Healthcare Support Workers, All Other	337
18. Engineering Managers	314
19. Microbiologists	281
20. Psychologists, All Other	271

Michigan

Job	Federal Workers
1. Postal Service Mail Carriers	12,900
2. Postal Service Mail Sorters, Processors, and Processing Machine Operators	5,770
3. Business Operations Specialists, All Other	3,826
4. Management Analysts	2,392
5. Postal Service Clerks	2,270
6. Compliance Officers, Except Agriculture, Construction, Health and Safety, and Transportation	1,884
7. Logisticians	1,483
8. Registered Nurses	1,458
9. Claims Adjusters, Examiners, and Investigators	1,007
10. Purchasing Agents, Except Wholesale, Retail, and Farm Products	819

Michigan

Job	Federal Workers
11. Detectives and Criminal Investigators	812
12. Tax Examiners, Collectors, and Revenue Agents	779
13. Postmasters and Mail Superintendents	760
14. Mechanical Engineers	683
15. Lawyers	406
16. Engineering Managers	398
17. Air Traffic Controllers	391
18. Eligibility Interviewers, Government Programs	370
19. Biological Technicians	320
20. Biological Scientists, All Other	281

Minnesota

Job	Federal Workers
1. Postal Service Mail Carriers	6,740
2. Postal Service Mail Sorters, Processors, and Processing Machine Operators	3,480
3. Business Operations Specialists, All Other	1,428
4. Registered Nurses	1,235
5. Postal Service Clerks	1,160
6. Management Analysts	848
7. Claims Adjusters, Examiners, and Investigators	821
8. Compliance Officers, Except Agriculture, Construction, Health and Safety, and Transportation	661
9. Postmasters and Mail Superintendents	660
10. Air Traffic Controllers	648
11. Licensed Practical and Licensed Vocational Nurses	422
12. Forest and Conservation Technicians	411
13. Correctional Officers and Jailers	394
14. Tax Examiners, Collectors, and Revenue Agents	367
15. Biological Technicians	316
16. Detectives and Criminal Investigators	291
17. Biological Scientists, All Other	251
18. Microbiologists	231
19. Loan Officers	190
20. Financial Examiners	184

Mississippi

Job	Federal Workers
1. Postal Service Mail Carriers	3,040
2. Business Operations Specialists, All Other	2,054
3. Management Analysts	1,243
4. Postal Service Mail Sorters, Processors, and Processing Machine Operators	790
5. Registered Nurses	713
6. Postal Service Clerks	620
7. Claims Adjusters, Examiners, and Investigators	505
8. Civil Engineers	460
9. Engineering Technicians, Except Drafters, All Other	457
10. Electrical and Electronic Engineering Technicians	455
11. Postmasters and Mail Superintendents	360
12. Teachers and Instructors, All Other	341
13. Biological Technicians	340
14. Biological Scientists, All Other	336
15. Purchasing Agents, Except Wholesale, Retail, and Farm Products	318
16. Industrial Engineering Technicians	307
17. Education, Training, and Library Workers, All Other	297
18. Geoscientists, Except Hydrologists and Geographers	296
19. Natural Sciences Managers	296
20. Physical Scientists, All Other	296

Missouri

Job	Federal Workers
1. Postal Service Mail Carriers	7,750
2. Business Operations Specialists, All Other	4,396
3. Postal Service Mail Sorters, Processors, and Processing Machine Operators	4,220
4. Management Analysts	2,556
5. Eligibility Interviewers, Government Programs	1,791
6. Claims Adjusters, Examiners, and Investigators	1,619
7. Registered Nurses	1,617
8. Postal Service Clerks	1,260
9. Tax Examiners, Collectors, and Revenue Agents	1,249
10. Compliance Officers, Except Agriculture, Construction, Health and Safety, and Transportation	937

Missouri

Job	Federal Workers
11. Postmasters and Mail Superintendents	840
12. Accountants and Auditors	795
13. Museum Technicians and Conservators	695
14. Teachers and Instructors, All Other	638
15. Lawyers	497
16. Licensed Practical and Licensed Vocational Nurses	447
17. Purchasing Agents, Except Wholesale, Retail, and Farm Products	425
18. Detectives and Criminal Investigators	384
19. Civil Engineers	361
20. Procurement Clerks	333

Montana

Job	Federal Workers
1. Forest and Conservation Technicians	1,686
2. Business Operations Specialists, All Other	1,099
3. Postal Service Mail Carriers	870
4. Postal Service Mail Sorters, Processors, and Processing Machine Operators	700
5. Management Analysts	663
6. Biological Technicians	557
7. Biological Scientists, All Other	445
8. Microbiologists	442
9. Registered Nurses	372
10. Detectives and Criminal Investigators	350
11. Compliance Officers, Except Agriculture, Construction, Health and Safety, and Transportation	298
12. Postmasters and Mail Superintendents	290
13. Postal Service Clerks	280
14. Conservation Scientists	265
15. Maintenance and Repair Workers, General	247
16. Industrial Machinery Mechanics	240
17. Zoologists and Wildlife Biologists	202
18. Engineering Technicians, Except Drafters, All Other	170
19. Electrical and Electronic Engineering Technicians	169
20. Civil Engineers	167

Nebraska

Job	Federal Workers
1. Postal Service Mail Carriers	2,310
2. Business Operations Specialists, All Other	1,297
3. Postal Service Mail Sorters, Processors, and Processing Machine Operators	1,220
4. Management Analysts	948
5. Compliance Officers, Except Agriculture, Construction, Health and Safety, and Transportation	738
6. Postal Service Clerks	490
7. Registered Nurses	484
8. Postmasters and Mail Superintendents	460
9. Claims Adjusters, Examiners, and Investigators	278
10. Biological Technicians	270
11. Civil Engineers	244
12. Agricultural Inspectors	172
13. Biological Scientists, All Other	157
14. Microbiologists	154
15. Forest and Conservation Technicians	146
16. Conservation Scientists	144
17. Purchasing Agents, Except Wholesale, Retail, and Farm Products	143
18. Licensed Practical and Licensed Vocational Nurses	136
19. Tax Examiners, Collectors, and Revenue Agents	129
20. Aircraft Mechanics and Service Technicians	126

Nevada

Job	Federal Workers
1. Postal Service Mail Carriers	2,360
2. Business Operations Specialists, All Other	1,257
3. Postal Service Mail Sorters, Processors, and Processing Machine Operators	970
4. Management Analysts	783
5. Registered Nurses	545
6. Postal Service Clerks	510
7. Forest and Conservation Technicians	356
8. Compliance Officers, Except Agriculture, Construction, Health and Safety, and Transportation	352
9. Biological Technicians	315
10. Tax Examiners, Collectors, and Revenue Agents	249

Nevada

Job	Federal Workers
11. Air Traffic Controllers	231
12. Biological Scientists, All Other	229
13. Claims Adjusters, Examiners, and Investigators	217
14. Microbiologists	196
15. Detectives and Criminal Investigators	172
16. Industrial Machinery Mechanics	119
17. Maintenance and Repair Workers, General	119
18. Social Scientists and Related Workers, All Other	117
19. Hydrologists	112
20. Conservation Scientists	110

New Hampshire

Job	Federal Workers
1. Postal Service Mail Carriers	1,620
2. Postal Service Mail Sorters, Processors, and Processing Machine Operators	920
3. Business Operations Specialists, All Other	600
4. Postal Service Clerks	530
5. Air Traffic Controllers	519
6. Compliance Officers, Except Agriculture, Construction, Health and Safety, and Transportation	469
7. Management Analysts	316
8. Postmasters and Mail Superintendents	210
9. Registered Nurses	141
10. Claims Adjusters, Examiners, and Investigators	115
11. Tax Examiners, Collectors, and Revenue Agents	96
12. Biological Scientists, All Other	66
13. Forest and Conservation Technicians	63
14. Detectives and Criminal Investigators	59
15. Microbiologists	58
16. Civil Engineers	56
17. Electrical and Electronic Engineering Technicians	49
18. Engineering Technicians, Except Drafters, All Other	49
19. Natural Sciences Managers	48
20. Physical Scientists, All Other	48

New Jersey

Job	Federal Workers
1. Postal Service Mail Carriers	11,390
2. Postal Service Mail Sorters, Processors, and Processing Machine Operators	7,760
3. Business Operations Specialists, All Other	3,951
4. Postal Service Clerks	2,930
5. Management Analysts	2,612
6. Compliance Officers, Except Agriculture, Construction, Health and Safety, and Transportation	1,788
7. Electrical Engineers	1,344
8. Engineering Managers	1,285
9. Electronics Engineers, Except Computer	1,183
10. Mechanical Engineers	985
11. Logisticians	915
12. Tax Examiners, Collectors, and Revenue Agents	817
13. Purchasing Agents, Except Wholesale, Retail, and Farm Products	746
14. Registered Nurses	728
15. Claims Adjusters, Examiners, and Investigators	678
16. Computer and Information Scientists, Research	528
17. Computer and Information Systems Managers	528
18. Detectives and Criminal Investigators	507
19. Postmasters and Mail Superintendents	480
20. Engineering Technicians, Except Drafters, All Other	437

New Mexico

Job	Federal Workers
1. Business Operations Specialists, All Other	2,704
2. Detectives and Criminal Investigators	1,937
3. Management Analysts	1,586
4. Postal Service Mail Carriers	1,510
5. Registered Nurses	1,070
6. Postal Service Mail Sorters, Processors, and Processing Machine Operators	840
7. Forest and Conservation Technicians	726
8. Engineering Managers	664
9. Eligibility Interviewers, Government Programs	634
10. Electrical and Electronic Engineering Technicians	628

New Mexico

Job	Federal Workers
11. Engineering Technicians, Except Drafters, All Other	628
12. Teachers and Instructors, All Other	618
13. Education, Training, and Library Workers, All Other	581
14. Purchasing Agents, Except Wholesale, Retail, and Farm Products	510
15. Postal Service Clerks	490
16. Compliance Officers, Except Agriculture, Construction, Health and Safety, and Transportation	481
17. Electrical Engineers	457
18. Industrial Engineering Technicians	454
19. Air Traffic Controllers	447
20. Electronics Engineers, Except Computer	418

New York

Job	Federal Workers
1. Postal Service Mail Carriers	22,950
2. Postal Service Mail Sorters, Processors, and Processing Machine Operators	12,750
3. Business Operations Specialists, All Other	5,857
4. Postal Service Clerks	5,790
5. Compliance Officers, Except Agriculture, Construction, Health and Safety, and Transportation	5,022
6. Management Analysts	3,794
7. Registered Nurses	3,198
8. Tax Examiners, Collectors, and Revenue Agents	3,121
9. Claims Adjusters, Examiners, and Investigators	2,710
10. Detectives and Criminal Investigators	1,853
11. Eligibility Interviewers, Government Programs	1,757
12. Lawyers	1,612
13. Postmasters and Mail Superintendents	1,340
14. Air Traffic Controllers	1,115
15. Accountants and Auditors	890
16. Licensed Practical and Licensed Vocational Nurses	775
17. Correctional Officers and Jailers	726
18. Healthcare Support Workers, All Other	684
19. Purchasing Agents, Except Wholesale, Retail, and Farm Products	637
20. Microbiologists	612

North Carolina

Job	Federal Workers
1. Postal Service Mail Carriers	10,350
2. Business Operations Specialists, All Other	4,760
3. Postal Service Mail Sorters, Processors, and Processing Machine Operators	4,100
4. Management Analysts	2,810
5. Postal Service Clerks	2,500
6. Registered Nurses	2,252
7. Teachers and Instructors, All Other	1,403
8. Claims Adjusters, Examiners, and Investigators	1,081
9. Biological Scientists, All Other	753
10. Microbiologists	717
11. Compliance Officers, Except Agriculture, Construction, Health and Safety, and Transportation	709
12. Postmasters and Mail Superintendents	650
13. Logisticians	624
14. Correctional Officers and Jailers	600
15. Licensed Practical and Licensed Vocational Nurses	581
16. Aircraft Mechanics and Service Technicians	577
17. Education, Training, and Library Workers, All Other	522
18. Maintenance and Repair Workers, General	508
19. Purchasing Agents, Except Wholesale, Retail, and Farm Products	494
20. Industrial Machinery Mechanics	491

North Dakota

Job	Federal Workers
1. Postal Service Mail Carriers	880
2. Business Operations Specialists, All Other	670
3. Postal Service Mail Sorters, Processors, and Processing Machine Operators	510
4. Compliance Officers, Except Agriculture, Construction, Health and Safety, and Transportation	384
5. Management Analysts	347
6. Biological Technicians	320
7. Postmasters and Mail Superintendents	300
8. Registered Nurses	287
9. Teachers and Instructors, All Other	188
10. Detectives and Criminal Investigators	174

North Dakota

Job	Federal Workers
11. Postal Service Clerks	160
12. Conservation Scientists	144
13. Biological Scientists, All Other	132
14. Microbiologists	116
15. Maintenance and Repair Workers, General	111
16. Education, Training, and Library Workers, All Other	108
17. Forest and Conservation Technicians	108
18. Industrial Machinery Mechanics	107
19. Zoologists and Wildlife Biologists	94
20. Licensed Practical and Licensed Vocational Nurses	88

Ohio

Job	Federal Workers
1. Postal Service Mail Carriers	14,230
2. Postal Service Mail Sorters, Processors, and Processing Machine Operators	6,450
3. Business Operations Specialists, All Other	6,214
4. Management Analysts	3,251
5. Postal Service Clerks	2,490
6. Registered Nurses	2,320
7. Purchasing Agents, Except Wholesale, Retail, and Farm Products	2,204
8. Accountants and Auditors	1,895
9. Claims Adjusters, Examiners, and Investigators	1,410
10. Electrical Engineers	1,319
11. Electronics Engineers, Except Computer	1,137
12. Aerospace Engineers	1,022
13. Logisticians	1,007
14. Engineering Managers	1,006
15. Tax Examiners, Collectors, and Revenue Agents	985
16. Postmasters and Mail Superintendents	900
17. Air Traffic Controllers	844
18. Eligibility Interviewers, Government Programs	714
19. Compliance Officers, Except Agriculture, Construction, Health and Safety, and Transportation	667
20. Lawyers	588

Oklahoma

Job	Federal Workers
1. Business Operations Specialists, All Other	5,044
2. Postal Service Mail Carriers	4,100
3. Management Analysts	2,774
4. Aircraft Mechanics and Service Technicians	2,038
5. Sheet Metal Workers	1,574
6. Postal Service Mail Sorters, Processors, and Processing Machine Operators	1,560
7. Logisticians	1,466
8. Claims Adjusters, Examiners, and Investigators	1,314
9. Engineering Technicians, Except Drafters, All Other	1,065
10. Registered Nurses	1,053
11. Electrical Engineers	1,047
12. Electronics Engineers, Except Computer	1,021
13. Electrical and Electronic Engineering Technicians	825
14. Postal Service Clerks	730
15. Purchasing Agents, Except Wholesale, Retail, and Farm Products	725
16. Procurement Clerks	615
17. Postmasters and Mail Superintendents	560
18. Painters, Construction and Maintenance	420
19. Industrial Engineering Technicians	376
20. Licensed Practical and Licensed Vocational Nurses	376

Oregon

Job	Federal Workers
1. Postal Service Mail Carriers	3,560
2. Forest and Conservation Technicians	2,266
3. Business Operations Specialists, All Other	2,122
4. Postal Service Mail Sorters, Processors, and Processing Machine Operators	1,750
5. Management Analysts	1,330
6. Registered Nurses	1,070
7. Biological Scientists, All Other	991
8. Postal Service Clerks	920
9. Microbiologists	718
10. Biological Technicians	715
11. Zoologists and Wildlife Biologists	481

Oregon

Job	Federal Workers
12. Claims Adjusters, Examiners, and Investigators	382
13. Compliance Officers, Except Agriculture, Construction, Health and Safety, and Transportation	359
14. Civil Engineers	337
15. Foresters	330
16. Electrical and Electronic Engineering Technicians	309
17. Engineering Technicians, Except Drafters, All Other	309
18. Postmasters and Mail Superintendents	290
19. Maintenance and Repair Workers, General	280
20. Industrial Engineering Technicians	266

Pennsylvania

Job	Federal Workers
1. Postal Service Mail Carriers	15,730
2. Business Operations Specialists, All Other	8,363
3. Postal Service Mail Sorters, Processors, and Processing Machine Operators	8,060
4. Management Analysts	4,916
5. Postal Service Clerks	3,590
6. Eligibility Interviewers, Government Programs	2,502
7. Claims Adjusters, Examiners, and Investigators	2,395
8. Tax Examiners, Collectors, and Revenue Agents	2,348
9. Registered Nurses	2,335
10. Purchasing Agents, Except Wholesale, Retail, and Farm Products	2,157
11. Logisticians	2,003
12. Electrical and Electronics Repairers, Commercial and Industrial Equipment	1,713
13. Correctional Officers and Jailers	1,548
14. Postmasters and Mail Superintendents	1,540
15. Compliance Officers, Except Agriculture, Construction, Health and Safety, and Transportation	1,502
16. Procurement Clerks	943
17. Lawyers	894
18. Detectives and Criminal Investigators	845
19. Engineering Technicians, Except Drafters, All Other	776
20. Accountants and Auditors	752

Rhode Island

Job	Federal Workers
1. Postal Service Mail Carriers	1,350
2. Electrical Engineers	915
3. Electronics Engineers, Except Computer	901
4. Postal Service Mail Sorters, Processors, and Processing Machine Operators	700
5. Business Operations Specialists, All Other	615
6. Mechanical Engineers	463
7. Management Analysts	345
8. Computer and Information Scientists, Research	332
9. Computer and Information Systems Managers	332
10. Registered Nurses	330
11. Postal Service Clerks	320
12. Teachers and Instructors, All Other	260
13. Claims Adjusters, Examiners, and Investigators	204
14. Engineering Technicians, Except Drafters, All Other	167
15. Electrical and Electronic Engineering Technicians	166
16. Healthcare Support Workers, All Other	124
17. Computer Hardware Engineers	119
18. Industrial Engineering Technicians	118
19. Purchasing Agents, Except Wholesale, Retail, and Farm Products	116
20. Engineering Managers	100

South Carolina

Job	Federal Workers
1. Postal Service Mail Carriers	4,570
2. Business Operations Specialists, All Other	2,308
3. Management Analysts	1,366
4. Postal Service Mail Sorters, Processors, and Processing Machine Operators	1,360
5. Registered Nurses	943
6. Postal Service Clerks	890
7. Claims Adjusters, Examiners, and Investigators	739
8. Compliance Officers, Except Agriculture, Construction, Health and Safety, and Transportation	624
9. Correctional Officers and Jailers	617
10. Electrical Engineers	505

South Carolina

Job	Federal Workers
11. Electronics Engineers, Except Computer	480
12. Teachers and Instructors, All Other	423
13. Electrical and Electronic Engineering Technicians	377
14. Engineering Technicians, Except Drafters, All Other	377
15. Purchasing Agents, Except Wholesale, Retail, and Farm Products	335
16. Postmasters and Mail Superintendents	330
17. Logisticians	277
18. Healthcare Support Workers, All Other	268
19. Procurement Clerks	256
20. Engineering Managers	250

South Dakota

Job	Federal Workers
1. Postal Service Mail Carriers	1,020
2. Business Operations Specialists, All Other	774
3. Registered Nurses	648
4. Postal Service Mail Sorters, Processors, and Processing Machine Operators	560
5. Management Analysts	430
6. Postmasters and Mail Superintendents	310
7. Forest and Conservation Technicians	308
8. Biological Technicians	244
9. Teachers and Instructors, All Other	232
10. Education, Training, and Library Workers, All Other	199
11. Licensed Practical and Licensed Vocational Nurses	173
12. Maintenance and Repair Workers, General	170
13. Postal Service Clerks	170
14. Industrial Machinery Mechanics	169
15. Conservation Scientists	163
16. Biological Scientists, All Other	114
17. Microbiologists	109
18. Medical Records and Health Information Technicians	100
19. Social Scientists and Related Workers, All Other	98
20. Claims Adjusters, Examiners, and Investigators	97

Tennessee

Job	Federal Workers
1. Postal Service Mail Carriers	6,930
2. Postal Service Mail Sorters, Processors, and Processing Machine Operators	3,040
3. Business Operations Specialists, All Other	2,599
4. Registered Nurses	1,823
5. Management Analysts	1,621
6. Postal Service Clerks	1,330
7. Tax Examiners, Collectors, and Revenue Agents	1,205
8. Eligibility Interviewers, Government Programs	954
9. Claims Adjusters, Examiners, and Investigators	896
10. Air Traffic Controllers	702
11. Teachers and Instructors, All Other	530
12. Postmasters and Mail Superintendents	480
13. Licensed Practical and Licensed Vocational Nurses	466
14. Compliance Officers, Except Agriculture, Construction, Health and Safety, and Transportation	455
15. Healthcare Support Workers, All Other	373
16. Detectives and Criminal Investigators	313
17. Accountants and Auditors	300
18. Lawyers	300
19. Maintenance and Repair Workers, General	270
20. Civil Engineers	267

Texas

Job	Federal Workers
1. Postal Service Mail Carriers	22,560
2. Business Operations Specialists, All Other	16,143
3. Postal Service Mail Sorters, Processors, and Processing Machine Operators	10,680
4. Detectives and Criminal Investigators	10,281
5. Management Analysts	9,850
6. Compliance Officers, Except Agriculture, Construction, Health and Safety, and Transportation	7,974
7. Registered Nurses	5,015
8. Postal Service Clerks	4,190
9. Tax Examiners, Collectors, and Revenue Agents	3,260
10. Claims Adjusters, Examiners, and Investigators	2,720

Texas

Job	Federal Workers
11. Eligibility Interviewers, Government Programs	2,174
12. Purchasing Agents, Except Wholesale, Retail, and Farm Products	2,086
13. Air Traffic Controllers	1,946
14. Aircraft Mechanics and Service Technicians	1,844
15. Teachers and Instructors, All Other	1,747
16. Correctional Officers and Jailers	1,729
17. Lawyers	1,728
18. Accountants and Auditors	1,651
19. Licensed Practical and Licensed Vocational Nurses	1,546
20. Engineering Managers	1,484

Utah

Job	Federal Workers
1. Business Operations Specialists, All Other	3,690
2. Tax Examiners, Collectors, and Revenue Agents	2,284
3. Postal Service Mail Carriers	2,090
4. Management Analysts	1,956
5. Logisticians	909
6. Forest and Conservation Technicians	903
7. Aircraft Mechanics and Service Technicians	875
8. Postal Service Mail Sorters, Processors, and Processing Machine Operators	810
9. Eligibility Interviewers, Government Programs	756
10. Electrical Engineers	673
11. Electronics Engineers, Except Computer	651
12. Engineering Technicians, Except Drafters, All Other	622
13. Postal Service Clerks	550
14. Sheet Metal Workers	539
15. Purchasing Agents, Except Wholesale, Retail, and Farm Products	526
16. Registered Nurses	497
17. Biological Technicians	486
18. Electrical and Electronic Engineering Technicians	435
19. Air Traffic Controllers	430
20. Electrical and Electronics Repairers, Commercial and Industrial Equipment	389

Vermont	
Job	**Federal Workers**
1. Compliance Officers, Except Agriculture, Construction, Health and Safety, and Transportation	1,183
2. Postal Service Mail Carriers	820
3. Business Operations Specialists, All Other	519
4. Postal Service Mail Sorters, Processors, and Processing Machine Operators	450
5. Management Analysts	362
6. Postal Service Clerks	300
7. Postmasters and Mail Superintendents	250
8. Detectives and Criminal Investigators	192
9. Registered Nurses	168
10. Claims Adjusters, Examiners, and Investigators	69
11. Aircraft Mechanics and Service Technicians	61
12. Purchasing Agents, Except Wholesale, Retail, and Farm Products	61
13. Tax Examiners, Collectors, and Revenue Agents	61
14. Biological Scientists, All Other	60
15. Biological Technicians	48
16. Microbiologists	45
17. Healthcare Support Workers, All Other	40
18. Forest and Conservation Technicians	38
19. Lawyers	38
20. Licensed Practical and Licensed Vocational Nurses	35

Virginia	
Job	**Federal Workers**
1. Business Operations Specialists, All Other	31,751
2. Management Analysts	23,865
3. Postal Service Mail Carriers	8,490
4. Purchasing Agents, Except Wholesale, Retail, and Farm Products	4,703
5. Postal Service Mail Sorters, Processors, and Processing Machine Operators	3,820
6. Compliance Officers, Except Agriculture, Construction, Health and Safety, and Transportation	2,921
7. Engineering Technicians, Except Drafters, All Other	2,850
8. Electrical and Electronic Engineering Technicians	2,838
9. Logisticians	2,810
10. Lawyers	2,600

Virginia

Job	Federal Workers
11. Social Scientists and Related Workers, All Other	2,506
12. Accountants and Auditors	2,476
13. Engineering Managers	2,392
14. Electrical Engineers	2,200
15. Economists	2,138
16. Postal Service Clerks	2,050
17. Industrial Engineering Technicians	2,011
18. Political Scientists	2,009
19. Registered Nurses	1,959
20. Budget Analysts	1,660

Washington

Job	Federal Workers
1. Business Operations Specialists, All Other	6,540
2. Postal Service Mail Carriers	6,370
3. Management Analysts	3,581
4. Postal Service Mail Sorters, Processors, and Processing Machine Operators	3,090
5. Registered Nurses	1,995
6. Compliance Officers, Except Agriculture, Construction, Health and Safety, and Transportation	1,705
7. Engineering Technicians, Except Drafters, All Other	1,603
8. Electrical and Electronic Engineering Technicians	1,593
9. Postal Service Clerks	1,470
10. Industrial Machinery Mechanics	1,272
11. Industrial Engineering Technicians	1,269
12. Claims Adjusters, Examiners, and Investigators	1,190
13. Biological Scientists, All Other	1,139
14. Eligibility Interviewers, Government Programs	1,125
15. Detectives and Criminal Investigators	1,027
16. Forest and Conservation Technicians	979
17. Purchasing Agents, Except Wholesale, Retail, and Farm Products	841
18. Electrical Engineers	781
19. Maintenance and Repair Workers, General	723
20. Civil Engineers	715

West Virginia

Job	Federal Workers
1. Postal Service Mail Carriers	1,760
2. Business Operations Specialists, All Other	1,592
3. Management Analysts	1,224
4. Postal Service Mail Sorters, Processors, and Processing Machine Operators	1,010
5. Registered Nurses	875
6. Correctional Officers and Jailers	822
7. Postmasters and Mail Superintendents	660
8. Postal Service Clerks	460
9. Claims Adjusters, Examiners, and Investigators	373
10. Accountants and Auditors	302
11. Licensed Practical and Licensed Vocational Nurses	244
12. Maintenance and Repair Workers, General	236
13. Biological Scientists, All Other	222
14. Microbiologists	208
15. Purchasing Agents, Except Wholesale, Retail, and Farm Products	206
16. Industrial Machinery Mechanics	197
17. Engineering Managers	196
18. Social Scientists and Related Workers, All Other	163
19. Civil Engineers	159
20. Healthcare Support Workers, All Other	154

Wisconsin

Job	Federal Workers
1. Postal Service Mail Carriers	7,150
2. Postal Service Mail Sorters, Processors, and Processing Machine Operators	2,990
3. Postal Service Clerks	1,300
4. Registered Nurses	1,299
5. Business Operations Specialists, All Other	1,180
6. Claims Adjusters, Examiners, and Investigators	821
7. Management Analysts	712
8. Postmasters and Mail Superintendents	650
9. Biological Technicians	344
10. Tax Examiners, Collectors, and Revenue Agents	299
11. Licensed Practical and Licensed Vocational Nurses	277

Wisconsin

Job	Federal Workers
12. Healthcare Support Workers, All Other	268
13. Compliance Officers, Except Agriculture, Construction, Health and Safety, and Transportation	260
14. Biological Scientists, All Other	243
15. Microbiologists	197
16. Forest and Conservation Technicians	174
17. Eligibility Interviewers, Government Programs	171
18. Pharmacists	164
19. Air Traffic Controllers	147
20. Conservation Scientists	147

Wyoming

Job	Federal Workers
1. Business Operations Specialists, All Other	557
2. Forest and Conservation Technicians	536
3. Postal Service Mail Carriers	400
4. Postal Service Mail Sorters, Processors, and Processing Machine Operators	350
5. Management Analysts	340
6. Biological Technicians	286
7. Registered Nurses	271
8. Biological Scientists, All Other	220
9. Postal Service Clerks	200
10. Microbiologists	196
11. Maintenance and Repair Workers, General	152
12. Industrial Machinery Mechanics	149
13. Conservation Scientists	143
14. Postmasters and Mail Superintendents	140
15. Engineering Technicians, Except Drafters, All Other	124
16. Electrical and Electronic Engineering Technicians	123
17. Industrial Engineering Technicians	104
18. Zoologists and Wildlife Biologists	99
19. Social Scientists and Related Workers, All Other	75
20. Healthcare Support Workers, All Other	63

Appendix D: Best Jobs with Largest Work-forces, by Agency

Perhaps there's a federal agency whose mission particularly appeals to you. In this appendix, you can find the 20 best jobs with the largest number of workers in that agency. I include all 15 cabinet-level agencies, plus the Postal Service.

Department of Agriculture	
Job	**Federal Workers**
1. Forest and Conservation Technicians	16,423
2. Biological Technicians	9,276
3. Management Analysts	6,581
4. Biological Scientists, All Other	5,987
5. Conservation Scientists	5,311
6. Loan Officers	3,888
7. Agricultural Inspectors	3,339
8. Foresters	1,833
9. Veterinarians	1,731
10. Zoologists and Wildlife Biologists	1,517
11. Soil and Plant Scientists	1,329
12. Engineering Technicians, Except Drafters, All Other	1,299
13. Industrial Engineering Technicians	1,299
14. Civil Engineers	1,286
15. Business Operations Specialists, All Other	1,159
16. Accountants and Auditors	1,070

(continued)

(continued)

Department of Agriculture

Job	Federal Workers
17. Purchasing Agents, Except Wholesale, Retail, and Farm Products	996
18. Compliance Officers, Except Agriculture, Construction, Health and Safety, and Transportation	981
19. Life, Physical, and Social Science Technicians, All Other	885
20. Budget Analysts	741

Department of Commerce

Job	Federal Workers
1. Management Analysts	7,370
2. Biological Scientists, All Other	1,495
3. Zoologists and Wildlife Biologists	1,117
4. Business Operations Specialists, All Other	1,034
5. Lawyers	1,009
6. Natural Sciences Managers	862
7. Physical Scientists, All Other	862
8. Life, Physical, and Social Science Technicians, All Other	560
9. Electrical and Electronic Engineering Technicians	531
10. Economists	489
11. Statisticians	425
12. Accountants and Auditors	400
13. Physicists	384
14. Chemists	305
15. Compliance Officers, Except Agriculture, Construction, Health and Safety, and Transportation	303
16. Electronics Engineers, Except Computer	298
17. Budget Analysts	291
18. Hydrologists	289
19. Geoscientists, Except Hydrologists and Geographers	276
20. Purchasing Agents, Except Wholesale, Retail, and Farm Products	266

Department of Defense

Job	Federal Workers
1. Management Analysts	67,157
2. Business Operations Specialists, All Other	35,470
3. Purchasing Agents, Except Wholesale, Retail, and Farm Products	24,603
4. Logisticians	24,343
5. Electronics Engineers, Except Computer	17,286
6. Aircraft Mechanics and Service Technicians	15,502
7. Engineering Managers	14,300
8. Accountants and Auditors	12,262
9. Engineering Technicians, Except Drafters, All Other	12,166
10. Industrial Engineering Technicians	12,166
11. Mechanical Engineers	10,781
12. Procurement Clerks	10,142
13. Fire Fighters	8,649
14. Registered Nurses	8,425
15. First-Line Supervisors/Managers of Police and Detectives	8,106
16. Education, Training, and Library Workers, All Other	7,806
17. Civil Engineers	7,797
18. Budget Analysts	7,413
19. Sheet Metal Workers	7,202
20. Electrical and Electronics Repairers, Commercial and Industrial Equipment	6,056

Department of Education

Job	Federal Workers
1. Management Analysts	1,582
2. Lawyers	409
3. Education, Training, and Library Workers, All Other	378
4. Accountants and Auditors	268
5. Compliance Officers, Except Agriculture, Construction, Health and Safety, and Transportation	214
6. Detectives and Criminal Investigators	101
7. Purchasing Agents, Except Wholesale, Retail, and Farm Products	91
8. Budget Analysts	58
9. Business Operations Specialists, All Other	42
10. Social Scientists and Related Workers, All Other	39

(continued)

(continued)

Department of Education

Job	Federal Workers
11. Public Relations Managers	22
12. Public Relations Specialists	22
13. Statisticians	11
14. Paralegals and Legal Assistants	9
15. Writers and Authors	5
16. Economists	4
17. Operations Research Analysts	4
18. Motor Vehicle Operators, All Other	3
19. Producers and Directors	3
20. Administrative Services Managers	2

Department of Energy

Job	Federal Workers
1. Management Analysts	3,110
2. Engineering Managers	1,667
3. Business Operations Specialists, All Other	1,028
4. Purchasing Agents, Except Wholesale, Retail, and Farm Products	678
5. Natural Sciences Managers	664
6. Physical Scientists, All Other	664
7. Lawyers	630
8. Accountants and Auditors	576
9. Electrical Engineers	529
10. Budget Analysts	263
11. Nuclear Engineers	250
12. Political Scientists	233
13. Civil Engineers	223
14. Economists	173
15. Environmental Scientists and Specialists, Including Health	148
16. Biological Scientists, All Other	107
17. Electronics Engineers, Except Computer	101
18. Public Relations Managers	96
19. Public Relations Specialists	96
20. Detectives and Criminal Investigators	90

Department of Health and Human Services

Job	Federal Workers
1. Management Analysts	12,347
2. Registered Nurses	5,620
3. Health Diagnosing and Treating Practitioners, All Other	5,124
4. Biological Scientists, All Other	3,674
5. Occupational Health and Safety Specialists	2,858
6. Healthcare Support Workers, All Other	2,612
7. Chemists	1,836
8. Business Operations Specialists, All Other	1,743
9. Microbiologists	1,508
10. Accountants and Auditors	1,458
11. Social Scientists and Related Workers, All Other	1,372
12. Purchasing Agents, Except Wholesale, Retail, and Farm Products	1,211
13. Medical Records and Health Information Technicians	895
14. Pharmacists	756
15. Lawyers	712
16. Medical Scientists, Except Epidemiologists	691
17. Budget Analysts	630
18. Detectives and Criminal Investigators	606
19. Maintenance and Repair Workers, General	596
20. Medical and Clinical Laboratory Technologists	577

Department of Homeland Security

Job	Federal Workers
1. Compliance Officers, Except Agriculture, Construction, Health and Safety, and Transportation	44,742
2. Detectives and Criminal Investigators	30,946
3. Management Analysts	26,661
4. Business Operations Specialists, All Other	2,669
5. Biological Scientists, All Other	2,268
6. Lawyers	1,971
7. First-Line Supervisors/Managers of Police and Detectives	1,516
8. Purchasing Agents, Except Wholesale, Retail, and Farm Products	1,472
9. Accountants and Auditors	1,178
10. Political Scientists	1,062

(continued)

(continued)

Department of Homeland Security

Job	Federal Workers
11. Media and Communication Equipment Workers, All Other	588
12. Logisticians	584
13. Tax Examiners, Collectors, and Revenue Agents	499
14. Paralegals and Legal Assistants	475
15. Administrative Law Judges, Adjudicators, and Hearing Officers	450
16. Maintenance and Repair Workers, General	446
17. Engineering Managers	355
18. Budget Analysts	304
19. Education, Training, and Library Workers, All Other	257
20. Public Relations Managers	205

Department of Housing and Urban Development

Job	Federal Workers
1. Management Analysts	2,309
2. Accountants and Auditors	475
3. Lawyers	433
4. Compliance Officers, Except Agriculture, Construction, Health and Safety, and Transportation	416
5. Detectives and Criminal Investigators	276
6. Business Operations Specialists, All Other	237
7. Budget Analysts	95
8. Purchasing Agents, Except Wholesale, Retail, and Farm Products	94
9. Economists	76
10. Paralegals and Legal Assistants	70
11. Administrative Services Managers	63
12. Engineering Managers	55
13. Architects, Except Landscape and Naval	30
14. Environmental Scientists and Specialists, Including Health	29
15. Real Estate Sales Agents	28
16. Social Scientists and Related Workers, All Other	26
17. Public Relations Managers	18
18. Public Relations Specialists	18
19. Loan Officers	14
20. Financial Managers	10

Department of the Interior

Job	Federal Workers
1. Management Analysts	5,548
2. Biological Scientists, All Other	4,932
3. Biological Technicians	4,314
4. Maintenance and Repair Workers, General	4,080
5. Zoologists and Wildlife Biologists	2,973
6. Education, Training, and Library Workers, All Other	2,562
7. Life, Physical, and Social Science Technicians, All Other	1,873
8. Hydrologists	1,614
9. Forest and Conservation Technicians	1,605
10. Business Operations Specialists, All Other	1,180
11. Purchasing Agents, Except Wholesale, Retail, and Farm Products	1,122
12. Civil Engineers	999
13. Conservation Scientists	977
14. First-Line Supervisors/Managers of Police and Detectives	865
15. Real Estate Sales Agents	831
16. Accountants and Auditors	783
17. Engineering Technicians, Except Drafters, All Other	780
18. Industrial Engineering Technicians	780
19. Budget Analysts	721
20. Compliance Officers, Except Agriculture, Construction, Health and Safety, and Transportation	670

Department of Justice

Job	Federal Workers
1. Detectives and Criminal Investigators	25,438
2. Correctional Officers and Jailers	17,580
3. Lawyers	10,678
4. Management Analysts	9,349
5. Political Scientists	4,092
6. Compliance Officers, Except Agriculture, Construction, Health and Safety, and Transportation	3,353
7. Paralegals and Legal Assistants	2,373
8. Social Scientists and Related Workers, All Other	1,943
9. Business Operations Specialists, All Other	1,710

(continued)

(continued)

Department of Justice

Job	Federal Workers
10. First-Line Supervisors/Managers of Correctional Officers	1,670
11. Accountants and Auditors	1,101
12. Electrical and Electronic Engineering Technicians	768
13. Maintenance and Repair Workers, General	734
14. Registered Nurses	713
15. Budget Analysts	681
16. Interpreters and Translators	638
17. Purchasing Agents, Except Wholesale, Retail, and Farm Products	606
18. Media and Communication Equipment Workers, All Other	524
19. Psychologists, All Other	521
20. Forensic Science Technicians	511

Department of Labor

Job	Federal Workers
1. Compliance Officers, Except Agriculture, Construction, Health and Safety, and Transportation	2,578
2. Management Analysts	1,996
3. Economists	1,298
4. Lawyers	654
5. Life, Physical, and Social Science Technicians, All Other	466
6. Accountants and Auditors	260
7. Detectives and Criminal Investigators	227
8. Business Operations Specialists, All Other	183
9. Purchasing Agents, Except Wholesale, Retail, and Farm Products	108
10. Statisticians	100
11. Industrial Engineers	99
12. Budget Analysts	88
13. Paralegals and Legal Assistants	82
14. Political Scientists	61
15. Administrative Services Managers	41
16. Civil Engineers	39
17. Electrical Engineers	39
18. Chemists	35

Department of Labor

Job	Federal Workers
19. Engineering Managers	35
20. Health Diagnosing and Treating Practitioners, All Other	32

Department of State

Job	Federal Workers
1. Management Analysts	2,543
2. Political Scientists	2,166
3. Compliance Officers, Except Agriculture, Construction, Health and Safety, and Transportation	1,482
4. Business Operations Specialists, All Other	602
5. Budget Analysts	237
6. Lawyers	216
7. Accountants and Auditors	164
8. Public Relations Managers	149
9. Public Relations Specialists	149
10. Purchasing Agents, Except Wholesale, Retail, and Farm Products	147
11. Media and Communication Equipment Workers, All Other	104
12. Detectives and Criminal Investigators	103
13. Administrative Services Managers	100
14. Engineering Managers	87
15. Logisticians	82
16. Education, Training, and Library Workers, All Other	60
17. Teachers and Instructors, All Other	55
18. Interpreters and Translators	54
19. Paralegals and Legal Assistants	49
20. Natural Sciences Managers	48

Department of Transportation

Job	Federal Workers
1. Air Traffic Controllers	20,445
2. Business Operations Specialists, All Other	7,327
3. Management Analysts	6,025

(continued)

(continued)

Department of Transportation

Job	Federal Workers
4. Transportation Inspectors	4,298
5. Civil Engineers	1,504
6. Engineering Managers	1,173
7. Electronics Engineers, Except Computer	896
8. Aerospace Engineers	771
9. Compliance Officers, Except Agriculture, Construction, Health and Safety, and Transportation	711
10. Lawyers	578
11. Electrical and Electronic Engineering Technicians	562
12. Engineering Technicians, Except Drafters, All Other	493
13. Industrial Engineering Technicians	493
14. Purchasing Agents, Except Wholesale, Retail, and Farm Products	454
15. Accountants and Auditors	347
16. Logisticians	332
17. Environmental Scientists and Specialists, Including Health	268
18. Operations Research Analysts	234
19. Computer and Information Research Scientists	223
20. Computer and Information Systems Managers	223

Department of the Treasury

Job	Federal Workers
1. Tax Examiners, Collectors, and Revenue Agents	34,706
2. Eligibility Interviewers, Government Programs	12,377
3. Management Analysts	8,546
4. Detectives and Criminal Investigators	3,181
5. Financial Examiners	2,662
6. Lawyers	2,377
7. Accountants and Auditors	1,088
8. Administrative Law Judges, Adjudicators, and Hearing Officers	943
9. Compliance Officers, Except Agriculture, Construction, Health and Safety, and Transportation	823
10. Paralegals and Legal Assistants	821
11. Business Operations Specialists, All Other	792

Department of the Treasury

Job	Federal Workers
12. Administrative Services Managers	648
13. Economists	532
14. First-Line Supervisors/Managers of Police and Detectives	512
15. Purchasing Agents, Except Wholesale, Retail, and Farm Products	490
16. Budget Analysts	375
17. Engineering Managers	269
18. Public Relations Managers	248
19. Public Relations Specialists	248
20. Political Scientists	200

Department of Veterans Affairs

Job	Federal Workers
1. Registered Nurses	52,998
2. Licensed Practical and Licensed Vocational Nurses	12,866
3. Management Analysts	12,864
4. Healthcare Support Workers, All Other	8,144
5. Pharmacists	7,019
6. Health Diagnosing and Treating Practitioners, All Other	5,179
7. Medical and Clinical Laboratory Technologists	4,363
8. Psychologists, All Other	4,320
9. Pharmacy Technicians	4,032
10. Radiologic Technologists and Technicians	3,185
11. First-Line Supervisors/Managers of Police and Detectives	2,916
12. Purchasing Agents, Except Wholesale, Retail, and Farm Products	2,741
13. Medical Records and Health Information Technicians	2,717
14. Business Operations Specialists, All Other	2,715
15. Health Technologists and Technicians, All Other	2,384
16. Social Scientists and Related Workers, All Other	2,233
17. Procurement Clerks	2,069
18. Physician Assistants	1,914
19. Physical Therapists	1,469
20. Motor Vehicle Operators, All Other	1,435

Postal Service

Job	Federal Workers
1. Postal Service Mail Carriers	343,340
2. Postal Service Mail Sorters, Processors, and Processing Machine Operators	179,890
3. Postal Service Clerks	75,780
4. Postmasters and Mail Superintendents	25,570

Appendix E: Foreign Job Opportunities

About 36,000 federal workers (1.7 percent of the workforce) are employed in foreign countries. An additional 15,000 federal workers are employed in United States territories, such as Puerto Rico and Guam. If you have a sense of adventure or want a drastic change of scene, you may consider work in one of these locations.

You should know that positions in foreign locations are most often filled by career federal workers who are transferred from similar positions they already have in the United States. Vacancies are less commonly filled through the open examination process. That happens only when federal employees are not available for transfer overseas and qualified United States citizens cannot be recruited locally.

In addition, a small number of positions are normally filled by first-time federal workers: attaché office clerk-translator, translator, interpreter, Foreign Service, and Peace Corps volunteer.

Qualifications. Generally, the qualification requirements for foreign assignments are the same as those established for positions in the United States. Applicants may, however, be required to meet certain additional or higher standards. For example, the ability to speak and read a foreign language, while not required in all federal jobs overseas, would obviously be a valuable qualification.

Earnings. Overseas employees are paid the same base salaries as federal employees in the continental United States. In some locations, employees may receive a post differential or cost-of-living allowance.

Finding federal jobs overseas. On the USAJobs website, you can use the name of a foreign location, such as "Germany," as one of the keywords in a search. You also can go to the USAJobs page for International Search, which offers a Location Search menu. United States territories are listed alphabetically among the states; foreign countries are listed alphabetically at the bottom of the menu.

Another strategy is to focus on a federal agency, such as the Department of Defense Dependents Schools or the Peace Corps, that employs many workers in foreign locations.

The following two sections of this appendix provide detailed information about these two agencies.

Department of Defense Schools

On the list of foreign jobs with the largest workforce (later in this appendix), you'll note that the biggest job by far is Teachers and Instructors, All Other, with 7,907 federal workers in September 2010. Another 327 federal workers in this occupation are employed in United States territories. Most of these workers (and many in other occupations) are employed by the Department of Defense (DoD) in schools that the DoD operates overseas for minor dependents of active-duty military and civilian personnel. The schools enroll students from kindergarten through grade 12 and are modeled on American public schools.

Some of these workers are spouses of military or civilian DoD employees stationed overseas; typically they begin in time-limited appointments and may be able to move to a permanent position with experience and appropriate teaching licensure. Others have no marital connection to a DoD employee and apply from the United States.

To qualify for one of these positions, you need a teaching license from one of the 50 states. The DoD certifies you in a field and level that match the certification in your original state as closely as possible. You usually need to sign a mobility agreement that says you are willing to work wherever the DoD needs you. To apply for a teaching position that starts with the following school year, you generally begin the process between September and January 15.

If you are an education major at a college that has an agreement with the Department of Defense Dependents Schools (DoDDS), you may be able to do your student teaching as a federal employee. Some students majoring in school psychology, counseling, nursing, library media, vocational education, or school administration are also eligible for student teaching for DoDDS. Ask your academic advisor about such opportunities. If you apply for spring placement, the deadline is October 31st; for fall placement, it is April 30th.

For further information about opportunities at DoD Dependents Schools, visit the DoDEA (Department of Defense Education Activity) Recruitment website at www.dodea.edu/offices/hr/default.htm or phone DoDEA's Recruitment Center at (703) 588-3983.

The United States Peace Corps

The Peace Corps was founded in 1961 by President John F. Kennedy. Volunteers serve in 77 countries in Africa, Asia, the Caribbean, Central and South America, Europe, and the Middle East. Peace Corps volunteers live, learn, and work with a community overseas for 27 months. The Peace Corps trains volunteers with necessary skills in language, cultural awareness, and technical tasks.

Volunteers provide technical assistance in several program areas:

- *Education* volunteers introduce innovative teaching methodologies, encourage critical thinking in the classroom, and integrate issues such as health education and environmental awareness into English, math, science, and other subjects.

- *Youth and community development* volunteers engage in a wide variety of outreach projects concerning at-risk children or youth, adult literacy, health or HIV/AIDS education, environmental awareness, development of libraries and resource centers, and information technology.

- *Health* volunteers educate and promote awareness about issues such as malnutrition and safe drinking water.

- *Business development* volunteers work in education, private businesses, public organizations, government offices, cooperatives, women's and youth groups, and other organizations.

- *Information and communications technology* volunteers teach computer and multimedia skills, develop regional databases, and implement networks for nongovernmental organizations, businesses, and government offices.

- *Agriculture* volunteers work with small farmers to increase food production while promoting environmental conservation practices.

- *Environment* volunteers work on a wide variety of activities, from teaching environmental awareness to planting trees within a community.

In addition, many volunteers contribute to HIV/AIDS initiatives during their service, regardless of their area of expertise. Also, 40 percent of volunteers are involved in some capacity to support food security through projects in health and nutrition, agriculture, and the environment.

Volunteers must be at least 18 years of age, and there is no upper age limit. A four-year college degree is necessary for some positions, but for many positions some other combination of education and work experience will qualify you. Although you may be able to express some geographical preference (such as a continent of interest), the Peace Corps places you where you're needed most.

The Peace Corps provides you with a living allowance that allows you to live in a manner similar to the local people in your community. Understand that volunteers usually live in poor communities. The Peace Corps also provides complete medical and dental care and covers the cost of transportation to and from your country of service. To assist with the transition back home, volunteers are paid $7,425 (before taxes) at the close of 27 months of service. The money is yours to use as you wish: for travel, a vacation, making a move, or securing housing. It is sometimes possible for volunteers to obtain deferment or even partial cancellation of student loans.

For up to 18 months after you return from service, you have access to an affordable health insurance plan. Your career also gets a boost because employers value the technical skills you have acquired and the work habits of initiative and resourcefulness that the Peace Corps experience instills in volunteers. If you apply for some other federal position, you may be eligible for an appointment that bypasses the standard competitive process, and you will get credit toward retirement equivalent to your time in the Peace Corps.

Peace Corps service can also pave the way for a master's degree. More than 80 grad schools offer programs that consist of study on campus, usually for one year, followed by two years of Peace Corps work in a related project. Most of these schools provide students in this program with opportunities for research or teaching assistantships, scholarships, or tuition waivers for the credits earned while serving in the Peace Corps.

The Paul D. Coverdell Fellows Program offers returned volunteers scholarships or reduced tuition, stipends, and internships at more than 50 participating campuses in a variety of subject areas, combining graduate study with substantive, degree-related internships that help meet the needs of underserved American communities. Fellows teach in public schools, work in public health facilities, and contribute to community development projects at nonprofit organizations. Volunteers can apply for this program any time after they complete their Peace Corps service.

Peace Corps service can also make you a more attractive candidate for other fellowships, teaching assistantships, or research assistantships that can pay for graduate study.

The Peace Corps accepts applications on a rolling basis. Recruiters, all of whom served in the Peace Corps themselves, can tell you what it's really like to volunteer, whether or not you qualify, and how to work through the application process. Find your regional recruitment office at www.peacecorps.gov/index.cfm?shell=meet.regrec or phone 800-424-8580 to contact your local recruiter.

Where the Jobs Are

The following lists show the occupations and locations where the largest number of federal workers are employed offshore.

Occupations with the Largest Number of Federal Workers in Foreign Locations

Job	Employees
1. Teachers and Instructors, All Other	7,907
2. Social and Community Service Managers	2,792
3. Business Operations Specialists, All Other	2,382
4. Computer and Information Systems Managers	1,778
5. Education, Training, and Library Workers, All Other	1,444
6. Management Analysts	998

Occupations with the Largest Number of Federal Workers in Foreign Locations

Job	Employees
7. Compliance Officers, Except Agriculture, Construction, Health and Safety, and Transportation	917
8. Logisticians	909
9. Lawyers	847
10. Purchasing Agents, Except Wholesale, Retail, and Farm Products	615
11. Detectives and Criminal Investigators	539
12. Motor Vehicle Operators, All Other	496
13. Registered Nurses	487
14. Engineering Managers	413
15. Engineers, All Other	413
16. Social Scientists and Related Workers, All Other	382
17. Budget Analysts	352
18. Accountants and Auditors	313
19. Recreational Therapists	272
20. Civil Engineers	259
21. Natural Sciences Managers	239
22. Media and Communication Equipment Workers, All Other	225
23. Transportation, Storage, and Distribution Managers	196
24. Combined Food Preparation and Serving Workers, Including Fast Food	192
25. Procurement Clerks	181
26. Engineering Technicians, Except Drafters, All Other	173
27. Healthcare Support Workers, All Other	167
28. Market Research Analysts	141
29. Public Relations Managers	128
30. Public Relations Specialists	128
31. Political Scientists	116
32. Fire Fighters	114
33. Medical Records and Health Information Technicians	106
34. Financial Managers	102
35. Health Diagnosing and Treating Practitioners, All Other	93
36. Construction and Building Inspectors	92
37. Instructional Coordinators	92
38. Air Traffic Controllers	77
39. Mechanical Engineers	75

(continued)

(continued)

Occupations with the Largest Number of Federal Workers in Foreign Locations

Job	Employees
40. Psychologists, All Other	74
41. Environmental Engineers	73
42. Licensed Practical and Licensed Vocational Nurses	68
43. Transportation Inspectors	62
44. Architects, Except Landscape and Naval	57
45. Electrical Engineers	56
46. Electronics Engineers, Except Computer	56
47. Pharmacists	53
48. Physical Scientists, All Other	53
49. Eligibility Interviewers, Government Programs	48
50. Security Guards	48

Occupations with the Largest Number of Federal Workers in United States Territories

Job	Employees
1. Security Guards	1,060
2. Compliance Officers, Except Agriculture, Construction, Health and Safety, and Transportation	878
3. Social and Community Service Managers	845
4. Registered Nurses	727
5. Eligibility Interviewers, Government Programs	369
6. Business Operations Specialists, All Other	354
7. Detectives and Criminal Investigators	346
8. Natural Sciences Managers	346
9. Teachers and Instructors, All Other	327
10. Lawyers	309
11. Claims Adjusters, Examiners, and Investigators	269
12. Licensed Practical and Licensed Vocational Nurses	248
13. Computer and Information Systems Managers	222
14. Biological Technicians	197
15. Management Analysts	181
16. First-Line Supervisors/Managers of Police and Detectives	174

Occupations with the Largest Number of Federal Workers in United States Territories

Job	Employees
17. Purchasing Agents, Except Wholesale, Retail, and Farm Products	169
18. Education, Training, and Library Workers, All Other	164
19. Correctional Officers and Jailers	150
20. Air Traffic Controllers	136
21. Tax Examiners, Collectors, and Revenue Agents	126
22. Procurement Clerks	122
23. Fire Fighters	119
24. Motor Vehicle Operators, All Other	106
25. Logisticians	99
26. Transportation, Storage, and Distribution Managers	92
27. Combined Food Preparation and Serving Workers, Including Fast Food	84
28. Civil Engineers	83
29. Maintenance and Repair Workers, General	83
30. Pharmacists	79
31. Paralegals and Legal Assistants	75
32. Loan Officers	73
33. Accountants and Auditors	67
34. Health Diagnosing and Treating Practitioners, All Other	67
35. Engineering Managers	62
36. Engineers, All Other	62
37. Pharmacy Technicians	62
38. Engineering Technicians, Except Drafters, All Other	61
39. Social Scientists and Related Workers, All Other	59
40. Medical and Clinical Laboratory Technologists	56
41. Environmental Engineers	50
42. Medical Records and Health Information Technicians	48
43. Psychologists, All Other	48
44. Life, Physical, and Social Science Technicians, All Other	46
45. Conservation Scientists	45
46. Occupational Health and Safety Specialists	43
47. Budget Analysts	40
48. Recreational Therapists	37
49. Aircraft Mechanics and Service Technicians	36
50. Radiologic Technologists and Technicians	35

Locations with the Largest Number of Offshore Federal Workers

Location	Employees
1. Germany	14,318
2. Puerto Rico	11,142
3. Japan	7,024
4. Korea, Republic of	3,333
5. Guam	2,720
6. Italy	2,528
7. United Kingdom	1,619
8. Belgium	703
9. Virgin Islands	703
10. Afghanistan	508
11. Canada	439
12. Spain	358
13. Kuwait	352
14. Bahrain	313
15. Iraq	312
16. Netherlands	257
17. Turkey	255
18. Cuba	242
19. Saudi Arabia	187
20. Northern Mariana Islands	186
21. Singapore	156
22. Portugal	147
23. Mexico	124
24. American Samoa	116
25. Egypt	111
26. China	93
27. Thailand	93
28. Kenya	86
29. Philippines	84
30. South Africa	84
31. Greece	78
32. Colombia	65
33. Pakistan	62
34. Russia	58
35. India	57
36. El Salvador	56

Locations with the Largest Number of Offshore Federal Workers

Location	Employees
37. Israel	56
38. France	54
39. Qatar	54
40. Bahamas	53
41. Peru	53
42. Honduras	49
43. Panama	49
44. Marshall Islands	48
45. Senegal	48
46. Indonesia	43
47. Guatemala	41
48. Dominican Republic	39
49. Uganda	39
50. Ghana	36

Index

B

C

E

F

J

K

L

M

N

O

Q

R

X–Z